SUMMITS

ALSO BY DAVID REYNOLDS

The Creation of the Anglo-American Alliance:
A Study in Competitive Cooperation, 1937–1941

An Ocean Apart: The Relationship between Britain and America
in the Twentieth Century (with David Dimbleby)

Britannia Overruled: British Policy and World Power
in the Twentieth Century

The Origins of the Cold War in Europe (editor)

Allies at War: The Soviet, American and British Experience, 1939–1945
(co-edited with Warren F. Kimball and A.O. Chubarian)

Rich Relations: The American Occupation of Britain, 1942–1945

One World Divisible: A Global History since 1945

From Munich to Pearl Harbor: Roosevelt's America and
the Origins of the Second World War

In Command of History: Churchill Fighting and Writing
the Second World War

From World War to Cold War: Churchill, Roosevelt and
the International History of the 1940s

SUMMITS

*Six Meetings That Shaped
the Twentieth Century*

DAVID REYNOLDS

BASIC
BOOKS

A Member of the Perseus Books Group
New York

Books published by Basic Books are available at special discounts for
bulk purchases in the United States by corporations, institutions, and other
organizations. For more information, please contact the Special Markets
Department at the Perseus Books Group, 2300 Chestnut St., Philadelphia, PA
19103, or e-mail special.markets@perseusbooks.com.

DESIGN BY JANE RAESE
Text set in 12.5-point Bembo

Cataloging-in-Publication Data is available from the Library of Congress.

ISBN-13: 978-0-465-06904-0
ISBN-10: 0-465-06904-5

10 9 8 7 6 5 4 3 2 1

FOR MY MOTHER

CONTENTS

MAPS

ILLUSTRATIONS

It is not easy to see how things could be worsened
by a parley at the summit.
—Winston Churchill, Feb. 14, 1950

It is far better that we meet at the summit
than at the brink.
—John F. Kennedy, Oct. 1, 1959

It's always the same with these conferences . . .
The Great Men don't know what they're talking about
and have to be educated.
—Sir Alexander Cadogan, Yalta, Feb. 6, 1945

If great princes have a desire to continue friends,
in my judgment they ought never to meet.
—Philippe de Commines, c. 1490

INTRODUCTION

THE TERM "SUMMIT" was coined by Winston Churchill. Speaking in Edinburgh on February 14, 1950, in the dark days of the Cold War, he called for "another talk with the Soviet Union at the highest level," adding that it was "not easy to see how matters could be worsened by a parley at the summit." What prompted Churchill to apply "summit" to diplomacy is not clear, but the word was popping up in British newspapers because expeditions to scale Mount Everest, the world's highest peak, had resumed in the late 1940s. Repeating his call for "a conference on the highest level" on May 11, 1953, Churchill appealed for a will to peace "at the summit of the nations." He delivered this speech to the House of Commons while the eighth attempt on Everest was in progress: the summit was finally conquered at the end of that month. [1]

The Everest obsession helps explain why Churchill's metaphor rooted itself in popular consciousness. A conference of the American, Soviet, British and French leaders in Geneva in July 1955 was billed as a "Parley at the Summit" by *Time* magazine, and "summit" was picked up as an official term by the U.S. State Department. Cartoonists portrayed world leaders eyeing a peak or perched uncomfortably on its top (figure I-1). By 1958 the term "summit" had become a heading in the *New York Times* annual index—a useful barometer of usage—and today it is a routine part of our political vocabulary, with equivalents in many languages.[2]

Yet familiarity breeds insensitivity. It is worth reflecting for a moment on Churchill's arresting phrase "a parley at the summit." The archaic "parley," much used by Shakespeare, evokes a hazardous encounter between enemies to broker terms. In *Titus Andronicus,* for instance, the scheming Empress Tamora tells the Roman noble, Aemilius:

> Go thou before, be our ambassador:
> Say that the emperor requests a parley
> Of warlike Lucius[3]

And "summit" conjures up the heritage of European Romanticism—the mountain peak as both perilous and sublime—celebrated, for example, by the poet William Wordsworth, the novelist Thomas Mann or the painter Caspar David Friedrich. The mountain is a place of danger, its "conquest" a moment of personal triumph and liberation. In the lines of Lord Byron:

> All that expands the spirit, yet appals,
> Gathers around these summits, as to show
> How Earth may pierce to Heaven, yet leave vain man below.[4]

From the top one sees the world in a new and different way, for good or ill, because a mountain is a magical place. Shelley was overwhelmed by his first visit to the Alps in 1816. "The immensity of these arial summits excited, when they suddenly burst upon the sight, a sentiment of extatic wonder, not unallied to madness."[5]

Churchill's "summit" also echoes the sacred mountain of Judaeo-Christian tradition—Moses ascending Sinai to bring back God's law to his people, Christ tempted by visions of an earthly kingdom or transfigured in a flash of divine approval. Standing on a bare mountain, at the mercy of nature, human beings experience a moment of judgment in which they are reduced to their true size in the cosmos. J.M.W. Turner's epic painting of Hannibal's army crossing the Alps in a snowstorm depicts the great commander as a minuscule silhouette clinging to his elephant at the bottom of the apocalyptic skyscape. Painted in 1812, it has even been interpreted as a premonition of Napoleon's downfall.[6]

Despite the dangers, many climbers find it hard to keep away from the summits. After his first expedition to Everest in 1921,

Figure I-1 After the conquest of Mount Everest, statesmen go for the final summit. Here Anthony Eden (Britain), Dwight Eisenhower (U.S.), Nikolai Bulganin (USSR) and Edgar Faure (France) prepare for the Geneva meeting of July 1955. (*Daily Mirror,* June 7, 1955, Mirror Syndication International, University of Kent Cartoon Library)

George Mallory wrote that "the highest of mountains is capable of severity, a severity so awful and so fatal that the wiser sort of men do well to think and tremble on the threshold of their high endeavour." Yet Mallory did not heed his own words: he returned to Everest in 1922 and again in 1924. Asked why by a reporter, he uttered the immortal line: "Because it's there."

For Mallory, like many others, the summit became a fatal attraction. He was last glimpsed on June 8, 1924, through a fleeting gap in the clouds—a tiny black speck near the base of the final pyramid going for the top. His body was found seventy-five years later, petrified in the snow: whether or not he reached the summit remains a tantalizing mystery. One of his colleagues in 1924, Francis Younghusband, speculated that Mallory's ego had triumphed over his reason. "Of the two alternatives, to turn back a third time, or to die, the latter was for Mallory probably the easiest. The agony of the first would be more than he as a man, as a mountaineer, and as an artist could endure ..."[7]

When Churchill first spoke of a diplomatic parley at the summit, these were some of the cultural associations that his words evoked: a perilous encounter between two adversaries. A dramatic act of will, opening up spectacular new vistas. A moment when a leader risks all before the gaze of the multitudes. A chance to make or break his reputation. A journey from which, once started, it is painfully hard to turn back.

It is this epic quality that lures statesmen to the summit. Having surmounted the foothills of domestic affairs, they are drawn almost magnetically to the peaks of international politics. Instinctively many of them espouse the opinion of Thomas Carlyle in 1840 that what has been accomplished in the world is "at bottom the History of the Great Men who have worked here." The closer they get to the top, however, the more they also understand what Karl Marx meant when he claimed that "human beings make their history but they do not make it ... under circumstances of their own choosing."[8]

THIS IS A BOOK ABOUT the human dramas of summitry—about what it was like to clamber to the top, parley at the summit and come down to earth again. It explores the "great man" philosophy that animates diplomatic summiteers as much as their mountaineering counterparts—and questions whether these human beings did make history or whether they were the victims of circumstances beyond their comprehension, let alone control.

Summitry, for all its high drama, is rooted in ordinary human encounters: it has similarities with a first date, a game of cards or a business meeting to clinch a deal. What illusions did each leader have about the other? How well did he play his hand? Who got the better of the negotiation? The way leaders conduct themselves at the table is another theme of *Summits*.

Understood in this manner, summitry might seem as old as human history; indeed, examples date back to the Bronze Age in Babylon. And yet to a surprising degree, leaders generally shied away from top-level meetings until the twentieth century, for reasons of both security and status. Summitry is really a recent invention—made possible by air travel, made necessary by weapons of mass destruction and made into household news by the mass media of newsreels and television.

In its classical sense, as an intimate business meeting between two or three heads of government, summitry flourished in the half-century from the late 1930s to the end of the 1980s. Thereafter those three conditions have been less applicable because of changes in the technologies of communication and weaponry. In the post–Cold War world, summitry has become institutionalized in arenas such as the G8 and the European Council. Yet its personal core, the human encounter, still endures—as the tortured story of George Bush, Tony Blair and the Iraq War makes clear.

I have built this book around six case studies that illustrate different facets of summitry. The first is Munich—more accurately the three encounters between Neville Chamberlain and Adolf Hitler in September 1938. Usually viewed simply as part of the run-up to World War II, they actually inaugurated modern summitry, with that oft-derided figure, Chamberlain, as its unlikely impresario.

Although "Munich" has become a synonym for abject surrender, by looking at the full sequence of three summits it is possible to discern a more complex picture in which the initiative kept shifting to and fro between Britain and Germany. In fact war was averted in September 1938 because Hitler, not Chamberlain, lost his nerve under the pressures of summitry.

In 1945 Churchill, Roosevelt and Stalin met in the Crimea to determine the shape of postwar Europe. Like Munich, Yalta has been depicted as a sell-out, especially by the American right, but critics have focused on one country—Poland—whose fate had already been largely decided on the battlefield. When we consider the full agenda, particularly the overriding issue of Germany, the dynamics of the conference look more balanced. In many ways Yalta was not a bad summit for the West: the real problems stemmed from prior assumptions and subsequent developments. Beforehand Roosevelt and Churchill each created a fundamentally flawed image of Stalin; after Yalta, both Churchill and Stalin panicked about the rush of events. Summits have to be seen in context.

During the early Cold War summitry was under a cloud, not least because of the stigma attached to Munich and Yalta. But in 1961 America's new president, John F. Kennedy, met the pugnacious Soviet leader Nikita Khrushchev in Vienna. Their ill-tempered encounter, which degenerated into a test of virility, constitutes a classic example of how not to do summitry. It also had far-reaching consequences, helping precipitate the Cuban missile crisis and America's quagmire war in Vietnam. Both of these defining episodes of the Cold War had deeper structural roots, of course, but to a frightening extent they grew out of the battle of egos in Vienna.

Much more productive was the Moscow summit of 1972, when Richard Nixon and Leonid Brezhnev signed a series of major agreements and started a real thaw in the Cold War. This was the result of months of intricate secret diplomacy, masterminded at the American end by Henry Kissinger, which involved playing off Russia against China. Without Kissinger's drive and dexterity, the summit would probably not have happened. But the back channels and backstabbing that made Moscow possible also served to undermine its achievements and, indeed, the Nixon presidency.

In 1978 Camp David, the presidential retreat in Maryland, was chosen by Jimmy Carter for his idealistic, high-risk bid to broker a peace settlement between Menachem Begin of Israel and Anwar Sadat of Egypt. Like Yalta, a three-man summit has a different dynamic from a bilateral meeting, allowing two of the participants to lean on the other. Yet that did not guarantee victory. Begin was able to resist Carter and Sadat because of his instinctive skill as a summiteer. Shifting adroitly between courtesy and obduracy, he also held the trump card in any summit meeting—the conviction that he could come down from the mountain empty-handed and still survive back home.

Geneva in 1985 began a new round of superpower summitry, between Ronald Reagan and Mikhail Gorbachev. Its immediate achievements were less striking than Moscow in 1972, but Geneva was based on firmer foundations and it started a process of summitry that helped bring the Cold War to a peaceful end. The growing trust between the two leaders was buttressed by cooperation with and between their foreign ministries, led by George Shultz and Eduard Shevardnadze. This partnership was particularly important on the American side. Nixon and Kissinger got to their summit by marginalizing everyone else—and they eventually paid the price. Reagan and Shultz harnessed the diplomats and that is an important reason why their successes were more enduring.

In writing the book, I came to see these meetings as falling into three loose categories. Two encounters were essentially *personal summits* in which the main object was to forge a relationship between the two leaders. Chamberlain embarked on summitry to find out for himself if Hitler was clinically mad. He then came back confident that the German leader was a man of his word and based his diplomacy, disastrously, on that personal assessment. At Vienna in June 1961 the aim for Kennedy and Khrushchev was, more modestly, mutual reconnaissance. But Khrushchev believed that he could bully the young president while Kennedy, equally confident about his powers of persuasion, thought he could reason with the volatile Soviet leader.

In what I call *plenary summits* the dynamics of personal encounter are balanced and complemented by the presence of specialist advisors and there is also a concerted effort to resolve substantive problems. Yalta in 1945 and Camp David in 1978 fall into this category and in themselves both were successful. But they rested on false assumptions which undermined the implementation of the agreements. And this was because, at a deeper level, neither was rooted in a truly cooperative diplomatic relationship. Deals made at the summit did not stick when the statesmen came back to earth.

Progressive summits, my third category, involve personal and plenary elements but in addition the single meeting became part of a series, both between leaders and also among lower-level specialists. The summit in Moscow in 1972 tried to start such a process but failed, largely because of Nixon and Kissinger's Machiavellian methods. In contrast the sequence that began with the Geneva summit of 1985 was successful thanks to that rare but absolutely vital combination: rapport between leaders *and* teamwork with their advisors.

These meetings also open a larger window into the general conduct of international relations. Summitry constitutes one form of diplomacy, which is essentially dialogue between states. Such dialogue cannot be taken for granted: alien societies are often shunned as the embodiments of evil, particularly in the twentieth century—notoriously the era of total war, or at least preparedness for total war. But it was also an era in which the alternatives to war were explored as never before, prompted initially by the haunting legacy of the conflict of 1914–18 and the looming menace of airborne destruction.

Munich and Yalta were variants on the diplomacy of appeasement, understood in the traditional sense of that term as the peaceful satisfaction of grievances. But after 1945 appeasement became a dirty word, not least because of the perceived consequences of Munich and Yalta. Cold War America committed itself to a policy of containment—standing firm and not negotiating with the Soviets.

Kennedy tried talking in 1961 and the results were disastrous. In 1972, however, Nixon successfully developed a policy of détente, a relaxation of tension, predicated on the assumption that the Soviet empire was America's equal and a fact of international life. It took a bizarrely radical Cold Warrior, Ronald Reagan—abetted by the even more visionary Mikhail Gorbachev—to move beyond détente and transform the Cold War world. And so, through these philosophies of appeasement, containment, détente and transformation, as practiced at the summit, we can trace some less familiar contours of the century of hate.

So although these summits may seem clichéd, there is much to say about them that is both novel and important. This is because I have gone back to the original records of what was discussed. For most of the meetings we have detailed minutes, sometimes almost verbatim transcripts, from at least one country. In many cases, such as Chamberlain and Hitler or Reagan and Gorbachev, there are records from both sides. I have tried to read these and related documents carefully and imaginatively.

Carefully, for the words used were important. Precise formulations were intended to suggest certain interpretations and preclude others, while unguarded asides shed light into the recesses of leaders' psychology, such as Khrushchev's comment before Vienna in 1961 that John Kennedy was younger than his son would have been had he lived.

But we also need to read the documents imaginatively because they were written as an aid to current business, not to enlighten future historians. Record keepers were usually more interested in the decisions that were agreed than in how they were arrived at. They glossed over points, often those made by their own leader, that were very familiar; they rarely conveyed the tone of the speaker or his body language; and they did not take time to reflect on who spoke first, who held back, in what order key issues were raised and what was deliberately left unsaid. These records were also political documents, disseminated to colleagues at home and allies abroad. Sometimes the text was touched up to put a better gloss on a statesman's performance. One is reminded of an anonymous verse circulating in Whitehall during the Second World War:

> And so while the great ones depart to their dinner,
> The secretary stays, growing thinner and thinner,
> Racking his brains to record and report
> What he thinks that they think that they ought to have thought.[9]

It is essential to read between the lines of the documents and to compare the official records with the diaries of participants and even their memoirs (despite the distortions of hindsight). The fundamental point to remember is that government records are not themselves the historical reality: they enable historians to reconstruct the reality. Or, more accurately, they enable us to construct a reality that no participant could have known at the time because he could not see the other man's cards or know how the game turned out.

Although my chapters are not burdened with jargon, they rest on reading in the literature of political science about bargaining and negotiation. In each case I reflect on three stages of summitry: *preparation*, *negotiation* and *implementation*. How leaders get to the summit and what baggage they take with them. How they engage with each other and how well they withstand the rigors of high-altitude personal diplomacy. And finally what happens when they come down from the summit and have to present their achievements to skeptical, sometimes hostile, audiences at home, and among allies. At the end I suggest a few lessons that I think leaders themselves might consider, should they have the time to do so amid the frenzy of events.

The book is intended to stimulate debate on an important subject that has been strangely neglected by scholars and pundits.[10] Yet for all its complexities international summitry remains essentially a human drama. The stories that follow are about skilled and self-assured men who meet in order to understand and manipulate each other. They have taken huge risks to get to the negotiating table and they operate under immense stress—political, physical and psychological—that exposes their deeper flaws. But, like Mallory contemplating Everest, they cannot stay away. They climb high and dangerously in the belief that at the summit they can change the world.

1

TOWARD THE SUMMIT

From Babylon to Versailles

Although Winston Churchill coined the word in 1950, the practice of summitry has much earlier antecedents. Indeed one might assume that it is as old as diplomacy itself, rooted in some primeval form of negotiation between tribal chieftains. Yet summits have had a checkered and erratic historical career, often being shunned as unnecessary, unwise and even dangerous. To understand why summitry flourished in the twentieth century, we need to look at why it didn't during most of previous history.

The origins of diplomacy date back at least to the Bronze Age in the Near East. Caches of documents from the Euphrates kingdom in the mid–eighteenth century BC and from Akhenaten's Egypt four centuries later reveal a regular exchange of envoys with neighboring states, prompted by the need for trade and the danger of war. This was hardly a fully fledged diplomatic "system." Envoys were not resident ambassadors and they were not protected by agreed rules of immunity—but it was a recognizable form of diplomacy.

Summitry, as we would understand it, was rare, being mostly confined to visits by minor rulers to pay homage at the courts of their overlords. This is hardly surprising because of the travel time

required—six weeks for even a fast courier from Egypt to Babylon—and because of the hazards and insecurities en route. For a
ruler to undertake such a journey was therefore a sign of his inferior status. Rulers of great powers, though they might address each
other in letters as "dear brother," would never meet unless one of
them had become the booty of battle, which was not summitry but
submission.[1]

Diplomacy also flourished in classical Greece, in the fifth and
fourth centuries BC. It proved a necessity for small city states in
proximity to powerful neighbors, each keen to maintain its independence but unable to do so unaided. Hence the frequent use of
envoys to forge alliances and negotiate peace treaties. These men
were not professional diplomats but prominent political figures with
persuasive tongues who operated under strict instructions, leaving
little scope for serious negotiation. And they dealt not with a sole
ruler but with the sovereign body of the other power, such as the
Spartan oligarchs or the standing council of the Athenian assembly.[2]

Imperial Rome, of course, did have a hegemonic ruler—by the
middle of the first century AD the senate had granted the emperor
authority to make treaties—but in the heyday of the empire the
pattern of diplomacy was similar to that of the Bronze Age in the
Near East. To maintain security at its margins, the empire relied on
satellite states but, rather than conducting summit meetings on
equal terms, their rulers came to Rome, often in circumstances that
demonstrated their subordination—in detention, for instance, or as
refugees from intrigues at home.[3]

By the late second century, however, the Roman frontiers were
increasingly precarious and emperors spent more and more time
personally waging war. As a consequence the imperial court moved
from the heartland of Italy to the northern or eastern borderlands
where the campaigns were taking place. Starting with Marcus Au-
relius and Lucius Verus in the 160s, it also became a frequent practice to appoint co-emperors, located on different frontiers. And as
the empire became increasingly insecure its rulers dealt not only
with foreign envoys but also directly with foreign counterparts. In
369 the emperor Valens met Athanaric, leader of the Goths, on the

Danube. Five years later, in 374, Valentinian I joined the Alamanni king Macrianus for a peace conference on the Rhine.

Such summits were testimony to the growing fragility of the late Roman Empire and thus the relative equality of the emperor and his barbarian foes. They often took place on an imperial river boundary—the Danube, Rhine or Euphrates—because this was a no-man's-land; it confirmed the parity of the two leaders by showing that neither had gone to the court of the other. In 374 Valentinian actually negotiated from a boat on the Rhine, with Macrianus standing on the bank. In 615 the Byzantine emperor Heraclius and the Persian leader Shahin moored their ships side by side in the Bosphorus to engage in their version of an equal "parley at the summit."[4]

In the heyday of the Byzantine Empire its rulers tried to manage affairs from Constantinople, either bringing foreign rulers to their court or conducting negotiations by letters and by envoys who acted as the self-styled "voice of kings."[5] In 1096 and 1097 the emperor Alexis Comnenos made a point of meeting the leaders of the First Crusade in his own palace, as did Manuel Comnenos when the Second Crusade arrived in 1147. But when Byzantium spiralled into decline in the fourteenth century, its emperors became as mobile as those of the late Roman Empire, and much less potent. Emperor Manuel II was reduced to touring the courts of Italy, France, Germany and England for help against the Ottoman Turks, handing out precious books and pieces of the supposed tunic of Christ as inducements. This was the diplomacy of desperation: Byzantium fell to the Turks in 1453, less than thirty years after Manuel's death.[6]

In the post-Roman West personal diplomacy was more normal, for instance when family members were vying to divide up a kingdom, as portrayed dramatically in the opening scene of Shakespeare's *King Lear*. A notable example was the series of summits in Carolingian France after the death of Louis the Pious, particularly those at Verdun in 843 and Meersen in 870. The outlines of these territorial settlements were laboriously thrashed out months in advance by commissioners who surveyed the terrain and gathered data. But plenty of scope still remained for face-to-face haggling by the principals—their in-person meetings guaranteed the agreements by an exchange of oaths and sometimes of hostages. On other occasions, summits concluded carefully prepared peace agreements, as when Frederick Barbarossa and Pope Alexander III met in Venice in 1177. This conference took place on neutral territory; others, as with late Roman practice, were conducted in the borderlands. In either case, the location was chosen to ensure the status and/or security of each ruler.[7]

The importance of status is vividly illustrated by perhaps the most celebrated summit in German history: the meeting at Canossa in 1077 between Pope Gregory VII and Holy Roman Emperor Henry IV. In German this is known as *der Canossagang*, the journey to Canossa; more aptly in Italian as *l'umiliazione di Canossa*, for it was truly a humiliation. In the Investiture Controversy—the power struggle between pope and emperor over the right to appoint bishops—Henry had renounced Gregory as pope, only to find himself excommunicated. This papal edict not only imperilled Henry's immortal soul, it also laid him open to revolt by the German nobility. He sought a meeting with Gregory who, fearing violence, retreated to the castle of Canossa, in safe territory south of Parma. This forced the emperor to come to him.

What exactly happened is shrouded in legend, but supposedly Henry arrived in the depths of winter, barefoot and in a pilgrim's hair shirt, only to be kept waiting by Gregory for three days. When he was finally admitted to the castle on January 28, 1077, the emperor knelt before the pope and begged forgiveness. He was absolved and the two most powerful figures in Christendom then shared the Mass.

The reconciliation was short-lived. After being excommunicated a second time Henry crossed the Alps with his army and replaced Gregory with an "antipope" of his own. But the events themselves matter less than the myth that grew up around them. During the German Reformation Henry was lionized as the defender of national rights and the scourge of the Catholic pope, often being dubbed "the first Protestant." And during Chancellor Otto von Bismarck's struggle to rein in the Catholic church, he famously declared in the Reichstag on May 14, 1872: "We will not go to Canossa, neither in body nor in spirit." He was voicing the new German Reich's resolve to accept no outside interference in its affairs—political or religious. As a result Henry IV shivering outside the gates of Canossa became a familiar figure in late-nineteenth-century German art; the phrase "to go to Canossa" (*nach Canossa gehen*) entered the language as a synonym for craven surrender—almost the equivalent of "Munich" to the British and Americans.[8]

Throughout history, security as much as status has been an obstacle to summitry. In 1419 France was in turmoil from war with the English and a power struggle provoked by the periodic insanity of King Charles VI. On September 10 the dauphin, Charles' son, conferred on a bridge near Rouen with their archrival, John, Duke of Burgundy. Both men were well attended by guards and a barrier had been erected in the middle, with a wicket gate bolted on either side to allow passage only by mutual consent. During the conference Duke John was persuaded to come through the gate—only to be cut down by the dauphin's bodyguard.

The dauphin, inheriting the throne as Charles VII, recovered much of France from the English. When his son, Louis XI, met the Yorkist king Edward IV at Picquigny near Amiens in 1475 to conclude a peace treaty, the fate of Duke John was much in mind. The chronicler Philippe de Commines tells how this conference was held on a bridge over the Somme. Louis insisted that across the middle of the bridge and along its sides his carpenters should build "a strong wooden lattice, such as lions' cages are made with, the hole between each bar being no wider than to thrust in a man's arm." The two kings somehow managed to embrace between the holes and conducted their meeting in secure cordiality.[9]

Summitry was now reaching its premodern heyday, for reasons relevant to our larger story. Although by about 1500 several strong national states had emerged in Europe, they remained greatly dependent on their monarchs. This kind of personalized power is at the heart of summitry. One of the most famous encounters took place on the so-called Field of the Cloth of Gold in June 1520, bringing together Henry VIII of England and François I of France. The young English monarch, whose titles still included "King of France," had resumed the old struggle in 1512. But his advisor Cardinal Thomas Wolsey secured a truce and then arranged a summit to consummate an enduring peace.

It took place on the edge of Calais, the last English enclave in France, in a shallow dip known as the Val d'Or. Both sides of the valley were carefully reshaped to ensure that neither party enjoyed a height advantage. A special pavilion was constructed for the meeting and festivities, surrounded by thousands of tents and a three-hundred-foot-square timber castle for the rest of those attending. Henry's entourage alone numbered more than five thousand, while the French crown needed ten years to pay off its share of the cost.

At the appointed hour on June 7, 1520, the Feast of Corpus Christi, the two monarchs with their retinues in full battle array appeared on the opposite sides of the valley. There was a moment of tense silence—each side feared an ambush by the other. Then the two kings spurred their horses forward to the appointed place marked by a spear in the ground and embraced. The ice was broken. They dismounted and went into the pavilion arm in arm to talk. Then began nearly two weeks of jousting, feasting and dancing that culminated in a High Mass in the open air. Choirs from England and France accompanied the mass and there was a sermon on the virtues of peace.[10]

In both choreography and cost, the Field of the Cloth of Gold resembles contemporary summits. In a further similarity, style was more important than substance: by 1521 the two countries were at war again. In many ways they were natural rivals, whereas Henry was bound—by marriage and interest—to France's enemy Charles V, king of Spain. Both before and after the Cloth of Gold Henry met Charles for discussions of much greater diplomatic magnitude. And although Wolsey hoped the meeting of the British and French elites might build bridges, this soon proved an illusion.

As the Cloth of Gold demonstrated, egos were everything in these summits, with each side alert to any hint of advantage gained by the other. Commines was implacably opposed to such meetings for this very reason. It was, he said, impossible "to hinder the train and equipage of the one from being finer and more magnificent than the other, which produces mockery, and nothing touches any person more sensibly than to be laughed at."

Even when summitry ended without mutual recrimination, Commines believed it rarely produced anything worthwhile: despite the cordiality of Louis XI and Edward IV at Picquigny in 1475, "scarce anything was performed that was promised there, but all their whole business was hypocrisy and dissimulation." In short, Commines concluded, it was "the highest act of imprudence for two great princes, provided there is any equality in their power, to admit of an interview . . . It were better that they accommodated their differences by the mediation of wise and faithful Ministers." His prescient remarks echo right through the twentieth century, capturing what might be called the bureaucrat's view of summitry.[11]

In any case, an alternative to summit meetings was emerging. For centuries it had been customary to send envoys on specific, short-term missions. But by the mid–fifteenth century the tightly knit but feuding city states of northern Italy—Venice, Florence, Milan and Rome—kept permanent ambassadors in key cities in order to gather intelligence and foster alliances. In due course their governments created chanceries to manage the mounting mass of paper.

From 1490 the great powers of Europe followed suit, led by Spain. It became normal to have at each of the major courts a resident "ambassador"—a word defined by the English poet and diplomat Sir Henry Wotton in a punning epigram as "a man sent to lie abroad for his country's good." Given the time required for travel, and the hazards en route—especially in an age of dynastic and religious warfare—permanent ambassadors offered a convenient substitute for personal summitry. And their detailed reports required the attention of specialist secretaries who oversaw foreign affairs, such as Francis Walsingham in Elizabethan London or Antonio Perez at the court of Philip III. Day-to-day diplomacy tended to slip out of the hands of rulers.[12]

This diplomatic revolution, part of the growing bureaucratization of government, was complemented by a revolution in political ideas that we can measure in the changing use of the term "state." In the fourteenth century the Latin term *status* (and vernacular equivalents such as *estat* or *state*) was mainly used with reference to the standing of rulers themselves, much as we would today use the term "status." Thus the chronicler Jean Froissart, describing King Edward III entertaining foreign dignitaries in 1327, recorded that his queen "was to be seen there in an *estat* of great nobility."

Gradually, however, usage was extended to include the institutions of government. In the works of Machiavelli, written in the 1510s, *lo stato* becomes an independent agent, separate from those who happen to be its rulers. In a similar vein, Thomas Starkey, the English political commentator of the 1530s, claimed that the "office and duty" of rulers was to "maintain the state established in the country" over which they ruled. The thrust of such arguments was to limit the power of kings by postulating their higher obligation to the common good. In radical hands this implied that subjects had the right to overthrow tyrannical rulers, which is what happened in the English civil wars of the 1640s and Europe's bitter wars of religion.

Responding to this crisis of governance, Thomas Hobbes moved the debate to a different level, defining the state as "an artificial man" abstractly encapsulating the whole populace, who enjoys absolute sovereignty (his "artificial soul . . . giving life and motion to the body") which is exercised in practice through a sovereign ruler. This gradual but dramatic word shift, from the medieval state of princes to the person of the Hobbesian state, was hugely important for political thought. It also reinforced the decline of dynastic summitry: diplomacy, like governance, was no longer regarded as the sole prerogative of princes.[13]

The religious wars were not settled at the summit. The treaties collectively known as the Peace of Westphalia in 1648 were the result of conference diplomacy—detailed negotiations lasting five years and conducted by 176 plenipotentiaries acting for 109 European rulers.[14]

After Westphalia brought peace to Europe, the second half of the seventeenth century saw a further spread of resident ambassadors, with Louis XIV's France leading the way, and French replaced Latin as the lingua franca. There was, however, still scope for summitry, for instance during Peter the Great's tour of Western Europe in 1697–8. His meetings with William III of England helped bring Russia belatedly into the European diplomatic orbit. In due course, the czar created a "Diplomatic Chancellery" and a network of foreign embassies on the European model.[15]

Ambassadors, except from England and the Dutch Republic, were predominantly aristocrats, chosen to represent their monarch in appropriate style. They usually regarded such service as a form of exile, undertaken in the hope of eventual preferment. Meanwhile back home the specialist secretaries of the sixteenth century grew into fully fledged foreign ministers with departments of their own by the eighteenth century. Again France led the way—its Foreign Ministry dates from 1626—while Britain was relatively late, in 1782. The new United States followed suit in 1789, although the title "Department of Foreign Affairs" was quickly changed to "Department of State."[16]

The development of foreign ministries further restricted the scope for summitry. But rulers often retained their own private diplomatic networks. Louis XV was a prime example, while Frederick the Great of Prussia created his own *Kabinett*, or private office, and took over the most important business from the Foreign Office. Not surprisingly, Frederick also tried his hand at summitry: seeking a rapprochement with Austria after the Seven Years War, he met the emperor Joseph II at Neisse in 1769 and Neustadt in 1770.[17]

War was often the stimulus for personal summitry and this was particularly true in the era of Napoleon, a natural autocrat who regularly intervened in diplomacy because it was intertwined with the waging of war and because he was impatient for immediate solutions. After Russia's defeat at Friedland in June 1807, Czar Alexander I needed peace while Napoleon wanted to turn back west against Britain. They met in person, like the late Roman emperors, on a raft on the Niemen River, the border of their respective domains. The French constructed two wooden pavilions, draped with white linen and inscribed with the two imperial monograms: N and A. The first meeting on June 25 was an emotional occasion: the insecure czar, though a good six inches taller, was captivated by Napoleon's magnetism, while the little ex-corporal had never before been accepted so fully as a brother sovereign by one of the great dynasties of Europe. Frederick William III of Prussia, humiliated by Napoleon the previous year at the battle of Jena, could only watch from the bank in the pouring rain.

The ceremonial raft was dismantled after a couple of days but the two leaders talked for over a week, with Napoleon buttering up Alexander at every stage. "In one hour," the emperor declared, "we shall achieve more than our spokesmen in several days."[18] Russia accepted French terms for an anti-British alliance—including the abandonment of its ally, Prussia—and got virtually nothing in return. The treaties signed at Tilsit in July 1807 marked the zenith of Napoleon's power. They also showed the seductions of summitry: by meeting face to face, Alexander had put himself in the hands of a man who was master of the personal interview.[19]

The crisis generated by Napoleon's inveterate war-mongering forced his European neighbors into real cooperation. In the later stages of the conflict monarchs and ministers accompanied the armies, making it relatively easy to confer. Alexander I left Russia with his troops in January 1813 and did not return until August 1814; the British foreign secretary, Lord Castlereagh, virtually lived on the continent for a year and a half in 1814–15. This collaboration was institutionalized in the Congress of Vienna, the long-running peace conference to wind up the Napoleonic wars. Although almost all of Europe was represented, the real work was done by the foreign ministers of the four leading Allied powers (Britain, Russia, Austria and Prussia) plus the French, leaving most of the delegations with little to do but amuse themselves.

For a few years after the Congress of Vienna in 1815 allied ministers continued to meet in a series of congresses, building on contacts forged in war. Prince Clemens von Metternich, the Austrian foreign minister, remarked before conferring with Castlereagh in

October 1821: "I shall achieve more in a few days . . . than in six months of writing." But during the 1820s diplomacy slipped back into more formalized channels. The personal ties forged by the Napoleonic wars had been broken; moreover Europe was at peace and there seemed little need for personal diplomacy. Occasional crises were usually settled by conferences of ambassadors chaired by the foreign minister of the host country.[20]

At this time ambassadors remained essential due to the slowness of communications. It could take a month for a letter to travel from London to St. Petersburg; in 1822 the record for an urgent dispatch to Vienna was one week. But in the 1840s and 1850s railways started to spread across the Continent, while steamships dramatically reduced the duration of sea voyages. After the introduction of the electric telegraph in the 1870s, ciphered telegrams replaced written dispatches for urgent business. Now that messages could be sent and answered within hours, the embassies in far-flung capitals could be subject to daily supervision. In 1904 the British diplomat Sir Francis Bertie complained that an ambassador had been reduced to the status of a "damned marionette," with the Foreign Office pulling the wires.[21]

The communications revolution was profoundly important for summitry. Not only did it emasculate the role of ambassadors, it also allowed heads of government to take center stage once more. The Congress of Berlin in 1878 is in many ways a precursor of modern summits.

Bismarck, the German chancellor, acted as host. Prince Alexander Gorchakov, the ailing Russian chancellor, and Count Gyula Andrassy, his Austro-Hungarian counterpart, were also there. The British delegation was led by the Tory prime minister, Benjamin Disraeli, recently ennobled as Lord Beaconsfield. In protracted sessions in June and July 1878 the congress resolved a Balkan crisis that threatened to plunge Europe into war. All the leaders played a part, notably Bismarck, but the British side is especially important because of the lasting images of summitry it generated.[22]

Much of the groundwork for the agreement was laid by Lord Salisbury, Disraeli's foreign secretary, who worked behind the scenes before the conference in negotiations with Russia, Turkey and Austria. Salisbury, from one of England's great landed families, distrusted Disraeli as a cynical opportunist—"the Artless Dodger"—and complained that the prime minister had only "the dimmest idea of what is going on" in Berlin. He "seemed to have forgotten the various agreements we had made" and needed constant memoranda by way of reminders.[23]

But it was Disraeli who hit the headlines. Tory propagandists presented him as an aging hero, now seventy-four and wracked by asthma and gout, making a last, valiant bid for peace. He was praised for his tough, anti-Russian speeches, deliberately delivered in English rather French, the language of diplomacy. And for his brinkmanship in ordering a train to be prepared for his return home, which supposedly brought the Congress to heel.[24]

Disraeli returned to London on July 16, 1878, to a triumphant welcome all along the flag-draped route from Charing Cross station to 10 Downing Street. There, from an upstairs balcony, he told the cheering crowds that he had brought back from Germany "peace with honour." It was one of the great dramatic moments of Victorian politics. It lodged in the public memory—with fateful consequences sixty years later.

So Disraeli got most of the credit, while Salisbury did much of the work. Though, to be fair, the prime minister insisted that his foreign secretary should share his open carriage from the station. And when Disraeli accepted the Order of the Garter from his adoring queen, he asked that Salisbury also be a recipient (prompting one Radical MP to sneer that they had actually obtained "peace with honours").[25]

Disraeli and Salisbury made a good team—the urbane prime minister combining his smooth social round with tough talk at the business sessions, the cerebral foreign secretary laboring behind the scenes to craft the deals and manage the details. This kind of teamwork, as we shall see, is at the heart of successful summitry.

The Congress of Berlin was made possible in large measure by the railway. Disraeli took four days to travel out from London to Berlin, but that was because he wished to conserve his energie with overnight stops; the return journey, fuelled by success, was completed in less than three. Heads of government were not the only ones to take advantage of improved communications. So too did monarchs, many of whom were related through the far-flung marriages of Queen Victoria's children and grandchildren.

The most notorious practitioner of dynastic diplomacy was Wilhelm II of Germany who, within two years of becoming Kaiser in 1888, had sacked the veteran Bismarck and claimed: "I am the sole master of German policy and my country must follow me wherever I go."[26] He went off in all directions, literally and metaphorically. He loved to travel by rail and sea to confer with his monarchical relatives but lacked a consistent policy as he veered off on one tack and then another. His personal diplomacy was a real headache for his ministers; one of them, Count Philipp zu Eulenburg, said wearily that "a discussion between two princes is propitious only when it confines itself to the weather"—and they had to work hard to manage his moods and offset his interventions.[27]

The most striking of the kaiser's diplomatic forays was his summit near Björkö in the Gulf of Finland in July 1905 with Czar Nicholas II of Russia. Cousin Willy and Cousin Nicky moored their royal yachts alongside each other, had a long and emotional talk over dinner and next morning signed a treaty pledging alliance if either were attacked by another power. The kaiser was ecstatic at his diplomatic triumph, but his chancellor, Bernhard von Bülow, threatened to resign, while the czar's advisors pointed out that the Treaty of Björkö was at odds with Russia's bedrock alliance with France, Germany's inveterate enemy since the French defeat in 1870. The Russian foreign minister, Count Vladimir Lambsdorff, told the czar that it was "inadmissible to promise at the same time the same thing to two governments whose interests were mutually antagonistic." Nicholas replied lamely: "I didn't understand the Treaty of Björkö as you do." The whole idea was soon dead in the water.[28]

Such spasms of dynastic diplomacy were now of little significance. Meetings between kings and emperors gradually metamorphosed into largely ceremonial state visits.[29] By the beginning of the twentieth century diplomacy was firmly in the hands of Europe's foreign ministries.

But the diplomats and the ministers failed to resolve the crisis in July 1914, allowing Europe to slide into its first great war in a century. Nor, as the death toll mounted, were they able to negotiate peace. Consequently there was a public backlash against this old diplomacy conducted by aristocrats behind closed doors in a web of secret treaties designed to make war. Critics demanded a new diplomacy that took into account the demands of democratic electorates and, instead of promoting narrow national interest, sought lasting international peace. These ideas were promulgated in Britain by left-wing intellectuals such as Norman Angell and Bertrand Russell but, across the Atlantic, they were adopted with messianic fervor in the White House.

THROUGHOUT THE NINETEENTH CENTURY the United States remained outside the main orbit of international diplomacy. To a country three thousand miles from the feuding states of Europe, diplomacy seemed like an old-world affectation, irrelevant to national security. Nonprofessionals ran missions and consulates and the top jobs were part of the spoils system—a payback from the president for political or financial support during an election campaign. Until the twentieth century the U.S. government did not own any diplomatic buildings abroad and a new ambassador had to find and rent something suitable when he took up his post.[30]

Things began to change in the 1900s, both in the professionalization of diplomacy—competitive exams on the European model—and also through new American involvement in world affairs after the Spanish-American War of 1898. In August 1905, following intricate secret exchanges, President Theodore Roosevelt brought together the belligerent parties in the Russo-Japanese war at the U.S. naval base at Portsmouth, New Hampshire. The president did not attend the conference in person, but he monitored the negotiations assiduously, on several occasions summoning the negotiators down to his home on Long Island. The eventual Treaty of

Portsmouth owed a great deal to TR's personal diplomacy and earned him the Nobel Peace Prize in 1906.[31]

Although Roosevelt's goal was similar to that of his European counterparts—a regional balance of power—he did not simply adopt the old-world approach to diplomacy. On the contrary, he conceived himself as playing a distinctively American role in world affairs. "The more I see of the Czar, Kaiser, and the Mikado," he declared, "the better I am content with democracy."[32]

Woodrow Wilson, Democratic president from 1913 to 1921, had a particularly profound sense of America's moral mission. He kept his country neutral in 1914 as "the one great nation at peace, the one people holding itself ready to play a part of impartial mediation and speak the counsels of peace and accommodation."[33] Wilson did not believe that Germany was solely to blame for the conflict. Even after its all-out U-boat warfare forced him to enter the war in April 1917, he did so self-consciously as an "Associate" power—joining the Allies to eliminate German militarism but determined to impose a new world order on them as well. "England and France have not the same views with regard to peace that we have by any means," he told his advisor Colonel Edward House in July 1917. "When the war is over we can force them to our way of thinking, because they will, among other things, be financially in our hands . . ."[34]

Wilson's agenda for a new international order, adumbrated in his Fourteen Points of January 1918, centered on a "League of Nations" to keep the peace. Instead of old-world power politics, he wanted open diplomacy, freedom of the seas, and the maximum possible disarmament "consistent with domestic security." There should also be "a free, open-minded and absolutely impartial adjustment of all colonial claims," in which "the interests of the populations concerned" would be weighed equally against the demands of the imperial powers.[35] Wilson's vision captured the imagination of liberals around the world, but Allied leaders were skeptical. "God gave us Ten Commandments, and we broke them," remarked Georges Clemenceau, the French premier, dryly. "Wilson gives us Fourteen Points. We shall see."[36]

The autumn of 1918 was Wilson's moment, with American supplies, finance and troops playing a decisive role in the Allied victory. "Never," wrote John Maynard Keynes, "has a philosopher held such weapons wherewith to bind the princes of this world."[37] When Germany and its partners finally collapsed, they appealed directly to Wilson over the heads of the European powers, and the armistice of November 11 was explicitly based on the Fourteen Points.

Britain and France were furious but House had warned them that otherwise they would be left to carry on the fight alone. In the end David Lloyd George, the British prime minister, secured a couple of reservations, allowing them to discuss freedom of the seas and reparations from Germany at the peace conference. He hoped that the rest of the Fourteen Points were "wide enough to allow us to place our own interpretation upon them."[38] Wilson had ended the war on virtually his own terms. But could he determine the peace as well?

This did not necessarily mean attending the peace conference in person, however. No U.S. president had previously left the western hemisphere while in office: William McKinley wanted to tour Europe after the Spanish-American War but did not feel legally entitled to be outside the country for an extended period of time. Initially, Wilson seems to have intended to pull the strings from afar. "House will be there," he told his brother-in-law, and "I shall be able to keep well informed of the daily proceedings," adding that it was not customary for heads of state to negotiate.[39]

Many senior Democrats concurred, favoring a scenario rather like Teddy Roosevelt managing the Portsmouth conference from Long Island. If Wilson went to Paris, the newspaper editor Frank Cobb warned House, "instead of remaining the great arbiter of human freedom" he would become "merely a negotiator dealing with other negotiators." By staying in Washington he could adjudicate from "a commanding position" as "a court of last resort, of world democracy."[40]

Firm advice was often counterproductive with Wilson: the wave of negative arguments helped persuade him he must go to Paris. He argued that personal prestige was worthless if it could not be used as a diplomatic weapon. "If it is so sensitive a plant that it cannot be exhibited in public, it will wither anyhow, and the sooner the better."[41] He also assumed that he would be attending only the preliminary conference, to thrash out the main outlines of the peace settlements, so his time in Europe would be relatively short.[42] Wilson was aware that Clemenceau and Lloyd George, his principal rivals, would play an active role at the peace conference—the former on his home turf in Paris, the latter handily placed in London for frequent cross-Channel visits—and felt that his presence was necessary to counter their machinations. "I am going over to Europe because the Allied governments don't want me to come," he remarked privately.[43]

But ultimately Wilson went to Paris because he was intoxicated by power. He had come to believe that he spoke not only for America but also for the people of the world. The rapturous receptions he received in Paris, London and Rome in December 1918 confirmed his belief that he was engaged on a special mission and that he could quickly translate his personal prestige into a lasting, democratic peace. The president was drawn to the peace conference, said one cynical British diplomat, like a debutante "entranced by the prospect of her first ball."[44]

It turned into a very long diplomatic dance. The president was actually away for over six months, spending only two weeks in the United States between December 3, 1918, and July 8, 1919—an absence unique in the history of the U.S. presidency.[45] Because the Allies were not ready, the peace conference did not begin for nearly a month after his arrival in Europe. And, although the preliminary conference proved the only one, the complex issues at stake and the conflicting interests of twenty-eight delegations made agreement very hard to reach.

In retrospect it is easy to criticize Wilson's approach to the negotiations. Confident that "if necessary, I can reach the peoples of Europe over the heads of their rulers,"[46] he was slow to forge the human contacts and build the diplomatic combinations that would help secure his goals. Although he had established a think tank of academics and journalists known as "The Inquiry" back in September

1917, which drew up a multitude of useful background papers, he made much less use of his technical advisors than did the British. He also proved surprisingly vague about some of his key ideas, such as the concept of self-determination or the structure of his cherished League of Nations.[47] On the latter, he was therefore obliged to work with a largely British draft. Far from being a "philosopher" in Keynes' famous phrase, he proved "only a prophet."[48] As such he was not particularly adept at the cut and thrust of parliamentary-style debate when the conference settled down to hard bargaining within the Council of Four (Wilson, Clemenceau, Lloyd George and Vittorio Orlando, the Italian leader). Here, as Frank Cobb had warned, he became only a negotiator—and not a very nimble one at that.

On the other hand, Wilson's position was weaker than it appeared. America's leverage over the Allies diminished once the armistice had been agreed and Germany fell apart in revolution. Wilson's threat to leave Britain and France to fight on alone if they did not like his terms was now immaterial: the German armed forces were a broken reed. What's more, contrary to the president's belief that European public opinion was behind him, it actually swung dramatically to the right in the British and French elections of late 1918. Clemenceau and Lloyd George were being pushed to demand a draconian peace. And whereas they had popular mandates, the American midterm elections of November 1918 had produced Republican majorities in both houses of Congress. Wilson would need the support of two-thirds of the Senate to ratify any peace treaty, which argued for a bipartisan approach to peacemaking. Yet the delegation he took to Paris included no prominent Republican politicians. Once again, he remained confident he could bulldoze his way through any obstacles.

So Wilson was actually playing a rather weak hand. And what seems at first glance to have been mere intransigence on his part did reflect a recognition of his predicament. A major reason why the preliminary conference did not end quickly was because the president insisted that the League of Nations must be built into any peace treaty. Although this stalled business for several weeks, Wilson believed that otherwise he could not get either the Allies or the

U.S. Senate to accept the concept. He knew that Lloyd George and Clemenceau needed a peace treaty and he was gambling that Republican critics of the League would not push their opposition to the point of jeopardizing the whole peace settlement. Nor was Wilson's League entirely utopian—it was intended to be a universal instrument of American influence that at the same time would preserve his country's freedom of action. The United States, he told a British audience in December 1918, was "not interested in European politics" directly; it sought a "partnership of right between America and Europe." In other words, American guidance behind the scenes.[49]

Wilson won the first round: by mid-February the Covenant of the League was firmly established. But at a price. Immediately afterward Wilson returned home to handle urgent domestic business, where he discovered the depths of opposition on Capitol Hill. He returned to Paris in mid-March obliged to seek various amendments, notably to ensure that America's dominance in the western hemisphere—as articulated in the Monroe Doctrine of 1823—would not be subject to League interference. For a president who had inveighed against balance of power politics and spheres of influence, this was acutely embarrassing. It also opened him up to Allied pressure for concessions in return. Their strategy was neatly encapsulated by the Australian premier, Billy Hughes: "Give him a League of Nations and he will give us all the rest."[50]

Wilson did not concede everything, but he had to give ground on key Allied concerns—including reparations from Germany, a fifteen-year occupation of the Rhineland and an Anglo-American guarantee of French security. The president was now tired and, for a while, stricken by the influenza now sweeping the world. He, like Lloyd George, was also conscious of the need to settle the peace and start reconstructing Germany before revolution took hold. House noted in his diary on March 22: "Bolshevism is gaining ground everywhere. Hungary has just succumbed. We are sitting upon an open powder magazine and some day a spark may ignite it."[51]

So a peace treaty was simply imposed on the Germans and its terms were a far cry from Wilson's Fourteen Points. There was an outcry in Germany. Eventually the Germans were instructed to accept within twenty-four hours or face invasion. On June 28, in the Hall of Mirrors in the Palace of Versailles, two quaking Germans signed on the dotted line in front of a thousand hostile delegates.

For the French, the moment was particularly sweet: in 1871 the victorious Bismarck had ended the Franco-Prussian war in this same Hall of Mirrors. Yet the vast gulf between Wilson's liberal agenda and this imposed peace created lasting resentment in Germany, fuelling talk of a "stab in the back" on which Hitler would later play so skillfully. Allied leaders recognized the problem: after the ceremony Lloyd George commented presciently that "we shall have to do the whole thing over again in twenty-five years at three times the cost."[52]

Moreover Wilson's failure to secure a two-thirds majority for the Treaty in the U.S. Senate meant that the United States failed to join the League of Nations—crippling the new international organization at birth. Despite being exhausted from months of transatlantic travel, the president had made a last frenzied appeal to the American people through an eight-thousand-mile speaking tour of the American heartland. This brought on a near-fatal stroke in October 1919 that left him paralyzed for the rest of his presidency. It was a sobering reminder of the dangers of personal diplomacy, and his fate haunted many of his successors. It has been said of Franklin Roosevelt, himself a wheelchair president, that "the tragedy of Wilson was always somewhere within the rim of his consciousness." And when Lyndon Johnson's presidency collapsed in 1968 over the Vietnam War, he frequently dreamed that he was lying paralyzed like Wilson in the Red Room of the White House. LBJ would awake, terrified, and stumble down the corridors to find Wilson's portrait. Touching it persuaded him that Wilson was dead and he was still moving.[53]

What of the effect on summitry itself? Paris 1919 is often seen as the first modern summit, yet that may be misleading. For the first couple of months the conference was run by the Council of Ten (the leaders and foreign ministers of America, France, Britain, Italy and Japan) together with their advisors and secretaries. On March 24, when the numbers present reached over fifty (and the leakage of news became a flood), Wilson proposed that to expedite business the leaders of the Big Four, excluding Japan, should meet alone except for an interpreter. It was not until mid-April that they added a minute taker (Maurice Hankey, the British Cabinet Secretary) to ensure some kind of record of what had been agreed.[54] Even then specialist commissions rather than the politicians often resolved the big issues. Moreover Versailles was only one of five treaties with the defeated powers, in a conference that was not concluded until January 1920—a year after it opened. In many ways Paris was a hybrid: a summit grafted uneasily onto an old-fashioned conference.

And in the 1920s there was a backlash. The "supreme disadvantage" of "democratic diplomacy," according to the disillusioned British ex-diplomat Harold Nicolson, was that national representatives were "obliged to reduce the standards of their own thoughts to the level of other people's feelings." Thus Lloyd George, "for all his essential liberalism and vision," was responsible and responsive to a Commons dominated by what Nicolson sniffily called "a *Daily Mail* type of mind."[55]

Lloyd George made several more forays into personal diplomacy (particularly when the meetings could be arranged in congenial Mediterranean resorts). His efforts were reinforced by a new prime ministerial secretariat—known as the "Garden Suburb" because it was housed in temporary buildings in the grounds of 10 Downing Street. Its members met foreign leaders and crafted policy with little reference to the Foreign Office: the foreign secretary, Lord Curzon, several times considered resigning in protest at "the Lloyd George dictatorship."[56] But after the "Welsh Wizard" lost power in October 1922, the Foreign Office regained control over the conduct and content of diplomacy. Apart from occasional flurries—such as Ramsay MacDonald's meeting with President Herbert Hoover in October 1929 in an attempt to resolve Anglo-American naval rivalry—foreign ministers, not heads of government, were generally in charge. Rather like the era after 1815, once again the world seemed safe enough to leave diplomacy to the diplomats.

The most famous and significant conference of the 1920s took place at Locarno, on Lake Maggiore in northern Italy, in October

1925. The principals were the foreign ministers of Britain, France and Germany—Austen Chamberlain, Aristide Briand and Gustav Stresemann. Their great achievements were to guarantee the Rhineland borders of France and Germany and to bring Germany into the League of Nations. The so-called spirit of Locarno became a benchmark for diplomacy.

In retrospect, however, Locarno looks more ambiguous. Stresemann had succeeded in bringing Germany in from the cold without abandoning any of its demands for lost territory in the east. These demands, particularly over Poland, were to prove the fuel for the next war.

But at the time praise was showered on Chamberlain for brokering the deal. On his return from Locarno, he received a special welcome at Victoria Station and, in further similarity to Disraeli in 1878, was immediately made a Knight of the Garter. Prime Minister Stanley Baldwin praised him for resolving an issue that had "so far defied the efforts of every statesman since the war." One of Baldwin's predecessors, Lord Arthur Balfour, said that Chamberlain's name would be "indissolubly associated" with this probable "turning point in civilisation." A few months later Chamberlain was awarded the Nobel Peace Prize.[57]

For a politician who had grown up in the shadow of his famous father, "Radical Joe," it was an intoxicating apotheosis. "I am astonished and a little frightened by the completeness of my success and by its immediate recognition everywhere," Chamberlain told his sister.[58] On October 22, 1925, he dined alone with his younger half-brother Neville, who noted in his diary that Austen

> talked almost without stopping from 8 till 11.00 on Locarno. Very naturally, perhaps, the rest of the world does not exist for him . . . Looking back he felt that no mistake had been made from beginning to end.[59]

Neville found it hard to conceal his envy at Austen's success. Nor, as we shall see, did he forget it.

ALTHOUGH PARIS IN 1919 might seem the start of modern summitry, the hybrid nature of the peace conference and the 1920s
backlash against personal diplomacy suggest that we should not
make such an unequivocal judgment. More important still, some of
what I consider to be summitry's key ingredients were not yet in
place.

The most important of these was the airplane. The Wright
Brothers made their pioneering flight in 1903, but both the first
scheduled air passenger service (in Florida) and the first regular airmail service (in German colonial Africa) date from 1914, so the airplane came of age with World War I. By the end of the conflict the
major powers had developed large fleets of fighters and bombers.

Airmen such as Giulio Douhet in Italy, Hugh Trenchard in Britain, and the American Billy Mitchell predicted that strategic bombing could prove a decisive weapon in future wars, extrapolating
from some surprise raids on London by German Gotha bombers in
1917–18 that caused panic and mob violence. These raids set a
(misleading) standard for possible casualties, and this was then mul-
tiplied astronomically by military planners in the 1930s as single-
winged planes made of steel greatly enhanced the power and range
of aircraft.

Yet the airplane was a means of communication as well as conflict. Airmail was its main stimulus, but passenger travel also developed: in 1934 nearly two billion air passenger miles were logged,
and major airlines had been established such as American and
United in the United States and the European national carriers, Air
France, Lufthansa, and Imperial Airways in Britain. Air travel entered popular mythology in May 1927 when Charles Lindbergh
became the first pilot to fly the Atlantic solo, turning him into an
international icon.[60]

Politicians also began to grasp the potential of air travel. For the
second round of German elections of March 1932—restricted by
the government to one week to minimize Nazi violence—Adolf
Hitler chartered a plane in order to speak in twenty-one cities,
even flying into Düsseldorf when a ferocious storm had grounded

all other aircraft. This unprecedented, futuristic use of air travel made an enormous psychological impression, giving another meaning to the Nazi slogan "The Führer over Germany," as the country's self-proclaimed savior literally descended from the heavens to address his people.[61]

A few months later, in July 1932, Franklin Roosevelt took his cue from Hitler after winning the Democratic presidential nomination. Instead of following tradition (candidates were supposed to sit on their front porch and await a party delegation), FDR flew straight to Chicago to address the Democratic convention. It was a brilliant gesture, demonstrating that he was not bound by his physical infirmity and dramatizing his convention pledge of "a New Deal for the American people." The next day one cartoon showed a frail farmer looking upward at a plane emblazoned with "New Deal" on its undercarriage. On the other hand, the journey from Albany, New York, to Chicago took more than nine hours, in turbulent headwinds, with two stops. Roosevelt did not fly again until his Casablanca summit with Churchill in 1943.[62]

The airplane was the essential precondition for modern summitry—in both its manifestations. As a means of communication it allowed political leaders to visit foreign counterparts in a matter of hours, not days (as in the era of railways and steamships), let alone weeks or even months (in the case of Canossa). And as a military weapon the airplane became one of the principal reasons for modern summits, because it could deliver weapons of mass destruction on the civilian population. And so in September 1938 a British prime minister took to the air to stop the threat from the air.

The talkies—films and newsreels that had emerged from the silent era—provided the other essential ingredient of summitry. In October 1927, a few months after Lindbergh had flown the Atlantic, Warner Brothers staged the New York premier of its movie *The Jazz Singer*, in which Al Jolson pronounced the immortal line "You ain't heard nothing yet" with near perfect synchronization between his lips on film and his voice recorded on a disc.[63] By the early 1930s synchronized sound became the norm in cinemas across America and Europe.

Film served as a vehicle for news as well as entertainment. The appeal of Woodrow Wilson and the impact of the Paris peace conference were in large measure due to the images spread around the world on the silent screen. And radio was already bringing politicians' words into people's homes, Franklin Roosevelt proving a master of the "fireside chat." Then in the 1930s the newsreel combined image and word. In 1934 Britain had some forty-three hundred cinemas with an average weekly audience of 18.5 million and newsreels served as trailers to the feature films.[64]

As with the airplane, the impact of newsreels was double-edged. They helped, for instance, to etch the air raid on Guernica in April 1937 into global consciousness. Gaumont, one of the major newsreel companies, took the lead with a segment on "the most terrible air raid modern history yet can boast . . . a hell that raged unchecked for five murderous hours. This was a city and these were homes, like yours." Over the next eighteen months Gaumont ran a succession of newsreel stories about mock bombing exercises and air-raid precautions in Britain, accompanied by lurid lines about planes "darkening the skies" or swarming "like armies of locusts." These films help explain the paranoia about bombing in London in 1938.[65]

From newsreels British audiences developed not only their image of the ranting Hitler, later satirized to devastating effect by Charlie Chaplin in *The Great Dictator*, but they also derived firm impressions of their own politicians. It is impossible, for instance, to appreciate the vast national appeal of Stanley Baldwin, the Conservative leader of the 1920s and 1930s, without reference to the newsreels. Like FDR, Baldwin was a superb performer—talking naturally as if addressing an individual rather than haranguing a meeting, keeping his sentences short and simple and making good use of his homely pipe. (During one early radio broadcast he had paused in midsentence to strike a match in front of the microphone.) Voters felt that, thanks to film, they knew Baldwin better than any previous premier. These lessons were not lost on Baldwin's successor as premier, Neville Chamberlain.[66]

AND SO THE STAGE WAS SET for modern summitry—made possible by air travel, made necessary by weapons of mass destruction and made into household news by the new mass media. The curtain rose dramatically on September 15, 1938.

2

MUNICH 1938

Chamberlain and Hitler

"M UNICH" IS ONE OF THE notorious clichés of modern diplomacy. From the Suez crisis of 1956 to the Iraq War of 2003 statesmen have cited the sell-out of Czechoslovakia to Hitler as a dreadful reminder of what happens if democracies fail to stand up to dictators.[1] Yet the Munich conference of September 29–30, 1938, was not an isolated event; it followed earlier meetings at Berchtesgaden in the Bavarian Alps on the 15th and Bad Godesberg on the Rhine (September 22–23). Munich was the culmination of two epic weeks during which Neville Chamberlain, in a dramatic gamble, invented modern summitry.[2] The prime minister saw a personal meeting with Hitler as the only way to save London from annihilation by weapons of mass destruction. Yet ironically peace was preserved in 1938 because Hitler, not Chamberlain, lost his nerve at the last moment under the pressures at the summit.

TO GRASP WHAT WAS AT STAKE, we need first to understand the vastly different ways that Chamberlain and Hitler viewed the problem of Czechoslovakia.

The collapse of the Austrian, German and Russian empires in 1917–18 had created a huge power vacuum in Central and Eastern Europe. Ethnic groups previously under imperial rule rushed to create their own states. In the process, they became overlords of subordinate national groups: post-1918 Poland, on territory formerly belonging to Germany and Russia, was ethnically only two-thirds Polish. In Czechoslovakia, barely half the population was Czech and nearly a quarter was German.

The growing agitation of the Sudeten Germans for full civic rights gave Hitler an excuse for intervening in Czech affairs. He started by demanding devolution for the Sudetenland, but his real goal was to bring the German-speakers into the Reich and thereby undermine the Czechoslovak state.

Czechoslovakia was allied to Germany's archenemies, France and the Soviet Union. Taking control of it would eliminate that threat. What's more, its raw materials and industrial plant would feed Germany's rapacious war economy. General Ludwig Beck, the army chief of staff, insisted that Czechoslovakia in its current, post-Versailles form was "intolerable" and that "a way must be found to eliminate it as a danger spot for Germany, if necessary through a military solution."[3]

During 1937, on Hitler's instructions, the army drew up a contingency plan—Case Green—for a possible lightning attack. But Beck, most senior officers, and even ardent Nazis such as Hermann Göring, head of the air force, wanted to squeeze the Czech state gradually out of existence. To break it up by war would plunge Germany into a premature conflict with France and Britain—soon to be joined, they assumed, by the United States. Not only were Germany's armed forces unready for such a struggle, rapid rearmament had created a serious cash-flow crisis that could only be offset by massive borrowing. To fight in 1938, the Finance Ministry warned, would destroy the Reich's credibility in the money markets and thus any chance of sustaining an eventual world war.[4]

Despite the weight of advice, however, Hitler was determined to destroy Czechoslovakia at once and by force. His desire for war was as fundamental to the ensuing crisis as Chamberlain's desire for peace. In the German part of the Hapsburg Empire, where he had grown up, hatred of the Czechs was endemic. At a deeper level, he

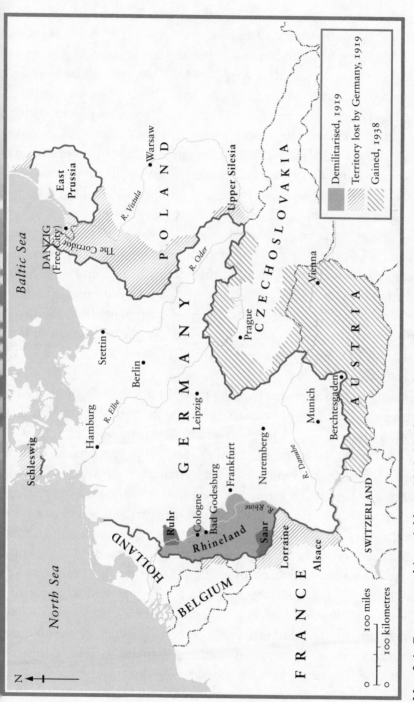

Map 2-1 Germany and its neighbors, 1919–38, showing losses after World War I and gains from Austria and Czechoslovakia in 1938.

regarded war as natural and desirable—testing and strengthening races in the international struggle for survival.

Hitler also had more immediate reasons for wanting to force the pace. Over the weekend of May 20–22, 1938, rumors of German troop movements toward Czechoslovakia and incidents between Czechs and Sudeten Germans prompted fears across Europe that war was imminent. The Czech government partially mobilized its reserves. Lord Halifax, the British foreign secretary, told Berlin that, if Germany invaded Czechoslovakia, France would be obliged by its treaty obligations to intervene and Britain "might be forced in by circumstances or by political necessity."[5]

This was hardly a categorical warning; Germany was not about to invade, but the fact that nothing happened was attributed in the international press to Hitler backing down in the face of Czech and British firmness. The Führer, always sensitive about his image, was furious. On May 30 he instructed his generals: "It is my unalterable decision to smash Czechoslovakia by military action in the near future." Case Green must be implemented by October 1 "at the latest."[6]

Domestic pressures also played a part in Hitler's decision making. In February 1938 he had replaced Constantin von Neurath, foreign minister since 1933, by Joachim von Ribbentrop, former ambassador to Britain. Ribbentrop, in earlier life a wine salesman, had been a long-standing Anglophile, with a penchant for bowler hats and umbrellas. But in London his wooden manner and aggressive Nazism turned people off. Worse still, his frequent gaffes, such as greeting the king with a Nazi salute, made him a laughing stock as "Ambassador Brickendrop." As a result Ribbentrop's Anglophilia turned into visceral hatred of Britain. Once foreign minister, he seized every opportunity to incite Hitler to war and to persuade him that the Western powers would not fight.[7]

In February 1938 Hitler had also taken advantage of scandals in the officer corps to assume supreme command of all the armed forces. The former corporal was determined to impose his will on the generals; Czechoslovakia would be the first real test.[8] Over the course of the summer of 1938 Hitler drove toward war despite

Beck's objections, finally forcing the chief of staff to resign in mid-August. Hitler also intervened repeatedly, almost gratuitously, in the detailed war planning for Case Green; this obliged the irritated generals to shift from a frontal attack on the Czechs' well-defended western border to a pincer attack from north and south. Hitler was genuinely obsessed with the risk of the German army "bleeding to death," as it had against the French at Verdun in 1916, but these displays of amateur generalship were also part of his battle for supremacy over the armed forces.[9]

By the summer of 1938 Hitler was convinced that the Czech problem had to be resolved by war: this had become for him a test of personality. At the same time, across the North Sea, a mirror-image situation was developing: for Chamberlain the search for peace had become almost an ego trip.

In London, like Berlin, there was intense anxiety about the Czechoslovak question. Few policymakers opposed some kind of autonomy for the Sudeten Gemans in the face of Czech discrimination. This reflected a general British conviction that the European order legitimized by the Treaty of Versailles was no longer tenable. Germany could not indefinitely be denied its rights as a major European power or rebuffed in its claims to bring ethnic Germans into the homeland—hence the lack of British protests when Germany reoccupied the Rhineland in April 1936 and united peacefully with Austria in March 1938. British conservatives also disliked Czechoslovakia's alliance with the Soviet Union. Less than two decades after the Bolshevik Revolution, communism seemed to many on the right a greater threat than Nazism.

But liberals and the left read the bigger issues very differently. Across a continent where dictatorships were on the rise, Czechoslovakia stood out as one of the last functioning democracies. And the rapid buildup of German airpower posed a direct and novel threat to Britain, whose navy was no longer a sufficient defense—as it had been in the days of Philip II's Spain, Napoleonic France or the Kaiser's Germany. Prodded by parliamentary critics such as Winston Churchill, from 1934 the national government embarked on a major program of air rearmament. The issue of Czechoslovakia therefore became part of a larger debate about the security and stability of Europe as a whole. Was Hitler simply trying to right the wrongs of Versailles? Or was he another Napoleon in the making, who should be nipped in the bud? On these questions, British opinion was divided.

Unlike the French government, Britain had no formal obligations to Czechoslovakia. A cardinal axiom of British foreign policy was not to get entangled in France's alliance system in Eastern Europe, designed to threaten a resurgent Germany with war on two fronts. However, the French coalition government led by Édouard Daladier was itself bitterly split over Czechoslovakia, with one group willing to honor France's obligations, another favoring peace at almost any price, and Daladier shifting uneasily between them. At root, a weakened and divided France would not go to war without Britain: for much of the Czech crisis, Paris therefore followed London—its "English governess," in the words of one historian.[10]

And London, in essence, meant Neville Chamberlain, aged sixty-eight, who had succeeded Stanley Baldwin as prime minister in May 1937. Although he came from one of the great political families of the day, his was an unlikely progress. His father, Joseph, was the titan of late-Victorian liberal politics, but never made it to the premiership. His half-brother, Austen, six years older, was groomed to take up the torch: he read history at Cambridge, went straight into politics and was chancellor of the exchequer at forty.

Neville, in contrast, studied metallurgy at home in Birmingham as prelude to a career in business and civic politics. His belated entry into national politics as wartime director of National Service was a disaster, though largely for reasons beyond his control. But in 1924–9, his energy, industry and reforming zeal were employed to the full as minister of health. And in the 1930s, as Austen's career fizzled out, Neville ascended first to the chancellorship and then the premiership.

Nearly six years at the Treasury had confirmed Chamberlain's reputation as an energetic and capable administrator. Although primarily concerned with Britain's economic recovery from the Slump, he had been an early supporter of air rearmament. He was also an accomplished performer on the newsreels, addressing the camera in a formal but conversational manner that commanded attention. Chamberlain entered 10 Downing Street determined to reshape British foreign policy in order to confront the mounting threats to European peace. In January 1938 he managed to move Sir Robert Vansittart, the fiercely anti-Hitler permanent undersecretary at the Foreign Office, into a high-sounding but innocuous post as the government's chief diplomatic advisor. Chamberlain replaced him with the more pliant Sir Alexander Cadogan.

The following month, Chamberlain's highly strung foreign secretary, Anthony Eden, resigned in irritation at the prime minister's personal diplomacy. His successor was Lord Halifax, a tall, lugubrious Tory peer, whose basic instinct—whether as Viceroy of India dealing with Gandhi or as foreign secretary facing the dictators—was to seek a peaceful compromise. Chamberlain would later discover that Halifax had a will of his own, but initially they formed an effective team. "I give thanks for a steady unruffled Foreign Secretary who never causes me any worry," the prime minister wrote privately that spring.[11]

After securing a rapprochement with Italy in April 1938, Chamberlain hoped to move on to an agreement with Germany, trading territorial concessions in Europe and colonial Africa for firm restrictions on the growth of German military power. This was all part of what he and his colleagues called the "appeasement" or pacification of Europe. And after the war scare of May 1938, it was clear that the Sudeten problem had to be resolved before further progress could be made. Accordingly the British government emerged from France's shadow as would-be mediator.

In early August a British mission, headed by the industrialist and former government minister Lord Runciman, arrived in Prague in an effort to bring the two sides together and hammer out agreement on some form of autonomy for the Sudetendeutsch. But there was also debate in Whitehall about whether to reiterate, more firmly than in May, that Britain was unlikely to stand aside if France went to war, in the hope that Hitler would again back off. Some diplomats and politicians believed that, if an unequivocal statement of this sort had been issued by the British government in the July crisis of 1914, Germany might not have continued down the road to war.

Opponents of Hitler in Berlin shared this belief. And one striking feature of the Czech crisis was the extent to which British leaders were well informed about the basics of Hitler's policy thanks to members of the secret German opposition. In the middle of August, Ewald von Kleist-Schmenzin, a Prussian conservative acting as informal emissary of Beck and other army moderates, visited London and talked with both Vansittart and Churchill. He insisted that war was now "a complete certainty," with the date set for the end of September, but added that "there was nobody in Germany who wanted war except H[itler] who regarded the events of May 21 as a personal rebuff whose recurrence he must avoid and whose memory he must obliterate." Von Kleist explained that because Ribbentrop had persuaded Hitler that London and Paris would do nothing, the Führer would only be stopped by a categorical warning that Britain would not stand aside. This would also strengthen those elements in Germany who were "sick of the present regime" and ready to overthrow it.[12]

Chamberlain and Halifax received accounts of these conversations but the prime minister felt that, because von Kleist was "violently anti-Hitler'" and keen "to stir up his friends in Germany" to overthrow the Nazi regime, "we must discount a good deal of what he says."[13] Other informed sources suggested that Hitler had not yet made up his mind for war, particularly Sir Nevile Henderson, the British ambassador in Berlin, who was in touch with Göring. The air minister, a wartime flying ace but now a bloated sybarite, was among those who wanted to avoid a conflict with Britain, at least until Germany was really ready. Anxious to concentrate for the moment on economically beneficial expansion in Eastern Europe, he did his best to counter Ribbentrop's war-mongering, feeding British contacts soothing words about Hitler in the hope of avoiding a confrontation.

At a specially convened meeting of Cabinet ministers on August 30, Halifax and Chamberlain reviewed the conflicting intelligence.

They concluded that the German leader, while determined to re-solve the Sudeten question in 1938, had not as yet made up his mind to do so by force. For Britain to threaten war, said Halifax, would probably divide opinion at home and across the empire (on which Britain relied for much of its military manpower). And if it failed as a deterrent there was nothing Britain and France could do to stop Hitler overrunning Czechoslovakia.[14]

In his own remarks Chamberlain laid bare two precepts of his diplomacy. First, he said that no democratic state "ought to make a threat of war unless it was both ready to carry it out and prepared to do so." He had been "fortified" in this belief over the summer when reading *The Foreign Policy of Canning* by Professor Harold Temperley. "Again and again," noted Chamberlain in a letter a few days later, Britain's foreign secretary in the 1820s had laid down "that you should never menace unless you are in a position to carry out your threats." Second, Chamberlain told the Cabinet that, al-though a firm warning might work with some statesmen, "Herr Hitler was withdrawn from his Ministers and lived in a state of ex-altation." Writing to his sisters, he was more candid: "Is it not posi-tively horrible to think that the fate of hundreds of millions de-pends on the man and he is half mad."[15]

When Chamberlain and his colleagues talked of the dangers of war, they did not simply mean a conflict in Central Europe or even a German attack on France. They believed that Hitler's Luftwaffe could and would mount an immediate and massive attack on the London area. Not only was this home to a fifth of the population, it was also the center of government and finance, a major port and the hub of the rail network. Moreover for most of the 1930s it was assumed that, in Baldwin's words, "the bomber will always get through."

The fear of "a knockout blow" from the air haunted the popular imagination, featured in books and films, and was also ingrained in official thinking. The military Joint Planning Committee had esti-mated in October 1936 that there would be 150,000 casualties within the first week. (This was more than Britain's total from all forms of bombing during the whole of the Second World War.) In retrospect it is clear that official estimates were wrong at almost every point about the Luftwaffe—exaggerating the number of planes, the size of their bomb loads and the likely casualties per ton of bombs. In 1938 Nazi bombers lacked sufficient range to reach London from Germany: this only became possible in 1940 when Hitler controlled the coasts of Belgium and France. Here was a massive intelligence failure about weapons of mass destruction. It skewed defense policy toward airpower and diplomacy toward isolationism.[16]

Critics of appeasement also overestimated the threat from the air. In 1934 Winston Churchill talked of 30,000 to 40,000 casualties in the first ten days; by 1936 he was even implying 150,000 after the first all-out attack.[17] Such alarmism encouraged the government to concentrate on home defense rather than committing aircraft and troops to France. By September 1938 Churchill was urging the government to take a firm line with Germany and call Hitler's bluff. But he was out of office. It was Chamberlain who would bear the moral and political responsibility if he read Hitler wrongly and London was devastated. This weighed heavily on the prime minister's conscience and on his policy.

On August 30 the Cabinet followed the lead set by Chamberlain and Halifax and agreed to avoid a formal warning. Instead the British would "try to keep Germany guessing" about their intentions.[18] Nevertheless several junior members of the Cabinet expressed unease, favoring some other display of firmness such as accelerating the planned naval maneuvers. This policy was urged most vocally by Duff Cooper, the fiery first lord of the admiralty. He and four other dissentients emphasized "the importance of Czechoslovakia in the general picture." If it crumbled, then other countries in Eastern Europe would fall into the German orbit. And, in any case, they argued, France was likely to go to war if Czechoslovakia were invaded, making this a general European war from which Britain could not stand aside. Chamberlain and Halifax, in contrast, carefully framed the issue very narrowly as to whether British opinion would be willing to fight in defense of Czechoslovakia.[19]

Cooper began leaking accounts of Cabinet discussions to parliamentary critics such as Churchill. So in early September Chamber-ain shifted policy discussions to an inner group of four: himself, Halifax, Sir John Simon and Sir Samuel Hoare. As chancellor and home secretary, Simon and Hoare held the other two principal offices of state, and each had been foreign secretary earlier in the 1930s. Chamberlain valued their loyalty and Simon, in particular, was a notorious placeman: Lloyd George said he had "sat on the fence so long that the iron has entered into his soul."[20]

Yet Chamberlain's closest counselor on foreign affairs was not a diplomat or a politician but the government's chief industrial advisor, Sir Horace Wilson. A career bureaucrat, Wilson had made his name as a statistical wizard and then as an effective labor negotiator. He looked, according to the *Daily Herald*, "rather like an ageing and unsuccessful clerk whose firm expects to be bankrupted next week." But Chamberlain had come to rely on Wilson while at the Treasury and, once prime minister, gave him an office next to his own, consulting him on all aspects of policy, including foreign affairs. "Sir Horace Wilson is *big*," noted the *Herald* sagely. "But not popular."[21]

And so, with the crisis mounting, the prime minister shifted decision making into channels that he felt confident he could control. Yet even this inner circle was not rock solid. Halifax was being deluged by eloquent notes from Vansittart, who argued that "if a firm declaration on our part is now accompanied by a very good offer of home rule [for the Sudeten Germans] . . . German opposition will then become too strong for Hitler to disregard." Vansittart also observed tartly that Britain had succeeded in keeping Germany guessing in the July crisis of 1914, but "they ended up by guessing wrong, and war followed."[22]

By September 4 Vansittart's advocacy had unsettled Halifax, who prepared a warning for Ambassador Henderson to deliver to Hitler stating that if France honored its obligations to Czechoslovakia, Britain would enter the war. But Chamberlain and other senior ministers held the line, strengthened by florid warnings from Henderson: "The form of Hitler's genius is on the borderline of madness . . . A second 21st May will push him over the edge." With Hitler about to address the party faithful, they did not want to "run the risk of provoking him to something wilder than he might otherwise say."[23]

In his speech at the Nuremberg rally on September 12, Hitler declared that "the misery of the Sudeten Germans defies description" and that the situation had become "unbearable."[24] But, still two weeks before his military deadline, he did not take the final step. "Sound and fury but no bridge broken," noted Hoare,[25] but the relief in London was short-lived. Hitler's speech sparked new rioting among the Sudeten Germans. On September 13 the Prague government imposed martial law, whereupon Konrad Henlein, the Sudeten leader, broke off negotiations and fled to Germany. The French, fearful that war was imminent, seemed to have lost their nerve: Daladier proposed that he and Chamberlain should meet with Hitler to resolve the crisis peacefully. This proposal did not appeal to Chamberlain. Late that evening the prime minister decided to implement "Plan Z." He would go to see Hitler alone.

THE IDEA HAD FIRST been discussed at the end of August among Chamberlain and his inner circle. Its exact origin is unclear but prominent British politicians such as Lloyd George and Halifax had already met the Führer. In late August Halifax was toying with sending "some eminent person" to see Hitler "in order to facilitate the acceptance of a reasonable solution on the German side." Runciman's name was suggested but he had declined.[26]

So Plan Z was not entirely novel but in Chamberlain's words "it rather took Halifax's breath away" when he first broached the idea.[27] One reason was the prime minister's insistence on flying. The plan would be put into operation only at the last minute if it seemed Germany was about to invade Czechoslovakia. In such circumstances, he could not afford to waste several days traveling by boat and train, like Disraeli in 1878. Chamberlain wanted a dramatic gesture to stop Hitler in his tracks and seize the initiative. As he told his sisters, a visit by the Führer to London "would not have suited me, for it would have deprived my coup of much of its dramatic force." And he thought it "might be agreeable to his [Hitler's vanity that the British Prime Minister should take so unprece-dented a step."28

Chamberlain also believed it vital that the two of them meet in person: "you could say more to a man face to face than you could in a letter." And he was sure that "doubts about the British attitude would be better removed by discussion than by any other means." After all, Hitler was clearly not normal. Chamberlain's fear that he might be dealing with some kind of "lunatic" underpinned his wish to meet the reclusive dictator. Not only would he be able to form his own judgment of Hitler's sanity, he might also penetrate the wall of malevolent advisors, notably Ribbentrop, and divert the German leader from some crazy act.29

Chamberlain also had an eye on the impact at home. In June 1938 Sir Joseph Ball, director of the Conservative Research De-partment, had warned that if the present political mood in the country continued "there would probably be a landslide against the Government" in the next election, which he assumed would take place in the autumn of 1939.30 Chamberlain surely saw the poten-tial impact of a personal diplomatic triumph on his government's popularity.

Diplomacy and politics aside, however, it is clear that peacemak-ing had become a personal mission about which Chamberlain de-veloped quite hubristic aspirations. In October 1937 he wrote pri-vately of "the far-reaching plans which I have in mind for the appeasement of Europe & Asia and for the ultimate check to the mad armaments race." As chancellor, he told his sisters, "I could hardly have moved a pebble: now I have only to raise a finger & the whole face of Europe is changed." Acknowledging the publication of H.A.L. Fisher's new *History of Europe* in March 1938, he replied: "At the present moment I am too busy trying to make the history of Europe to read about it."31

Chamberlain even entertained hopes of resolving a problem that had vexed British politics for centuries, telling his sisters: "It *would* be another strange chapter in our family history if it fell to me to settle the Irish question' after the long repeated efforts made by Fa-ther and Austen."32 This revealing remark takes us into the deepest recesses of Chamberlain's character. To the outside world, the Chamberlains were united by powerful clan loyalty, yet Neville, the late developer, was always measuring himself against his father and brother. When he had introduced the epoch-making bill for a system of Imperial Preference in February 1932, he presented it explicitly as "setting the seal" on the project of tariff reform that his father had started twenty-nine years before but had left unfinished.[33]

After the flight to Berchtesgaden, Neville's sister Hilda wrote to express "an immense pride" for his brilliant coup. She was convinced that "our father was the only other man whom I could imagine either conceiving it or carrying it out!" Hilda was "quite right," Neville replied. "It was an idea after Father's own heart."[34] Surely he cannot have forgotten that long evening back in 1925 sitting through Austen's self-congratulatory monologue after Locarno?[35] As the marginal man in this fiercely proud family, Neville would have been less than human if he did not sense a chance to outdo his father and his brother in the battle for reputation.

The prime minister was careful to keep Plan Z under wraps. His initial intention was not to inform even the Germans of his visit until he was in the air, but Henderson warned that, if Hitler did not want to meet Chamberlain or felt his hand was being forced, he could easily say he had a cold, thereby administering a humiliating rebuff. Heeding this advice, Chamberlain asked Hitler in advance but not his own Cabinet.[36] In early September a few trusted ministers had been brought into the secret, but under strict instruction not to mention it "either in or out of the Cabinet." Chamberlain had already been told by a furious Vansittart that "it was like [the Emperor] Henry IV going to Canossa [all] over again" to grovel before the pope.[37]

On September 13, just before sending Chamberlain's message to Hitler, Horace Wilson had an attack of constitutional cold feet. "Do you think it would be wise to summon Cabinet before doing this?" he asked Simon in a hastily scribbled note. "I do *not* think it is necessary," the chancellor replied. "Cabinet will back P.M. S.H[oare] agrees."[38] Chamberlain did not inform his Cabinet until 11 a.m. on September 14, when awaiting Hitler's reply. "Approval was unanimous and enthusiastic," according to Duff Cooper.[39] Even Chamberlain's critics were, like Halifax, taken aback by the prime minister's audacity.

Chamberlain's message was delivered by Henderson to the German Foreign Ministry very late on September 13. It read as follows:

> In view of the increasingly critical situation I propose to come over at once to see you with a view to trying to find a peaceful solution. I propose to come across by air and am ready to start tomorrow. Please indicate earliest time at which you can see me and suggest place of meeting. I should be grateful for very early reply.[40]

Hitler was at the Obersalzberg, Ribbentrop in Munich, a hundred miles away, and neither was an early riser. At 9:30 a.m. on September 14 Ernst von Weizsäcker, the state secretary or senior diplomat at the Foreign Ministry, phoned the message to Ribbentrop. At 12:15 an agitated Henderson phoned the Foreign Ministry for news, to be told that Ribbentrop was driving down to see Hitler in person. It was not until 2:40 in the afternoon that Ribbentrop called von Weizsäcker to say that Hitler "would naturally be pleased to receive Chamberlain."

There had been some debate about whether the Führer should offer to visit London or to meet on his yacht in the North Sea but both ideas were dropped. Chamberlain was therefore invited to Berchtesgaden on the 15th (with his wife if he wished); Henderson should go there independently from Berlin.[41]

What was Hitler's reaction when Ribbentrop drove up the mountain on the morning of September 14 with the astonishing message that Chamberlain wanted to pay a visit?[42] Two weeks before the Führer had said privately that he did not expect British military intervention in the crisis, adding that if this did occur he was confident of Germany's superiority. He felt Britain was bluffing, playing for time, and declared that he would refuse a visit from any British minister.[43]

But Chamberlain was not "any" British minister. Hitler later admitted to the Polish ambassador in Berlin that he had been somewhat taken aback by Chamberlain's gambit. He said it was of course impossible for him to refuse to meet the British prime minister, but he had thought "Chamberlain was coming to make a solemn declaration that Great Britain was ready to march."[44]

There was similar uncertainty among senior German policymakers. On September 14, reflecting on "the great sensation" of Chamberlain's proposal, the propaganda minister Josef Goebbels reckoned that "the crafty English" were trying to protect themselves with "a moralistic alibi," seeking to pin the guilt on Germany if it came to war. On the Foreign Ministry's hastily arranged special train from Berlin to Munich, von Weizsäcker's mood was somber. "Tomorrow at Berchtesgaden it will be a matter of war or peace."[45]

At 9 p.m. on the evening of September 14, the London press was summoned to a special briefing at Number 10, carefully timed to ensure coverage on the evening radio news and in next morning's papers. Excited newspapermen dashed out of Downing Street, filling every available phone box as they communicated the news to their editors, while crowds pressed against the glass, desperate to hear. "There is still hope," said a woman standing at the foot of the Cenotaph, London's memorial to the dead of 1914–18.[46]

The veteran journalist Beverley Baxter wrote of how reports of Chamberlain's démarche had suddenly dispelled the clouds of apparently inevitable war. "I have spent nearly all my life in the midst of the thrill and stress of journalism, but I can never remember receiving any news so overpoweringly dramatic, so electric and so moving."[47] Theo Kordt, the German chargé d'affaires in London, was similarly impressed, telling Berlin: "Never have I witnessed such a sudden change of atmosphere . . . It is no exaggeration when the newspapers report that men and women wept for joy in the streets."[48]

Across the Atlantic, the New York Times called it a "breathtaking decision . . . no Prime Minister has ever made a gesture so unconventional, so bold and in a way so humble." Not so much humble but humiliating in the view of the Italian dictator, Benito Mussolini. "There will be no war," he exclaimed. "But this is the liquidation of English prestige . . . England has hit the canvas."[49]

Figure 2-1 The news that Chamberlain would fly to meet Hitler seemed like a revolution in diplomacy. (*Daily Express,* September 16, 1938, Express Newspapers)

Next morning the visit was the main story in the British press. Its impact was heightened by reports—often also on the front page—that Beck had resigned because the German army was not ready for general war, and by reminders of Disraeli's journey to Berlin in 1878. Almost all the editorial comment was favorable. "This dramatic event, without precedent in history, transforms the whole international situation," trumpeted the Tory *Daily Mail.* "This momentous step is being taken on the initiative of Mr. Chamberlain itself. It is the outstanding example in his great career of his wisdom, his vision, and his straightforward methods."[50]

Even the *News Chronicle*—a Liberal paper generally critical of government policy and uncertain whether the meeting would "save peace" or "betray democracy"—acknowledged in its front page editorial that "Britain's Prime Minister wins credit today for one of the boldest and most dramatic strokes in modern diplomatic history. In whatever guise, the name of Neville Chamberlain is now assured of a place in history."[51]

The turnaround in national mood over the night of September 14–15 set the British public on an emotional rollercoaster that helps explain why the next two weeks etched themselves so deeply into popular memory. Chamberlain left Number 10 early on Thursday, September 15, making time for photographs on the steps. "The Prime Minister was dressed exactly as for his morning stroll in the park," noted an *Evening Standard* reporter, "and he carried a rolled umbrella."[52]

The umbrella, taken as emblematic of Chamberlain's caution, was noted the world over and later became something of a joke, but the *Star* reminded its readers that "it was an old Chamberlain trick to make your turn effective with some good 'props.'" Neville's father, Joe, sported an orchid and eyeglass to impress himself on Victorian politics. Like Churchill with his cigar and Clement Attlee with his pipe, Chamberlain had his own trademark and it suited his image. The *Star* predicted that the umbrella, "stiff, straight, rigid, and tightly rolled up, rather like its owner, may take its place in history."[53]

From Downing Street Chamberlain was driven to Heston airfield, in West London. He posed for more photos on the steps of his plane—a specially chartered British Airways Lockheed Electra—and made a brief statement for the newsreels, which further raised expectations: "My policy has always been to try to ensure peace, and the Führer's ready acceptance of my suggestion encourages me to hope that my visit to him will not be without results."[54]

Traveling with the prime minister were Horace Wilson and William Strang, head of the Foreign Office's Central Department (which dealt with Germany and France). A second plane carried two female secretaries and Chamberlain's two detectives. Although Strang was one of the FO's rising stars, like the others he did not speak German.[55] Chamberlain was relying on the German Foreign Ministry to provide a translator and record taker; this was to cause problems later. But the simplicity of the visit, especially compared with later summits, underlines what Chamberlain had in mind—a personal encounter between two leaders to build a personal relationship.

Most newspapers stated that Chamberlain had never flown before. This was not literally true: he had once taken a spin around Birmingham airfield on a brief demonstration flight[56] but that was a far cry from a four-hour journey over the Channel and down the length of Germany. The little plane took off at 8:35, as he recalled a few days later:

> I must confess to some slight sinkings when I found myself flying over London and looking down thousands of feet at the houses below, but that soon wore off and I enjoyed the marvellous spectacle of ranges of glittering white cumulus clouds stretching away to the horizon below me. As we neared Munich we entered a storm and for a time flew blind through the clouds which the aeroplane rocked and bumped like a ship in the sea. Then the steward came to say that we were going down & I had some more nervous moments while we came down over the aerodrome. But I was reassured when I saw a pilot plane showing us the way and in a minute or two we taxied to the main buildings . . .[57]

This extract comes from one of Chamberlain's weekly letters to his spinster sisters, in which he always presented himself in the best light, so we may assume that his emotions were even more intense in reality.

There were also regular progress reports for the anxious Mrs. Chamberlain:[58]

- 'Machine passed over Dunkirk 9.20.'
- '10.35. 38km past Köln. Going well. Weather clear.'
- '11.15 Frankfurt. Going well.'

At noon, dressed in black, Anne Chamberlain walked alone down Whitehall to Westminster Abbey to attend a special service of prayers for peace. Recognized only by the vergers, she sat with other worshippers around the Tomb of the Unknown Warrior, with its wreath of Flanders poppies. She went again in the evening, after her husband had met Hitler—one of nearly four thousand people who visited the Abbey that day.[59]

The stress was intense, but all observers agreed that when the prime minister landed at Munich aerodrome at 1:35, he looked remarkably fresh and unperturbed. Ambassador Henderson, part of the reception party, commented on his appearance, and Chamberlain simply replied, "I'm tough and wiry." He was equally understated when Ribbentrop offered a formal welcome:

"I greet you in the name of the Führer and in the name of my country."

"I thank you."

"Ach! Did you have a good trip?"

"Yes, thank you. It was quite all right."

The *Daily Express* correspondent, Selkirk Panton, was struck by the relatively informal and "un-German" nature of the reception, with few uniforms, no bands and little heel-clicking—probably due to the hastiness of the arrangements. There were some Nazi salutes and shouts of "Heil," to which Chamberlain raised his gray homburg hat in what Panton called "a democratic salute."[60]

The group took a special train from Munich to Berchtesgaden, arriving there shortly after 4 p.m. There was another welcome party, more "Heils" from the crowd (mostly in Bavarian dress), and more hat-raising in response. Then a short drive to the town's Grand Hotel, from which holidaymakers had been abruptly evicted to provide twenty-four rooms for the British guests and German ministers, including Ribbentrop.

Chamberlain was given the Royal Suite, usually reserved for the wife of the ex-Kaiser, which had a bedroom, sitting room and breakfast room. But he made little use of the facilities, beyond freshening up and swapping his gray hat for a black one. Wilson just had time to phone 10 Downing Street and give messages to Chamberlain's secretary using the direct line that had been kept open for the British party.

Half an hour later, the prime minister, Ribbentrop and their two staffs swept off in a fleet of cars to Hitler's retreat on the Obersalzberg, high above the town. As the *New York Times* put it, Mahomet was going to the mountain.[61]

HITLER HAD FALLEN IN LOVE with the Bavarian Alps back in the winter of 1922–3. Their soaring peaks and sheltered valleys on the German-Austrian border became his favorite holiday destination. He stayed regularly at a hotel on the Obersalzberg, dictating some of *Mein Kampf* there, and in 1928 took out a lease on a nearby house. After he became chancellor, this was converted into the grandiose Berghof, around which leading Nazis such as Göring built their own residences. By the mid-1930s the Obersalzberg had become the regime's second headquarters.[62]

The drive up from Berchtesgaden took about fifteen minutes. This might have given Chamberlain a few moments to catch his breath and relax but probably, like most summiteers, he was too fired up with excitement. At 4:55 p.m. the car drew up outside the Berghof. Although he did not commit Halifax's faux pas a year before of initially mistaking Hitler for a footman, ready to receive his hat and coat,[63] Chamberlain, like Halifax, was not impressed. He told his sisters that Hitler looked "entirely undistinguished. You would never notice him in a crowd, and would take him for the house painter he once was." To the Cabinet Chamberlain was more candid: "the commonest little dog I have ever seen."[64]

After some words of welcome, translated by the Foreign Ministry's premier interpreter, Dr. Paul Schmidt, the two men walked up the steps to the house and into its conference hall decorated with paintings, tapestries, fine furniture and many nude sculptures (Chamberlain noted censoriously). Its most celebrated feature was a huge picture window in place of one wall. On a good day the view toward Salzburg was superb but it rained throughout Chamberlain's visit and only the valley bottoms were visible.

Over tea Chamberlain tried to break the ice only to find, like many others, that Hitler was not one for small talk.

"I have often heard of this room, but it's much larger than I expected."

"It is you who have the big rooms in England."

"You must come and see them sometime."

"I should be received with demonstrations of disapproval."

"Well, perhaps it would be wise to choose the moment."

At this Hitler managed the shadow of a smile. After more desultory conversation he abruptly asked how Chamberlain would like to proceed. Should two or three others from each side be present? The prime minister said he wished to talk one to one. This ploy had been agreed in advance to exclude the baleful Ribbentrop and was a major reason why Halifax, his opposite number, was not in the British party. So, accompanied only by Schmidt, at 5:20 the two leaders went upstairs to Hitler's sitting room. To Chamberlain's surprise they were there for the next three hours.[65]

After mutual expressions of desire for improved Anglo-German relations, Chamberlain started to lay his cards on the table.[66] He suggested they devote the rest of the afternoon to "a clarification of each other's point of view so that each might know exactly what the other had in his mind." Then they could consider Czechoslovakia next day. Chamberlain wanted to move gradually from the general to the particular, sensing out his opponent before they got into the hard stuff. This fitted his overall strategy, which was to tie a settlement of the Sudeten problem into a general easing of European tensions.

But Hitler quickly knocked Chamberlain off course, insisting that Czechoslovakia was "very urgent and could not wait" because that day three hundred Sudeten Germans had been killed and many more injured. Such a situation demanded an instant solution. The claim of three hundred dead was totally untrue and probably a deliberate lie, but it allowed Hitler to take the initiative. "All right," said Chamberlain. "Go ahead."[67]

The diatribe that followed was rambling and at times very excited—Hitler rarely moved in straight, smooth lines. But the gist of what he wanted to convey was clear. He insisted that he was not a dictator because his position was based on the confidence of the nation which, in turn, rested on promises he had given. These included liberating his country from the fetters of Versailles and bringing Germans in neighboring territories into the Reich. This had already been done in the case of seven million in Austria; all that now remained were the three million Germans in Czechoslovakia. The Führer was at pains to say that Germans farther afield were a different case—he could distinguish between "the possible and the impossible."

Thus far Chamberlain had let Hitler talk and Schmidt translate, but now he pushed at a critical point. "Hold on a moment," he interjected. "You said that the three million Sudeten Germans must be included in the Reich; would you be satisfied with that and is there nothing more that you want? I ask because there are many people who think that is not all; that you wish to dismember Czechoslovakia."

Hitler replied that if the demands of the Sudeten Germans were met, the Polish, Hungarian and Ukrainian minorities would also secede,[68] implying that Czechoslovakia would fall apart of its own accord. But he insisted that all he was interested in were Sudeten Germans: he spoke of this issue as "the spearhead" in his side and moved on to the emotional high point of the meeting:

> I want to get down to realities. Three hundred Sudetens have been killed and things of that kind cannot go on; the thing has got to be settled at once: I am determined to settle it: I do not care whether there is a world war or not.[69]

Chamberlain was again taken aback. But he seized on Hitler's statement about bringing a final three million Germans into the Reich. This, he said, meant that "thereafter no territorial demands could exist any longer in other regions, which might give rise to conflicts between Germany and other countries." He also said dryly to Hitler that it ought to be possible for the two of them "to prevent a world war on account of these 3 million Sudeten Germans."[70]

The prime minister then proposed they address a joint appeal to both parties in Czechoslovakia to refrain from violence, thereby creating the atmosphere for constructive discussions. But Hitler angrily brought up the three hundred dead again, demanding that the problem be settled immediately. Whereupon Chamberlain, losing his own cool for the first time, said he was wondering why Hitler had let him come to Germany if the Führer's mind was set so firmly. "I have wasted my time."[71]

For a moment Hitler backed off, saying that today or tomorrow they should consider whether a peaceful settlement was still possible. But when Chamberlain pressed yet again about an armistice, Hitler asked bluntly whether Britain would agree to the secession to the Reich of the regions inhabited by the Sudeten Germans. This, he asserted, was in line with the right of self-determination embodied in the Treaty of Versailles.

Officially the Runciman mission was still exploring the idea of autonomy for the Sudeten Germans within the Czech state, so Hitler's demand moved the goalposts dramatically. Tactically it would have been shrewd for Chamberlain to say that this proposal created a new situation, which he would have to discuss with his Cabinet. But he had no problem with the idea in principle,[72] and was ready to concede the point without haggling because he feared that war was imminent over an issue in which Britain had no serious interest.

The prime minister therefore told Hitler he personally accepted the idea of a transfer of population and territory; however, he would have to consult his colleagues and the French and examine the practicalities of what would be a complicated business. In the meantime he asked Hitler to do his best to prevent the situation from deteriorating further.

The Führer spoke about Germany's great military machine, warning that once set in motion it could not be stopped (echoes again of the July crisis in 1914). But eventually they agreed, in Chamberlain's words, that "I would do my best to influence the Czech Government, if the Führer would do his best to keep his people quiet."[73]

They then concocted a brief press communiqué stating that there had been "a comprehensive and frank exchange of views about the present situation," and that Chamberlain would return to Britain next day to confer with his Cabinet. "In the course of a few days a further conversation will take place."[74]

Going downstairs Hitler was much friendlier than when they went up, proposing a further visit to see the scenery "when all this is over."[75] Collecting the rest of the British party—who were sitting in embarrassed silence, having long since run out of chit-chat—Chamberlain left at 8:15 to spend the night at the Grand Hotel before flying home. He would never see the Berghof again.

IT HAD ALL TURNED OUT very differently from British expectations. The press had assumed a visit of three or four days; Cabinet colleagues and even Chamberlain's wife read with "complete surprise" in next morning's papers that he was on his way home.[76]

Chamberlain himself had planned a general conversation that afternoon, and serious talks about Czechoslovakia next day. Instead he had virtually conceded the secession of the Sudetenland in a couple of hours. Little wonder that Hitler clapped his hands in satisfaction afterward. Even the loyal Horace Wilson confessed it was "something of a shock" to learn over dinner that "there were to be no more talks there and then."[77]

Yet Chamberlain had not been a complete pushover. Schmidt the interpreter was favorably impressed with the British prime minister. Like Chamberlain's brother Austen—for whom Schmidt had translated at Locarno in 1925—his face gave little away. But "Neville Chamberlain had nothing of his brother's aloof frigidity. On the contrary, he dealt in lively manner with individual points brought up by Hitler," looking his protagonist full in the face. Moreover Schmidt noted in surprise, when Hitler moved to his calculated climax about being ready to risk world war, Chamberlain's testy "Why did you let me come?" actually made him back off.[78]

Given Hitler's professed determination to settle the Sudeten question by force by the end of September, his half-promises to Chamberlain about restraint and delay represented at least a shift of mood. In that sense, Chamberlain had gained the breathing space he wanted.

Nevertheless Hitler's demands had dramatically escalated from autonomy for the Sudeten Germans to a transfer of territory. The prime minister could not be sure how his colleagues would respond. To strengthen his case, he described the meeting in the starkest terms to his inner circle on the evening of September 16 and to the full Cabinet before and after lunch the following day.

On arrival at Berchtesgaden, he said, it became clear that the situation was "one of desperate urgency. If he had not gone he thought that hostilities would have started by now. The atmosphere had been electric." And he presented his threat to go home as "perhaps the turning point of the conversation," after which "Herr Hitler became quieter in his manner" and a more rational discussion ensued. With senior colleagues backing up the prime minister, the discussion turned to the practicalities of staging a plebiscite and winning over the Czech government.[79]

Duff Cooper did express the fear that "even if a solution of the present problem was found, it would not be the end of our troubles, and that there was no chance of peace in Europe so long as there was a Nazi regime in Germany." But there were few other notes of dissent, and Cooper himself had no alternative to suggest at this stage, admitting that "war in modern conditions was a terrible affair."

Nevertheless he had put his finger on the crucial issue. Was the Sudeten question "the end" of what Hitler was aiming at, or "only a beginning"? The prime minister said this was "a matter on which one could only exercise one's judgment": his own view was that Hitler was telling the truth. He said he had seen "no signs of insanity but many of excitement." Occasionally Hitler "would lose the thread of what he was saying and go off into a tirade. It was impossible not to be impressed with the power of the man . . . he would not brook opposition beyond a certain point." But—and this was "a point of considerable importance" declared Chamberlain—he had formed the opinion that Hitler's objectives were "strictly limited."[80]

Chamberlain's words were carefully chosen and of great significance. He was dismissing the view, which he himself had entertained before Berchtesgaden, that Hitler might be mad. Instead, he presented the German leader as a determined, difficult and volatile opponent but someone who entertained limited aims and would keep his word—a man with whom one could conduct meaningful negotiations. More than that—a man with whom he, Neville Chamberlain, was ideally suited to do business.

He made a point of telling the Cabinet about the Führer's parting words proposing another visit, adding that "information from other sources" (actually German Foreign Ministry officials buttering up Horace Wilson) showed that Hitler had been "most favourably impressed" with the prime minister. This, Chamberlain told the Cabinet, was "of the utmost importance, since the future conduct of these negotiations depended mainly upon personal contacts." The prime minister saw himself as pioneering a diplomatic revolution. He told the Cabinet that he "attached great importance to the dramatic side of the visit, since we were dealing with an individual, and a new technique of diplomacy relying on personal contacts was required."[81]

Even some of Chamberlain's closest colleagues were skeptical. Sir Thomas Inskip, the minister for the Co-ordination of Defence, who in Cabinet criticized Cooper, noted privately: "The impression made by the P.M.'s story was a little painful . . . It was plain that H[itler] had made all the running: he had in fact blackmailed the P.M."[82] But, like Cooper, none of Chamberlain's cabinet was willing on September 17 to sacrifice London for the sake of Prague.

With the Cabinet supportive, or at least acquiescent, Chamberlain sought approval from the French. Next day, Sunday, September 18, Prime Minister Édouard Daladier arrived in London with his principal colleagues and advisors. (They too had flown—another reminder that the plane was replacing the train as the vehicle of crisis diplomacy.)

Earlier, when Daladier had been informed that Chamberlain was going to Berchtesgaden, he "did not look very pleased," telling the British ambassador in Paris that he had refused several proposals for talks à deux with Hitler because he felt a British representative should be present.[83]

But the Anglo-French meetings on September 18 were cordial and, for Chamberlain, productive. The French did not want a plebiscite on the Sudetenland, fearing that Germany would then try to use this mechanism to resolve other minority disputes in Europe, including Alsace and Lorraine. But they agreed to a transfer of Czech territory in areas where Germans constituted more than half the population. In return they persuaded the British (hitherto, unlike France, not bound to Czechoslovakia by any treaty) to join them in guaranteeing the rump Czechoslovak state against "unprovoked aggression."[84]

After a gruelling day of formal meetings and private huddles, running from eleven in the morning until after midnight, the two governments sent a joint message to President Eduard Beneš in Prague early on September 19 outlining their proposals. They requested a reply by September 21 at the latest, because that was when Chamberlain planned to meet Hitler again.

When the Czech government protested that their state would be "completely mutilated," it was told that any delay would simply prompt a German invasion. The British and French ministers in Prague were instructed to deliver this message "immediately on receipt at whatever hour," so they arrived at the Hradschin Palace at 2 a.m. on September 21 to pressurize Beneš. By the end of the day the Czechoslovak government and the main political parties had all caved in.[85] Yet virtually nothing of this appeared in the British press. Chamberlain had given Hoare the task of keeping the press barons on side and nearly all of them played along.[86]

Prior to the British and French ultimatum, Beneš had already accepted in principle the idea of a limited cession of territory, hoping thereby to preempt larger German demands. Daladier learned of this concession in the utmost secrecy on September 17 and then shared it with Chamberlain, who used Prague's acquiescence to justify his own policy. And the Anglo-French message of September 21 was delivered after Czech premier Milan Hodža had secretly asked the French for an ultimatum to help justify capitulation in the eyes of domestic opinion.[87]

The Czechoslovak leadership could therefore be seen as a willing victim. Yet that was only because it was clearly going to be sacrificed by the British and French. The pressure applied by the two Western powers was brutal in the extreme: Halifax, usually circumlocutory in his language, wanted it stated "pretty bluntly that if Dr. Benes did not leave himself in our hands we should wash our hands of him."[88]

On September 20 Chamberlain's inner circle expressed unease that the British government was now so deeply implicated. Why could Britain not simply transmit the Czech reply to Berlin and leave Beneš and Hitler to sort out the details? Horace Wilson said this "would be inconsistent with the leading part which the Prime Minister had hitherto played in this matter."

But, if Chamberlain was going to remain the prime mover, his colleagues suggested that from the point of view of British public opinion it would be "very desirable" for him "to obtain some concessions" from Hitler in return for "the large concessions which were being made to him." What about raising the criterion for areas to be transferred from 50 percent German-speaking to 80 percent? Or persuading Hitler to reduce the tension by demobilizing some of his troops? The following day Hoare confirmed that several press barons agreed it would be "desirable" from the angle of public opinion for Chamberlain to return from his second trip to Germany "able to show that he had obtained some concession from Herr Hitler."[89]

By taking the Czech crisis to the summit, the prime minister had exposed Britain's status and prestige to an alarming degree.

CHAMBERLAIN LEFT HESTON AIRFIELD at 10:45 on Thursday, September 22. As before he stressed to the waiting pressmen that a peaceful settlement of the Sudeten problem was "an essential preliminary" to better Anglo-German relations, which in turn was the "indispensable foundation" for what he was really aiming at— "European peace." Theo Kordt of the German embassy in London, who again saw him off, reported that opposition was growing. He cited speeches the previous day by Churchill and Eden and demonstrations by the Labour Party and the trades unions in support of Czechoslovakia. There was a growing public feeling, voiced in Whitehall by the press barons, that the Anglo-German negotiations had become one-sided. Chamberlain left "under a heavy load of anxiety" Kordt told Berlin.[90]

This time, the British had to fly only to Cologne, from where they were driven to the spa town of Bad Godesberg, just south of Bonn, and ensconced in the superb Hotel Petersberg with its bird's-eye view of the Rhine. Hitler was on the opposite bank in the riverside Hotel Dreesen—one of his favorite haunts.

Chamberlain's party included not only Wilson and Strang but also Sir William Malkin, head of the Foreign Office's Legal Department. Henderson again joined them from Berlin, this time bringing Ivone Kirkpatrick, his first secretary—a fluent German speaker who had assisted at the Hitler-Halifax talks the previous year. At the Berghof, Chamberlain had relied entirely on the official German interpreter Paul Schmidt. He was furious afterward to be denied a copy of Schmidt's notes of the meeting and had to construct his own account from memory. There has been some dispute whether the ban was imposed by Ribbentrop in pique at his exclusion from the talks or, more probably, by Hitler himself in an effort to maximize his freedom of maneuver, but it left a nasty taste in Chamberlain's mouth.[91]

Only after vehement protests via Henderson and the intercession of Göring, Ribbentrop's archrival, was a transcript grudgingly provided.[92] Although Schmidt continued to interpret the meetings at Godesberg, Kirkpatrick was brought in to verify his accuracy and keep a proper British record of what was said. It was a sign that Chamberlain's approach to summitry was becoming a bit more professional.

Unlike their first meeting, the weather that Thursday afternoon at Godesberg was beautiful. At 4 p.m. Chamberlain and his party drove down to the Rhine and crossed on the ferry, in full view of a huge crowd of newspapermen and spectators—the scene reminded Henderson of the excited throngs at the Oxford-Cambridge boat race.[93]

At the Dreesen, Hitler shook hands with Chamberlain. Accompanied by Schmidt and Kirkpatrick, the two immediately went upstairs. In the conference room there was a long table covered with green baize, with chairs for at least twenty people. Hitler stalked to the top end of the table, Chamberlain sat on his right, Schmidt and Kirkpatrick on his left. After a moment's silence, Hitler gestured to Chamberlain as if to say, "Your move."[94]

The prime minister launched into a prepared summary of current position. He spoke of the impasse when they last met and of all he had achieved during the intervening week. He outlined the idea—now accepted in London, Paris and Prague—of an agreed transfer of territory, overseen by an international commission, and he identified the practical problems that still needed to be cleared up. Then he sat back, Schmidt recalled, with "an expression of satisfaction," as if to say, "Haven't I worked splendidly?"[95]

Hitler said he was grateful to Chamberlain for his great efforts to achieve a peaceful solution. He then asked whether the Czechoslovak government had agreed to these proposals.

"Yes," said Chamberlain.

"I'm terribly sorry," Hitler replied, "but that's no longer any use."[96]

Chamberlain sat up with a start, his face flushed with anger,[97] as Hitler began a diatribe about how the situation had changed, making much of the escalating clashes between Czechs and Germans in the Sudetenland. This problem, he said, must be "finally and completely solved" by October 1 at the latest.

By the time Hitler finished and his words were translated, Chamberlain had collected himself. Using diplomatic language he said that he was "both disappointed and puzzled" by the Führer's statement. At their last meeting Hitler had said that if he, Chamberlain, could arrange for a settlement on the basis of self-determination, Germany would be willing to discuss procedure. Ticking off how he had worked to bring round his Cabinet, the French and the Czechs, the prime minister said he had in fact "got exactly what the Führer wanted and without the expenditure of a drop of German blood." In doing so, he went on with mounting indignation, he had "been obliged to take his political life in his hands." He contrasted the rapturous reception of news of his first trip to Germany with the critical mood that day, when he had actually been booed at Heston airfield. Why, he asked, were these proposals no longer acceptable?

Hitler backtracked a little—Kirkpatrick surmised that he did not want an early breakdown[98]—and said there was only one way to resolve the situation peacefully. They must agree a new frontier immediately, following "the language line, based on existing reliable maps," and the territory must be occupied by German troops at once. This was a far cry from what Chamberlain thought they were discussing—an agreed transfer of territory under international supervision.

Eventually the two leaders went downstairs and joined Ribbentrop, Wilson and Henderson to inspect a map showing where Hitler proposed to draw his line. Chamberlain tried to pin him down to specifics but Hitler kept exploding about the iniquities of the Czechs. (Throughout the meeting he had received reports of new border incidents.) Tired and no doubt hungry, the two men eventually agreed to resume in the morning.

Before retiring both Hitler and Chamberlain made revealing comments. Chamberlain, harking back to his main theme, said it was difficult to see why, if Hitler could obtain all he wanted by peaceful means, he was willing to risk a war and loss of German life. And as they parted Hitler said he had never believed a peaceful solution could be reached; he admitted that he had never thought Chamberlain could have achieved what he had.[99]

Once again Hitler had pulled the rug from under Chamberlain's feet. At Godesberg, as at the Berghof, the prime minister had arrived with what he considered a sensible and attractive package, but each time the Führer simply upped his demands. Hitler had outlined his strategy for the Godesberg meeting in advance to Goebbels, anticipating after Chamberlain's performance the previous week that there would be little resistance. "The Führer will show Chamberlain his map," Goebbels noted in his diary, "and then that will be the end of it, basta!"[100]

Yet despite his second tactical victory over the British prime minister, Hitler's policy was now not as clearcut as a few weeks before. On the one hand, he was still talking of war and preparing for it, sticking to his deadline of the end of September. His psychological need to assert himself as supreme commander and to redeem the May humiliation had not diminished.

On the other hand, Britain and its leader had become much more actively involved in the crisis than Hitler had expected; that complicated matters, despite his continuing hunch that they wouldn't go to war. The map and plebiscite strategy he outlined to Goebbels suggests that Hitler had come to envisage a phased approach to eliminating Czechoslovakia, rather than military destruction in a single blow.[101] Both routes were possible and only time would show which one Hitler would choose.

On the other side, Chamberlain's puzzled comment about why Hitler wanted war if he could get all he said he wanted peacefully reveals the prime minister's fundamental blind spot. He had returned from Berchtesgaden convinced Hitler was not mad and had acted on that assumption with characteristic energy. Yet now Hitler was behaving in a way that defied rationality; he was also making demands that were unacceptable to both Cabinet colleagues and public opinion. The prime minister went to bed exhausted and, in Wilson's words, "much disturbed."

While Chamberlain slept, Kirkpatrick and a secretary worked until 4 a.m. on a transcript of the meeting. When the group reconvened at breakfast the mood among the British was grim: there was clearly a real prospect that the talks would break down completely.

Chamberlain cancelled the planned 11:30 meeting and sent over a letter spelling out exactly why Hitler's new proposals would not be acceptable to public opinion in Britain, France "and indeed in the world generally." Wilson claimed later that the idea came from his own previous experience of industrial negotiations, being designed both to force the other side to define their ideas and also to have something for future publication and self-defence if the talks did collapse.

After the letter was dispatched across the river, Chamberlain could do nothing but wait. The weather was again beautiful and the panorama spectacular, but the sight of the British delegation pacing the terrace with their cars standing idly by the door fuelled press speculation about a breakdown. Chamberlain spoke to Wilson for the first time of the likely fate of his premiership if the talks collapsed.

At 3:35 p.m. Schmidt arrived with Hitler's reply, but for the most part it contained only a reiteration of his grievances. So Chamberlain wrote back saying that he could not put any proposals to the Czechoslovak government without a memorandum and map setting them out in detail. At 5:45 p.m. Henderson and Kirkpatrick went across to the Dreesen to make this clear to Ribbentrop in person. They returned two hours later only when promised that the memorandum would be ready for discussion later that evening.[102]

Throughout his visit to Godesberg, Chamberlain was under mounting pressure from London. At 3 p.m. on Thursday, September 22, before his first meeting with Hitler, the inner Cabinet had discussed what measures should be taken if the talks broke down and war ensued.

During the evening they became increasingly frustrated by the lack of hard information about the talks. They had received that day only cryptic phone calls from Wilson and Chamberlain saying negotiations had been "pretty difficult" and "most unsatisfactory." Nor were they enlightened next morning by Wilson's message: "Fog all round, but it may clear during the day—in fact, it will one way or the other."[103]

Meanwhile pressures intensified to mobilize Czech and British forces. Hitherto the Czechs had been warned very firmly by Britain and France not to mobilize, for fear of provoking Hitler, but the French now wanted to withdraw this advice and it was only in deference to Chamberlain that London held the line on September 22. The following day the inner Cabinet felt it could no longer justify discouraging Czech mobilization and Chamberlain had to concur. The British armed forces were also chafing at the bit. They needed a precautionary stage of forty-eight hours in order to prepare for hostilities.

On the afternoon of September 23 the inner Cabinet cabled Chamberlain asking for authority to act in his absence. After dinner

Wilson phoned to say that, since they would return tomorrow, precautionary measures could wait. But he set off new ripples by saying he would soon be going to collect the German memorandum for transmission to Prague. Halifax told the inner Cabinet at 9:30 p.m. that he felt the talks should end on a simple and strong statement. Backed by Hoare, still in close touch with the press lords, he sent a message to Chamberlain stressing that "great mass of public opinion seems to be hardening in sense of feeling that we have gone to the limit of concession." Hitler should be told so, "if possible by special interview"; he should be warned that, after the concessions made by the Czechs, a German declaration of war would be "an unpardonable crime against humanity."[104]

The text was phoned through to Godesberg without taking the time to encode it. Halifax wanted Chamberlain to receive it before he crossed the river, but he probably intended the Germans to get the message as well.

Wrong-footed by Hitler and harried by his own colleagues, Chamberlain must have been very tense as he entered the Hotel Dreesen that night for round two of the Godesberg summit. This time the two leaders and their interpreters met in a downstairs salon, around a low table, with Henderson, Wilson, Ribbentrop and von Weizsäcker also in attendance.[105]

Discussion got going soon after 11 p.m. Hitler made an effort to be pleasant, but Chamberlain quickly cut through the civilities, saying that they had come to discuss the German memorandum. Ribbentrop produced the memo and Hitler said it represented essentially the ideas he had made in person and by letter over the past day or so. As before, he suggested that if their efforts to reach a peaceful solution succeeded, it might be a turning point in Anglo-German relations, adding that it was "the last question that remained open."

But Chamberlain would no longer be fobbed off. Echoing the warning from Halifax, he said he must be able to show the British people something in return—hitherto there had been "very little response" from the Führer. Hitler contested this vehemently but Chamberlain stuck to his guns, citing the German deadline of

October 1. "I can't believe that the Führer will be prepared to gamble away the chances of collaboration," he said, "just for the sake of a few days."

As the temperature rose, a message was brought in. Ribbentrop glanced at it, then announced portentously that the Czechoslovak government had announced general mobilization. That settles it, Hitler exclaimed. Why? asked Chamberlain: mobilization was a precaution, not necessarily an offensive measure. They got into an argument about who had mobilized first—Germany or Czechoslovakia—and Hitler became steamed up again about the need for an immediate settlement.

As at Berchtesgaden, Chamberlain now played his ace, asserting that there was clearly no point in negotiating further: he would go home with a heavy heart, he said, but also a clear conscience. But this time he was trumped by Ribbentrop who pointed out that Chamberlain had not taken the trouble to read the memorandum that he and his emissaries had been clamoring for all afternoon.

The British were of course at considerable disadvantage, since they had not seen this paper in advance of the meeting and Kirkpatrick, their best Germanist, was busy taking a record of the conversation. But Henderson had scribbled down in English the main points and Wilson noted that the memo clearly stated that the Czechoslovaks must evacuate the territories in question between September 26 and 28.

"The memorandum is an ultimatum and not a negotiation," exclaimed Chamberlain.

"*Ein Diktat*," interjected Henderson[106]—tossing in the word Hitler had made notorious in English by his ranting about the "Diktat" of Versailles.

"It has the word 'Memorandum' at the top," retorted Hitler.

"I am more impressed by the contents than the title," Chamberlain shot back. The whole memorandum would, he said, have a very bad effect on British opinion. It would make people say that Hitler was "behaving like a conqueror."

"No," the Führer cut in, "like the owner of his property."

Hitler and Ribbentrop reiterated that the British had not read the German memorandum in its entirety. Perhaps at this stage—though the minutes are confused—the British withdrew for "a short private conversation."[107] It was then agreed that Schmidt would translate the entire document orally into English. As he did so, Chamberlain sniped away at the most objectionable points.

Hearing the phrase "the following demands are made by the German Government," the prime minister said this was precisely the kind of language that public opinion would find offensive. Hitler said he had did not mind replacing "demands" with "proposals," which was duly done.

Chamberlain also inveighed against the document's "peremptory and rigid time-table," including a start date that was less than forty-eight hours away. Hitler backed off a bit, agreeing to completion by October 1.

And the British worked to minimize the area that would be occupied immediately by German troops. Eventually Chamberlain said he would submit the proposals to Prague as soon as possible and the talks ended at 1:45 a.m., having lasted nearly three hours.[108]

In his memoirs Kirkpatrick recalls that near the end of the meeting Hitler looked at Chamberlain "with a penetrating stare and said in a hoarse disgruntled voice: 'You are the first man to whom I have ever made a concession.'"[109] Kirkpatrick's official record gives the impression that the meeting then ended abruptly and coldly.[110]

But according to Schmidt's memoirs, which contained a similar line from Hitler about the rarity of his making concessions, the air had now been cleared and the two leaders "parted in a thoroughly amiable atmosphere after talking alone, with my assistance, for a short time." His official note at the time recorded these exchanges in the entrance hall, when Chamberlain "bade a hearty farewell to the Führer" and spoke of "the relationship of confidence" that had grown up between them in the last few days, allowing each to speak very frankly without the other taking offence. Again he expressed his hope that once the present crisis was over they could discuss the "greater problems" still outstanding in the same spirit. His sentiments were echoed by Hitler and Chamberlain took his leave, according to Schmidt, "with a hearty *Auf wiedersehen.*"[111]

The tone of Godesberg was therefore ambiguous. Chamberlain, again taken aback when Hitler moved the goalposts, this time played a much harder game, forcing the Führer first to put his demands on paper and then to modify them.

Yet Hitler was still behaving dictatorially and Chamberlain had not broken off negotiations. Instead he and his advisors decided to transmit the proposals to Prague. The prime minister still hoped to resolve the Sudeten question and move on toward an Anglo-German settlement. In any case, having staked his political future on the success of summitry, he had climbed too far to turn back.

AFTER A FEW HOURS' SLEEP (except for Kirkpatrick, who again had to compose a record of the meeting) the British party left Godesberg on Saturday morning, September 24. Henderson and Kirkpatrick were driven to Cologne to take a train back to Berlin. Killing time, they visited the great medieval cathedral where a despondent Henderson knelt in the nave to pray for peace.[112] Meanwhile, Chamberlain and the others flew back to London, arriving at lunchtime.

The prime minister reported to his inner Cabinet at 3:30 p.m. and to the full Cabinet two hours later.[113] On both occasions, he gave a lengthy account of the visit, making clear the impasse on the first day, the difficulties of eliciting a written statement from the Germans and the peremptory nature of its contents. But he then summed up the summit in a positive way, admitting his indignation on the first day when Hitler upped his demands but saying that, after further conversation, he had modified his views.

"In order to understand people's actions," Chamberlain told the Cabinet solemnly, "it is necessary to appreciate their motives and to see how their minds work." He felt he could now speak with greater confidence on this point than after his first visit. According to the Cabinet minutes, Chamberlain said:

Herr Hitler had a narrow mind and was violently prejudiced on certain subjects; but he would not deliberately deceive a man whom he respected and with whom he had been in negotiation, and he [Chamberlain] was sure that Herr Hitler now felt some respect for him. When Herr Hitler announced that he meant to do something it was certain that he would do it . . . The crucial question was whether Herr Hitler was speaking the truth when he said that he regarded the Sudeten question as a racial question which must be settled, and that the object of his policy was racial unity and not the domination of Europe. Much depends on the answer to that question. The Prime Minister believed that Herr Hitler was speaking the truth. Herr Hitler had also said that, once the present question had been settled, he had no more territorial ambitions in Europe. He had also said that if the present question could be settled peaceably, it might be a turning-point in Anglo-German relations.[114]

Here was Chamberlain's whole justification for summitry. He was claiming that he had forged a personal relationship with Hitler, that the German leader could be trusted to honor his word, that his aims were limited and that a settlement of the Sudeten question could pave the way to a much larger agreement. He told his colleagues he could see no hope for a peaceful solution except on the basis of the Godesberg memorandum, as modified in their late-night negotiation.

The Cabinet would have to decide whether the differences between these proposals and those he had taken to Godesberg were sufficient to justify Britain going to war. To underline his point Chamberlain spoke movingly of flying home to Britain that morning up the Thames. He had imagined a German bomber on the same course and asked himself what protection the government could give to the thousands of homes spread out beneath him. He said he felt in no position to justify waging war today in order to prevent a war later.[115]

Chamberlain wanted the Cabinet to adjourn so colleagues could read the terms and reflect on them. He got his way, though not before Duff Cooper had demanded immediate mobilization. The first lord of the admiralty said that instead of a choice between war and peace with dishonor, he now foresaw a third option—"war with dishonour," with the government being kicked into it by "the boot of public opinion."[116]

That evening Chamberlain, Halifax and the inner circle had further meetings, including one with the Labour leadership to try to sell the Godesberg terms. Meanwhile Wilson was drawing up proposals to render the immediate transfer of Czechoslovak territory more palatable to public opinion. He was especially concerned to "stage the 'occupation' as measures to guarantee the fulfillment of an agreement already made."[117]

Over the previous week Chamberlain had wrenched diplomacy out of the hands of the diplomats, but now the bureaucrats fought back. Apart from their professional irritation at being bypassed, many in the Foreign Office were convinced that he was taking the country down a dangerously slippery slope. One of them was Sir Alexander Cadogan, the permanent under-secretary at the Foreign Office—by appearance a buttoned-up bureaucrat but also a man of strong emotions, as is evident from the diary he scrawled each evening to unburden himself.

When Britain was pushed after Berchtesgaden from "autonomy" to cession of territory, Cadogan had salved his conscience by stipulating it should be an "orderly" affair under international supervision. He had written a note for Chamberlain before Godesberg stressing that "we have gone to the limit to try to satisfy what Hitler said was his claims" and that if he asked for more "there will be nothing more to be done but to oppose them."[118]

On the afternoon of Saturday, September 24, attending the meetings of the inner Cabinet in case his advice was required, Cadogan sat in horrified silence as the politicians apparently moved like sleepwalkers to "total surrender." Not only had Hitler "hypnotised" Chamberlain, he noted in his diary, "P.M. has evidently hypnotised H[alifax]." The foreign secretary told the inner Cabinet that "notwithstanding the political difficulties, he doubted whether the disadvantages of acceptance of Herr Hitler's proposals were so great as to justify us in going to war." And Simon, that political weathervane, was swinging with the wind. Having in Cadogan's words been "bellicose," almost "berserk" at times while

Chamberlain was at Godesberg, Simon now said it was really a question of "modalities." [119]

Cadogan was appalled at the Cabinet's pusillanimity. At 10:30 p.m. he drove Halifax home: "Gave him a piece of my mind, but didn't shake him," he scribbled before going to bed. "I know we are in no condition to fight: but I'd rather be beat than dishonoured. How can we look any foreigner in the face after this? How can we hold Egypt, India and the rest? . . . I've never had such a shattering day, or been so depressed and dispirited." [120]

Like most of his colleagues, Cadogan had little affection for the Czechs. His concern was with what would now be called "soft power"—the way Britain's standing in the world depended to a considerable extent on reputation. This, he was sure, Chamberlain was now fatally squandering. Next day, Sunday, September 25, he waited miserably while the Cabinet deliberated. Finally he caught up with Halifax at 6 p.m.

"Alec," said the foreign secretary, "I'm very angry with you. You gave me a sleepless night. I woke up at 1 and never got to sleep again. But I came to the conclusion that you were right, and at the Cabinet, when P.M. asked me to lead off, I plumped for refusal of Hitler's terms."

Cadogan was impressed and relieved.

"Did you know," asked Halifax severely, "that you would give me an awful night?"

"Yes," said Cadogan, "but I slept very well myself." [121]

That morning at the 10:30 Cabinet, Chamberlain had reiterated the case for the Godesberg terms: an immediate occupation of the Sudeten areas by the German army. Contrary to what he told Cadogan, Halifax didn't exactly "lead off" with his dissent: the first mutterings came from Hoare, who having questioned the lack of German concessions in the inner Cabinet, now suggested it would be "a tremendous responsibility" to advise the Prague government to accept. [122] But it was indeed Halifax who made the decisive intervention, all the more devastating in its impact because of his typically judicious, low-key manner.

The previous day, Halifax told his Cabinet colleagues, he had felt that the differences between the Godesberg scheme and the one they had agreed to a week earlier did not seem sufficient justification for going to war. Now he was not quite sure. There was perhaps "a distinction in principle between orderly and disorderly transfer, with all that the latter implied for the minorities in the transferred areas." The language was deliberately opaque but the message was clear: having slept on it, Halifax was saying that the Godesberg terms were a license for ethnic cleansing.

Warming to his theme, the foreign secretary said he could not rid his mind of the fact that Hitler "had given us nothing and that he was dictating terms, just as though he had won a war but without having had to fight." Becoming ever blunter, Halifax then stated that his "ultimate end" was "the destruction of Nazi-ism. So long as Nazi-ism lasted, peace would be uncertain. For this reason he did not feel that it would be right to put pressure on Czechoslovakia to accept." And, mindful of the noises from the German opposition, he suggested that if Hitler was driven to war "the result might be to help bring down the Nazi *regime*."[123]

Halifax said that he offered his opinions not as "final conclusions" but "provisionally" and "tentatively" as an expression of his own "hesitations." Despite all the circumlocution, however, the thrust of his remarks was devastating. Halifax admitted that although he had "worked most closely with the Prime Minister throughout the long crisis," he "was not quite sure that their minds were still altogether as one."[124]

Chamberlain felt betrayed. As other ministers weighed in, he wrote his foreign secretary a hasty note—"your complete change of view since I saw you last night is a horrible blow to me"—and hinted at possible resignation if the French dragged Britain into war.

"I feel a brute," Halifax scrawled back, "but I lay awake most of the night, tormenting myself . . ."

Back came the tart reply: "Night conclusions are seldom taken in the right perspective."[125]

Instinctively Halifax sought the middle ground between conflicting parties, and could be flexible, even casuistic, about means and ends—hence his nickname "Holy Fox."[126] But he was also a High

Anglican of stern morals and, when convinced that a real issue of principle was at stake, he dug in hard. On September 4 he had toyed with the idea of sending Germany a clear warning, but was over-ruled; on the 25th, unlike Chamberlain, he concluded that they were not dealing with a rational man with whom one could negoti-ate. Having stayed in London during both of Chamberlain's trips to Germany, he was more aware than the prime minister of the swelling tide of criticism, in the country and his own party. And as a shrewd politician he must have been emboldened by the knowledge that, after Eden's controversial resignation, Chamberlain could not afford to lose a second foreign secretary within the year.[127]

In a protracted Cabinet meeting that continued after lunch that Sunday, some ministers made clear their support for Chamberlain. Others took their cue from Halifax, voicing their previously sup-pressed anxieties, and there was talk of possible resignations. Mean-while the Czechoslovak government dismissed the Godesberg terms as "absolutely and completely unacceptable." The rejection note—delivered to the Foreign Office that afternoon by Ambas-sador Jan Masaryk, son of the founder of the Czech Republic—proclaimed that "[t]he nation of St. Wenceslas, John Hus and Thomas Masaryk will not be a nation of slaves" and called on Brit-ain and France "to stand by us in our hour of trial."[128]

Playing for time, Chamberlain told the Cabinet that they should reconvene after he had ascertained the attitude of the French lead-ers, because Britain would certainly not go to war if France, Czechoslovakia's formal ally, stood aloof. Sir Eric Phipps, the am-bassador in Paris, was close to the peace party in France. He sent a message, which Chamberlain read out, stating that "all that is best in France is against war, *almost* at any price" and warning of the "extreme danger of even appearing to encourage small, but [a] noisy and corrupt, war group here." Phipps's assessment appalled senior figures in the Foreign Office, who were now ready to stand firm: Sir Orme Sargent, the assistant under-secretary, considered it "unfair and misleading" and Vansittart, Phipps's brother-in-law, called it "hysterical."[129]

Nor did it square with the line taken by the French leaders in discussions late that evening with the inner Cabinet. Daladier said that he and his ministers regarded Hitler's new terms as an attempt to "destroy Czechoslovakia by force, enslaving her." Chamberlain tried to find out whether France would resist. "Each of us will have to do our duty," Daladier equivocated. Sir John Simon tried to pin him down. Would French troops stay defensively on the Maginot Line, or would they attack Germany? Would the French air force also engage in offensive operations? Simon was an eminent barrister and his cross-examination infuriated Daladier. He tried to turn the tables on his British inquisitors. Did they accept Hitler's plan? We are just intermediaries, Chamberlain replied disingenuously.[130]

Simon described the meeting as "rather unpleasant." Strang, a silent observer, called it "one of the most painful which it has ever been my misfortune to attend."[131] Each side was trying to pass the buck. Daladier probably hoped his rhetorical defense of the Czechoslovak cause would enable him to pin any sellout on the treacherous English, while Chamberlain and Simon sought to expose France as unwilling to fight seriously for Czechoslovakia so they could use that information to silence Cabinet hawks.

After two hours of inconclusive argument, Chamberlain adjourned at 11:40 p.m. to meet his Cabinet again. He tried to present the French as completely indecisive but Halifax came close to contradicting him. Opinion among ministers had hardened since the afternoon and the prime minister decided he must shift ground. He told the Cabinet he would send Horace Wilson to Berlin with a final appeal, asking Hitler to reconsider the idea of an international commission. If the Führer refused Wilson would warn him verbally that if Germany attacked Czechoslovakia and the French offered "active measures" in support, this would bring Britain into the war.[132]

The next morning, Monday, September 26, Chamberlain and Daladier patched up their differences in private. The French endorsed Wilson's mission, and General Maurice Gamelin, the French chief of staff—flown over specially from Paris—said enough about their military plans to reassure the British without committing themselves explicitly to going on the offensive against Germany.

Afterward, however, Halifax notified Wilson, who had just landed in Berlin, that "French have definitely stated their intention of supporting Czechoslovakia by offensive measures if latter is attacked. This would bring us in: and it should be made plain to [the] Chancellor that this is inevitable alternative to a peaceful solution." The foreign secretary also approved a communiqué for the press stating that if despite all Chamberlain's efforts for a peaceful settlement Germany attacked Czechoslovakia, "the immediate result must be that France will be bound to come to her assistance" and Britain would "certainly stand by France." Downing Street was furious. The communiqué, like the message to Wilson, was further evidence that prime minister and foreign secretary were now on very different tracks.[133]

Hitler met Wilson at 5 p.m. on Monday, September 26 in the Chancellery building in Berlin. He presented a letter from Chamberlain and Schmidt began to translate. The Führer was in an explosive mood, working himself up for a major speech he was to give that evening at the Berlin Sportpalast. He repeatedly interrupted Schmidt and Wilson with what Kirkpatrick's official notes called "gestures of dissent" and "exclamations of disgust." Eventually Hitler agreed to see a Czech representative to discuss the territorial transfer, but only if Prague accepted the Godesberg terms and promised to vacate the area by October 1.

Schmidt recalled it as "one of the most stormy meetings that I have ever experienced," frustrating even his impressive ability to maintain an orderly flow of talk and translation. Given Hitler's mood Wilson decided not to deliver the verbal warning, fearing that this might provoke Hitler in his speech to announce that the Wehrmacht was marching into Czechoslovakia. Instead he secured another meeting the following morning. Cabinet dissenters in London were furious when they learned of his action. Chamberlain told Wilson: "We do not consider it possible for you to leave without delivering special message, in view of what we said to French, if you can make no progress. But message should be given more in sorrow than in anger."[134]

Wilson's second meeting took place at 1:15 p.m. on Tuesday the

27th.[135] Hitler had delivered his Sportpalast speech, vitriolic in tone but containing little new, yet he had not budged from his position on the Sudetenland. "[T]hat morning it was quite impossible to talk to Hitler reasonably," Schmidt recalled. Wilson rose reluctantly to his feet and read out the warning. If Germany attacked Czechoslovakia and if France, fulfilling her treaty obligations, "became engaged in active hostilities against Germany," then the British government "would feel obliged to support her."

As Chamberlain had predicted, Hitler chose to interpret the message as a threat that France was going to attack Germany and declared that he had no intention of invading France. So, slowly and clearly, Wilson repeated the whole formula, again interrupted by Hitler. The Führer of course was playing his own game, seeking to depict the French as aggressors. But the Chamberlain government had finally issued the warning that hardliners had been demanding for weeks. Although its impact may have been somewhat dulled by Wilson's parting whisper—"I will still try to make those Czechos sensible"—the British had now done what they failed to do in the July crisis of 1914, namely to tell Berlin clearly they would not stand aside if Germany and France went to war.[136]

Yet Hitler was still intent on invading Czechoslovakia on Saturday, October 1. At 1:20 p.m. that Tuesday, soon after Wilson left, he ordered the units that would spearhead the invasion of Czechoslovakia to start moving, so they would be in their assembly areas on the 30th. At 6 p.m. he approved mobilization of the active and reserve divisions in the West, facing France.[137] Announcement of general mobilization was scheduled for 2 p.m. on Wednesday the 28th.

In London too events were surging toward a climax. The prime minister finally agreed to the mobilization of the fleet. This was announced in the press next morning, further ratcheting up the tension.

Chamberlain, though now exhausted—"I'm wobbling about all over the place," he said at one point[138]—had not abandoned hope. Closing his radio broadcast to the nation at 8 p.m. on September 27, he promised: "I am going to work for peace to the last moment." He also uttered his now notorious exclamation: "How horrible, fantastic it is that we should be digging trenches and trying on gas-masks here because of a quarrel in a far-away country between people of whom we know little. It seems still more impossible that a quarrel which has already been settled in principle should be the subject of war."[139]

But, fantastic and impossible as it might seem, on Wednesday, September 28, 1938, Britain was preparing for an apparently suicidal war. Fighter Command had twenty-nine functional squadrons, but only five of these were equipped with modern Hurricanes and none of those could operate above fifteen thousand feet. The radar chain along the coast was only partly complete and radio links were primitive, while a mere third of the barrage balloons, antiaircraft guns and searchlights deemed necessary to protect London were actually in place.[140]

During the week beginning September 26 the government delivered to homes and offices in the capital a forty-page illustrated booklet entitled "The Protection of Your Home against Air Raids." This contained advice on such matters as making blackout curtains, creating a special "refuge-room" and stocking up appropriate provisions. Local authorities improvised nine hundred first-aid posts and dug about a million feet of trenches as emergency shelter from bomb blast. There was also a mad rush to shore up basements: in Birmingham alone this produced air-raid accommodation for ten thousand people. Yet as Hoare admitted in his postcrisis review of air-raid precautions, "the country was not ready" and the "defects of detail were numerous and widespread."[141] These included lack of air-raid personnel and firefighting equipment and serious shortages of doctors, nurses, ambulances and hospital beds. Although the rail authorities were confident they could evacuate four million people from major cities in three days, half of them from London, no operational plans existed.[142]

And there was a real fear of gas attacks, evoking all the horrors of the Western Front in 1914–18. Thirty million gas masks were distributed to the public, but there were as yet no special respirators for babies and small children.

Anyone reading through the official booklet at the breakfast table on Wednesday morning must have been left with an overwhelming sense of futility. There were, for instance, precise instructions about how to reinforce rooms with a row of posts from floor to ceiling—"but it would be best to take a builder's advice before setting to work." Suggestions such as sealing the "refuge-room" against gas using sticky tape, putty or "a pulp made up of sodden newspaper" were hardly reassuring, as was the advice: "If there is a fire-place, stuff the chimney with paper, rags or sacks. Do not, of course, light a fire in the grate afterwards."[143]

In October, after the crisis had passed, the historian Arnold Toynbee reflected on the panic in an apocalyptic letter to an American friend:

> It is probably impossible to convey what the imminent expectation of being bombed feels like in a small and densely populated country like this. I couldn't have conveyed it to myself if I hadn't experienced it in London the week before last (we were expecting 30,000 casualties a night in London, and on the Wednesday morning we believed ourselves, I believe correctly, to be within three hours of the zero hour). It was just like facing the end of the world. In a few minutes the clock was going to stop, and life, as we had known it, was coming to an end. This prospect of the horrible destruction of all that is meant to one by 'England' and 'Europe' was much worse than the mere personal prospect that one's family and oneself would be blown to bits. Seven or eight million people in London went through it.[144]

On the morning of Wednesday, September 28, Chamberlain made one last effort to avert armageddon. At 11:30 he sent a telegram to Hitler, offering to come yet again to Germany to discuss the transfer of territory. If helpful, he suggested, the French and Italian leaders should also be present. He said he was convinced that "you can get all the essentials without war and without delay." In a parallel message the prime minister asked Mussolini to urge Hitler to accept another meeting.[145]

Then Chamberlain set about finalizing his statement for the House of Commons that afternoon, intended to accompany and explain the government's publication of key documents from the crisis. Chamberlain had to choose his words carefully. He wanted to show just how far he had gone, and was still willing to go, in the search for peace. But he knew he might also be setting out the government's case for war.

Earlier that morning Wilson had told the press advisor at the German embassy that Chamberlain still wished to "leave the door open" in his speech. But if Germany marched at 2 p.m., Wilson explained, the prime minister would announce a declaration of war.[146]

IN LONDON the turning point in the crisis came over the weekend of September 24–25, when Halifax led the Cabinet revolt against the Godesberg terms, and belatedly set parameters for Chamberlain's summit diplomacy. In Berlin the crux occurred the following Tuesday and Wednesday, September 27–28. It was then that Hitler, against all expectations, drew back from starting a European war.

Most of Tuesday afternoon a German mechanized division rumbled through the streets of Berlin and along the Wilhelmstrasse, passing the Chancellery, the Foreign Ministry and the British embassy. Hitler loved watching his army, which he had created from the ashes of Versailles; he stood at the window for three hours that afternoon.

The whole event had been staged to impress foreign diplomats and journalists with Germany's military might, but what struck them (and Hitler himself) was the mood of the Berliners. There was virtually no cheering; people averted their eyes or ducked into doorways. Germans, it seemed, had no stomach for another European conflict, and war, as Hitler had said again and again, was about will as much as materiel. For the Führer, it was a chastening experience.[147]

The following morning pressures on him mounted. The British position was now clear thanks to the Foreign Office communiqué,

Wilson's reluctant warning and news that the Royal Navy had been mobilized. In another well-publicized move, the French called up reservists.

That morning the Chancellery building in Berlin was even more chaotic than usual; officers and officials milled around, excitedly trading the latest gossip. The mood was definitely against risking a European war; among Hitler's inner circle the only obdurate hawks were Ribbentrop and Heinrich Himmler, head of the SS. Göring pressed his arguments for peace at length on Hitler and later accused Ribbentrop to his face of war-mongering. "I know what war is like," he shouted, and if the Führer ordered it, "I shall be in the first plane. But you must be in the seat next to me."[148]

Von Neurath, the former foreign minister, and Goebbels also weighed in. "We have no jumping-off point for war," the propaganda minister noted in his diary. "One can't wage a world war over points of detail (*Modalitäten*)."[149]

At 11:15 the French ambassador in Berlin, André Francois-Ponçet, who had so far played a minor role in the crisis, arrived to warn Hitler that an invasion of Czechoslovakia would set Europe ablaze. His remarks had even more impact because he spoke fluent German, without an interpreter.

At 11:40 Hitler received the Italian ambassador, Bernardo Attolico, hot-foot with an urgent message from Mussolini. This urged the Führer to delay his war plans and to accept Chamberlain's proposal for a four-power summit.

Schmidt translated. Hitler reflected and then said: "Tell the Duce that I accept his proposal." It was almost noon—two hours before the 2 p.m. trigger for general German mobilization.[150]

Which of the many pressures bearing down on Hitler was ultimately decisive remains a matter of dispute. Some commentators believe it was the belated sign of British resolve.[151] Schmidt, who was in attendance for much of Wednesday morning, felt that Francois-Ponçet's powerful performance prepared the ground for Attolico's decisive démarche. Göring said later that what turned Hitler around was doubt about the mood of the German people and fear that Mussolini might leave him in the lurch.[152] Or possibly the Italian proposal provided him with a convenient pretext for pulling back.[153]

Whatever Hitler's precise motives, his action astonished the inner circle in Berlin after months of his bellicose talk. "One cannot grasp this change," wrote one senior officer in his diary. "Führer has now finally given way—what's more fundamentally."[154]

Hitler may have lost face, but in doing so he probably saved his life. During the summer, opposition had mounted within the military to his apparently suicidal determination to risk a war with Britain and France over Czechoslovakia, for which Germany was not yet prepared. This opposition did not abate with the resignation of General Beck as army chief of staff at the end of August.

Beck's successor, General Franz Halder, also appalled at Hitler's obduracy, was drawn into a plot concocted by conservative politicians and dissident officers to seize control of Berlin, surround the Chancellery and overthrow the Führer. Conservative senior figures such as Beck wanted to take him alive and put him on trial, whereas younger elements believed he must be killed. These radicals secretly assembled an assassination squad in various Berlin apartments—mostly junior officers but also some students and trade unionists.

On the morning of Wednesday, September 28, General Erwin von Witzleben—who was to confront Hitler in the Chancellery—saw Hitler's answer rejecting Chamberlain's final message. He showed it to Halder, who in turn took it to General Walther von Brauchitsch, the army commander in chief. Although both professed themselves convinced of the need for "action," Brauchitsch wanted to be absolutely sure that Hitler was going to war; he went down in person to the Chancellery.

Meanwhile Erich Kordt from the Foreign Ministry was primed to ensure that the great double doors at the entrance of the Chancellery were kept open. The death squad was ready to burst in, and there was no special security to protect Hitler. But then came the bombshell news that mobilization had been postponed and another conference would take place. The plotters had no choice but to stay their hand.[155]

There was of course no guarantee that the putsch would have succeeded. On the other hand, this was probably the best laid of all the conspiracies to overthrow Hitler—certainly more coordinated than the celebrated bomb plot of July 20, 1944. After the war, some of the conspirators laid the blame entirely on Chamberlain, even making the misleading claim that all was prepared by mid-September and that his first trip to Berchtesgaden sabotaged their plans.[156]

Undoubtedly Chamberlain's refusal to encourage the resistance in August with firm public warnings was a serious deterrent to the plotters. But by the end of September they were nerved and ready. At root, Hitler saved himself. The plotters needed war to justify mounting a coup, and it was the Führer who pulled back at the very last moment from invading Czechoslovakia.

None of this was known in London, however. The House of Commons, officially adjourned until November 1, had been recalled specially on September 28 to debate the international situation. Millions of British civilians awoke that Wednesday morning fearful that war was only a few hours away; older people recalled Sir Edward Grey's statement to the Commons on the fateful fourth of August in 1914.

The chamber was packed to hear Chamberlain lead off the debate. His wife was in the gallery, together with several members of the royal family. The archbishops of Canterbury and York sat in the Peers' Gallery, together with Halifax and Stanley Baldwin, Chamberlain's predecessor as premier; the ambassadors of all the interested powers were crammed uneasily in the diplomatic seats.

As they waited, many were fascinated by what MP Harold Nicolson described as "a strange metal honeycomb" in front of the prime minister. This was a microphone specially installed on the assumption that Chamberlain's speech would be broadcast over the radio—a historic first. But at the last moment the party leadership balked at setting a precedent, so the microphone was not switched on. Further heightening the tension, the House followed its established rituals: Prayers at 2:45, notice of recent deaths among MPs, then some questions and answers on mundane topics such as unemployment benefit.[157]

At 2:54 Chamberlain rose and embarked on a long and detailed account of the Czechoslovak crisis, of his visits to Hitler and of their correspondence—some of which was contained in the White Paper that was being issued simultaneously. The House listened closely and in silence, the tension rising with Chamberlain's relentless chronology. At important points during the speech, the prime minister took off his pince-nez and raised his head toward the skylight. It was all compelling theater, but Chamberlain must have been painfully aware that he lacked a punchline.

Just before he left Downing Street, Henderson had phoned to say that Hitler had agreed to postpone mobilization for twenty-four hours but did not see any need for a further visit by the prime minister. Chamberlain therefore had a sliver of good news up his sleeve but it hardly constituted a clear, let alone happy, ending.[158]

Instead the denouement was, as Chamberlain wrote later, "a piece of drama that no work of fiction ever surpassed."[159] At 3:30 p.m. Henderson phoned the Foreign Office with news that Hitler had invited Chamberlain, Mussolini and Daladier to meet him at Munich the next morning and that the Italian leader had already accepted. Cadogan took the message and then virtually ran with it to the Commons—not, however, forgetting his umbrella even at this moment.

Getting the news to Chamberlain was no easy task because at every turn it had to be passed via Commons messengers. Cadogan had the paper delivered to Halifax in the Peers Gallery; the two of them then hurried downstairs to the door behind the speaker's chair. Another messenger took it to Horace Wilson, sitting in the officials' box.

On the back of Henderson's message, the foreign secretary had written: "You should see this urgently. I think P.M. should announce at the end of his speech. I presume we can take French agreement for granted."[160] Wilson beckoned to Lord Dunglass, Chamberlain's private secretary and (as Sir Alec Douglas-Home) a future prime minister, who passed the paper to Sir John Simon, sitting near the prime minister on the front bench.

The whole Chamber could see that something important was

happening but Chamberlain was deep in his text and Simon did not wish to throw him off balance. He passed it over during a burst of applause.[161]

It was about 4:15 p.m. and the prime minister had just reached the passage about his final appeals that morning to Hitler and Mussolini. He broke off, adjusted his pince-nez, and read the paper. Then, said Nicolson, "His whole face, his whole body, seemed to change . . . he appeared ten years younger."[162] The prime minister told the House that, in response to Mussolini, Hitler had deferred mobilization for twenty-four hours. Raising his face to the sunlight, he smiled:

> This is not all. I have something further to say to the House yet. I have now been informed by Herr Hitler that he invites me to meet him at Munich tomorrow morning. He has also invited Signor Mussolini and Monsieur Daladier. Signor Mussolini has accepted and I have no doubt that Monsieur Daladier will also accept. I need not say what my answer will be.

The Commons erupted. Many MPs stood on the seats, throwing their Order Papers in the air. Amid the cheers the prime minister proposed an adjournment for a few days, after which "perhaps we may meet in happier circumstances." It was an amazing piece of brinkmanship. Chamberlain later called it "the last desperate snatch at the last tuft on the very verge of the precipice."[163]

NEXT MORNING, Thursday, September 29, the atmosphere in London was like that of two weeks before, when Chamberlain made his first flight to Germany. There was almost an explosion of relief that war had been averted, at least for the moment.

The whole Cabinet was at Heston to see Chamberlain off. "When I come back," he told reporters, "I hope I may be able to say, as Hotspur says in *Henry IV,* 'out of this nettle, danger, we pluck this flower, safety.'" He also recalled "as a little boy" repeating the maxim: "If at first you don't succeed, try, try, try again."[164]

Figure 2-2 Get out on the streets! To ensure that the people of Munich gave a warm welcome to the Führer and his guests, the Nazi party printed thousands of notices giving details of the route they would follow on the morning of September 29, 1938. (U.S. National Archives)

Jaundiced critics rendered it: "If at first you don't concede, fly, fly, fly again." But, that Thursday, the critics did not speak out. Though fearful that the prime minister would sacrifice the Czechs, they were obliged to wait impotently on events.

As a summit, Munich was very different from Berchtesgaden and Godesberg. For one thing Daladier and Mussolini were present—the French premier subdued and ill at ease, the Italian leader relishing his role as broker. Over dinner on the overnight train from Rome, he had been full of contemptuous sociological observations about the British, ascribing the country's passion for peace to its gender imbalance after the Great War. "Four million sexually deprived women . . . Being unable to embrace a man, they embrace all of humanity."[165]

In further contrast to the earlier summits, arrangements at Munich were shambolic.[166] Chamberlain arrived at the airport at noon, with the inevitable Wilson, and also Strang and Malkin. They drove straight to the *Führerbau*—the Nazi party's headquarters near Königsplatz in the northwest of Munich—and were told that proceedings would start at once. Chamberlain had not consulted with Daladier in advance, whereas Hitler and Mussolini had talked at length. Both dictators were also supported by their foreign ministers, whereas Halifax had again been left at home. The participants did not sit around a table but on chairs in a large circle, with the British too far away from the French to concert business—not that Chamberlain had any desire to do so.[167]

Schmidt, acting as master of ceremonies, announced that the discussions would be interpreted as necessary into English, French and German (Mussolini understood all three languages and liked to think of himself as an accomplished linguist).[168] The Duce read out a memorandum he had prepared as a basis for discussion. It soon became clear that this was based on the German response to the last Anglo-French proposals—essentially a reiteration of the proposals made at Godesberg. Chamberlain and Daladier agreed to work through it clause by clause, though it was some time before written copies were produced.

After adjourning for a very late lunch at 3:15 p.m., discussions resumed at 4:30 p.m. and continued through the evening, breaking only briefly for dinner. (Chamberlain and Daladier declined the invitation to dine with Hitler and Mussolini.)

The British focused on the timetable for territorial transfer and the precise areas in question, but there were also protracted debates about the nature of the Anglo-French guarantee and the compensation to be paid by Germany for Czech state property.

Malkin and Henderson were brought into the discussions, the former heading a small drafting committee which attempted to clean up the phrasing cobbled together by the principals. There were long delays even in getting short drafts typed up and distributed.

The agreement was finally ready for signature at 2 a.m. on September 30. The four delegations trooped into Hitler's office, where an enormous desk was topped off by a massive inkpot. In an apt finale, Hitler dipped in his pen, only to discover that there was no ink. Another inkpot had to be produced before the document could be signed.[169]

The Czechs had not been involved in the discussions. Chamberlain's last appeal to Hitler on September 28 had mentioned them as participants, but that idea disappeared in the headlong rush for an agreement. Eventually Daladier and Chamberlain saw the two representatives from the Czech Foreign Ministry, who had been waiting for hours at their hotel. They were given what Wilson called "a pretty broad hint" that, given "the seriousness of the alternative," it would be best for their government to accept.[170]

At the summit, leaders often seize what is within their grasp at that moment: their paramount aim is agreement rather than breakdown. But afterward the content of the agreement has to be justified. And in September 1938 there wasn't much difference between the Munich agreement and the Godesberg terms already rejected by the British Cabinet. The area to be transferred was somewhat smaller and the process would take place over ten days, rather than being completed on October 1, but these were changes of detail not substance. Chamberlain knew he needed to take back more than this to London.

And so, at 1 a.m., while waiting for the draftsmen to finish their work, he asked Hitler for a private talk the following morning, Friday. September 30. This took place in the Führer's apartment overlooking Prinzregentenplatz, a fashionable suburb on the east of Munich.

Beforehand Chamberlain asked Strang to prepare a short statement on future Anglo-German relations, which he hoped Hitler would sign. Strang worked this up over breakfast at their hotel. His draft stressed that consultation rather than war was the best way to resolve differences between the two nations. Chamberlain revised it, adding the sentence: "We regard the agreement signed last night and the Anglo-German Naval Agreement as symbolic of the desire of our two countries never to go to war with one another again." Strang said that the 1935 naval agreement (which freed the German navy from the constraints of the Versailles treaty) was not something to be proud of. On the contrary, Chamberlain replied, it was exactly the type of agreement Britain should try to reach with Germany. He also brushed aside Strang's suggestion about informing the French. The text was retyped, and Chamberlain slipped two copies into his jacket pocket before leaving to see Hitler.[171]

The prime minister intended this meeting to be their oft-postponed *tour d'horizon* of current problems. This is clear from Schmidt's record and from Chamberlain's own pencil notes as he went along, on fourteen pages of a little white notepad, using the abbreviation "HH" for "Herr Hitler."[172]

They talked about the Spanish civil war, southeastern Europe, Germany's fears of economic encirclement, and how to promote disarmament. Hitler spoke about his desire to confine aerial bombing to combatants: "Hates idea of little babies being killed by gas bombs," Chamberlain scribbled, apparently discerning in such remarks evidence of the Führer's essential humanity.

Eventually Chamberlain told Hitler that he wouldn't detain him any longer but thought it would be a pity if the Munich meeting "passed off with nothing more than the settlement of the Czech question." Accordingly he had drafted a short statement about their mutual desire to improve Anglo-German relations and thereby en-

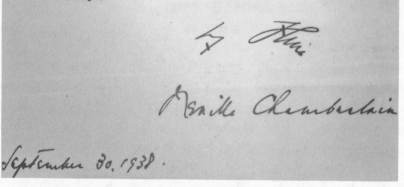

We, the German Führer and Chancellor and the British Prime Minister, have had a further meeting today and are agreed in recognising that the question of Anglo-German relations is of the first importance for the two countries and for Europe.

We regard the agreement signed last night and the Anglo-German Naval Agreement as symbolic of the desire of our two peoples never to go to war with one another again.

We are resolved that the method of consultation shall be the method adopted to deal with any other questions that may concern our two countries, and we are determined to continue our efforts to remove possible sources of difference and thus to contribute to assure the peace of Europe.

September 30. 1938.

Figure 2-3 The notorious "piece of paper" signed by Chamberlain and Hitler at Munich. (Birmingham University Library)

hance European stability. Pulling it out of his pocket, he asked if Hitler would sign.

The notorious "piece of paper" was, in Chamberlain's mind, not an isolated event but the climax of his September summitry—a sign that the two leaders were ready to move on toward the European settlement that was the prime minister's ultimate dream.

Writing to his sisters later, Chamberlain said that Hitler had "jumped at the idea" of a private talk, that the conversation had been "very pleasant and friendly," and that the Führer was very keen to sign the piece of paper. Schmidt, in contrast, felt that Hitler had accepted the wording with reluctance and signed only to please Chamberlain. According to Schmidt, Hitler was "pale and moody" throughout the meeting, "listened absent-mindedly to Chamberlain's remarks," and contributed "comparatively little" to the conversation. This he attributed to the massive and spontaneous displays of enthusiasm for Chamberlain by the people of Munich.[173]

Wherever the prime minister went he was cheered through the streets, and his hotel had been deluged with floral tributes. Hitler was never one to share the limelight and that may have been one reason for his morose mood that morning.

But, more deeply, he was now surely coming to terms with what he had done by losing his nerve at the last minute. His anger toward Chamberlain was not because he wished to share the credit as peacemaker. On the contrary, he resented being cheated out of the glory of victorious war. Even more galling, he knew he had cheated himself.

But he signed. Chamberlain gave one copy of the text to Hitler and put the other in his jacket. Back at his hotel, the prime minister patted his pocket in satisfaction and told Strang: "I've got it." As they flew home that afternoon he asked Strang to draw up a comparison of the Godesberg and Munich terms: it was politically essential to show that he returned with something better than Hitler's final demands.[174] Daladier knew there was little difference: he flew back to Paris in trepidation, only to be bowled over by the wave of cheering when his plane door opened. "The people are crazy," he muttered.[175]

Chamberlain's reception was even more remarkable. Despite pouring rain when he landed at Heston at 5:40 p.m. that Friday evening, the crowds were vast and ecstatic, caring only that war had been averted. He read out the paper that he and Hitler had signed. Then he drove to Buckingham Palace, where he was thanked by the king and, in an unprecedented gesture, invited to acknowledge cheering Londoners from the front balcony overlooking the Mall. Finally, and with great difficulty, the car took him back to Downing Street where he spoke to another dense crowd from a first-floor window.

Then Chamberlain made a fatal slip. In justification he was exhausted from several very late nights and from two weeks of intense drama. (Next day, he told his sisters, he came nearer to a nervous breakdown "than I have ever been in my life."[176]) But he was also exultant at having, as he had hoped, plucked the flower from the nettle, and the scenes that evening in London would have gone to any man's head.

In the entrance hall of 10 Downing Street, someone urged him to repeat Disraeli's famous words on returning from the Congress of Berlin sixty years before. Chamberlain retorted icily: "No, I do not do that sort of thing." But when he went upstairs to acknowledge the crowds, he was conscious that he was standing at the window from which Disraeli had spoken. Very possibly impelled by that deep desire to go one better than his father and brother, he let his emotions get the better of his reason. "My good friends," he said, "this is the second time in our history there has come back from Germany to Downing Street peace with honour. I believe it is peace for our time."

His former parliamentary private secretary, Alec Douglas-Home, commented bleakly years later: "He knew at once that it was a mistake, and that he could not justify the claim. It haunted him for the rest of his life."[177]

AFTERWARD STRANG, like many in the Foreign Office, described Munich frankly as a "débâcle."[178] And there is no doubt that Chamberlain's personal diplomacy looks profoundly amateurish by the standards of later summits. No psychological profiles of his opponent had been prepared; there was no sign of what would now be called "position papers" or "briefing books." The prime minister kept professional diplomats at arm's length, including his foreign secretary, and went to Berchtesgaden without even his own interpreter and record keeper. He did not think through his bottom line and tended to throw away bargaining chips without gaining anything in return.

But Chamberlain's basic problem was not one of method but of assumptions. He flew to Berchtesgaden because he feared that the fate of Europe was in the hands of a madman; he came back with the illusion that he was forging a personal relationship with Hitler and that this would bear fruit because, at root, the Führer was a man of his word.

More dangerous still was the idealism (and hubris) of a politician who believed he could bring peace to Europe and, perhaps, the ambition of a marginalized younger son determined to outdo his father and his brother. But none of this would have mattered if Chamberlain and most of his colleagues had not convinced themselves that war over Czechoslovakia would mean the devastation of much of London. Not for the last time a British prime minister got it profoundly wrong about weapons of mass destruction.

It is also clear that, left to themselves, Chamberlain's political colleagues would eventually have undermined his summitry. To bypass Cabinet critics he moved key discussions into an inner circle, and his dramatic flight to Berchtesgaden silenced the skeptics. But his weakness there as a negotiator—conceding Sudeten secession on the spot—disconcerted many in the Cabinet. Even his inner circle warned that the next meeting must involve concessions by Hitler as well and they kept him under pressure throughout the Godesberg meeting.

The revolt led by Halifax after Chamberlain returned is not surprising when one remembers that, as early as September 4, the foreign secretary had been inclined to issue a warning to Hitler. What does remain puzzling is Halifax's failure to keep reasserting himself during the rest of the crisis. Having seen what happened when he was twice excluded from summitry, he might have been expected to claim a seat on the plane to Munich. But perhaps the euphoria in the Commons on September 28 carried all before it, catapulting Chamberlain back to the dominant position he enjoyed on the eve of Berchtesgaden.

What about Hitler as a summiteer? He had not sought the initial meeting: when Chamberlain invited himself to Berchtesgaden, it knocked the Führer off balance. For a moment he thought it might presage the threat of war. Like Chamberlain, Hitler did not prepare himself for the meetings—he was a politician of instinct. But across the table he proved much more skilful, using calculated rants to unsettle his opponent and extract concessions. Chamberlain was not a complete pushover, as interpreter Paul Schmidt realized at Berchtesgaden, but he tended to concede matters of substance whereas Hitler yielded on points of detail.

Until September 28, that is. Just at the moment when Halifax and Hoare turned the Cabinet against further concessions, Hitler lost his nerve. Until then he was set on war, not diplomacy. But at the brink—pressed by Britain and France, swayed by Mussolini, and shaken by the antiwar mood in Berlin—he pulled back and accepted a further summit. In doing so he may have unwittingly saved his own life. At Munich, aided by Mussolini, he engineered a peaceful settlement of the Sudeten secession on virtually the Godesberg terms.

In short, Hitler was a much more effective negotiator than Chamberlain, but he never wanted to negotiate, whereas Chamberlain, a less skilled tactician, got what he really wanted—peace not war.

Yet it was a hollow victory, because Hitler never intended to honor the Munich agreements. He was soon kicking himself for losing his nerve at the end of September. In March 1939, when he seized the rest of Czechoslovakia, he was not only going beyond his professed aim of simply bringing Germans within the Reich, he had also torn up what had been signed at Munich. A disenchanted Chamberlain was forced into a complete U-turn, offering guarantees to Poland, Romania and other countries possibly on the Nazi hit-list in a belated and panicky effort to deter further German expansion.

That summer Chamberlain still hoped for peace but Hitler was now bent on having a war over Poland, determined not back down a second time. He felt he had the measure of his opponents. "Our enemies are small worms," he told his generals in August 1939. "I saw them in Munich."[179]

He believed that the Nazi-Soviet pact, cobbled together by Ribbentrop, would deter Britain and France from fighting for Poland. But now the worms had turned, and it was Hitler's turn to act on misperceptions. He finally got his war over Poland but at the price of British and French belligerency years earlier than expected.

In the final weeks of his life, Hitler convinced himself that he should have gone to war in September 1938—"it was the last chance we had of localizing the conflict"—and that he had been taken for a ride by "that arch capitalist bourgeois, Chamberlain, with his deceptive umbrella" who traveled all the way to the Berghof knowing "very well that he really intended to wage ruthless war against us." Chamberlain "was quite prepared to tell me anything which he thought might serve to lull my suspicions," Hitler railed. "His one and only object in undertaking the trip was to gain time."[180]

That of course was not true: Chamberlain hoped and worked for a real change in Anglo-German relations. But gaining time *was* a subordinate goal in a worst-case scenario, because he was sure the country was not ready for war in 1938. Chamberlain's defenders later stressed that the year's grace allowed Britain to develop radar and to deploy its new Hurricanes and Spitfires, which were crucial for the Battle of Britain in 1940. But as we now know, British intelligence greatly exaggerated the strength of the Luftwaffe and the likely casualties from aerial bombardment. Hitler was simply not capable of delivering a devastating knockout blow on London in 1938.

Had Chamberlain been so inclined, he could have called Hitler's bluff. But Chamberlain was no gambler. He believed a statesman should not bluff unless he had the power to act decisively if his bluff was called. But Churchill, who was equally deluded about the Luftwaffe's ability to mount devastating attacks on London, was a compulsive card-player. Convinced that Hitler would back away from war if Britain bluffed it out firmly, he favored a firm Anglo-French front, ideally with Russian support. He called Chamberlain's visit to the Berghof "the stupidest thing that has ever been done," and was one of the few MPs to remain seated when the Commons exploded in delight at news of another conference at Munich. Eventually he did walk over to wish the prime minister "God speed" but added, to Chamberlain's deep irritation, "You were lucky."[181]

In the Commons on October 5 Churchill described the Munich settlement as "a total and unmitigated defeat," insisting that the differences between Berchtesgaden, Godesberg and Munich were minimal: "£1 was demanded at the pistol's point. When it was given, £2 were demanded at the pistol's point. Finally, the dictator consented to take £1 17s 6d and the rest in promises of goodwill for the future." Summitry as practiced by Chamberlain was not diplomatic negotiation but highway robbery.[182]

After Chamberlain's speech there was a tart exchange of letters with the prime minister in which epithets such as "unworthy" and "offensive" were exchanged.[183] Relations improved in the autumn of 1939, when Chamberlain brought Churchill into his War Cabinet; after Churchill became premier in May 1940 he found his predecessor to be a loyal and industrious colleague. Churchill particularly admired Chamberlain's fortitude and dignity in struggling with bowel cancer.

By the time Chamberlain died in November 1940, his reputation lay in ruins and "Munich" was well on the way to becoming a term of abuse. "Few men can have known such a tremendous reverse of fortune in so short a time," Chamberlain reflected sadly just before his death.[184]

But Churchill did not drive in the knife. The valedictory tribute he delivered in the Commons was one of his noblest orations, partly because of his newfound respect for Chamberlain but also because he too had been stretched on fortune's wheel. "The only guide to a man is his conscience; the only shield to his memory is the rectitude and sincerity of his actions," Churchill told a packed and silent House. "Herr Hitler protests with frantic words and gestures that he has only desired peace. What do these ravings and outpourings count before the silence of Neville Chamberlain's tomb?"[185]

Summitry had made Chamberlain's name and then destroyed it. Churchill believed the prime minister should have stood firm and stayed at home, rather than flying off to woo the dictator with a Czech dowry. But this did not mean that Churchill was opposed to summitry in principle; on the contrary, as premier he made it almost a way of life. And before the war ended, he would be accused of perpetrating another Munich.

3

YALTA 1945

Churchill, Roosevelt and Stalin

D URING THE COLD WAR the Yalta conference of February 1945 became notorious. In Gaullist France it was depicted as the moment when the superpowers divided Europe between them into two blocs. In America it was cited by Republicans as another example of craven appeasement, in which millions in Poland and eastern Europe were consigned to communist oppression. Sixty years on, President George W. Bush was still coupling Yalta with Munich as historic turning points when "the freedom of small nations was somehow expendable." This "attempt to sacrifice freedom for the sake of stability," the president declared, actually "left a continent divided and unstable. The captivity of millions in Central and Eastern Europe will be remembered as one of the greatest wrongs of history."[1]

Bush, like most Republicans, blamed Franklin Roosevelt for selling out to Stalin at Yalta. Yet the agreements were also negotiated by his great hero, Winston Churchill. To understand why, we need to comprehend both men's remarkable confidence in Stalin. And we must move beyond the conventional focus on Poland and look at the whole agenda of the conference. Yalta's problems lay in its preparation and implementation rather than in the parley at the summit itself.

NEVILLE CHAMBERLAIN PIONEERED modern summitry, but Winston Churchill made it almost routine. He was even readier than Chamberlain to take personal charge of foreign relations. In the first month of his premiership, Churchill flew across the Channel five times in an increasingly desperate effort to stop the French from surrendering.

Once Britain was left to fight Germany alone, Churchill turned his formidable attention on America. "No lover ever studied every whim of his mistress as I did those of President Roosevelt," he remarked later.[2] The courtship was conducted through nearly two thousand telegrams and letters,[3] but also face to face. Because Franklin Roosevelt was "the wheelchair president"—stricken with polio in his forties and henceforth unable to move unaided—Churchill usually traveled to North America.[4]

After their seaboard meeting off Newfoundland in August 1941, famous for the Atlantic Charter, they met three times in Washington and twice in Quebec, as well as at Casablanca, Cairo and Malta. They also conferred on two occasions with Josef Stalin—at Teheran in November 1943 and Yalta in February 1945—and Churchill went twice to Moscow, in August 1942 and October 1944.

President and prime minister both enjoyed these trips, which provided a welcome respite from the pressures of politics at home—especially when the meetings were held in warm and exotic locations. Plumping for North Africa rather than Alaska in January 1943, FDR told Churchill: "I prefer a comfortable oasis to the raft at Tilsit." FDR's allusion to Napoleon and Alexander I on the Niemen River in 1807 reveals the degree to which these leaders self-consciously thought of themselves as successors to the potentates of the past. Harold Macmillan, Churchill's emissary in North Africa and a lover of classical allusions, depicted Churchill and Roosevelt at Casablanca as an encounter between the Emperor of the East and the Emperor of the West, because it seemed "rather like a meeting of the later period of the Roman Empire."[5]

Yet these modern emperors traveled very differently. Churchill's first two visits to Roosevelt were by ship but he returned from America in January 1942 on a flying boat, which opened up new

Figure 3-1 During World War II, in the era of air travel, modern summitry took off. David Low depicts Churchill and Roosevelt flying across the Mediterranean for their January 1943 meeting at Casablanca, while Hitler and Mussolini look on, enraged, from the toe of Italy. (*Evening Standard,* January 28, 1943, Solo Syndicate, University of Kent Cartoon Library)

possibilities. "Perhaps when the weather gets better," he cabled the president in April, "I may propose myself for a weekend and flip over. We have so much to settle that would go easily in talk." After that Churchill flipped around in a big way. In all he flew 107,000 miles during the war, much of the time in unheated, unpressurized converted bombers that were frequently under threat from enemy planes.[6] After his ten-thousand-mile round trip to Moscow via Cairo and Teheran in August 1942, the American general Douglas MacArthur, no Anglophile, remarked that Churchill deserved the Victoria Cross for the journey alone. At Teheran, when someone said that Churchill, Roosevelt and Stalin were like the Trinity, the

Soviet leader quipped that Churchill was the Holy Ghost: "He flies around so much."[7]

Of the two "Big Three" summits of the war, Teheran has often been neglected. Yet in crucial respects it marked the turning point in the wartime alliance,[8] when America and Russia became dominant. What was agreed there is essential background to what transpired at Yalta.

During the first two years after Pearl Harbor, the British were the senior partner in the Anglo-American alliance. With more troops available for the European theater, they were able to override the preference of the U.S. military for an early, direct invasion of France, instead drawing the Allies into North Africa. FDR went along with this because he believed that some kind of action against Germany was essential that year in order to head off "Pacific first" sentiment at home. By November 1943, however, U.S. mobilization was almost complete. American preparedness, along with the presence of Stalin, meant that Churchill was outvoted at Teheran, where the Allies confirmed the invasion of Normandy, code-named Overlord, for the following spring.

D-Day on June 6, 1944, therefore occurred two years later than the most ardent American planners had wished; there has been debate ever since about whether the Western Allies could have landed earlier in France.[9] Probably they could have made a serious attempt in the summer of 1943, but only by husbanding their resources, particularly scarce merchant shipping and landing craft. Such an effort would have come at the expense of the Pacific war, where Japan was running amok, and would have precluded the landings in Morocco and Algeria in autumn 1942. Doing virtually nothing in 1942 was never a serious political option.

But the real point is that Britain and America did *not* invade France until 1944. As a consequence, the land war in Europe was decided largely on the Eastern Front. Between June 1941 and June 1944 (from Hitler's invasion of the Soviet Union up to D-Day), 93 percent of Germany's combat losses were inflicted by the Red Army. In cold figures that meant 4.2 million German dead, wounded or missing on the Eastern Front, against 329,000 in North Africa and Italy.[10]

Once the Soviets turned the tide at Stalingrad in January 1943 and then began the rollback at Kursk the following July, it was almost inevitable that they would end up deep in Eastern Europe. Stalin's influence at Teheran, indeed his readiness to leave his lair and meet Roosevelt and Churchill, reflected these new geopolitical realities.

June 1944 saw not only the great invasion of Normandy by America, Britain and their allies but also the massive Soviet summer offensive, code-named Bagration after one of Russia's generals in the war against Napoleon. In the West this operation is virtually unknown, yet its achievements were as significant as Overlord and came much more quickly. In a bare five weeks, while the Allies were still bogged down in the hedgerows of Normandy, the Red Army drove nearly five hundred miles across Belorussia and Poland. It destroyed thirty German divisions—more than the whole force engaged by the Allies in Italy—and inflicted double the losses of Stalingrad. By the end of July Soviet troops were on the outskirts of Warsaw.[11]

Bagration was only one of five great offensives mounted by Soviet forces during the summer and early autumn of 1944, in the course of which they recaptured the Baltic States and secured Romania, Bulgaria, Yugoslavia and much of Poland. This dramatic shift in the European balance of power was the stimulus for Churchill's second visit to Moscow in October 1944 and his so-called percentages deal with Stalin. On a piece of paper he itemized the percentages of influence each country would have in southeastern Europe. Precisely what the prime minister had in mind by the numbers is unclear, but Churchill's general aim was to highlight those Balkan countries in which the British felt a particular interest—notably Greece (supposedly 90 percent British) and Yugoslavia (fifty-fifty).

Churchill did not intend to imply that Britain had no interest elsewhere but Stalin seems to have understood his 90 percent stake in Romania and 80 percent in Bulgaria and in Hungary to signify virtually a free hand in these countries. They had all been conquered by the Red Army, unlike Greece (where British troops intervened) and Yugoslavia (liberated by Tito's partisans). As Stalin observed in April 1945: "Everyone imposes his own system as far as his army has the power to do so."[12] So Churchill and Stalin had very different understandings of spheres of influence and this mattered enormously during and after Yalta.

By February 1945, when the Big Three convened at Yalta, the Soviets were in control of much of Eastern Europe. They could not be evicted except by force, and it was politically impossible for Britain or America to turn on their ally in this way. The French and American myths about Yalta gloss over these realities. *If* the Western Allies can be said to have forfeited Eastern Europe, it was by their strategy in 1942–3 rather than their diplomacy in 1944–5.

The interesting issue about Yalta is not the things that Roosevelt and Churchill conceded (Stalin had most of them already) but their belief that it was possible to build a cooperative and durable relationship with the Soviet leader. As with Munich, this fundamental misjudgment takes us into the realms of perceptions, politics, and also hubris.

THE PRESIDENT WAS a "feely" politician, operating on a blend of intuition and experience, and this approach shaped his views of both Hitler and Stalin. FDR knew Germany well, or at least the Kaiser's Germany before the First World War. From school and travel there he derived firm opinions about the German "character" which lasted all his life. In 1940 FDR said that he had "little patience with those who seek to draw a clear distinction between the German government and the German people." He recalled how in 1893 his German school class started on "Heimatkunde"— geography lessons centered on home. The first year, they moved out from the village and local towns to cover the whole province of Hesse-Darmstadt. The following year they learned what could be seen "on the way to the French border." He did not take the course the year after, but understood that the class was "conducted" to France, "all roads leading to Paris."[13]

Holding as he did these stereotypes about German militarism, rooted in Prussia, Roosevelt was against Hitler from the start. He read the abridged English edition of *Mein Kampf* soon after entering the White House in 1933 and wrote caustically on the flyleaf: "This translation is so expurgated as to give a wholly false view of what Hitler really is or says. The German original would make a different story."[14]

In the mid-1930s the president, preoccupied with the Depression, left the problem of Nazi Germany primarily to Britain and France, but the Czech crisis of September 1938 marked a fundamental shift in his attitude. Whereas talking to Hitler persuaded Chamberlain that the Führer was not a lunatic, the vivid reports from U.S. ambassadors in Europe about the British and French meetings with Hitler had the opposite effect on the president.

Speaking to senators in January 1939, Roosevelt described the German leader as a "wild man," walking up and down the room for hours on end, "pounding the table and making speeches." What, asked the president, can be done about someone like that? "We would call him a 'nut.' But there isn't any use in calling him a 'nut' because he is a power and we have to recognize that."[15]

These perceptions about Germany and Hitler were fundamental to the president's worldview.[16] They pushed Roosevelt into rearmament in 1938–9, spurred him into backing Britain in 1940–1, and drove him by 1943 to demand Germany's "unconditional surrender." Only the demise of Hitler and radical reform in Germany, he believed, could create a peaceful and secure Europe: one could not negotiate with such a man or such a people.

The animosity was mutual: the eugenicist Führer despised the American president as the crippled leader of a mongrel race. The contest between Roosevelt and Hitler became very personal, whereas Churchill's animus was directed at German militarism and autocracy.

About the Soviet Union, Roosevelt knew little and feared even less. He viewed Russia historically as a continental power without colonial ambitions—like America, in his opinion, and unlike Britain and France. He was never much worried about the expansion of Bolshevism; he viewed the revolution as a temporary reaction to oppression and inequality, and moved quickly to recognize the Soviet Union once president in 1933. In April 1943 he expressed his belief that "the revolutionary currents of 1917 may be spent in this war" and predicted that the Soviet Union would develop along "evolutionary constitutional lines" in the future, probably toward a form of state socialism. He told a British diplomat in December 1944 "that he was not afraid of Communism as such. There were many varieties of Communism and not all of them were necessarily harmful."[17]

Roosevelt's approach was typical of liberal American opinion at this time. Stalinism was seen as a very different entity from Bolshevism and even the right, though fearing Russian expansion, believed that the Soviet Union was no longer bent on world revolution.[18]

Roosevelt's main wartime priority was to overcome Russia's suspicion of the outside world and draw it into a durable postwar international community. He intended that the new United Nations would depend on the leading powers, what he called the "policemen" of world politics, which was why he needed to get around the table with the Soviet leader. In typically breezy tones he told Churchill in March 1942: "I think I can personally handle Stalin better than either your Foreign Office or my State Department. Stalin hates the guts of all your top people. He thinks he likes me better, and I hope he will continue to do so."[19] Convinced of his personal powers of persuasion, the president worked tirelessly in 1942–3 to arrange a meeting with Stalin. He was not particularly bothered about Eastern Europe, recognizing he had no real influence there. "I don't care two hoots about Poland," he joked during the Teheran conference. "Wake me up when we talk about Germany."[20] And in May 1944 he told Averell Harriman, his ambassador in Moscow, "that he didn't care whether the countries bordering Russia were communized." His overriding aim was to achieve a settlement that would satisfy Stalin and stabilize Europe without offending American opinion. Harriman considered the president disturbingly optimistic that he could "persuade Stalin to alter his point of view on many matters" that Harriman was sure Stalin would "never agree to."[21]

At first glance Churchill's attitude to the Soviet Union seems very different. A vehement critic of "the foul baboonery of Bolshevism" during the Revolution, he became the leading British advocate of aid to Lenin's enemies. In the early 1930s he was also an outspoken critic of Stalin's camps: "The conditions there are tantamount to slavery. That Government has despotic power."[22] Churchill never lost his hatred of Soviet ideology or his lurking fears of Russian imperialism. "It would be a measureless disaster" he told his foreign secretary Anthony Eden in November 1942, "if Russian barbarism overlaid the culture and independence of the ancient States of Europe."[23]

Britain's proximity to the Continent meant that Churchill, with his keen sense of the balance of power, could not be indifferent if the Soviets absorbed Eastern Europe. And, unlike Roosevelt, Churchill also felt special responsibilities toward the Poles. In 1939 the British government had guaranteed Poland's independence—indeed this was the immediate reason for its declaration of war—and London became the home of the Polish government in exile after Hitler and Stalin had overrun Poland. As prime minister, Churchill worked to secure a Polish settlement that would satisfy the Soviet-backed communists and the London Poles; he pushed unsuccessfully for a fifty-fifty deal when in Moscow in October 1944.

For all these reasons, Churchill was much more engaged than Roosevelt in the Soviet question. His mood was also more volatile. In April 1943, although acknowledging that "the overwhelming preponderance of Russia" would be "the dominant fact" of Europe's future," he asserted "we shall certainly try to live on good terms with her." During a difficult moment at Teheran in November, however, he speculated about another "more bloody war" in which "man might destroy man and wipe out civilization."[24]

But Churchill was nonetheless steadfast in his conviction that the Soviet leader was amenable to negotiation. He remarked in January 1944 that "if only I could dine with Stalin once a week, there would be no trouble at all. We get on like a house on fire."[25]

Why did Churchill, so hard-headed about Hitler, maintain such illusions about Stalin's tractability? In large part it was because the two dictators were viewed very differently in the West. In contrast with the plenitude of information available on Nazi Germany in the 1930s, the Soviet regime had remained virtually a closed book during this period. Diplomatic staff had minimal opportunity for contacts with Russian officials, let alone the ordinary population. Even ambassadors rarely met Stalin; they dealt with his foreign minister, Vyacheslav Molotov, renowned as a hard-faced "Mr Nyet." Moreover the Soviet press provided virtually no useful political intelligence, in stark contrast with the media in Washington, which offered endless insights into the White House and Capitol Hill. Churchill spoke aptly in 1939 of Soviet policy as "a riddle wrapped in a mystery inside an enigma."[26]

Then suddenly the Soviets needed outside help and the doors to the Kremlin were flung open. In the second half of 1941, Roosevelt's emissaries Harry Hopkins and Averell Harriman and Churchill's right-hand men Max Beaverbrook and Anthony Eden all spent hours with Stalin. Churchill met him for extended summits on five occasions, joined by Roosevelt for two of them.

Although all Stalin's visitors were conscious that they were talking to a ruthless autocrat who had sent hundreds of thousands to their deaths, that was not how he seemed in the flesh. At five foot five, an inch or so smaller than Churchill, with a pockmarked face and withered arm, the Soviet leader lacked charisma. He spoke quietly and to the point, not wasting his words, and also displayed a dry wit. At Teheran, for instance, when Churchill admitted that the British political complexion had changed during the war, becoming, if not red, at least "a trifle pinker," Stalin shot back: "That is a sign of good health."[27] The nickname "Uncle Joe" by which Roosevelt and Churchill referred to Stalin in their private correspondence reflected this almost avuncular image.

Stalin's dress was also unassuming. One of Churchill's entourage in Moscow in 1942, Colonel Ian Jacob, described his "lilac coloured tunic, buttoned up to the neck, his cotton trousers stuffed into long boots" and "rather shambling walk." Jacob summed Stalin up as a "little peasant, who would not have looked at all out of place in a country lane with a pickaxe over his shoulder." During that same visit Churchill also referred to Stalin privately as "a peasant" whom he knew exactly how to handle. In reality Stalin was wearing standard Communist Party dress, but the idea that he was a provincial yokel who had hacked his way to the top helped British interlocutors to explain away his rough edges. As one Foreign Office official put it, not entirely tongue-in-cheek: "It's too bad that Stalin and Mol[otov] were not at Eton and Harrow, but what can we do about it?"[28]

Later in the war Stalin's attire changed dramatically. By the summer of 1943, after the great victories at Stalingrad and Kursk, he had adopted the uniform of a field marshal, associating himself with the Red Army now that it was on a winning streak. Perceptive visitors to his office in the Kremlin also noted that the portraits of Marx, Engels and other communist luminaries had been replaced by generals from the "Patriotic War" against Napoleon, after which the current "Great Patriotic War" was named.[29]

And yet this transformation of Stalin from "Boss" to "Generalissimo" did not unsettle his Western allies. Whereas Hitler in military dress looked sinister, and Mussolini comical, Marshal Stalin's manner in conferences remained calm and wry as he sat doodling and puffing his pipe. There was no sign of the Hitler rants or Mussolini bombast that many British diplomats had endured before the war. Even in uniform Stalin did not seem like a dictator.[30]

Of course the Soviet leader could be difficult at times. In 1941–2 Harriman and Beaverbrook, Eden and then Churchill were all subject to the one-two-three treatment, in which a bruising middle meeting was sandwiched between cordial opening and closing sessions. Equally important, this "nasty second-session ploy" became familiar to Stalin's visitors and was accepted as one of his negotiating tactics.[31] It was less evident in the conferences in the second phase of the wartime alliance, from Teheran onward, and this itself was taken as a sign of deepening trust.

Good relations with Stalin seemed doubly important to Churchill and Roosevelt because so little was known about Soviet decision making. Even men at the very center of power in Washington and London had only the most rudimentary sense of Kremlinology. When Stalin suddenly emerged into the spotlight after mid-1941, this threw into relief the continued darkness shrouding the rest of Moscow, making him seem even more reassuring and important. In March 1943 Churchill told Eden of "the feeling which has for some time been growing in my mind that there are two forces to be reckoned with in Russia: (a) Stalin himself, personally cordial to me. (b) Stalin in council, a grim thing behind him, which we and he have both to reckon with."[32] This supposed polarity helped Churchill make sense of the ups and downs of his correspondence with the Kremlin. Friendly telegrams were interpreted as personal messages from Stalin, nasty ones as products of "the Soviet machine" which, Churchill told FDR in October 1943, "is quite convinced it can get everything by bullying."[33]

Nor was this way of thinking peculiar to the British. Harriman, as ambassador to Moscow, developed his own two-camps theory of Soviet policy making. "Many of Stalin's counsellors," he told the State Department in September 1944, "see things to a degree at least as we do, whereas others are opposed . . . Through our actions we should attempt to encourage his confidence in the advice of the former group and make him realize that the others get him into trouble when he follows their advice."[34] Both Harriman and Roosevelt were prone to blame Soviet displays of truculence on unfriendly factions in the Politburo or on the failure of the Foreign Ministry or Soviet intelligence to provide the Kremlin with accurate information. Stalin himself was almost always given the benefit of the doubt.[35]

For Churchill, his second visit to Moscow in October 1944 confirmed his favorable impression of Stalin. "I have had v[er]y nice talks with the Old Bear," he scribbled to his wife. "I like him the more I see him. Now they respect us here & I am sure they wish to work w[ith] us."[36] Churchill's litmus test was Stalin's promise to respect British predominance in Greece—the heart of his percentages deal. Once in place, the agreement freed Churchill to send British troops into Athens when the Germans left in order to prevent the communists taking power. In December 1944, in messages to Eden, he called Stalin "that great and good man" and said that "I am increasingly impressed (up to date) with the loyalty with which, under much temptation and very likely pressure, Stalin has kept off Greece in accordance with our agreement."[37]

How did the Soviet leader view his Western partners? They were of course vastly different from him in background, both being from comfortable landed families in capitalist societies whereas the young Josef Vissarionovich Dzugashvili came from a broken home in dirt-poor rural Georgia. Those early years were profoundly important. Although Stalin had a sharp mind and a prodigious memory, he always had an inferiority complex about his lack of formal education; he was also deeply xenophobic, often lashing out at signs of Russian subservience to "cosmopolitan" Western culture. Sixteen years on the run as a revolutionary terrorist had confirmed his isolated, brutal nature, which was evident again and again as he maneuvered his way to the top of the Bolshevik party after Lenin's death and disposed of his enemies, real or imagined, in the purges of the 1930s. As a Marxist-Leninist, Stalin—his revolutionary pseudonym, meaning "man of steel"—had no doubt about the underlying enmity of the capitalist West, which had tried to strangle Bolshevism at birth by aiding its enemies in the civil war of 1918–21. The main foe, he believed, was Britain and its vast empire: in 1941 he was more afraid of the British trying to entice him into war against Germany than he was of an attack from Hitler, even though the Nazi buildup was plain for all to see.[38]

For Stalin, even more than for his partners, the wartime alliance constituted a marriage of convenience. He never shook off his fear that the British and Americans might sign a separate peace with Hitler—he even alluded to this concern obliquely during Churchill's visit in October 1944[39]—and their delays in opening a second front were seen as sinister confirmation. Having turned the Nazi tide by its own efforts, the Soviet Union, he believed, must also provide for its own postwar security; for Stalin, that meant preventing Germany from becoming a threat once again, probably by dismembering the country into small states on the pre-Bismarck

model. It also required a quiescent, client state in Poland—historically the gateway for German aggression. More generally, Stalin
wanted to regain Russian territories lost in World War I, including
eastern Poland and the Baltic states, and to expand into traditional
czarist areas of influence, particularly around the Black Sea (Russia's gateway to the Mediterranean) and on the Pacific. The concept
of territorial security was therefore fundamental to his regime.[40]

So Stalin was very different from Hitler, a true megalomaniac
who lusted for world domination. But, because of both his personal
background and recent Soviet experience, Stalin's craving for security was "insatiable"—he was always seeking more territory and
more influence—and this lay at the root of growing friction with
the West.[41] Furthermore, as a Marxist-Leninist, Stalin never abandoned the hope of eventual international revolution. He recognized that in the modern world change could come by political
means—"today socialism is possible even under the English
monarchy"[42]—but believed that the vast upheavals of the war were
part of the structural "crisis of capitalism." For the moment, he said
in January 1945, the Soviet Union had joined the "democratic"
faction of capitalists against the "fascist" faction, because Hitler
posed the greater threat, but "in the future" the Soviets would confront their former allies.[43]

In the winter of 1944–5, however, Stalin was still concentrating
on victory in Europe and then on entering the war against Japan to
secure his territorial aims. Moreover he knew that his shattered
country was in no position for a new conflict in the immediate future. In fact he anticipated substantial economic aid, indirectly via
agreed reparations from Germany and directly through a peacetime
version of American lend-lease. This meant staying on good terms
with his wartime allies. The Italian and French communist parties,
both strongly placed because of their prominence in the wartime
resistance, were warned against a revolutionary bid for power because Italy and France were both firmly in the British and American sphere. Stalin took the same line on Greece once Churchill had
made clear Britain's special interest. On the other hand, he treated
the rest of the percentages deal as giving him the carte blanche he

desired in Romania, Bulgaria and Hungary. Guided by Marxist-Leninist ideology about the innate antagonisms of the capitalist powers, he was also ready to exploit policy differences between Britain and America. Roosevelt's ostentatious digs at Churchill during the Teheran conference—intended to relieve Stalin's suspicions of a combined Anglo-American front—seemed to confirm the aptness of this tactic. He felt he could work with the Allies while playing one off against the other.

On November 6, 1944, in his widely publicized speech on the anniversary of the Bolshevik Revolution, Stalin dwelt on the value of the "anti-German coalition." He insisted that it was "based not on casual and transient motives, but on vitally important and longstanding interests," particularly to prevent fresh aggression from Germany. Hence the need for an organization of "peaceful states" that could employ armed forces as needed to prevent aggression.[44]

Even allowing for wartime rhetoric, Stalin's commitment to a continued alliance was probably genuine. Stalin did not want another hot war, or even cold war. He favored continuing dialogue with the West but on his terms, hopeful that these would be accommodated by Western leaders who were now clearly wooing him enthusiastically. He did not have a clear diplomatic blueprint, but entertained a spectrum of aims.[45] At the minimum these included essential security issues such as Poland and Germany. Stalin's maximum aims were desirables whose realization would depend on circumstances. Like Roosevelt, Stalin's diplomacy was a mix of gut instincts and skillful opportunism. Churchill was also ready to seize the moment but he preferred to pin things down on paper: the percentages deal exemplifies both these features of his diplomatic style.

From the documentation now available, it would seem that Roosevelt and Churchill were right to feel that Stalin was a man with whom they could conduct meaningful negotiations. Chamberlain was mistaken on that point about Hitler. But the American and British leaders were wrong to believe that they were developing a real rapport with the Soviet leader, because he viewed the world in fundamentally different terms. Once again a summit would be built on fallacious assumptions.

IT WAS AGAINST THIS BACKGROUND that planning for Yalta began in earnest in the fall of 1944. Although the State Department disliked Churchill's percentages deal, the agreement suited Roosevelt's broad objective of preventing European territorial problems from disrupting the Big Three alliance. He cabled Harriman on October 11, 1944, that his main interest was to take "such steps as are practicable" to "insure against the Balkans getting us into a future international war."[46]

But the president still believed that he was much better suited than Churchill to drawing the Soviet leader into a harmonious postwar relationship and he was anxious to launch the new United Nations Organization before the end of the war. FDR therefore redoubled his efforts for a second Big Three summit but pressure of business in Washington made it impossible until after his inauguration for a fourth term on January 20, 1945.

On the location, Stalin held sway. He rejected various Mediterranean venues—Cyprus, Sicily, Alexandria, even Jerusalem—and insisted instead on the Black Sea, which the British and Americans considered too remote, a health hazard and still dangerous for warships because of mines.[47] Stalin justified his obduracy on the grounds that "his health was beginning to fail him"—it had taken two weeks to get over his trip to Teheran—and his doctors did not like him to fly. He said only someone with the robust health of Churchill—"that desperate fellow"—could stand such journeys.[48]

Stalin's health did deteriorate during the war, including heart problems, but this was an excuse. He was in fact petrified of flying and also wary of going outside the security net of the NKVD, his brutal secret service. With the Red Army surging across Eastern Europe and Soviet help deemed vital for the Pacific war, Churchill and Roosevelt needed the summit more than Stalin. So, reluctantly they agreed to go to him. Because of the epic nature of the journey, Churchill proposed "Argonaut" as the conference code name—an allusion to classical mythology and the intrepid search for the Golden Fleece.

Roosevelt set out from Washington on January 22 for a ten-day five-thousand-mile sea journey to Malta; Churchill traveled there by air, leaving London on January 29. The two leaders had lunch and dinner together on Malta on February 2 but Roosevelt, as before Teheran, did not want to give Stalin the impression of an Anglo-American front and evaded all Churchill's efforts to get down to serious business. Eden, the foreign secretary, warned Harry Hopkins, Roosevelt's confidant, that "we were going into a decisive conference and had so far neither agreed what we would discuss nor how to handle matters with a Bear who would certainly know his mind."[49] This did not worry the president, however. True to his conception of summitry, he had told Stalin: "I like to keep these discussions informal, and I have no reason for formal agenda."[50] He also arranged that the press were excluded entirely from Yalta, except for a few service photographers from each country to generate official publicity.

Nevertheless Yalta was very different in scale and form from Chamberlain's personal summits in 1938 because it also brought together the foreign ministers and the military staffs. And, despite Roosevelt's cold-shouldering of Churchill, their two foreign ministers met beforehand in Malta and thrashed out a common line on most of the main issues for the conference. Thus the personal encounters that the two leaders loved were embedded in formalized diplomacy.

Initially the British and Americans had talked of bringing 35 people apiece, but that was utopian: at Malta their joint party had already swollen to 700.[51] During the night of February 2–3 a succession of transport planes took off on the fourteen-hundred-mile flight to the Crimea. Each government also sailed a headquarters ship into the Black Sea and moored it at Sevastopol—the *Franconia*, a converted British cruise liner, and the *Catoctin*, a U.S. naval auxiliary—to handle essential communications with home. Their crews further swelled the total complement of "Argonauts"—the British group alone totalled 750, of whom 200 were the delegation proper, another 300 were officers and other ranks from Air Transport Command, and the rest were marines, drivers, medics and naval communications personnel.[52]

Churchill and Roosevelt both flew from Malta to Saki, on the west coast of the Crimea. The flight took more than seven hours, followed by another four and a half hours by car over the snow-covered mountains to Yalta on the southeast coast, once the czar's summer resort. Along the way they saw frequent signs of the savage fighting the previous year to drive out the Nazis.

The mountains shielded Yalta from the north winds but the temperature in February was still only a few degrees above freezing.[53] The area had been systematically looted by the Germans, so the Soviets had to organize everything from scratch in a few weeks. Ambassador Harriman's daughter (who was in the Soviet Union as his embassy hostess) wrote home:

> All the Moscow hotels have been stripped of their staffs, furniture and plates, china, kitchen utensils to look after us . . . Besides that, the country nearby is being scoured for such things as shaving mirrors, coat hangers and wash bowls . . . We've just found one ashtray that advertises a china factory "by appointment of" five Czars!![54]

When the British queried the single bed provided for Churchill—he worked in bed and liked to spread out his papers—the Soviets grudgingly had a double bed shipped down from Moscow. It arrived just before the prime minister.[55]

The conference sessions took place in the Livadia Palace, south-west of Yalta, built for Nicholas II in 1911 with panoramic views over the Black Sea. In consideration of Roosevelt's disability, the Americans also stayed in the palace, with the president accommodated on the ground floor near the czar's ballroom where the plenary sessions were held. Churchill and the British were allocated the Vorontsov Palace, twelve miles south down the coast—a bizarre mix of Moorish and Gothic architecture—while Stalin and his party stayed in the old Yusupov Palace, known now as the Koreis villa, which was midway between the two.

The three delegations took turns hosting communal meals in appropriate style: on February 5, for instance, Stettinius entertained his fellow foreign ministers to a six-course lunch that included Grapefruit aux États Unis, Chicken Consommé à la Washington, nd Tambole à la Californie (a creamy apple dessert).[56]

However grand the menus, the living conditions were primitive. Most of the British and Americans, even senior military, shared rooms and had to line up like ordinary soldiers to use the scarce toilets and baths. They also tried in vain to get rid of the bedbugs by spraying with large quantities of DDT.

Bugs of another sort were also pervasive. The accommodations of both delegations were fitted with NKVD microphones; daily summaries of what was said were provided to Stalin. The Soviets also received a steady stream of top-level policy background from highly placed agents in London and Washington, one of whom, Alger Hiss, was a member of the State Department delegation at Yalta. All this might suggest that Stalin knew so much about the minds of his conference partners that the meetings were almost a formality, but this assumption is debatable. So pervasive were conspiracy theories in the Kremlin that the Soviet moles were suspected, by this stage in the war, of being Allied double agents: their information seemed too good to be true. Moreover Stalin had become more confident that he "knew" his adversaries. He took much less interest in the daily summaries at Yalta than he had at Teheran, where he cross-examined the eavesdroppers intently each morning on the detail and tone of Allied conversations.[57]

On their side, the British and Americans were now well aware of the danger of bugging and took precautions at Yalta, for instance, by holding confidential conversations out of doors. They also protected the communications they sent home. Messages between Yalta and the relay ships at Sevastopol had to be transmitted by teletype and, after a few days of what was euphemistically called "wire trouble," U.S. engineers laid a completely new landline, some eighty miles in length. Churchill, for his part, was warned that security considerations made it impossible for him to receive his usual daily diet of Ultra decrypts of Axis signals.[58]

Even if Stalin could read some of Roosevelt's and Churchill's cards, this did not give him a decisive advantage: what really counted was how each man played his hand at the conference table. But Churchill and Roosevelt had both been weakened by the summit in Teheran. The prime minister had contracted severe pneumonia, with heart fibrillations, and for a time there were fears for his life. Roosevelt's health never recovered from Teheran. Chronically ill in the early months of 1944, he was eventually persuaded to have a thorough medical checkup with a cardiologist who concluded that the president was in "God-awful" condition, suffering from anemia, high blood pressure and heart disease.[5] FDR agreed to cut down on smoking and alcohol, but his gray gaunt face, loss of weight, and wavering attention were all signs of serious deterioration.

In early 1945 Churchill's doctor, Lord Moran, found the prime minister ill and run down; Churchill's staff complained that he was working much less efficiently than earlier in the war, while Cabinet colleagues were now extremely irritated by his rambling verbosity.[60] During the Yalta conference Eden was infuriated at times by Churchill's long speeches and failure to grasp key details.[61] And Moran was frankly appalled when he saw Roosevelt at Saki airport. He "looked old and thin and drawn . . . he sat looking straight ahead with his mouth open, as if he were not taking things in." Most of the British delegation commented on the way FDR "had gone to bits physically" and "seemed to have little grip on things."[62] Summitry requires quick wits and mental stamina. Arriving at Yalta, neither Churchill nor Roosevelt seemed at their best.

UNLIKE THE IMPROVISED SUMMITS of September 1938, Yalta followed a set routine.[63] Each afternoon there was a plenary session involving the Big Three and about twenty advisors, sitting around a circular table in the hall of the Livadia Palace. The meeting usually began at 4 p.m. and lasted for three or four hours. Even with a break for tea, imbibed Russian-style from large glasses in silver holders, these were long and taxing affairs, during which tempers sometimes became frayed. It became a conference joke that Churchill's consumption of cigars rose in proportion to his agitation. Both he and Roosevelt listened intently to Stalin. Churchill watched the Soviet leader even when his words were being translated, while the president often nodded his head or changed his expression in response to what Stalin said.[64]

There were in all eight plenaries, each day of the conference from Sunday, February 4, to Sunday the 11th. Both the three military delegations and the foreign ministers also held meetings, usually over lunch, with the venue rotating around the three palaces. The military were concerned with plans for the last phase of the European war, including how to avoid bombing each other's forces as they all converged on the heart of the Reich. The U.S. and Soviet military also discussed the Red Army's entry into the Pacific war. Meanwhile the foreign ministers and their staffs were tidying up the problems thrown up by the Big Three and haggling over the wording of key documents: they often met again after dinner as well as holding many informal meetings with their leaders.

Roosevelt and the Americans had two main priorities. First, on the diplomatic side, to clear up the remaining differences about the constitution of the United Nations Organization, so that a founding conference could be convened as soon as possible. The president himself was not too bothered about specifics, but the UN was politically essential as the means of tying the American public into a postwar order and avoiding another isolationist backlash as had occurred after 1918. FDR also believed that a Soviet commitment to the UN, in contrast with its alienation from the League of Nations after World War I, would be a token of its willingness to cooperate in postwar security.

Roosevelt's other priority was to get Stalin to commit to an early entry in the war against Japan. Although Roosevelt had been informed at the end of 1944 that the first atomic bomb would be ready in August,[65] no one could yet envisage it as a war-winning weapon. American planners still believed they would have to mount a full-scale invasion of the Japanese home islands. Since this invasion could not begin before the spring of 1946, because of the vast redeployment of troops and supplies from Europe, U.S. Army Chief of Staff George C. Marshall was anxious for Soviet help. Stalin had made a general promise at Teheran that he would join the war against Japan after Germany had surrendered. At Yalta the American military wanted to tie down the details, while the State Department sought to establish Stalin's territorial demands. Roosevelt hoped these could be tied to his larger goal of a strong, united China as a bulwark of postwar Asia.

The British deemed the future of Europe to be more important than the UN. With the Red Army already occupying half of Poland, it seemed vital to settle the borders of the new Polish state and to agree on a government that would satisfy the émigré leadership exiled in London. For Roosevelt the exact details were less important—his overriding aim was to prevent the Polish question from undermining Allied unity—but he too could not simply rubber-stamp the existing communist government in Warsaw.

The British were also anxious to avoid repeating what they considered the mistakes of the Versailles settlement on Germany, particularly the punitive reparations that had destabilized the international economy and the substantial losses of territory that provoked German demands for restitution. The Foreign Office, mindful of another "lesson" of World War I, was skeptical that the United States would play a major role in postwar European security. Eden therefore pressed Churchill to ensure that the French were given a full role with the Big Three in the occupation and control of Germany as part of rehabilitating France as a major power.

The British were also anxious for a formal agreement on procedures for repatriating Allied prisoners of war. The Red Army had liberated many British soldiers from German captivity, while thousands of Soviet citizens were now in the hands of the Western Allies. In principle, an exchange seemed simple but beneath it lurked both practical and moral problems.

Stalin's priorities at Yalta are harder to pin down because less Soviet documentation is available; nonetheless, one can sense them clearly from his behavior at Yalta. In most of the sessions his interventions were short and to the point; Churchill and Roosevelt wanted more from him and tended to make the running. But Stalin did take the initiative in raising the question of whether Germany should be dismembered—broken into a number of smaller states—

nd he presented precise demands for substantial reparations from he defeated enemy. The Polish question was also very important, as ndicated by the unusually long speeches Stalin delivered on this ubject.

Aside from the long-term issue of Soviet territory and security, Stalin wanted to ensure order and a friendly government in the rear of the Red Army as it drove into Germany: he kept harping on about attacks by Polish partisans on Soviet troops. These complaints were not entirely unreasonable but, under cover of the need for security in a war zone, the NKVD was systematically eliminating the noncommunist Polish leaders. The question of Japan also mattered greatly to Stalin but he let the Americans take the initiative, as they were clearly ready to do.

The Big Three came to the table with a range of very different aims and priorities. Churchill and Stalin differed about key issues, and the likelihood of clashes between them was therefore higher than between Roosevelt and Stalin. On some matters, such as the dismemberment of Germany and the future of France, the Americans and Soviets took a very similar line but, conversely, the British shared some of Stalin's skepticism about American plans for the UN. Conference diplomacy is about resolving differences through an interlocking set of compromises and tradeoffs, in which no party gains everything but all get something and concede something. This is what happened at Yalta. Over the first two days the Big Three brought most of the diplomatic issues to the table. From Wednesday, February 6, the deals began to be made.

FRICTION OVER THE United Nations Organization dated back to the Dumbarton Oaks conference of August–October 1944. This lengthy gathering in Washington, D.C., established the outline structure of the new body, including a General Assembly of all members and a Security Council, or executive, whose inner core would comprise five permanent members: the Big Three plus France and China. The latter two were allies of Britain and America respectively. Moreover the British Dominions, such as Australia

and Canada, would be voting members and the Americans were
trying to pack the Assembly with Latin American clients who had
not formally declared war on the Axis. All this alarmed the Soviets,
who wanted to be absolutely sure that their interests could not be
overridden in the new international body. They sought assurances
on the principle of unanimity in the Security Council—an effective veto—and demanded seats for the sixteen Soviet republics on
the fiction that they, too, were autonomous entities. The United
States tried to clarify the proposed voting procedures in a message
from Roosevelt on December 5, 1944, but the Soviets remained
obdurate on both questions and these had to be resolved at Yalta
before the UN could convene.

Stalin was never particularly bothered about the United Nations
as an institution; he was convinced that security would depend on
military strength and on deals among the great powers. But, given
the importance attached by the Americans to it, he was ready to
play along and extract concessions in return. At Yalta he moved
with considerable dexterity, exploiting the fact that neither Roosevelt nor Churchill was particularly committed to the detailed blue-
prints of the State Department.[66]

At the start of the plenary session on February 6, Edward R.
Stettinius Jr., the U.S. secretary of state, read out a detailed clarification of the voting procedures. Stalin and Molotov used his admission that there had been "a minor drafting change" from earlier
proposals to ask for time to study the document. During the session
the Soviets maintained their demand about seats for the sixteen Soviet republics.[67]

At next day's plenary, however, Stalin announced that the voting
proposals were acceptable and that the Soviets would now ask for
only two or three republics to be original members of the Assembly. It is likely that Stalin and his advisors had already concluded
that these were acceptable, and they gave a delayed and apparently
grudging approval at Yalta, as well as dropping their implausible demand for sixteen seats, in order to gain credit for use on other issues. The fact that Stalin and Molotov made these concessions jus

before making Soviet proposals on the Polish question strengthens the impression of a bargaining ploy.

For Roosevelt, however, the way the Soviets had come round on the UN represented "real progress"—he said he was "much gratified" by the Soviet change of heart—and FDR's chief of staff, Admiral Leahy, noted in his diary that February 7 represented "a major victory for the President."[68] With the UN structure largely in place, Roosevelt was able to secure agreement for its founding conference to be held in San Francisco on April 25.

On the question of extra Soviet votes, the State Department tried to reserve the American position, fearful of a backlash back home, but in the foreign ministers' meeting on February 8 Eden backed the Soviet compromise proposal. He had ulterior motives: India had been a member of the League of Nations, even though still a dependent part of the British Empire, and the British wanted Soviet support in perpetuating this anomaly.[69] They quietly secured Roosevelt's agreement to the additional Soviet votes behind the backs of American diplomats.

The conference's final protocol therefore stated that the United States and the United Kingdom "would support a proposal to admit to original membership" of the UN the two Soviet republics of the Ukraine and Belorussia. When FDR warned Stalin of a possible outcry back home, the Soviet leader said he was willing to support a proposal for the United States to have three General Assembly votes in return.[70]

On the Pacific war, the outcome was also satisfactory for the Americans. The Soviets not only confirmed their plans to enter the war but also agreed to detailed and regular discussions with the U.S. military mission in Moscow. Stettinius remarked to Marshall as they were leaving Yalta, with its ubiquitous bedbugs and rudimentary plumbing, that the general would doubtless be glad that the week was over. "For what we have gained here," Marshall replied, "I would gladly have stayed a whole month."[71] In parallel with the military discussions, Averell Harriman elicited the Soviet territorial demands—mostly allowing Stalin to regain Russian territory lost to Japan or economic concessions in China from czarist times.

Roosevelt accepted these with virtually no demurral when he met Stalin alone on February 8.

Stalin, as we now know, was desperately anxious to get into the Pacific war as soon as he could extricate his combat troops from Europe.[72] Yet Roosevelt was convinced that Soviet entry had to be bought. The Americans seem to have been frankly naïve about Stalin's intentions and objectives. But the deal was all part of binding the Soviets—the suspicious odd-man-out of interwar diplomacy—into a network of international cooperation. And Roosevelt probably saw the concessions as relatively small in consequence. Concluding an agreement now had the advantage of forestalling possibly larger Soviet gains later, once the Red Army was unleashed into Manchuria, particularly if a deal could be tied into his larger Asian policy. FDR accomplished this linkage in the final agreement by indicating that the concessions in China had to be approved by Chiang Kai-shek's nationalist government and that the Soviet Union was ready to sign a pact of "friendship and alliance" with Chiang.[73]

Although Churchill was excluded from the Far Eastern deal making at Yalta and later distanced himself from it in his memoirs, he readily assented to the terms when talking privately with Stalin on February 10.[74] Nor was his approval given on impulse. In October 1944 he had told Eden that Stalin's promise during their Moscow conference to "march on Japan" had been "the most important statement" of the whole visit (which included his percentages accord over the Balkans). And a few days before Yalta, he informed his foreign secretary:

A speedy termination of the Japanese war, such as might be procured by the mere fact of a Russian declaration against Japan, would undoubtedly save us many thousands of millions of pounds. The Staffs see no particular harm in the presence of Russia as a Pacific Power. I should not be able to oppose the kind of Russian wishes you mention, especially as the *quid pro quo* far outvalues anything we are likely to get out of China.[75]

While Churchill and Roosevelt convinced themselves of the need to buy Stalin's entry into the war against Japan, the British Foreign Office was far more realistic. Eden told Stettinius on February 1 that if the Soviets entered the Pacific war it would be because they considered it in their interests to do so rather than leaving victory to America and Britain. Consequently "there was no need to offer a high price for their participation." If the Western powers did accept Soviet territorial demands they should obtain "a good return" through concessions on issues that mattered to the West. Eden's perception of the situation was shrewd, but it was not acted on at Yalta.[76]

On the United Nations and East Asia, Roosevelt therefore got what he wanted but in ways that also suited Stalin. On Germany, the outcome was different. Stalin did not leave Yalta very satisfied with the conference decisions, whereas Churchill came away with a good deal of what he had sought.[77]

In 1943–4 preliminary Soviet plans for postwar Germany had assumed a single German state, albeit under tight Allied control.[78] In the winter of 1944–5, however, Stalin took up the idea of dismemberment, probably because it seemed his Allies were moving in this direction. At the Quebec conference in September 1944, Roosevelt and Churchill had endorsed proposals by Henry Morgenthau, the U.S. Treasury secretary, for a fragmented and "pastoralized" Germany. Stalin knew about this from his Western moles. Although they backtracked in private on the Morgenthau Plan, the following month, in Moscow, Churchill spoke out vehemently in similar vein for "hard terms" and a "divided" Germany. In December Stalin told the French he expected the British would take a hard line against Germany.[79]

At Yalta Stalin therefore sought to pin things down. How would Germany be broken up? Would each part be self-governing, or would there still be a central German government? He asked for a decision in principle at the conference. But it soon became clear that Roosevelt and Churchill had not come with any clear proposals about dismemberment and, indeed, were not of one mind. The president favored breaking Germany into five or even seven states. Churchill envisaged fewer units and was less keen to make commitments—part of his strategy now of keeping open as many options as possible on the German question. Stalin probed for some time on February 5 but, seeing that there was no clear Western policy, he eventually cut through the verbosity with three points: that they agree in principle that Germany should be dismembered, refer the details to a commission of the foreign ministers, and state a commitment to dismemberment in the surrender terms. Churchill wriggled on the last point but, under pressure from Roosevelt, he eventually agreed.[80]

The foreign ministers had to tie up the loose ends. Eden, unhappy with Churchill's concession, tried to water down what was to be said in the surrender terms (favoring the word "dissolution" not "dismemberment"). Molotov wanted to toughen the wording, while Stettinius sought to broker a compromise. After a difficult lunchtime meeting on February 6, the foreign ministers bounced the issue back to their leaders that afternoon but Molotov, on instructions from Stalin, then withdrew his stronger language. The general commitment to "dismemberment" became Allied policy but British officials felt that "we still have a great deal of elbow room."[81]

On the issue of dismemberment the Soviets tried to elicit an Anglo-American policy but on reparations they came to Yalta with clear proposals of their own. A commission under Ivan Maisky, the former ambassador in London, had already estimated that the Soviet Union's "direct material losses" from the war surpassed the national wealth of Britain and were one-third of that of the United States. But Maisky warned Stalin that the Allies would resist extravagant claims for reparations, and so at Yalta on February 5 he pitched the Soviet case conservatively, proposing a total Allied bill of $20 billion, half of which would go to the USSR because of the magnitude of its war losses. All would be payments in kind—industrial plant, goods and raw materials—with half the $20 billion removed immediately after the war and the rest in annual payments over ten years. Maisky justified his proposals with a detailed explanation of why and how he thought Germany could pay.[82]

Despite the calculated moderation of the Soviet case, his allies were not happy, and they had more leverage than Stalin expected because they had not tried to sell him a package on dismemberment.[83] The British and Americans refused to make any decision on reparations at Yalta: it was agreed that the issue would be examined by a commission sitting in Moscow. Molotov asked that the figure of $20 billion serve as a basis for these discussions. Stettinius was agreeable but Eden and Churchill were not. Stalin was struck that the president did not confront the British on the issue—he began to fear a common front.[84]

In the plenary session on February 10 Churchill and Eden continued to oppose naming any figure, even as a basis for discussion. This was the only occasion during the conference when Stalin became visibly annoyed; several times he rose up from his chair and spoke with real emotion. He even told the British that if they did not want the Soviet Union to get any reparations they should say so openly.[85] So fixated was Stalin on this issue that at the final dinner that evening—supposedly just a social occasion full of grandiloquent toasts—he reopened the issue and extracted agreement that the final communiqué would at least state the principle that Germany should pay for damage caused and would mention the work of the Reparations Commission.[86]

In the plenary on February 10 Churchill was assisted by what he called a "very severe" telegram on reparations from his colleagues in London, which he read out to Stalin and FDR.[87] This followed a lively discussion at the War Cabinet in which the chancellor of the exchequer, Sir John Anderson, called the Soviet case "fantastic"; there was general agreement that any reparations should be extracted quickly in two years after the war, rather than over a whole decade as in the 1920s.[88] The reparations issue was sensitive in Britain because of the debt tangle after World War I which, it was widely felt, had undermined the German economy, forcing Britain to help out, and also provoked an extremist backlash in Germany that aided the Nazi party. Churchill, however, was not renowned for his punctiliousness about consulting colleagues: diplomatic tactics as much as constitutional propriety motivated his decision to ask the Cabinet for its opinion. It was a ploy he used at several war-time conferences: cabling the Cabinet at difficult points in negotiations in order to strengthen his hand at the table.

The other German issue at Yalta was the role of France in the Allied zones of occupation and again Stalin did not get his way. The French leader, Charles de Gaulle, had not been invited to Yalta—partly because of France's inferior status after the humiliating defeat of 1940 but mostly because all three agreed that his presence would cause complications. De Gaulle was a notoriously prickly nationalist and even Churchill, the most Francophile of them, felt that "the whole character of our discussions would be destroyed if de Gaulle were present."[89]

Prodded by Eden, however, the prime minister pressed for France to have a zone of occupation in Germany after the war. Roosevelt and Stalin agreed, though they considered this an act of "kindness" rather than recognition of France's true status. But the Soviet leader indicated in the plenary on February 5 that he opposed Churchill's notion of granting France a seat on the Control Commission to run occupied Germany, which would have put France on the same footing as the Big Three. Roosevelt agreed with Stalin. When Churchill tried again, arguing that a zone required a seat, he got nowhere: his other two allies wanted to let the matter lie for the moment. Behind the scenes, however, the president was strongly pressed to concede on this point by Harry Hopkins and by Freeman Matthews, head of the State Department's European desk, who had served in Vichy during the war and understood French sensitivities. On February 10, having informed Stalin in advance, FDR announced that he had changed his mind, whereupon the Soviet leader said he had no objection; all then agreed to give France a place on the Control Commission. Although there is less evidence to explain Stalin's change of heart than Roosevelt's, the Soviet leader was usually sensitive to majority opinion on matters that were of secondary importance to him. But none of this would have occurred without the persistence of Churchill, pressed by Eden.[90]

Reviving France was important to Churchill in the wake of Roosevelt's admission at Yalta that he did not expect the U.S. Congress to keep an army in Europe for long after the war: "two years would be the limit."[91] The president had said as much at Teheran—but the reiteration strengthened Churchill's desire to find another European partner to keep Germany down and, perhaps also, as some British military planners had argued, to offset the growing power of Russia.

So Stalin's tactics on Germany had not worked. He seems to have come to Yalta assuming that the Western Allies wanted agreement on dismembering Germany, which he was ready to trade in return for substantial reparations. But this basic assumption about Allied policy was wrong, which greatly reduced his leverage on reparations, the issue that really mattered to him. And he ended up letting Britain secure a larger role for France in the occupation of Germany than he had probably intended.

Stalin seemed to recognize that he had been outmaneuvered. On February 5 he conceded to the British on a French zone in Germany; on the 6th he told Molotov to stop pressing the obdurate Eden for stronger language than "dismemberment." Later that day, Stalin walked up to the British foreign secretary and said cryptically: "You have won again."[92] It is of course sometimes a clever tactical ploy to suggest to an adversary that one has conceded more than is actually the case. Nevertheless Stalin's language to Eden, coupled with his genuine anger over the reparations compromise, suggest that on Germany he felt he had come off worse than his allies.

The dynamics of the conference were very different, however, on the issue of Poland. There, as Roosevelt and Churchill well knew, the Soviets were in a strong position with their troops occupying half the country and their clients already forming a provisional government. Speaking to senators in private on January 11, the president said that "the occupying forces had the power in the areas where their arms were present and each knew that the others could not force things to an issue." He also stated that "the Russians had the power in Eastern Europe, that it was obviously impossible to have a break with them and that, therefore, the only practicable course was to use what influence we had to ameliorate the situation."[93]

Churchill was even more conscious of the limits of Western influence, at times bleakly pessimistic. "Make no mistake," he told his private secretary on January 23, "all the Balkans, except Greece, are going to be Bolshevised; and there is nothing I can do to prevent it. There is nothing I can do for poor Poland either."[94] But that was not his considered policy: like the president, indeed with far more energy, he intended to "ameliorate" the situation as far as he possibly could, on the two big issues for Poland—frontiers and government.

It was symptomatic of the power balance that Stalin waited for the others to raise the issue of Poland, which they did not do until February 6. And then their case was little more than a plea for some concessions by Stalin to help them with domestic opinion.

Poland's eastern border had already been settled in principle at Teheran, when the Western Allies accepted the so-called Curzon Line, which had originally been proposed by the British foreign secretary in 1920. Implementing this decision would bring the Soviet Union one or two hundred miles closer to Germany than in 1938; it was roughly the line followed by the Nazi-Soviet Pact of August 1939. On February 6, 1945, Roosevelt spent some time arguing that the city of Lwow and its surrounding oilfields, east of what was generally regarded as the Curzon Line, should be conceded to Poland—"it would make it easier for me at home . . . I hope Marshal Stalin can make a gesture in this direction." But Stalin did not budge: after all, he said disingenuously, the Curzon Line originated as a British proposal.[95]

In return for losing its eastern territories, Poland was to be compensated in north and west—a point also accepted in principle at Teheran. Stalin wanted to maximize Poland's westward expansion, probably because it would weaken a postwar Germany economically and because the consequent German anger would force any Polish government to depend on Moscow. Fearing this, the Americans and British tried to limit Poland's gains in the west: as Churchill put it, "I do not wish to stuff the Polish goose until it dies of German indigestion."[96] They blocked Stalin's demands for a Polish-German border up the River Oder and then the Western Neisse. The British were willing to accept a more easterly line all the way

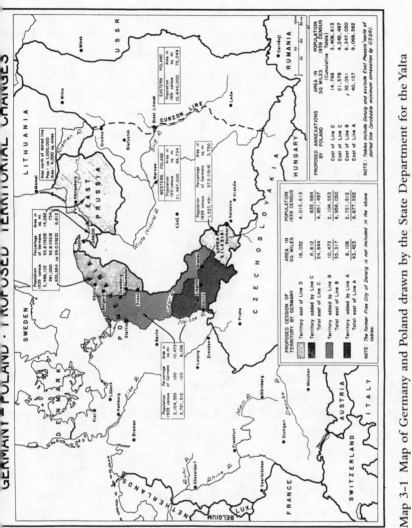

Map 3-1 Map of Germany and Poland drawn by the State Department for the Yalta conference, showing the different proposals for postwar boundaries and the consequent transfers of territory and population. (U.S. State Department)

up the Oder to Breslau—saving eight thousand square miles and most of the Silesian coalfield for Germany, and avoiding a further two to three million German refugees. But Roosevelt did not want anything formalized until the eventual peace conference; this was also the preference of the British War Cabinet, whom Churchill had consulted. Nevertheless the prime minister reopened the issue at the plenary on February 10 and secured a statement in the final communiqué that, in return for conceding the Curzon Line with minor modifications in the east, "Poland must receive substantial accessions of territory in the North and West."[97]

Churchill's last-minute move was motivated by a desire to show how hard he had fought on Poland's border—necessary because he had achieved limited success on the issue of the future Polish government. By now what the West called "the Lublin Poles" had been installed by the Soviets as the provisional government in Warsaw. This was much to the dismay of London and Washington: they wanted a new government, involving noncommunists from within Poland as well as figures from the exiled Polish government in London, that would prepare the way for full and free elections. The only (small) leverage they had was that Stalin wanted them to recognize a new Polish government.

In the plenary sessions Churchill and Roosevelt made clear the sensitivity of this issue back home. Aware of this, some of the Soviet delegation, including Lavrenti Beria, the head of the secret police, favored a coalition of communists and "bourgeois" politicians to start with, until the communists could seize power outright, but Stalin was unyielding.[98] He also blocked repeated Western requests to bring the Polish communist leaders to Yalta, claiming implausibly that it had proved impossible to reach them by phone. On February 7 his carefully timed "concession" on the United Nations was clearly intended to extract something in return over Poland; during protracted arguments over the next three days, the Western leaders gradually backed down.

First, they retreated on the question of a genuinely new interim government: instead the existing regime would be "reorganized on a broader democratic basis."

By February 9 FDR had decided that the composition of the current government was less important than the principle that the elections, likely within a couple of months, must be validated as "free and unfettered" by the British and American ambassadors.

Churchill fought even harder for such monitoring, making use of the strong views expressed by the War Cabinet at its meeting on February 8. But when the Americans eventually capitulated, the most he could get—after a private meeting with Stalin on February 10—was a line in the conference communiqué that London and Washington would be "kept informed about the situation in Poland" by their ambassadors.[99]

The Americans, again, were more interested in moral statements than in hard detail. The Declaration on Liberated Europe, which the State Department had proposed and drafted, enunciated the overriding principles of "sovereign rights and self-government" that should prevail in all the countries freed from Axis rule. The British and Soviets accepted the Declaration but much less enthusiastically. When Churchill gained the erroneous impression that the Declaration might oblige Britain to give independence to parts of its empire, he blew his top, shouting, "Never, never, never." Molotov also emasculated the original American proposal that the Allies "immediately establish appropriate machinery" for implementing the principles of the Declaration. Instead the final version simply stated that in such cases the Allies would "immediately consult together on the measures necessary." Although Roosevelt stressed the applicability of the Declaration to Poland, in its final form it was largely vague generalities.[100]

The Americans did not follow through on the tactic agreed with Eden in advance—to let the deadlock over Poland continue rather than rubber-stamp the Lublin regime.[101] Ultimately Churchill accepted that he could do no more. Of course both leaders had stipulated that the existing Lublin government must be "reorganized," but that was another loose term. Likewise the ambassadorial oversight of the elections from Moscow was vestigial: all would depend on establishing an official diplomatic presence in Poland and thereby finding out what was going on.

But Churchill could only open an embassy in Warsaw when he had formally recognized the "reorganized" Polish government. Not only would this be a gain for Stalin, it required Churchill to sever all links with the exiled government in London, as well as alienating one hundred thousand Polish troops who had fought courageously with Britain during the war. For Churchill the costs of the Polish settlement were immediate and immense, whereas Stalin conceded little in exchange. The Soviets had committed themselves on paper to reorganizing the existing government "on democratic lines, by including democratic leaders from Poland itself and from abroad," and to holding "free and unfettered elections as soon as possible on the basis of universal suffrage and a secret ballot." These phrases, Churchill wrote later in his memoirs, were "the best I could get." According to Admiral Leahy, who remonstrated with his boss about the elasticity of the agreement, FDR said much the same thing to him at Yalta: "It's the best I can do for Poland at this time."[102]

STALIN WAS CLEARLY a hard man to bargain with, but in a completely different way from the unpredictable and emotional Hitler. A month before Yalta, Eden had expressed fears about the summit: "Stalin being the only one of the three who has a clear view of what he wants and is a tough negotiator. P.M. is all emotion in these matters, F.D.R. vague and jealous of others." Reflecting on the conference in 1965, Eden had not changed his opinion: "Churchill liked to talk, he did not like to listen, and he found it difficult to wait for, and seldom let pass, his turn to speak. The spoils in the diplomatic game do not necessarily go to the man most eager to debate." As for Stalin, Eden wrote that "after something like thirty years' experience of international conferences of one kind or another, if I had to pick a team for going into a conference room, Stalin would be my first choice." This of course was in part retrospective wisdom but it paralleled the verdict at the time of Sir Alexander Cadogan of the Foreign Office:

I must say I think Uncle Joe much the most impressive of the three men. He is very quiet and restrained. On the first day he sat for the first hour or so without saying a word—there was no call for him to do so. The President flapped about and the P.M. boomed, but Joe just sat taking it all in and being rather amused. When he did chip in, he never used a superfluous word, and spoke very much to the point.

High praise indeed from a cynical British diplomat who had a low opinion of politicians in general and foreigners in particular.[103]

Yet that was not Cadogan's overall verdict on Yalta. "I think the Conference has been quite successful," he wrote home on February 11. "We have got an agreement on Poland which may heal differences, for some time at least, and assure some degree of independence for the Poles." Not exactly a ringing endorsement, but essentially optimistic and a reflection of his positive feeling about the meeting as a whole: "I have never known the Russians so easy and accommodating. In particular Joe has been extremely good."[104] General Ismay, Churchill's military secretary, on his fourth wartime conference with the Russians, was struck by the novelty of relatively free discussions with the Soviet high command, without Stalin and Molotov in attendance. He felt Yalta had been "a great success, not so much, perhaps, because of the formal conclusions that were reached, but because of the spirit of frank cooperation which characterized all the discussions, both formal and informal."[105] Similarly, Churchill cabled the Cabinet: "I am profoundly impressed with the friendly attitude of Stalin and Molotov. It is a different Russian world to any I have seen hitherto."[106]

On the American side, Leahy predicted that the peace terms outlined at Yalta would "make Russia the dominant power in Europe, which in itself carries a certainty of future international disagreements and prospects of another war."[107] But his was a rare note of pessimism. The dominant feeling in the U.S. delegation, including Roosevelt, was one of "supreme exaltation" as they left Yalta. Not only had the Americans achieved their two main objectives—on the UN and the Pacific war—they were also convinced that the conference had not been a one-way street. "The Russians have given in so much at this conference," Hopkins observed to FDR.[108] Stettinius claimed in 1949 that the Soviets "made greater concessions" than they gained in return and that Roosevelt did not surrender anything significant at Yalta that it was within his power to withhold (given the Red Army's position in Poland).[109]

And, despite the encomia from Cadogan and Eden for Stalin's terse diplomacy, one should remember that both were now utterly fed up by years of Churchillian monologues. In fact, the prime minister's obdurate long-windedness, which wore down opposition in Cabinet and the chiefs of staff in London, had paid dividends at Yalta on issues such as reparations and the western Polish border.

Did Roosevelt's health make a difference to the outcome? After the president's death two months later, newspaper editors went back over the Yalta photographs and featured those of FDR looking weary, drawn and even gaga (with open mouth). He was undoubtedly tired by the end of the conference, but so were all the participants after such a gruelling week: Hopkins took to his sick bed and "Pa" Watson, the president's aide, died on the voyage home. It has been suggested that Roosevelt's fatigue may have made him reluctant to haggle with Stalin about the Pacific. This may be the case, but he did take up the Polish issue with considerable firmness, and in the end his overriding priority was to keep the alliance intact. Most historians agree that deteriorating health did not fundamentally affect the positions FDR adopted—these had been defined long before—or change his diplomatic style, which was always informal and intuitive rather than based on detailed reading and analysis.[110]

More instructive than the debate about Roosevelt's health is the question of whether the Western Allies might have applied more pressure on Stalin at Yalta. It has been suggested, for instance, that they could have taken a tougher line on whether to hand over to Stalin "Soviet citizens" who had either fought for the Nazis or had become prisoners of war, as agreed in the documents signed at Yalta on February 11.[111] Implementation of this agreement meant that thousands of men, women and children were sent to their deaths or to the gulag because Stalin had a vendetta against ethnic groups such as the Cossacks; he regarded POWs as tantamount to deserters.

In fact the agreement drawn up at Yalta, mostly by diplomats and the military, reflected policies outlined months before. The British Cabinet had agreed to a handover the previous summer, aware that it probably meant consigning many to certain death. POW transfers had begun before Yalta; at one stage, it was proposed to send a thousand or so to the Crimea on the *Franconia*, the British communications ship for the conference.[112]

Callous though this seems in retrospect, the priority in both London and Washington at the time was to ensure safe return of their own soldiers freed from German POW camps by the Red Army. There were already reports that these men were being poorly treated by the Russians and Eden had effectively made a deal about mutual exchanges when he met Stalin in Moscow on October 11, 1944.

Undoubtedly in the Yalta agreement the term "Soviet citizens" could have been defined more closely—local Allied commanders tried to do that later, for instance, by not handing over those of Polish or Baltic nationality—and there could have been a more hard-headed reckoning of the imbalance between some two million Soviet POWs, on the one hand, and an estimated sixty thousand British and Americans, on the other. But on the essential point Churchill and Roosevelt saw little room for maneuver: the lives of their own citizens were at stake, and as democratic leaders they were not willing to use them as a diplomatic bargaining chip.[113]

More promising as potential leverage was the Soviet desire for postwar American economic aid. Lend-lease was a purely wartime expedient and Molotov had asked for six billion dollars in postwar credits to purchase American industrial equipment for its devastated economy. In January 1945 the U.S. Treasury advocated an open-handed approach, proposing to offer up to ten billion as a carrot to induce cooperation at Yalta. Harriman and the State Department wanted more of a quid pro quo approach, tying any aid much more closely to progress on America's diplomatic agenda. But all were agreed that the issue would come up at Yalta and Molotov did indeed broach the question at the foreign ministers meeting on February 5, saying it was "most important" for agreement to be reached at the conference on postwar credits as well as on reparations from Germany. Moreover Stalin, in what might well have been a heavy hint, twice went out of his way on February 8 to praise lend-lease as one of Roosevelt's "most remarkable and vital achievements . . . without which victory would have been delayed."[114]

The president had said in advance that he would discuss the issue of credits with Stalin at Yalta, but there is no sign that he did so. Perhaps this was because of second thoughts. He had told senators beforehand that "our economic position did not constitute a bargaining weapon of any strength"—meaning that the United States, facing a likely postwar recession, needed a deal as much as the Soviets.[115] And he also knew that any package would face a long, difficult and possibly uncertain passage through Congress. Insofar as aid was a viable diplomatic card, he felt it should not be played yet. "I think it's very important that we hold this back and don't give them any promises of finance until we get what we want," he told Henry Morgenthau on January 10.[116]

So prisoners of war and economic aid were not used as leverage at Yalta. What other options did the Western Allies have? At the time some insiders questioned the whole premise underlying the conference, that postwar cooperation with the Soviet Union was possible. From the U.S. embassy in Moscow the diplomat George Kennan wrote a long, impassioned letter on these lines to Chip Bohlen just before Yalta. He argued that the United States should accept the reality of a Soviet predominance in Eastern and East-Central Europe but deny Moscow moral and political recognition of these gains and the economic aid it needed to consolidate its hold. This was "not a very happy program," Kennan admitted. It amounted to "a partition of Europe" but at least it had "the virtue of resting on the solid foundation of reality" rather than "staking the whole future of Europe on the assumption of a community of aims with Russia for which there is no real evidence except in our wishful thinking." In the long term, Kennan believed the Soviets would not be able to hold on to such a vast empire. But, in the short term, nothing could be done to stop their imperialism in eastern Europe and, equally, nothing should be done to endorse it. "Divide Europe frankly into spheres of influence—keep ourselves out of the Russian sphere and keep the Russians out of ours." That, said Kennan, would be the "best" and "most honest" line to take.[117]

A partition of Europe of course is what Gaullists in France claimed was actually done at Yalta. But not even Churchill in 1944–5 was advocating two separate spheres: his percentages agreement still sought to preserve some residual Western authority in countries such as Romania, where the Soviets were conceded 90 percent not 100 percent. And Kennan's hard-boiled realpolitik was certainly not the official line in Washington. The State Department's postwar planners drew a distinction between "exclusive" spheres of influence—which were unacceptable—and more open and informal spheres in which the Soviets would have the security of friendly governments tied to Moscow through pacts of mutual assistance. In return the USSR should give its neighbors pledges of noninterference in their internal politics and allow them to develop economic and cultural relations with the rest of the world. This is essentially what the Declaration of Liberated Europe was about. Moreover Kennan's prescription would have meant abandoning FDR's basic wartime goal of a cooperative postwar international order, based on the great powers. Whatever their doubts about Moscow, few policymakers in Washington or London were ready to go that far in early 1945. "Chip" Bohlen, the only Russian specialist whom FDR took to Yalta, responded to his old friend Kennan's critique of the conference in a chatty letter about the Russians:

> Either our pals intend to limit themselves or they don't. I submit, as the British say, that the answer is not yet clear. But what is clear is that the Soyuz [the Soviet Union] is here to stay, as one of the major factors in the world. Quarreling with them would be so easy, but we can always come to that.[118]

Bohlen's last sentence hints at something often forgotten about Yalta: it was not intended to be the last word on the future of Europe. Churchill and Roosevelt assumed that there would eventually be a full peace conference, a (better) version of Paris 1919. Their meeting in February 1945 was intended as a holding operation to address some urgent problems such as the Polish government, the Pacific war and the exchange of POWs. The overriding aim was to keep the alliance on track in the run-up to Nazi Germany's final defeat (which the American and British military did not expect before July at the earliest[119]) and then to victory over Japan (which might well take a further year).

Churchill and Roosevelt took it for granted that there would be more opportunities to haggle with Stalin. But in April Roosevelt died and in May Germany surrendered; the Potsdam summit was delayed by the new president, Harry Truman, until the end of July, and that proved to be only a few weeks before Japan's capitulation.

Taken in itself, Yalta, unlike Munich, was characterized by real give-and-take on all sides. The final agreements reflected Stalin's strong position in Poland but equally his much weaker position on Germany. Where Roosevelt and Churchill conceded more on paper than they probably needed to—on the Far East, for instance—this was part of the larger goal of Allied cooperation after the war as well as during it. Western diplomacy at Yalta was not flawless, but nor was it inept. The real problems occurred afterward, not least in the way the conference was oversold in the West.

CHURCHILL KNEW he would face severe problems explaining the Yalta agreements to the Cabinet and the Commons. The government's chief whip (business manager) had cabled that there was "a considerable body of responsible opinion, mainly Conservative, which is uneasy about Poland." As soon as the prime minister arrived back in London on February 19 he sought to reassure the War Cabinet with an upbeat account of the conference. He said he was sure that Stalin "meant well to the world and to Poland" and quoted the Soviet leader's statement that although Russia had often sinned in the past against the Poles it did not intend to do so in the future. Churchill said he felt certain about the sincerity of this remark, repeating his mantra that Stalin had "most scrupulously respected" their percentages agreement of October 1944 by keeping out of Greece. This strengthened his view that when the Russians "made a bargain, they desired to keep it."[120]

It was all very reminiscent of the way Chamberlain returned from his meetings with Hitler in September 1938, putting the best possible face on events. Churchill could not keep that parallel out of his mind or even out of his mouth. At a specially convened meeting of all ministers on February 23 he made the remarkable statement: "Poor Neville Chamberlain believed he could trust Hitler. He was wrong. But I don't think I'm wrong about Stalin." Yet that evening, in his cups, the prime minister was not so sure. His private secretary, Jock Colville, found him "rather depressed, thinking of the possibilities of Russia one day turning against us, saying that Chamberlain had trusted Hitler as he was now trusting Stalin (though he thought in different circumstances)." When Churchill was preparing his speech on Yalta for the Commons he even included the sentence, "Soviet Russia seeks not only peace, but peace with honour." On the draft Colville scribbled: "? omit. Echo of Munich." The words were duly cut.[121]

On February 21 Churchill acknowledged to the War Cabinet that all depended on whether the Russians kept to the agreement on Poland. He thought they would; if not, however, "our engagement would be altered." Developing a fallback position, he said he wanted to offer citizenship to those Polish soldiers who had fought with the British forces and did not wish to return home and live under the new government.[122] Nevertheless in the Commons on February 27 he made a lengthy and bullish statement—not denying the "imponderables" and admitting that "in all this war I never felt so grave a sense of responsibility as I did at Yalta"—but insisting that on both frontiers and government this represented a good deal for Poland: "The impression I brought back from the Crimea, and from all my other contacts, is that Marshal Stalin and the Soviet leaders wish to live in honourable friendship and equality with the Western democracies. I feel also that their word is their bond."[123]

Quoting these words a few years later in his memoirs, Churchill wrote defensively: "I felt bound to proclaim my confidence in Soviet good faith in the hope of procuring it." But at the time his hopes probably outweighed his fears, if only because the alternative was too grim to contemplate. During Yalta he had read a pessimistic paper from the Moscow embassy arguing that only "common enmity to Germany" had held the alliance together and proposing a postwar Western European bloc. On the memo Churchill scribbled:

Query? Moral!

1. The only bond of the victors is their common hate.
2. To make Britain safe she must become responsible for the safety of a cluster of feeble states.

We ought to think of something better than these.[124]

That "something better" was what Churchill had worked for at Yalta. The alternative was a divided, hostile Europe—in short, Cold War.

The government whips had favored an adjournment debate about Yalta, which would allow the Commons to ventilate its feelings without a vote. But Churchill, as always in the war, believed that a full-scale division was the best way to deter critics by making it, in effect, a vote of confidence in his government.[125] Even so, critics put down an amendment regretting "the decision to transfer to another power the territory of an ally." On March 1 the government had a majority of 396 to 25 on the amendment, but those numbers concealed the depth and significance of the opposition—eleven government ministers abstained and one resigned. The most vocal critics of Yalta had been strong backers of Munich, including Lord Dunglass (Alec Douglas-Home), Chamberlain's parliamentary private secretary in 1938. After his speech, Churchill chuckled with Harold Nicolson, a fellow anti-appeaser, about the way "the warmongers of the Munich period have now become the appeasers, while the appeasers have become the warmongers." but he was "overjoyed" by the final vote—in Nicolson's words "like a schoolboy."[126]

In America the initial spin was applied by the influential Southern Democrat James F. Byrnes, whom FDR took to Yalta to help sell the conference to Congress and the public. The White House press office staged a major press and radio conference for Byrnes on February 13. However, although presented to the American media as a source from the heart of Yalta, Byrnes had actually been on the margins of the conference. He had taken detailed notes there (having been trained in shorthand), but had attended only the plenary sessions, lunches and dinners. Not having participated in the foreign ministers' meetings, he did not understand the unresolved differences behind the scenes on Poland and reparations. Nor did he sit in on Roosevelt's personal meetings with Stalin, when the Far Eastern agreements were reached. He had also left the conference early, on February 10, in advance of the final Western concessions on Poland.

Because Byrnes had witnessed so little of the actual negotiating at Yalta, his upbeat press conference on February 13 gave a glossy, one-sided account of the summit. He highlighted the Declaration on Liberated Europe and the Polish settlement as signs of a new era in the making. In retrospect it is clear that his optimistic presentation encouraged dangerous public illusions; at the time, however, it was exactly what the president needed from his advance man. The White House reported to FDR a "magnificent press reception" and "enthusiastic approval" from political leaders of both parties.[127]

On March 1, the day after returning to Washington, Roosevelt presented the Yalta agreements to a joint session of the U.S. Congress. On similar occasions in the past, he had walked down the aisle on an aide's arm, his legs locked in iron braces. This time he allowed himself to be wheeled into the chamber. And instead of standing stiffly at the podium, he sat on a chair, asking the indulgence of the Congress for that "unusual posture" because it "makes it a lot easier for me in not having to carry about ten pounds of steel around on the bottom of my legs." It was the most public sign Roosevelt had ever given of his deteriorating health. Nor was his address flawless. Speechwriter Sam Rosenman was "dismayed at the President's halting, ineffective delivery" and the unusual amount of ad-libbed remarks, "some of them almost bordered on the ridiculous." On the other hand, the informal, sit-down style made the speech seem more conversational and persuasive.[128]

The president emphasized how important it was to deal once and for all with the curse of German "militarism" and to lay the foundations of postwar peace at the impending San Francisco conference. He insisted that the United States must accept its share of the responsibility for keeping the peace; he stated candidly that decisions in this area would "often be a result of give-and-take compromise" with neither America, nor Russia nor Britain always having its way "a hundred percent." As an example, he cited the settlement on Poland's eastern boundary at Yalta—"I did not agree with all of it, by any means" but neither, he said, did Stalin or Churchill. Roosevelt did not mention the deal to give Stalin three seats in the General Assembly and he held up the agreement on the Polish government as "one outstanding example of joint action by the three major Allied powers." He also hyped the conference as "a turning point" in American history and in "the history of the world." The decisions reached at Yalta, he proclaimed in Wilsonian rhetoric, "ought to spell the end of the system of unilateral action, the exclusive alliances, the spheres of influence, the balances of power, and all the other expedients that have been tried for centuries—and have always failed. We propose to substitute for all these, a universal organization in which all peace-loving Nations will finally have a chance to join."[129]

In their speeches about Yalta, both Churchill and Roosevelt had put the best possible gloss on the agreements and papered over the cracks. The prime minister made extravagant professions of faith in Stalin. The president spoke about abolishing spheres of influence, whereas he had admitted privately before Yalta that he could hope only to "ameliorate" Soviet control of Eastern Europe. So both leaders were sticking their necks out a long way.

For Churchill and Roosevelt the stakes were very high. The prime minister feared that the fragile Polish settlement might be wrecked by the London Poles and their parliamentary allies; the ailing president was determined that nothing should imperil the launch of the United Nations on April 25. Both men believed that their improving relationship with Stalin would help resolve further problems as and when these arose over the next few months. Roosevelt of course did not intend to die on April 12, nor did Churchill anticipate his election defeat three months later. Both expected to stay at the helm, steering the Grand Alliance to victory and into more peaceful waters.

As CHURCHILL AND ROOSEVELT were overselling Yalta to the West, the agreements made there broke down in Eastern Europe during the month after the conference. The Soviets dragged their feet on repatriating prisoners of war. They did not send representatives to London to start up the new Control Commission for Germany. In Romania they forced the king to appoint a new government dominated by communists. In Poland they allowed the communist provisional government to veto candidates for its own "reconstruction" and to exclude Western observers, while potential rivals in Poland were butchered or sent to the camps. Stalin also said that Molotov was too busy to come to San Francisco and that the Soviet delegation to the UN founding conference would be led by Andrei Gromyko, then a midlevel diplomat. This was taken not only as a blatant snub but also as a real threat to the whole structure of postwar cooperation.

Putting all this together during March 1945, British and American leaders detected a fundamental and sinister shift of Soviet policy. Why it had happened, however, seemed less clear. Most attempts at explanation took as their premise the continued good faith of Stalin himself: that seemed to be one of the lessons of Yalta, indeed of wartime summitry as a whole. Therefore the change of heart was presumed to lie with his advisors—those sinister forces supposedly swirling around in the shadowy recesses of the Kremlin. British Cabinet Minister Ernest Bevin (soon to become foreign secretary) suggested that blame for the turnaround should be ascribed to Molotov. Alternatives postulated by the Foreign Office were the "Party bosses behind the scenes" or "Army marshals at the front" who were throwing their weight about amid the chaos of

Eastern Europe.[130] Churchill was similarly unwilling to blame Stalin. On 5 April he wrote darkly to FDR about "the Soviet leaders, whoever they may be."[131]

In Washington speculation ran on similar lines: putative causes of the Soviet turnaround included a Politburo review or the resurgence of anti-American, xenophobic elements. According to Bohlen, by May all the State Department officials who had been at Yalta "felt that the Soviet failure to carry out the agreement reached there had been due in large part to opposition inside the Soviet government which Stalin encountered on his return."[132] Roosevelt himself may have toyed with the same idea. The president is said to have told an American editor at the end of March 1945 that, although he had genuinely believed what he told Congress at the beginning of the month about having confidence in the agreements worked out with Stalin, this was no longer the case. FDR "said that either Stalin was not a man of his word or else Stalin did not have the control of the Soviet government which he [Roosevelt] had thought he had."[133]

Even more perplexing was the question of how to respond to the Soviets' apparent betrayal of Yalta. Of the two leaders, Churchill was more hard-line and often highly emotional. Starting on March 8 he subjected Roosevelt to a steady barrage of telegrams. The prime minister recognized that Britain's hands were tied in Romania because of his percentages agreement with Stalin the previous autumn, so he urged FDR to take the lead in protesting about Soviet actions there. On Poland, where he was already talking about a sinister "veil" or "curtain" coming down over events ("there is no doubt in my mind that the Soviets fear very much our seeing what is going on") Churchill urged an early joint appeal to Stalin as "the only way to stop Molotov's tactics." He insisted that Poland was "the test case between us and the Russians of the meaning which is to be attached to such terms as Democracy, Sovereignty, Independence, Representative Government and free and unfettered elections." Churchill kept emphasizing the political sensitivity of the Polish question in Britain. He had gone out on a limb in the Commons on February 27, advising critics of Yalta to trust Stalin, and he warned Roosevelt repeatedly during March that, if the Polish deadlock was not resolved, he would have to report this openly to MPs and leave them to draw their own conclusions.[134]

Roosevelt wanted to play things long and calmly. His declining health had certainly affected his diplomacy, but it was not a determining factor. Although by now he rarely composed his messages to Churchill himself, he read the drafts with attention and only signed when satisfied with the contents.[135] The president authorized American protests about Romania, invoking the Declaration on Liberated Europe, but reminded Churchill that it was "not a good place for a test case." On Poland, Roosevelt persuaded the prime minister to give their ambassadors in Moscow more time to sort things out, saving up a message to Stalin as the last resort. When he finally did address the Soviet leader directly on Poland, at the end of March, Roosevelt was at pains to pin his arguments closely to the Yalta agreement, rather than introducing extraneous complaints. But Stalin simply replied on April 7 that it was he who was adhering to the Yalta statement about reorganizing the existing provisional government. This rejoinder exposed the ambiguities of the compromise wording at Yalta, noted at the time by critics such as Admiral Leahy.[136]

The only point at which Roosevelt lost his cool was when Stalin protested about peace feelers made by the German army in Italy to U.S. emissaries in Bern. In a message received on April 3, the Soviet leader accused the Americans and British of negotiating a deal behind his back whereby the Germans would allow them to advance unopposed in return for softer peace terms. Only such a deal, he insinuated, could explain the rapid Allied advance in the West while the Red Army was still facing savage resistance.

When Roosevelt read Stalin's message, he was furious—face flushed, eyes flashing. Bohlen recalled: "It was one of the few times that I saw him angry." The president's reply used such phrases as "bitter resentment" and "vile misrepresentations." A jubilant Churchill described Roosevelt's message as "about the hottest thing I have seen so far in diplomatic intercourse." And it seems to have had an effect because Stalin backed off on April 7 with assurances that he never questioned the "integrity or trustworthiness" of either Roosevelt or Churchill.[137]

Stalin's April 7 messages on Poland and Germany were received on the 10th; Roosevelt died of a cerebral haemorrhage two days later. In those final days of his life the president was mulling over his policy toward the Soviet Union. But his penultimate message to Churchill early on April 12 stated: "I would minimize the general Soviet problem as much as possible because these problems, in one form or another, seem to arise every day and most straighten themselves out as in the case of the Bern meeting. We must be firm, however, and our course thus far is correct." The fact that this was one of very few messages in those last weeks that FDR actually drafted himself suggests that this was indeed Roosevelt's authentic voice.[138]

Even more instructive is another message sent by the president on April 12 in which he thanked Stalin for his "frank explanation" of the Soviet view of the Bern incident which "now appears to have faded into the past." He added that "there must not, in any event, be mutual distrust, and minor misunderstandings of this character should not arise in the future." Ambassador Harriman in Moscow queried the adjective "minor," cabling Roosevelt: "I confess that the misunderstanding appeared to me to be of a major character." Back came the firm reply, just hours before FDR died: "I do not wish to delete the word 'minor' as it is my desire to consider the Bern misunderstanding a minor incident."[139]

These cables to Churchill and Stalin point in the same direction: Roosevelt was still determined to keep the alliance intact, even if that meant gliding over issues of disagreement. Perhaps his policy would have shifted after the United Nations was safely launched, but there would still have been other pressing reasons for avoiding a total breach with the Soviet Union.

Significantly, Harry Truman pursued essentially the same policy on Poland as his predecessor. Although on April 23 he told Molotov repeatedly in a brusque meeting that he expected the Soviets to honor the Yalta agreements, this did not mark a new hard line.[140] Within weeks he (and Byrnes) realized that those agreements were more ambiguous than had been presented to the American public after the conference, and at the end of May Truman sent the ailing Hopkins to Moscow to stitch up a compromise. Hopkins' instructions, the president wrote in his diary, were to make clear to Stalin that

> Poland, Rumania, Bulgaria, Czeckosovakia [sic], Austria, Yugo-Slavia, Latvia, Lithuania, Estonia et al made no difference to U.S. interests only so far as World Peace is concerned. That Poland ought to have "free elections," at least as free as [Frank] Hague, Tom Pendergast, Joe Martin or [Robert] Taft would allow in their respective bailiwicks . . . Uncle Joe should make some sort of gesture—whether he means it or not to keep it [—] before our public that he intends to keep his word. Any smart political boss will do that.[141]

Truman's language reveals his assumption that Stalin operated like an American machine politician and that this was acceptable as long as he made the necessary genuflections to democratic pieties over Poland. FDR would not have put the point so crudely, but his successor was working on essentially Rooseveltian lines.

Despite some ups and downs, American policy after Yalta was more consistent and logical than Churchill's. The Yalta agreement was a fudge—Roosevelt knew this and Truman discovered it, whereas Churchill seems to have closed his eyes to the fact and then woken up in horror. His almost panicky telegrams in March need more explaining than the steady-as-she-goes attitude of Roosevelt.[142] Was the prime minister's U-turn motivated by domestic politics? The wartime coalition was crumbling and an election was likely in the summer. But the weightiest opposition on Poland came from within his own Conservative party. At root, Churchill seems to have felt his whole political credibility was at stake. This was partly because of the special sensitivity of the Polish question for Britain: if the Soviet hard line continued, he would be forced to abandon the Polish government in London or rupture the alliance with Moscow. Yet the intensity of Churchill's reaction surely also reflected the fact that he had so publicly staked his faith on Stalin.

Although realizing the eerie parallels with Chamberlain's rhetoric about Hitler, Churchill was nonetheless unable to resist the same language in describing Stalin.

Churchill's diplomacy had been based quite fundamentally on summitry, on forging personal relations with the leaders of the countries that mattered. But in March and April 1945 that was all called into question—his rapport with Stalin no longer seemed the key to the Kremlin, while FDR was harder to influence and then suddenly dropped dead.

Churchill did not change policy in the early spring of 1945; rather, he experienced a crisis of confidence. A little-noticed subplot of the political drama that was unfolding—his wife's visit to the Soviet Union that spring—takes on new relevance in this context.

Clementine Churchill had been invited by the Russian Red Cross to see what had been done with the supplies and equipment she had helped provide as patron of the Aid to Russia Fund. She spent the first week of April in Moscow, exactly when Stalin was accusing Roosevelt and Churchill of doing a deal with the Nazis. Yet none of this clouded the visit. Molotov, who was then being obnoxious over Poland, received Clementine "most amiably" in the Kremlin; he and his wife also hosted a "lovely banquet" in her honor. Stalin personally welcomed her and cabled Churchill that she had made a "deep impression" upon him. The prime minister, who had considered postponing his wife's trip because of the crisis, found it very hard to read the conflicting signals. In a message to his wife on April 6 he detailed the great difficulties about Poland, Romania and the Bern affair, but also noted "there is no doubt your visit is giving sincere pleasure." The previous day the Soviet ambassador Feodor Gusev had called on Eden, who had braced himself for another assault, but instead Gusev relayed a message from Moscow praising Clementine's work and asking if they might offer her the Order of the Red Banner of Labour. "What puzzles me," Churchill told his wife, "is the inconsistency."[143]

So what *was* going on in Moscow in those critical weeks after Yalta? There is no evidence of serious debate within the Kremlin: that image of Stalin balancing between shadowy power blocs was a

Western delusion. Bohlen's mature judgment nearly thirty years on was that "Stalin changed his own mind" after realizing through intelligence reports from Poland that free elections would yield an anti-Soviet government.[144] But Stalin's enmity toward the Poles had been formed long before and his liquidation program was already well advanced when Yalta commenced.

More likely, as both the British and U.S. embassies in Moscow kept arguing, Stalin had assumed at Yalta that he could have his cake and eat it too. The Soviets wanted to establish a *cordon sanitaire* in key areas of Eastern Europe and had come to believe that they could do so without jeopardizing continued good relations with America and Britain.[145] Churchill's percentages deal in October 1944 would have seemed to Stalin a clear statement of spheres of influence, revolving around Romania for the Soviets and Greece for the British. At Yalta he sought similar recognition of his paramount interest in Poland. The Soviet leader must have discerned that Roosevelt and Churchill did not want to give him an entirely free hand there, but he never seems to have grasped the American distinction between open and exclusive spheres. And why should he? Churchill's and Roosevelt's repeated reference to opinion in Parliament and the Congress made no sense to the leader of a one-party state based on terror. Indeed Stalin seems to have treated such comments as implausible and irritating.

Neither Churchill nor Roosevelt went to Yalta with illusions that they could do much for Poland; the ambiguously worded concessions they extracted from Stalin were regarded as ideological fig leaves—albeit politically essential. Stalin twisted that language the way he wanted without realizing that he might in the process be tearing the fabric of the Grand Alliance. When Molotov complained privately at Yalta that the American draft of the Declaration of Liberated Europe was "going too far," Stalin told him not to worry: "We can deal with it in our own way later. The point is the correlation of forces."[146]

So it is conceivable that Stalin misunderstood his Alliance partners as badly as they misunderstood him. And he was probably also shaken by developments in the weeks after Yalta: by March 1945 the "correlation of forces" no longer seemed as favorable as they had been when the conference convened. In late January the Red Army was nearing the River Oder, some forty miles from Berlin, whereas the Western Allies, still recovering from the Battle of the Bulge, had not even set foot in Germany. But in early February Stalin and his high command accepted that, before they could attack the German capital, they had to clear their flanks in Pomerania and Silesia, and this took several weeks. They were also delayed by a German counter-offensive in Hungary in early March.[147] Meanwhile Allied troops started to cross the Rhine in strength on March 23 and in the first half of April they raced across Germany against little resistance. Hitler had pulled his best troops and armor back to face the Red Army; moreover Germans expected better treatment if they surrendered to the Western Allies—Soviet rape and plunder across East Prussia seemed to confirm Nazi propaganda about the barbarous Asiatic hordes. On April 12 advance American units crossed the River Elbe, the last big natural obstacle before Berlin, seventy-five miles away.[148]

Stalin's testy exchanges with Roosevelt and Churchill in early April therefore coincided with a real crisis of confidence in Moscow. It must have seemed to the Soviet leader that he had only a brief window of military opportunity, now closing, to impose his will on eastern Germany and perhaps even Poland. On March 29 he told Marshal Georgii Zhukov that the German front in the West had "collapsed completely" and showed him the reports of German negotiations with the Western Allies. According to Zhukov, Stalin said: "I think Roosevelt won't violate the Yalta agreements, but as for Churchill, that one's capable of anything."[149]

On March 31 Stalin received a message from Eisenhower, intended to improve coordination between their armies. The Allied commander stated that his troops were now thrusting toward Leipzig, south of Berlin, rather than the German capital. Given the mindset in the Kremlin, the message was probably dismissed as sinister disinformation. Next day Stalin summoned Zhukov and Ivan Koniev, his two top marshals, and asked: "Who is going to take Berlin: are we or the Allies?" There was one only possible answer, and Koniev gave it immediately: "It is we who shall take Berlin, and we will take it before the Allies." With his flanks now secured, Stalin cannily unleashed Zhukov and Koniev—two bitter rivals—in their own personal race for Berlin. That same day, April 1, he cabled Eisenhower that Berlin had "lost its former strategic importance" and that the Soviets would send only second-rate forces against it, sometime in May. "However, this plan may undergo certain alterations, depending on circumstances." Historian Antony Beevor has described this message as "the greatest April Fool in modern history."[150]

It seems likely that in all three Allied capitals there was a fear by early April that the Yalta accords were breaking down.[151] Moscow was as worried as London and Washington, though for very different reasons. The crisis was eventually patched up—in June Truman and a reluctant Churchill recognized the Polish government after a few token noncommunists were added—but the damage caused by the row to mutual trust was lasting.

At the end of July the Big Three met for a final time at Potsdam, on the edge of Berlin, but this was a very different summit from Yalta. Roosevelt was dead and Churchill was voted out of office during the conference, being replaced by the new Labour leader, Clement Attlee, whose contribution was limited. Byrnes, now Truman's secretary of state, fixed up a deal—despite British objections—by which the Soviets got their way on the western border of Poland (following the Oder and Western Neisse). But, in return, the Western powers refused to set a total figure for what the Soviets would receive in reparations from Germany. Instead each ally would take what it wanted in equipment, food and raw materials from its zone of occupation and the Soviets would also receive some transfers from the western zones. This deal on reparations did more than the decisions at Yalta to divide Soviet-controlled eastern Germany from the west.[152]

But it was Yalta that became a dirty word in the United States, even before the Potsdam conference began. Reports of the offer of three Soviet seats in the UN General Assembly appeared in the American press on March 29, after the president had briefed the American delegation to San Francisco, supposedly in strictest secrecy. This news and the apparent cover-up prompted critical comment from usually friendly papers and commentators. "From then on," wrote Robert Sherwood, "the very word 'Yalta' came to be associated in the public's mind with secret and somehow shameful deals."[153] At the end of August congressmen started asking why Soviet troops had been allowed to occupy the Kurile Islands, and Byrnes felt obliged to mention for the first time the secret Yalta agreement on the Far East. Both FDR and Stettinius had denied that any such agreement had been made. In the extreme Republican press, the equation of Yalta with appeasement and deception was already clear in 1945.[154]

In Washington lessons were also being learned about summitry. On April 10, 1945, before Roosevelt's death, Averell Harriman concluded that FDR's decision to go to Yalta had been a mistake. The president "at great inconvenience and risk to himself" accepted Stalin's choice of venue. "It seems clear," wrote Harriman, "that this magnanimous act on his part has been interpreted as a sign of weakness and Stalin and his associates are acting accordingly."[155] In June 1945 George Kennan wrote a lengthy indictment of the Western failure to stand up to the Russians. Those in Moscow who believed they could always get their way by assertive policies, he said, "can point to the unshakable confidence of the Anglo-Saxons in meetings between individuals, and can argue that Russia has nothing to lose by trying out these policies, since if things at any time get hot all they have to do is allow another personal meeting with western leaders, and thus make a fresh start, with all forgotten."[156]

WHERE THEN SHOULD BE the verdict today on Yalta? Unlike the summits of September 1938, these were multifaceted negotiations from which each party came away with something. Roosevelt secured his priorities—agreement on the UN and a Soviet pledge to enter the war against Japan. Churchill managed to avoid firm commitments about Poland's western border, German dismemberment and reparations—the latter to Stalin's undisguised irritation. The British also secured a larger role for France in postwar Europe than

either of their partners wanted. Stalin, for his part, gained acceptance of his main territorial goals in Asia and agreements that
seemed to recognize his predominance in Poland. Each of the Big
Three left with the belief that the wartime alliance would continue
after the war. That indeed had been their major goal for the conference. Building on Teheran in 1943, they hoped to turn summitry
into a process.

Unlike Chamberlain's summits, the leaders came to Yalta with
detailed briefing books and a body of specialist advisors, including
all three foreign ministers, and in many cases they acted on policies
already laid down. The deals on prisoners of war, for instance, or
Soviet territorial demands in Asia had already been established in
outline, while Maisky's presentation on reparations followed the
lines of a report he had drawn up over the winter.

At a number of key points, however, the leaders took their own
line. Stalin rejected the advice of Beria and others to offer the West
more fig leaves on the Polish government. Ignoring his advisors,
FDR succumbed to British pressure to accept three Soviet votes in
the UN. And Churchill batted aside Eden's apt questions about
why the Western Allies needed to buy Soviet entry into the Far
Eastern war.

But the British foreign secretary was very effective in obtaining a
greater role for postwar France than any of the Big Three, left
alone, would have preferred. In September 1938, Halifax had—
belatedly—exerted influence in Cabinet, but he never appeared at
the conference table. Eden, in contrast, was a real presence at
Yalta—vocal if rejected over the Far East, influential over France,
and backing up Churchill robustly on Germany. He was far more
significant at Yalta than his counterparts, particularly Stettinius.

As Eden and Cadogan remarked, Stalin was indeed a skilful negotiator, letting the others do the talking and saving his succinct remarks for the right moment. Nevertheless Churchill's more bombastic approach should not be underrated: it wore down the other
two over France and German reparations. And Roosevelt pushed
harder on Poland than the myths might suggest.

The real problems lay not in negotiation but in assumptions.

Churchill and Roosevelt—who were right about Hitler from afar—were both captivated by Stalin when they met him in the flesh. Hopeful that the Soviet Union was gradually shedding its revolutionary skin, they saw a man of business with whom they could conduct meaningful negotiation. Both hoped and, to a large extent, believed that he could be trusted. Whenever doubts welled up, particularly for Churchill, he looked into the abyss, recognized that confrontation, let alone war, was "unthinkable," and pushed on with the search for cooperation.[157]

Contrary to French mythology, Yalta was not the moment when the big powers crudely divided Europe. Churchill and FDR were still resisting a stark separate-spheres deal of the sort advocated by George Kennan. Nor was Yalta a sellout of Eastern Europe to the Soviets, as claimed by the Republican right: it was already clear that the Soviet Union would be the predominant influence in Eastern Europe. That had been decided on the battlefields of Russia in 1942–3, by the Allied failure to mount a second front until June 1944, and by the understandings already reached at Teheran in November 1943 and Moscow in October 1944. When they went to Yalta, Churchill and Roosevelt sought only to "ameliorate" Soviet influence.

To compensate for their intrinsically weak hand over Poland, both hoped that Stalin would offer cosmetic concessions because he wanted to maintain the alliance. They were right on the latter point but wrong on the former. Poland was a fundamental, even visceral, issue for Stalin and his expectations of a free hand had been fostered by Churchill's blatant spheres-of-influence approach in Moscow the previous autumn. He could not begin to comprehend the limiting conditions that his democratic partners wished to set on his influence in key countries in Eastern Europe. Their need for some degree of political pluralism and openness in order to persuade domestic opinion made no sense to this ruthless dictator. The misapprehensions at Yalta occurred on both sides, not just in the West.

But the failures of implementation were equally important. Both Churchill and Roosevelt oversold the agreements and especially the "spirit" of Yalta when they got home. This would create grave credibility problems for them in the weeks that followed. Churchill's desperate public hyperbole about trusting Stalin over Poland is particularly remarkable, given his trenchant critique of Chamberlain in 1938. Many were appalled by it at the time, but Churchill repackaged himself as a fierce Cold Warrior with his "Iron Curtain" speech in March 1946, whereas Roosevelt, being dead, could not retrieve his reputation. Yet Stalin overreacted as well. As the Western Allies surged into Germany in March 1945, his fears revived that they were negotiating a separate peace with the Nazis. This would threaten his position in Germany on which—portentously, it now seemed—Churchill had been so uncooperative at Yalta. Stalin knew much more about his Allies than they did about him—thanks to well-placed agents—but, as with the intelligence failures of 1938, interpretation matters as much as information. If Churchill and FDR were seduced by their hopes, Stalin was the victim of his own paranoia.

The summitry of 1938 changed history decisively. It saved Hitler's regime and postponed world war for a year, by which time the Nazi-Soviet pact tilted the balance against the Western Allies. In contrast Yalta in 1945 was less significant than American and French stereotypes have made it out to be. The West's surrender of Eastern Europe to the Soviets, if that is what it can be called, occurred earlier and by default, because of Anglo-American delays in mounting a Second Front. The formal partition of Europe came later, in 1947–9, with the Marshall Plan, the establishment of two German states, and the creation of NATO.

But the aftermath of Yalta *did* play a significant part in the breakdown of the Grand Alliance, engendering a sense of betrayal on both sides. And the interpretations about why that happened shaped the history of summitry. The Soviets harked back to a golden age of cooperation with Roosevelt that was abandoned by his successors. And in America the political sensitivity of the Yalta myths haunted policymakers for decades, deterring them from a parley at the summit to thaw the Cold War.

4

VIENNA 1961

Kennedy and Khrushchev

THE COLD WAR froze out serious summitry for a generation. This was not Churchill's wish: he coined the term in 1950 as part of his quest for an easement of tension—what was later called détente. But Britain, its empire fast disintegrating, was no longer in the same league as the United States and the Soviet Union. By the end of the Second World War it was not so much the Big Three as 'the Big 2 ½," to quote one despondent British diplomat.[1] In the West, America's leaders called the shots. Reflecting their country's essentially Manichean view of the world—a struggle between good and evil—they were skeptical of any kind of negotiations with the Soviets. And the lessons drawn from Munich and Yalta suggested that parleys at the summit were particularly dangerous.

In June 1961 the disastrous meeting at Vienna served to confirm that precept. The bruising encounter between John F. Kennedy and Nikita Khrushchev constitutes almost a textbook lesson in how *not* to do summitry. And their meeting helped spark two of the most dangerous confrontations of the Cold War: the Cuban Missile Crisis and America's quagmire war in Vietnam.

POTSDAM IN JULY–AUGUST 1945 was the last wartime summit. Meetings of foreign ministers continued for a couple of years but in the summer of 1948 America and Britain came close to war with the Soviets over Stalin's blockade of Berlin, still under Allied occupation. For nearly a year the Allies airlifted supplies into the beleaguered city, meanwhile turning the British, American and French zones of occupation into a West German state. The Berlin blockade also spurred the United States into an unprecedented peacetime alliance with Western Europe: the North Atlantic Treaty of 1949. In May 1955 West Germany became a member of NATO, while East Germany joined the Soviet-led Warsaw Pact. Exactly a decade after the end of Hitler's Reich, Europe had been divided into two armed camps, with the fault line running through Germany.

The two blocs were also nuclear arsenals. In August 1949 the Soviet Union tested an atomic bomb, signalling an end to America's monopoly. Then in 1953–4 tests of hydrogen bombs by both sides presaged weapons of far greater power. Reading reports of America's H-bomb tests, Churchill murmured that the world was now as far from the era of the atomic bomb as the atomic bomb had been from the bow and arrow.[2] The launch of *Sputnik*—the first artificial earth satellite—in 1957 showed that the Soviets now possessed a missile of sufficient range to land a nuclear warhead on the United States within thirty minutes. For the first time, continental America was vulnerable to weapons of mass destruction, creating public paranoia comparable to that which had gripped Britain in the 1930s. Both blocs in the Cold War raced to build up their nuclear arsenals. While each side sought to deter the other from outright attack or nuclear blackmail, the cost of the arms race imposed grave burdens on their economies.

Stalin's death in March 1953 brought a new, reforming leadership to power in the Kremlin—initially led by the troika of Nikolai Bulganin, Nikita Khrushchev and Georgi Malenkov—and this offered hopes of a relaxation of tension. In 1953–4 Churchill, prime minister again, tried to arrange another Big Three meeting, picking up from where he had left off in 1945; across the Atlantic, President Dwight D. Eisenhower was keen to restrain the nuclear arms race. But both the British Foreign Office and the U.S. State Department

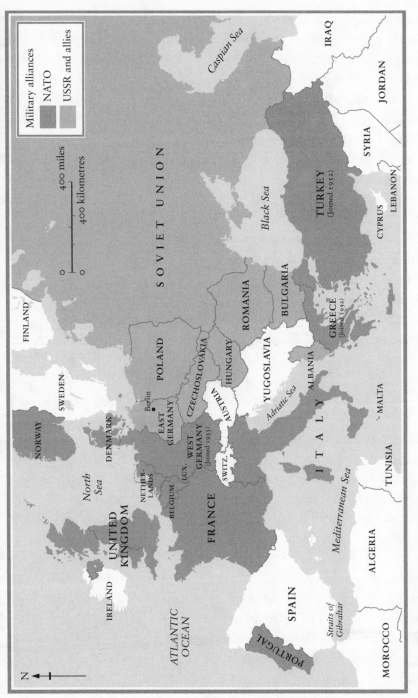

Map 4-1 Cold War Europe, 1949.

applied the brakes, insisting that a summit should occur only if and when specialist diplomats had prepared the ground for a real breakthrough. No such breakthrough occurred, but the political pressures for some kind of meeting became hard to resist.

Consequently the first Cold War summit, in Geneva in July 1955, was a carefully staged affair. The American, Soviet, British and French leaders, flanked by their advisors, sat around a square of tables in the Palais des Nations, reading prepared statements. They had brought some twelve hundred people to Geneva, making this more like an old-fashioned international conference than the intimate "parley at the summit" envisaged by Churchill. And it was all largely for propaganda purposes. The intended audiences were public opinion in the West, alarmed at nuclear war, and Moscow's uneasy satellites in Eastern Europe.[3]

The "spirit of Geneva" proved ephemeral and summitry remained under a cloud in the West. "I'm not enamoured of this individual business," Ernest Bevin, the British foreign secretary, snorted after Churchill's 1950 speech. "It was tried by Mr. Chamberlain with Hitler and it did not work very well. It was tried at Yalta and did not work very well."[4] In the United States Republicans made Yalta a centerpiece of their attacks on the Democrats' foreign policy. The "Yalta sellout," declared Senator William Jenner, turned communism "loose around one-half of the world." The Republican party platform in 1952 became almost an attack on summitry itself. Teheran, Yalta and Potsdam, it said, were the scenes of "tragic blunders"; Roosevelt and Truman "traded our overwhelming victory for a new enemy and for new oppressions."[5]

The Republicans were playing politics but, at a deeper level, the whole American approach to the Cold War militated against not merely summitry but any kind of negotiation. The Truman Doctrine of March 1947 depicted a world in which "nearly every nation must choose between alternative ways of life" and the choice was "too often not a free one." One way of life was "based upon the will of the majority" and was distinguished by "free institutions, representative government" and other basic liberties. The second was "based upon the will of a minority forcibly imposed upon the majority," backed by "terror and oppression." Truman committed the United States to "support free peoples who are resisting attempted subjugation" anywhere in the world.[6]

The Truman Doctrine helped define the Cold War as a global and total struggle in which there could be little or no compromise. And, especially after the Chinese Revolution of 1949, the perceived threat became communism rather than simply Soviet expansion. In response American policymakers developed the policy of "containment." Its prime author was the diplomat George Kennan, building on his bleak analysis of Yalta, who described containment as being "designed to confront the Russians with unalterable counter-force at every point where they show signs of encroaching upon the interests of a peaceful and stable world." Kennan was confident that eventually the Soviet Union would collapse under the weight of its own imperial repression, presciently suggesting that this might happen during a power transition when a new leader tried to mobilize popular support. But in the meantime the United States simply had to tough it out. "The issue of Soviet-American relations," Kennan argued, "is in essence a test of the overall worth of the United States as a nation among nations." This was an almost Darwinian struggle for the survival of the fittest.[7]

This American worldview left little scope for international dialogue, especially at the top, whereas Churchill's enthusiasm for summitry was predicated on his basic faith in diplomacy. He was not even afraid to use what was now a dirty word in the United States. "Appeasement from weakness and fear is alike futile and fatal," he warned in December 1950, but "[a]ppeasement from strength is magnanimous and noble and might be the surest and perhaps the only path to world peace."[8] Consistently after 1945 he looked to negotiate from a position of strength with the Soviets—that was the thrust of what is usually known as his "Iron Curtain" speech of March 1946 (his title was "The Sinews of Peace"). In May 1953 he told Eisenhower that he was ready to undertake a "solitary pilgrimage" to Moscow to meet the new Soviet leaders—few of whom had "any contacts outside Russia"—to talk with them "frankly and on the dead level." Referring to the American stance, he said he found it "difficult to believe that we shall gain anything by an attitude of pure negation."[9]

Churchill was also sure that the West should work for greater social contacts with the Soviet bloc. "If the Iron Curtain were lifted," he declared in October 1948, "if free intercourse, commercial and cultural, were allowed between the hundreds of millions of good hearted human beings who dwell on either side, the power of this wicked oligarchy in Moscow would soon be undermined and the spell of their Communist doctrines would be broken."[10]

Churchill's would-be mission to Moscow, though partly an ego trip, had a clear rationale: parleys at the summit would help thaw the Cold War and gradually erode the Iron Curtain. This was a very different approach from the no-negotiation, hang-in-there philosophy of containment.

This divide between the American and British attitudes to diplomacy was not absolute, of course. Diplomats on both sides were skeptical about letting their leaders loose at the summit, and not all Americans believed that dialogue with the Soviets was pointless. But Republican exploitation of the Cold War and of the Yalta myths made it particularly difficult for U.S. policymakers to show much flexibility in the 1950s, whatever their inclinations. Consequently the initiative for summitry tended to come from Europe.

On the Western side in the late 1950s it was Harold Macmillan, the British prime minister, who made the run for a summit—rather surprisingly, it might seem, considering his past. In 1938 he had been one of the few Tory opponents of Munich. He felt Yalta had been "a failure and a disaster" because "in an atmosphere of fervid rush and hurry, vast decisions were reached in a few crowded days." And he noted in his diary in February 1957, weeks after taking office: "I am said to have lost touch with public opinion in England because I have not already set out for Moscow to see Khrushchev. All this is pure Chamberlainism. It is raining umbrellas." But, as Churchill once observed, "how much more attractive a top-level meeting seems when one has reached the top!"[11] Once into his stride as premier, Macmillan saw the political benefits of summitry and in February 1959 he contrived a personal visit to Moscow. Politically the trip was a great success, helping Macmillan win an election by a landslide later that year. But Britain, like France, was no longer a serious presence at the top table. The real momentum for a summit in the late 1950s came not from Western capitals but from the Kremlin.

Born in 1894, Nikita Khrushchev was the son of poor peasants in southern Russia. Clever, ambitious yet uneducated, he wanted to become an engineer but, after the Bolshevik Revolution of 1917, he threw himself into politics instead, rising rapidly up the hierarchy to become Ukrainian party boss in 1938. As Khrushchev later acknowledged, he was Stalin's "pet." Energetic and loyal, he was also unthreatening because of his poor background, chatty exuberance and diminutive stature—at five foot one, he was even shorter than the self-conscious dictator.[12] By the early 1950s Khrushchev was part of the inner circle in Moscow; he took over as party secretary after Stalin's death yet none of his colleagues in the new collective leadership regarded this coarse little man as a real threat. Like Stalin after Lenin's demise, he outmaneuvered his rivals to become the clear leader of his country by 1955.

Khrushchev retained a huge inferiority complex about his lack of education and culture and was always alert to condescension, real or imagined, at home and abroad. Stalin too had such a complex, but Khrushchev was not as good at concealing it. Nor, unlike his patron, could Khrushchev control his explosive temper: within seconds he could shift from good humor to foul-mouthed abuse. At their first meeting in Geneva in 1955, the Soviet leader seemed a frankly "obscene figure" to the elegant, urbane Macmillan, who wondered how "this fat, vulgar man, with his pig eyes and his ceaseless flow of talk" could really be the head of a great country.[13]

At home Khrushchev wanted to free his people from the nightmare of Stalinism. Addressing the worst abuses of Stalin's rule, he liberated millions from the gulags. A genuine believer in the potential of communism, he strove to improve living standards through better food, housing and consumer goods. But that meant taking on the Soviet military-industrial complex, geared for three decades to arms production, its depredations justified by repeated war scares.

Increasingly the success of Khrushchev's domestic program turned on foreign policy. If he could pressure the West to ratify the Soviet position in Eastern Europe, especially Germany, that would give his country greater security. And if he could represent the Soviet Union as winning the Cold War by peaceful means, then he could hold his domestic critics at bay and reduce arms spending. That is why he seized with glee on the new missile program, unveiled to the world with the launch of *Sputnik* in 1957. Now the Soviets could strike directly at the United States, and this justified slashing cuts in conventional forces. "In our country," he boasted in January 1960, "the armed forces have to a considerable extent been transformed into rocket forces."[14] These were heady days for the Soviet leader, even more prone than usual to shoot his mouth off. "We will bury you," he warned the West, explaining later that this should be understood ideologically not literally: "I meant that capitalism would be buried and that Communism would come to replace it."[15]

Yet world communism was no longer a unity. By the late 1950s there was an open rupture between the Soviet Union and the People's Republic of China, led by Mao Zedong. This split involved personal animosity between the two erratic autocrats and Chinese resentment at Soviet efforts to stop them developing an atomic bomb. But its core was ideology: Khrushchev's doctrine of "peaceful coexistence" with the West. By this he meant not an end to rivalry but continued Soviet expansion without the risk of World War III, and he was confident that his country's new strength made the goal more feasible. Indeed his whole program, at home and abroad, depended on a measure of détente with the United States.

Mao, on the other hand, was still full of the rhetoric of armed struggle, even countenancing nuclear war on the grounds that the communist bloc had a much larger population. Even if "900 million are left out of 2.9 billion," he told party leaders chillingly in 1958, "several Five Year Plans can be developed for the total elimination of capitalism and for permanent peace."[16] Khrushchev thought Mao was utterly crazy but the Chinese were now bidding for leadership of the communist bloc and the developing world; they argued that the Soviets had become reactionary. So Khrushchev's relations with the West had to be conducted with one eye on the East.

Khrushchev had virtually no experience in foreign affairs while Stalin was alive. "The rest of us were just errand boys," he recalled. From his boss he acquired an essentially Stalinist view of the world: the West had always been out to undermine the Soviet Union, plotting encirclement during the civil war, trying to bleed them dry with no Second Front during World War II and then fostering German rearmament. But Khrushchev was also determined to outdo his master by getting his country out of the isolation of the early Cold War and showing the West, as Stalin had not, that the Soviet Union was impervious to nuclear intimidation.[17]

That was a major reason for his enthusiasm about summitry: he needed to take the measure of his adversary, and he left Geneva in 1955 elated to sense that "our enemies probably feared us as much as we feared them." Watching U.S. Secretary of State John Foster Dulles passing Ike a stream of notes, which the president "read conscientiously like a schoolboy," strengthened his self-confidence. Summitry was also about status. At Geneva airport Khrushchev had been utterly humiliated that his two-engine Ilyushin looked like an "insect" next to the four-engine monsters carrying the other delegations. Thereafter he used the latest versions of Tupolev jet, flaunting them before Westerners, and he proudly displayed a model of the giant Tu-114 on his Kremlin desk.[18]

What Khrushchev really wanted was an invitation to the United States. If he could browbeat the Americans into arms control, then he might win a real breathing space for reform at home. But Dulles and the State Department continued to block a summit unless and until the foreign ministers had made progress on the big issues. So Khrushchev decided to apply some "shock therapy" by engineering a new crisis over Berlin.[19]

Although Germany itself had been divided, the former capital, deep within East Germany, remained under four-power occupation: America, Britain, France and the Soviet Union each administered a zone. The Western powers still refused to recognize the East German government of Walter Ulbricht, backing instead the principle of eventual German reunification. So in November 1958 Khrushchev demanded that, if they did not conclude a German peace treaty within six months, he would hand over all their rights in Berlin to the Ulbricht government, with whom the West would then have to deal if it wanted to maintain its access to West Berlin. He acted on his own authority, impatient to cut through the endless arguments with the West. But key allies such as Anastas Mikoyan were appalled at the risk he was taking and at this "flagrant violation of party discipline." Their struggle over policy was not known in Washington, where even the CIA thought Khrushchev now called all the shots, but it helps explain the on-off nature of the Berlin crisis over the next few years.[20]

Khrushchev's hope was that the Soviets would either get a formal German treaty that recognized the new order or else the West would have to extend effective recognition to the East German regime. "Berlin is the West's balls," he remarked. "Every time I want to make the West scream, I squeeze on Berlin."[21]

But the city was also a vulnerable part of Moscow's imperial anatomy. East Germans who got to the Western sectors of Berlin could take planes or trains to West Germany, where they had the right of citizenship, and they were now fleeing in great numbers. Between September 1949 and August 1961 some 2.7 million East Germans went west, making the country the only member of the Soviet bloc to experience a net decline in population during the 1950s.[22] Moreover those who fled were mostly the young and better educated, whose skills and energies were economically vital. Ulbricht wanted to annex West Berlin but this, Khrushchev knew, could spark a major crisis. Yet the Soviet Union had to do something or its showcase country in Eastern Europe might collapse from within.

Khrushchev was also afraid of growing West German rearmament. In 1941 the Soviet Union had suffered a devastating surprise attack by Germany; not surprisingly fear and suspicion ran deep. If West Germany became a nuclear power, following Britain and France, then Khrushchev's arms reduction program would lose all credibility at home.

So Berlin was a high-stakes issue for both sides. Initially Khrushchev's brinkmanship achieved results. In London Harold Macmillan was persuaded that the Soviet leader showed signs of megalomania. "Could Khrushchev do as foolish things as Hitler did?" The need to dissuade him helped justify Macmillan's visit to Moscow, rather like Chamberlain's flight to Berchtesgaden.[23]

In their meetings the Soviet leader was often blustering and aggressive—telling one shocked aide that he had "fucked" Macmillan "with a telephone pole." He did drop the six-month deadline and proposed a foreign ministers' conference to resolve the crisis but this got nowhere. Eisenhower, with only eighteen months left in office, was anxious for real progress on nuclear arms control. The death of Dulles in May 1959 removed a skeptical voice, and Khrushchev was invited to America in September. The Soviet leader was jubilant. "Who would have guessed, twenty years ago, that the most powerful capitalist country in the world would invite a Communist to visit? This is incredible," he told his son. "Today they *have* to take us into account. It's our strength that led to this."[24]

During the visit Eisenhower also agreed to a four-power summit. Khrushchev, now confident about reaching agreements on Berlin and arms control, cut Soviet conventional forces even further. Though admitting that there were still ardent Cold Warriors in "very influential circles," he believed Ike had realized that Dulles' policies had got America into a "dead end street."[25]

In early 1960, however, hopes waned of any diplomatic breakthroughs. And on May 1, just two weeks before the scheduled summit in Paris, the Soviets shot down an American U-2 spy plane over the Urals and captured its pilot. Khrushchev gave Ike the opportunity to blame the flight on "Pentagon militarists" but the president declined to pass the buck. The Soviet leader flew to Paris to torpedo the summit for which he had agitated for years. Contrary to administration suspicions, Khrushchev genuinely wanted a summit: he believed Ike had shared this desire but was undermined by the CIA and Pentagon.[26]

Khrushchev also withdrew his invitation for Ike to visit the Soviet Union. This was all set for June 10–19, with five days of talks in

Moscow, side visits to Leningrad and Kiev, and three speeches on Soviet TV and radio.[27] The president was chagrined at losing the chance of a Moscow summit to crown his administration, but Khrushchev was equally a loser. The progress he sought on Berlin and the arms race would have to await a new U.S. president.

ON JANUARY 21, 1961, John F. Kennedy delivered his inaugural address in front of the U.S. Capitol. It was a richly symbolic moment. The forty-three-year-old president, bareheaded and without an overcoat despite the biting cold, announced that "the torch has been passed to a new generation of Americans—born in this century." His predecessor, old enough to be Kennedy's father, listened in silence as the new president promised, in the kind of language that Ike had sedulously avoided, to "pay any price, bear any burden" to "assure the survival and the success of liberty." Such phrases could be read as a clarion call to Cold War confrontation. But Kennedy also pledged to "begin anew the quest for peace, before the dark powers of destruction unleashed by science engulf all humanity in planned or accidental self-destruction."[28]

Kennedy's inaugural kept his options open. Khrushchev, who had wrong-footed the West for years, was now the man left guessing.

The new president's view of the Soviet Union had evolved over the years. He had visited it only once, in the summer of 1939, when he discovered "a crude, backward, hopelessly bureaucratic country." A decade later, representing an ethnic, Catholic district in Boston, he mouthed the language fashionable at the time, blasting a "sick" Roosevelt for selling out China at Yalta. After the Geneva conference of 1955 he had warned that "the barbarian may have taken the knife out of his teeth to smile, but the knife is still in his fist."[29] Privately and more reflectively in August 1959, he pondered the motivation behind Soviet policy. Was it merely a search for security or was it "evangelical" with the aim of eventually achieving "world revolution"? Kennedy guessed it was probably a combination of the two, which meant that there was no "magic solution," no "button that you can press" to reach a lasting accommodation.

Instead America was engaged in a "constant day-by-day struggle with an enemy who is constantly attempting to expand his power." Perhaps, Kennedy mused, "the desire of everyone to be independent" would "screw the Russians ultimately."[30] He also spoke of education as a promoter of change: "Once the Pandora's box of learning is opened, truth will be loose in the land of the Soviets—and the truth may make them free."[31]

Kennedy was clearly feeling his way beyond mere containment. But these were prescriptions for the long term and in the nuclear age humanity's chances of surviving the short term did not seem high. This was the main reason why Kennedy came out cautiously but firmly in favor of a summit—as a form of damage limitation. In a speech on October 1, 1959, just after Khrushchev's visit, he acknowledged that "the real roots of the Soviet-American conflict cannot easily be settled by negotiations." Substantive change would depend on Soviet "deeds, not words." But Kennedy believed that a summit could help prevent Soviet-American competition escalating from cold war to hot war: "It is far better that we meet at the summit than at the brink." And he discerned in Khrushchev's speeches the "germs" of some "potential common interests." These included avoiding the horror of nuclear war, the pollution of nuclear tests and the crushing economic burden of the arms race.[32]

The Paris summit, Kennedy claimed in June 1960, had been "doomed" long before the U-2 crashed onto Soviet soil because the Eisenhower administration had consistently failed "to build the positions of long-term strength essential to successful negotiations."[33] Kennedy had pondered this issue years before, in 1940: he wrote a Harvard senior thesis titled "Appeasement at Munich," later published as *Why England Slept*.[34]

Kennedy's basic interpretation of Munich was strategic rather than personal; he wanted to shift responsibility away from individuals and dispel the American stereotype of Chamberlain as "a doddering old man being completely 'taken in.'" He argued that the prime minister had "a double-barrelled policy": to build up Britain's defenses while seeking to remove potential causes of war. And although ultimately Chamberlain allowed his "sincere and strong hopes" for peace to unbalance his policy, Kennedy insisted that in September 1938 the British leader "could not have fought, even if he had wanted to . . . Munich was inevitable on the grounds of lack of armaments alone."[35]

This was a structural explanation for appeasement, rooted in the balance of power, elements of which foreshadowed later revisionist histories of the 1930s.[36] In consequence, however, it played down the more personal aspects of Chamberlain's summitry, particularly his weaknesses as a negotiator. Moreover the book was published in 1940 when the world was in awe at the apparent might of the Nazi military machine. Kennedy did not appreciate that in 1938 Germany was as unprepared as Britain for world war. Bluff at the summit was critical in 1938. And it would matter as much in 1961.

From his undergraduate reading of Munich Kennedy drew two enduring lessons. The first was the deficiency, in the short term, of democracy as a decision-making system when competing with totalitarian rivals. Being peace loving and consensual, a democratic people take longer to gear up for war. Yet, secondly, readiness for war is essential to secure a lasting and secure peace. Otherwise you will be unable to bargain on equal terms with your opponent.[37] These were the lessons that Kennedy (or rather Theodore Sorensen, his speechwriter) distilled so memorably in the Inaugural Address twenty years later: "Let us never negotiate out of fear. But let us never fear to negotiate."[38]

Kennedy therefore came to power with a clear and somewhat Churchillian philosophy of summitry. But his approach was never merely cerebral; it was also intensely personal. His father, Joseph P. Kennedy, a ruthless multimillionaire, was determined to get his family into the White House. When his eldest son, Joe Junior, was killed in the war the mantle of parental ambition fell on Jack. But whereas Joe seemed a natural politician—dynamic, sociable and easygoing—Jack, as his father admitted, was rather shy, withdrawn and quiet." "If Joe had lived," Jack said later, "I probably would have gone to law school."[39]

He didn't enter politics simply to satisfy his father's ambitions—having seen other politicians close up, he thought himself at least as capable—yet climbing the political ladder involved a huge effort of will. It was also physically taxing because Jack, despite his good looks and athletic appearance, was often virtually a cripple. Since his teens he had suffered from ulcers and humiliating diarrhea; the drugs he took for these probably exacerbated a severe adrenal condition known as Addison's disease. He had a weak lower back, into which a metal plate was inserted in 1954. He also suffered from repeated urinary and bladder problems, the result of his promiscuous sex life and probable venereal disease, and was prone to sinus and respiratory infections.[40]

Kennedy therefore became dependent on a daily cocktail of drugs, administered by various physicians with little knowledge of the likely side effects. He had to endure excruciating pain, finding it difficult at times to even put on his shoes or sit in a chair. Any of these ailments would have been the excuse for a quiet life, yet they seemed to have driven Kennedy on. Instead of using his health and a politically influential father to avoid the draft in World War II, he not only entered the U.S. Navy but volunteered for hazardous duty as the commander of a motor torpedo boat in the Pacific. The heroism he displayed when his vessel was sunk in August 1943—hours swimming in the water and helping his men—made him a national hero. A decade later, while recuperating from back surgery, Kennedy finished a book entitled *Profiles in Courage,* about eight U.S. senators who risked their careers by taking unpopular stands. As with most of Kennedy's books, the research was done by others, but the underlying ideas were his own. The product of a ferociously competitive family, Kennedy was fascinated by moral and political courage. This personal dimension, as much as an intellectual approach to summitry, would shape his encounter with Khrushchev.

The two men met briefly on September 17, 1959, during Khrushchev's visit to the United States, when he spoke to the Senate Foreign Relations Committee. "Tan suit—French cuffs—short, stocky, two red ribbons, two stars," Kennedy noted. Only senior senators had a chance to ask questions but, shaking hands afterward, Khrushchev told Kennedy that he had heard of him as an up and coming politician, observing that he looked too young to be a senator. This was the comment that stayed with Kennedy, always sensitive to hints that he lacked gravitas and experience.[41] The session disabused Kennedy of any lingering image of the Soviet leader as a "vodka-drinking politician-buffoon." In his speech on October 1 he portrayed Khrushchev as "a tough-minded, articulate, hard-reasoning spokesman for an ideology in which he was thoroughly versed and in which he thoroughly believed."[42]

Khrushchev paid more attention to Kennedy after he won the Democratic nomination in July 1960. A profile by the Soviet embassy in Washington stressed Kennedy's belief that the superpower relationship was one of "constant struggle" and noted his "bellicose" position on Berlin. But it also emphasized his interest in arms control and a nuclear test ban, motivated by the desire for "a mutual effort to avoid nuclear war. For this reason," said the embassy, "Kennedy, in principle, advocates talks with the Soviet Union."[43]

Within days of the presidential election on November 8, 1960, Khrushchev started pressing for a summit. The Soviet ambassador in Washington, Mikhail Menshikov, lobbied Averell Harriman, the veteran American statesman and Kennedy insider; Menshikov explained that Khrushchev hoped for "a return to the spirit of Soviet-American co-operation which we had during the war" when Harriman was U.S. ambassador in Moscow. Harriman relayed the message to Kennedy.[44] The ambassador kept up Khrushchev's pressure for a summit, badgering all who would talk to him.

On January 10, 1961, the president-elect asked George Kennan why the Soviet leader was so keen. The intellectual architect of containment suggested that Khrushchev's political position had been weakened by the U-2 episode, the failure of the Paris summit and growing tensions with communist China. He thought there was now "a real urgency in Moscow about achieving agreements on disarmament" and surmised that the Soviet leader hoped, by concluding such a deal personally, to recoup "his failing political fortunes." But Kennan urged Kennedy not to rush into a summit: advocates of such a meeting, he said, should show why the issues in dispute "could not be better treated at lower and more normal levels."[45]

This was the traditional line from diplomatic professionals. Secre-

The summiteer as hero and visionary. Modern summitry drew on the passions of nineteenth-century Romanticism. Caspar David Friedrich, *Der Wanderer über dem Nebelmeer* (c. 1818).

The raft at Tilsit. Napoleon greets Alexander I of Russia for a specially contrived meeting in the middle of the Niemen River, June 1807.

Taking off for the first modern summit. This picture of Chamberlain's plane at Heston aerodrome, West London, September 15, 1938, conveys something of the euphoria aroused by his dramatic gamble. (*Birmingham University Library*)

Chamberlain, Hitler and interpreter Paul Schmidt. Photographed in Hitler's study at the Berghof, September 15, 1938. (*U.S. National Archives*)

Discord on the Rhine. This undistinguished boardroom in the Hotel Dreesen at Bad Godesberg was the venue for the second Chamberlain–Hitler summit, September 22–23, 1938. (*Münchner Neuste Nachrichten*)

Muddle at Munich. The shambolic final round took place in Hitler's office in the Führerbau on September 29, 1938. Mussolini's bald head is center; Hitler, to the left, obscures Chamberlain; and French premier Daladier is on the extreme right. (*akg-images*)

The Livadia Palace, venue for the Yalta conference of February 1945. (*Government of the Ukraine*)

The Big Three at Yalta. This picture, taken on February 9, 1945, shows Roosevelt's deterioration since Teheran. Immediately behind are the three foreign ministers: Anthony Eden (GB), Edward R. Stettinius (USA), and Vyacheslav Molotov (USSR). Sir Alexander Cadogan (Foreign Office) is between Stettinius and Molotov; to the right of the latter is Averell Harriman (U.S. Ambassador to Moscow). (*Franklin D. Roosevelt Library*)

The Soviet Enigma. Molotov (center) harangues Stettinius; Andrei Gromyko (Ambassador to the USA) is second from the left. Many British and Americans believed that Molotov was the Soviet hard man and Stalin the moderate. (*RIA Novosti/akg-images*)

Around the table. Churchill is bottom left and Stalin top left. To the left of Roosevelt are Admiral William Leahy and General George Marshall. (*Ullstein/akg-images*)

Keeping it in the family. Badly shaken by official incompetence over the Bay of Pigs invasion of Cuba, President Kennedy used his brother Bobby as a back-channel to Moscow before the Vienna summit. (*PA Photos*)

Taking advice. Llewellyn ("Tommy") Thompson, the U.S. ambassador to Moscow, encouraged a summit but wanted Kennedy to show flexibility on Berlin. During their talk in the Oval Office, the president sits in his rocking chair to ease his bad back. (*John F. Kennedy Library*)

Vienna day one. Kennedy and Khrushchev meet on the steps of the U.S. ambassador's residence, June 3, 1961. To the right of Khrushchev is Soviet interpreter Viktor Sukhodrev, then Foreign Minister Andrei Gromyko talking to U.S. Secretary of State Dean Rusk. Above Sukhodrev is Soviet diplomat Anatoly Dobrynin. (*John F. Kennedy Library*)

Vienna day two. On June 4 the venue shifted to the Soviet Embassy in Reisnerstrasse, and Khrushchev continued to dominate. (*John F. Kennedy Library*)

After the summit—the Wall. The confrontation at Vienna led directly to the final division of Berlin. The Wall separated the Brandenburg Gate from the ruined Reichstag, from where this picture was taken. (*Presse- und Informationsamt der Bundesregierung, Berlin*)

After the summit—the abyss? Kennedy's conduct at Vienna encouraged Khrushchev to try installing medium-range ballistic missiles in Cuba, but he was caught by U.S. spy-planes. The ensuing confrontation was the most dangerous moment in the Cold War. (*Corbis*)

tary of State Dean Rusk was also against such an encounter so early in the new presidency. In an article the previous year, before the Paris meeting, Rusk set out the classic argument against summits.

Picture two men sitting down together to talk about matters affecting the very survival of the systems they represent, each in a position to unleash unbelievably destructive power . . . Is it wise to gamble so heavily? Are not these two men who should be kept apart until others have found a sure meeting ground of accommodation between them?[46]

On the other hand, Democratic doves such as Adlai Stevenson told Kennedy "the most important first thing" the administration had to do was "discover what is in K[hrushchev]'s mind." Stevenson offered himself as a high-level emissary, a proposal that held no appeal for Kennedy. He shared Stevenson's sense of priorities but was determined to do the discovering himself.[47]

On January 6 Khrushchev gave a major speech about foreign affairs to party workers. In line with his slogan of peaceful coexistence, Khrushchev argued that the impending economic victory of socialism over capitalism would exert "a revolutionizing influence" around the globe; he insisted that world war in the nuclear age would be "the most destructive war in all history." He also warned against letting the "imperialists" stir up "local wars," which he said could easily develop into global nuclear conflict. To retain his ideological credentials against China, Khrushchev identified a special category of local wars, those of "national liberation" such as in Vietnam, Algeria or Cuba, which should be supported "wholeheartedly" by communists as "just wars." Peaceful coexistence, he stated, "helps the national liberation movement to gain successes."[48]

The U.S. ambassador in Moscow, Llewellyn "Tommy" Thompson, advised Washington that the speech "should be read in its entirety by everyone having to do with Soviet affairs" because it brought together in one place Khrushchev's point of view as a "communist and a propagandist." Yet, Thompson added, "there are other sides to him." The ambassador also noted that much of the speech was clearly directed at China, a point underlined in a State Department analysis for the president.[49] But Kennedy, who received the translated text of the speech just after his inauguration, was inclined to take it as a definitive statement of Khrushchev's foreign policy. "You've got to understand it," he told his top officials. "This is our clue to our future with the Soviet Union."[50]

How far the Soviet leader would go in supporting wars of national liberation became one of the big questions for Kennedy. Small crises could easily escalate—like Macmillan, he had much in mind the July crisis in 1914, which started as a strike by Serbian nationalists against the Austrian empire.[51]

To sort out his thinking about the Soviet Union, Kennedy arranged a special Saturday-morning seminar in the Cabinet Room of the White House on February 11, 1961. He wanted to pick the brains of three veteran U.S. envoys to Moscow—Harriman, Kennan and "Chip" Bohlen—as well as hear from Thompson, who had been summoned home for the purpose. The ambassador—who had enjoyed unusual access to the Soviet leader, even spending a family weekend at his dacha—emphasized that Khrushchev was the man who mattered: "While the Government is a collective enterprise, it is increasingly a collective enterprise of Khrushchev's supporters." Thompson believed Khrushchev wanted "a generally unexplosive time in foreign affairs" so as to concentrate on economic progress; the Soviet leader therefore needed some specific diplomatic successes in 1961. Thompson felt Soviet interest in arms control was genuine, likewise its concerns about Germany and China. On the other hand, as Bohlen emphasized, Germany was "an excellent crowbar to pry at the seams of the Atlantic alliance." Similarly in the Third World, the Soviets were exploiting "targets of opportunity" such as Laos, the Congo and Cuba. This "double character" of Soviet policy, warned Bohlen, would require both "courtesy" and "firmness," the latter being essential over Berlin.[52]

At the February 11 seminar there was "considerable feeling among the experts that a meeting in due course, for an exchange of courtesies and the opportunity of becoming personally acquainted, might be useful." But the experts also agreed that "nothing approaching a summit, in terms of serious negotiations, should be considered favorably for the present." Over the next ten days, however, momentum built up. The principal reason was probably the president's own impatience to get a sense of his main adversary. As Bohlen remarked later, on these matters "he really felt he had to find out for himself."[53] And, as Thompson had already observed, a meeting would enable Kennedy to set the tone of his relationship with Khrushchev. He could convince the Soviet leader that he did not intend to seek solutions by force and was ready for serious negotiations. If the encounter occurred soon, the president could avoid substantive discussion because he could not yet be expected to have formulated positions on controversial issues. An additional concern, raised particularly by Bohlen, was to head off a possible visit by Khrushchev to the United Nations General Assembly in March. When he attended in October 1960 he had used the occasion for propaganda purposes, famously banging his shoe on the lectern for emphasis. If Kennedy offered to go east, this might pre-empt a repeat performance.[54]

A mixture of these considerations probably explains why the president decided to push ahead. In a letter to Khrushchev dated February 22 he expressed the hope that "before too long" they could "meet personally for an informal exchange of views" on some of the questions in dispute between them. Of course, he said, such a meeting would depend on such preconditions as "the general international situation at the time" as well as on "our mutual schedules." He asked Ambassador Thompson to deliver the letter on his return to Moscow and to discuss the question of a meeting with Khrushchev.[55]

Bohlen also urged on Kennedy some further, private conditions. He should not talk to the Soviet leader until he had met with America's principal European allies. The president should be in Europe anyway because a special trip would heighten expectations. And for reasons of equality it was desirable to meet in a neutral country, such as Austria or Switzerland.[56]

Ambassador Thompson had some problems delivering Kennedy's

letter. Khrushchev was engaged in a lengthy tour of Soviet agriculture, and Thompson eventually caught up with him on March 9, in the Siberian city of Novosibirsk, some two thousand miles from Moscow. By then, the State Department had made progress in fixing talks with Allied leaders; Thompson was able to suggest a meeting in Vienna or Stockholm on the back of Kennedy's proposed trip to see President Charles de Gaulle. (The prickly French leader was less ready than his British and West German counterparts to cross the Atlantic for an audience in the White House.) Khrushchev told Thompson that he would need to study Kennedy's letter but indicated agreement in principle, with a preference for Vienna. The Soviet leader was "obviously pleased with the President's initiative," Thompson reported.[57] Khrushchev confirmed his willingness for a summit when he saw Thompson on April 1[58] and news started to leak into the American press.[59]

BUT, JUST WHEN the "mutual schedules" were falling into place, Kennedy's other precondition for a summit, "the general international situation," took a decided turn against the United States.

On April 12 the Soviet Union became the first country to put a man into space—Yuri Gagarin circled the earth for ninety minutes before landing safely. The handsome young cosmonaut, with his telegenic smile, became a national and international status symbol. Although the American astronaut Alan Shepard evened the score on May 5, his was only a fifteen-minute flight, blasted like a cannonball from the Florida coast into the Atlantic; it could not offset the basic point that, as with the so-called missile gap, the Americans were again seen to be lagging behind in high technology.

The reality of course was very different. Key areas of the Soviet military-industrial complex were indeed precocious, but its underlying economic base was far inferior to that of the United States. On the day that Gagarin was received in triumph at the Kremlin, the British ambassador to the Soviet Union, Sir Frank Roberts, had to drive from Moscow to Leningrad. There were only two gas stations on his 430-mile route and, at the one where Roberts stopped, the automatic pumps failed. While staff filled his Rolls-Royce by hand, Roberts looked at the posters of Gagarin and savored the irony.[60]

But perceptions mattered as much as reality. "In the eyes of the world," Vice President Lyndon Johnson warned, "first in space means first, period; second in space is second in everything." Hitherto Kennedy had shown little interest in the issue but on April 19, a week after Gagarin's flight, he asked Johnson to identify a space program that "promises dramatic results in which we could win."[61] Backed by strong defense and aeronautical lobbies, Johnson pushed the project to land a man on the moon. Eisenhower had refused to make space into a race but his young successor saw no alternative. That was not just because of Gagarin's success, humiliating though it was for America; this coincided with a diplomatic fiasco nearer home, for which only the president could be blamed.

In January 1959 the guerrilla leader Fidel Castro had seized power on the island of Cuba, ninety miles off the Florida coast, toppling a corrupt dictatorship in pawn to American economic interests. Castro was not initially a communist but the growing opposition of the Eisenhower administration drove him into the Soviet camp. For more than a century the United States claimed South America as its sphere of interest, regularly intervening to replace governments that it opposed—most recently in a full-scale invasion of Guatemala in 1954. In Eisenhower's last months, the CIA drew up a plan to end the Castro regime and this landed on the new president's desk when he entered the White House.

Although initially sympathetic to the Cuban revolution, Kennedy had come to see Castro as the Latin American vanguard of Khrushchev's plans to promote communism globally. The president's response to this challenge was the Alliance for Progress, a massive development program for the continent that he unveiled in March. He was also wary of committing the United States overtly in toppling Castro. The CIA therefore turned what had been a conventional invasion centered on U.S. forces into an operation by Cuban exiles with the minimum possible American support. The State Department and some senior advisors continued to voice opposition but over the Easter weekend of April 1–3, the president made up his mind. He spent the break at his father's house in Palm Beach, Florida, and returned to Washington on the 4th fired up with determination.

Exactly what tipped the balance is not clear but various factors played a part. The CIA, backed by the joint chiefs of staff, had now made the plan politically acceptable and the veteran CIA director, Allen Dulles, assured Kennedy that its prospects were even better than those for Guatemala in 1954. An inexperienced new president would find it hard to demur. In any case Kennedy wanted Castro overthrown, and the operation appealed to his sense of daring. A weekend with his macho father probably had an effect. While at Palm Beach Kennedy received Ambassador Thompson's telegram confirming Khrushchev's willingness to meet in Vienna after his Paris trip at the end of May. With the road to the summit now open, Kennedy perhaps felt freer to deal with the problem of Castro.[62]

The CIA's critics were still not convinced. Arthur Schlesinger, the Harvard historian who was special assistant to the president, presciently warned that the plan would probably fall between two stools. "No matter how 'Cuban' the equipment and personnel, the U.S. will be held accountable for the operation, and our prestige will be committed to its success." At the same time, without real American firepower, the operation would fail to topple Castro and would "turn into a protracted civil conflict."[63]

Schlesinger was right. A "deniable plan" led to an "undeniable fiasco."[64] Landing on the remote Bay of Pigs on April 17 with virtually no air support, the Cuban exiles crumbled within a couple of days. By April 19 Kennedy could conceal neither their failure nor American involvement. Publicly and with dignity he accepted "sole responsibility."[65] But in private his mood was angry and distressed; on several occasions he could not control his tears. Acute diarrhea and another urinary tract infection added to his misery. Bobby Kennedy, the president's brother and now attorney general, berated JFK's inner circle: "All you bright fellows have got the President into this, and if you don't do something now, my brother will be regarded as a paper tiger by the Russians."[66]

On April 18, 1961, Khrushchev sent Kennedy a fierce message casting doubt on his professed wish to improve relations and warning that "any so-called 'little war' can touch off a chain reaction in all parts of the globe." Kennedy fired back a robust reply about the right of the Cuban people to seek freedom from "the Castro dictatorship," only to receive a long and rambling lecture dated April 22 about "the very dangerous road" he was treading.[67]

In May 1960 the U-2 fiasco had given Khrushchev justification for sabotaging the Paris summit and the Kennedy administration recognized that this could happen again. In the wake of the Bay of Pigs, Kennedy could not seem too eager for a meeting—that might look like appeasement. But if he backed away from the proposed encounter, it would suggest he was a coward. And if the idea lapsed altogether, he would lose the chance to convince the Soviet leader that, despite Cuba, he was no soft touch.[68] Whereas initially it was Khrushchev who had wanted a summit more than Kennedy, after the Bay of Pigs the balance was much more equal.

On May 4 Moscow broke silence. Thompson was asked to call on the Soviet foreign minister, Andrei Gromyko, who said he would not like to repeat Khrushchev's comments about the Bay of Pigs. But, Gromyko went on, the recent "discord" over Cuba underlined the fact that "we live on one planet" and "bridges have to be built" to link the two countries. He asked Thompson to ascertain whether Kennedy genuinely wanted a personal meeting, making clear that the Kremlin still thought this would be "useful" for both sides. The White House was quick to respond. "The President remains desirous of meeting Khrushchev," Gromyko was told. "He hopes that it will be possible to adhere to the original schedule of early June in Vienna but is not at the moment in a position to make a firm decision." The Soviets were promised a definite reply within the next two weeks.[69]

Kennedy's message indicated that the prospects for a summit would be helped by progress toward a peaceful settlement of the crisis in Laos. There an American-backed military government was under attack from the communist Pathet Lao, aided by North Vietnam. Laos was poor, tiny and landlocked—hardly a country of

great strategic importance. Nor was it a credible ally. The economist John Kenneth Galbraith, Kennedy's ambassador to India,
scoffed that in military terms "the entire Laos nation is clearly inferior to a battalion of conscientious objectors from World War I."
Seen in a Cold War context, however, Laos took on larger significance because North Vietnam was backed by communist China. To
many in Washington, the United States would have to draw a line
against Chinese expansion sooner or later. Admiral Arleigh Burke,
deputy chairman of the joint chiefs of staff, warned that "each time
you give ground it is harder to take a stand next time" and said that
abandoning Laos could mean having to fight for South Vietnam or
Thailand. But the military's fevered talk about troops, air strikes and
even nuclear war alarmed Kennedy, especially after the Bay of Pigs
fiasco had undermined his respect for so-called expert advice. His
preferred solution was a genuinely neutral Laos and, to that end, an
international conference was convened in Geneva in April. Hence
his warning to Gromyko that progress at Geneva would make a Vienna summit "easier from the point of view of public opinion" at
home and abroad.[70]

Laos was partly reason, partly pretext for procrastinating about
the summit. On May 9, three days after the reply was sent to
Gromyko, Bobby Kennedy met secretly in Washington with
Georgi Bolshakov from the Soviet embassy. Ostensibly a newsman,
Bolshakov actually worked for Soviet military intelligence and was
a close friend of Khrushchev's son-in-law. Their meeting, arranged
through an American journalist, Frank Holeman, took place at 8:30
p.m. at the back entrance to the Justice Department. The two men
walked out onto the Mall.

Bobby Kennedy started very firmly, referring to recent events in
Cuba and Laos. The Soviets, he said, seemed to be underestimating
the capabilities of the United States and the president. If this continued the administration would "have to take corrective action,
changing the course of its policies." Having laid that on the line,
Bobby then indicated that his brother held out hopes for real
progress at Vienna, above all a treaty banning nuclear tests. Officially
this issue was deadlocked because it depended on verification and

the Americans demanded twenty on-site inspections a year whereas the Soviets stuck at three. Now, secretly, Bobby said that the administration was willing to compromise on ten inspections, if it were made to seem like a Soviet offer. The United States wanted the details to be fleshed out through diplomatic channels in the next few weeks so the two leaders could sign an agreement in Vienna. He made it clear that the president was "not interested in a summit where leaders just exchange views."[71]

Bobby Kennedy's meeting with Bolshakov on May 9 was enormously important. It was the first of a series of regular encounters between the two men, lasting until December 1962, which created a back channel between the White House and the Kremlin. It was also a sign of the president's growing reliance on his brother as a foreign policy advisor, after the damaging shock of the Bay of Pigs.

Bobby said later of the Bolshakov channel that "unfortunately, stupidly . . . I didn't write many of the things down. I just delivered the messages verbally to my brother and he'd act on them, and I think sometimes he'd tell the State Department, and sometimes, perhaps, he didn't."[72] This was disingenuous: the informality was exactly what the Kennedys needed to operate outside the trammels of official diplomacy. The May 9 conversation made clear how far Kennedy's hopes for Vienna had diverged from those of the State Department. The February 11 seminar at the White House had endorsed a chance of "becoming personally acquainted" but advocated "nothing approaching a summit, in terms of serious negotiations."[73] Bobby Kennedy, however, was now passing the word to Khrushchev that his brother wanted concrete agreements, not a social chat. The president was raising the stakes.

From then on preparations for Vienna proceeded along two channels: the official diplomatic one managed by Ambassadors Thompson and Menshikov, and the back channel operated by Bolshakov and Bobby. On May 12 Khrushchev sent the president a formal letter, picking up on the Gromyko-Thompson conversation eight days before. Using the same language about the need to build "bridges of mutual understanding," he confirmed his readiness to meet in Vienna on June 3–4; he also highlighted Laos, disarmament and the German question as key issues for discussion. Menshikov delivered this letter to the White House on May 16. Not surprisingly Kennedy redefined the second topic as nuclear testing, saying that this was an easier area on which to make progress. He was also anxious that "the hopes of the peoples not be disappointed by false expectation of concrete results from a meeting" and therefore proposed that it be publicly presented as merely "an opportunity for a general exchange of views." Quoting from the end of Khrushchev's letter, Menshikov said this was also the Soviet position.[74]

In this meeting Kennedy admitted he was now "doubtful that any agreement on Laos or on nuclear testing would be reached by the time of his visit to Europe."[75] There had been no reply along the back channel and when it came, a few days later, the tone was discouraging. Khrushchev was still out of Moscow, touring Central Asia, so the Foreign and Defense Ministries had prepared Bolshakov's reply. On the idea of a neutral Laos, Bolshakov was told to make encouraging noises about "the coincidence of the viewpoints of our governments." But on nuclear testing and on Berlin, he was instructed to reiterate traditional Soviet policies, stressing the obstacles to a test ban agreement and threatening a unilateral Soviet treaty with East Germany. Bolshakov delivered these messages to Bobby Kennedy.[76]

Yet the president refused to be deterred. Having campaigned for a test ban treaty long before he entered the White House, he pressed skeptics in the Pentagon and the Atomic Energy Commission to rethink American positions. He especially wanted them to reconsider the number of inspections and the Soviet demand that they be conducted not by a single international administrator but by a "troika" comprising a representative of the communist world, another from the West and a neutral. Whether or not Vienna would yield a firm agreement, Kennedy still intended to make real progress. Indeed he probably felt it vital to achieve some kind of success after the fiasco in Cuba and the fudge over Laos.[77]

Khrushchev, though equally set on a summit, approached it quite differently. "I don't understand Kennedy," he told his son after the Bay of Pigs. "What's wrong with him? Can he really be that indecisive?" The president's failure to unleash American power against Castro reinforced the Soviet leader's belief that now was the time for a meeting; the surprising willingness of the weakened president to go ahead with a summit made him even more confident.[78] Like Kennedy, Khrushchev wanted more than a chat at Vienna, but his agenda was quite different. As the instructions to Bolshakov made clear, the Kremlin saw little prospect of a nuclear test ban and this was low on its list of priorities. The top issue for the Soviets was still Berlin. Yet Bobby told Bolshakov on May 21 that the president "will discuss this subject with Khrushchev in Vienna, but only to discuss it and not to seek any kind of agreement at this meeting."[79] Both leaders were now marching boldly toward the summit, but following totally different maps.

ON MAY 17 Thomas Finletter, the U.S. ambassador to NATO, briefed Allied envoys about the summit. He stressed that the intention was "solely to have an exchange of views and not to negotiate or reach agreement on major problems, regarding which there would be full consultation with allies." But the Belgians thought the distinction between exchange of views and full negotiations was "nebulous." The West Germans and the Dutch wanted to know more about the topics on the agenda. And the French ambassador, recalling original American caution about an early personal meeting, asked slyly what had happened to make the president change his mind. Responding, the State Department threw the onus on the Soviets, stressing Gromyko's initiative on May 4; they asserted that the administration did not want to be seen to "rebuff this Soviet overture."[80]

This account considerably underplayed Kennedy's own enthusiasm for a meeting but, as Bohlen emphasized to the president, it was important to give the impression that on the American side the idea of a summit was "not a backwash of recent events" and that there was no "anxiety or desperation" in the White House.[81]

A similar line was struck in the formal press announcement on the morning of May 19:

The President and Chairman Khrushchev understand that this meeting is not for the purpose of negotiating or reaching agreement on the major international problems that involve the interest of many other countries. This meeting will, however, afford a timely and convenient opportunity for the first personal contact between them and [for] a general exchange of views on the major issues which affect the relationships between the two countries.[82]

Following up with an off-the-record press briefing, Bohlen had to fend off skeptical questions such as, why meet when Khrushchev "has got us over a barrel"? Bohlen insisted the event should be regarded as "a rather normal thing: two guys in this big ring who haven't met." It would be "not a summit in the gobbledegook sense that has collected around this word" but a "conference at the summit . . . without trying to reach an agreement." Wasn't the latter what Churchill had originally meant, asked one newsman, when he spoke of "a parley at the summit"? Playing at semantics Bohlen insisted that a summit now meant a conference where "you would have specific questions you would try to settle"; he went on to deny the label to Macmillan's visit to Russia, Khrushchev's visit to America, and even Paris in May 1960. The official line was that Vienna would be "a size-up" not "a summit."[83]

Even for this supposedly low-key chat the logistics were immensely complex, yet they had to be arranged in less than three weeks. Although rumors of a meeting in Vienna or Stockholm had been circulating for a month or so, the State Department didn't approach the Austrian government until May 16, after Ambassador Menshikov's visit to the White House.[84] A special advance party headed by Kenneth O'Donnell and Pierre Salinger, the president's appointments and press secretaries, descended on Vienna for reconnaissance and planning meetings on May 23–24. The group numbered thirty-nine, and it flew in Air Force One, the president's Boeing 707, so that the pilot could practice landings and takeoffs while the discussions took place.[85]

Agreement was quickly reached that Kennedy and Khrushchev would stay at the official residences of their respective ambassadors, both located in the southwest suburbs of Vienna. This reduced the security headache for the Austrians, but they were still asked to find nearly one hundred top-class hotel rooms for the American party at two weeks' notice during the peak tourist season. Eventually they commandeered the Hotel Bristol for the American official party and the Hotel Imperial for the Soviets, with the American overflow housed in two other hotels. The media were also accommodated, though not in such style. The Fasangarten Barracks, also in the southwestern suburbs, had space for five hundred men and sixty women in shared rooms. Shuttle buses took them to the press center, established in the Neue Hofburg, the late-nineteenth-century addition to the Imperial Palace where the Congress of Vienna had been held in 1814–15. The Neue Hofburg now housed the International Atomic Energy Commission and therefore had a large auditorium equipped for simultaneous translation, with several radio and TV studios and some 130 phone and telex lines—to which the Austrians added many more.[86]

The American advance party also had intensive discussions about the agenda with their Soviet counterparts, led by General Nikolai Zakharov. On the first day meetings would be held in the U.S. ambassador's residence, on day two at the Soviet embassy in the center of Vienna. The latter was naturally more spacious and the Soviets could offer several rooms for the American delegation accompanying the president, whereas the Americans could offer only one for the Soviets at their residence. "Will that be adequate?" asked the U.S. ambassador, H. Freeman Matthews. "In the short space of time you cannot build a house" was the reply. "We will be content with whatever you're able to give."[87]

On June 1 both sides spent an afternoon checking out the two venues. The Soviets wanted to choreograph everything minutely and expressed "consternation" at the president's request that the meetings at the U.S. residence be "completely informal," with no seating plan. There was even more "consternation" at the American desire for photo opportunities inside the Soviet embassy. But both matters were settled to American satisfaction and the discussions, lubricated by various toasts to the success of the conference, re-

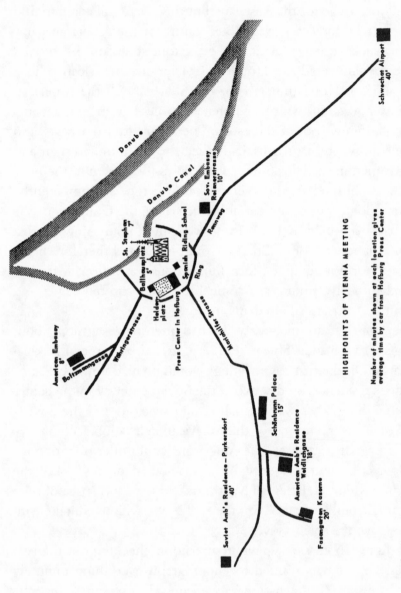

HIGHPOINTS OF VIENNA MEETING

Number of minutes shown at each location gives
average time by car from Hofburg Press Center

Map 4-2 The U.S. Information Agency distributed this map for journalists covering the Vienna summit. (John F. Kennedy Library)

mained cooperative and good humored. On the other hand, it became clear that the Soviet advance men were mainly concerned with VIP security, whereas the big consideration for Salinger and his colleagues was to "get the 'story' out" to the media.[88]

The Americans also insisted that they must establish their own communications system to keep the president in full and secure contact with Washington. It was essential that he could, if necessary, launch America's nuclear forces at any time. In an era before mobile phones, this required a completely separate, state-of-the-art land-line telephone network wherever the president went. Salinger claimed that the phone system in Brasilia, the new capital of Brazil, was "originally installed by the White House Signal Agency" for Eisenhower's visit there in 1959. Even in an advanced European capital like Paris, which Kennedy was to visit immediately before Vienna, special White House phones had to be installed. They were placed not only in the hotel rooms of all key staff but along the president's routes through the city. There was one even at the Arc de Triomphe, near which Kennedy was to lay a wreath honoring France's war dead. In Vienna the Soviets agreed that a phone could be installed temporarily in a study in their own embassy, where the second day of talks were to take place. Doubtless they were aware that this could allow Kennedy to call down missiles upon Moscow.[89]

WHILE VIENNA WAS CAUGHT UP in this feverish activity, the two principals tried to prepare for their encounter. Kennedy found it particularly hard to focus amid other distractions. He had privately ruled out American military intervention in Laos, but the Geneva conference was going badly and the prospects for guaranteed neutrality seemed slim. At home he was preoccupied with the racial crisis in Alabama where Freedom Riders, seeking to challenge segregation on public transport, were being beaten up by white thugs. This raised larger issues about the line between federal responsibility and states' rights. And on May 17, during a visit to Ottawa, the president damaged his fragile back while stooping to plant a ceremonial tree. He was in acute pain and, in private over the next few weeks, resorted to crutches for the first time in years.

Prospects for the summit also looked less rosy than a couple of weeks before. The Soviets had not responded positively to Kennedy's overtures about a nuclear test ban, and now the president was under intense pressure from the military to end the current informal moratorium and resume American testing. Kennedy had also offered to collaborate in space, but again the reaction was cool. On May 21 Bobby Kennedy saw Bolshakov to confirm the president's personal acceptance of the troika proposal for nuclear inspections. He had further meetings on May 23 and 24 to urge progress on testing and space before Vienna, adding that his brother was losing patience with Soviet unresponsiveness. Bobby also expressed the president's concern at Ambassador Thompson's latest conversation with Khrushchev on May 23.[90]

In this the Soviet leader stated categorically that American access to Berlin would be blocked under the proposed treaty with East Germany, telling Thompson that disarmament was "impossible" as long as the problem of Berlin existed. But the effect of this remark may have been blunted by Thompson's supplementary telegram saying that Khrushchev was "deeply troubled" about how to handle the German problem at Vienna; Thompson suggested that Kennedy try to discuss it alone, except for interpreters. The implication conveyed by the ambassador's message was that Khrushchev might be more malleable on Berlin than his hawkish colleagues.[91]

Kennedy had already given the annual State of the Union address on January 30. But in an effort to shore up his prestige after the Bay of Pigs and as a build up to Vienna, he decided to deliver a special message to a joint session of Congress on May 25. He insisted that he was going to Vienna to "make clear America's enduring concern for both peace *and* freedom," but his emphasis was predominantly on defending and expanding freedom in what had become a global struggle. Kennedy requested new appropriations for the armed forces and for civil defense—a nationwide program of fallout shelters—and finished by espousing "the goal, before this decade is out, of landing a man on the moon and returning him safely to earth." He insisted that this was not simply an adventure story; it was an integral part of "the battle that is now going on around the world between freedom and tyranny" because of the immense psychological impact of being first in space. So vast would be the commitment required, he said, that it would "not be one man going to the moon" but "an entire nation."[92]

While Kennedy talked tough in public, Khrushchev was even more intransigent in private. In preparation for Vienna, the Foreign Ministry had drawn up position papers. Although correctly identifying American priorities for the meeting, these offered no positive responses; they simply reiterated standard Soviet lines on testing, space and Germany. They were approved with little comment at a meeting of the ruling Presidium on May 26.[93]

"I attach a lot of significance to the meeting with Kennedy," Khrushchev told his colleagues, "because we are approaching the moment when we must solve the German question." Feelers via Thompson and Bolshakov had made it clear that Kennedy was no more inclined than Eisenhower to move on Berlin. The Soviet leader said he was ready to sign a treaty with the East German government and then turn over control of all access to the city, including air traffic, the Western lifeline in the blockade of 1948–9. "The risk that we are taking is justified," Khrushchev assured his colleagues; "there is more than a 95% probability that there will be no war." Only Anastas Mikoyan argued back. He renewed the criticisms he had made of Khrushchev's saber rattling in 1958, predicting that NATO would not be deterred. And he questioned Khrushchev's whole approach to Vienna: instead of backing Kennedy into a corner, he suggested taking some of the president's proposals more seriously. At this Khrushchev lost his temper, blustering that he would not only close the air corridor but would shoot down any Allied plane that tried to land in West Berlin. Although Gromyko and others may have shared Mikoyan's doubts, all were cowed into silence. At the end of the meeting Khrushchev was asked about the gifts to be given to the president and his wife, including cans of the best caviar and a silver coffee service. The Soviet leader gave his approval: "Presents can be made even before a war."[94]

Khrushchev portrayed Vienna as a great opportunity to pressurize a weak president. Here he was influenced not only by recent
American setbacks but also by his reading of the country and its
president. According to Georgii Kornienko, a counsellor at the Soviet embassy in Washington in 1961, Ambassador Menshikov (feeding Khrushchev what he thought the Soviet leader wanted to hear)
kept telling Moscow that Jack and Bobby Kennedy talked tough,
but when pushed would cower and back down.[95] And, following
Marxist-Leninist dogma, Khrushchev believed that Kennedy, like
Eisenhower, was a puppet of the Pentagon, Wall Street and the
American military-industrial complex. The Bay of Pigs debacle underlined for him the lesson of the U-2 affair. He even told the
journalist Walter Lippmann in April that the forces behind the government could be summed up in one word: "Rockefeller." Reporting this in his column Lippmann dryly observed that "the view that
he is running the Kennedy administration" would be "news" to
Nelson Rockefeller, the Republican governor of New York.[96]

Khrushchev's contempt for Kennedy had personal as well as ideological roots. Talking to Thompson on May 23 he said he had not
met Kennedy before—a revealing lapse of memory considering
how much impact their brief meeting in September 1959 had
made on the American senator. Thompson also recorded Khrushchev's remark that Kennedy was "younger than his son would
have been had he lived."[97] This cryptic aside was revealing. Leonid,
Khrushchev's eldest son, was born like John Kennedy in 1917. A
daredevil pilot during World War II, he was finally shot down and
killed in 1943. His father rarely talked about it, perhaps from grief
but more likely because Leonid's pre-war life had been a decadent
chronicle of drink and debauchery. So much so that in 1937 Khrushchev practically evicted him from the household.[98] For the Soviet leader to compare Kennedy to Leonid was therefore hardly a
compliment. Not merely was the president his junior by twenty-
three years, as Khrushchev must have known from KGB reports,
Kennedy was also an inveterate womanizer. If the Soviet leader
subconsciously saw his own son across the table in Vienna, it helps
explain why he found it hard to take Kennedy seriously.

The CIA's personality sketch of Khrushchev, part of Kennedy's background reading for Vienna, made reference to Leonid's war story but did not mention his date of birth. If Kennedy had seen the year 1917 it might have told him how he was likely to be viewed by the Soviet leader. Even so the briefing papers from the CIA and the State Department left no doubt about Khrushchev's pugnacity, quick-wittedness and debating skill—particularly his ability to put others on the defensive by sudden explosions of anger, real or feigned. "He has an uncanny ability of making people depart evaluating their own performance rather than describing his," noted the CIA. The briefing papers also emphasized Khrushchev's pride as a self-made man who outwitted better-educated rivals to reach the top, and his sensitivity to any slights on his origin or on the newly attained stature of the Soviet Union. Although a man of action rather than an ideologue, Khrushchev was said to be inspired by his "political faith"; he saw the world "through Marxist-Leninist spectacles" and was probably genuinely convinced, as he often told Westerners, that their grandchildren would live under a communist system.[99]

The president should therefore have been under no illusions; he faced a demanding opponent whose manner could oscillate from the "cherubic" to the "choleric."[100] The briefing papers also made it clear that Berlin was likely to be Khrushchev's priority and that the situation there was working up to a crisis. "In order that the possibilities of a disastrous miscalculation be reduced," the State Department advised, "it is absolutely vital for the USSR to understand that Berlin is of paramount importance to the U.S." National Security Advisor McGeorge Bundy noted that "everyone agrees on this"—from hawks like Dean Acheson to moderates like Walter Lippmann—and now Khrushchev "must have it from you."[101]

Sounding tough on Berlin was the fundamental message of all the papers about Germany that Kennedy took with him to Vienna. Rather like the Soviet briefings for Khrushchev on nuclear testing, they showed no flexibility on the issue or even willingness to explore the other side's motivations. Yet Khrushchev was becoming increasingly strident. From Moscow Ambassador Thompson told

Washington on May 25 that, having talked with his British, French and West German colleagues, all four of them were "fully convinced" that Khrushchev would take steps before the end of the year to conclude a separate treaty with East Germany and that this would bring on a "major crisis."[102]

The crisis for which America and its allies were preparing was essentially a repeat of the 1948 Soviet blockade of the city. But now there was a grim recognition that, in the missile age, attempts to keep open access routes could easily escalate into nuclear war. Khrushchev's diatribe to the Presidium revolved around the same 1948 scenario, though he believed nuclear weapons meant that this time the Soviets could win. What is striking in view of what actually transpired is the lack of reference in all the American briefing papers to the principal cause of Khrushchev's urgency: the flood of East German refugees through West Berlin. The State Department stated flatly that there was "nothing in the present situation in Germany and Berlin really intolerable" to either side. "The Soviet Union cannot really believe that the continued existence of West Berlin offers any threat to Soviet security—or indeed to the continued existence of the East German regime."[103]

Yet this was exactly the point Walter Ulbricht was pressing on Khrushchev. In the first half of 1961, a hundred thousand East Germans fled west. Khrushchev's aides joked grimly that soon no one would be left in the country except Ulbricht and his mistress. The Soviet ambassador in Berlin warned Gromyko on May 19 that "our German friends" wanted to close "the door to the West" immediately. They intended to block the sector boundary between East Berlin and the rest of the city, even though this would create a crisis with the Western powers and complicate the real Soviet goal of a German settlement. Khrushchev didn't want a showdown over Berlin; he hoped to use the city as leverage to force the West into serious negotiations about Germany.[104]

The only senior U.S. policymaker who apparently sensed Khrushchev's mind was Ambassador Thompson. Playing a role analogous to that of Mikoyan in Moscow, he had for some months been urging Washington to show some flexibility on Germany, offering

Khrushchev the hope of a phased agreement over Berlin. One of his reasons was that the present situation threatened the stability of the East German regime, causing pressure on Moscow from Ulbricht. Thompson used Khrushchev's edgy conversation on May 23 to again urge Washington to develop "a better position on the German problem." But even Thompson was not aware of the scale of the exodus; when he asked Khrushchev on May 23 whether the refugee problem was the most important aspect of Berlin, the Soviet leader "brushed this aside." The hypersensitive Khrushchev was reluctant to reveal his Achilles heel: on another occasion he had sniggered dismissively that the whole population of West Berlin was equivalent to "one night's work" in bed by Soviet couples.[105]

The U.S. briefing papers were generally upbeat. It was assumed that tough talk from Kennedy would show he couldn't be pushed around, thus making Khrushchev more tractable. The State Department believed that despite tactical shows of "anger and bluster" Khrushchev would "generally assume an attitude of reasonable firmness," preferring that "the talks end on a note of accord." It was expected that if the meeting went well the Soviets would invite Kennedy to visit Moscow, reviving the offer to Eisenhower that had been revoked after the U-2 affair.[106]

Each leader was going with his own list of priorities and with a confidence that, if he played it tough, the other man would come around. Each had fundamental blind spots about his adversary. The world had moved a long way since the days of Hitler and Chamberlain—communications had been transformed and information was much fuller—yet the psychological barriers to summitry were much the same.

THE TWO-DAY SUMMIT was scheduled to start on Saturday, June 3.[107] Khrushchev left Moscow the weekend before. He took a break in Kiev, then traveled by train via Lvov and Bratislava, where he talked with Czechoslovak leaders. He arrived in Vienna at 5 p.m. on Friday, June 2. For Kennedy the preceding week was much less leisurely. He spoke at a dinner in New York on Tuesday, May

30, then flew out on Air Force One, arriving in Paris at 10:30 the following morning. This was the start of an intense two-day state visit to President de Gaulle, for which Kennedy had done as much homework as for his meeting with Khrushchev.

On many matters the two allies did not see eye to eye. From bitter French experience, de Gaulle gave Kennedy a particularly stern warning about becoming entangled in Indochina. But there was immense relief in the American camp that the two men clicked. "For the first time," noted the French ambassador to Washington, "de Gaulle found an American he could talk to." Nevertheless the visit was a huge strain for the president: he often felt at sea in a francophone atmosphere, whereas his bilingual wife was in her element. Both de Gaulle and the French public were charmed by Jackie, so much so that Kennedy introduced himself at a press lunch on June 2 as "the man who accompanied Jacqueline Kennedy to Paris."[108]

Throughout the visit Kennedy was in acute pain from his back. Whenever possible he took long hot baths in his gold bathtub in the Palais d'Orsay. White House physician Dr. Janet Travell administered injections of procaine into his lower back, as well as a range of assorted drugs to control his diarrhea, insomnia, adrenal insufficiency, urinary infections and other ailments. In addition Kennedy had secretly asked Dr. Max Jacobson—a New York physician whom he had used during the election campaign—to fly to Paris and Vienna. Jacobsen's speciality was amphetamines, which he injected daily to keep Kennedy off crutches during his European tour. Bobby was skeptical of Jacobson's remedies (his New York nickname was "Doctor Feelgood") but the president breezily declared: "I don't care if it's horse piss. It works."[109] He insisted he would not meet de Gaulle or Khrushchev as a cripple.[110] Back in 1949 Kennedy had criticized a "sick" Roosevelt for his conduct at Yalta; he didn't need the same label being stuck on him at Vienna.

In Paris Kennedy was given final advice about his meeting with Khrushchev. Stand firm on Berlin, said de Gaulle. "That is the best service you can make to the entire world, Russia included." Make it clear that "we are not asking for anything. It is he who seeks a change." The French leader was convinced that the on-off Soviet ultimatums showed Khrushchev was bluffing: "If he had wanted war over Berlin he would have acted already."[111] But Averell Harriman, the veteran Soviet watcher, offered different advice about Khrushchev: "Remember that he's just as scared as you are . . . His style will be to attack, and then see if he can get away with it. Laugh about it, don't get into a fight. Rise above it. Have some fun." A memo from Kennedy's speechwriter and confidant Ted Sorensen took a position somewhere between de Gaulle and Harriman. "Do not challenge him in public—for this makes him tougher in front of the crowd . . . Watch the translation. If your sentence has an unfriendly opening, his mind may close and refuse to hear the rest." And remember, wrote Sorensen, "Khrushchev is above all a counter-puncher, who will be frustrated and angered by bland, non-commital [sic] and silent approach, or by issues that are not simply black and white."[112]

With this contradictory advice swirling around in his mind, Kennedy flew on to Vienna on Saturday, June 3—poring over his briefing papers all the way there.[113] He landed at 10:45 a.m. and was met by Dr. Adolf Schärf, the Austrian president. Despite the rain, Kennedy was greeted by cheering crowds—again as interested in his wife as himself. Like Paris, Vienna had "a new goddess," gushed *Time* magazine.[114] But a group called Young Europe distributed leaflets with a "warning" from history:

> Yalta, 1945: Roosevelt sold East Europe to Stalin.
> Vienna, 1961: Kennedy will sell Western Europe to Khrushchev.
> Mr. Kennedy—Europe does not forget Yalta.[115]

Schwechat airport lay to the southeast of Vienna. It was well after noon when Kennedy arrived at the U.S. ambassador's residence in Hietzing, on the southwest of the city and Khrushchev was due at 12:45. But there was just time for Dr. Jacobson to administer a quick injection. "This could go on for hours. I can't afford any complications with my back," Kennedy told him.[116] As soon as the Soviet motorcade drew up outside, Kennedy—tanked up by excitement and no doubt by the drugs—strode down the steps, apparently the model of youthful vitality. Shaking hands, the portly Khrushchev—aged sixty-seven to the president's forty-three—came up to his chin. As they posed for press photographs, the two men joked about the age gap. When Kennedy mentioned their brief meeting in 1959, Khrushchev, whose memory had apparently improved since talking to Ambassador Thompson in April, recalled telling Senator Kennedy that he had heard of him as "a young and promising man in politics." Yes, said Kennedy, adding that Khrushchev had also said that he was very youthful in appearance.[117]

The ambassador's residence was a stucco villa situated in several acres of grounds. The first day of meetings would take place in the music room, whose glass doors overlooked the garden. The two leaders sat on opposite sides of a coffee table, with an interpreters and advisors on either side. The Americans were Dean Rusk, the secretary of state, Ambassador Thompson, Chip Bohlen and Foy Kohler, assistant secretary of state for European affairs. Flanking Khrushchev were Ambassador Menshikov and Anatoly Dobrynin, chief of the Americas division of the Foreign Ministry.[118]

After initial pleasantries about their mutual desire for peace, Khrushchev seized the initiative.[119] The West, and the United States as its leader, must recognize one fact he said: "Communism exists and has won its right to develop." Kennedy hit back, arguing that the Soviet Union was trying to eliminate free governments allied to the United States and that this was a matter of "very serious concern" to the United States.

And so the two men launched into an ideological argument, conducted through lengthy speeches that became even more ponderous because of the consecutive translation.

Khrushchev hammered on about the Soviet belief that communism would triumph not by force of arms but as a law of historical development. Just as capitalism had challenged feudalism, so communism was now challenging capitalism. We cannot regard all this as historical inevitability, insisted Kennedy, "our position is that people should have free choice."

Khrushchev suggested the United States "wanted to build a dam preventing the development of the human mind and conscience," likening this to the philosophy of the Spanish Inquisition. Kennedy tried again to explain the American positions on historical inevitability and political freedom, emphasizing the danger of "miscalculation" on both sides.

This triggered an explosion from Khrushchev about the way the West kept using this term. It looked as if the United States wanted the Soviet Union to do nothing, sitting "like a schoolboy with his hands on his desk."

Kennedy tried to explain miscalculation as the "failure to foresee with precision what other countries would do." He mentioned "certain misjudgements" by America, such as "the Cuban situation" and, further back, the failure to anticipate Chinese entry into the Korean War. The object of their meeting, he said, was to obtain a clearer understanding of where both sides were going.[120]

Khrushchev said he could agree with that. It was virtually their only moment of convergence during the whole morning. And so, after seventy-five minutes, they adjourned at 2 p.m. for a late lunch.

"Is it always like this?" Kennedy whispered to Thompson. "Par for the course" was the light-hearted reply, but privately the ambassador was shaken that Kennedy seemed to be taking one hit after another from the Soviet leader.[121] In an effort at rational discussion the president had ended up on the defensive in an ideological argument, even conceding that the Bay of Pigs had been a misjudgment.

Over a lunch of Coquilles de Foie Gras and Beef Wellington, washed down with three fine wines, the conversation was lighter in tone. At one point Khrushchev asked: "How do you get on with Gromyko?"

"All right," replied Kennedy. "My wife thinks he has a nice smile. Why do you ask?"

"Well," said Khrushchev, "a lot of people think that Gromyko looks like Nixon."[122]

During lunch the president scored a few points of his own. After chatting about Gagarin's space flight, Kennedy asked why the two countries couldn't collaborate in a moon mission. Taken off guard, the Soviet leader muttered something about space flight being used for military advantage, but then said: "All right, why not?"[123]

Kennedy also asked him about the array of medals on his jacket. "This one is the Lenin Peace Prize," replied Khrushchev, touching his chest with his chin. "I hope you get to keep it," Kennedy shot back—or so his press office quickly told reporters. As one of Kennedy's biographers observed: "There were two summits, the private and the public: what was happening and what the world saw and was told was happening. The president was winning in public" but in private the story was rather different.[124]

After lunch and a stroll around the garden the two men returned to the music room, this time alone except for interpreters.[125] Possibly Kennedy had in mind Ambassador Thompson's suggestion that Khrushchev might be more tractable away from his entourage.

But instead of moving on to specifics, such as Laos, Germany and nuclear tests, the president said he wanted to "come back to the general thesis" about historical change. He probably wanted to warn Khrushchev, after his January 6 speech, that Soviet support for wars of "national liberation" could easily escalate through miscalculation into a general crisis. When "systems are in transition" he stated, "we should be careful, particularly today when modern weapons are at hand." Kennedy again admitted he had "made a misjudgement with regard to the Cuban situation" and reiterated his desire to ensure "greater precision" so that both countries "could survive this period of competition without endangering their national security."

This time Khrushchev did not flare up but turned Kennedy's points to his advantage. The president, he said, believed that "when people rise against tyrants, that is a result of Moscow's activities," but this was not so. In Iran the people were "so poor that the country has become a volcano and changes are bound to occur sooner or later." By supporting the shah, the United States generated "adverse feelings" toward itself and "favourable feelings" toward the Soviet Union. Likewise in Cuba, U.S. support for the "oppressive" Batista regime created anti-American feeling, and Kennedy's attempted landing "only strengthened the revolutionary forces and Castro's own position."

The president was back on the defensive, saying that the shah needed to reform and that he personally held no brief for Batista. But Khrushchev warmed to his thesis that "the United States supports old, moribund, reactionary regimes."

Kennedy tried to get back to generalities. A basic American interest was that all peoples should enjoy "free choice" through free elections. But forced by Khruschchev to address the case of Franco's Spain, where America had military bases and there was no prospect of elections, he said that a second interest was strategic: to maintain regional balances of power. This, added Kennedy, was why the United States was concerned about the growth of China.

Khrushchev exploited that as an opening to attack the United States for supporting Taiwan and blocking the People's Republic's claim to its seat at the UN. "What kind of United Nations is it when it does not have among its members a nation numbering 600 million people?"

Moving on around the world, Khrushchev kept Kennedy on the back foot: in the Congo, Angola and Algeria the United States was supporting European colonial powers against the people's struggles for freedom. The only thing on which the two leaders seemed able to agree was the need for a peaceful settlement in Laos.

The afternoon meeting ended after three and a half hours. Meanwhile Rusk, Gromyko and the diplomats had been discussing disarmament, without much sign of movement. All in all it had been a grimly unproductive day.

Bohlen had advised Kennedy that "ideological topics" and the "general threat of communism" should "not be dealt with *per se* but as a function of and in relation to Soviet state policy."[126] Instead the president not only allowed himself to get into an ideological debate with a diehard Marxist-Leninist, he kept pursuing that general line of argument—in the afternoon as well as the morning—rather than moving on to specifics. When they had finally turned to world affairs, Khrushchev zeroed in on several embarrassing cases where the United States seemed on the side of reactionary forces opposed to "freedom." In the process Kennedy conceded that "Sino-Soviet forces" and those of the United States and Western Europe were "more or less in balance"—an important goal of Soviet diplomacy.[127] Because of their lengthy debate about generalities, nearly all the big issues were left for discussion on the second day.

Thompson admitted later that "there hadn't been worked out any very clear scenario" in advance for the discussions. He regretted that they had got into ideology, on which Khrushchev could not have yielded even if he wanted to: "I don't think that the president quite appreciated the fact." Bohlen felt that Kennedy "got a little bit out of his depth."[128] As for Khrushchev, according to his aide Oleg Troyanovsky, he returned from the first day's meeting asserting that "this man is very inexperienced, even immature." Compared to Kennedy, he added scathingly, Eisenhower was "a man of intelligence and vision."[129]

The discussions finished at 6:45 p.m.—forty-five minutes late. At 8 p.m. the two leaders and their wives were due at the Schönbrunn Palace, as guests of honor at a formal dinner and concert hosted by the Austrian president. Both men must have been tired; Kennedy in particular was surely in acute pain from his back. There was only a short time for a hot bath and, presumably, another dose of speed from Dr. Feelgood, before the car whisked him off to the palace. He arrived five minutes late and at one point nearly sat on Mrs. Khrushchev's lap when she changed seats abruptly.

The Soviet leader stole the limelight by turning up in a business suit rather than black tie (no bourgeois affectations for him and his comrades). And he spent much of the time chatting up Jackie Kennedy, alternating between far-fetched anecdotes and recitations of Soviet achievements. "Oh, Mr. Chairman, don't bore me with statistics," she exclaimed at one point. During a lecture on the Soviet space effort, Khrushchev mentioned that a dog they had used had now given birth to puppies. "Why don't you send me one?" Jackie asked. Two months later Ambassador Menshikov and two aides arrived at the White House with a terrified dog. How come? asked the president. "I'm afraid I asked Khrushchev for it at Vienna," his wife apologized. "I was just running out of things to say."[130]

NEXT MORNING, Sunday, June 4, the president went to nine o'clock mass at St. Stephen's Cathedral, while Khrushchev paid his respects at the Soviet War Memorial. (Its enormous statue was unaffectionately known to locals as Ivan the Plunderer.) Both men were then driven to the Soviet embassy, an elegant late-eighteenth-century mansion on nearby Reisnerstrasse, where the summit resumed at 10:15 a.m. in a first-floor conference room.

Compared with the previous afternoon there were two important changes. Both men were again flanked by their advisors—with Gromyko now joining the Soviet side—and Kennedy finally got down to specifics. But his tone was still one of firm but rational discussion as he tried to explain and justify American policy, whereas Khrushchev kept scoring debating points. This happened even on Laos, a rare point of convergence on day one, and eventually Kennedy proposed that they leave that to their foreign ministers.[131]

Discussion then moved to nuclear testing, on which Kennedy had hoped for some breakthrough. Instead Khrushchev stuck to the Soviet position—a three-man control commission and only three inspections a year—emphasizing that these conditions would be dropped only if there were "general and complete disarmament." It was clear, despite all the president's hopes, that there would be no breakthrough to kickstart the formal talks in Geneva. As a result Kennedy probably concluded that he would have to resume nuclear tests.[132]

And so they turned, finally, to Germany.[133] Khrushchev began with a lengthy statement about the need to draw a line under World War II with a peace treaty with Germany. If the United States declined the Soviets would sign one with East Germany. This would end all Western rights of access to Berlin unless they were renegotiated with the Ulbricht government. Kennedy had come with no new proposals on Berlin and, as advised, sat tight on the status quo. A firm line seemed even more important after his performance the previous day.

As the two men thrashed around, their language became more hyperbolic. Kennedy insisted that if the United States accepted the loss of its rights in Berlin, "no one would have any confidence in

U.S. commitments and pledges . . . If we were to leave West Berlin Europe would have to be abandoned as well." Khrushchev, for his part, said that Hitler had spoken of Germany's need for Lebens-raum to the Urals; he claimed that some of "Hitler's generals" were now "high commanders in NATO."

The Soviet leader also kept bringing up in distorted form inconvenient American statements from the past: at Yalta Roosevelt had said that American troops would stay in Europe only a couple of years and at Geneva Eisenhower had admitted that the situation in Berlin was "abnormal."

The exchanges also exposed raw emotions. Twice Khrushchev mentioned the twenty million Soviet dead from World War II, one of whom, he added cryptically, was his own son. Mikoyan had also lost a son, he said, and Gromyko two brothers. The president responded quietly that he too had lost a brother in the war. Khrushchev acknowledged that "American mothers mourn their sons just as deeply as Soviet mothers" but made a point of noting factually that the American death toll was 350,000.

Tired and frustrated, the two men began to talk about the danger of open conflict. "If the U.S. wants to start war over Germany let it be so," said Khrushchev. "A peace treaty denying us our contractual rights is a belligerent act," Kennedy replied. With the Soviet leader adamant that he would sign a peace treaty with East Germany, the two sides moved into their final lunch.

The Soviets laid on an even grander spread than the Americans; it included caviar, fish pie, chicken and ice cream, lubricated by four choice wines.[134] The tone was lighter than during the formal session, with both leaders toasting the benefits of face-to-face meetings even though, as Khrushchev admitted, "no understanding" had been reached between the two sides.[135]

Kennedy, doubtless keen to get something tangible from the meeting, asked again about a cooperative effort in space. But Khrushchev now withdrew the hesitant approval he had given over lunch on Saturday: a flight to the moon was very expensive, he said. America "should go there first because it is rich and then the Soviet Union will follow." The president ended his remarks with yet another reference to their relative ages. Last night, he said, he had asked the Soviet leader what post he had occupied at age forty-four. Head of the Moscow Planning Commission, Khrushchev told him. Kennedy said that when he was sixty-seven, Khrushchev's present age, he hoped to be head of the Boston Planning Commission.

Perhaps head of the Planning Commission of the whole world, Khrushchev interjected—jabbing away right up to the end. No, insisted the president, only Boston.

Lunch was scheduled as the last act of the summit.[136] But at 3:15 p.m. when Kennedy was supposed to leave the Soviet embassy, he asked Khrushchev for a few words in private. They went back upstairs with only their interpreters, and the president reverted to Berlin. This session was "the nut-cutter," Kennedy recalled later, unconsciously echoing Khrushchev's comment that Berlin was the "balls" of the West.[137]

Of course, said the president, decisions about East Germany were a Soviet matter. But the issue of Western access to Berlin deeply affected American interests and he reiterated his hope of avoiding "confrontation" between the two governments. Again Kennedy tried to sound firm yet reasonable, but Khrushchev flared up that "the U.S. wants to humiliate the USSR and this cannot be accepted." According to the official American record the final moments of the summit went as follows:

The president said he had gained the impression that "the USSR was presenting him with the alternative of accepting the Soviet act on Berlin or having a face to face confrontation."

"If the U.S. wants war, that is its problem," Khrushchev shot back. "It is not the USSR that threatens with war, it is the U.S."

Kennedy retorted that it wasn't he but Khrushchev who wanted to force a change.

"It is up to the U.S. to decide whether there will be war or peace," replied the Soviet leader. The decision to sign a peace treaty was "irrevocable" and he would do so in December if there was no agreement.

As reported in the American record: "The President concluded the conversation by observing that it would be a cold winter."[138]

KENNEDY HAD GRANTED a special postsummit interview with James Reston of the *New York Times,* one of America's most influential journalists. This took place at the U.S. embassy a few minutes after his farewell to Khrushchev. The blinds were drawn to help keep the meeting secret from the American press corps. The president, unusually, was wearing a hat and he did not take it off. Slumping into a couch, he tipped the hat over his eyes and heaved a deep sigh.

"Pretty rough?" asked Reston.

"Roughest thing in my life," Kennedy replied. He told Reston how, knowing Khrushchev's contempt at Eisenhower's reliance on Dulles, he had been determined to talk man to man. He had tried to hold out his hand, saying in effect: "I propose to tell you what I can do, and what I can't do, what my problems and my possibilities are, and then you can do the same." Instead Khrushchev had launched a series of violent attacks on the United States, on American imperialism and especially on its policy over Berlin.

> I think he did it because of the Bay of Pigs. I think he thought that anyone who was so young and inexperienced as to get into that mess could be taken, and anyone who got into it, and didn't see it through, had no guts. So he just beat hell out of me. So I've got a terrible problem. If he thinks I'm inexperienced and have no guts, until we remove those ideas we won't get anywhere with him.[139]

An hour or so later the Austrian chancellor, Bruno Kreisky, saw Kennedy off at the airport. "The President was very gloomy," he told Khrushchev later. "He seemed upset and his face had changed." On Air Force One the mood was silent and depressed. One aide said it was like riding with the losing team after the World Series.[140]

In London, Kennedy's first stop, the formal talks were cancelled and the president poured out his experiences to Macmillan, who found Kennedy "much concerned and even surprised by the almost brutal frankness and confidence of the Soviet leader." Some of this, reflected the prime minister, was "an act—as always with

Khrushchev." Nevertheless Kennedy was clearly "shocked." In a letter to the queen Macmillan said it "reminded me in a way of Lord Halifax or Mr. Neville Chamberlain trying to hold a conversation with Herr Hitler."[141]

While the president rushed to Vienna airport that Sunday afternoon, Pierre Salinger and his Kremlin counterpart, Mikhail Kharlamov, gave a joint briefing to more than a thousand newsmen in the Hofburg press center. Their agreed statement said that the talks had been "useful" but the only concrete subject mentioned was the two leaders' reaffirmed support for "a neutral and independent Laos." The White House press secretary declined to use the adjective "fruitful" about the talks, and he ducked a question about whether the world could "breathe more freely now."[142]

It soon became clear that the Soviets were putting a distinctly more positive spin on the meeting than the Americans. Khrushchev spoke of "a very good beginning" and Kharlamov claimed the atmosphere was "equally agreeable" on both days. U.S. sources, in contrast, admitted "tension" during the discussions about Berlin, and Reston's piece in the *New York Times*—clearly well sourced, though naturally not mentioning that it came from the horse's mouth—said that "the conference, which started well yesterday, ended in hard controversy today." Over the next week the American press contrasted Kennedy's somber postsummit mood with Khrushchev's return to Moscow in "bubbling good spirits." On June 6 the Soviet leader sang, danced and played a drum at a sixtieth birthday party for President Sukarno of Indonesia, "fresh from what he obviously considered his diplomatic success in Vienna." One veteran correspondent said that Khrushchev looked "more exuberant and relaxed" than in years.[143]

The Central Committee issued a decree praising Comrade Khrushchev for his "fruitful work" in Vienna and for conducting the talks "with great skill and in an aggressive spirit." This was given wide circulation among communist and leftist leaders around the world.[144]

Kennedy's radio and television report to the American people on June 6 spoke of "a very full and frank exchange of views" on the major issues that divided the two countries. It was, he said, "a very sober" two days. Khrushchev had made it clear that "the present test ban negotiations appeared futile." And on Germany and Berlin, "our most somber talks," both sides simply set out their divergent positions. But Kennedy represented all this as being in line with expectations: "No major decision was either planned or taken; no spectacular progress was either achieved or pretended." This kind of "informal exchange," he said, "may not be as exciting as a full-fledged summit meeting with a fixed agenda and a large corps of advisors, where negotiations are attempted and new agreements sought, but this was not intended to be and was not such a meeting, nor did we plan any future summit meetings at Vienna." Nevertheless, he continued, the meeting had been "extremely useful"; it was of "immense importance" that he now had a firsthand sense of Khrushchev and that the Soviet leader, in turn, understood the "policies" and the "strength" of the United States.[145]

Khrushchev"s post-Vienna broadcast on June 15 was much more positive. Top-level meetings were, he said, "indispensable" because "questions which defy solution through conventional diplomatic channels insistently require meetings between heads of government." He stated that "on the whole" he was "pleased" with Vienna: "Neither side evaded bringing up and discussing the most acute questions." Each listened attentively to the other and he particularly felt that Kennedy understood "the great responsibility" for peace that lay with "the governments of two such powerful states." Reviewing the topics discussed, however, the Soviet leader acknowledged that little progress had been made. He was more blatantly propagandist than Kennedy about the reasons; for instance, blaming the deadlock over disarmament on "capitalist monopolies" that were making "huge profits" from the arms race. On Germany he made public the memorandum given to Kennedy, insisted that a peace treaty "must be attained this year," and warned darkly of the indistinct borderline between cold war and hot war. "Surely it is clear that a cold war is a period of preparation, of accumulating forces for war."[146]

Most of those who met with Kennedy in those first days after Vienna found him shaken and worried. Bobby Kennedy thought it was "the first time the President had ever really come across somebody with whom he couldn't exchange ideas in a meaningful way." Jack told a friend it was "like dealing with Dad—all give and no take." The Munich analogy preyed on his mind.[147]

The president's back pain was now so excruciating that he had to take a complete rest in Florida. On June 8 Salinger had to admit to the press that that president was on crutches; as Kennedy had feared, this news added to the general perception of weakness. While he was in Florida publication of the Soviet memorandum left no doubt that the situation in Berlin was building to a crisis. Kennedy reflected that, after botching the Bay of Pigs and backing down over Laos, he couldn't afford a third defeat. Yet he was appalled at the possible cost of standing firm. Immediately after arriving back in the White House, he had asked for statistics on how many Americans might die in an all-out nuclear exchange with the Soviets. The Pentagon estimated seventy million—about half the nation. And what if one missile got through and landed near a city? Six hundred thousand was the answer. Kennedy reflected that this was comparable to total losses in the American Civil War. "And we haven't gotten over that in a hundred years."[148]

The president's top priority after Vienna was to review military planning for a crisis in Berlin. It was clear that this would be a moment of truth for his leadership.[149] Hard-liners in the Pentagon had an eloquent spokesman in Dean Acheson, President Truman's secretary of state and now head of a special task force on Berlin. He insisted that this had become a test of "resolution" between the superpowers, "the outcome of which will go far to determine the confidence of Europe—indeed, of the world—in the United States." Until "this conflict of wills" was resolved, any attempt to solve the Berlin issue by negotiation was not merely "a waste of time and energy" but was frankly "dangerous": talking would reinforce Khrushchev's perception that America and its allies would "not do what is necessary to stop him" getting his way. To change that perception, insisted Acheson, required America being ready to undertake nuclear war if necessary.[150]

More moderate policymakers, including Rusk and White House staffers Sorensen and Schlesinger, had been scarred by the Bay of Pigs and were now, like the president, very wary of military advice. They believed firmness should be balanced by negotiation, to help Khrushchev back down. The gravity of the refugee crisis in East Germany was belatedly becoming clear to the Americans. During June twenty thousand East Germans crossed into West Berlin, in July thirty thousand. Not only was the flood undermining the East German economy—with mounting labor shortages in the food, building and transport industries— it was also posing a huge problem for the authorities in West Berlin. Desperately the East Germans increased their checks on movement between the two halves of the city and on the autobahn going west; they also established a ring of troops around the whole city.[151]

The Berlin "escape hatch" was going to be closed, but how was not clear. Most of official Washington still expected a replay of the past. Perhaps the Soviets would try to seal off the whole city (as in 1948), necessitating military action by air or land to keep open access to West Berlin. Another possibility was that the Soviet crackdown would spark a popular uprising (as in 1953), which could inflame the German question to war fever. Only a few officials, mostly in West Berlin, thought the East German target might be the sector boundary between East and West Berlin, and even these predicted tighter frontier controls rather than a physical barrier. Straws in the wind—such as Ulbricht's bluff assertion at a press conference on June 15 that "nobody has the intention of building a wall"—were lost in the background noise.[152]

Although Kennedy shared his staffers' unhappiness with Acheson's hard-line proposals, he agreed that he had to win a battle of wills with Khrushchev. That had been his refrain ever since talking with Reston just after the summit. Still on crutches, he hobbled to the Oval Office on the evening of July 25 to speak over radio and television to the American people, his first such address for nearly six weeks. Berlin, he said, had become "the great testing place of Western courage and will" and "we cannot separate its safety from our own." The president dismissed claims that West Berlin was "militarily untenable." So was Bastogne, he said, "and so, in fact, was Stalingrad," making calculated reference to the iconic American and Soviet sieges of the previous world war. "Any dangerous spot is tenable if men—brave men—will make it so." He announced another three billion dollars for the armed forces (the third supplemental appropriation in four months), increased calls for draftees and reservists, and substantial new spending on civil defense. "We seek peace," Kennedy declared, "but we shall not surrender. That is the central meaning of this crisis."[153]

The speech was acclaimed at home: after weeks of apparent drift Kennedy had reasserted American leadership. And his words seem to have rattled Khrushchev. Before Vienna the Soviet leader had told his Presidium and Czech communists that there was only a 5 percent chance of the West going to war over West Berlin. But when Warsaw Pact leaders convened in Moscow on August 3, he admitted that war was "possible," blaming this on American reactionaries gaining the upper hand over their weak president.[154]

The Soviet leader was now backing away from the idea of a separate peace treaty with East Germany, against which Kennedy had inveighed at Vienna. Instead he concentrated on solving the Berlin crisis by less inflammatory means. During the Moscow meeting Khrushchev gave Ulbricht the go-ahead for plans to seal East Berlin from West Berlin. He warned him to start with barbed wire, monitoring the Western reaction before proceeding to a concrete wall.[155]

The barbed wire went up in the early hours of August 13, with Ulbricht presenting it as a necessary measure to block Western "recruiters" and "saboteurs." There was outrage in West Germany but silence from the White House. In part this was because the president, like his advisors, was surprised by the Soviet solution. More important, Kennedy, though officially pledged to a free and united Germany, could see benefits in this outcome. As he remarked privately, it gave Khrushchev a way out of his predicament, which threatened to destabilize the whole of Central Europe. And, he quipped, "a wall is a hell of a lot better than a war." His July 25 speech, with its reiterated commitment to *West* Berlin, may have been signalling to Khrushchev that he could have a free hand in his part of the city.[156]

The Wall became a propaganda triumph for the West. To those around the world who professed not to understand "what is the great issue between the Free World and the Communist world," Kennedy declared in June 1963: "Let them come to Berlin."[157]

Yet in August 1961 Kennedy did not feel triumphant. His reinforcement of West Berlin led to some anxious face-offs, notably between U.S. and Soviet tanks across "Checkpoint Charlie" in October. Moreover West Germans felt betrayed and West Berliners were demoralized. Despite official rhetoric, Kennedy had not stood up for the unity of their country and its historic capital. The mayor of West Berlin, Willy Brandt, wrote later that in August 1961 "a curtain was drawn aside to reveal an empty stage."[158]

And although Khrushchev had momentarily lost his nerve—rather like Hitler at Munich—he did not change his reading of Kennedy. The fact that the president had accepted the Wall seemed to confirm his susceptibility to pressure. This reading of events inspired the most dangerous gamble of Khrushchev's reckless career: installing nuclear missiles in Cuba. Although what he called the idea of throwing "a hedgehog down Uncle Sam's pants" did not take shape until the spring of 1962 and its denouement came only in October, it was rooted in Khrushchev's conclusions at Vienna in June 1961. Yet, as over Berlin, Kennedy struck a balance between firmness and provocation: he rejected air strikes on Cuba and his blockade of the island gave Khrushchev time and diplomatic room to remove the missiles. The two superpowers had come eyeball to eyeball and Moscow blinked first. Khrushchev's bluff had been called: he knew that his nuclear arsenal was vastly inferior to Kennedy's—220 warheads compared with about 4,000. Only after the Cuban crisis, as Khrushchev's aide Oleg Troyanovksy recalled, did the Soviet leader stop doubting the president's "will and intellect": at last bullying gave way to the kind of negotiation that Kennedy had hoped for at Vienna. By then, however, it was too late. Khrushchev's colleagues knew he had been humiliated in the

missile crisis and this was a major reason for his overthrow in October 1964.[159]

The missile crisis dramatized Kennedy's warnings at Vienna
about miscalculation. It is therefore interesting that the president
took no action during the summit about one very practical proposal that could have helped. Both the U.S. embassy in Moscow
and the Soviet embassy in Washington communicated with home
in coded cables using commercial telegraph companies. Neither
government would permit installation of the huge roof aerials necessary for radio communication, fearful that these could be used for
local intelligence eavesdropping. Khrushchev had suggested a
phone link between the White House and the Kremlin—what he
called a "white telephone"—and in May 1961 a high-level American group, headed by Professor Thomas Schelling of Harvard, concurred. It favored a direct phone line from the State Department to
the U.S. embassy in Moscow; this could be used for communication between heads of government in an emergency but without
being so designated.

On May 25, 1961, Rusk advised Kennedy to discuss this idea at
Vienna, as part of his theme about "the risk of war by miscalculation." But nothing was done, presumably because of the lack of
constructive dialogue at the summit. In consequence the climax of
the Cuban Missile Crisis had to be settled almost farcically via
commercial telegram messages delivered by Western Union bicycle
boys or even statements transmitted over Radio Moscow. One positive outcome of the crisis was agreement in June 1963 to install a
twenty-four-hour telegraph link between the two centers of government, known as the "hot line" to Americans and the "red line"
to the Russians. Neglecting this issue at Vienna had fortunately not
proved fatal.[160]

There was a much more serious miscalculation on the American
side, almost on a par with Khrushchev and Cuba. During Kennedy's surreal meeting with James Reston at the U.S. embassy immediately after the summit, the conversation touched on Vietnam—the crucible of the struggle for Indochina now that Laos had

been settled. Reston recalled Kennedy remarking that "we have a problem in trying to make our power credible, and Vietnam looks like the place." Subsequently Reston modified his account, claiming that this was his own inference, not Kennedy's exact words.[161] Historians remain divided about how Kennedy would have handled Vietnam had he not been assassinated in November 1963. Some highlight the president's recurrent wariness about committing U.S. troops to back the shaky South Vietnam government. "It's like taking a drink," Arthur Schlesinger recalled him saying in November 1961. "The effect wears off and you have to take another."[162] Kennedy kept insisting that the war could only be won by the South Vietnamese. On the other hand, there is no evidence that Kennedy was planning to withdraw from Vietnam. On the contrary, he had increased America's commitments greatly during his presidency, both in economic aid and through sixteen thousand military "advisors." He also gave the nod to the overthrow of South Vietnam's problematic leader, Ngo Dinh Diem, just before his own assassination.[163]

The imponderable question is what Kennedy would have done when the South Vietnamese state crumbled in the winter of 1964–5 in the face of Vietcong guerrillas from within and military offensives from communist North Vietnam. Would he have Americanized the war, through bombing the north and the introduction of combat troops, the policy of his successor Lyndon Johnson? Or would he have sought some kind of negotiated withdrawal? After the successful outcome of the Cuban Missile Crisis, of course, Kennedy enjoyed much greater domestic and international clout than in 1961—far more than LBJ. So perhaps he could have backed away without loss of face. Yet throughout his presidency (and even as a senator), Kennedy had constantly put the spotlight on Vietnam as a test case of America's will and credibility in the Cold War. Even if he did not say those words to Reston, they encapsulated his attitude. However warily, President Kennedy did treat Vietnam as the place to try to make America's power credible, and this was in large part because of his need after Vienna to prove he could not be pushed around. At the very least JFK made it much harder for either himself or his successor to pull out of Vietnam. The Vienna summit marked a fateful step into America's quagmire.

AT A STRATEGIC LEVEL both Kennedy and Khrushchev were ready for summitry in 1961. The Soviet leader had an interest in getting Western approval for the Cold War order in Europe, especially Germany, and this could only be secured, if at all, by a meeting at the highest level. The American president shared Churchill's conviction that containment was not enough in the nuclear age. Hence his aphorism about it being better to meet at the summit than at the brink, and the declaration in his inaugural that America must not negotiate out of fear but, equally, never fear to negotiate.

Tactically, however, neither man was properly prepared for their encounter in Vienna. Kennedy persuaded himself that Khrushchev was a rational leader, susceptible to argument and capable of appreciating Kennedy's priorities and limits. He failed to grasp the rigidity of Khrushchev's ideology and the extent of the Soviet dilemma over Berlin. Or to appreciate that Khrushchev was likely to perceive him as being on a par with his own son, Leonid. The Soviet leader in turn believed, after Cuba and Laos, that Kennedy could be bullied and, somewhat inconsistently, that he was simply a pawn of American capitalists. Both leaders ignored minority voices urging the need to come up with serious policies on issues that mattered to the other side—Mikoyan on testing and Thompson on Berlin. And they also closed their eyes to apparently clear evidence from direct and back channel contacts that they were likely to run into a brick wall if they pressed ahead on their chosen issue. Clear, that is, in retrospect. But prior to Vienna each probably believed in his persuasive powers, powers that had got him to the top of his own political tree. Or perhaps when the contradictory evidence became apparent it was, as so often with summitry, too late to turn back.

Kennedy's health probably weakened his performance at the summit. What we know now about the president's reliance on a cocktail of medicines is alarming. It has been justly observed that Kennedy was even more promiscuous with drugs than he was with women. Yet there is no evidence that the medicines per se affected his conduct at Vienna: like the dying Roosevelt at Yalta, his line of approach was clear long before.[164] But the problems that the drugs were used to treat, especially his crippled back, surely contributed to his poor performance; for instance, failing to change tack and get out of the ideological argument on that long first afternoon in Vienna. Nor did it help that he had flown in that morning after a gruelling summit in Paris. On health grounds he probably should have called off the whole European trip after damaging his back in Ottawa. But that would have been abhorrent to the Kennedy self-image and a further loss of face after the Bay of Pigs. At the very least the official schedule should have taken account of his physical limitations, with greater time for recuperation, but the cover-up about them lay at the heart of the Camelot myth.

One might also ask with hindsight whether Kennedy was wise to accept Khrushchev's pressure for an early meeting. Of course the official rhetoric was that Vienna was simply a chance for the two leaders to get acquainted: Chip Bohlen had tied himself in semantic knots trying to avoid the word "summit," insisting that this term should be reserved for full-scale negotiations with formal agendas and phalanxes of advisors. Whatever the rhetoric, however, both leaders came for more than a chat. Indeed it would be almost impossible for any such meeting to avoid the substance of policy. Each hoped for a breakthrough in his key area—nuclear testing for Kennedy and Berlin for Khrushchev—only to be gravely disappointed. After Vienna they insisted in public that the meeting had been beneficial, enabling firsthand contact and frank discussion. Kennedy certainly came away with a powerful conviction of the need to show Khrushchev he could not be pushed around. But that was only necessary because the Soviet leader had succeeded in doing so at Vienna.

Yet one can also make this point more positively. If, as Bobby Kennedy had suggested, the meeting made clear Khrushchev's totally alien mentality, then it did serve an essential purpose for the president. In September 1938 Chamberlain encountered a leader who saw the world in totally different ways, but he persuaded himself that Hitler was a man with whom he could negotiate. In June 1961 Kennedy hoped to meet a leader with whom he could negotiate and came away deeply disillusioned. Now thoroughly convinced that a contest of wills had to be won before they could embark on rational discussion, he set his course on Berlin, Cuba and, most fatefully, Vietnam. It is unlikely that this would have happened so clearly and categorically if he had not followed his instinct to size up the Soviet leader in person.

In Moscow judgments on the Vienna summit shifted dramatically over time. The initial mood of triumphalism—the diminutive Khrushchev pushing around another Western leader—had to be revised after the Cuban Missile Crisis. Doubters like Mikoyan had been proved right. The Vienna face-off had backed Kennedy into a corner from which he came out strongly to humiliate the Soviets in October 1962. Once again a summit had turned to a large extent on bluff. But whereas Munich in 1938 showed how much a leader with strong nerves could get away with, Vienna, as viewed after Cuba, showed the dangers and limitations of bluff. Khrushchev's successors would spend the rest of the decade building up their missile strength, so as not to be outfaced again in another crisis. They also knew that his recklessness at Vienna and over Cuba had proved counterproductive. In future the Kremlin would play it firm but avoid bluster.

After June 1961 no new American president rushed into an early meeting with his Cold War adversary. And never again did a Soviet leader try to browbeat his American counterpart. But for Americans Vienna seemed to confirm the verdicts on Munich and Yalta: that summitry is risky and often counterproductive, that dealing with dictators does not work. In Moscow the lesson of Vienna and Cuba was the one that Kennedy had learned from Chamberlain: negotiate only when in a position of military strength. It would be another decade before the superpowers tried summitry again in earnest.

5

MOSCOW 1972

Brezhnev and Nixon

Although Eisenhower, Kennedy and Johnson all hoped for a summit in Moscow, none of them pulled it off. But in May 1972 Richard Nixon flew to the Soviet capital on the first visit by a U.S. president. The Strategic Arms Limitation Treaty (SALT) he signed with Leonid Brezhnev was the first superpower accord to regulate the nuclear arms race. The two leaders also concluded other agreements for economic and social cooperation. Underpinning this most productive Cold War summit to date was the belief of both the White House and the Kremlin that they had now moved beyond confrontation to negotiation. The world seemed to be entering a lasting era of détente—relaxation of tension. But these hopes were soon dashed. In fact the preparations for Moscow in 1972 sowed the seeds of détente's decline. Both the triumphs of the summit and its fatal flaws are largely attributable to one of the most remarkable yet bizarre partnerships in modern diplomacy, between Richard Nixon and Henry Kissinger.[1]

RICHARD NIXON HAD BEEN a keen observer of the 1961 debacle in Vienna. In a press conference on February 6, 1969, the newly inaugurated president said he took a dim view of "instant summitry," particularly when there were "very grave differences of opinion" between the participants. He was not against a "well-prepared summit" but said it would take time to identify the areas where progress might be possible.[2]

Yet although Nixon had made it clear that unlike in 1961 there would be no rush to the summit, both superpowers had powerful incentives to reduce mutual tension.[3]

Nixon's biggest headache was Vietnam, where half a million U.S. troops were bogged down in a conflict that had bitterly divided American society. President Johnson's efforts to pay for the war by stealth—borrowing rather than taxation—had fuelled inflation and undermined the once-mighty dollar. And by the spring of 1968 his war was so unpopular that Johnson decided not to run again for a second term. Extricating America from the Vietnam quagmire was therefore essential, not just to clear the way for foreign policy initiatives but also to salvage the presidency itself. "I'm not going to end up like LBJ," Nixon told an aide after the election of November 1968, "holed up in the White House afraid to show my face on the street. I'm going to stop that war. Fast."[4]

Yet this was easier said than done. LBJ had made Vietnam a public test of America's credibility in the global struggle against communist expansion, invoking the "lessons" of appeasement: "We learned from Hitler at Munich that success only feeds the appetite of aggression."[5]

Nixon therefore had to avoid any withdrawal being seen as a defeat: in his oft-repeated Chamberlainesque phrase America needed not just peace but "peace with honour." In March the president approved secret bombing raids on communist guerrilla sanctuaries in neighboring Cambodia. Over the next fourteen months the United States dropped 110,000 tons of bombs—50 percent more than the tonnage dropped on Britain during the whole of the Second World War.[6]

Together with military escalation he applied diplomatic pressure, seeking to detach North Vietnam's communist backers: China and the Soviet Union. A cardinal principle of his diplomacy was therefore "linkage"—tying concessions in one aspect of superpower relations, such as arms control, to progress on priority issues for

America, notably Vietnam. In a benchmark statement at the beginning of his presidency, he told Cabinet members that "the Soviet leaders should be brought to understand that they cannot expect to reap the benefits of cooperation in one area while seeking to take advantage of tension or confrontation elsewhere."[7]

Nixon's capacity for leverage was, however, weaker than Kennedy's in October 1962 because the nuclear arms race had moved into a new phase. Determined not to be outfaced again, as in the Cuban Missile Crisis, Khrushchev's successors had systematically built up the Soviet nuclear arsenal. By 1969 the USSR had more land-based intercontinental ballistic missiles (ICBMs) than the United States. On the other two legs of the strategic "triad"—submarine-launched ballistic missiles (SLBMs) and nuclear-capable bombers—the United States still enjoyed substantial superiority. But overall by 1969 its nuclear arsenal was only double that of the Soviets, compared with a four-to-one advantage in 1964—and the gap was shrinking every month.[8]

Two other developments were also unsettling. Now that it was possible to envisage a system of antiballistic missile (ABM) defense, the Soviets had begun building a local one around Moscow. The delicate balance of terror, on which nuclear deterrence was believed to depend, could be upset by successful missile defense. And in 1968 the Pentagon began testing multiple, independently targetable reentry vehicles (MIRVs)—missiles with several nuclear warheads, each of which could be directed at a separate target. Like ABM technology, MIRVs might encourage one side to risk a first strike on the other. The Nixon administration urgently needed to address these new technologies and the arms race in general.

The Vietnam quagmire and the Soviet nuclear buildup were signs that America's relative power had diminished during the 1960s. But Moscow had problems of its own. The Soviet command economy remained intrinsically inefficient. Agriculture was a notorious black spot, with low productivity; its inadequate output could not satisfy the people's growing expectations. In years of bad weather and poor harvests the Soviets were obliged to import massively from the capitalist world—and 1972 was a very bad year. Industrial growth was also slowing and the Soviet Union clearly lagged behind the West in advanced technology. In contrast with Khrushchev's bullish economic nationalism, his successors wanted to promote technology transfers from the West. And, given the overall economic problems and rising consumer expectations, a reduction of the arms burden was desirable. These were all powerful reasons for détente.[9]

Tensions with the People's Republic had also increased dramatically during the Khrushchev era. Mao Zedong denounced Soviet talk of "peaceful coexistence" and called for renewed "armed struggle" against capitalism. His support for the North Vietnamese obliged the Soviets to follow suit or lose face in the communist world. In October 1964 the Chinese joined the nuclear club, after an all-out bid to develop a weapon that they deemed essential for their country's security and status. And in 1966 Mao's efforts to clean out party hacks and rejuvenate his revolution unleashed waves of student violence, backed by the army, that threw the country into chaos. By the time the Great Proletarian Cultural Revolution had abated in 1969, half a million people had died and China was gripped by xenophobic nationalism.

Relations with every country suffered, but the Soviet Union was the prime target, especially after the Red Army invaded Czechoslovakia in August 1968. The Chinese feared they could be next on the Soviet list and both sides massed forces across their long, disputed border. In March 1969 Chinese incursions in the east on the Ussuri River resulted in several hundred casualties. In response the Soviets gave the impression they were planning a preemptive nuclear strike. Although probably bluff, the war scare had a profound effect on the Chinese. In October Mao and most of the party and military leadership fled Beijing, fearful of a Soviet nuclear attack; those remaining operated for several months from an underground command center in the western suburbs. Eventually the Chinese backed down and agreed to talks about the border.[10]

But the long-term security situation deeply alarmed the Soviets, given that China's booming population was already three times the size of their own. With typical black humor, one Moscow joke imagined the party secretary, Leonid Brezhnev, calling President Nixon on the phone: "I hear you have a new super-computer that can predict events in the year 2000." Nixon proudly confirms this, whereupon Brezhnev asks, as a test question, who will be the members of the Soviet Politburo at the start of the new millennium. There is a long pause. "So," Brezhnev crows, "your super-computer isn't so sophisticated after all." "Oh no," Nixon replies, "the names came up all right. But I can't read Chinese."[11]

By 1969 Beijing felt more threatened by Russian "revisionists" than by American "imperialists." For China to improve relations with the United States might therefore be a way to unsettle the Soviet Union. Moscow likewise viewed the prospects of détente with Washington within this triangular context—as a means of isolating China. And the United States, no longer so dominant in world politics, could benefit from more stable relations with the maverick Chinese communists. A rapprochement might help detach them from Hanoi, thereby enabling America to extricate itself from Vietnam.

Nixon had been alert for some time to the chances of an opening: "Taking the long view," he wrote in 1967, "we simply cannot afford to leave China forever outside the family of nations." And in January 1969 Mao took the unprecedented step of authorizing the Chinese press to print the whole of Nixon's inaugural address (albeit coupled with critical commentaries), apparently because the new president had said that the United States wanted good relations with *all* the countries of the world.[12]

On paper, therefore, it was possible to discern compelling reasons for improvement in both American-Soviet relations and American-Chinese relations. But politics are about people, not paper. For such changes to occur something approaching a psychological revolution was needed, or at least a tipping of the political balance in all three capitals against hard-line Cold Warriors. These domestic realignments, involving intricate maneuvers and power plays, were essential before any summit could take place.

RICHARD NIXON HAD MADE his name in Congress as a dema-gogic anticommunist. His lead role in the hearings that exposed Al-ger Hiss as a Soviet agent helped catapult him to the rank of Eisen-hower's vice president. But then defeat by John Kennedy in the presidential election of 1960 apparently signalled the end of his po-litical career. For a few years he returned to corporate law. But, modelling himself on Churchill (one of his heroes), he came back from the political wilderness to reach the pinnacle of power.

The new Nixon was a self-styled realist, arguing that post-Viet-nam America had to adapt to a more even distribution of world power. This meant burden-sharing with its allies—what became known as the Nixon Doctrine: "We cannot supply all the concep-tions and all the resources."[13] It also required, in his view, a new re-lationship with the Soviet empire, accepting that it was a fixture on the international scene. "After a period of confrontation, we are en-tering an era of negotiation," he declared in his inaugural address in January 1969. "Let all nations know that during this administration our lines of communication will be open." Here was a new twist to Kennedy's Cold Warrior rhetoric eight years before: "Let every na-tion know, whether it wishes us well or ill, that we shall pay any price, bear any burden, meet any hardship, support any friend, op-pose any foe to assure the survival and the success of liberty." By June 1963, sobered by the missile crisis, Kennedy spoke of "accom-modation," of helping "make the world safe for diversity"; in Janu-ary 1969 Nixon asked Americans to "make the world safe for mankind." Both men had moved a long way from Woodrow Wil-son's universalist slogan in 1917 about making the world "safe for democracy."[14]

Yet Nixon was still ready to apply America's power with calcu-lated ruthlessness, as his secret bombing of Cambodia in 1969 showed. And he had no doubt about the global superiority of the American way. Indeed he considered Wilson "our greatest Presi-dent of this century" because he had the "greatest vision of Amer-ica's world role." Wilson failed, insisted Nixon, because "he wasn't practical enough."[15]

A practical foreign policy, in Nixon's judgment, required a strong, assertive presidency. However, America's constitutional separation of powers left the president frequently at the mercy of Congress. Worse still, the country's politicized bureaucracy and aggressive press made it hard to formulate a coherent policy and keep it confidential. Nixon therefore came to power convinced that he must conduct foreign policy in maximum secrecy. His temperament pushed him in the same direction. An insecure loner with few close friends, he brooded obsessively on politics; he was convinced from bitter experience that "they" were out to get him and that he must therefore strike first. His copies of the daily White House news summaries were full of annotations such as "hit him," "cut him," "fight him."[16] And, as a compulsive reader of history and political biography, he was determined to leave his mark on world affairs. This also seemed to require a centralization of power in the White House.

As secretary of state, Nixon appointed his old law partner William Rogers. But this was purely a front. Nixon's all-important advisor and collaborator was Henry Kissinger, a Jewish refugee from Nazi Germany whose intellect and ambition won him a place on the Harvard faculty. Kissinger's doctoral dissertation on Metternich and the Concert of Europe after the Napoleonic wars expressed his enduring belief in geopolitics, realpolitik and the virtues of a balance of power. Equally revealing, it celebrated the capacity of a gifted statesman to perceive realities and shape events. A best-selling book on nuclear strategy made his name as a defense intellectual, and he served as a part-time consultant to the Kennedy administration. During the 1968 campaign the ambitious Kissinger kept open links to both Democratic and Republican camps. But he was openly disparaging about Nixon, calling him a "disaster" who was "unfit to be president."[17] Yet after the election was over he was appointed national security advisor. "I don't trust Henry, but I can use him," Nixon remarked privately.[18] Thus began a formidable marriage of convenience spiced with mutual suspicion and resentment.

On the face of it, as Nixon later admitted, it was an "unlikely" combination: "the grocer's son from Whittier and the refugee from

Nazi Germany, the politician and the intellectual."[19] Moreover Kissinger had a sense of humor that Nixon conspicuously lacked, joking even about his own vanity:"I have been called indispensable and a miracle worker. I know, because I remember every word I say." And he sedulously cultivated his image as a "swinger," dating movie stars such as Liv Ullman and Jill St. John, mostly it seemed for PR purposes. "I just don't think Henry was interested in sex," said one girlfriend. "He didn't have time for it. Power for him may have been the aphrodisiac, but it was also the climax."[20] Behind Kissinger's back Nixon made snide comments about his "girls" and his thick German accent, while Kissinger regaled intellectual friends with gossip about Nixon's maladroitness and his liking for the bottle. Yet despite all their differences and rivalry Kissinger shared Nixon's insecurity and solitariness. "I'd never seen finger-nails bitten so close to the quick," recalled John Ehrlichman, Nixon's top domestic aide. "I've always acted alone," Kissinger observed in an unusually candid interview in November 1972, likening himself to "the cowboy who rides all alone into the town with his horse and nothing else."[21]

Like his boss Kissinger was convinced that the White House must keep tight control over foreign policy. "It is no accident," he wrote in 1961, "that most great statesmen were opposed by the experts in their foreign offices, for the very greatness of the statesman's conception tends to make it inaccessible to those whose primary concern is with safety and minimum risk."[22] With similar condescension Nixon told senior U.S. diplomats in 1969: "If the Department of State has had a new idea in the last twenty-five years, it is not known to me."[23]

On inauguration day the president issued a memorandum, drafted by Kissinger, asserting the central role of the National Security Council and its head. On February 17 Nixon invited the Soviet ambassador, Anatoli Dobrynin, to bypass the State Department on important issues and deal directly and secretly with Kissinger. This back channel between the White House and the Kremlin— prefigured by Bobby Kennedy's contacts with Georgii Bolshakov but far more systematic—became the main conduit for Soviet-

American relations during the Nixon years. Dobrynin usually met Kissinger in the ground-floor Map Room (established by FDR during World War II), his car coming and going through the service entrance to avoid reporters.

In his memoirs Dobrynin reflected that the extensive use of this back channel was "unprecedented in my experience and perhaps in the annals of diplomacy." He also credited it with many of the achievements of the détente era.[24] But the price was high. The back channel excluded the State Department and the Pentagon from the most important messages and discussions about key issues, such as Vietnam, arms control and summitry. So much so that specially sanitized copies of telegrams between the White House and the Kremlin were prepared for general Washington consumption in order to preserve the secret. The back channel also turned the U.S. embassy in Moscow into a backwater. Since Soviet leaders knew that Dobrynin was the avenue for all the important diplomatic traffic, they had little incentive to take the U.S. ambassador Jacob Beam, a career diplomat, seriously.

In fact the back channel played into the power struggle that was going on in Moscow. Although the Soviet Union is often depicted as a one-man dictatorship, that was only true in Stalin's heyday. At many points in its history the country was managed by a bureaucratized collective leadership in which several senior figures jockeyed for power. This was particularly evident during the succession struggles after Lenin, Stalin and Khrushchev, and was aided by the USSR's complex constitutional structure. In 1964 Leonid Brezhnev assumed Khrushchev's place as party leader, Alexei Kosygin took over as prime minister and within a year Nikolai Podgorny became head of state.

To begin with, Kosygin seemed first among equals within the troika. As chairman of the Council of Ministers he had a commanding role over economic policy. And as head of the government he conducted most of the foreign policy initiatives, including correspondence with Lyndon Johnson. In fact the two men met briefly at Glassboro, New Jersey, in June 1967 after Kosygin had visited New York to address the UN. But LBJ's hopes of a full-scale summit in the Soviet Union were dashed by the Vietnam War and the Soviet invasion of Czechoslovakia in August 1968. A technocrat by background, Kosygin was also a strong believer in arms control and the economic benefits of détente for the struggling Soviet economy. Although Podgorny seemed a less powerful figure—both in personality and because of his more ceremonial position—he was an instinctive Cold Warrior who headed a powerful faction in the Ukraine that was well represented in Moscow.

Initially it was Brezhnev who seemed the least substantial of the triumvirate—vain, boozy and a lover of flashy cars. But, like Stalin and Khrushchev in their time, he used the underrated position of party secretary to extend his power base and make allies in important places. By the end of the decade Brezhnev began to challenge Kosygin's dominance of foreign policy, gradually taking over his mantle as an exponent of détente. This was a delicate business, because he could not afford to rupture his close ties with the defense establishment. He also had to protect himself from Podgorny and other hard-liners such as the influential party ideologist Mikhail Suslov, who had masterminded the 1964 coup against Khrushchev. All sides were looking to the next party congress, scheduled for 1970, where rankings would be confirmed and publicized to the country and the world. The Soviet power struggle was therefore entering a delicate stage as Nixon developed his back channel with Moscow during 1969.[25]

This conduit into Kremlin politics was controlled by Andrei Gromyko, a professional diplomat who had been foreign minister since 1957. "Grim Grom" was seen in the West as a humorless automaton. Khrushchev joked that, if so ordered, his foreign minister would drop his trousers and sit on a block of ice for a month. But Gromyko was committed and hard working, always master of his brief in a negotiation and famed for his dogged patience in extracting one small concession after another. At Vienna in 1961 he was regarded by the Americans as little more than an "errand boy"[26] but his influence grew after Khrushchev's demise. Gromyko saw merits, given the friction with China, in a more stable relationship with the United States. The Kissinger-Dobrynin back channel enabled him to conceal moves toward détente from hard-liners and the military, rather as the White House excluded the rest of official Washington. His Foreign Ministry staff prepared the papers for the Politburo— like Nixon and Kissinger, sanitizing anything inappropriate. Kosygin was in the loop of course, but so too was Brezhnev, whom Gromyko had cultivated ever since Khrushchev's time. During the 1960s Gromyko helped Brezhnev move into foreign affairs, even assigning him some of his own aides such as Andrei Alexandrov-Agentov. Gromyko's enthusiasm for duck hunting began as a tactic for keeping close to the party leader through his favorite sport.[27]

IN NOVEMBER 1969 the two superpowers began Strategic Arms Limitation talks, alternating the sessions between Helsinki and Vienna. Although they made some progress, the real agenda was being shaped privately in the back channel. (Nixon's embittered principal arms negotiator, Gerard Smith, argued that this uncoordinated "double-track" negotiating process resulted in "doubletalk."[28]) Dobrynin found Kissinger evasive about a summit, seeking to link this to progress on other issues including Vietnam and Berlin. As we have seen, Nixon was skeptical about the value of summitry in resolving issues and, temperamentally, he shied away from face-to-face confrontation. He had also watched Johnson's poll ratings soar at the time of Glassboro and then slump dramatically when nothing significant came of the meeting. For all these reasons there was no rush to a summit in 1969.[29]

During 1970 the frustrated Soviets pursued détente in Europe, taking advantage of the new center-left coalition in Bonn headed by the Social Democrat leader Willy Brandt. Hitherto the Christian Democrats (CDU) had followed Adenauer's policy of ignoring the East German (GDR) regime and waiting for the day when Germany reunified on Western terms. But Brandt, formerly mayor of West Berlin, had watched impotently as the Wall went up in 1961: he believed that, without abandoning hopes of eventual unity, bridges should now be built across the Cold War divide. The object, declared his foreign policy advisor Egon Bahr, was "change through rapprochement"; "small steps are better than none" (a pun in German: *kleine Schritte sind besser als keine*).[30]

In dramatic minisummits during 1970, Brandt reached out to the leaders of Poland, East Germany and the Soviet Union; he signed agreements that accepted in practice the truncated 1945 borders of his country and negotiated a natural gas pipeline from Siberia, using West German technology and credits. Particularly momentous was Brandt's visit to the East German town of Erfurt on March 19, 1970, to meet the GDR premier Willi Stoph. Despite the efforts of the secret police, a crowd of more than fifteen hundred people broke through barriers to surround Brandt's hotel, chanting his name. The Erfurt meeting was a spectacular public relations disaster for the East German leaders and a graphic reminder of how unpopular their regime really was.[31]

In the winter of 1970–1 the four occupying powers and the two Germanys started to negotiate agreements to open up access between West Germany and West Berlin. They also wanted to allow controlled visits by West Berliners to the eastern half of the city. These would mark a milestone in the Cold War, finally removing the danger of war over Berlin. Yet Kissinger was unhappy about Brandt's enthusiastic *Ostpolitik*. Not only did his initiatives breach the administration's principle of linkage—tying the resolution of German problems to progress on America's global agenda—it also seemed the thin end of a dangerous Soviet wedge. One of the Kremlin's great aims was formal acknowledgment of the division of Europe into two blocs. The Soviets wanted a European security conference, rounding off Yalta and Potsdam, to accept the borders of 1945 and renounce the use of force as a means of changing them. "This is a nightmare," Kissinger warned the president. He feared the Soviets would "use the climate of détente to argue that NATO is unnecessary."[32]

Nixon was also unsettled by the pace of détente in Europe because it contrasted jarringly with the escalating war in Vietnam. Kissinger's secret talks with the North Vietnamese in Paris were getting nowhere. In the spring of 1970 the president sent troops into neighboring Cambodia to neutralize communist sanctuaries.

His announcement on April 30 stressed that this was a short-term operation to sap North Vietnam's resistance at the negotiating table, but the invasion of Cambodia provoked new waves of protest across America. On May 4 four students were shot dead by National Guardsmen at Kent State University in Ohio. And the following weekend protestors descended en masse on Washington, clearly visible (and audible) from the White House.

Just before dawn on Saturday, May 9 a restless Nixon ordered his driver to take him down to the Lincoln Memorial where he engaged in a rambling conversation with the students. Trying to get on their wavelength, the president said he knew exactly how they felt; he recalled his excitement at their age when Chamberlain came back from Munich talking about "peace for our time." In 1938, fresh out of law school, he thought Chamberlain was "the greatest man alive" and Churchill "a madman" for criticizing him. But now, he told the students, he believed that whereas Chamberlain was "a good man," Churchill was "a wise man." His policies, though unpopular, had been right.[33]

Yet privately that spring Nixon was lurching into Chamberlain mode. The roadblocks to peace and the massive domestic protests prompted him to make a dramatic leap toward a summit. He believed this would outflank the antiwar lobby and help his party in the midterm elections that autumn. Kissinger was skeptical, conscious that the administration was still unprepared on the big issues and had not established effective linkage as leverage over the Russians. But Nixon was adamant, so on April 7, 1970, Kissinger hinted to Dobrynin that a summit might be acceptable soon if some major breakthrough were in hand. As Kissinger predicted, the Soviets used Nixon's eagerness to demand concessions on key issues—including cooperation against China. The Kremlin had overreached itself; to Kissinger's relief Nixon eventually backed off, recognizing that a summit at any price would leave him looking more like Chamberlain than Churchill.[34]

In any case the Soviets had problems of their own, because the power struggle in Moscow was reaching its decisive phase. In December 1969 Brezhnev bemoaned the state of the Soviet economy in a speech to the full Central Committee of the party. This was coded criticism of Kosygin's stewardship and the first shot in Brezhnev's battle to gain effective control of the Council of Ministers. Aware of his political subtext, Suslov and others derided such "hysterics," whereupon Brezhnev quoted Lenin's condemnation of "factionalism." In June 1970 Brezhnev opened a new front with a major address on foreign policy. And when Kosygin, in poor health, broached the idea of retirement, he used this to bid for control of the premiership, in fact if not in name. In July the Politburo decided that Kosygin should stay on, but by then it was too late to stage the 24th Party Congress that year.[35] On September 25 Dobrynin told Kissinger that Moscow preferred to hold a summit after the congress in the following spring.

The 24th Party Congress opened on March 30, 1971, with a six-hour keynote address by Brezhnev, the only speech to be televised in its entirety. He outlined a program of "peaceful coexistence" that included measured détente with the West. The speech set the direction of foreign policy and confirmed that Brezhnev was now the dominant figure in Soviet leadership. After the congress ended on April 9, the Politburo met to review the question of a summit. Dobrynin, whose back channel role had helped him rise to full membership of the Central Committee, advised the meeting that the omens for a beneficial summit were now propitious. Kosygin and some others agreed but then, to Dobrynin's surprise, Gromyko urged them to take advantage of Nixon's continued eagerness. They should first press the president to complete negotiations on West Berlin which, he said, had been "passed on from one American administration to another." Brezhnev agreed, and most of the Politburo then concurred that "a meeting with Nixon can wait." Afterward Brezhnev told Dobrynin privately that the majority decision was correct and must be respected, but added that the ambassador should proceed on the assumption that a summit would be held in 1972.[36]

Possibly all this was another ploy by Gromyko and Brezhnev to isolate Kosygin, but it also reflected Gromyko's confidence that he was playing a strong hand against the White House. If so, he overreached himself. On April 12 an American table tennis team was invited to Beijing.

PING-PONG WAS CHINA'S FAVORITE SPORT, but the guardians of the Cultural Revolution had barred Chinese teams from international competition in recent years. In 1970, however, Mao and his prime minister, Zhou Enlai, personally authorized participation at the world championships in Nagoya, Japan, the following spring. China won four of the seven gold medals. During the competition there were several friendly talks between Chinese and U.S. players, and the question was raised about an American visit to Beijing. Foreign Ministry officials concluded that the time was "not yet mature"; Zhou agreed and so did Mao, but then he changed his mind. An invitation was hurriedly issued and the White House gave its approval. National and world television featured the American visit and on April 14, 1971, the players were received by Zhou in the Great Hall of the People. To general amazement, he spoke of "a new chapter" in Sino-American relations, predicting that "this beginning again of our friendship will certainly meet with majority support of our two peoples.[37]

In reality this unlikely demarche did not come out of the blue. For a couple of years American and Chinese diplomats had met on and off clandestinely in Warsaw. Feelers were also extended via the governments of Romania and Pakistan. But progress was slow and there was serious opposition in both capitals. The "China lobby" was well entrenched in the U.S. Congress. It was constantly reminding the administration of America's commitment—ever since the communist takeover in 1949—to the rump Nationalist regime that had fled to the offshore island of Taiwan. Officially the United States still recognized the Nationalists as the rightful government of China. In Beijing many felt that Taiwan and Vietnam proved the impossibility of compromise with American imperialism. Lin Biao, the reclusive but powerful head of the People's Liberation Army, was fundamentally opposed; as Mao's designated heir he was now increasingly impatient to ease out the old man.

And so in Beijing, like Moscow, foreign policy fed into the struggle for power. Despite the perceived threat from the Soviet Union, Mao and Zhou had to move carefully in overtures to the United States. In this context table tennis provided a sudden and safe opportunity. It was possible to send the desired signals to Washington, Moscow and—given the national passion for the sport—to the Chinese people as a whole, but in a way that hard-liners would find hard to criticize. Ping-Pong diplomacy caught the imagination of the world. As Zhou put it: "A small ball shakes the big ball."[38]

On April 12 Kissinger predicted that the table tennis visit would unsettle the Soviets and "play in our favor for a SALT agreement and a Summit conference." But when Dobrynin came in for another talk on April 23, the ambassador stuck to the line established by Gromyko at the recent Politburo meeting, linking a summit to progress over Berlin. Kissinger angrily refused.[39]

On May 20, after a flurry in the back channel about SALT, the two governments suddenly announced that they would concentrate on two areas: antiballistic missile systems and a freeze on missile launchers. These negotiations would be linked: deadlock in one would preclude agreement on the other. But the announcement contrasted with the earlier American insistence on a comprehensive agreement to limit all offensive and defensive weapons. Nixon's climb down indicated his political need for some kind of progress. It also reflected his concern that a similar idea was being aired in the official negotiations, which he wanted to preempt in order to get the credit.[40]

Doubtless thinking that Nixon was on the defensive, Gromyko continued to link the summit and Berlin. This was reiterated in a message of July 5, which suggested the end of the year as the earliest possible date for Nixon to visit Moscow. Kissinger's deputy, General Alexander Haig, described this as transparently "a holding action" and an effort to put further pressure on the United States about Berlin.[41]

By then, however, Sino-American relations had raced ahead. Just days after the Ping-Pong visit Zhou sent a message via the Pakistani government, indicating that further progress could only be made by direct discussions. He said that Kissinger, Rogers or even Nixon would be welcome to come publicly to Beijing. On May 10 the president proposed a preliminary trip by Kissinger to prepare the way but stressed that this must be "strictly secret." Zhou probably preferred an open visit because of the likely effect on Moscow. He certainly doubted that the news could be kept under wraps, but replied guaranteeing secrecy on the Chinese side.[42] Kissinger therefore conducted his summer exchanges with Dobrynin about a Moscow summit knowing that he was about to visit China. He was content to let the Soviets drag their feet, because it would strengthen his leverage when the news came out.

Kissinger concealed his China odyssey under an official visit to Pakistan. Once in the capital, Islamabad, he pleaded the Pakistani equivalent of Delhi belly. President Yahya Khan (postman for White House messages to Zhou) offered him the use of a presidential retreat in the mountains in order to recuperate. That was the cover story. In reality, Kissinger was en route to Beijing. Early on July 9 America's national security advisor, sporting a hat and dark glasses, was spirited away in a Pakistani plane flown by Yahya's personal pilot, but guided by Chinese navigators. For Kissinger, with his profound sense of history, it was probably one of the most dramatic moments of his life, flying over the Himalayas, disconcertingly close to K-2, across the Chinese deserts and into the unknown heart of Mao's communist empire. He traveled with only three aides and two Secret Service men, relying—like Chamberlain at Berchtesgaden—on his host for interpreters.

There followed seventeen hours of talks with Zhou Enlai. Here was a man of intellect, culture and charm, who bargained hard yet, unlike Gromyko, thought big. "There was none of the Russian ploymanship, scoring points, rigidity or bullying," Kissinger later told Nixon. Zhou "spoke with an almost matter-of-fact clarity and eloquence," nearly always without notes. "He was equally at home in philosophical sweeps, historical analysis, tactical probing, light repartee. His command of facts, and in particular his knowledge of

American events, was remarkable." Zhou Enlai, gushed Kissinger, "ranks with Charles de Gaulle as the most impressive foreign statesman I have met."[43]

As we now know, Zhou was treated by Mao as his round-the-clock diplomatic factotum, forced at times to grovel even more basely than Gromyko did before Khrushchev. In 1972 Mao denied Zhou treatment for bladder cancer lest his premier outlive him, and even refused to pass on a full diagnosis. The statesman who dazzled Kissinger was in reality Mao's "blackmailed slave."[44]

On the question of a summit, Kissinger detected a real ambivalence in Beijing. The prospect of Chairman Mao sitting down with the arch imperialist was hard for veteran revolutionaries to stomach. Yet he believed they were "deeply worried about the Soviet threat to their national integrity" and saw the United States as "a balancing force." Zhou tried to represent the Americans as suitors for a summit; eventually the two men agreed upon wording for a communiqué that stressed a mutual desire to address questions of concern to both sides. Zhou pressed hard to stage Nixon's visit in the summer of 1972 *after* the president had been to Moscow. He said they were "not afraid of anyone" but were "not looking for unnecessary trouble." Kissinger judged this "perhaps the most significant" sign of "Chinese worries about their confrontation with the USSR."[45]

The Americans preferred the exact opposite sequence: a summit in China—strong on symbolism but certainly short on substance given the intractable problem of Taiwan—would strengthen America's bargaining position for the more substantive negotiations with Moscow. Nixon bluntly told Kissinger on his return: "We're doing the China thing to screw the Russians and help us in Vietnam . . . And maybe down the road to have some relations with China."[46]

Despite their cynical tone both Nixon and Kissinger were delighted with the breakthrough. The national security advisor called the talks "the most intense, important, and far reaching of my White House experience." A jubilant Nixon replied that "if we play the game to the hilt from now on out, history will record your visit [as] the most significant foreign policy achievement of this century. When you return," he added with no discernible irony, "I intend to give you a day off in compensation for your superb service to the nation."[47]

On the evening of July 15 Nixon delivered a brief radio and TV address in which he stated that Kissinger had held talks with Zhou Enlai in Beijing and that he had accepted an invitation to visit China in person "at an appropriate date before May 1972."[48]

Although the news unsettled Taiwan, Japan, South Korea and other Asian allies, most of the world (and nearly all Americans) applauded. To Nixon's distress, however, the praise was largely directed at Kissinger, who really took off as a media celebrity, lauded as a "Modern Metternich" and "Superkraut." Furious, the president demanded that Kissinger stop talking to the media; when that failed (like trying to dam Niagara Falls) he touted his own credentials as a man "uniquely prepared" for the summit and on the same historical plane as Zhou Enlai. Consider the similarities, he noted:

Cool. Unflappable. A tough bold strong leader. Willing to take chances where necessary. A man who takes the long view, never being concerned about tomorrow's headlines but about how the policy will look years from now. A man with a philosophical turn of mind. A man who works without notes.

Kissinger assured the president that he was doing his bit. For instance, he had told some right-wing congressmen, fearful of a sellout at the summit, that Nixon was exactly the man needed—"tough, unemotional, precise." Most Americans at summit conferences got carried away with a "sense of euphoria" because of the social occasions. But that couldn't happen to Nixon, Kissinger told the congressmen in a typically backhanded compliment—the president "doesn't have any social occasions, he works all the time."[49]

BEFORE NIXON'S BROADCAST on July 15, 1971, Kissinger had phoned Ambassador Dobrynin to emphasize that détente with China was not directed against the USSR. But he clearly implied that Soviet foot-dragging about a Moscow summit had played into the hands of Beijing. "In my heart of hearts," Dobrynin wrote later, "I could only agree with him."[50]

The precise impact of the China opening on Soviet policy is a matter of dispute, with some scholars questioning Nixon's and Kissinger's claims that it made Moscow more accommodating.[51] But when Dobrynin met Kissinger on July 19, just after the president's broadcast, he found the ambassador "for the first time in my experience with him, totally insecure."[52] And although it is true that superpower agreements on Berlin and SALT were already taking shape, many details still remained to work out. Gromyko could easily have used those as an excuse for dragging his feet about the summit; instead by his former standards, he now positively hurried to fix the date.

Nixon also had to minimize the offense to Secretary of State Rogers, still aggrieved at being kept in the dark about Kissinger's trip to China. Eventually the president exploited a meeting with Gromyko at the White House on September 29 to pretend that the Soviet foreign minister had offered a surprise invitation to visit Moscow. On October 12 Nixon announced in a news conference that a summit would be held in late May 1972. He said he would be meeting with the Soviet "leaders," in the plural, but admitted that Brezhnev was "the major center of power." Since August, on Dobrynin's advice, he had been addressing his messages to Brezhnev instead of Kosygin.[53]

During the autumn, preparations for his visit to Beijing moved rapidly, assisted by a dramatic tilt in China's internal politics. On September 13 a plane carrying Lin Biao, his family and entourage crashed in Mongolia. The story remains murky but officially it was claimed that the army leader was fleeing after a failed coup. His son certainly seems to have concocted an inept assassination plot. The death of Mao's handpicked heir amid accusations of betrayal was a damaging blow to his image of infallibility. This sparked a crisis of faith among millions of Chinese about the "continuous revolution" to which they had been subjected so brutally for two decades. A foreign policy triumph was now even more important for Mao. Lin was supposedly an opponent of détente with the United States. Certainly his death and disgrace strengthened Zhou Enlai, even though strong opposition remained to Nixon's visit from Mao's estranged wife, Jiang Qing, and from radicals in Shanghai.[54] Zhou pushed ahead with arrangements and in October Kissinger paid a second visit to China—this time in public—to agree the agenda and draft the all-important communiqué.

The president's arrival in Beijing on the morning of February 21, 1972, was timed for maximum effect back home—as prime-time Sunday-night viewing. The advance men had made sure that TV cameras would be positioned at all key points. Still chafing at Kissinger's self-promotion, Nixon stressed on numerous occasions during the flight that no one else must be in view when he and his wife descended from Air Force One. Just to make sure, a burly Secret Service agent blocked the aisle after they landed. Mindful that in 1954 John Foster Dulles, Eisenhower's secretary of state, had refused to shake hands with Zhou Enlai at the Geneva conference on Indochina, Nixon walked down the steps with arm outstretched. "Your handshake came over the vastest ocean in the world," Zhou said later, "twenty-five years of no communication."[55]

Although Nixon, like Kissinger, was impressed by Zhou, the highlight of the trip for both of them was a courtesy call on Mao. Born in 1893 and so twenty years older than the president, the ailing Chinese leader had nearly died that winter from congestive heart failure. His legs swelled up, his blood pressure was dangerously high and he coughed incessantly from fluid in the lungs. With immense difficulty doctors overcame Mao's peasant suspicion of antibiotics and got him well in time for Nixon's visit. Even so he needed help to sit and walk after months in bed, and a new suit and shoes had to be ordered for his bloated body. But on the day his visitors arrived, Mao's doctor recalled, he was "as excited as I have ever seen him." Staff dismantled his bed, hid the oxygen cylinders in a huge lacquered trunk and moved other emergency equipment behind potted plants, out of sight but ready for any crisis.[56]

The effort was worthwhile and the Americans were duly taken in. Mao turned in a superb performance, avoiding all substantive issues and sparring deftly with his guests. Kissinger felt that the ba-thetic setting of an untidy, book-lined study was a more effective place to show off the innate power of this "colossus" than if he had received them in the pomp and circumstance of a formal state oc-casion.[57] Nixon was particularly struck by Mao's long and friendly handshake (immortalized of course on film). And toasts at the offi-cial banquets replicated the positive mood. Behind the scenes Kissinger, despite his assurances to Dobrynin, passed on high-grade intelligence about Soviet weaponry and dispositions along the Chi-nese border.[58]

In the business sessions, conducted with Zhou Enlai, Nixon's ap-proach was to seek a "tradeoff" over Taiwan and Vietnam. He took the line that

1. Your people expect action on Taiwan.
2. Our people expect action on V. Nam.
Neither can act immediately—But both are inevitable.[59]

Nothing could be said explicitly on either side. Nixon insisted that he must be able to go home and say that he had made no "se-cret deals" over Taiwan. But he made it equally clear that his long-term goal was to normalize relations between their two coun-tries—"If I should win the election, I have five years to achieve it"—and this could only be done by pulling out of Taiwan. Zhou for his part insisted that if the war in Vietnam did not stop, it would be "impossible to relax tensions in the Far East." The People's Re-public would be "forced to continue aid" to North Vietnam's "just struggles . . . We do not have a right to interfere in their position . . . We have no right to negotiate for them." But the following month, when briefing North Vietnamese leaders on Nixon's visit, he warned that "if the problem of Indochina is not solved, it will be impossible to realize the normalization of China-U.S. relations."[60]

The Beijing summit was about symbolism more than substance. The tradeoff over Vietnam and Taiwan was understood, not formal-ized. Kissinger and Zhou had broadly settled beforehand the pa-rameters of the discussion. During their detailed summit talks they

With respect, Mr. President, with a flick of the wrist you've just put back U.S.-Chinese relations another 23 years.

Figure 5-1 Beware of banquets at the summit: Kissinger (right) warns Nixon of the perils of chopstick diplomacy. (*Birmingham Post*, February 25, 1972, Bert Hackett, University of Kent Cartoon Library)

also finalized the communiqué. The two sides agreed to set out their divergent views on many of the issues under discussion. But wording on Taiwan took hours of haggling. This, like Kissinger's previous meetings with Zhou and his advisors, was done without input from the State Department. Rogers was taken to the summit but kept off the peak, excluded from the meeting with Mao and fobbed off with negotiating minor issues such as visas. Only near the end of the visit were the secretary of state and his staff shown the draft communiqué. Some of their criticisms were resentful nit-picking, but they did identify two serious errors.

Kissinger had affirmed that "all Chinese on either side of the Tai-wan Strait maintain that there is but one China and that Taiwan is a part of China. The United States Government does not challenge that position." This apparently bland statement, U.S. diplomats pointed out, ignored the powerful Taiwanese independence move-ment. Secondly, the draft communiqué reaffirmed America's defense commitments to Japan and South Korea, but neglected to mention those to Taiwan. It was widely believed in Washington that Secretary of State Dean Acheson's 1950 failure to name South Korea as lying within America's defense perimeter in Asia had encouraged the communists to mount their fateful attack. These omissions were sufficiently serious that Kissinger, to Nixon's fury, had to reopen the communiqué. The Chinese dug in on the first point but yielded on the second, predictably extracting a concession elsewhere. The whole affair was a reminder that no man, however able, not even "Superkraut," could keep in mind all the issues at stake. This problem was to recur in Moscow a few months later.[61]

NIXON CALLED HIS VISIT to Beijing "the week that changed the world." The British ambassador in Washington detected a "distinct whiff" of "peace in our time" in the air.[62] But by the time the euphoric Americans returned home, there was almost open warfare between Nixon's secretary of state and his national security advisor. As Nixon put it later: "Rogers felt that Kissinger was Machiavellian, deceitful, egotistical, arrogant, and insulting. Kissinger felt that Rogers was vain, uninformed, unable to keep a secret, and hopelessly dominated by the State Department bureaucracy."[63]

Despite stringing Kissinger along at times, the president basically sided with him. Having been marginalized in the Vietnam negotiations and at the China summit, a humiliated Rogers was desperate to take over planning for Moscow. On March 17 Nixon had to tell Dobrynin in person that Kissinger remained in charge. On many occasions separate sets of specially edited documents about the summit were prepared for Rogers, who was apparently still unaware of the back channel. Kissinger even briefed the Soviet ambassador on exactly what the U.S. secretary of state did and did not know about the diplomacy he was supposed to oversee.[64]

The summit was now coming into view and it looked alluring to both sides. Several useful bilateral agreements were close to completion on issues such as health, space and the environment. Discussions were also under way to settle the USSR's unpaid lend-lease debts from World War II. This would unlock new credits and increased trade, including a mutually beneficial agreement to sell surplus American grain. The SALT talks were progressing and both leaders, eyeing their domestic critics, wanted to sign an agreement when they met in May. If all this came off, the summit would be the most substantive ever and it would lay the groundwork for further agreements in future meetings. In the words of Dwight Chapin, deputy assistant to the president, Moscow was going to be "more of a business trip, whereas China was just opening a channel."[65] Yet as a canny politician Nixon sought to dampen media speculation; otherwise, he told Kissinger, "when we do make the formal agreements there will be no real news value to them." He even wanted to promote "a line of pessimism with regard to what may be accomplished," particularly on SALT, to prevent his bête noire Gerry Smith claiming credit for it before the summit.[66]

Brezhnev shared Nixon's concern that everything should come to the boil nicely at the summit. He instructed his official arms control negotiator, Vladimir Semyenov, to draw out the SALT talks while keeping him informed.[67] A grain deal was now particularly important: in March the Central Committee had held emergency discussions about the poor crop of winter wheat. Like the White House, however, the Kremlin also saw more at stake than a few substantive deals that would yield economic and political benefits. It seemed clear that the Nixon administration was now willing to take the Soviet Union seriously as an equal partner, and this represented a dramatic tilt in the balance of the Cold War.

Looking beyond merely an arms control agreement, Brezhnev and Gromyko hoped to conclude a pact renouncing nuclear war and another articulating the basic principles of Soviet-American relations. Coupled with the Berlin agreements, signed in September 1971 and now awaiting ratification by the West German Bundestag, these would reduce the danger of war in Europe and signal a Soviet-American condominium in international affairs. That would be a lesson to the Chinese and also evidence to the world that the Soviet Union had come of age. The Kremlin also hoped for a summit agreement on the Middle East, to offset Israel's new power after the 1967 war and further demonstrate the Soviet Union's global role.

Some of Moscow's goals were utopian. The White House had no interest in renouncing nuclear war—its possibility was the underlying premise of deterrence and the bedrock of NATO. Nor was it ready, particularly in an election year, to lean on Israel, given the importance of the Jewish lobby in American politics. On March 17 Dobrynin complained that Kissinger was "producing one red herring after another to avoid facing concrete issues" about the Middle East.[68] Yet whether or not the Soviets came down from the summit with their whole package, the meeting with Nixon promised Brezhnev huge benefits.

But on March 30 the North Vietnamese army mounted a new offensive into the south. Not only did it achieve large territorial gains, but whole units of the South Vietnamese army fell apart. Nixon was deeply shaken. Convinced of the need to wind down the war before the election, he had been planning to follow up his Moscow summit with an announcement that most American troops would be out by November.[69] This strategy was now in jeopardy. Moreover the north's breakthrough showed that it was still receiving substantial logistic support from Moscow and Beijing. So much for his hopes that they would both restrain Hanoi in the interests of improved relations with Washington. The president ratcheted up the bombing. But he also had to address a more fundamental question: should he call off the Moscow summit as well? How could he clink glasses in the Kremlin while Soviet-made tanks were rolling over an American ally?

For Nixon Vietnam and reelection were the overriding priorities. He had no doubt that if his administration was seen to fail in Vietnam, it could not survive politically. If the Soviets would help, fine; if not, as seemed to be the case that spring, then he wanted to bomb North Vietnam into serious negotiations regardless of the effect on the summit.[70] Kissinger, in contrast, gave the summit higher priority, partly because he believed that the U.S. could still exert leverage on Hanoi through Moscow. But also because he reckoned that, politically, two successful summits would outweigh disaster in

Vietnam. On a more personal level, the Moscow meeting would surely cap his career as a diplomat. Given the ups and downs of his relationship with Nixon and the animosity he engendered throughout the administration, he could not be sure that the president would keep him on beyond the first term.[71]

These tensions came into the open over whether Kissinger should visit Moscow to resolve the agenda for the May summit. The Soviets had been pressing for this since the previous autumn, partly to match Kissinger's presummit meetings in Beijing. Although the idea had practical merits, Nixon was afraid of further antagonizing Rogers and kept stalling.[72]

After the North Vietnamese offensive Dobrynin increased the pressure, arguing that the visit would be an opportunity to discuss Indochina as well as the summit. On April 12 Nixon agreed on this basis—a convenient pretext to placate Rogers—providing the visit was conducted in secret. Over the next few days, however, the president shifted his emphasis, instructing that in Moscow Vietnam must be the priority. Only if the Soviets made a "solid proposal" was Kissinger authorized to discuss the summit. Otherwise "you get the hell out of there." Fearful that Vietnam would destroy his presidency, like LBJ's, he worked himself into a frenzy. "We will bomb the living beejezus out of North Vietnam and then if anybody interferes we will threaten the nuclear weapon." Kissinger's evident keenness to go to Moscow fuelled Nixon's innate suspicions. "Henry wants to talk about the summit," he told H. R. Haldeman, the White House chief of staff. "He just loves this excuse for going over there." Nixon wobbled to and fro over the next few days. Eventually he allowed the visit to go ahead, but a final Vietnam-first injunction from the president was relayed to Kissinger en route. "Please assure him it will be carried out meticulously," his advisor cabled back.[73]

As with Beijing in July 1971, the trip was concealed from most of the administration; Rogers was informed only a few hours before Kissinger took off. Adopting the usual spy-novel subterfuge, Kissinger, Dobrynin and a Soviet navigator were smuggled into Andrews Air Force Base and flown across the Atlantic, refuelling secretly at a U.S. airfield in Britain. Once in Moscow Kissinger was accommodated in a Soviet government guest house on the Lenin Hills, just outside the city. The U.S. embassy knew nothing of his trip until Kissinger summoned Ambassador Jacob Beam just before flying home to Washington. But although reliant on Russian hospitality, Kissinger could not of course trust his hosts. To guard against the inevitable bugs he used a "babbler"—a cassette tape of a dozen voices talking gibberish simultaneously. This was played during confidential American discussions in the guest house, but only for short periods because of the damage to one's sanity. Kissinger's staff had also brought old-fashioned manual typewriters, lest the KGB read the "telemetry" of electric machines. And because the embassy was out of the loop, messages to and from Washington had to be transmitted via special equipment on his plane, now an hour's drive away.[74]

The stakes were high for Brezhnev as well as Kissinger. This was the Soviet leader's first formal encounter with a top-level American and he was palpably on edge when they met on the morning of April 21. Throughout their conversation he was always doing something—flicking ash from an ever-present cigarette, suddenly offering refreshments or interjecting a tangential anecdote. At times during the consecutive translation he would get up and walk around, occasionally even leaving the room without explanation. Once during their talks he returned carrying a toy cannon. When it failed to fire he seemed to ignore his guest until he could make it work, whereupon he strutted around in jubilation. Some of this restlessness was a tactical ploy to unsettle his interlocutor, but it was all a far cry from the urbane sophistication of Zhou Enlai. In further contrast with Zhou, the Soviet leader spoke from notes. Kissinger reported that Brezhnev was "very forceful, extremely nervous, highly unsubtle, quite intelligent but not in the class of the other leaders we have met."[75]

The first meeting, some five hours long, was largely devoted to Vietnam. Kissinger was encouraged by the relative mildness with which Brezhnev criticized recent American bombing. He also noted the Soviet leader's enthusiasm for the summit, especially

Brezhnev's comment that "certain forces in the world" would "gloat" to see the Chinese summit come off while the Soviet summit did not.[76]

Next day, April 22, they had another five-hour session. Kissinger outlined proposals he wished to submit if the North Vietnamese agreed to a private meeting in Paris on May 2. Essentially he suggested a return to the status quo before March 30, an immediate exchange of long-term prisoners and a serious effort to negotiate a settlement within a set period of time. Brezhnev, transparently keen to get on to summit business, promised to submit these proposals to Hanoi. In his memoirs Kissinger presented all this as a victory for his toughness.[77] He did not mention the carrot he had also offered to Hanoi. The United States, he told Brezhnev the previous day, had two principal objectives in Vietnam: "to bring about an honorable withdrawal of all our forces" and "to put a time interval between our withdrawal and the political process which would then start. We are prepared to let the real balance of forces in Vietnam determine the future of Vietnam . . . We are not committed to a permanent political involvement there." In other words the Nixon administration would tolerate a united, communist Vietnam as long as this did not seem the direct result of American withdrawal.[78]

Kissinger was operating way beyond his instructions. On the night of the 21st, in fact, Nixon instructed Alexander Haig to tell Kissinger that the "summit is not to be discussed further until Vietnam is settled."[79] The president had retreated to Camp David to help conceal Kissinger's absence, leaving him nothing to do but fret, especially when communications problems delayed reports of Kissinger's meetings. The presence of his crony Bebe Rebozo and plenty of booze did not help his mood. The result was a succession of fractious telegrams, which usually arrived hours after they were relevant. Being outside the official State Department communications system played into Kissinger's hands. He was free to play his favorite role, that of the Lone Ranger.[80]

Brezhnev had promised only to submit Kissinger's proposals to Hanoi, not to press for their acceptance. But, judging that he could make no further progress on Vietnam, Kissinger ignored Nixon's orders and let Brezhnev present his scenarios for the summit, reasoning that the president could always reject them if he wanted a showdown.[81] This was probably right. Face to face across the table, he could sense, in a way Nixon could not, the Soviet leader's keenness to meet the president.

But Kissinger needed to discuss the summit for more personal reasons. In the back channel he had made a serious mistake over arms control, and the situation had to be retrieved before final negotiations.

Nixon's May 20, 1971, statement about SALT indicated that the two sides would seek agreements in two linked areas: limiting the deployment of antiballistic missile systems (ABMs) and what was vaguely described as "certain measures with respect to the limitation of offensive strategic weapons."[82] Most of Kissinger's attention in 1971–2 had been devoted to ABMs, partly because of divergent Soviet and American priorities but also because of the divisions on the issue within Washington. During his talks with Brezhnev the outlines of a deal were confirmed: each country would be allowed two ABM systems, one of them to protect its capital. More difficult was pinning down the other element of a SALT agreement, a freeze on "offensive strategic weapons." In the back channel this phrase had become a synonym for land-based intercontinental ballistic missiles (ICBMs), on which Kissinger focused because of the Pentagon's concern about the Soviet arsenal. He had not explicitly included submarine-launched ballistic missiles (SLBMs), apparently failing to realize that American building programs were in limbo pending decisions about a new Trident system, while Soviet SLBM construction was surging ahead. Here was another sign of the dangers of his Lone Ranger approach. When the gravity of his omission became clear, Kissinger hoped that the Pentagon would accept an agreement covering only ICBMs. It refused, leaving him with a real problem in the spring of 1972.[83]

What Kissinger did, according to arms control expert Raymond Garthoff, was to make the Soviets "an offer they could not refuse" by including SLBM launchers in the draft agreement but "at such a high level that in practice the Soviet Union would not actually have to constrain its SLBM buildup." In March Kissinger had suggested to Dobrynin a total of 950 SLBMs, and it was this that Brezhnev accepted on April 22. A relieved Kissinger seized on it without further haggling, exclaiming: "The figures are agreed. There is no problem with figures. I will show you what a bad diplomat I am." In Washington afterward Kissinger covered his tracks by setting this figure against much higher estimates of the likely Soviet buildup if there were no arms control agreement. Fortunately for Kissinger, the Pentagon's normal tendency to exaggerate possible threats played into his hands.[84]

Kissinger's intervention in SALT was the second time he had seriously upstaged the official U.S. negotiator, Gerard Smith. After the May 1971 agreement Smith thought seriously of resignation; when informed of the April 1972 discussions he was "flabbergasted that Kissinger once again had gone off on his own and by-passed the delegation," giving the negotiations "a random lurch in an unprepared direction." Smith's attempts to refine what had been agreed in Moscow infuriated Kissinger, and Nixon called one proposed modification "bullshit." Rightly Smith sensed that the Brezhnev-Kissinger arrangement was "a fait accompli."[85]

The deal on SALT was sketched in outline on the second day of Kissinger's talks with Brezhnev. On Sunday the 23rd, day three, he spent several hours with Gromyko, successfully resisting Soviet pressure for a summit agreement on the Middle East. On the final day he and Gromyko had a strained meeting, much of it pacing up and down, about the wording of the final communiqué about his talks with Brezhnev. Despite Nixon's wishes[86] this made no explicit mention of Vietnam. But Kissinger did ensure that it said they had "discussed international issues of interest to both governments" before mentioning talks about "bilateral matters preparatory to the meeting" between Nixon and the Soviet leaders in May. That enabled him to claim they had discussed Vietnam before the summit. He also wanted to say that the talks were "frank and useful." Gromyko pointed out that "frank" implied "disagreement" which of course was exactly the note Kissinger wanted to sound in Washington and the Soviets did not wish to convey to Beijing. On this point Kissinger had to concede, but his unusually petulant outburst to Gromyko—"You know, you have a habit that when someone drops a nickel you will do anything to get that nickel, even if you lose a million dollars of goodwill in the process"—revealed the pressure he was under.[87]

The other summit document Kissinger and Gromyko discussed was a statement of "Basic Principles" of Soviet-American relations. Dobrynin had been pressing this in the back channel for some months; on March 17, with Nixon's approval, Kissinger gave him a first draft. Nothing more was heard of the matter until April 22, when Brezhnev produced a Soviet revision, flavored with what Kissinger called "Pravda-like rhetoric," and invited him to "strengthen" it. The national security advisor and two of his staff produced a rewrite overnight. With some amendment, this was accepted by Gromyko and carried over for final approval at the summit. For Kissinger, these Basic Principles were a minor issue: he dismissed them in his memoirs as a form of verbiage to which the Soviets were "much addicted . . . Perhaps there is something in Russian history that leads them to value ritual, solemn declarations, and visible symbols."[88]

For the Kremlin, however, the statement really mattered as a way to enshrine the new equality of superpower relations. It was to cause America considerable embarrassment later on. The point to be emphasized here is that once again, for good or ill, the national security advisor was making up U.S. policy on his own. As we shall see, his cavalier handling of the Basic Principles would come back to haunt him.

Kissinger flew home on April 24. It was a long and taxing day, not just because Washington was eight hours behind Moscow time but also because he was scheduled to meet the president as soon as he arrived at Camp David. Kissinger was returning with, essentially, the outlines of the summit, but he had negotiated most of them on his own initiative having ignored Nixon's instructions to sort out Vietnam before anything else. The crossfire between the two men had continued throughout the trip. Kissinger's repeated insistence that Brezhnev wanted a summit at almost at any cost was dismissed (once again) by the president as "bullshit." Nixon kept instructing Haig to cable back that a Vietnam settlement was far more important than the Soviet summit. "I despair of making position here clear to Washington," Kissinger replied on April 23, adding with remarkable disingenuousness: "So far they have made all the concessions; we have made almost none." He sought to play up the visit's achievements—trumpeting "great progress" which "practically guarantees the success of the Summit"—without feeding Nixon's jealousy. "My role can easily be eliminated. I want the result not the credit." Nixon was not taken in. He was afraid that Kissinger would come home and immediately brief the press, claiming credit for the SALT deal now, rather than waiting for the summit. So he insisted that the national security advisor go straight to Camp David.[89]

Aware that he faced a very difficult interview that evening, Kissinger decided that attack was the best form of defense. He told Haig in advance that he felt "sabotaged and undercut" by the carping cables from Washington and he behaved "very frostily" on arrival at Camp David. The president, said Haldeman, was "all primed to really whack Henry" but, when faced with a real confrontation, he characteristically backed off. (The fact that he had forgotten to zip up his trousers did not enhance the president's gravitas.) What started as a "pretty tense" meeting ended "in good spirits." After reading Kissinger's full report on the visit, Nixon scribbled, "Superb job!" This "might have reflected his real judgment," Kissinger noted later, or "his acceptance of a fait accompli."[90]

DURING KISSINGER'S SECRET VISIT to Moscow the White House advance men were also there, openly headed by Dwight Chapin. "First 24 hours in Moscow have gone very well," he cabled Haldeman on April 20. "They are cooperating and have been told from on high not to play games and get the job done."[91]

One tough issue was the size of the American media presence—an essential part of election-year summitry as far as Nixon was concerned, but abhorrent to the leaders of a closed society. The Americans had wanted to bring three hundred; the Russians con-

sidered this "completely out of reason" and proposed one
hundred.[92] Eventually they split the difference. Other problems
were harder to settle. The Soviets wanted the president's broadcast
on Soviet TV and radio to be videotaped in advance; the Americans demanded it go out live to preclude Soviet censorship. The
Soviets also wanted him to use Soviet planes and automobiles for
internal travel. This was partly on grounds of national pride but, as
the Americans were well aware, also to eavesdrop on the president's
conversations. Chapin's negotiations were not helped by the fact
that Kissinger was having his own discussions on these matters,
thereby getting wires crossed. In the end, after Chapin's return
home, a compromise package resolved these issues. The president
would have his live broadcast and use his car for drives of any distance, but he would fly to Leningrad and Kiev on Soviet planes.[93]

On both the substantive and logistical levels, the summit was
therefore taking shape. But then everything fell apart once more.
On May 1 General Creighton Abrams, the U.S. commander in
Vietnam, bluntly warned that the South Vietnamese army might
have lost the will to fight. Nixon suddenly had to face the possibility of total defeat in Indochina. Next day Kissinger held his secret
meeting in Paris with Le Duc Tho, the chief North Vietnamese negotiator. The first such meeting for eight months, it proved a complete waste of time: "Ducky" simply recited his hard line without
modification or explanation. For the second time in a week
Kissinger had to fly back across the Atlantic after a gruelling day to
face a difficult meeting with the president.

The North Vietnamese evidently thought victory was so close
that they did not need even to pretend to negotiate. Equally disturbing for Nixon and Kissinger, Soviet pressure was irrelevant: either Hanoi felt able to ignore it or Moscow was not exerting any. A
message from Brezhnev, which Nixon received on May 1, strengthened the latter impression: the Soviet leader urged American restraint in Vietnam to expedite negotiations and save their meeting.
Nixon did not want U.S. policy in Vietnam to be held hostage by
the summit. He had to be free to bomb North Vietnam with the
gloves off, but that would make it very difficult for the Moscow

meeting to take place. In which case his political instinct was to call off the summit before the Soviets pulled the plug on him. He convinced himself that Khrushchev's humiliating cancellation of the projected 1960 Moscow summit had damaged the Republicans domestically and helped cost him the election. This was the line he adopted on the evening of May 2 when Kissinger returned from Paris. His national security advisor agreed with him.[94]

Nixon was in an emotional state, as usual when big decisions were pending. The White House tapes record a succession of angry, rambling discussions with his aides over the next few days. But the president began to have second thoughts about the idea of cancelling the summit before Brezhnev did it to him. Possibly this had always been, as Haig suspected, a "devil's advocate position" to draw out Kissinger. But the latter held fast on preemptive cancellation backed by massive escalation. Nixon and Haldeman believed that Kissinger was furious at having bet on Brezhnev to deliver Hanoi, only to be humiliatingly rebuffed. His wish to cancel was "a bravado act basically," the president said. "Because he's failed, I mean because they did not come true as he had hoped they would in both Moscow and Hanoi, he wants to say in effect 'goddamn you, you can't do this to us.'" Exactly what was going on is hard to determine—Nixon always enjoyed Kissinger's moments of discomfiture—but, if he was right, Kissinger's mood would be understandable given the intensity of the previous two weeks. Summitry—and that's what Kissinger was engaged in—is a ferocious physical and emotional experience, during which it is hard to maintain one's equilibrium.[95]

Two other advisors exerted decisive influence on Nixon's thinking at this crucial moment. On the president's instructions Haldeman had commissioned an opinion poll, which showed that 60 percent of Americans wanted the summit to go ahead regardless of the situation in Vietnam. This, the chief of staff argued against Kissinger, showed "the people want hope, not just blood, sweat, and tears all the time." Equally important was John Connally, the Treasury secretary, a savvy Texan politician and one of the few Cabinet members whose opinion Nixon valued. Connally was positive that cancellation would gain Nixon nothing domestically; the administration should take whatever actions it deemed necessary and leave the dilemma to the Soviets. He did not think it a foregone conclusion that they would cancel the summit. This robust line from Haldeman and Connally had a steadying effect. Abruptly reversing his reading of history, Nixon now decided that "it didn't hurt Eisenhower when the Russians cancelled the summit in 1960 . . . Goddammit, the American people don't like to be kicked."[96]

On May 8 the president spoke to the nation, announcing "decisive military action to end the war." America could not stand by "in the face of a massive invasion" by North Vietnam and its "complete intransigence at the conference table." The "only way to stop the killing," he said, was "to keep the weapons of war out of the hands of the international outlaws of North Vietnam." To that end he announced that the entrances to all its ports were being mined. This was Kissinger's main contribution to the debate: he persuaded Nixon that blockade would be better than bombing—a novel twist instead of more of the same.[97]

But in private Kissinger was very depressed at the impasse they were in. Unlike Connally he expected the Soviets to cancel the summit: on May 5 he talked of it as 75 percent likely; on May 8 he spoke of a "better than even chance" of cancellation. He told one of Nixon's speech writers that "we are wrecking in twenty minutes what it has taken three and a half years to build." He was also leaking his feelings to the press. Aware of Kissinger's equivocations, Nixon staged a last-minute spasm of doubt by Haldeman, intended to force Kissinger into a firm statement of support for escalation, which was then captured on the president's secret tapes.[98]

American press reaction to the president's speech was largely critical. The *New York Times* feared for the SALT treaty; the *Washington Post* predicted that the summit was in the balance. Nixon could only watch and wait. "Still no reaction from the Soviets," Haldeman noted in his diary on May 9, "we're kind of sweating that one out." On May 10 Dobrynin called with the inevitable message of protest. The White House was relieved that it was delivered via the back channel, not publicly, and that it was relatively mild in tone. Next

Figure 5-2 Mine and Yours: After Nixon blockaded North Vietnam's ports, British cartoonist Keith Waite speculates on how Brezhnev (seated) and Kosygin (to the left of him) would welcome the U.S. president to Moscow. (*Sunday Mirror,* May 14, 1972, Keith Waite, University of Kent Cartoon Library)

day a courtesy call on Nixon by the Soviet trade minister went ahead as planned, in a warm atmosphere. It became clear that the Soviets intended business as usual. "The general feeling now, even on Henry's part," Haldeman wrote on May 11, "is that the Summit is going to be on rather than off." On the 12th Kissinger and Dobrynin discussed the gifts the two leaders would exchange.[99]

Dobrynin's memoirs later claimed that in Moscow "the summit literally hung in the balance." William Bundy, in his study of Nixon's foreign policy, claims similarly that in "the latter part of the Cold War, there may have been equally important decisions, but none more dramatic."[100] From what we know now about the mood in the Kremlin, it is clear that Kissinger's original instincts during his April visit were correct. Brezhnev wanted a summit at almost any price—on policy grounds such as SALT, trade and the China angle, and politically, because he had staked his new position on advocacy of détente. On May 9, when Gromyko's staff was drafting Moscow's response to Nixon's speech, the line from the Kremlin was "keep it calm, firm, a strong condemnation," but don't talk of possible retaliation. The summit was of overriding importance. "It will go ahead as scheduled. No matter what."[101]

On the other hand, even with the support of Kosygin and Gromyko, Brezhnev had to move carefully. The military, led by Marshal Andrei Grechko, was against the summit; so too was President Podgorny. Many hard-liners, allergic to America at the best of times, could not stomach the idea of welcoming the U.S. president while he was bombing one of the USSR's principal allies. "I will not shake the hand that has been bloodied in Vietnam," declared Pyotr Shelest, the Ukrainian party boss and rival of Brezhnev. However, Hanoi had acted cavalierly, failing to inform Moscow of its plans or to synchronize them with Soviet diplomatic priorities. If the Politburo cancelled the summit it would be allowing Hanoi to dictate Soviet policy: the tail would be wagging the dog. A further consideration was the German treaties, currently being steered through the parliament in Bonn despite ferocious criticism from the opposition Christian Democrats. The final votes on ratification were scheduled for May 17 and 19 and the Soviet leadership did not want anything to derail them.[102]

Even with majority Politburo support on May 10, Brezhnev sought to cover himself. He had received several cables from regional party secretaries, full of anti-American rhetoric, demanding that the summit be cancelled. "I do not want to take all the blame," he told an aide. So he called a special session of the Central Committee on May 19, three days before Nixon was due to arrive. In his speech Brezhnev acknowledged that America was the "main force of imperialism" but insisted that "the more stable and normal our relations with the United States, the less the threat of world nuclear war." Cancelling the summit, he argued, would damage dé-

tente without helping Vietnam. He insisted the "correlation of
forces between the Soviet Union and the United States, both in
terms of international influence and prestige, and in the military
sphere, is now more favourable for us than ever before." Despite
such an authoritative statement from the party leader, Shelest
voiced his opposition openly in the Central Committee. But
Brezhnev's easy victory there enabled him to remove Shelest from
his position as Ukrainian party leader within a week.[103]

The Kremlin followed up with a discreet campaign to educate
party members. Doubters recalled Khrushchev's decisive act of cancellation in 1960, when American aggression was less blatant than
Nixon's against North Vietnam. The official response was that "it
would have been the path of least resistance to give way to emotions and call off the summit." This would have been short-sighted
because in contrast to their Chinese "fishing trip," the Americans
were "giving absolute priority to reaching concrete agreements
with the USSR." Consequently it was "worth Moscow's while to
go ahead with the visit." A cornucopia of deals was outlined, including "great possibilities" in trade and especially grain—a real issue for ordinary Russians after the winter's poor harvest. Critics
were also promised that the president's reception would be "restrained" and there would be "very tough negotiations on Indochina."[104]

On May 14 the president asked why Kissinger and most of the
inner circle, including the CIA, had failed to predict the Soviet attitude correctly. Kissinger admitted that "we had underestimated
how badly they wanted the Summit." But he discerned an "omi-
nous" side as well. "I think they are determined to hit China next
year . . . They want to get their rear cleared and then they are going
to jump China."[105]

On May 18 Nixon, a movie fanatic, watched the classic James
Bond film *From Russia with Love* at Camp David. Two days later Air
Force One took off for Moscow. The mood was buoyant, almost
elated. "This has to be one of the greatest diplomatic coups of all
time!" Kissinger told the president. "Three weeks ago everyone
predicted it would be called off, and today we're on our way."[106]

ALTHOUGH DELIGHTED to be the first U.S. president to visit Moscow, Nixon did not feel the same buzz as in Beijing. He had been to the Soviet capital three times before—as vice president in July 1959 and as a private citizen in April 1965 and March 1967. Each time he had come as a militant Cold Warrior, most famously in 1959 when he sparred with Khrushchev about the merits of their two systems across the set of an American ideal home exhibit. This "kitchen debate" had boosted Nixon's image at home as the man who stood up to Khrushchev, but many in Moscow still regarded him with suspicion.[107]

En route to the summit the American party spent two nights in Salzburg, adjusting to jet lag. During the flights Nixon, with characteristic diligence, pored over his briefing books. But he also spent a good deal of time on the "Rogers problem," pondering with Kissinger and Haldeman how to bring the secretary of state up to speed on the presummit deals and documents without revealing the Dobrynin back channel or repeating the outbursts generated in Beijing. Nixon even joked that he wished Gromyko were "working for us." Kissinger agreed: "He's the sort of Secretary of State you would want"—methodical and hard-working but "never tries to upstage."[108]

Nixon landed at Vnukovo airport in Moscow at 4 p.m. on Monday, May 22. He was met by Podgorny and Kosygin in a restrained reception, calibrated to be diplomatically polite without giving egregious offense to North Vietnam, still being battered by American bombs. The president and his wife were then driven to a suite of ornate fifteenth-century rooms in the Armoury Palace, on the opposite side of the Kremlin complex from Red Square. This was an unusual honor—in 1966 de Gaulle had been given only a night in the Kremlin before being housed elsewhere—and was intended to show how seriously the Soviets were treating their new relationship with America.[109]

Barely had the Nixons settled in when the president was invited to meet Brezhnev. The Soviets liked to throw surprises during summits, to keep opponents off balance. But in this case the summons probably reflected the eagerness of Brezhnev, like Mao in February, to get face to face. Their first encounter took place in the office where Nixon had met Khrushchev in 1959. Brezhnev, a Khrushchev protégé, had stood near his boss during the notorious "kitchen debate" during that visit.[110]

Brezhnev had made a point of inviting Nixon alone, to Kissinger's chagrin. This suited the president, however: after Kissinger's role in setting up the summit he did not want to seem dependent on his advisor. Nixon also wanted to avoid a repetition of Rogers's anger in Beijing, when Kissinger had participated in the historic meeting with Mao. Despite pressure from Rogers the president refused to use an American interpreter, relying instead on the Soviet veteran Viktor Sukhodrev, who had translated for Kennedy and Khrushchev in Vienna. Nixon thought Brezhnev might be more forthcoming that way, but he also wanted to keep his talk confidential from the State Department. The interpreting throughout the summit was consecutive: according to Kissinger, Nixon had once tried simultaneous translation but stopped after five minutes because the system "made him nervous."[111]

Brezhnev began with Vietnam, stressing how difficult it had been for him to hold the summit after recent American actions. Having performed what Nixon sensed was a necessary ritual, the Soviet leader warmed up, talking of the need for a personal relationship between the two of them and of the Soviet people's cordial memories of FDR. Nixon said he had studied the relations between the Big Three during the war and had noted how differences between subordinates were usually overcome by agreement at the top. That, he said, was the "kind of relationship I should like to establish with the General Secretary." Brezhnev replied that he would be only too happy. "If we leave all the decisions to the bureaucrats," Nixon went on, "we will never achieve any progress." Brezhnev laughed heartily and banged the table: "They would simply bury us in paper!" After making common cause against their officials, the two leaders shared their problems about political colleagues. Brezhnev explained that it would be necessary to bring Podgorny and Kosygin to most of the meetings. Indicating that Rogers knew nothing about the draft Basic Principles Nixon asked Brezhnev to help introduce the document into their discussions.[112]

Having bonded as fellow politicians, the two men went on to the state banquet, delayed until 8 p.m. because of their impromptu meeting. All the Soviet leadership was assembled in the Great Hall of the Granovitaya Palace. Pointing to a huge mural of Christ and the apostles, Brezhnev joked: "That was the Politburo of those days." In which case, Nixon responded, "the General Secretary and the Pope have much in common." Brezhnev guffawed and pumped his hand.[113]

Behind the scenes of course the Cold War was still being waged, not least through the pervasive and virtually open bugging. On one occasion a member of Nixon's staff remarked to his secretary that he fancied an apple. Within minutes a Russian maid walked in and placed a bowl of apples on the table. Kissinger and Gromyko even joked about the surveillance. When an American Xerox machine broke down, Kissinger says he asked if he could hold some documents up to a chandelier and get copies made. Gromyko replied that the cameras had been installed by the czars and were adequate for photographing people but not papers. American defenses against the bugging were a little easier to arrange than during Kissinger's April visit. With the U.S. embassy in the loop, it was possible to have secure and speedy communications with Washington. But Nixon could not stand the "babbler"; his important conversations with Kissinger took place in the presidential limo parked outside on the (hopeful) assumption that its bullet-proof windows would offer protection.[114]

At 11 a.m. on Tuesday, May 23 the two sides got down to business with their first plenary session, held in the rose and silver splendor of St. Catherine's Hall. They sat face to face across a long table covered in beige felt, divided by crystal glasses and bottles of mineral water. The atmosphere was cordial, with much banter. Nixon mentioned his reputation as "a very hard-line, cold-war-oriented anti-communist," whereupon Kosygin remarked dryly: "I had heard this sometime back." When the talk got onto trade, the Soviets urged Nixon to import Russian vodka—far better, they said, than the émigré stuff produced in America—and Brezhnev suggested he and Kissinger set up a company. Much of the substance was formulaic: Brezhnev gave a good deal of time to Kosygin and Podgorny; he and Nixon also went over a lot of ground already agreed in the back channel (without admitting as much) to bring most of the U.S. delegation up to speed. The president suggested that the two foreign ministers should concentrate on European security. This was a sop to Rogers, but it implied that Kissinger would handle the rest. Taking his cue Brezhnev suggested that Gromyko should work with Kissinger on SALT and coyly proposed that the two of them also give some thought to basic principles for Soviet-American relations. Kissinger was impressed at his adroit way of getting the draft document onto the agenda.[115]

This first plenary meeting set the tone for the summit. Many of the big issues had been settled in advance and were now being formalized in a politically acceptable way. Nearly every evening there was a ceremony to conclude one of the bilateral agreements for economic and social cooperation. These had all been agreed beforehand but Nixon brought along the relevant departmental head to sign the document and enjoy a carefully modulated media moment. As for Rogers: by involving the secretary of state in discussions on economics as well as Europe, Nixon avoided the anger aroused in Beijing; this ensured that he and Kissinger kept their grip on SALT, Vietnam and the Middle East.

On his side, Brezhnev also controlled the big issues but left Kosygin to manage discussions on his own terrain of economics. Brezhnev was also careful that the record of the summit sent to senior party officials stated that negotiations were conducted by all three of them, naming Nixon as the American spokesman but usually masking his own comments as those of "the Soviet side." Yet his colleagues were not completely tamed. During the first plenary Brezhnev took the line that economic relations were important in their own right and should not be linked, as Nixon wanted, to SALT. Suddenly Podgorny intervened to say that SALT was more important than trade. Brezhnev was not able to dissuade him and Kosygin weighed in as well. This dispute reflected a genuine difference of view within the Kremlin, but the way Podgorny and then Kosygin aired it at the first plenary was probably intended to show that they were not Brezhnev's stooges.[116]

The Soviets' most consummate piece of theater was staged on the evening of Wednesday, May 24. After the 5 p.m. signing ceremony, this time for an agreement on space, Brezhnev propelled Nixon into his Zil and raced off to a state dacha in the woods above the Moscow River. Kissinger and frantic U.S. Secret Service agents followed as best they could. The Soviet leader, in high spirits, then insisted on a hydrofoil ride—again at frenetic speed. By the time they returned to the dacha Kosygin and Podgorny had arrived, whereupon the mood changed abruptly as each of the troika denounced Nixon for his policies in Vietnam. Emotionally, often pounding the table, Brezhnev blasted this "shameful war" of "pure aggression," making several unsubtle allusions to Hitler. Kosygin was "glacially correct," but Kissinger thought that in substance he was the most combative of the three. Podgorny's language was scathing. "You are murderers," he exclaimed at one point. "There is blood of old people, women and children on your hands. When will you end this senseless war?" In response Nixon was firm but cool, addressing specific points without being aroused.

Then suddenly, after three hours, the mood changed again. At 11 p.m., all sweetness and light, the Soviet leaders took their guests upstairs for a four-course dinner, punctuated by incessant toasts. Kosygin seemed particularly keen to drink the Americans under the table, picking on anyone who did not keep emptying his cognac glass. At the end Nixon could hardly find his way out of the room. But Brezhnev insisted that Gromyko was waiting for Kissinger back in Moscow, to discuss SALT. Nixon, by that stage "feeling no pain," did not dissent.[117]

The drinking contest was of course a familiar feature of Soviet summits, as American and British participants had learned to their cost during World War II. And the evening as a whole was reminiscent of the old Stalin one-two-three technique—shifting from niceness to toughness and back again to amiability. After a while, Kissinger notes in his memoirs, he also realized that the diatribes about Vietnam were being delivered for the record, so as to satisfy hard-liners at home and to propitiate Hanoi. As one of Brezhnev's aides has confirmed, the whole performance was staged out at the dacha—"almost in secret" rather than in front of the two delegations—to avoid spoiling the overall atmosphere of the summit.[118]

Kissinger does not, however, draw attention to the concessions he made on Vietnam during the summit. Building on his remarks the month before, he told Gromyko on May 27 that the Americans were ready to withdraw if the war stopped and then "leave the struggle to the Vietnamese . . . All we ask is a degree of time so as to leave Vietnam for Americans in a better perspective." In other words, not Nixon's much-trumpeted "peace with honor" but a face-saving interval. "We will not leave in such a way that a Communist victory is guaranteed. However, we are prepared to leave so that a Communist victory is not excluded."[119]

The big issue was the SALT negotiations: with an eye on public relations, Nixon and Brezhnev had deliberately left some loose ends for themselves to tie up at the summit. The Soviet leader was particularly keen to show off his skills as a negotiator, so he met Nixon and Kissinger for two sessions before and after dinner on May 23. He was accompanied only by Alexandrov-Agentov, who never spoke, and by Sukhodrev the interpreter—Gromyko did not attend. According to Kissinger, in the first meeting Brezhnev firmly adopted a position diametrically opposite to the official Soviet stance on the volume of ICBMs and the size of their silos. In the second he and Nixon haggled about the distance between the two ABM sites, using figures at odds with those already agreed. Brezhnev became very irritated by Kissinger's interventions, eventually declaring that he should "sit still and be quiet and the president and I will finalize all the outstanding points." Kissinger was reduced to passing notes to his boss. One of them read simply: "I get his goat." Next morning Gromyko cancelled a follow-up meeting in order to review the mess and regroup. It was, said Kissinger, the last time the Americans encountered Brezhnev in a SALT negotiation without advisors. The two meetings, in his opinion, "demonstrated that heads of government should not negotiate complex subjects."[120]

But the same criticism can be made of national security advisors As we saw earlier, Kissinger had fumbled the issue of submarine-launched missiles and had to retrieve matters covertly during his visit to Moscow in April. That should have taught him the value of having expert advice on hand, but it didn't. It is likely that the mix-ups about ICBMs and silos took place in his own mind as well as in those of the two leaders.[121] Throughout the Moscow summit the official SALT negotiators were completing their own deliberations in Helsinki. Much of the confusion occurred because deals were being struck separately in two places and the decisive ones, in Moscow, were handled by amateurs. Kissinger himself admitted during an argument about the treaty texts: "I don't have a Russian expert on my staff."[122]

There was of course a simple answer: bring the Soviet and American arms control delegations to Moscow, so they could work in conjunction with the summit. But, as Kissinger put it in his memoirs: "Given Nixon's feelings about who should get the credit, I doubt that he would have agreed if I had proposed it. We shall never know because I did not put forward the idea, not uninfluenced by vanity and the desire to control the final negotiation."[123]

Kissinger's disarming remarks only hint at the truth. He and Nixon had absolutely no intention of bringing Gerard Smith and the U.S. SALT delegation to Moscow, except for a token role in the signing ceremony. Otherwise Smith, to whom they were allergic would steal their thunder. So throughout the summit week, messages went back and forth between Kissinger in the Kremlin and Smith in Helsinki—a process made all the more difficult by the usual political imperative to bypass State Department channels of communication. Smith's resentment was, not surprisingly, intense and he could not conceal it years later in his memoirs. But Semyenov and the Soviet delegation were also kept in Helsinki and given even less information than Smith. Brezhnev, as much a Nixon, wanted to portray himself as a diplomatic virtuoso and take political credit for the eventual agreement.[124]

But the botched discussions between the two leaders on May 2 created some serious problems because of their overriding desire to sign the SALT agreement at the summit. The timetable was now seriously out of joint. Hence the early-hours meeting between Kissinger and Gromyko on Thursday, May 25, after the face-off about Vietnam at the dacha. There were more nocturnal discussions that night when the two sides haggled over the definition of a "heavy" missile and tried to agree on baseline figures for their current submarine fleets. And the Politburo had to spend most of Friday morning in special session reviewing the final proposals. At noon Smith was told to fly to Moscow—with only a few of his delegation—for the signing ceremony at 11 p.m. He, Semyenov and their staffs spent the afternoon turning what had been agreed in Moscow into acceptable treaty language, finishing off the paperwork on the plane. In Moscow, alerted by Rogers, Smith turned up at the presigning press conference. Covering his dismay Kissinger invited the tired, irate and hungry SALT negotiator to explain an agreement he had not negotiated. When the results were predictably less than ideal, Nixon and Haldeman—panicking about the effect on coverage of the treaty back home—had Smith banned from further contact with the media. Kissinger retrieved matters with an impromptu press conference at 1 a.m. in a Moscow nightclub, where he was celebrating his forty-ninth birthday.[125]

Afterward Smith and Raymond Garthoff, the SALT delegation's senior expert on Russia, were scathing about the process—and justly so. Kissinger's one-man-band approach meant that, as with the China summit, mistakes were made. The policy of using Soviet interpreters made it hard for the Americans to clarify key points or to establish a documented record. And the White House determination to keep Smith and his colleagues out of the Moscow limelight not only hampered negotiations but also descended, by the end, to a pathetic pettiness. But Smith and Garthoff's criticisms of the process are undercut by their admission that the summiteers were haggling mostly about "secondary, not central issues" and that the Moscow treaty was the best that could be negotiated at that time.[126] SALT I was only a partial and interim agreement: the real problem, as we shall see, was that the momentum of arms control was not maintained.

At his first meeting with Nixon, Brezhnev said he considered the Basic Principles of Soviet-American relations to be even more important than the SALT treaty, but the president took the opposite view. He paid virtually no attention to the document and Kissinger regarded it as having been "essentially agreed" during his visit in April.[127]

The crucial point was principle number one, which affirmed that both sides would "proceed from the common determination that in the nuclear age there is no alternative to conducting their mutual relations on the basis of peaceful coexistence." Apparently innocuous, this wording had been accepted with little more than stylistic changes by Kissinger in April, yet it was interpreted very differently in Moscow and in Washington. "Peaceful coexistence," an old Leninist term, had been adopted as the centerpiece of Brezhnev's "peace program" at the party congress in 1971. Slotting it into the summit documents was therefore politically important for Brezhnev to use against his hard-line critics. And although it reflected a genuine Soviet desire to avoid nuclear war, it was understood to mean that nuclear parity now made the world safer for class conflict and the ultimate triumph of Marxism-Leninism. As Brezhnev had declared back in 1964, "A situation of peaceful coexistence will enable the success of the liberation struggle and the achievement of the revolutionary task of peoples."[128]

Given this interpretation of peaceful coexistence, veterans of the Ministry of Foreign Affairs' American desk did not believe that Washington would accept the Basic Principles. The new Policy Planning Staff was more optimistic and it was they who pushed the document. After the summit a report for the Central Committee highlighted its importance. Not only had the principle of peaceful coexistence now been placed on a "juridical basis," the fact that Nixon felt obliged to sign a document so advantageous to the Soviet Union demonstrated how far the "correlation of forces" between the two sides had shifted. Above all it showed an underlying equality between the two powers—an enormous boost not only to Brezhnev but also to Soviet prestige and self-esteem.[129]

Little of this seems to have been appreciated by Kissinger. Had he worked with a Soviet specialist from the State Department, his antennae might have been more sensitive, but he only brought in Martin Hillenbrand, the assistant secretary for European affairs, at the end to avoid a repeat of the row with Rogers in Beijing. This is not to say that Kissinger should have refused to sign the Basic Principles: on the contrary, they had value as a token of détente and clearly mattered politically to Brezhnev. But he should have been more careful about the drafting, as British diplomats immediately complained. Unlike the Franco-Soviet declaration, for instance, there was no reference to a freer exchange of people and information.[130] And, as was done with the SALT agreement, Kissinger should have issued a statement setting out the U.S. understanding of key terms such as "peaceful coexistence." Without this the Soviets could and did claim American acceptance of their interpretation, and they also drew conclusions about the relative weakness of the United States in this new era of détente.[131]

At the time, however, these flaws were concealed. By the end of the summit both sides were very pleased with what had been achieved. Complementing SALT and the Basic Principles, they signed six bilateral agreements on environmental protection, public health, the use of outer space, science and technology, avoiding incidents at sea, and establishing a joint economic commission. These promised a new era of cooperation in world affairs. Settlement of the lend-lease debts, concluded after some final bargaining on interest rates, drew a line under a long-standing row and opened the prospect of new credits and trade. The two leaders announced that Brezhnev would visit the United States the following summer, signifying the continuance of the process of summitry.

On a personal level, the visit was consummated with an exchange of gifts. Brezhnev was known for his love of flashy cars, so Nixon presented him with a Cadillac. The Soviets had more of a problem because no one, even American specialists at the Foreign Ministry, could find out if Nixon had any hobbies. "I think what he'd really like," said Gromyko, "is a guarantee to stay in the White House forever." Eventually they decided to give Nixon a hydrofoil, because Brezhnev had one and loved it.[132]

Although never throwing off their suspicions of the impenetrable Nixon, the Soviet leaders did conclude that he could be dealt with on the level of realpolitik. "You can do business with Nixon," Brezhnev declared after the summit. "It is time to prepare for a return visit to the United States." And although he enjoyed needling Kissinger, he also rather liked "smart Henry." So did Gromyko's staff at the Foreign Ministry; they called him *kisa*—pussycat—not because he was a softie but as an affectionate nickname. Their boss was a bit more ambivalent: Gromyko respected Kissinger as a diplomat but envied his cult status.[133]

For his part Nixon was struck by Brezhnev's physical presence and sheer "animal magnetism," reminiscent of LBJ. He "couldn't help thinking that Brezhnev and Johnson would have been quite a pair if they had met at Glassboro." Nixon considered Kosygin to be "all business . . . with very little outward warmth. He is by Communist terms, an aristocrat; while Podgorny is more like a Midwestern senator; and Brezhnev like a big Irish labor boss." Nixon was also struck that all three lacked the inferiority complex about their country that he sensed when in Moscow in 1959. Unlike the self-consciously proletarian Khrushchev, they all dressed well, Brezhnev being a bit of "a fashion plate" with his gold cigarette holder and lighter. Kissinger, lacking experience of fifties Russia and still infatuated with Beijing, found the Soviet leaders cruder and more insecure than Mao and Zhou. But he enjoyed the banter and appreciated little courtesies such as the cake baked for his birthday. These personal touches, though superficial, seemed to presage a more rounded, more human relationship between the two superpowers.[134]

In Moscow the media trumpeted the summit as a great success for Soviet policy, rebuffing the "aggressive efforts of imperialism" while showing "a constructive approach to international problems." This was taken as vindication of Brezhnev's line at the 24th Party Congress that "businesslike cooperation" with the United States was possible. *Pravda* ran a series of letters under the heading "People Support Party's Policy." Although these were obviously orchestrated, one should not be too cynical. In a country imbued with the fear of attack, any progress to reduce tension was likely to be welcome. The specific agreements on trade, played up by the media, also struck a chord. There was a genuine sense of optimism that summitry could literally deliver the goods to the people.[135]

Although most of the groundwork had been done by Kissinger and Gromyko in April and Brezhnev had not shown himself exactly an accomplished negotiator when let loose on SALT, it was he who gained the political credit. This dramatic success helped keep him in power for another decade. Unlike Khrushchev there would be no attempt to remove Brezhnev, despite increasingly failing powers.

Nixon traveled home via Iran and Poland, arriving back in Washington on the evening of Thursday, June 1. For weeks White House aides had debated how best to present his trip to the American people. Should he give a televised speech on landing at Andrews Air Force Base, as had happened after the China summit? Or would a grand reception on the South Lawn of the White House be more effective? The latter, however, ran into security objections, given all the anti-Vietnam demonstrators in Washington. It was Haldeman who suggested that the president should go straight to the Capitol to address a joint session of Congress, thereby ensuring symbolism and security. Chapin was enthusiastic: "Good drama, good TV," and the best time for television and news magazines. But Ehrlichman thought the Thursday night idea "too stagey"; other aides feared that Congress would feel exploited, especially in an election year. The debate went on until May 31 when Nixon plumped decisively for Haldeman's view.[136]

On arrival at Andrews the president flew immediately by helicopter to the Capitol. Although exhausted by his sixteen-thousand-mile, thirteen-day odyssey, Nixon pulled out the stops in a bid to shape the verdicts of the public and of posterity. Avoiding Chamberlain's language after Munich, he said he did not bring back from Moscow "the promise of instant peace"; he spoke instead of "the beginning of a process that can lead to a lasting peace." Unlike previous Cold War summits that had produced only "a brief euphoric mood," he said that Moscow had been "a working summit" in-

tended to establish a "solid record of progress on solving the difficult issues." The president listed the various agreements signed, of
which the "most important" were the arms accords. "Three-fifths
of all the people alive in the world today have spent their whole
lifetimes under the shadow of a nuclear war which could be
touched off by the arms race among the great powers. Last Friday
in Moscow we witnessed the beginning of the end of that era
which begun in 1945." If the country seized this "unparalleled opportunity" for peace, he ended with a Churchillian flourish, "the
historians of some future age will write of the year 1972, not that
this was the year that America went up to the summit and then
down to the depths of the valley again, but that this was the year
when America helped to lead the world up out of the lowlands of
constant war, and onto the high plateau of lasting peace."[137]

Nixon was delighted with the reaction to the summit, even better than the response after his visit to Beijing. He felt that Moscow
went to "the heart of what people are worried about"—world
peace—and therefore created "a greater reaction." On a report
about opinion among America's allies, he wrote "good" against a
comment that "the Moscow meeting was not seen as a contest
with victors and losers but as an understanding from which both
sides gained."[138]

In America itself even habitual critics such as the *New York Times*
and the *Washington Post* paid tribute. Veteran columnist James Reston lauded Nixon's "efforts to reach an accommodation with the
communist world" as "the bravest diplomatic initiative of the postwar generation." *Time* admitted that the Moscow summit had been
"stage-managed" but said it was likely to "change world diplomacy." And the defense intellectual Zbigniew Brzezinski argued
that the Soviet-American agreements, "while not terminating the
rivalry, do involve a significant codification of 'the rules of the
game.'" Once again, however, Nixon had to share the credit with
Kissinger, a man who in the words of the *Chicago Sun-Times* was no
longer merely "a phenomenon" but "a legend." As "a reputed
ladies' man" he had "given aid and comfort to every squat, owl-
eyed, overweight and middle-aged bachelor in the land."[139]

For the Moscow meetings, like those in Beijing, Kissinger had done the indispensable groundwork in secret beforehand. Nevertheless only a ruthless right-winger like Nixon could have sold the two summits to the Republican party. And he was right to say that Moscow was the most productive summit of the Cold War to date, promising a more stable era of Soviet-American relations after the crises of the past. The ABM Treaty, if honored, was particularly important: it removed the temptation for either side to develop defensive systems. Such systems would jeopardize the balance of mutually assured destruction on which deterrence was based. The SALT I freeze on offensive missile launchers was much less satisfactory, with many loopholes and a distinct tilt in favor of the Soviets, but the United States still retained more than a two-to-one advantage in total warheads.[140]

SALT I was intended as the platform for a more substantial agreement that would actually reduce nuclear arsenals. These negotiations were to start in the autumn and Nixon wanted to sign a SALT II agreement when Brezhnev visited America in 1973. Vietnam of course was still unresolved, but Kissinger hoped that the inducements offered behind the scenes would have an effect. The May crisis certainly proved that the Soviets would not allow North Vietnam to hold their diplomacy at ransom. The year 1972 did indeed mark a moment of détente in the Cold War. Despite the election-year hyperbole, the president was justified in seeing it as a chance for more substantial progress during his second term.

On Friday, June 16, Nixon flew off to the Bahamas. He took with him *Triumph and Tragedy*, the last volume of Churchill's memoirs, because he wanted to ponder the British war leader's analysis of Yalta. "What we must not do is to repeat history," Nixon noted. "Yalta led to an improvement of relations, but then to a sharp deterioration thereafter. Reading about Yalta gives one great pause because it was not what was agreed at Yalta, but the failure of the Soviets to keep the agreement, which led to all the troubles after that time." For Nixon, as he reflected that weekend, the Moscow summit was indeed the beginning of a process; he was already thinking ahead to Brezhnev's return visit to America the following summer.

Beyond that he anticipated annual summits and regular interaction across the top levels of both governments.[141]

That night as the president slept, police in Washington arrested five men attempting a break-in at the offices of the Democratic National Committee.

IT IS UNLIKELY that Nixon knew about Watergate before the arrests. But thereafter he participated actively and illegally in the cover-up—suppressing evidence, funneling hush money to the accused and using federal agencies to obstruct the investigation. Moreover the original break-in stemmed directly from the ethos of the Nixon White House. A prime target of the president's paranoia was Lawrence O'Brien, chairman of the Democratic National Committee, whom he feared had got hold of some serious dirt about his financial dealings. Nixon's constant injunctions to find out prompted his underlings—rather like the story of King Henry II and Thomas Becket—to plant bugs in O'Brien's Watergate office.[142]

Watergate did not inflict immediate damage on the Nixon presidency. Although the burglars were financed by Nixon's reelection campaign, the White House successfully managed to insulate itself during the summer. While the Democrats feuded, "every effort was made to create an economic boom for the 1972 election," Defense Secretary Melvyn Laird recalled. His department did its bit by ordering a two-year supply of toilet paper.[143]

In November Nixon duly won his second term, carrying every state except Massachusetts and the District of Columbia. And after another ferocious bombing campaign over Christmas, North Vietnam finally agreed to a ceasefire, allowing Nixon the political cover to extricate U.S. troops. It was, the president kept insisting in another Chamberlainesque phrase, "peace with honor."[144]

During 1973, however, Watergate became all-consuming news, thanks to the federal court case and televised Senate committee hearings. To save their own skins, lower-level operatives started to implicate their superiors. In April, as the trail came ever closer to the Oval Office, Nixon forced Haldeman and Ehrlichman, two of his closest aides, to resign. And in July a White House staffer confirmed that Nixon had taped most of his private conversations, prompting demands that he release the evidence. Although Nixon fought a stubborn rearguard action for another year, from that point his presidency was doomed.

So too was his foreign policy. In June 1973 Brezhnev spent a week in the United States visiting Camp David, Washington, and Nixon's California home in San Clemente. The two leaders got on well again and Brezhnev, a fan of John Wayne, loved playing with Nixon's gift of a six-shooter and holster. At the level of substance, the summit continued the détente process and produced a few more concrete agreements in areas such as aviation, agriculture and the peaceful use of atomic energy. But there was nothing on the scale of the ABM Treaty; moreover no real progress was made on a full-scale arms control agreement—SALT II. Above all a week's exposure to the American media demonstrated to the Soviets that Nixon was now under massive political pressure over Watergate. So Brezhnev started to distance himself on a personal level: there was no point in linking his prestige to that of a failing president. And, at a time when the Soviet leader was consolidating Moscow's commitment to détente—in April he removed Shelest, his main critic, from the Politburo and elevated allies such as Gromyko to full membership—it seemed that détente was being undermined in Washington, as critics exploited the president's growing weakness. On arms control the Pentagon blocked further negotiations, angry at the inequality of the SALT I interim freeze. And Senator Henry Jackson, a noted hawk, allied with Jewish leaders and human rights groups to tie progress on trade relations to Soviet concessions on Jewish emigration.[145]

In foreign policy the main beneficiary of Watergate was Kissinger. *Time* magazine had made him and Nixon joint Men of the Year for 1972, much to the president's fury. Even Kissinger begged the editors not to do it. If Watergate had not exploded, Kissinger might well have been a casualty of Nixon's jealousy in the second term. Instead, with key staffers being forced out in the deepening political crisis, "Super K" became essential to help polish the administration's tarnished image; in September 1973 Nixon appointed him secretary of state in succession to William Rogers. Since Kissinger would never have tolerated a national security advisor doing to him what he had done to Rogers, Nixon kept him on in that role as well, making Kissinger the only person to hold both jobs simultaneously. But the president's lack of enthusiasm was transparent: announcing the news to the press, he lavished hypocritical praise on Rogers and then said simply that Kissinger's qualifications were "well known by all of you." At the swearing-in ceremony Nixon stated pointedly that success in any area, "particularly foreign policy," did not come "simply from the activities of one person." In fact, by appointing Kissinger the president acknowledged that he had lost the battle. For the rest of the second term Nixon's foreign policy was essentially Kissinger's.[146]

But, given the deepening political crisis, that policy was largely one of damage limitation. The White House prepared for another Soviet summit, but Nixon, politically and physically on his last legs, had little to offer Brezhnev. His defense secretary, James Schlesinger, was now openly defiant on SALT. A week before the summit Nixon warned in an NSC meeting that Brezhnev would reject the Pentagon's hard-line proposals. "But, Mr. President," Schlesinger sneered, "everyone knows how impressed Khrushchev was with your forensic ability in the kitchen debate. I'm sure that if you applied your skills to it you could get them to accept this proposal."[147]

Nixon's final Soviet summit in June 1974 was therefore a complete anticlimax. In his public remarks the president kept stressing how much détente depended on his personal relations with Brezhnev. The Soviets omitted such comments from the official record and Brezhnev, for his part, pointedly emphasized the Soviet Union's relationship with Congress and the people of the United States. To the very end the public relations aspect of summitry obsessed Nixon. Brezhnev wanted some of their meetings to take place in Yalta: he had a dacha there and it would be the equivalent of his 1973 visit to San Clemente. But Nixon had made his name blasting Roosevelt for selling out Eastern Europe to Stalin at Yalta. On this matter at least the Soviets couldn't rewrite history, so they decided to emend the cartography. Since the formal meetings took place at the Oreanda Hotel on the seafront in Yalta, the area was re-named the "town of Oreanda," with some freshly painted signposts to prove the point. Officially 1974 was known as the Moscow-Oreanda Summit.[148]

It was all a far cry from those heady days of June 1972 when Nixon came back from Moscow predicting annual summits and a steady strengthening of détente. Instead of reaching the "high plateau" of "lasting peace" he had descended from the summit into the "valley" of despair. In his memoirs Nixon asserted that Water-gate was not a serious factor in what happened, blaming "American domestic political fluctuations, most of which had preceded Water-gate." Kissinger, in contrast, admitted that "Nixon's capacity to lead collapsed as a result of Watergate." Otherwise he "might have been able to translate the very tangible foreign policy successes of his first term into permanent operating principles." This was closer to the truth, but in Kissinger's account Watergate signified a political problem on the margins of foreign policy. In fact the ruthless, para-noid style of government that produced Watergate was integral to Nixon and Kissinger's conduct of diplomacy.[149]

In his memoirs—volumes that match Churchill's for their supple reshaping of history—Kissinger defended his personal, secret diplo-macy as a necessary response to the leaks, feuding or inertia of Washington. The way, for instance, that he bypassed the U.S. ambas-sador when visiting Moscow in April 1972 was attributed to "our strange system of government"; his persistent sidelining of Gerard Smith in the SALT talks was blamed on "the administrative prac-tices of the Nixon Administration." It is "difficult," he argued, "for a President to make new departures through the 'system.'"[150]

There is some justification for this line. Without the back chan-nel Nixon would probably not have got to Beijing and Moscow—the domestic opposition would probably have been too strong. But Kissinger pushed his argument too far. These "administrative prac-tices," as he called them dismissively, were rooted in personality as well as pragmatism—and Kissinger's personality as much as Nixon's. For instance, the taping system that ultimately brought down the president was a practice started by Kissinger. It was not unusual for important phone conversations to be recorded—Johnson and Rusk had done so—but Kissinger did it systematically, using professional transcribers to generate copy overnight. Nixon began recording his own phone calls and conversations in February 1971, partly with an eye to his memoirs but also to cover himself against Kissinger, who was prone to say one thing—obsequiously—to the president while taking a more caustic line with reporters. Kissinger did not learn about the president's tapes until 1973, when he reacted with outrage, apparently oblivious to the irony of the situation.[151]

The back channel procedures were a reflection of this endemic paranoia as much as a way to conduct a vigorous foreign policy under the constraints imposed by the American political system. This mistrust also undermined the agreements thereby reached. Having marginalized the State Department, Kissinger could not expect much support from its embittered staff. Becoming secretary of state did help, but excluding the Pentagon from the serious negotiation of SALT I almost guaranteed its hard-line attitude to SALT II, and even Kissinger couldn't take on the post of defense secretary as well. Given Nixon's paranoia, senior members of Congress, even from his own party, were also excluded from meaningful consultation. This made it harder to win their support for the agreements reached at the summit. Yet "the acid test of a policy," as Kissinger himself argued in his study of Metternich and Castlereagh, "is the ability to obtain domestic support."[152]

In the end Nixon and Kissinger each remained a "Lone Ranger," maneuvering all the while to relegate the other to the role of Tonto.[153] Their methods may have helped to win major diplomatic successes in the short term, but they also undermined long-term support for administration policies—and ultimately for the administration itself. The way Nixon got to the summit virtually ensured that he would not stay there.[154]

The ultimate beneficiary of Nixon's summitry was Leonid Brezhnev. The Soviet party leader had staked his bid for outright leadership on a policy of peaceful coexistence with the United

States. That made sense for economic and defense reasons, not to mention the looming threat from China. In the spring of 1972 Brezhnev let nothing, not even the American mining of North Vietnam, get in the way of a summit. The arms control agreements signed in Moscow in May silenced his critics and apparently confirmed the Soviet Union's equality with the United States. The statement of Basic Principles also suggested that the Americans were accepting détente on Soviet terms.

Had Nixon remained potent in the second term he might have held the Kremlin to account, as he believed had not been done after Yalta. Instead his crumbling presidency gave the Soviets and their allies an increasingly free hand to act as they pleased. By the middle of 1975 communist forces controlled all of Indochina. Over the next few years the Soviets extended their influence in eastern and southern Africa, in ways that fitted their understanding of détente—a world made safe for class struggle—but also undermined support for the process in the United States. In 1976 Gerald Ford, Nixon's successor, banned the word "détente" from the official diplomatic lexicon.[155]

Nixon's failure, in other words, relegated not merely summitry but diplomacy to the back burner. Dialogue with Moscow atrophied. And after the Brezhnev Politburo sent troops into Afghanistan at the end of 1979, Soviet-American relations degenerated into what was dubbed a "new cold war."

One of the most outspoken Republican critics of détente as "a one-way street" was Ronald Reagan. In 1976 he denounced Kissinger for a policy of "weakness and retreat," for behaving as if America's day was done and that it was now "the day of the Soviet Union."[156] And during the early years of his presidency, in 1981–3, superpower relations were as tense as in the days of Kennedy and Khrushchev. Yet as we shall see, rather like Churchill—that trenchant critic of Chamberlain—Reagan could not keep away from summitry when he eventually had his chance.

6

CAMP DAVID 1978

Begin, Carter and Sadat

R ONALD REAGAN HOPED to be the Republican candidate in
the election of 1976. Instead he had to wait on the sidelines as
Gerald Ford tried and failed to win a popular mandate for his care-
taker presidency. The winner in November 1976 was the Democratic outsider, Jimmy Carter. His passion for world peace would
lead him into one of the most risky summits of the twentieth century at Camp David in September 1978. Carter brought together
the key players in the Arab-Israeli conflict—Menachem Begin of
Israel and Anwar Sadat of Egypt—investing the full measure of
America's prestige and influence in a bid for Middle East peace.
Camp David was probably the best-prepared American summit of
the twentieth century. Yet its outcome was ultimately determined
not by Carter but by Begin's consummate skill as a negotiator.

CAMP DAVID WAS AN ATTEMPT to settle thirty years of bitter conflict. At issue was the state of Israel, founded in 1948 when the
British evacuated Palestine and left its inhabitants to fight for supremacy. Since 1919 Britain had held the area as a mandate from
the League of Nations, in preparation for eventual independence.
The mandate's main condition was that the British government
honor its wartime promise, under the Balfour Declaration of 1917,

to promote "the establishment in Palestine of a national home for the Jewish people" without prejudice to "the civil and religious rights of the existing non-Jewish communities."[1]

But the two parts of this pledge proved incompatible: migration from Nazi Germany in the 1930s pushed up the Jewish population to nearly a third of the total and provoked a backlash from the Arabs. After 1945 British efforts to restrict the influx of Holocaust survivors sparked a Jewish revolt and a brutal spiral of terror and counterterror. When the British withdrew in May 1948 the Jewish settlers, led by David Ben-Gurion, triumphed in the ensuing war with the Palestinians and neighboring Arab states. Their new state of Israel was helped enormously by rapid diplomatic recognition from the Americans—because of the strong Jewish lobby and the deep sympathy for Jews after the Holocaust—and by the Soviets, out of a desire to weaken Britain, still the predominant Western power in the Middle East. Soviet help was short-lived, but its weapons were a crucial factor in Israel's victory over the Arabs, which left it with 80 percent of the old Palestine mandate (Jordan held most of the rest).

The first Arab-Israeli war of 1948–9 founded the state of Israel but also created its endemic insecurity. More than six hundred thousand Palestinians fled or were expelled by Israeli forces; they ended up in squalid refugee camps in Jordan and the coastal Gaza Strip. The latter, only twenty-eight by five miles, contained some two hundred thousand refugees and became the seedbed for future Palestinian terrorist organizations. Moreover Israel's victory in 1948 created permanent and embittered enemies in the neighboring Arab states, Egypt, Jordan and Syria, who rejected Israel's right to exist. The tiny new country—only nine miles wide at its narrowest point—was in a permanent state of siege. It was threatened by renewed war and harassed by guerrilla raids from Egypt, led by Gamal Abdel Nasser. In the autumn of 1956 Ben-Gurion entered into a secret alliance with Britain and France, anxious to topple Nasser who had now taken over the Suez Canal. Their invasion of Egypt failed, making Nasser a superstar in the developing world,

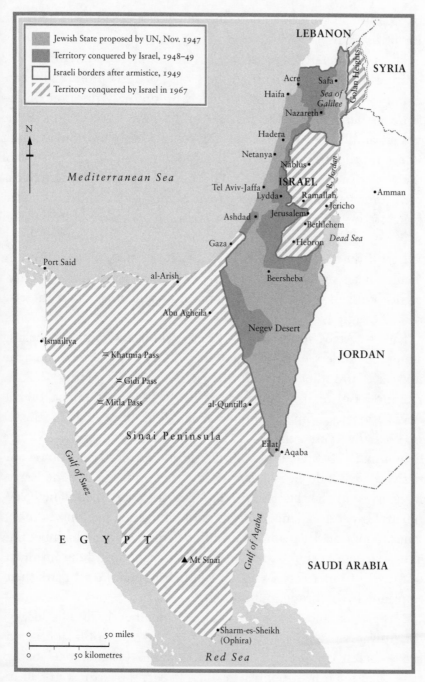

Map 6-1 Israel before and after the 1967 War.

but the Israelis were able to destroy the guerrilla bases and quiet the Egyptian army.

For a decade after 1956 Israel developed its economy in relative peace. But Nasser's pressure in the spring of 1967 prompted a pre-emptive Israeli attack, masterminded by the new minister of defense, General Moshe Dayan, hero of the 1956 war. On June 5 the Israelis annihilated most of the Egyptian, Syrian and Jordanian air forces on the ground, and went on to drive the Egyptians out of the vast Sinai Peninsula right up to the Suez Canal. They also occupied Jordanian territory west of the River Jordan and took complete control of the holy city of Jerusalem, whose eastern section had been held by the Jordanians since 1948. Finally they drove Syria off the Golan Heights, a vital strategic plateau commanding Galilee. The Six-Day War of June 1967 won Israel some twenty-eight thousand square miles of territory, tripling its area at the cost of 759 lives.

But the Arabs continued a war of attrition by raids and shelling along the borders. And, instead of negotiating away some of the land for peace, as outlined in UN Security Council Resolution 242, Israel hung on to all its gains and began building settlements on the new territories, home to a million Arabs. This third Arab–Israeli war in 1967 thus raised the stakes dramatically. The superpowers were drawn in: the Soviets broke off diplomatic relations with Israel and threw their weight behind Syria and Egypt. America became Israel's main arms supplier but also tried to mediate a settlement. The Palestinians now lost patience with the frontline states, flocking in thousands to join the Palestinian Liberation Organization, which became almost a state within a state in Jordan. When King Hussein drove out the PLO in 1971, it relocated in Lebanon and used bases there to plague Israel throughout the 1970s.

Nasser, sick and shattered, died in September 1970. His successor, Anwar Sadat, inherited a country on the brink of financial collapse—bereft of vital revenue from the Suez Canal yet unable to raise taxes for fear of popular revolt. His secret overtures in February 1973 for a diplomatic solution were rejected by Henry Kissinger and the Israelis. In April Sadat warned that "everything in

this country is now being mobilized for the resumption of the battle—which is now inevitable," but Kissinger dismissed Sadat as a
"bombastic clown."[2] Frustrated, the Egyptian leader plotted a limited war for diplomatic ends, aiming to recover the Suez Canal and
drag the superpowers into the peace process.

After three victories, especially the stunning triumph of 1967, Israel had become complacent. One joke envisaged this exchange
between Defense Minister Dayan and General David Elazar, his
chief of staff:

DAYAN: There's nothing to do.
ELAZAR: How about invading another Arab country?
DAYAN: What would we do in the afternoon?[3]

But Israelis suffered a rude awakening on October 6, 1973. It was
Yom Kippur, the Day of Atonement, their most solemn festival of
the year. That afternoon Syrian tanks drove the Israelis off the
Golan Heights, while the Egyptians—in a superbly planned and
executed operation—forced their way across the Suez Canal and
drove several miles into Sinai. In Cairo crowds numbering hundreds of thousands acclaimed Sadat as "Hero of the Crossing."

Within days, however, the surprised Israelis regrouped, regaining
the Golan Heights and thrusting north toward Damascus. In
Sinai—after the biggest armored battle since Kursk in 1943, which
involved some two thousand tanks—the daring Israeli general Ariel
Sharon exploited a gap in the Egyptian lines, established a bridge-
head across the Canal and encircled the whole Egyptian Third
Army. Meanwhile the superpowers were sucked even deeper into
the Middle East. The Soviets mounted a major airlift to supply
Egypt and Syria; the Americans did the same for Israel.

On the night of October 24–25 Kissinger placed U.S. forces
worldwide on Defense Condition Three, the highest state of nuclear alert short of imminent attack. How far he was motivated by
fear of Soviet military intervention, and how far by the desire to assert America's authority (and his own) at a time when Nixon was
sinking in the morass of Watergate remain in dispute. What matters

here is that the Middle Eastern conflict had become a global issue. Although the Americans engineered a cease-fire, the crisis deepened as Arab oil producers embarked on economic warfare against friends of Israel—quadrupling prices in three months and imposing a total ban on oil exports to the United States.

Although Sadat lost the war tactically, he secured his strategic aim: the Americans were being drawn into active regional diplomacy because the nuclear face-off and the oil crisis underlined the need for a Middle Eastern settlement. During 1974–5 Kissinger, after intense shuttle diplomacy, converted the fragile cease-fires into firm disengagement agreements in Sinai and the Golan. In return the Arabs lifted their oil embargo.[4] But disengagement was not peace. That became Jimmy Carter's priority when he took office in January 1977.

A FORMER GOVERNOR of Georgia, Carter was America's first president from the Deep South since before the Civil War. He had deliberately run as a critic of the Washington establishment, which helped him in an era of intense disillusion about the Republicans and Watergate. On the other hand, his status as an outsider made it hard to get things done against the suspicions of Congress and the bureaucracy. The so-called Georgia Mafia on whom he relied had few ties with the movers and shakers of Washington. There was also a good deal of patronizing back-chat: when his wife asked the White House staff if they could prepare Southern dishes that the family enjoyed, she was told, "Yes, Ma'am, we've been fixing that kind of food for the servants for a long time."[5]

Carter was an idealist who advocated a more ethical foreign policy in the wake of Vietnam, with human rights high on his diplomatic agenda. He also evinced a special interest in the Middle East. A devout Southern Baptist steeped in the Bible, he viewed the Holy Land as almost his own land. A family visit to Israel in May 1973 was therefore a memorable experience that opened his eyes to the smallness and fragility of the Jewish state. More than a decade later he still recalled his first sight of the River Jordan:

All our lives we had read about this river, studied and sung about it, so we visualized a mighty current with almost magical qualities. We were amazed. In fact, it was not as large as many of the tributary creeks that flow into the small rivers of Georgia.[6]

This tour of Israel left Carter with a keen sympathy for the Zionist cause and deep admiration for Israeli democracy. By contrast he had met only one Arab before his presidency, and that was casually at a Florida racetrack. Yet, unlike many American friends of Israel, he was deeply moved by the Palestinians' predicament, seeing in them a Middle Eastern analogue to the American blacks of the civil rights movement. The Cold War and the oil crisis added practical incentives but, at root, Carter's commitment in the Middle East stemmed from his faith and his personality. Trained as a naval engineer, he was a doer who liked to tackle difficult problems, confident that his capacity for hard work and attention to detail would achieve results. He was convinced that he had to make progress on the Middle East in his first year, before the pressures of midterm elections in 1978 and a second-term campaign in 1980 began to bite.[7]

The president had a distinguished foreign policy team. Cyrus Vance was his secretary of state, a lawyer with a long-standing interest in international affairs who had served in the Johnson administration. Vance was a patient negotiator with an eye for essential detail, widely respected for his "principled pragmatism." Zbigniew Brzezinski, the new national security advisor, was in contrast a man for big, bold ideas. An immigrant from Poland, he was a professor of international politics with a gift for synthesis and conceptualization. He was also a political manipulator and often became frustrated with Vance's legalistic approach to problems. Over policy toward the Soviet Union, relations between the two men would become increasingly strained. But on the Middle East they agreed about the need for a comprehensive settlement that took seriously the Palestinian issue. And, in contrast to the Nixon administration, their two staffs worked closely together.[8]

By the time of Carter's inauguration, Anwar Sadat had become an international figure. He had been raised in a village north of

Cairo; his mother was Sudanese, hence his dark skin. From an early age he was passionately determined to overthrow British rule, and his eclectic group of nationalist heroes included Gandhi and even Hitler. As an army officer in 1942 he was involved in an inept conspiracy to turn the Egyptian forces over to Rommel. This resulted in his first spell in prison; another followed in 1948 after complicity in terrorist activities. He then tried various careers in journalism and business, even advertising himself in a Cairo magazine: "I go in for comic acting, and am ready to play any role in the theatre or cinema." Drawn back into politics in the 1952 Free Officers coup, he became Nasser's loyal lieutenant, earning himself the derisory nickname "Major Yes Yes" (*Bikbashi Sah*). The "self-deprecating, almost comical part" he played did reflect his subservience to Nasser, but it was also a deliberate role. Once he succeeded to the presidency in 1970, Sadat showed that his theatrical range included high melodrama as well as low comedy. The 1973 war was a huge gamble, but it succeeded in pulling America seriously into the peace process. Sadat recognized that only the United States had the capacity to put pressure on Israel, because of its massive economic aid.[9]

Extricating himself from the Soviet orbit, Sadat secured massive Western loans to cover the spiralling costs of defense and welfare: over half his 1975 budget was funded by borrowing. But aid came at a price: when the International Monetary Fund demanded spending cuts as a quid pro quo, the government was forced to cut subsidies on basic foodstuffs. On January 18, 1977, Cairo awoke to newspaper headlines announcing that the price of bread had doubled. "Bread" is known as *aish* in Egypt, the Arabic word for "life." Hundreds died in the riots that followed. The popular mood was now very different from the adulation of Sadat back in October 1973. *Ya Batl al-Ubuur, Feen al-Futuur*, ran one rhyming chant— "Oh Hero of the Crossing, Where Is Our Breakfast?"[10]

The riots coincided almost exactly with Carter's inauguration on January 20, 1977. When the two men met in Washington on April 4 and 5—Carter's first encounter with an Arab leader—Sadat must have seemed somewhat tarnished. The Egyptian for his part was uneasy about Carter, who had made some strongly pro-Israel remarks during the election campaign.[11] But they hit it off personally, in marked contrast to Carter's frigid meeting with Israeli premier Yitzhak Rabin the previous month. Since the Carter-Sadat relationship is an essential part of this story and it became romanticized after the Egyptian leader's assassination in 1981, it is worth spending a moment on its chemistry.

"There was an easy and natural friendship between us from the first moment," Carter wrote in his 1982 memoirs. "It soon became apparent that he was charming and frank, and also a very strong and courageous leader . . . extraordinarily inclined toward boldness." Sadat, shortly before he died, wrote that "Jimmy Carter is my very best friend on earth." Tasheen Basheer, longtime spokesman for Sadat, recalled in 1995 that his boss warmed to three things about Carter: "First, that he was a small-town farmer type. Sadat did not like slick city boys. Second, that he was a religious man of principle. He has a spiritual core uncontaminated by politics. Third, he was a military man. So was Sadat."[12]

Undoubtedly there were elements of mutual distortion here. Carter, true to the log-cabin vocabulary of American politics, was prone to talk himself up as a hard-working peanut farmer, even though his father ran a profitable supply business and had enough political clout to secure Jimmy a place at the U.S. Naval Academy. Sadat, similarly, loved to recall that he was "peasant-born," even though his father was a local civil servant and his taste for good living and elegant clothes (in marked contrast with Nasser) won him inclusion in a 1977 list of the world's ten best-dressed men. He was also prone to emotional displays of amity: kissing Henry Kissinger in January 1974 he declared: "You are not only my friend, you are my brother."[13]

So Carter and Sadat each saw in the other what he wanted to see. That said, their relationship was from the start both close and potent. At that first meeting, in April 1977, Sadat showed two traits that proved to be durable features of his diplomacy. First, he wanted quick results and was impatient with details. Second, he was willing to reveal at least part of his negotiating hand to Carter, urging the president to extract comparable concessions from Israel. Although the Americans did not fully grasp this, Sadat seems to have regarded the best road to peace to be through a joint ambush of the Israelis.[14]

But history had made any Israeli politician wary of ambushes, even more so after the Israeli elections of May 17, 1977. To the surprise of most foreign observers, the Labour Party—which had ruled the country since independence in 1948—was ousted by the *Likud* (Unity) center-right alliance led by Menachem Begin. After the coalition-building that was obligatory in Israel's fragmented politics, Begin was able to form a government with a decent working majority in the Knesset, Israel's parliament.

This political transition from Labour to Likud marked deeper shifts in Israeli society. Begin's core supporters were Sephardic Jews from the Mediterranean and the Middle East, who had felt like second-class citizens in a state created and run by European Zionists. Even more important, Begin was outspokenly committed to holding on to all of Israel's gains from the 1967 war—what he called the biblical heritage of Judaea and Samaria. In short, he rejected the principle of trading "land for peace" on which both UN Security Council Resolution 242 and Carter's diplomacy were based.

Begin and Sadat had one thing in common—in earlier life they had both been terrorists against the British—but their paths to power were very different. Begin was a Polish Jew born in 1913 in Brest-Litovsk, then on the borderlands of the Czarist Empire. He took a law degree at Warsaw University but never practiced, captivated instead by the person and ideals of Vladimir Jabotinsky, founder of the Zionist Revisionist Movement. Breaking with moderate Zionists, Jabotinsky wanted an immediate Jewish state— one covering the whole of the Palestine Mandate and guarded by "a wall of bayonets" against the Arabs. Begin threw himself into organizing the Revisionist's militaristic youth movement in Poland. But all this came to an end with World War II, a searing experience for Begin—his father, mother, brother and two nephews were all victims of Hitler's Final Solution. A iron resolve that the Jewish people never again suffer in this way animated his subsequent career. He would regularly refer to Munich in 1938 as evidence of what happened to a small country if it looked to others for security, rather than relying on its own strength.[15]

Begin's war experience pointed in the same direction. Captured by Stalin's secret police in September 1940, he survived nine months in an NKVD prison, despite regular sleep deprivation and relentless interrogation. Determined to make it through, he treated the whole experience as a deadly game of chess in which he tried to outwit his captors, maintaining his self-belief by refusing to admit the errors of Zionism. Night after night he argued back, stubbornly and pedantically. Not only Begin's survival instinct but also his negotiating style were honed in those months in Vilna prison. "I never want to see you again," his interrogator yelled at the end of their war of verbal attrition.[16]

Survival did not mean freedom. Shipped off to one of Stalin's camps, Begin endured months of back-breaking work before suddenly being released under an agreement between Stalin and the Polish government in London. Begin joined the Polish army, got to Palestine and in 1943 took command of the Irgun Zvai' Le'umi—the Revisionists' military wing in the battle against the British authorities.

His most notorious operation was blowing up the King David Hotel in Jerusalem, headquarters of the British administration, in July 1946. Ninety-one people were killed, two-thirds of them Arabs and Jews. Begin sanctioned a tit-for-tat policy when the British executed or whipped his men. This included hanging two British sergeants and booby-trapping their bodies, an episode that provoked an international outcry. Throughout his life Begin was unrepentant about Irgun's campaigns, but the British regarded him as simply a terrorist. David Ben-Gurion, Israel's founding father, even likened him to Hitler, as the leader of a quasi-fascist movement that imperilled Israel's fledgling democracy.[17]

After independence Begin entered mainstream politics, but his Herut (Freedom) Party remained on the margins. Losing eight elections in succession over nearly three decades, he seemed like a natural man of opposition—jealous of his principles, relishing a fight, almost paranoid in his animosities. It was his followers who pushed him into cross-party deals and widened his political base to make victory possible in 1977.

Begin totally rejected UN Security Council Resolution 242, especially its goal of "withdrawal of all Israeli forces from territories occupied in the 1967 conflict," which was regarded in the wider world as a precondition of Middle Eastern peace. He had also repeatedly abused Sadat—the "Egyptian tyrant"—warning that his image of a would-be peacemaker was "a deception."[18] Nor did he forget the Egyptian leader's earlier idolization of Hitler: in 1953 Sadat had written in a Cairo magazine that, although the Führer had "made some mistakes, such as opening too many fronts," he should be forgiven on account of his faith in his country and his people.[19] To an Israeli leader haunted by the Holocaust, this kind of comment was obscene.

Yet once he came into office Begin started making more encouraging noises about talking to Egypt. To general surprise he also appointed Moshe Dayan, hitherto a Labour stalwart, as foreign minister. Dayan disliked Begin's bombast and extremism; he could imagine a land-for-peace deal on the West Bank if it really enhanced Israel's security. These underlying tensions between the two would surface in due course. But in the short term Dayan's appointment sent a powerful signal to the world, legitimizing Begin's government and suggesting it was not totally opposed to peace.

The Carter administration was as taken aback as anyone by Begin's victory. In a letter of congratulation Brzezinski admitted that, when Begin told him a year before that he expected to win the 1977 election, "I was somewhat less than convinced."[20] NSC staffers struggled to find any biographical background information, eventually coming up with a history of the Irgun entitled *Terror Out of Zion*. Brzezinski passed this on to the president, marking a few pages including Begin's dictum "We Fight, Therefore We Are."[21] The president himself had been frankly "shocked" by Begin's victory. When the new Israeli leader was interviewed on American television, Carter noted in his diary: "It was frightening to watch his adamant position on issues that must be resolved if a Middle Eastern settlement is going to be realized."[22]

Even before Begin's election, Carter was running into problems over Israel. In March 1977 he had stated that, although "the first prerequisite of a lasting peace" was recognition by Israel's neighbors of the country's right to exist, another essential element was "a homeland provided for the Palestinian refugees who have suffered for many, many years." No previous American president had made such a commitment, and it caused a storm both in Israel and among Jewish-Americans.[23]

Belatedly Hamilton Jordan, assistant to the president, acknowledged that the administration had underestimated the Jewish lobby. In a lengthy memo he reminded Carter that its fund-raising capacity was immense: in 1976 the American Red Cross had raised $200 million, whereas Jewish charities netted $3.6 billion. Through the American Israel Public Affairs Committee (AIPAC), which represented more than thirty organizations, Jewish-Americans had an "unsurpassed" ability to mobilize political pressure across the country, playing on sympathy for Israel and memories of the Holocaust. With an estimated 31 "hard" votes in the 100-strong Senate, and 43 others that could be counted on in "a showdown," it exerted an effective veto in the upper house. AIPAC operated in a "vacuum," noted Jordan, because there was "no political counterforce" to agitate for the Arabs or Palestinians. One might think that all this represented the obvious facts of American political life, particularly for Democrats. But it was "not a part of our Georgia and Southern political experience," Jordan told the president, "and consequently not well understood."[24]

During the summer the White House developed a new strategy toward the Jewish lobby: cultivating key leaders and ensuring that the president did not do all the administration's speech-making about the Middle East. On the face of it, the elevation of a hardline Israeli leader made Carter's search for peace even more difficult. But, as both Jordan and Brzezinski noted, many Jewish-Americans were equally unsettled by Begin, fearing that he could jeopardize America's special relationship with Israel. His extremism might make them more receptive to a balanced peace plan from Carter.[25]

Much clearly depended on Begin's first meetings with the president, held at the White House on July 19–20. Beforehand Samuel Lewis, the U.S. ambassador to Israel, sent a series of background telegrams, and William Quandt of the NSC underlined their key points for Brzezinski: Begin's "deep convictions and principles," how it was "impossible to overestimate the Holocaust's impact" on him and the way his legal training had influenced his style and approach to negotiation. After their first day of meetings Carter noted in his diary: "I think Begin is a very good man and, although it will be difficult for him to change his position, the public-opinion polls that we have from Israel show that people there are quite flexible . . . and genuinely want peace." Begin delivered his standard historical lecture on the Jewish people's right to all Judaea and Samaria; he was unyielding on the question of settlements, unrolling a "national security map" to show how much of Israel was in range of Arab artillery. But Carter did not press him really hard—in line with the new and more conciliatory strategy toward Israel and the Jewish lobby. Begin's courtly manner also helped conceal the extent of their differences, for the moment.[26]

There was an inclination in the White House to assume that Begin's extremism was a compound of dated ideas, election rhetoric and tactical ploys, and that it would be eroded in negotiation. With Begin, as with Sadat, Carter tended to see what he wanted.

After Begin's visit Vance shuttled around the key Middle Eastern capitals during August 1977. The Americans sought a comprehensive regional settlement involving all the main parties and backed by the two superpowers. They were working toward an international conference at Geneva, the basis of Kissinger's diplomacy back in 1973–4. But this ran into serious difficulties. Carter was clear that there had to be some kind of Palestinian representation, but Begin would not talk to the Palestine Liberation Organisation (PLO) while it refused to recognize Israel's right to exist. The president also wanted Israel to negotiate with a single Arab delegation but, leaving aside Begin's reservations, Sadat had no time for King Hussein of Jordan and open contempt for President Hafiz al-Assad of Syria. Soviet foreign minister Andrei Gromyko told Vance that expecting the Arabs to adopt a united view would be like waiting "for the Second Coming of Christ."[27]

In fact Sadat never really liked the idea of a multilateral conference at Geneva: his preference, as indicated to Carter in April, was for direct American pressure on Israel. The president persevered and the U.S. and Soviet governments issued a joint communiqué on October 1 about the framework for peace. But this included "the resolution of the Palestinian question, insuring the legitimate rights of the Palestinian people"—a phrase that upset not only AIPAC but also ardent Cold Warriors who opposed any Soviet involvement in the Middle East.[28]

Carter's subsequent attempts at damage limitation gave the impression, as Brzezinski noted, that the president was "susceptible to pressure" from Israel and its friends. Sadat was certainly disconcerted. On October 21 Carter sent him a handwritten note indicating that they had reached "a crucial moment" in the search for peace and making "a very personal appeal for your support." The president's goal, as he said, was still that of "advancing all parties to Geneva," but Sadat seems to have seen the letter as a cry of desperation. A few days later he suggested to the White House a summit of all the interested parties together with the leaders of the permanent member states of the UN Security Council, to be held in East Jerusalem. The idea that the Israelis would welcome the Soviet and Chinese leaders, not to mention Yasser Arafat of the PLO, to the sacred heart of their 1967 conquests was, as Brzezinski noted with heavy irony, "somewhat droll." Carter sent a polite rejection. Next time Sadat spoke out, he did not consult the White House in advance.[29]

ON NOVEMBER 9 Sadat addressed the annual opening of the Egyptian parliament. His speech was typically rambling but in the middle he dropped a bombshell: he declared his willingness "to go to the ends of the earth" for peace, even to the Israeli parliament— "to the Knesset itself." It was a few days before Begin took the proposal seriously but eventually he issued a formal invitation, and the visit was arranged. Sadat had taken another dramatic gamble, akin to his crossing of the Suez Canal in 1973, and it showed how desperately he needed peace. But the cost was high. His foreign minister, Ismail Fahmi, resigned and the visit was condemned as apostasy across the Arab world.[30]

Yet on the evening of November 19 Sadat descended the steps of his Boeing 707 at Tel Aviv's Ben-Gurion airport to shake hands with a beaming Begin and to banter with Ariel Sharon, the general who had turned the tables on him in 1973. It seemed almost unreal. "President Sadat is now inspecting a guard of honour of the Israeli Defence Forces," gasped one Jewish reporter. "I'm seeing it, but I don't believe it." The whole visit was conducted with one eye on the Western media—Sadat gave interviews to the three main American TV networks during his half-hour flight—and the events of November turned him into a media superstar. In the battle for American opinion, Begin now had to play to the gallery as well, presenting himself in a softer light. "Never mind the Nobel Peace," exclaimed the former Israeli premier Golda Meir, "give them both Oscars."[31]

Sadat's two days in Israel personalized the peace process and gave it a momentum of its own. "Egypt and Israel became hostage to each other," notes one of Begin's biographers. "The failure of the peace process was liable to inflict heavy damage on one, or both, of them."[32] Although Sadat was taking greater risks—threatened with isolation in the Arab world—Begin had been sucked into the spiral of soaring expectations.

Yet neither leader had shifted his central positions. In Sadat's historic address to the Knesset on November 20 he spoke movingly of his passion for peace—"any life that is lost in war is a human life, be it that of an Arab or an Israeli"—and of the need to break through the "psychological barrier" of mutual suspicion that he described as "seventy percent of the whole problem." But, to the anger of Begin and his Cabinet, he called unyieldingly for withdrawal from all "the Arab territories occupied in 1967," including East Jerusalem, and recognition of the "fundamental rights of the Palestinian people," including "the right to establish their own state." These must be an integral part of any agreement: there could be no separate peace between Egypt and Israel. Responding, Begin expressed his desire for "real peace with complete reconciliation between the Jews and the Arab peoples" and proposed that "everything be open to negotiation." Yet most of his speech set out the lessons of the Holocaust and the war for independence in 1948 for "this generation of extermination" who had pledged "we would never again put our people in danger."[33]

On December 25, 1977, Begin paid a return visit to Egypt, where he and Sadat conferred in Ismailia on the Suez Canal. Begin proposed a phased military withdrawal from Sinai, but insisted that the Jewish settlements must remain. He also offered a plan for self-rule for Palestinians in the West Bank and Gaza, allowing them to elect an administrative council with limited powers. Although the issue of sovereignty was left vague in the plan, it became clear that Begin did not intend to relinquish control or to concede the applicability of UN Resolution 242. Sadat, who seems to have expected that by breaching the "psychological barrier" he would elicit dramatic Israeli concessions, was bitterly disappointed.[34] At Ismailia he agreed that two committees—one military, the other political—should explore the issues at stake but he rejected virtually all Begin's substantive proposals. "I cannot agree to surrender a single inch of Arab land. It is sacred," he exclaimed. "Mr. President," Begin retorted, "I cannot give up a single inch of *Eretz Yisrael*. It is sacred."[35]

For Carter the dramatic events of late 1977 redrew the parameters of his Middle Eastern diplomacy. The Americans had been informed but not consulted about Sadat's visit to Jerusalem, which seemed for a while to push them to the sidelines. And Begin's autonomy plan for the West Bank and Gaza, despite its manifest inadequacies for the Egyptians and Americans, became the document on the table. Brzezinski in particular thought it might prove the basis for transitional arrangements acceptable to all parties.[36]

The idea of reconvening the Geneva conference under American-Soviet aegis was also dropped: the best prospects obviously lay now in direct talks between Egypt and Israel. But the Ismailia talks were hardly encouraging. On January 18, 1978, the first meeting of the new political committee, held in Jerusalem, broke down when

Sadat ordered the Egyptian delegates back to Cairo, complaining bitterly that Begin wanted land rather than peace. It became clear that the two leaders were not willing or at least not able to achieve a radical breakthrough on their own.

And so the White House resorted to summitry. Two days later, on January 20, Carter and Brzezinski discussed bringing Begin and Sadat to Camp David for a summit. Carter was keen; his notes show that he also wanted to "open [the] door to Hussein's involvement," aware that Jordan's participation was essential to making progress on the West Bank.[37]

But at a meeting on January 23 Vance came out strongly against a summit with Begin and Sadat, fearing that it was premature and politically risky. And Brzezinski backed off, influenced by a warning from the U.S. ambassador in Cairo that Sadat was losing faith in America's commitment to an even-handed peace process. To address this "crisis of confidence" Brzezinski now favored meeting only with the Egyptian leader. Hamilton Jordan was left as the lone advocate of a joint summit, telling the president that "by just having Sadat here, you help him. But Sadat is *not* the problem, Begin is the problem." Yet Brzezinski's new strategy took this on board. He and his staff wanted to use the meeting to help Sadat craft a reasonable proposal into which the Egyptian leader would insert a few extreme demands. The United States could then "persuade" him to drop these, urge Israel to make similar "concessions" and eventually introduce an American "compromise" on lines already agreed with Sadat. Vance, more cautious, wanted to use an American-Egyptian summit to find out Sadat's real sticking points. Despite this difference of emphasis, the State Department went along with the NSC's strategy, at least for the moment.[38]

Sadat went to Camp David with his own agenda. At his first substantive meeting with Carter, on the morning of February 4, he described all he had done to advance the cause of peace since his dramatic visit to Jerusalem. He also vented his mounting disillusion with Begin, especially on the issue of Jewish settlements. Bitterly he declared that he was now sure Begin did not want peace and said he would therefore announce an end to the military and political talks agreed on at Ismailia. In his memoirs Carter presented the story of February 4 as a successful effort to bring Sadat back from the brink. More likely, as Brzezinski believed, Sadat the actor had gone to Camp David with the intention of forcing Carter's hand and drawing him actively into the negotiating process. This of course the Americans were now ready to do. During a day of meetings they fleshed out with the Egyptians the plan they had previously concocted, including a rough timetable leading up to a comprehensive U.S. compromise proposal by early April.[39]

This first Camp David summit therefore ended in apparent victory for Brzezinski's strategy of orchestrated American-Egyptian pressure on Israel. The private meetings and dinners between Carter, Sadat and their wives also deepened the personal rapport. And when Begin came to Washington for talks on March 21–22, Carter was unusually blunt in his criticisms of Israeli policy—partly to increase the pressure but also because the president was genuinely angry when he learned that Begin had interpreted his patient manner as a sign of weakness. In a meeting that Begin's circle considered the low point of the whole negotiating process, Carter clinically set out all the negatives in Begin's position. There was no hint of his trademark toothy smile. He also briefed key congressmen, who soon leaked Begin's "six no's" to the American press.[40]

During the spring, however, Carter backed away from Brzezinski's gambit, for several reasons. Sadat, impatient with details, was hardly the ideal partner for such a carefully calibrated strategy. A successful but bruising fight over an arms package to Israel, Egypt and Saudi Arabia forcibly reminded Carter of the potency of the Jewish lobby on Capitol Hill. And, most important, Carter began to toy with the idea of a bilateral peace between Egypt and Israel rather than the comprehensive regional agreement to which he originally aspired. At this stage there was no clear-cut decision— the president simply got the NSC to explore the implications—but both Brzezinski and Quandt, one of the NSC staffers, believe the seeds of a bilateral deal were sown in his mind at Camp David when he found that Sadat was not going to push really hard for Israeli withdrawal on all fronts.[41]

If that is true, Vance's strategy of using the summit to ascertain the Egyptian bottom line had paid off. But Sadat's approach alarmed his Foreign Ministry, now headed by Mohamed Ibrahim Kamel, who wanted to keep open links with the Soviets and the Arab world in search of a comprehensive Middle Eastern settlement.[42]

By the summer of 1978 it was clear that the peace process had run out of steam. "I don't see any way through the next several months without Cy devoting a substantial amount of his own time to the Mideast," Hamilton Jordan told Carter on July 10, adding that it would require "the very personal diplomacy that Kissinger used so successfully."[43]

But Vance's meeting with the Egyptian and Israeli foreign ministers in England on July 17–19 made little progress. At a breakfast meeting the following morning the president told his advisors that he was reviving the idea, cast aside in January, of a summit with both Begin and Sadat. Carter went into his study and started looking at a globe. According to Brzezinski, he said "that for political reasons he would like to have a rather dramatic meeting, perhaps somewhere abroad." He wanted "a historically proper setting." Whereupon Brzezinski proposed Morocco, mentioning the Roosevelt-Churchill summit at Casablanca in 1943.[44]

It was a revealing exchange. For Carter politics were now as important as principle. During 1978 his approval ratings continued to slide, down to 38 percent in June compared with a high of 64 percent in April 1977. The midterm elections were coming in November. Already there was speculation about his reelection campaign in 1980, when he was likely to be challenged by Senator Edward Kennedy. In an effort to improve his image, on July 1 Carter appointed Gerald M. Rafshoon, a successful advertising executive from Atlanta who had advised on Carter's gubernatorial and presidential campaigns, to be his assistant for communications. One of Rafshoon's tasks was to clarify the "themes of the presidency" especially through what he called "media events." A summit clearly fell into that category.[45]

On July 30 Carter returned to the summit idea, now favoring Camp David as a venue because he would be able to control the environment and minimize leaks. The State Department was convinced that the recent meeting in England had been ruined by constant briefings from Egyptians and Israeli participants to hovering journalists.[46] And so the president sent Begin and Sadat similar handwritten letters, each dated August 3, suggesting that the time was right for the three of them "to make a renewed effort at the highest level and with the greatest determination."[47]

In these letters Carter said he had "no strong preference about the location, but Camp David is available" and he referred to the benefits of "relative seclusion." Back in February, when he had met alone with Sadat at Camp David, Carter had toyed with Brzezinski's idea of America and Egypt trying to pressure Israel into an agreement. But having dropped that approach his intention was now to work through Begin rather than against him.[48] That may not have been entirely clear to Sadat, however. Carter's letter to him said that the president wanted to "search for additional avenues for peace as we planned at Camp David." This difference in their approaches was to prove important at the conference.

Vance personally delivered these letters to Begin and Sadat and secured their consent. On the morning of August 8, Jody Powell, the president's press secretary, told astonished reporters that the three leaders would convene at Camp David on September 5 "to seek a framework for peace in the Middle East." Each, he said, would be accompanied by a small number of principal advisors and "no specific time" had been set for the duration of the meeting.[49]

With the news out in the open, the White House moved into top gear. Vacations were cancelled; staffers worked round the clock. They had less than a month to prepare a summit of peculiar complexity. The nearest precedent they could find was 1905 when, as we saw in Chapter One, Teddy Roosevelt brought the Russians and Japanese together at Portsmouth, New Hampshire. But TR then stayed on Long Island and took no part in the actual negotiations.[50] This time an American president intended to host and to manage the whole meeting. The risks were very high, not only for the Middle East but also for Carter's presidency.

CAMP DAVID LIES some seventy-five miles northwest of Washington, in the Catoctin Mountains of Maryland. Built in 1939 as a New Deal recreation camp, it was commandeered in 1942 by President Roosevelt, who wanted a retreat relatively near the capital. Not all his successors enjoyed its rustic cabins (Jackie Kennedy dubbed their style "early Holiday Inn") but Eisenhower, who named it Camp David in honor of his grandson, hosted Khrushchev and several other foreign leaders there. And it was often used by Nixon, who updated many of the facilities. A helicopter pad meant that Washington was only a thirty-minute journey away.

Although covering two hundred acres, Camp David was a military establishment, surrounded by a double security fence patrolled by marines. Access was via a single gate along a private road. The press could be kept outside the perimeter or, if necessary, allowed just inside into a special area screened by evergreens to watch the presidential helicopter land or take off. Military personnel handled food, cleaning and other services and, in this pre-cell-phone era, all outside calls went through a central switchboard, run by the Army Signal Corps. No phone conversations were tapped during the summit, but the Israelis and Egyptians could not be sure. All this helped maximize the chances of participants talking to each other, not to the outside world.[51]

Yet the White House knew that the media could not be silenced. Abhorring a news vacuum, they would simply fill it with gossip and rumor. The pressure of speculation mounted with each passing day, particularly for an event of such historical importance. In any case Carter's public relations men, hopeful that the summit would boost his ratings, were looking for safe ways to capitalize on the media interest. "The theme we should project at the meeting is CARTER IN CONTROL," Rafshoon told the president. He and Press Secretary Jody Powell proposed several camera opportunities inside Camp David each day and, later, substantive statements from the president. But Carter opposed anything that would prejudice the desired seclusion.[52]

So Powell and his staff decided to follow a practice used occasionally in the past and create a press center in the little town of

Thurmont, Maryland, some six miles away. Renting the American Legion Hall, a bargain at two hundred dollars a day, they established offices, a canteen downstairs and a briefing area upstairs. It was equipped with typewriters, telex machines and two hundred long-distance phones. For members of the press who did not fancy being marooned in the backwoods, a special bus from the State Department would enable them to commute each day. Vance suggested that Jody Powell be the only official spokesman at the summit. Despite some initial resistance—Powell's Israeli counterpart warned that his own press was "even more aggressive and sensationalist than the Americans"— both Sadat and Begin agreed. Much to Powell's surprise, but also relief, he ended up doing a solo daily briefing.[53]

While the media strategy was being crafted, Vance, Brzezinski and their staffs compiled briefing materials for the president. Camp David was one of America's most meticulously prepared summits, with a vast number of position papers and psychological profiles. Unlike Vienna in 1961, there was even a suggested day-by-day scenario for how to proceed.

At the end of August Vance submitted the bulky briefing book from the State Department. It assumed that the summit would last about six days and argued that the president should "allow as much as 2–3 days to talk on a broader scale about the issues before getting into detailed negotiations about them." The schedule, said Vance, lent itself to this approach because Sadat and Begin would arrive on Tuesday, September 5 and it would be "necessary to allow a quiet time from early Friday afternoon through sundown Saturday for the Moslem and Jewish sabbaths." This could serve as a transitional period of reflection between the general discussion and the hard bargaining. Vance and his staff had modest aims for the meeting: "Our main objective at Camp David is to break the present impasse at the highest political level so that ministerial-level negotiations can proceed towards detailed agreements. Our objective is not to achieve a detailed agreement."[54]

In the State Department's view the main need was to "begin to alter the Israeli and Egyptian mindsets about the nature of a Middle Eastern peace settlement and how it is arrived at." In other words, to help each side think more flexibly and creatively about its dogmatic slogans. Israel needed to see that it could ensure security in the West Bank and Gaza in other ways than through "sovereignty"; equally, Sadat must accept that Israeli "withdrawal" from the occupied territories could be a phased process rather than an abrupt exit. More generally, the State Department argued that total commitment to UN Resolution 242, still anathema to Begin, should be interpreted in light of all that had happened in the decade since it was passed. It particularly noted that the Israeli economy now depended on outside workers flowing through the increasingly open borders between Israel and its neighbors. This was a further sign that traditional notions of sovereignty had become outmoded and that a collaborative approach to security was required. The "essence of our job," said the State Department creatively, was "to find new ways of posing the old issues so that the discussion can focus on solving the problems as we now see them without getting tangled up in the language that has been used since 1967 to avoid facing the real issues."[55]

The State Department papers also contained shrewd comments about Begin and Sadat:

> Both men are master manipulators, utilizing basically two different personality styles in order to achieve power and control. Begin concentrates on tactics and details, whereas Sadat focuses on the grand strategy, often employing broad dramatic gestures. In each case, this allows them to avoid making hard decisions . . . In dealing with Begin, avoid entering into word definitions. Allow him to make his basic point without interference and then point him to the intended objective . . . In contrast, Sadat will need more guidance, direction, and limit-setting. Left alone, he may get involved in ambiguities and generalities.[56]

The State Department also paid attention to the makeup of the two delegations. "How do we use Dayan to manipulate Begin toward greater flexibility?" it asked. In contrast, referring to the Egyptian foreign minister: "How do we neutralize Kamel's cautious influence?" which could easily "derail a whole negotiating track." The State Department proposed a mix of "tetes-a-tetes among the leaders" and "slightly broadened meetings" including a few key advisors. It set out a possible schedule of meetings, from Tuesday evening arrivals to wrap up on the following Monday, broken down into morning, lunch, afternoon and evening segments with goals for each one.[57]

Despite all this planning, notable blind spots existed. Bearing in mind what actually happened at Camp David, it is striking how little emphasis the State Department placed on the problems of engineering an Israeli withdrawal from Sinai. This was discussed only in a perfunctory paragraph mainly devoted to estimating how tightly Sadat would tie this issue to progress on the West Bank, Gaza and Palestinian rights. State believed that this linkage would be the "pivotal issue" of the talks. Carter instead seems to have had a hunch, perhaps derived from talking with Sadat at Camp David in February, that the Egyptian leader needed less linkage than State imagined. On this Carter seems to have been right but, as we shall see, he too failed to anticipate how serious a stumbling block the intrinsic issues of Sinai would prove.[58]

The president focused more than the State Department on the basic psychology of the two leaders. He wanted to help transcend their mutual suspicions and persuade each to deal directly with the other. This he thought could be done by repeatedly stressing to Begin and Sadat the "consequence of failure." The president also had serious reservations about the State Department briefing book. He scribbled on the top page that he wanted "more ambitious goals." Though less contemptuous of the bureaucracy than Kissinger, he believed its usual tendency was to arrive at "the lowest common denominator of goals." It irritated him to see a paper headed "Fallback Options Should Camp David Produce a Deadlock." As he recalled in his memoirs: "We had already risked the possibility of total failure and great embarrassment. We could not lose much more by aiming at success."[59]

When Vance delivered the initial invitations to Sadat and Begin in early August, he found the Egyptian leader to be keener about the summit, especially when Vance promised the United States would be a "full partner"—the stance that Sadat had long wanted. But "having reached the moment of truth," Vance observed, "Sadat was not his normal ebullient self." He was conscious that unless Camp David was a massive success he would face an outcry in the Arab world. For his part Begin knew that Vance had brought an invitation that could not be refused, but he feared concerted pressure from Carter and Sadat.[60]

Yet despite the Israeli leader's forebodings his delegation came to Camp David, in the words of one of them, "without adequate preparation, without background material, and without alternative proposals." This was largely an expression of the prime minister's autocratic style, which Dayan was already finding intolerable, but it also reflected Begin's underlying assumption that the summit would be exploratory rather than decisive.[61]

In a speech to senior Israeli military on August 16 Begin remained adamant that there would be no territorial concessions on the West Bank and indicated that a comprehensive peace for the Middle East was unlikely. Instead, he said, he would be taking to Camp David the concept of "a permanent partial peace," meaning a separate agreement with Egypt, probably without a full-scale peace treaty, rather as the two Germanies had recently extended recognition at the de facto level. The concept of a "permanent partial peace" proved a good indicator of Begin's objectives for the summit.[62]

In Cairo too Sadat was playing things his own way. On August 28, Foreign Minister Kamel submitted a lengthy strategy memo to the president. Egypt's objective, he said, should be to reach a general consensus on the principles of a comprehensive settlement, including the West Bank, Gaza and Palestinian self-determination. Assuming a conference of about one week, the Egyptians should initially adopt "a relatively hard stand." Then they would "progressively show flexibility within limits previously agreed" in response to American initiatives, assuming that Carter acted as full partner rather than mediator. Such flexibility might include, for instance, a phased period of Israeli withdrawal from the occupied territories.[63]

Sadat was also taking a hard line in the preconference exchanges. On August 26 he told the U.S. ambassador in Cairo, Hermann Eilts, that there could be no separate peace; nor would he accept anything but total Israeli withdrawal from Sinai, with a dismantling of the Jewish settlements there. But, in an echo of Camp David in February, the Egyptian president also mentioned he would be giving Carter a statement of his position and strategy: the United States might not have to put forward a proposal of its own at this stage. In fact, said Sadat, he was thinking of "saving President Carter for a major coup" and spoke of an "exercise in brinkmanship" reminiscent of Eisenhower's secretary of state, John Foster Dulles. Although Sadat did not elaborate on these cryptic remarks, they also proved a good guide to his tactics at Camp David. Like Begin, he was a foreign policy autocrat.[64]

In his presummit analysis Brzezinski drew Carter's attention to the cable from Ambassador Eilts—"Sadat seems to be preparing more surprises"—and underlined the contrast in likely goals between the two leaders: "Sadat will define success in terms of substance, and in particular an Israeli commitment to the principle of withdrawal on all fronts. Begin will define success largely in terms of procedural arrangements and will be very resistant to pressures for substantive concessions." Like the State Department, Brzezinski seems to have underestimated the problems of Sinai, but he did make an astute overall observation: "Sadat cannot afford a failure and he knows it; both Sadat and Begin think that you cannot afford failure; but Begin probably believes that a failure at Camp David will hurt you and Sadat, but not him."[65]

It was a shrewd appreciation. An essential part of successful bargaining at the summit is the conviction that, if necessary, you can afford to go home empty-handed. That is a political judgment rather than a matter of "pure" foreign policy. Brzezinski, as a politically savvy aide, came closer to the heart of the matter than the Middle Eastern experts at Foggy Bottom, for all their creative thinking.

CARTER FLEW TO CAMP DAVID on Monday, September 4, the Labor Day holiday. He took with him a mass of briefing books, notes of previous meetings and his annotated Bible, which he (rightly) predicted would be essential in arguments with Begin. As far as possible Vice President Walter Mondale would handle all other business from Washington. Carter was ready to devote a full week, if necessary, to the summit. He spent Tuesday morning reviewing the papers, making notes of what seemed the main areas of agreement and difference. His wife, Rosalynn, arrived at lunchtime. At 2:30 p.m. Sadat flew in from Washington, followed by Begin and his wife, Aliza, later that afternoon. Jihan Sadat had stayed with a sick grandchild in Paris, to Carter's regret since he hoped that the three wives would help "ease some of the tension and create a more congenial atmosphere."[66]

As with all other aspects of the summit, Carter had given careful thought to the physical arrangements. On the top of the mountain, surrounded by a thick screen of trees, was a series of small but commodious lodges. The Carters stayed in "Aspen," Sadat in "Dogwood" and the Begins in "Birch." Members of their respective staffs doubled up in other cabins. The Egyptians and Israelis each had agreed to bring only eight senior ministers or aides, though there were additional security, communications and press personnel housed in the camp barracks.

The Americans had considered bugging the Israeli and Egyptian lodges but Carter—in what Brzezinski felt was "an excess of chivalry"—flatly forbade this, thereby denying himself the advantage Stalin had gained at Yalta. On the other hand, the other delegations assumed they were being bugged and tended to hold sensitive conversations outside on the porches. The three heads of government took meals in their own lodges but their staffs used the communal dining area in "Laurel," where kosher food was available and all pork items had been removed from the menus. The Begins also often dined in Laurel. Each delegation had a twenty-eight-foot trailer for office space, fitted with desks, chairs, photocopiers and typewriters (with Arabic or Hebrew script as appropriate). For

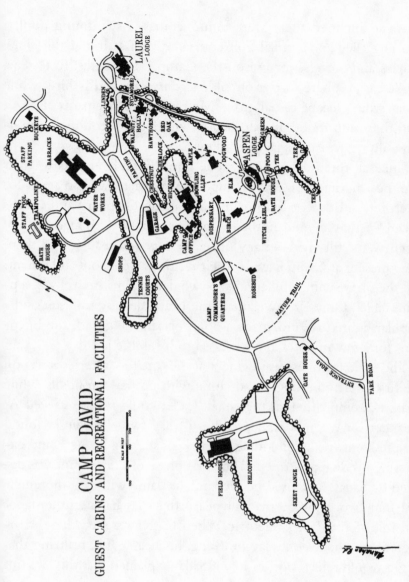

Map 6-2 Camp David as it was in 1978. (Jimmy Carter Library, Atlanta, Georgia)

those so inclined there were tennis courts, a swimming pool, a bowling alley and a small golf course, as well as round-the-clock movies and bicycles for use on the Camp David paths. To foster a relaxed atmosphere, Carter often dressed in jeans and T-shirts, while Sadat wore elegant casual attire. Most of the participants also got into the camp mood and dressed down: Begin was unusual in almost always wearing a jacket and tie.[67]

Since all three delegations spoke good English (thanks to their common heritage of British imperialism), there was no need for interpreters. But that did not mean that the Egyptians and Israelis talked freely with one another—on the contrary. With memories of recent wars still vivid—many of the leaders who had waged them were present at Camp David—their relations were cool and distant. On the first evening, in Laurel, the two delegations ate stiffly at separate tables. Only Ezer Weizman, the Israeli defense minister and a popular figure in Cairo, made a point of bantering with the Egyptians for a few minutes, but he failed to break the ice.[68]

The same frostiness was evident at the top. To Carter's dismay on the first afternoon, Begin had come with no new proposals, while Sadat was emphatic that the Israeli leader could not be trusted. At breakfast on Wednesday, September 6 (day two) Brzezinski found the president "really discouraged. He kept shaking his head and expressing his disappointment." The first phase of the summit was defined by Sadat. As hinted beforehand, he came with a comprehensive framework for permanent peace that was harsh, intransigent and full of anti-Israeli rhetoric. When Carter scanned the eleven-page memo on Wednesday morning, his heart sank, realizing that Begin would reject most of it, but Sadat explained that this was not his final position. He gave Carter a three-page list of concessions that the president could use at appropriate moments in their discussions. Sadat was clearly harking back to the strategy they had discussed at Camp David in February but then backed away from: to confront Begin with extreme Egyptian demands so that the Americans could then broker a compromise.[69]

Sadat had discussed this opening gambit with only one member of his delegation, Foreign Minister Kamel, who was appalled that

Sadat intended to show his hand so completely at the start. But the Egyptian leader was adamant. "In the end, all depends on whether Carter is really ready to undertake the role of full partner he has accepted, and exert pressure on Begin. If he is not ready, why waste time? I'll pack, and return to Egypt to prepare the next step."[70]

At three o'clock that Wednesday afternoon, Begin and Sadat both came to Carter's cabin for their first tripartite meeting.[71] The Israeli premier arrived first, giving the president a chance to warn that Sadat would present a "very aggressive" proposal, to which he asked Begin not to overreact. His two guests were clearly nervous, Sadat in particular fumbling for English words, but after agreeing on some procedural points they got down to business.

As Sadat read out his paper Begin sat silent and expressionless, but the tension was rising. The Egyptian proposal contained all his no-no's, such as "withdrawal of Israel from the occupied territories" and East Jerusalem, the removal of all Israeli settlements and a Palestinian state linked to Jordan. It even demanded that Israel pay "full and prompt compensation" for the damage caused by its armed forces and for its "exploitation of natural resources in the occupied territories."

When Sadat finished, there was silence. Carter tried to lighten the mood by telling Begin that if he would sign the document as written, that would save them all a lot of time.

There were gales of laughter. "Would you advise me to do so?" Begin asked. Smiling, Carter admitted it would probably be better if they all consulted their aides, and they duly set a full discussion for the following morning.

With studied courtesy Begin said how pleased he was to receive the document and how much he looked forward to reading it thoroughly. To Carter's delight the meeting ended after ninety minutes in light-hearted bonhomie, with the three leaders patting each other on the back.

At the time the president could not understand the mood. Later he decided that Sadat was relieved that Begin had not simply walked out, while Begin was relieved to find the paper "so ridiculously harsh."[72]

That was certainly the line Begin took next morning (Thursday, September 7), when he, Dayan and Weizman talked with Carter in a state of high indignation. Carter was at pains to say that this constituted Sadat's opening gambit. Eventually Dayan and Weizman, though still furious with Sadat, accepted Carter's explanation, but Begin did not. Maybe this reflected his paranoid streak; more likely, it suited his purpose to play up a sense of outrage and thereby strengthen his claim that there was no basis for serious negotiations. "This smacks of a victorious state dictating peace to the defeated!" he exclaimed at one point. He continued in the same vein when the three leaders convened again at 10:45. Carter sat behind his desk at Aspen, head down, taking notes. He had decided to withdraw from the discussion to make Begin and Sadat talk directly to each other.[73]

They did that with a vengeance for three hours.[74] The Israeli leader went through Sadat's paper point by point. He was "brutally frank," Carter noted. It was the Egyptian's turn to sit silent and impassive. But eventually he too exploded, hammering back on the "inadmissibility of acquisition by war," the heart of UN Resolution 242 to which Begin was so allergic. Leaning forward and pointing at Begin, he declared: "You want land."

Begin repeated that no Israeli leader could dismantle the Sinai settlements. "Security, yes! Land, no!" Sadat shouted. He pounded the table, insisting that Arab territory was not negotiable.

"All restraint was now gone," Carter recalled. "Their faces were flushed, and the niceties of diplomatic language and protocol were stripped away." The argument surged on to the West Bank and the Lebanon, with Begin characteristically retreating into detail and semantics. Sadat, also true to type, tended to fly off into abstract principles.

Near the end the Egyptian president stated bluntly that the good mood created by his visit to Jerusalem had been destroyed: "Minimum confidence does not exist anymore since Premier Begin has acted in bad faith." As they adjourned for an afternoon break, Begin announced that he had complete confidence in Sadat. The Egyptian leader, conspicuously, did not return the compliment.[75]

"I did not know where to go from there," Carter confessed later. During the afternoon he chewed things over with Vance, Brzezinski and Vice President Mondale, who had been talking with the two delegations and found things equally tough. Carter decided to meet Begin and Sadat again at 5 p.m.

The Israeli premier was open in his desire to keep all the big issues away from the summit, suggesting they hand negotiations over Sinai back to the military. Sadat said that would be a complete waste of time; no progress could be made without direction from the top. Begin did say that Sadat would get Sinai back, but his concept of a phased and conditional withdrawal—preserving the settlements and some of the Israeli airfields—was unacceptable to Sadat.

Although there were moments of shared emotion—for instance when Sadat declared, "I still dream of a meeting on Mount Sinai of us three leaders, representing three nations and three religious beliefs. This is still my prayer to God!"—they got nowhere. Finally Sadat stood up, announced angrily that a stalemate had been reached and stared hard at Carter. Desperately the president asked for time to bring forward some suggestions of his own, but his guests started moving to the door. Rushing to bar the way, he begged them not to break off the talks. Begin agreed readily. Carter looked hard at Sadat, who finally nodded. The Egyptian and Israeli leaders left without speaking to each other. In fact it proved the last Big Three meeting of the whole summit.[76]

That evening Carter had arranged an "entertainment." On the helicopter landing field the U.S. Marines who guarded Camp David performed precision maneuvers and drill. The president, flanked by his two guests, sat grimly in the front row of specially erected bleachers, with no vestige of his famous smile; Sadat and Begin did not exchange a word. Their body language was eloquent and word quickly got around that the talks had broken down.[77]

At 10:30 Carter and Sadat met with their principal advisors. The Egyptian leader was still emotional—"Begin is not ready for peace . . . The man is obsessed"—but during the two-hour meeting he made certain concessions, including allowing the Israelis two or three years to phase out the Sinai settlements. Vance's conversations during the day with Dayan and Weizman showed that not all the Israelis were as intransigent as Begin. On the other hand, most of the Egyptians were clearly more hawkish than their leader, Foreign Minister Kamel in particular fearing that Sadat was placing too much faith in Carter.[78]

The first three days of the Camp David summit were therefore a story of confrontation. Sadat's hard-line proposal had prompted a vituperative response from Begin, whereupon Carter, to salvage the summit, promised compromise suggestions of his own. (Sadat had also arranged publication of his proposal in the Egyptian press, to cover his backside against Arab criticism.) In many ways the meeting so far had gone according to Sadat's plan, and the one Carter had toyed with in February. But the Begin-Sadat argument had got totally out of hand: theatrics aside, the two men clearly could not stand each other and this undermined Carter's central aim, the creation of personal trust. (Interestingly the U.S. ambassadors to Egypt and Israel, who knew both men well, had urged Carter not to bring Begin and Sadat together at the start of the summit.[79])

So the president would now have to engage in shuttle diplomacy, bringing ideas to one side for comment, and then to the other. He also took account of the different dynamics of the two delegations, talking mainly to Sadat rather than his hawkish aides, yet including the more flexible Dayan and Weizman in his conversations with Begin. And so in this crablike manner they moved into what we might see as phase two of the summit: preparing American mediation.

Friday, September 8 (day four) was much quieter. The American delegation continued to probe the Israeli moderates, seeking room for maneuver. In the afternoon Carter and Vance talked for ninety minutes with Begin, Dayan and Weizman, and then had an hour alone with Sadat.

The president told both leaders of his plan to bring forward a comprehensive American proposal. Sadat of course was keen, saying that he would support anything Carter presented, as long as it did not prejudice his key demands about land, sovereignty in Sinai and the Golan Heights. Begin, in contrast, was most unhappy and—

sensing that he might be pressured into concessions or pilloried for rejecting them—begged Carter not to present a proposal. But the president was adamant. He said he would submit the plan first to Begin, so the Israelis would not feel ambushed. In light of their comments he would present a revised text to Sadat. And then, perhaps after further rounds, all three would convene for a "final" meeting.[80]

At the end of their discussion Begin invited the Carters to join the Israelis for their Friday-evening meal. What about Sadat? asked the president. "No, not this time," was the reply. Presumably Begin was trying to improve relations with Carter and avoid isolation. If so his ploy was successful. The food was good, the singing hearty and the amiable mood a complete contrast with the last couple of days. Carter felt much more encouraged as he walked back to Aspen. Meanwhile Harold Saunders, the assistant secretary for Near Eastern Affairs, started work on an American framework document. It would go through twenty-three drafts before the summit came to an end.[81]

Saturday, September 9 (day five) was even less eventful, with no formal meetings between the delegations. But Carter had to spend a good deal of time on the mounting crisis in Iran, where the shah's declaration of martial law on the 8th had provoked demonstrations in which several hundred were killed by police and troops. U.S. diplomats worked intensively on their peace proposals, discussing them with Vance, Brzezinski and Carter. The president had given his drafting team a list of the Necessary Elements of Agreement. These included

- The inadmissibility of acquiring territory by force
- Security for the nations involved
- Withdrawal of Israel on all fronts from the occupied territories
- Terminating the state of belligerency
- Freedom of navigation in the surrounding waterways
- Just settlement of the refugee problem
- Legitimate rights of the Palestinian people in all aspects

- Normal diplomatic relations
- A comprehensive settlement through the conclusion of a peace treaty between Egypt and Israel
- Return of Sinai to Egyptian sovereignty including withdrawal of Israeli airstrips and the removal of settlements[82]

Those not involved in the drafting tried to find ways to relax. Carter, a fitness addict, used tennis or cycling to work off some of the tension during the summit. He and his wife watched movies in their cabin on several evenings. Begin also liked movies; he had particularly asked to see the classic Western *High Noon*, which seemed an apt choice. Sadat's main relaxation was a brisk two-and-a-half-mile walk each morning. Both he and Begin, having suffered heart attacks, were also careful to get a rest after lunch. Vance and Brzezinski were keen tennis players, most of the Israelis preferred billiards and all the summiteers tried, with varying success, to catch up on their reading. At the start Dayan handed out copies of his new book, *Living with the Bible*. The only person to read it was Brzezinski, who said he had learned more from the book about Dayan than about the Bible.[83]

That evening Brzezinski went to play chess with the Israelis, conscious that they saw him, unlike Vance, as basically hostile. (Weizman thought that he reminded Begin of the Polish aristocrats who tyrannized his family back in Brest.) Brzezinski quickly demolished Weizman and then played Begin. Both men were ferocious competitors and their "social" encounter was no-holds-barred. Just as they were starting, Begin observed this was the first time he had played chess since the game in September 1940, during which the NKVD came to arrest him. It was a powerful and unsettling remark. Later, when his wife turned up and exclaimed, "Menachem just loves to play chess!" Brzezinski realized he had probably been the victim of another of Begin's exercises in psychological warfare.[84]

First thing on Sunday, September 10 (day six) Carter reviewed the current American draft with senior advisors and asked for another version that afternoon. In the meantime the president became anxious about the mounting sense of claustrophobia. For many of the Americans the venue brought back memories of teenage summer camp (each participant was given a windbreaker with CAMP DAVID emblazoned in gold on the back) but their guests, used to the arid, open spaces of the Middle East, found the dark, tree-covered hilltop very confining. Sadat recalled his days in a British prison; the Israelis joked somberly about the "concentration camp."[85]

So on Sunday morning, after worship, Carter took his campers on an excursion to Gettysburg, a forty-five-minute drive away. For two hours they toured the main sites of the brutal three-day battle in July 1863, the turning point of the American Civil War. Many of the Israeli and Egyptian military had studied Gettysburg at staff college and were fascinated to see the terrain. Begin was more interested in the cemetery where Abraham Lincoln had delivered his celebrated Gettysburg Address, which he greatly admired and seemed to know by heart. What struck Sadat (and also Dayan on the Israeli side) was the passion with which Carter, as a Southerner, spoke about the fighting; he interrupted the dry account of the official guide with stories of the suffering and courage of the bedraggled, often barefoot, Confederate soldiers. This forged another bond between the American and Egyptian leaders: Sadat felt Carter could understand what it meant to be involved in a terrible war and how difficult it was afterward to rebuild a people physically and spiritually.[86]

The Gettysburg trip was also intended to placate the increasingly frustrated newsmen. Even the most distinguished correspondents, such as Walter Cronkite of CBS, had been reduced to doing pieces-to-camera in front of the Camp David sign at the bottom of the hill. Or sitting each day in Jody Powell's half-hour lunchtime briefing in the American Legion Hall in nearby Thurmont. Or simply filming each other filming: "Have you ever seen anything so incestuous?" asked one disgruntled reporter. Powell's aim throughout was to provide the big beasts of the press with some morsels of red meat, but nothing they could really get their teeth into. He would explain in detail what meetings had taken place during the past twenty-four hours, adding trivial color such as "President Sadat went for a stroll yesterday afternoon and ran into Mrs. Begin and Mrs. Carter, who were touring the premises in a golf cart," but deflecting questions about the content and mood of the negotiations, or their likely duration. "We are only talking about a few days here," he stated on Thursday the 7th. That evening, however, the press were allowed into Camp David to watch the marine drill. Despite being kept on the opposite side of the parade ground, which only added to their fury, the body language of Carter, Begin and Sadat was both visible and eloquent. Media suspicions were further aroused when Powell stopped announcing any trilateral meetings. In an effort to control the speculation, on Saturday morning Powell offered an on-the-record statement: "Progress does seem to have been made in some areas. However, substantial differences still remain on other important issues."[87]

These two carefully crafted sentences helped keep reporters in a balancing act, despite their growing private doubts. The feature pieces in the Sunday papers and on television remained generally positive, though with an undertone of mounting drama about what was variously called the "Camp David political-mystery thriller" or a modern version of "Waiting for Godot." The Sunday trip to Gettysburg helped the White House divert the newsmen, who were allowed to film the leaders at designated points around the battlefield; they duly filled up columns of Monday's papers with stories and pictures.[88]

By Monday lunchtime, however, Powell faced a mounting wave of skepticism. "Why have there been no formal three-way meetings since Thursday?" he was asked. "Doesn't that show the conference is stalemated?" Treading water desperately, the press secretary replied: "I think neither optimism nor pessimism is justified at this time." Pressed on whether the summit would go beyond Wednesday, he answered, "I don't know."[89]

Neither, in all honesty, did his president, for on Sunday the participants hit not only the high water mark of the Confederacy but also of the Camp David summit. That afternoon Carter finally unveiled the American draft proposal, bringing the conference into a new phase of acute crisis.

HAVING GOT HIS CAMPERS BACK behind the wire, the president reviewed the latest American draft, refining and developing his "Necessary Elements," and further toned down some of its wording. Then at 4 p.m. he presented the Israelis with the American proposal for a comprehensive settlement. Begin was still unhappy about the whole idea: the Egyptians had presented a proposal, followed now by the Americans, and he said he wanted to draw up an Israeli paper so that each could be published. Carter refused, insisting that nothing was for publication until the final, agreed version. But he consented to an adjournment until after dinner so that Begin could examine the document more carefully.[90]

When they met again at 9:30 p.m., the Israelis ploughed through the whole draft point by point. Angry, as anticipated, about the reference to the inadmissibility of acquisition of territory by war, Begin wanted all allusions to UN Resolution 242 deleted from the document. Carter could not restrain himself from exclaiming that if Begin had openly disavowed 242 beforehand, he would not have been invited to Camp David. After a fruitless argument, Weizman suggested they move on, but there was little improvement. They continued until 3 a.m., stumbling over virtually every line of the document and often resorting to dictionaries when debating words such as "autonomy," "sovereignty" and "rights." The Israelis reopened issues already agreed and Begin even tried to add contentious wording of his own, such as "Jerusalem, the capital of Israel." It became clear to Carter that the Israeli leader was now doing what Sadat had done at the start: staking out an extreme position. The difference was that Sadat had privately told Carter his bottom lines, whereas Begin gave no hint of his priorities and haggled over every point.[91]

Carter got only four hours' sleep before resuming business on Monday, September 12 (day seven). Tired and now very angry with Begin—whom he privately called a "psycho" after the previous night's performance[92]—the president incorporated some Israeli comments in a revised draft; he showed this to Sadat during a two-hour meeting starting at 10:30. Although the Egyptian leader took it fairly well, his delegation was very unhappy when it met with Vance during the afternoon. In an effort to keep Begin in play, the Americans had sidelined the most contentious issues, notably the return of the West Bank, Gaza and East Jerusalem. Yet Foreign Minister Kamel and most of his aides considered these were the heart of the Arab case and could not imagine any agreement without them. Kamel, in particular, was convinced that Carter had caved in to pressure from Israel and the Jewish lobby and that Sadat, indifferent to detail, was his willing accomplice. Kamel wanted to bring at least King Hussein and also the Saudis into consultation. This was something that Sadat, who had little time for the other Arab leaders and a high sense of Egypt's special status, was reluctant to do, though eventually he talked with Hussein over the phone.[93]

During Monday night, Kamel worked up a lengthy memorandum for Sadat, urging him to walk away from the summit if Egyptian goals could not be realized and to make common cause with the other Arab states. The Egyptian delegation had a fierce discussion about it the following morning (Tuesday, September 12, day eight). This took place on the front porch of Sadat's cottage (presumably to avoid the supposed American bugs) and Carter happened to witness part of it as he returned from a bike ride. The president was even more concerned when Sadat arrived late and very agitated for their meeting. He carried a paper in his hand (possibly Kamel's memo) and Carter formed the distinct impression that Sadat had come to tell him that he was going home. To forestall this the president started a discussion on general Middle Eastern problems, particularly the danger of Soviet expansion. Although Sadat pulled the talk round to what he considered Israel's lack of good faith, he eventually left without delivering the message Carter had feared. But, when the Egyptians met Vance and Brzezinski that afternoon, they made clear in detail their fundamental objections to the American document and what they considered its bias to Israel.[94]

In the forty-eight hours since the Americans unveiled their comprehensive framework document on Sunday afternoon, they had got it in the neck, first from Begin and the Israelis and then from the Egyptian delegation who were clearly placing enormous pressure on the more tractable Sadat. And, lest Carter now expected some "give" from Begin, the Israeli leader went out of his way to be particularly difficult.

Late on Tuesday morning Begin took Brzezinski for a walk to chastize him for calling Israeli settlements a form of colonialism. Working himself up Begin shouted: "My right eye will fall out, my right hand will fall off before I ever agree to the dismantling of a single Jewish settlement." That evening he asked to call on Carter for what he termed "the most serious talk I have ever had in my life, except once when I discussed the future of Israel with Jabotinsky." This was a prelude to an impassioned speech about how he could never sign a document that included Resolution 242 language regarding no acquisition of territory by war. The same was true, he went on, about references to the dismantling of settlements or withdrawal from East Jerusalem. "Better my right hand should lose its cunning than I should sign such a document," he kept repeating. Begin of course naturally spiced his comments with biblical language; he was prone to emotion, even paranoia, when he felt his country was under threat. Yet it is hard to avoid the conclusion that these were deliberately melodramatic displays to keep Carter on the defensive at a time when, harangued by the Egyptians, he was likely to come back and try to squeeze the Israelis. The president certainly found it an exceedingly unpleasant evening, telling Brzezinksi later he was "not quite sure whether the fellow is altogether rational."[95]

The evening also provided further evidence, after his meeting with Sadat that morning, that both his guests felt under enormous pressure. The American proposal had created crisis not compromise. It would require radically new ideas to save the summit.

The next phase of Camp David may be characterized as working at a lower level in search of a split agreement. Engaging with Israelis and Egyptians below the heads-of-government level was a logical response to the impasse reached at the top. Begin was clearly the least flexible of the Israeli delegation, and Carter had already held some one-to-one talks with Dayan (who was privately threatening to go home because of Begin's intransigence). On the other side, the Americans had to find wording that satisfied Kamel and his colleagues, otherwise there would be a damaging, possibly fatal, rift among the Egyptians. But the crisis on Monday and Tuesday showed how difficult it would be to craft a single agreement whose content and language would satisfy both parties.

And so the idea emerged of a split deal in two separate documents: the outline of an Egypt-Israel treaty, focusing on Sinai, and a looser framework for an overall Middle Eastern peace. The first could then be made more precise to satisfy Sadat, the second increasingly vague in the hope of winning Begin's support.

The germination of this split-deal strategy can be sensed during a two-hour meeting on Monday evening between Carter, Dayan and Aharon Barak, the Israeli attorney general. Not having really talked before with Barak, the president found the Israeli lawyer a breath of fresh air, referring to him later as "a real hero of the Camp David discussions." Instead of rambling on emotionally like his leader about the Sinai settlements, Barak helped Carter to discern some credible reasons for Begin's obduracy. Not least of these was the precedent that any surrender in Sinai would set for the strategically more important settlements on the Golan Heights between Israel and Syria. After some discussion Carter proposed dropping Sinai altogether and concentrating on the more comprehensive framework for peace. But Dayan urged the president to sketch out his own proposal on Sinai and see how Sadat reacted. Carter got down to this on Tuesday afternoon, with maps and a yellow notepad. He produced a first draft in three hours. To his pleasure he got Sadat's approval, after a few changes, in less than twenty minutes. From then on Carter handled most of the revisions to the Sinai agreement as his personal project.[96]

What also encouraged Carter to pursue the idea of a split deal was his unique understanding of Sadat's mentality and intentions. At Camp David in February and again now in September (during meetings whose content have not yet been fully divulged) he seems to have gained the firm impression that Sadat's overriding aim was a peace treaty between Egypt and Israel. The larger Arab issues seemed secondary. The Egyptian leader needed some kind of agreement on the latter to avoid charges from the wider Arab world (and from his aides) about a separate peace, but it was not clear how precise that agreement needed to be. Sadat's tactic of informing Carter in advance about his likely concessions encouraged the president's sense that the Egyptian president would be flexible. Given Begin's obduracy, real and calculated, a split deal involving a bilateral treaty between Egypt and Israel and a general framework for regional peace began to seem the best possible outcome. But that made it all the more important to carry the Egyptian delegation along; their bottom line would be more important than Sadat's if the Americans wanted a united front.

And so the new phase of the conference took shape. The Americans would craft two agreements. First they would deal with Barak, the tough but realistic lawyer, for the Israelis. Then with Usama el-Baz, the Egyptian under-secretary for Foreign Affairs. El-Baz had taken the lead in critiquing the earlier American document and therefore could be assumed to speak for the Egyptian hard-liners. If the Americans could get these two to agree to appropriate wording, then there was a chance it might be sold to their two delegations.

Wednesday, September 13 (day nine of the summit) was almost entirely taken up with meetings among the Americans and with Barak and el-Baz. Carter found both of them "brilliant draftsmen, fluent in English," who helped find wording to patch over or avoid contentious issues. To deal, for instance, with Begin's aversion to any statements about territory being taken by force, the preamble to the framework document would make a general reference to UN Resolution 242, whose full text would then be appended. (Preamble and appendix were not regarded as integral parts of any treaty.) There was also the problem of the distinctive vocabulary used by Begin—"Judaea and Samaria"—whereas the Americans and Egyptians spoke of the West Bank and Gaza, or "Palestinian Arabs" because he was not willing to concede the idea of embryonic statehood incipient in the term "the Palestinian people." In the end they agreed to use Begin's language in the Hebrew text of the agreements, but not in the English and Egyptian versions.

During eleven hours of drafting considerable progress was made, yet there were limits. Barak refused to discuss the settlements issue and el-Baz, backed by Sadat, would not include a commitment to open borders and full diplomatic recognition. Moreover at the end, el-Baz took a surprisingly tough line on refugees in the West Bank, but when questioned admitted that he had not discussed the point with Sadat. This undermined some of the trust Carter had built up in him during the day.[97]

It also led to one of the most bizarre episodes of this strange summit. After the altercation with el-Baz the president had phoned Sadat, only to be told that the Egyptian leader had retired to bed, asking not to be disturbed. This was unusual—Sadat was normally a night owl—and the light was still on in his cabin. Carter went to bed but for once could not sleep. He started to worry about Sadat, thinking back over the row he had witnessed on the porch, the disturbing incident with el-Baz and the surprising response to his phone call. Finally at 4 a.m. the president phoned the Secret Service, then summoned Brzezinski (still in his pajamas). "Zbig," he said, "I am very much concerned for Sadat's life." It was agreed to instigate a close watch over who entered and left the Egyptian leader's cabin. Carter was greatly relieved to see Sadat emerge on Thursday morning, and said nothing about the episode. But his panic that Egyptian hard-liners might do away with their leader shows that the pressure was getting to Carter as much as his guests.[98]

Thanks to assiduous and imaginative drafting, a split deal was taking shape. But on Thursday, September 14 (day ten) the summit seemed on the verge of breakdown, most of all on a problem largely ignored beforehand: Sinai and the Israeli settlements. Not just Begin but most of the Israelis wanted that issue left open, whereas Sadat insisted that a commitment to dismantle them was the only basis on which he could negotiate a treaty. At lunch the president was very depressed. He told Vance and Brzezinski that the summit would end in failure and he would be made the scapegoat.

Even the normally controlled secretary of state got into a shouting match later with Begin. "Vance was very angry," Dayan recalled. The Americans started to plan a damage-limitation strategy, and Vice President Mondale was summoned from Washington to help. One possibility was an agreement between America and Egypt, which would clearly put the spotlight on Israel. Dayan's preference naturally was a statement of the differences between the two sides: when Carter started outlining this he was "heartbroken" at the smallness of the gap.[99]

But the president now had to face the prospect that they had come to the summit and would go back empty-handed. Anxious at least for an amicable exit, he sent a handwritten note to Begin and Sadat early on Friday, September 15 proposing "that today we receive your most constructive recommendations, that tomorrow (Saturday) be devoted to drafting efforts, and that we conclude the meeting at Camp David at some time during the following day."[100] Friday was day eleven and the pressure of deferred business in Washington had now become overwhelming. Not least was the mounting crisis in Iran.

Carter's hopes for at least an orderly retreat from the summit were soon dashed. Around noon on Friday Vance burst into Aspen, white-faced, to announce: "Sadat is leaving. He and his aides are already packed. He asked me to order him a helicopter." The president was aghast. After asking everyone to leave, he sat and prayed fervently for several minutes that somehow they could still find a way to peace. Then, after changing into more formal clothes because of the gravity of the moment, he marched down to Dogwood.[101]

Sadat and his entourage were on the porch; some of the Americans were also there, saying farewell. Carter walked into the cabin and Sadat followed. They looked at each other in silence for a while, the Egyptian leader drawn and nervous, the American genuinely unsure what to say. Eventually Carter spoke:

"I understand you're leaving."

"Yes."

"Have you really thought through what this means?"

"Yes."

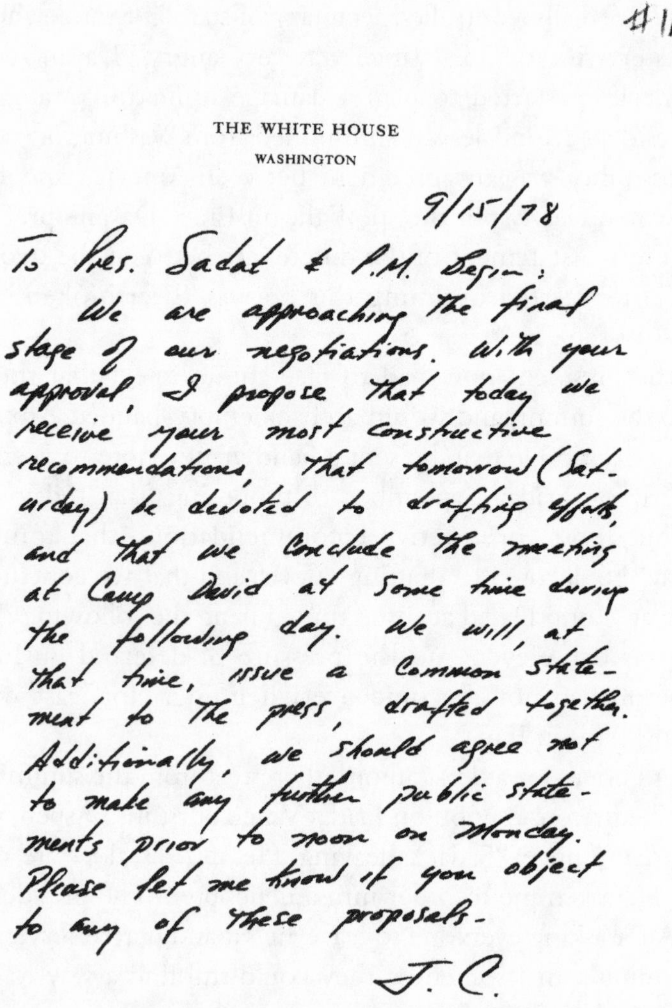

#1A

THE WHITE HOUSE
WASHINGTON

9/15/78

To Pres. Sadat & P.M. Begin:

We are approaching the final stage of our negotiations. With your approval, I propose that today we receive your most constructive recommendations, that tomorrow (Saturday) be devoted to drafting efforts, and that we conclude the meeting at Camp David at some time during the following day. We will, at that time, issue a common statement to the press, drafted together. Additionally, we should agree not to make any further public statements prior to noon on Monday. Please let me know if you object to any of these proposals.

J. C.

Figure 6-1 Carter's final appeal to Begin and Sadat at the climax of the Camp David summit, Friday, September 15, 1978. (Jimmy Carter Library)

"Then let me tell you," said Carter. "It will mean first of all an end to the relationship between the United States and Egypt. There is no way we can ever explain this to our people. It would mean an end to this peace-keeping effort, into which I have put so much investment. It would probably mean the end of my Presidency because this whole effort will be discredited. And last but not least, it will mean the end of something that is very precious to me: my friendship with you. Why are you doing it?"

Sadat was very shaken. He told Carter of a meeting with Dayan the previous day, intended as a bridge-building exercise, from which he had concluded that the Israelis would not sign any agreements and that it would be better for him to leave now. If he signed something with the Americans, then the Israelis could use those one-sided concessions as the basis for any future negotiations. Carter said that, if so, the Americans would make clear that any promises Sadat had made unilaterally would be null and void. Sadat was silent for a while. Then he said that on this understanding he would stay. To his frustrated aides, the Egyptian leader would only say extravagantly that Carter was "a great man" who had "solved the problem with the greatest of ease . . . I shall sign anything proposed by President Carter without reading it."[102]

Although Sadat had backed down, his threat to leave encouraged Carter to tilt more to his side. He asked William Quandt of the NSC to draft a speech that he could deliver to Congress if the talks failed. This stated that only two issues prevented agreement: Begin's resistance to giving up the settlements in Sinai and his refusal to acknowledge that eventual negotiations on the West Bank and Gaza would involve Israeli withdrawal, as set out in UN Resolution 242. And that on both points Carter sided with Sadat. The president reviewed Quandt's draft of what they called the "failure speech" and gave conditional approval. But he regarded it as a last resort, still hoping for a more positive outcome.[103]

During Friday the focus was on finding a solution on Sinai. Weizman and Harold Brown, his counterpart as U.S. defense secretary, managed to work out a deal whereby America would help Israel to build new airbases in the Negev desert to compensate for the loss of those in Sinai. This would cost the United States three billion dollars but, although Carter had been wary of "buying peace," he now agreed. Weizman also helped break the deadlock on the settlements. At the suggestion of General Avraham Tamir, director of Israeli army planning, they phoned Ariel Sharon (architect of the Likud alliance back in 1973 and also a leading advocate of the settlement policy) back in Israel in an effort to put pressure on Begin. A few hours later the prime minister, deeply moved, was telling his colleagues that Sharon had called to say that, if the settlements in Sinai were the only remaining barrier to peace with Egypt, he was in favor of relinquishing them. Crucially, however, the Israelis did not make that concession known immediately: on Saturday morning Dayan was still telling Carter that he would not dismantle them for twenty years and that Begin would never do so.[104]

On Saturday the 16th (day twelve), the Americans haggled with the Israelis over the West Bank and other issues, inclined to make concessions there in the hope of purchasing Begin's support over Sinai. In consequence they were receptive to the compromise suggestions made that morning by Barak, by now well established in their eyes as a "goodie." Israel's attorney general said he saw two possible ways forward. If they wanted to find a satisfactory resolution of the West Bank and Gaza, it would probably take another two weeks. Since going on that long was inconceivable, especially when Carter had already stated that the summit would end next day, it inclined everyone toward Barak's alternative: they would have to fudge the unresolved issues. In the case of Resolution 242 this meant finding language that the Americans and Egyptians would interpret as applying to the West Bank and Gaza, while Begin would not. On other contentious issues, such as Jerusalem or the interpretation of words such as "Palestinians" and "West Bank," each side would set out its own position in an exchange of letters appended to the agreement. Carter persuaded Sadat to agree.[105]

That evening Carter and Vance tried the new approach on Begin. On the Sinai settlements, the Israeli leader put up a tremendous performance—shouting words like "ultimatum" and "political suicide" in a stormy discussion that Carter thought would never end. Finally he agreed to submit to the Israeli parliament within two weeks the question: "If agreement is reached on all other Sinai issues, will the settlers be withdrawn?" Although Begin would not promise to vote in favor, under pressure from Carter he said he would allow his party members a free vote. When they turned to the larger Framework for Peace, the talk was "surprisingly amicable," Carter recalled. But of course Barak's breakthroughs that morning had already tilted the balance in the Israeli direction. For instance, when Begin, to Carter's jubilation, finally conceded the phrase "legitimate rights of the Palestinian people," the exchange of letters already agreed allowed him to gloss this as referring to the "Palestinian Arabs" and thus to incorporate them within his plans for perpetual autonomy within Israel's "Judaea and Samaria." The whole discussion lasted from 8 p.m. until well after midnight. Near the end an exhausted Carter believed he had extracted from Begin a commitment for a total freeze on all settlements during the negotiations over the West Bank and Gaza and that this would also be stated in an exchange of letters. On that positive note the discussions broke up.[106]

Summing up Saturday, Quandt noted that in such negotiations "there comes a time when one opts for clarity at risk of reaching no agreement at all, or settling for vagueness, which means postponing problems until a later date. On the West Bank and Gaza, we have chosen to postpone until a later date what cannot be solved today."[107] His memo offers an astute analysis of this last-minute breakthrough. Backing away again from a name-and-shame confrontation with Israel, Carter was getting close to an agreement—but on Begin's terms.

BELOW THE SUMMIT, meanwhile, the world's press was still waiting in vain for a glimpse of the tablets of stone. Powell had managed to maintain the blanket of cloud but the media mood was ugly. "We are tired of your lectures every day," one journalist shouted on Tuesday the 12th. When another asked whether "this essentially is still a non-news briefing," Powell replied: "That would be my assessment of it, yes." On Thursday the 14th Powell offered correspondents "a general comment about the situation." The goal, he said, was to produce a general framework for reaching peace in the Middle East. "There has been some progress and some flexibility, but we do not yet have such a framework." On the timing he was similarly balanced: the summit was probably in its "final stages" but, he added to laughter, "the final stage can be the longest stage." And so the speculation continued to ebb and flow. That evening NBC's *Nightly News* said that the summit would wind up on Friday or over the weekend, whereas its rival, CBS, suggested that hopes of progress had dampened and that the summit might drag on until Monday.[108]

At his lunchtime conference on Friday, Powell was asked whether there had been a point on the previous day or night when Sadat had been about to leave. Powell replied, "No, there was not." This was strictly true: it was only that morning that Sadat threatened to leave and Carter did not inform Powell until after his briefing. Powell's denial was just as well because the press was now convinced that Sadat and Begin were totally at odds, asking no less than thirteen questions about this on Friday. Even a wink from the White House Press Secretary would have encouraged them to go public. The formidable Helen Thomas was furious when Powell kept stonewalling about why there had been no tripartite meetings: "Don't tell us this is normal; don't give us the normal Camp David ————." When on Saturday the 16th Powell announced that the three delegations had agreed that Sunday would be the last day of the summit, there was applause from the assembled media. But he left them on a cliff-hanger: "There are still outstanding differences in important areas and serious efforts to resolve those differences continue . . . It is not possible to say at this point what time on Sunday the summit will conclude, or whether efforts to resolve differences will be successful."[109]

The uncertainty was not contrived. Throughout Sunday the 17th (day thirteen) new crises broke over the summit. The biggest concerned the agreed exchange of letters about Jerusalem. The American draft spelled out their standard position, articulated in speeches to the UN in 1967 and 1969, that East Jerusalem was not lawful Israeli territory. The Israelis were furious: Begin declared that he would not sign *any* document if the Americans wrote *any* letter to Egypt about Jerusalem. Again, with help from the resourceful Barak, the president gradually found a possible way out of the impasse: strike out all quotations from past U.S. statements, which would simply be cited by speaker and date. Carter agreed to try that on the Israeli prime minister. Meanwhile he had been autographing some summit photographs for Begin to give his grandchildren; his secretary, Susan Clough, obtained the names of each child so Carter could make the gifts more personal. The president took them with him for his final confrontation with Begin and they seemed to have some effect. The Israeli leader became emotional as he turned over the pictures, repeating the children's names and telling Carter a bit about each one. But then, calmly and without the usual histrionics, he said he was very sorry but he could not sign the American letter about Jerusalem. Carter gave him the revised wording, which Begin had not yet seen, and walked back dejectedly to his cabin. A few minutes later Begin phoned to say he would accept this formulation.[110]

During the afternoon there were further hitches. Begin's letter on the settlements in the West Bank and Gaza stated that they would be frozen only for the three months it was assumed would be required to negotiate the detailed Egypt-Israel treaty. That was not what Carter believed had been agreed and he read out his notes from the previous evening to Barak. But he then agreed that Begin could send the appropriate letter the following day, and his advisors did not demur. Later Carter admitted that this was "perhaps the most serious omission" of the summit; Quandt similarly called it the Americans' "most serious technical mistake."[111]

But it was now after 3 p.m. and Carter was hoping to get everyone to Washington that night to sign the Camp David Accords in the White House. So he concentrated on getting Sadat's consent to the final package, which took another two and a half hours. The Egyptian leader could see the limits of what he had achieved; most of his delegation was unhappy and Foreign Minister Kamel had already told Sadat that he intended to resign once the summit was over.[112]

No one was elated. The dominant mood was relief at finally being let out of "prison" and Begin, no less than Sadat, was genuinely worried about the reaction back home. But they managed a reasonably cordial conversation that afternoon, their first for ten days, and flew in the same helicopter to Washington for the signing ceremony. The flight, in a raging thunderstorm, brought the summit to an appropriately "Wagnerian" finale, recalled one American staffer.[113]

At 10:30 p.m. in the East Room of the White House, the cameras lingered on the empty chair where Kamel should have sat, but that did little to dampen the euphoria and mutual goodwill. Sadat was fulsome in praise of his "dear friend," the American president. Amid laughter Begin said the summit should be renamed "the Jimmy Carter conference . . . he worked harder than our forefathers did in Egypt building the Pyramids." Both the compliment and the backhander were typically Begin. Noting that the Accords committed him and Sadat to conclude their peace treaty within three months, Begin said they should promise to do so more quickly.[114]

Over the next few days Carter was deluged with praise for what even Henry Kissinger called a "very major achievement." *CBS News* announced on Tuesday evening that Carter's poll ratings had surged to 51 percent, up 13 percent since June. "With a single stroke," wrote Jack Germond and Jules Witcover in the *Washington Star*, "President Carter has transformed the political landscape." The *Washington Post* editorialized: "It was in truth Jimmy Carter's conference. We salute him: He did a beautiful piece of work."[115] For the beleaguered administration, this was heady stuff. "It goes without saying," exulted Stuart Eizenstat, Carter's chief domestic policy advisor, "that the Camp David Summit will go down in history as one of the great diplomatic achievements of the century."[116]

Even before Begin left Washington, however, he was telling the press that his country would never withdraw from the West Bank and Gaza or ever negotiate about statehood for the Palestinians. He insisted that all he had recognized were the rights of "Israeli Arabs." As for the adjective "legitimate," that was a "redundancy," he scoffed: "Is there such a thing as illegitimate rights?"[117]

More serious still, Begin failed to send Carter the confirmatory letter about a general freeze on settlements. Convinced that Begin had broken his word, the president sent him a memo setting out his firm understanding of what had been agreed on Saturday night. The Americans who had been there sided with Carter's interpretation; the Israelis either backed up Begin's denials or were vague about what had been agreed. Investigating the available evidence later, Quandt concluded that Begin probably did not make a categorical promise about the wording of the letter but allowed Carter to infer that he agreed. The problem was not so much Begin's habitual word games as the American failure to pin him down on what was one of the few big achievements that Sadat could claim with regard to larger Arab demands.[118]

On September 26 the Knesset approved the Accords, including an end to the Sinai settlements, and next day it was announced that Begin and Sadat would receive the 1978 Nobel Peace Prize (the White House was miffed at Carter's exclusion). But the detailed drafting of the Egypt-Israel peace treaty made slow progress. Negotiations began in Washington in October but Begin kept his team under tight rein and, instead of wrapping up things in a few weeks, as Carter had assumed, the haggling dragged on into the New Year. "You succeeded at Camp David because . . . you kept both parties under your control," Brzezinski told him. The agreements were "coming apart" because that was no longer the case. And because both leaders were now more intimidated by domestic opinion (in the case of Begin) and Arab criticism (in the case of Sadat) than they were by America. Echoing Brzezinski's analysis Hamilton Jordan told the president: "I feel strongly that you have to become personally involved"—probably by visiting the Middle East to put personal pressure on Sadat and Begin once again.[119]

With other problems absorbing his attention, notably the Islamic revolution that had erupted in Iran, Carter was only willing to do this as a last resort. He tried first to bring the Egyptian and Israeli foreign ministers to America for "Camp David II" in February 1979. When this got nowhere he invited Begin to Washington at the beginning of March, when the Israeli leader's obstructive tactics finally got Carter's blood up. A few days later he set out for a week of intensive shuttle diplomacy between Cairo and Jerusalem to pin down the details of an agreement. Once again Sadat, despite the opposition of his aides, made more concessions than Begin. They were enough to bridge the gap.

On March 26, 1979, a peace treaty between Egypt and Israel was signed on the White House lawn. All present found it a deeply moving occasion, particularly when Sadat embraced Ezer Weizman's son, a former paratrooper now permanently brain damaged after being shot in the head by an Egyptian sniper. Again there was praise for Carter's achievements: Kissinger said that the president was doing him out of his career of criticizing the government. For his part Carter wrote in his diary that he resolved "to do everything possible to get out of this negotiating business!"[120]

In personal terms, all three leaders paid a high price for Camp David. Although Carter's defeat in the 1980 election owed much to failures in domestic policy and politics, his intense engagement in high-level diplomacy such as Camp David and the Panama Canal treaty undoubtedly diverted his attention and energy from problems at home. The election defeat in turn affected the peace process: many observers have since echoed Sadat's faith that a second-term President Carter would have thrown himself into the search for a full Middle Eastern settlement.[121]

For the Egyptian leader the cost of Camp David was even higher—ostracism in the Arab world and then assassination by Islamic extremists in October 1981. His death cemented Carter's respect and affection. "Of almost a hundred heads of state with whom I met while president," Carter reflected in 2006, "he was my favorite and my closest personal friend."[122]

In contrast relations between Begin and Carter became frosty and distant: the former president believed the Israeli leader had reneged on solemn commitments he had made at Camp David, not least about settlements. But whatever satisfaction Begin gained from the 1978–9 agreements was short-lived. Continuing to strike out at Israel's enemies, real and imagined, he authorized Ariel Sharon's ruthless assault in June 1982 on Yassir Arafat's PLO base in Beirut. This in turn allowed Israel's Lebanese allies to massacre at least seven hundred inhabitants of the refugee camps. Initially Begin was characteristically defiant, likening the Israeli action to sending an army to Berlin "to annihilate Hitler in his bunker."[123] But as the protests escalated at home and abroad, he realized the damage done to Israel's image of superior, post-Holocaust morality. Sliding into a deep depression accentuated by the death of his beloved wife, he resigned the premiership in 1983, a broken man.

HOW SHOULD WE VIEW Camp David as a summit? The Americans were undoubtedly the best prepared. Carter had invested a great deal of time, energy and political capital in the Middle East peace process; he had also been thinking since January about a summit to break the deadlock. The strains between Vance and Brzezinski on Cold War issues were not apparent on the Middle East. Unlike the Kissinger-Rogers feud in the Nixon years, Brzezinski generally confined himself to the role of advisor and left Vance to do the negotiating—the Secretary of State often shuttling between the cabins at Camp David at high speed in his electric golf cart.[124] In fact the United States performed as an effective team at the summit—in marked contrast with the Egyptians (whose leader was far more dovish than his aides) and the Israelis (whose leader was much more of a hawk).

The United States also made the most careful preparations for the meeting. Its media strategy of isolation, skilfully executed by Jody Powell, stopped the tensions and deadlock from exploding in public. And the State Department's detailed briefing book displayed a shrewd sense of the two leaders and offered a thoughtful scenario for dealing with the "mindset problem" on both sides.

There was, however, tension between the State Department's approach and Carter's. First, the president wanted grander goals, at least as a target: nothing less than a comprehensive framework for regional peace. (He was to display the same ambition when approaching the Vienna summit with Leonid Brezhnev in 1979.[125]) Second, he suspected from earlier discussions that Sadat would settle for less than the State Department imagined on the wider Arab and Palestinian issues, as long as he could achieve an acceptable peace between Egypt and Israel. Although more a hunch than a clear strategy, this was to prove important later in the summit.

The State Department also seems somewhat naïve in believing

that the participants could be channelled into a preliminary general discussion followed by detailed negotiations, rather as Chamberlain had hoped at Berchtesgaden. The atmosphere at most summits is too turbulent. Such meetings only take place because dangerous issues cannot be resolved lower down, and this makes an early explosion by one of the participants very likely. At Camp David it was Sadat who fired first, partly because of this pressure but also because it suited his overall strategy. As the State Department observed, the Egyptian leader (a would-be actor in his youth) loved big, dramatic gestures, such as his visit to Jerusalem in November 1977. Seizing on Vance's promise that Carter would be a "full partner" in the talks, he set out the Egyptian position in the starkest terms, partly to protect himself from Arab criticism but mainly to ensure that Carter did come forward with his own compromise proposals.

Although high risk, Sadat's strategy was not ridiculous: indeed it had been encouraged by discussion with Carter at Camp David back in February. But it was flawed in several respects. First, in his bid for a novel partnership with America, Sadat did not grasp how deeply the United States was tied to Israel, for reasons of geopolitics, ideology and domestic politics. Although Carter flirted at times with the idea of confronting Begin, he always backed off. Second, as Foreign Minister Kamel argued, it was surely a mistake for Sadat to reveal most of his bottom line to Carter as early as day two. Ambassador Eilts thought Sadat was "mesmerized" by the American president: "The personal relationship between them was one I'd never seen between two leaders before." Even Carter wrote later that "Sadat seemed to trust me too much."[126] One wonders if Sadat really thought he had come to negotiate at all. The crux, in his view, seems to have been to trigger an initiative by Carter from which all else would follow.

Like Sadat, Begin was his own man, and apparently came even less prepared for the summit. Initially he was forced onto the defensive by Sadat's confrontational opening and then by Carter's determination to offer compromise proposals rather than, as Begin preferred, acting as mediator. There were also serious rifts within the Israeli delegation. But gradually the Israeli prime minister counter-

Nixon and Mao Zedong. The Soviets became more cooperative about a summit when Nixon secured an opening to their enemy, China. The president's historic handshake with the Chinese leader on February 29, 1972, was transmitted around the world. (*PA Photos*)

Nixon and Zhou Enlai. The Americans considered China's prime minister to be the consummate diplomatist, but Mao treated him as a "blackmailed slave." (*PA Photos*)

Allies and rivals. The fractious partnership between President Richard Nixon (center) and his National Security Advisor Henry Kissinger (right) made possible the summits of 1972. They are pictured with Kissinger's deputy, General Alexander Haig, in January 1973. (*Corbis*)

The fixers. Nixon in the Oval Office on March 13, 1970, with his Chief of Staff H. R. ("Bob") Haldeman (left) and Assistant for Domestic Affairs John Ehrlichman (right). Standing is Dwight Chapin, Deputy Assistant to the President, who was the advanceman for the summits in Beijing and Moscow. (*Corbis*)

Savoring SALT. Nixon clinks glasses with Soviet leader Leonid Brezhnev after signing the SALT I treaty in St. Catherine's Hall in the Kremlin. Alexei Kosygin is to the right of Brezhnev and Andrei Gromyko is next. (*Nixon Presidential Materials Project, U.S. National Archives*)

Nixon and Brezhnev aboard the presidential yacht *Sequoia* on June 19, 1973. The photo captures something of the Soviet leader's "animal magnetism," as Nixon put it, when Brezhnev was in his prime and also indicates the addiction to tobacco that eventually helped destroy him. (*Corbis*)

Welcome to Camp David. President Jimmy Carter looks on as Menachem Begin of Israel (right) greets Anwar Sadat of Egypt at the start of the summit on September 6, 1978. (*Jimmy Carter Library*)

The alternative to diplomacy. To remind his campers of the costs of war, President Carter (between Begin and Sadat) took them on a Sunday excursion to the Civil War battlefield of Gettysburg. Behind Carter are his wife, Rosalynn (left) and Mrs. Aliza Begin. (*Moshe Milner/Israel Government Press Office*)

Checkmate? Begin and Carter's National Security Advisor, Zbigniew Brzezinski, the two sharpest tacticians at Camp David, pit their wits over the chessboard. In the center is General Ephraim Poran, Begin's military secretary, with press spokesman Don Pattir to the right. (*Hulton Archive/Getty Images*)

Bridge builders. Israel's Foreign Minister, Moshe Dayan (left), and Defense Minister, Ezer Weizman, were more flexible than Begin. They maintained dialogue with Sadat and Carter, shuttling between the cabins at Camp David. (*AFP/Getty Images*)

Breaking the ice at Geneva. Ronald Reagan and Mikhail Gorbachev on the steps of Fleur d'Eau, November 19, 1985. Just before this first meeting and despite the freezing cold, the president removed his overcoat, making him seem Gorbachev's equal in age and vigor. (*RIA Novosti/akg-images*)

Fireside chat. When the formal session on one day got too heated, Reagan took Gorbachev down to a pool house by the lake where they continued their discussion in a more relaxed atmosphere. (*Corbis*)

Hands across the table. The two leaders say a hearty farewell in the Soviet Mission at the end of the Geneva summit, November 20, 1985. Gorbachev is still wired for simultaneous translation. White House Chief of Staff Donald Regan is to the right of Reagan. (*Corbis*)

The man who made summitry work. Essential to the success of the Reagan–Gorbachev summits was the teamwork between the two foreign ministers. Eduard Shevardnadze is pictured in the White House Rose Garden in September 1987. George Shultz (behind) was one of America's most effective secretaries of state. (*Diana Walker*/Time Life *Pictures*)

G8 summit, Birmingham, 1998. Anxious for a more informal atmosphere, host Prime Minister Tony Blair (in control, center) took his fellow leaders to the British government conference center at Weston Park. To the left are Boris Yeltsin (Russia) and then Bill Clinton (USA). Note the translator's booths behind. (*G8 2006 web site*)

Countdown to war. President George Bush and Prime Minister Tony Blair (in the background) at the White House, January 31, 2003, after their final summit before invading Iraq. (*Corbis*)

ttacked. On the Sunday (day six) he responded with an unyielding
tatement of Israeli views, giving no indication of his bottom line.
Moreover his advisors, though arguing with their leader in private,
ll played it tough in public, leaving the Americans and Egyptians
uncertain of how much Israel would concede. A central feature of
uccessful bargaining is the projection of uncertainty about one's
minimum goals, and here the Israelis were very effective. In contrast
"Sadat was a real amateur," observed Boutros Boutros-Ghali, a
member of his team at Camp David and a future UN secretary general. "He often moved hastily and predictably."[127]

Begin's other big asset proved to be his negotiating style. That
phrase sounds like a euphemism, since the Israeli leader tended to
harangue rather than negotiate, but his technique proved effective,
rather as Churchill's oratory and almost embarrassing obstructiveness forced concessions at Yalta. In his presummit assessment in August 1978, Samuel Lewis, the U.S. ambassador to Israel, said it was
impossible to decide in the abstract whether Begin's firmness was
that of "an intransigent hardliner" or just "a tough bargainer,"[128]
but the White House preferred to assume the latter. Indeed it was
only on that assumption that he was invited to Camp David.

In fact Begin proved both "an intransigent hardliner" and "a
tough bargainer." Harold Saunders, the U.S. assistant secretary of
state for Near Eastern Affairs, admitted later that they underestimated "the difficulty of moving Begin . . . We were persuaded that
we could work with him, and that we would not necessarily have
to expect to meet an ideological stone wall." Begin's legalism, his
obsession with terminology, his lengthy lectures on biblical history
and his emotional hyperbole all made it very unpleasant at times to
do business with him. The president was unusually patient but at
considerable cost in time and energy. "You cannot imagine how
difficult, how agonizing, it was to deal with Begin," Saunders said
later. "Carter dreaded having to deal with him." This telling comment, in Saunders' view, helps explain why the president failed to
pin Begin down on the settlements freeze.[129]

If Begin had been unremittingly obnoxious, that would have
been counterproductive. But on other occasions he could be

friendly and studiously courteous: some detected here traditional
Polish manners, others the influence of his idol, Jabotinsky. Cyrus
Vance, the American who got on best with Begin, saw him as "a
combination of Old Testament prophet and courtly European . . .
an odd mixture of iron will and emotionalism . . . harsh and acerbic
at one moment and warm and gracious the next." Begin's intransigence was in part a matter of calculation: Brzezinski was struck that
the Israeli leader, despite all the rhetoric about his right hand falling
off, eventually signed an agreement on the Sinai settlements.[130] But
Begin's conduct was also rooted deep in his personality and his
past, in the insecurity, even paranoia, engendered by the war and
the Holocaust. He could turn the emotion on or off, but the pressure was always there, pent up, just beneath the surface.

And so during the second half of Camp David, Begin and the Israelis wore down the Americans who in turn won over Sadat. Time
was also on Israel's side. The president's strategy of removing his
guests from Washington and isolating them at Camp David, which
initially paid dividends, eventually boomeranged because he could
not afford to stay out of the capital for a third week. At the start of
the summit Begin and Sadat were held hostage at Camp David; by
the end it was Carter.

And so the president allowed his sights to slip: some kind of
agreement was better than none and it had to be achieved soon.
With the obdurate Begin's bottom line unclear and the amenable
Sadat's largely disclosed, the Egyptian leader could be pushed
harder than the Israeli—an example of how it is often easier politically to squeeze your "friend" than your adversary. And with Begin
making a far bigger fuss than expected about the Sinai settlements,
Carter increasingly softened the larger framework for regional
peace to buy agreement on Sinai. So, in a fraught and convoluted
way, Begin ended up with something close to what he really
wanted: peace with Egypt and minimal concessions to the larger
Arab agenda.

Even so he was genuinely worried about how his surrender of
the Sinai settlements would be regarded by Likud supporters. His
foot-dragging about the treaty after he got back home was partly a

sign of how different the atmosphere is when one descends from the summit—domestic politics return with a vengeance—but it probably also reflected diplomatic calculation. As William Quandt has noted, by 1979 Carter was becoming preoccupied by his bid for reelection: the longer Begin dragged out negotiations on the treaty with Egypt, the less chance there was that Carter would do much on the more intractable issues of the West Bank, Gaza and the Palestinians.[131] If that was indeed Begin's strategy, it also paid off, for the general framework document proved largely a dead letter.

Nonetheless the treaty between Egypt and Israel has been the most notable breakthrough in Middle Eastern peacemaking since the state of Israel was born. In the quarter century between 1948 and 1973 there were four full-scale wars between Israel and its Arab neighbors; in thirty-five years since 1973 there have been none, largely because of the agreements of 1978–9. That was a huge achievement.

On the other hand, the underlying conflict had not been resolved: it simply metamorphosed into a different form as the Palestinians, feeling betrayed by Egypt and the other frontline states, took matters into their own hands through guerrilla operations and terrorism against Israel and Israelis. But, because Egypt, the most potent Arab state, had been detached in 1978–9, the tensions never escalated into another regional war that threatened to embroil the superpowers. That enhanced global stability but, conversely, it reduced the incentive for the great powers to address the Palestinian question. And by fighting so tenaciously on the issue of settlements, Begin protected Israel's principal means of colonizing the occupied territories and thereby ensuring their long-term retention.[132] Camp David therefore left an ambiguous legacy, anticipation of which made Sadat's delegation so opposed to his signing an almost separate peace.

All three leaders made signal contributions to the agreements at the summit. Sadat's dramatic visit to Jerusalem uncoupled the peace process from the superpower relationship and encouraged Carter to act on his own. It also broke the psychological barrier to peace in both Israel and Egypt. Yet Sadat was incapable of turning conception into reality. This was Carter's achievement; he brought them together for the carefully planned summit and micromanaged the negotiations after the initial deadlock. No other president has shown such personal concern for the Middle East or invested so much energy, thought and political capital in serious negotiations. But the actual content and balance of both the Camp David Accords and the eventual treaty owed more to Begin than the other two. As the most adept negotiator at the summit, the Israeli leader had protected what he regarded as key national interests. Whether his country became more secure is a question that Israelis and the world still debate.

7

GENEVA 1985

Gorbachev and Reagan

GENEVA IN NOVEMBER 1985 pitted a new, telegenic leader and an aging Cold War veteran in often stormy exchanges. Insults were traded about the American military-industrial complex and about Soviet violations of human rights. It sounds like Kennedy and Khrushchev at Vienna all over again. But this time the new boy was Russian, the grizzled Cold Warrior an American. And, despite the similarities with Vienna, Geneva turned out very differently. It began a process of summitry that would totally transform Soviet-American relations.[1]

At the heart of this story was the remarkable chemistry between Ronald Reagan and Mikhail Gorbachev. Each was almost a split personality, in which new thinking vied with traditional Cold War ideology. Their rapport at the summit helped draw the peacemaker out of the other. But that personal chemistry only developed into a chain reaction because of the partnerships between the two leaders and their foreign ministers. Teamwork, rather than Lone Ranger diplomacy, helped ensure lasting achievements. Geneva in 1985 is the story of how, implausibly and against the odds, summitry can sometimes work.

ONE PRECONDITION FOR effective bilateral summitry is a rough equality of power between the leaders and their countries. That was

true in the heyday of Nixon and Brezhnev in 1972, but not thereafter because the White House was crippled by Watergate and the
debacle in Vietnam. In November 1975 Nixon's successor, Gerald
R. Ford, met Brezhnev in Vladivostok and agreed to the outline of
a second SALT treaty. But by the time the treaty was ready for signing at the Carter-Brezhnev summit of June 1979, the Soviet leader
was in terminal decline. Their Vienna meeting was carefully chore-
ographed to accommodate his incapacity; its set speeches were a far
cry from the cut and thrust of Camp David the year before.

Another precondition for worthwhile summits is some degree of
mutual trust. The Soviets had been aggrieved at Carter's attempt to
renegotiate the bases of the SALT II. By the time the treaty was
signed in 1979 the president lacked the political clout to push it
through the Senate: this accentuated suspicions in Moscow. And
when the Red Army was sent into Afghanistan during Christmas
1979, to create a cooperative client government in the USSR's turbulent neighbor, Carter shifted his policy dramatically. He restricted trade and pressured U.S. athletes to boycott the Moscow
Olympics the following year. These sanctions reflected political calculation—Carter was struggling in the opinion polls ahead of the
November 1980 election—but at root the president's outrage was
genuine. He told an interviewer that the Soviet invasion had "made
a more dramatic change in my own opinion of what the Soviets'
ultimate goals are than anything they've done in the previous time
I've been in office," a comment that sounded so naive that the
White House kept it out of the public record.[2]

The man who defeated Carter, Ronald Reagan, seemed the ar-
chetypal Cold Warrior. In the mid-1940s, as a fading movie star, he
led the fight against communists in Hollywood. In the 1950s, disillusioned with Eisenhower's policy of containment, he argued that
America should intensify its economic and military pressure on the
Soviets because "in an all out race our system is stronger" and eventually the enemy would give up. His simple, stark belief in the superiority of American values made him ideal as General Electric's
roving ambassador in the 1950s. This experience of public speaking
all over the country, much more than his movie career, turned

Reagan into "the Great Communicator"; he used it as a spring-board into politics, serving as a two-term governor of California between 1966 and 1974. In foreign policy Reagan remained on the far right, openly critical of the SALT and ABM treaties once Nixon had resigned. In 1976, after failing to win the Republican nomination, he told his son: "I wanted to become president of the United States so that I could sit down with Brezhnev" to negotiate another SALT treaty. "I was going to listen to him for maybe twenty minutes, and then I was going to get up from my side of the table, walk around to the other side, and lean over and whisper in his ear, 'Nyet.' It's been a long time since they've heard 'nyet' from an American president."[3]

Like Nixon in 1969, the Reagan White House saw little point in an early summit. A meaningful meeting would require careful preparation and consultation with American allies; it would have to serve a "real purpose" and involve "legitimate negotiations." As Reagan put it in his typically folksy manner: "You don't just call up and say, 'Yes, let's get together and have lunch.'"[4] But Reagan's rhetoric in 1981 was far more hawkish than Nixon's when he was inaugurated. At his first press conference on January 29, 1981, he claimed that "so far détente's been a one-way street that the Soviet Union has used to pursue its own aims." Their professed goal was "the promotion of world revolution and a one-world Socialist or Communist state"; their leaders, he asserted, "have openly and publicly declared that the only morality they recognize is what will further their cause, meaning they reserve unto themselves the right to commit any crime, to lie, to cheat," in order to attain their goal. In May, at Notre Dame University, he stated flatly that "the West won't contain communism, it will transcend communism."[5]

Two years later, on March 8, 1983, the president denounced the Soviet Union as "an evil empire," in fact "the focus of evil in the modern world." He also prophesied that "communism is another sad, bizarre chapter in human history, whose last pages even now are being written." Although Anthony Dolan, an ultraconservative speechwriter, drafted much of the text, the phrase "evil empire" was Reagan's own: he had regularly used it in the mid-1960s.[6]

Even more dramatically, on March 23, 1983, he announced a program to develop a defensive system to intercept and destroy nuclear weapons. The White House called this the Strategic Defense Initiative (SDI), but critics dubbed the multibillion-dollar project "Star Wars" and that was the label that stuck. In Moscow, and much of Western Europe, SDI seemed to threaten an escalation of the arms race into space. And if it worked America might be able to mount a nuclear strike on the "evil empire" without fear of retaliation.

But there was another side to Reagan. This ardent anticommunist was also a passionate opponent of nuclear weapons. Reagan believed that the Cold War policy of deterrence based on mutually assured destruction (MAD) was truly insane. In July 1979 he was shown round the top-secret command center in Colorado that would coordinate U.S. defenses in the event of a nuclear war. It was a vast underground city, carved out of the Rocky Mountains and protected by steel doors several feet thick. Yet when asked what would happen if a Soviet missile landed outside, the commander shrugged, "It would blow us away." Reagan was shocked that even the nerve center of America's defenses was defenseless against nuclear missiles and this reinforced his desire to replace mutual destruction with mutual survival.[7]

In essence SDI was his own idea, which he sprung on an astounded State Department. Some Pentagon hawks backed the project as a way to strengthen America for a possible first strike on the Soviet Union. But Reagan was absolutely sincere in March 1983 when he said that his goal was to "render these nuclear weapons impotent and obsolete." His closest advisors in the White House doubted that he would have been willing to launch America's nuclear weapons even if the country were under attack.[8]

This side of Reagan is less well known. Critics scoffed at his black and white view of the world, his shakiness on details, his preference for storytelling rather than hard work. They dubbed him "the acting president"—a Hollywood cast-off who had exploited his name and face to secure "the role of a lifetime."[9] But Reagan's self-image was very different. Throughout his life his mind kept returning to summers as a teenage lifeguard on the Rock River in

Illinois. Enthroned on an elevated wooden chair commanding the beach, his tanned, well-tuned body made him into a cult figure. But, on his own reckoning, he also plucked seventy-seven people from near-death in the river. The "lifeguard" became the abiding motif of Reagan's inner life.[10]

It was, wrote one of his biographers, a role "perfectly suited to his personality. Lifeguards are solitary objects of adoration who intervene in moments of crisis and perform heroic acts without becoming involved in the lives of those they rescue."[11] Similarly, Robert McFarlane, one of Reagan's national security advisors, noted that he had "enormous self-confidence in the ability of a single heroic figure to change history."Yes, he was determined to resist the Soviet threat—hence the massive defense buildup of 1981–2—but he also hoped to transcend it, and summitry was the means to do so. In the words of another national security advisor, Frank Carlucci, Reagan was "convinced he could change the 'evil empire' to a 'good empire' through force of persuasion."[12]

Reagan had been raised by his mother as an evangelical Protestant, with a black and white view of the world. His faith, though very private, ran deep and it was strengthened by what happened to him on March 30, 1981, a little over two months into his presidency. After a speech at the Washington Hilton, Reagan was shot by a deranged gunman. A bullet lodged an inch from his heart and only his strong constitution plus quick action by surgeons saved his life. His quip on the operating table has gone down in American folklore: "Please tell me you're Republicans." But near death was a shattering experience. Afterward Reagan brooded over why God had spared him, eventually concluding it was to fulfill a providential mission. On Good Friday he told a visiting Catholic cardinal: "I have decided that whatever time I have left is left for Him." The following day, despite his public coolness toward an early summit, he drafted a personal message to Brezhnev about their mutual responsibility for world peace.[13]

Here was the central paradox of the Reagan presidency—on the one hand, the tough Cold Warrior; on the other, the would-be crusader for peace. The Soviets found it hard to decide which was the real Reagan, quite understandably because the president never resolved the confusion himself. He was, wrote Kenneth Adelman, his senior arms control negotiator, "a man singularly endowed with an ability to hold contradictory views without discomfort."[14]

To make matters worse, Reagan created an administration that mirrored his contradictions. Caspar Weinberger at the Pentagon and William Casey, head of the CIA, were vehement hawks, skeptical of every Soviet move. Even in 1990, after the velvet revolutions in Eastern Europe and the collapse of the Berlin Wall, the die-hard Weinberger was warning: "Just because General Secretary Gorbachev wears a smile and dresses fashionably does not mean there is any fundamental change in Soviet goals."[15]

But the State Department was more pragmatic, particularly after George Shultz took over in June 1982. The following February he finally got Reagan, for the first time, to meet Anatoly Dobrynin, the veteran Soviet ambassador in Washington and an influential advisor to the Kremlin. By the summer Shultz was pulling together a four-point negotiating agenda that sought to move beyond arms control into a much broader engagement to open up the Soviet Union's bunker mentality. "Strength and realism can deter war," the secretary of state told senators, "but only direct dialogue and negotiation can open the path toward lasting peace." Shultz believed that dialogue should begin at lower levels of government, building up from specialist officials, ambassadors and foreign ministers before reaching the summit. He also felt that the Nixon-era tactic of linkage was often counterproductive. America should make progress in superpower negotiations wherever that was possible; linkage, "if applied rigidly, could yield the initiative to the Soviets."[16]

Reagan's forte was simple: big ideas and their communication to the public through folksy, set-piece speeches. He was no good at formulating effective policies. "He knew what he wanted but he didn't know how to get there," observed aide Jack Matlock—and that was where Shultz came in.[17] An economist and professor, he was at home with ideas, able to take the long view and to analyze structural problems. Years as a labor-business mediator had made him an adept negotiator, able to balance toughness with humor. A former president of Bechtel, one of America's largest corporations, he knew how to run large institutions; as a veteran of the Nixon Cabinet, including a spell as Treasury secretary, he could survive in the Washington jungle.

But although the secretary of state eventually proved decisive in helping Reagan find his way to the summit, it was a tortuous and bloody process: the internecine struggle with Weinberger and the hawks brought Shultz to the point of resignation on at least four occasions.[18] Leaning to one side or the other and trying to establish some policy coherence was a succession of no less than six national security advisors, the greatest number to serve any U.S. president.[19]

THE SPLITS WITHIN Reagan's administration weren't the only reason why summitry was slow to get going: superpower relations were hardly propitious. The Red Army remained in Afghanistan; the Kremlin had forced the Polish communist government to suppress the new trade union, Solidarity. And in late 1983 the Soviets walked out of all arms control talks when NATO deployed cruise and Pershing missiles in Western Europe, in response to Soviet modernization of their own intermediate nuclear forces.

But what most inflamed relations in 1983, dashing Shultz's hopes for dialogue, was the fate of Korean Airlines flight KE 007 in the early hours of September 1, 1983. The plane had strayed badly into Soviet airspace and was shot down. All 269 passengers and crew, some of them American, were lost. The Kremlin initially denied responsibility. But after releasing tapes of the Soviet pilot's final exchanges with ground control, it then asserted that KE 007 was an American spy plane. The whole affair was a callous botch by a fumbling bureaucracy but Washington hard-liners gleefully played it up as "wanton, calculated and deliberate murder," a classic example of the evil empire at work.[20]

In any case the Soviet leadership was not up to summit diplomacy. Brezhnev, sick, senile and nearly blind, was on his last legs. During the 1979 summit with Carter in Vienna, two burly KGB men, each supporting one of his arms, had carried him in and out of the embassies.[21] Private jokes about the so-called era of stagnation abounded. In one Brezhnev greets Mrs. Thatcher on her arrival in Moscow. Reading his prompt card, he says: "We welcome you, Mrs. Gandhi." An aide whispers in his ear: "Mrs. Thatcher." Brezhnev brushes him aside: "We welcome you, Mrs. Gandhi." "Leonid Ilyich," hisses the aide," she is not Mrs. Gandhi, she is Mrs. Thatcher." "You fool," grunts Brezhnev, "I know that she is Mrs. Thatcher, but it says here 'Mrs. Gandhi.'"[22]

Brezhnev finally died in November 1982 and Reagan's hopes for a summit rose with the appointment of Yuri Andropov, former head of the KGB yet also a would-be reformer. Andropov was soon struck down by kidney failure, making effective government, let alone summitry, impossible. Despite dialysis several times a week, he died in February 1984. The Kremlin old guard then chose another geriatric, Konstantin Chernenko. After attending his second Soviet state funeral in fifteen months, Vice President George Bush quipped to U.S. embassy staff: "See you again, same time, next year."[23] He was wrong, but only by one month. Chernenko wheezed his last in March 1985.

The old men embodied an old mentality. That generation of Soviet leaders never forgot being invaded out of the blue by Hitler in 1941, starting a war that nearly destroyed their country and left twenty-eight million dead: one-seventh of the prewar population. They carried over the fear of surprise attack into a new era, the nuclear age, and against a new enemy, the United States. This paranoia peaked in November 1983. Rattled by Reagan's strong language and by the cruise and Pershing missile deployments, the Kremlin misinterpreted a NATO exercise (code-named "Able Archer") as a sign that U.S. bases had been placed on full alert. Maybe this was the prelude to an American first strike? The war scare wasn't simply official propaganda—Andropov genuinely believed it—and it spilled over into the public at large. The Soviet press depicted Reagan as the man willing and able to push the nuclear button, even as a modern version of Hitler.[24]

The president was genuinely shaken when he learned this from intelligence sources. For years he had been saying that the Soviet regime would stop at nothing, even war, to advance their ends. Now he discovered that they apparently believed exactly the same about him. The same month ABC television aired *The Day After*, a blockbuster movie about the impact of nuclear war on Lawrence, Kansas, a college town in the heartland of America. Its dramatic narrative and graphic images of burns, radiation sickness and famine left Reagan, in his own words, "deeply depressed" but also fortified in his determination "to see that there never is a nuclear war."[25]

Responding to these shocks, the president delivered his most conciliatory speech to date. In a special TV broadcast on January 16, 1984, he insisted: "The fact that neither of us likes the other system is no reason to refuse to talk. Living in this nuclear age makes it imperative." In an ending he wrote himself, he mused about what would happen if American couple "Jim and Sally" could sit and chat with "Ivan and Anya" from Russia. They would soon discover everyday interests in work, hobbies, families and, above all, peace that transcended nation and ideology. "They would have proved," declared the president, "that people don't make wars." That was the fault of governments.[26]

The following day Reagan met Suzanne Massie, author of *Land of the Firebird*, a vivid cultural history of pre-revolutionary Russia. White House advisors knew that their boss absorbed information more effectively when packaged in anecdotal form, with an eye to human detail. Even better if delivered not in a dry memo but by a charming and talkative woman. Reagan and Massie hit it off: this was the first of twenty-two meetings over the next five years of his presidency. Massie was passionate about her cause. "The Russians are human beings, for heaven's sake," she would say. "And they are very human beings."[27]

This new sense of Russians as people strengthened Reagan's bid for peace. So did his impending reelection campaign and a growing concern, fostered by his wife, about how his presidency would go down in history. Yet the president never resolved his contradictions. Testing a microphone before a radio broadcast on August 11, 1984, he remarked: "My fellow Americans, I am pleased to tell you I have signed legislation to outlaw Russia forever. We begin bombing in five minutes." When those lines leaked out, they accentuated doubts in Russia and the world about the president's real intentions. The administration claimed that critics were making too much of a light-hearted aside, but bombing Russia into oblivion was a strange thing for a would-be peacemaker to joke about.[28]

Nevertheless, by the time this almost schizoid president began his second term in January 1985, the peacemaker was definitely in the ascendant. George Shultz was beginning to impose some coherence over the policy process in Washington. Above all, after Chernenko's death in March, Reagan finally had someone to talk to in Moscow.

MIKHAIL GORBACHEV was born in 1931, making him thirty years younger than Brezhnev and Chernenko. Products of Stalinism and World War II, their approach to national security never escaped the paranoia of those years. Gorbachev, in contrast, was a member of the educated middle class that emerged under Khrushchev's reforms. Like Khrushchev, he believed that the Soviet system needed radical change, which above all meant reducing the arms burden. And that required a more peaceful and cooperative relationship with the West. Gorbachev was not as dogmatic a communist as Khrushchev, however. Extensive reading and, unusually, travel in Western Europe inclined him to think that Western socialism had much to teach the Soviet Union. "We can't go on living like this," he told his wife the night before he was nominated.[29] But he still believed the Soviets had plenty to teach the world, providing they overcame the gruesome legacies of Stalinism and got back to the true faith of Lenin. "You have to begin with him and end with him," he told party leaders in February 1986.[30]

If Reagan's image as a Cold Warrior obscures his true complexity, the way "perestroika" and "glasnost" echoed around the world in the late 1980s can give a distorted impression of Gorbachev when he came to power. His buzzword in 1985 was *uskorenie*—acceleration. Get the system going rather than scrapping it for something new.[31] Gorbachev's radicalism was learned on the job, and a big part of his education came from meeting foreign leaders.

His visit to London in December 1984, when still deputy general secretary, was an early milestone, helping erode his stereotypes about the East-West divide. Margaret Thatcher—the "Iron Lady"—was notorious in Moscow as an even more fervent Cold Warrior than Reagan, yet she and Gorbachev engaged in a genuine, if spirited, dialogue. Thatcher found Gorbachev clever, confident and articulate—a far cry from the Kremlin gerontocrats. "I like Mr. Gorbachev," she famously told the BBC. "We can do business together."[32]

Meeting Reagan at Camp David a few days later she said that Gorbachev was "an unusual Russian . . . much less constrained, more charming, open to discussion and debate." Though she added that "the more charming the adversary, the more dangerous."[33] Thatcher's briefing helped alert the Reagan administration to Gorbachev's significance.[34]

When Chernenko died in March 1985, Reagan sent Bush and Shultz to yet another Kremlin funeral, but this time bearing a personal letter for Gorbachev. "I would like to invite you to visit me in Washington at your earliest convenient opportunity," the president wrote. No strings or conditions were attached.[35] The new Soviet leader made a powerful impression on his American visitors. "Confident but not overbearing," Shultz told his staff. "Can decide things. Businesslike and bright. Sense of humor. Can be provoked," particularly on human rights, "but keeps control." Overall a "very different kind of person" from his predecessors. "Effortlessly in charge."[36]

In contrast Gorbachev considered the Americans "quite mediocre . . . This is not a very serious team." He noted scathingly that Bush "got lost" on anything outside his prepared text and complained that, although "the only issue the Americans kept pushing" was a summit, Reagan's letter on the subject was "quite amorphous and general."[37]

Nor could the Soviets forget overnight the president's Cold Warrior image. Advisor Alexander Yakovlev told Gorbachev that the summit invitation was largely propaganda to quiet Western critics of Reagan's hard line. Although the Soviet Union should agree to a meeting, if only to sense out Reagan at first hand, Yakovlev advised no haste and a venue in Europe, not America. All this would show that the president did not call all the shots. Yakovlev warned firmly against expecting any substantial change in U.S. policy, partly because of the "anti-Communist dogmatism of Reagan himself" but also because this was "a transitional period" for the United States. Although in the next quarter century America would remain "the strongest power in the world," Yakovlev predicted its gradual slide to a position of "dominant partnership" within the capitalist world and eventually "relative equality." American policy, Yakovlev suggested, was therefore the tough face of a power conscious of its long-term decline.[38]

These comments by Gorbachev and Yakovlev, a reformist party intellectual who believed in learning from the West, do not suggest a regime on its knees before American power. Nor does Gorbachev's essentially temporizing reply to Reagan's invitation to a summit. Although he said he had a "positive attitude" to the idea, he suggested that they "return again to the question of the place and time for the meeting." He also alluded to the president's Jekyll and Hyde image, reminding Reagan that "trust is an especially sensitive thing" and that it would "not be enhanced, for example, if one were to talk as if in two languages: one for private contacts and the other, as they say, for the audience."[39]

For a couple of months the Soviets played hard to get. When they finally started talking seriously about a summit, they proposed either Moscow or Geneva (like Vienna, a suitably neutral capital). Administration hard-liners such as Weinberger and Casey opposed a summit in principle. At the very least they wanted Gorbachev to come cap in hand to Washington. But Reagan, encouraged by Shultz, accepted Geneva and the two governments announced on July 3 that the summit would take place in November.

The Soviets coupled this with some even more surprising news. Andrei Gromyko, foreign minister for a quarter of a century, would be replaced by a virtual unknown, Eduard Shevardnadze, the party

Figure 7-1 Fatal Attraction? Cummings in the *Daily Express*, March 13, 1985, warns against holding a summit on top of a house of cards. (Express Newspapers, University of Kent Cartoon Library)

boss of Georgia. Gorbachev had phoned him out of the blue on June 30 and told him to report for duty in Moscow next morning. Shevardnadze protested his total lack of diplomatic experience. "Well, perhaps that's a good thing," Gorbachev replied. "Our foreign policy needs a fresh eye, courage, dynamism, innovative approaches." Many professional diplomats were scathing. "Our foreign policy is going down the drain," Ambassador Dobrynin told Shultz: "They have named an agricultural type."[40]

Shevardnadze's appointment was indeed a breathtaking change and a clear sign of Gorbachev's personal power. As long as Gromyko remained in charge he could not change foreign policy: he needed a committed reformer, personally loyal. And, as the new leader of an autocratic system, he could reshape the bureaucracy more quickly and radically than any American president. In May Gromyko had warned Shultz that Gorbachev had "a nice smile but iron teeth." But it was Gromyko who was the first to feel the new leader's bite.[41]

Shevardnadze, though initially out of his depth, proved a quick learner, putting in eighteen-hour days and losing twenty-four pounds in a few months.[42] Equally important, he soon forged a good working relationship with Shultz, his opposite number. Like Gorbachev, Shevardnadze engaged in real discussion, rather than reading out prepared positions. He was also ready to talk back. At their first meeting, in Helsinki on July 31, Shultz lectured him about the abysmal Soviet record on human rights. Shevardnadze took it with a smile and then asked: "When I come to the United States, should I talk about unemployment and blacks?" Learning Mrs. Shevardnadze was coming to Helsinki, Shultz brought his own wife. This was part of his project to break down barriers through personal relationships and in due course the two couples forged a genuine friendship.[43]

But in the summer of 1985 that was well in the future. The State Department said the Helsinki meeting "made apparent the deep differences in virtually all areas." Although eschewing "the polemics and detailed rebuttals that characterized Gromyko's style," Shevardnadze "restated Soviet positions with no changes."[44]

Meanwhile the advance men started worked on the logistics for the summit. As usual the Americans were more thorough than their Soviet counterparts, paying at least five visits to Geneva, but two pressures made them particularly assiduous. In the spring the president had been thrown off balance over his visit to the Bitburg military cemetery near Bonn. Intended as a sign that America and Germany had buried the wartime hatchet, the proposal provoked furor when it was revealed that the cemetery contained the graves of nearly fifty soldiers from the Waffen SS. Reagan went ahead with the visit on May 5 but coupled it with a trip to the Nazi death camp at Belsen. Although White House staffers had twice toured the Bitburg cemetery, they did so when the graves were covered with snow, accepting assurances from the Germans that there were no hidden embarrassments. The public relations disaster made them doubly careful over Geneva.[45]

Also breathing down their necks was the president's wife. Nancy Reagan, a former Hollywood starlet, had devoted the rest of her life to Ronnie. Fiercely protective, she saw the summit as essential in softening his image as a Cold Warrior. Nancy was also obsessed with astrology. After the president's near assassination in 1981, she insisted on checking all important journeys and venues with her favored star-gazer, Joan Quigley, in San Francisco. Driven almost to distraction by the First Lady's obedience to "My Friend," White House Chief of Staff Donald Regan resorted to a color-coded calendar on his desk to help remember which days were supposed to be "good," "bad" or "iffy." After Bitburg blew up, Nancy insisted that the White House follow Quigley's exact timings for the visit to West Germany; the court astrologer was also closely involved in planning for Geneva. In July White House advance men identified two possible residences for the Reagans to stay in but Nancy vetoed the first. After consultation with Quigley, she insisted they stay at Maison de Saussure, which Eisenhower had used for the 1955 summit. Don Regan was peeved at her interference but later admitted that she had been right. The elegant eighteenth-century château, with its view across Lake Geneva to Mont Blanc, was an ideal venue for the Reagans; even a ring of Swiss troops and an antiaircraft system at the front gate did not spoil its charm.[46]

Meanwhile Robert McFarlane, Reagan's national security advisor, was concerned about the president's "spotty" command of facts and his reliance on "generalities, even slogans" about the Soviet Union. (Most of his "quotations" from "Nikolai" Lenin were lifted from a right-wing tract published by the John Birch Society.) So Jack Matlock, the senior Soviet specialist on the NSC staff, put together a set of twenty-four papers for Reagan, each eight to ten pages. Matlock wrote three himself—on Soviet psychology, their view of the country's place in the world and whether the USSR was essentially Russian or communist (both, Matlock said). Most of the other papers came from researchers in the CIA and State Department and ranged over domestic and foreign policy, national security and Soviet-American relations; two were on Gorbachev and his aims for the summit. The result was virtually an introductory

college textbook—NSC staff nicknamed it "Soviet Union 101"—
and the president worked through the material carefully. Matlock's
papers shrewdly played on Reagan's interests and prejudices, engaging him in a way rarely achieved by normal briefing books:

> Yes, they lie and cheat. And they can stonewall in negotiations when
> it seems in their interests to strike a deal. They have a sense of pride
> and "face" that makes the proverbial Oriental variety pale in com-
> parison. Yet, in private, with people he trusts, the Russian can be
> candid to a fault—groveling in his nation's inadequacies—and so
> scrupulously honest that he can be irritating, as when he makes a
> big deal over having forgotten to return a borrowed pencil.[47]

Matlock also arranged meetings with specialists inside and outside government, particularly Suzanne Massie whose book Reagan
was reading on the plane to Geneva; he also arranged video presen-
tations on relevant topics such as Gorbachev as a public leader. In
the final weeks he secured some appropriate Russian movies from
the Soviet embassy. On the weekend of November 2–3 the president watched *Moscow Doesn't Believe in Tears,* the 1980 box-office
hit about three young women going to the metropolis in 1957. The
following weekend he saw *The Cranes Are Flying,* a classic fifties
movie about two young lovers caught up in World War II.[48]

But neither the advance men nor Reagan's tutors could address
the fundamental problem bedevilling American preparations for
Geneva—the failure to agree on policies. SDI was particularly contentious: the president clung to his vision of sharing the technology
with the Soviets. Weinberger and the Pentagon thought this crazy
and saw the project as a way to drive the Soviets into the ground
through a new arms race. McFarlane and, to some extent, Shultz
had come to see it as a potential bargaining chip to get big cuts in
Soviet nuclear forces. Shultz and McFarlane were themselves at
odds over whether SDI could be researched and tested without
breaching the 1972 ABM treaty, still a hallmark of détente; this argument exploded publicly in early October. On rare occasions
when State, the NSC and the Pentagon were in agreement, they

ran into opposition elsewhere. For instance, the FBI believed that cultural and educational exchanges—viewed as a good thing almost everywhere else in official Washington—would produce yet more Soviet spies.

And even though Shultz and McFarlane were moving in broadly the same direction—to make the summit a success despite hardliners in the White House and the Pentagon—they did not work well together. Shultz saw McFarlane and the NSC as ineffectual and even hostile, while McFarlane came close to a breakdown as he tried to mediate between Shultz and Weinberger. The national security advisor also attempted to dampen media expectations about the Geneva meeting; like Chip Bohlen before Vienna in 1961, he even tried to dissuade the media from calling it a summit.[49]

By October the Soviets were getting very fed up with American feuding and the consequent lack of progress on a firm agenda for Geneva. Their remedy was simple: revive the back channel through Dobrynin that had proved so productive in 1971–2. But the State Department was determined not to be bypassed again, insisting that the U.S. ambassador in Moscow be used equally.[50] And Kissinger's personal diplomacy was anathema in the Reagan administration, where all the national security advisors functioned as (would-be) coordinators rather than negotiators.

It was Shultz who stepped into the void, aware that the Soviets were beginning to doubt that America was serious about the summit. On October 10 he proposed, via Dobrynin, that he pay a flying visit to Moscow, ostensibly to discuss "housekeeping details" such as the exchange of gifts between the two leaders and the composition of the two delegations. But this was cover against the Washington hawks. In reality Shultz wanted to make a final effort to cut through the bureaucratic mess. Gorbachev, irritated that "we hear nothing from the Americans but generalities," agreed to the visit: the result was a mini summit.[51]

ON THE FACE OF IT, Shultz was playing the same role as Kissinger in April 1972. But the differences were fundamental. Shultz was acting as the official head of the American diplomatic establishment, not its jealous rival, and he also took with him McFarlane, the national security advisor. This was a far more satisfactory basis for summit preparation than the Lone Ranger diplomacy of 1972.

On November 4 George Shultz landed in Moscow for the first visit by a U.S. secretary of state in seven years. As he and Shevardnadze ploughed through lengthy briefing books, the atmosphere was cordial; Shultz broke things up with cracks such as: "The next page is blank. As a reward please excuse me to use [the] facilities." They agreed on a loose agenda for the two days at Geneva: on the first morning an overview of Soviet-American relations, in the afternoon a discussion of arms control. The second morning might focus on regional and bilateral issues, while the final afternoon would look to the future, including "guidance for our negotiators, and further summits." On the content of the meeting, however, their achievements seemed meager. A mere two weeks before the summit, only four issues could be categorized by the State Department as "Agreed or likely to be by November 19." Listed under the heading "Further work needed / Possibles but not clear" were seventeen issues, including human rights, the president's cherished agreement on social and cultural exchanges, and the opening of consulates in Kiev and New York. "Agreed language" was deemed "unlikely" on five hot chestnuts including Afghanistan, Berlin and nuclear testing. When discussing arms control issues, Shultz, Shevardnadze and their aides simply went through the motions. "The U.S. will not get chocolate until it gives sugar," warned Yuli Kvitsinsky, the senior Soviet negotiator, meaning no cuts in offensive weapons without an end to SDI.[52]

On November 5 Shultz, together with McFarlane, had a four-hour meeting with Gorbachev. The Soviet leader was in a feisty mood, lambasting the United States for its "disinformation" about the Soviet Union, for not honoring agreements such as SALT II and for the follies of its military-industrial complex. His language was often blunt: "You are inspired by illusions," "You ought to put that in mothballs." Both in tone and content he sought to dispel any impression that Moscow was being driven to the negotiating table by the arms race and economic weakness: "The Soviets know how to meet their challenges." And he was also emphatic that the precondition for an arms control agreement was a ban on the militarization of space. "If you want superiority through your SDI, we will not help you. We will let you bankrupt yourselves . . . We will engage in a buildup that will break your shield." Yet this was not just a Khrushchev-style rant. "The Geneva meeting is an important starting point," Gorbachev declared, "but using it as a get-acquainted meeting is too restricted. And so is just setting an agenda for the future . . . The great question is of war or peace . . . We should have as our intent the development of a dialogue to reduce confrontation and to encourage détente and peaceful coexistence."[53]

In this torrent of talk, Shultz and McFarlane were struck by the crosscurrents. The dead hand of communist dogma clearly shaped Gorbachev's distorted image of the United States and was reflected in old-style Leninist phrases such as "peaceful coexistence." It was also clear that he was preoccupied, almost neurotic, about SDI. And Gorbachev was probably letting rip to show he would not be a soft touch at Geneva. But the Americans also sensed a genuine willingness to talk, even on sensitive issues such as human rights. Moreover there were times when Gorbachev could listen as well as lecture. He was at his most receptive when Shultz delivered a carefully prepared homily about modern economics.

For some time the secretary of state had been groping for a way to get across the American message about human rights. Although obviously a powerful propaganda point for the West, Shultz saw it as the thin end of a wedge to prise open Soviet society. Without such an opening, he was convinced that there could be no lasting change in Soviet-American relations: the rise and fall of détente made that clear. Moreover, when lectured about human rights, Shevardnadze kept responding that the USSR would do what made sense for itself. So Shultz, donning his economist's hat, decided to give Gorbachev a tutorial on how the world was moving from the industrial age to the information age, driven by the ubiquitous computer that was revolutionizing science, finance, manufacturing, indeed everything. This new age depended on the free movement of people and ideas. "The successful societies are the open societies," Shultz argued, and that's why human rights mattered. Some American aides thought his tutorial, indeed the general harping on human rights, was misguided: "It's a classroom in the Kremlin," one of them complained. "It's condescending." But the secretary of state was unmoved and, when he made his pitch at the Kremlin meeting, "far from being offended, Gorbachev lighted up." On your next visit to Moscow, he told Shultz with a twinkle in his eye, "come as a businessman and economist."[54]

Shultz had hit the Achilles heel of the Soviet economy. Apple pioneered the personal computer in 1977 and IBM turned it into big business in the United States. So much so that *Time* magazine made the PC its Man of the Year for 1982, the first time in fifty-five years that a nonhuman had been given this accolade. The Soviets, in contrast, were marooned in computer prehistory, struggling with mainframe designs pirated from IBM. Their new twelve-year plan envisaged 1.3 million PCs in Soviet schoolrooms by 1995, but the Americans already had three million in 1985 and the principal Soviet PC, the Agat, was really an inferior version of the already outdated Apple II.[55]

The difference in information technology was apparent at the very top, in the Reagan-Gorbachev correspondence. The Soviets were still using electric typewriters, whereas Reagan's National Security Council had moved to an IBM data management system and even rudimentary email. Their 1980s IT looks primitive to twenty-first-century eyes—it operated on mainframes and was backed up by 5¼ floppy disks and microfiche—but it far surpassed the Kremlin's technology.[56] Little wonder that *informatizatsiya* (literally "informationization") became a buzzword of the Gorbachev era, or that the Soviet leader responded so positively to Shultz's tutorial. Here, he already saw, could be one benefit of a new relationship with America. It was an example of how meetings at the top can indeed help to change minds.

Shultz promoted another technological innovation that had a more immediate effect on Soviet-American relations: simultaneous interpreting. All previous summits described in this book, except

Camp David, had been interpreted consecutively: while one leader spoke, his interpreter took notes and then, at a suitable break, translated those words into the other language. The result was a very precise translation, but a lot of time was wasted. Although simultaneous interpreting dates back to the 1920s, it made its mark in international relations only with the Nuremburg trials of 1946. It was adopted at the United Nations but not at international conferences, and the U.S. government did not try simultaneous interpreting for bilateral meetings between the president and another head of government until 1981.[57]

At Helsinki in July 1985 Shultz persuaded Shevardnadze to try the simultaneous method, wearing headphones and listening to interpreters in sound-proof booths. How did you like it? Shultz asked afterward. "We got eight hours' work done in four," was the reply. Time was indeed one benefit of simultaneous interpreting. But, equally valuable, the listener could connect the speaker's words to his tone and body language, essential elements of a real conversation. When Shultz met Shevardnadze on November 4 in Moscow, the room had been set up for simultaneous interpreting: "I hope you like this bit of technology transfer," said Shevardnadze with a smile. They agreed to use it for plenary meetings at the Geneva Summit, though one-to-one meetings between the two leaders would still be interpreted consecutively. Sergei Tarasenko, Shevardnadze's senior aide, observed later that simultaneous interpreting set the conduct of Soviet-American relations "on a completely new road."[58]

To the president, Shultz offered a cautiously upbeat account of his visit to Moscow. He admitted that "we have a long way to go to achieve any basic understanding or results in negotiations on major issues": when reviewing the issues with Shevardnadze, there were "more question-marks than answers." Nevertheless the Soviets were committed to further summits in Moscow and Washington in "the nearest future to review progress and coordinate follow up measures aimed at reaching our goals." This, said Shultz, "could be the most important outcome of this summit as it could establish a process of decision-making." The administration should "view the meeting in Geneva as a beginning; a chance to start dealing with an enormous accumulation of problems." Above all, he told Reagan, what really mattered was that the two leaders "establish a relationship with each other." Their first tête-à-tête would be decisive in setting the mood, and Shultz was confident that Gorbachev would "do less posturing and more real discussion" when alone. The secretary was pleased, possibly relieved, when Dobrynin passed on a message that Gorbachev would not be as tough on Reagan as he had been on Shultz.[59]

Advice of a rather different sort came from that veteran summiteer of the 1970s, Richard Nixon, in the elite journal *Foreign Affairs*. In the lead article of its fall 1985 issue, the former president extolled the virtues of well-prepared superpower summits; he favored holding one every year to help leaders understand each other's political limits and get bureaucracies moving. But he warned against getting fixated about personal relationships. "Spirit and tone matter only when two leaders of nations with similar interests have a misunderstanding that can be resolved by their getting to know each other. Such factors are irrelevant when nations have irreconcilable differences, which is the case as far as the United States and the Soviet Union are concerned." Nixon concluded with what he called "the one absolute certainty about the Soviet-American relationship," namely that "the struggle in which we are engaged will last not just for years but for decades."[60]

Whereas Nixon believed that the Soviet Union was here to stay, Reagan was sure it was ready to go. And as an idealist he placed much more faith than Nixon the realist in personal relations as a way to effect this great transition. But even in his most utopian moments Reagan could not have foreseen the dénouement of the late 1980s.

What of the view from the Kremlin? Although liking Shultz's economic ideas, Gorbachev told the Politburo that Shultz "did not have serious baggage" for the summit. To some extent this was a tactical ploy by the Soviet leader to lower expectations, but it also reflected the mounting frustration in Moscow. Given the president's reputation as hard-line on policy yet soft on details, Gorbachev was felt in some quarters to be taking a serious risk in having a meeting so soon, especially with no sign of common ground on SDI. But the Soviet leader, like his American counterpart, had profound faith in his powers of persuasion. The latest Soviet offer was, broadly, a 50 percent cut in nuclear arsenals in return for an end to SDI. Whatever Shultz said in Moscow, Gorbachev hoped he might cajole and seduce Reagan into agreement on this basis in Geneva. If not, the meeting would still have been a valuable opportunity to meet his opposite number and the start of a process of real dialogue.[61]

But the Kremlin's hopes of meaningful discussion were shaken on the very eve of the summit. For some weeks the State Department and the Ministry of Foreign Affairs in Moscow had been roughing out the elements of a possible joint communiqué. This was standard practice for such international meetings, and also a convenient checklist for areas of agreement. Negotiating a draft communiqué had been the centerpiece of Kissinger's presummit visit to Moscow in 1972. Reagan had approved an outline in October 1985, which Shultz and Shevardnadze refined in Moscow.

Having delayed as long as he could, Shultz then gave a copy of the draft communiqué to Weinberger, whom the president was not taking to Geneva after combined pressure from Shultz, McFarlane and Don Regan. Weinberger vented his anger on the draft, nitpicking at phrases such as "serious differences can only be overcome by sustained dialogue." (Rubbish, said Weinberger, they could only be overcome by an arms race that forced the Soviets to change their ways.) More substantively, he persuaded the president that a "precooked" communiqué would impede a candid personal discussion with Gorbachev. This played on Reagan's bad memories of his early G7 summits in 1981, when he was appalled to find that the final statement had been written before the discussions started. On November 13, six days before the summit, a very embarrassed Shultz had to tell Dobrynin that there must be no further work on the communiqué. After an angry reaction from Moscow, Dobrynin warned Shultz that this was seen as evidence that the administration was not serious about the summit. Shultz wriggled and protested, but there was no shift in the U.S. position.[62]

Although this last-minute hitch was not publicly known, the media were well aware of the roadblocks on the way to the summit. "What's the headline?" demanded one reporter who accompanied Shultz to Moscow. "Stalemate on Eve of Summit," replied the secretary with a laugh. When a *New York Times* correspondent wanted to know if it was realistic to expect even a face-saving agreement in principle on arms issues at Geneva, Shultz responded: "I wouldn't bet *The New York Times* on it." Most reporters therefore surmised that Shultz's eleventh-hour trip to Moscow to engineer a presummit deal had failed. And the reason seemed obvious. At the end of August Gorbachev had told *Time* magazine that the world situation was "very tense," even "explosive." His main concern was SDI: "If the present U.S. position on space weapons is its last word, the Geneva negotiations will lose all sense."[63]

At a press conference on September 17, Reagan was asked directly if he would trade SDI for big cuts in Soviet nuclear arsenals. "Rather than that kind of negotiation," he said, the summit should take up the idea of "turning toward defensive weapons as an alternative to this just plain naked nuclear threat of each side saying we can blow up the other." He reiterated his hope that, if SDI proved practicable, "then we can realistically eliminate these horrible offensive weapons—nuclear weapons—entirely."[64]

The media therefore anticipated a direct clash between the two leaders over SDI. And there was a feeling in some quarters that the Great Communicator might be about to meet his match. Now seventy-four—twenty years older than Gorbachev—and recovering from an operation for bowel cancer in July, Reagan lacked his opponent's energy and concentration. He was also notoriously fuzzy on details. In a presummit interview he told the BBC that the Russians had no word for "freedom." They did have, of course—*svoboda*—as Matlock reminded him next day. "Gee, Jack," said Reagan cheerily, "you know, I guess I did mix that up." None of this boded well for the cut and thrust of a parley at the summit. Gorbachev was also superb at public relations; the Western media speculated about whether he and his chic, intellectual wife would upstage the senior citizens from Hollywood. Even White House staffers were privately worried. According to *Time* magazine, Reagan's aides knew he would "need a lot more than charm and amiability" when facing "the tough-minded Soviets at the higher-stakes show in Geneva."[65]

THE AMERICAN PARTY left Washington early on Saturday, November 16. The exact takeoff time was 8:35 a.m., apparently chosen for astrological reasons. The Reagans, together with Shultz, McFarlane, Regan, other close aides and some select journalists, flew in Air Force One. The main press plane had departed an hour earlier with two hundred members of the White House press corps, forty press aides and the newly appointed presidential biographer, Edmund Morris (another sign that the Reagans were eyeing his place in history). They arrived late Saturday evening, Geneva time. The president had a "thing" about jet lag and wanted a couple of days to recover; the White House physician had issued detailed instructions about how to shift his body clock as smoothly as possible, including alternating "feast days" and "fast days" in the run up to the summit.[66]

The Reagans stayed in Maison de Saussure, their astrologically approved château on the lake; senior staff were housed in the adjacent Villa Pometta. Both residences had been especially rented for the occasion. The president had Sunday and Monday for rest and final preparations, including a full-scale role-play with aide Jack Matlock speaking in Russian as Gorbachev, to provide experience communicating via an interpreter. Staff found Reagan tired and preoccupied, often staring at his shoes during final briefings. "Lord," he wrote in his diary, "I hope I'm ready and not overtrained." It was a revealing aside. During the first presidential debate of the 1984 election campaign, he had been tense, muddled and lacking in authority. His wife called it "the worst night of Ronnie's political career." The president explained afterward that he had felt "brutalized" by the rehearsals, his mind so jammed with facts and figures that he hadn't been able to focus on what his opponent, Walter Mondale, was saying. His diary entry on the eve of the summit possibly reflected lurking fears of a repeat performance.[67]

Meanwhile the usual media circus had converged on Geneva. Almost all its twelve thousand hotel rooms and two hundred private limousine drivers had been booked for months. The White House had taken over the Intercontinental Hotel, Geneva's top conference center, for staffers and press. Some thirteen hundred miles of phone cable had been laid down, serving more than three thousand special direct lines, and the bill for the Swiss was likely to be well over one million U.S. dollars. Lobbyists were also there in strength, particularly those concerned with nuclear weapons and human rights. Back in America, the Coalition to Free Soviet Jews took out an ingenious full-page advertisement in the *New York Times* showing Reagan and Gorbachev facing off in profile. Between them banner letters proclaimed: "FOR MILLIONS OF JEWS THIS COULD BE THE MOST IMPORTANT SUMMIT MEETING SINCE MT. SINAI." The ad explained that "Thou shalt not leave the Soviet Union" was a commandment sent down to two and a half million Jews from their government. "But it's not carved in stone. It can be changed . . . Mr. Gorbachev has the power. If only he can imagine the glory."[68]

Tuesday, November 19 dawned cold and gray, with periodic snow flurries. But the president was now lively and chatty; about to perform, the stage nerves had gone. He was driven a few miles to Fleur d'Eau, another lakeside chateau where the Americans were to host the first-day's sessions. He paced around its rooms, awaiting Gorbachev's arrival, as Secret Service agents relayed news of the Soviet cavalcade's progress. "He's two minutes away, Mr. President." Then: "He's coming through the gate." Reagan took a deep breath and stepped out onto the patio as the black limousines drove around the house and scrunched to a halt on the gravel. The handshakes were firm, the smiles warm, but what struck waiting journalists and TV viewers around the world was the way the two leaders looked. Gorbachev, muffled against the cold in coat, hat and scarf; Reagan supremely elegant in his dark navy suit—almost, it seemed, the younger man. Gorbachev got the message instantly, pulling off his hat, but that only revealed he had less hair than the president. His aides were furious at Reagan's public relations coup. The whole

FLEUR D'EAU
GROUND FLOOR - MEETING SITE
GENEVA, SWITZERLAND

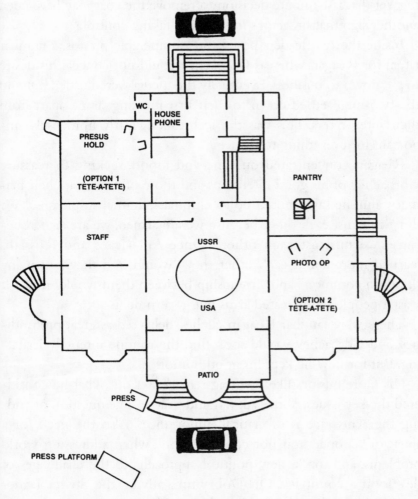

Map 7-1 *Fleur d'Eau,* the venue for day one of the Geneva summit. The patio is at the rear of the house, from where a lawn slopes gently down to the lake. The first meeting took place in the room marked "Option 1" and the plenary in the large room off the patio. (Ronald Reagan Library)

business was possibly less Machiavellian than they believed: the president had been bickering with staff beforehand whether or not to wear an overcoat; he hated the encumbrance but the cold was biting. Yet that last-minute decision to remove the coat may have been another sign that his actor's instinct was taking control.[69]

Inside the two leaders posed for innumerable photos, a familiar ritual for Reagan whereas Gorbachev could not conceal his desire to get down to business. Eventually the media were hustled out and the two men settled down to their first meeting, alone apart from their interpreters. This was the icebreaker, clearly immensely important for everything to come.[70]

Reagan concentrated on tone and mood, seeking to reassure Gorbachev of his good intentions and those of America. Their primary aim, he said, should be to eliminate mutual suspicions. "We don't mistrust each other because we are armed, we are armed because we mistrust each other." Once Americans and Russians learned more about each other they "would find they had many things in common" and "friendship between them would grow." It wasn't people who created arms but governments.

These were familiar Reagan clichés, delivered as great profundities, and Gorbachev would soon find the routine intensely irritating. But for now he kept his good humor.

His more businesslike opening remarks set out what he considered the key issues. Above all, war and peace: "The question of ending the arms race is of critical importance." Also the need for a spirit of "cooperation not confrontation" when addressing world problems, and for "a new political approach" to the challenges of developing countries. On Dobrynin's advice the Soviet leader avoided heavy detail and added plenty of humor.

Toward the end Reagan got in a few digs, noting that one cause of mistrust in the United States was the Soviet practice of "helping socialist revolutions throughout the world and the belief that the Marxist system should prevail." Gorbachev responded that "you should not think that Moscow is omnipotent and that I wake up every morning thinking about which country I wanted to start a revolution in."

Overall, though, the atmosphere remained cordial, with both men deliberately pulling their punches.

Fifteen to twenty minutes had been scheduled for this opening encounter. Since interpretation was consecutive, that was always likely to be unrealistic. Outside the room Americans and Russians milled around, chatting edgily and wondering how things were going. After half an hour Don Regan began to fret about the slippage in the timetable. When nearly an hour had elapsed he badgered Jim Kuhn, the president's principal aide, into asking Shultz whether he should go in and give Reagan an excuse to wind things up. "If you're dumb enough to do that," Shultz exploded to Kuhn, "you shouldn't be in your job." The secretary of state rightly appreciated that keeping to the timetable was far less important than a productive first encounter between the two leaders. But the asperity of his outburst probably reflected his own private anxiety.[71]

Eventually the two leaders emerged, all smiles, and the first plenary session began just before 11:30. After the one-on-one—"four eyes" in diplomatic slang—they moved to "wall-on-wall." One delegation was ranged facing the other across a sixteen-foot oval table especially flown to Geneva from the U.S. mission to the UN. As hosts the Americans generously allowed the Soviets the view toward the lake (and also the sun in their eyes if it happened to be shining). In the plenaries, for the first time in Soviet-American summits, interpretation would be simultaneous, so there was an interpreter and a notetaker on both sides. Gorbachev clearly relished the technology: intuiting the gist of many of Reagan's remarks, he often jumped in before the translator was finished. The president, in contrast, was very deaf in his right ear and wore a hearing aid. He had to switch that off in order to concentrate on the interpreter's voice plugged into his left ear and this reduced the impact of Gorbachev's performance.[72]

In substance the two leaders were mostly developing ideas they had articulated when alone, sticking close to their prepared talking points. Gorbachev, who spoke first for about half an hour, kept on about "war and peace" while Reagan's theme remained that of mutual suspicion. Overall "the language was restrained, the atmosphere polite," recalled Don Regan. "Neither side wished anything to go wrong before the summit had fairly begun." But at the end the president alluded to SDI, reiterating that they should share this "defensive" technology. He knew Gorbachev would have no time to reply before lunch and wanted the Soviet leader to reflect on his offer, in light of the trust he had tried to foster during the morning. But Gorbachev was not impressed. He complained to his staff during the break: "This man is a real dinosaur."[73]

Lunch was taken separately, giving each leader a chance to brief his aides, chew over the morning and fine-tune tactics for the afternoon. According to the loose agenda, the general topic for this second plenary session was to be arms control. The Americans expected an all-out attack on SDI and they were quite right.[74]

The Soviet leader denounced America's "primitive approach" to world problems, assuming all "hotbeds of conflict" around the world could be blamed on the Soviet Union. This was either an illusion or "deliberate distortion." He disputed Reagan's claims of a Soviet arms buildup, insisting that the United States still had more nuclear weapons. And he warned that SDI would lead to "an arms race in space which is not only defensive but offensive. Space weapons will be harder to verify and will feed suspicions and mistrust . . . We will not help you in your plans," he told the president; on the contrary, "we will build up in order to smash your shield."

This was powerful stuff. Gorbachev spoke in torrents, his grammar sometimes dissolving in the flood of words, which made it very hard to interpret. His body language was vigorous, often unrestrained: for emphasis he struck the edge of his hand rhythmically on the table. Sometimes he would point a finger accusingly; on other occasions he sat back in his chair, arms spread wide in a gesture of incredulity.

But Reagan gave as good as he got. Gorbachev's presentation, he said, illustrated "the lack of trust between us." Leafing through his prompt cards, he reeled off examples of Soviet double-dealing—from World War II to the present, from nuclear weapons to Afghanistan. "SDI is my idea," the president insisted, "I'm talking about a shield." That's what was being researched. "If a defensive system is found, we would prefer to sit down and get rid of nuclear weapons and, with them, the threat of war."

The atmosphere was getting heated. It seemed almost a replay of Kennedy and Khrushchev trading accusations at Vienna nearly a quarter century before. Indeed, reviewing the transcript a few years later, Gorbachev said it read like "the 'No. 1 Communist' and the 'No. 1 Imperialist' trying to out-argue each another."[75] Simultaneous translation was probably making matters worse by allowing each leader to react immediately and impulsively.

But then Reagan suddenly defused the tension by suggesting they take a walk outside. This had been planned beforehand for just such a moment and Gorbachev accepted with alacrity. Remembering his arrival that morning, though, he would not put on his overcoat until sure that Reagan was doing the same. Outside they chatted about Reagan's Hollywood years. The president had been piqued by a recent comment of Georgi Arbatov, head of the influential U.S.-Canada Institute in Moscow, that he was "a Grade B movie actor." "Tell Arbatov, I didn't just make B-movies," Reagan remarked. "I made a few good ones." Gorbachev had recently seen *King's Row* and said he liked it very much. This was a shrewd move because Reagan considered that his best movie, famous for his line on discovering both his legs had been amputated by a vindictive doctor: "Where's the rest of me?"[76]

All the time Reagan was testing Gorbachev's sense of humor, which he regarded as an important test of whether they would be able to get on. In one of his jokes an American and a Russian were debating freedom in their respective countries. The American claimed he could walk into the Oval Office, pound the table and say he didn't like the way Reagan ran the United States. "So what?" responds the Russian: "I can do exactly the same. I can walk into the Kremlin, pound the table and say I don't like the way Reagan is running the United States."[77] Most of the president's Russian jokes had an anti-Soviet sting in the tail. He didn't seem to appreciate that Gorbachev could have a sense of humor and yet not find these stories particularly amusing.

Back in the main house feelings were still high. Georgii Kornienko, the deputy foreign minister, was angry that Reagan had asserted that the Soviets did not allow U.S. bombers, after runs over German targets in 1944, to refuel on Russian soil, implying that this had caused unnecessary American loss of life. That claim wasn't true, Kornienko fumed, citing the huge Soviet airbase at Poltava. "I personally was a citizen defending that base, and was injured. Many died there. I know the U.S. general in charge . . . What kind of information is being given to President Reagan?" Shultz cut him off sharply: "If President Reagan is wrong, I will tell him. Let's turn to different things." But it was a fair point. Hurried cabling back to Washington that afternoon established that three such bases had been used to support at least fourteen missions in the summer of 1944 and that Soviet cooperation had been at least "sufficient." On the other hand, it had taken months to hammer out the wartime arrangements, which did not last long. The president's point was not devoid of truth but, as so often, the facts he cited were inaccurate. Kornienko's very personal intervention helps us understand the continued Soviet suspicions of Reagan.[78]

Meanwhile the two leaders had strolled down to a poolhouse by the lake where a roaring fire awaited them. Reagan handed Gorbachev a translation of the latest American arms control proposal and they quickly got back to SDI.[79]

The Soviet leader hammered away about the folly of "space weapons." Reagan kept insisting that SDI was purely defensive and that he would share the results. Gorbachev came back at him with real feeling. What, he asked, was the point of "deploying a weapon that is as yet unknown and unpredictable?" Where was the logic of "starting an arms race in a new sphere?"

Reagan returned to his favorite image of the spear and the shield. The two superpowers should "go forward to rid the world of the threat of nuclear weapons" but retain a shield in case "there was an unforeseeable return to nuclear missiles."

Eventually Gorbachev said he could understand the president's feelings "on a human level": clearly the idea of strategic defense had captured Reagan's imagination. But "as a political leader" Gorbachev couldn't possibly agree. There was a scientific consensus that strategic defense had threatening implications. America would be able to launch its nuclear spear, then use its shield as protection when the Soviets threw their own spear in retaliation. In other words, America would be in a position to mount a first strike against the Soviet Union. "I firmly believe," said Gorbachev, that "I must do everything in my power to stop this project from happening."

Before the summit, when Shultz warned that Gorbachev would go all-out against SDI, the president wrote in his diary: "Well, this will be a case of an irresistible force meeting an immovable object." But rather than letting the collision break up the summit, as happened over Berlin in 1961, the two leaders again backed off. Walking back from the pool house just before 5 p.m., Gorbachev said something about the value of further meetings; Reagan then extended an invitation to Washington. Gorbachev accepted and suggested a return visit to Moscow. The idea of future summits had been on the agenda but Reagan's advisors had told him not to broach the matter early on. Shultz and the others were therefore astonished when the president announced that he and Gorbachev had already fixed it all up. He ribbed them about his diplomatic "coup" for weeks afterward.[80]

When the two men parted on the gravel, they "locked hands and eyes with real affection," according to Reagan's official biographer. "I have rarely seen such mutuality." Gorbachev recalled a "spark of electric mutual trust which ignited between us, like a voltaic arc between two electric poles." In the morning, the Soviet leader told his aides, he had seen only "blank, uncomprehending eyes" as Reagan "mumbled certain banalities from his paper." But by the end of their talk in the pool house, they had managed a human conversation. He also recognized Reagan's sincerity about SDI, even though convinced it was totally misguided. The president was struck by the way Gorbachev had made several references to "God" during the day and wondered whether these were signs of closet Christianity.[81] He certainly enjoyed the Soviet leader's passion and directness. Most Western leaders, except Margaret Thatcher, treated him rather like an elderly relative, but Gorbachev was not in the least deferential. "You could almost get to like the guy," the president told Don Regan that evening. "I keep telling myself I mustn't do it, because he could turn."[82]

Their rapport strengthened during dinner at the Soviet mission, as they chatted easily about movies, travel and their families. Both men were relaxed and humorous; aware of Reagan's love of anecdotes, Gorbachev had come with some jokes of his own. One concerned a presummit cartoon of the two of them on either side of an abyss. "Gorby," shouts Reagan, "I am ready to go my part of the way." Gorbachev waves back: "Come on over."[83]

Their wives did not bridge the gap. The encounter between the First Ladies had been hyped up by the Western media for weeks beforehand. Not only was Raisa (in the unchivalrous cliché of the time) the first Soviet leader's wife to weigh less than her husband, she was also attractive, articulate and well dressed. "This is going to be probably as competitive a press arena as that of the negotiating table in Geneva," warned one White House aide.[84]

While their husbands were talking in the pool house that afternoon, Nancy Reagan entertained Raisa Gorbachev at tea in the Maison de Saussure. Although mutual invitations to visit America and Russia were issued and accepted, the conversation—about weather, jet lag and favorite flowers—was strained. The two women were like oil and water—an ex-Hollywood star who had devoted her life to her husband and a PhD in sociology who lectured on Marxism-Leninism. "Lectured" was in fact the operative word about Raisa. That evening at dinner she delivered a lengthy analysis of Russian history. She argued that having to act as Europe's buffer against the Asiatic hordes was the reason her country had fallen behind. She also had lauded Soviet achievements to the president, who listened gallantly. Nancy, no shrinking violet, had difficulty getting a word in edgewise. "Who does that dame think she is?" she exploded afterward.[85]

Robert McFarlane was sitting near Raisa at dinner and decided not to let her get away with her litany of Soviet accomplishments. After a lively exchange, McFarlane deemed it politic to shift to the pleasures of Switzerland, not least its chocolates. "We have excellent chocolates in the Soviet Union," Raisa insisted, and developed this

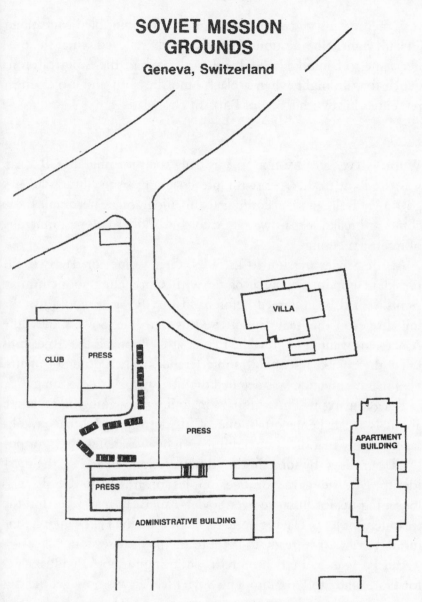

SOVIET MISSION GROUNDS
Geneva, Switzerland

Map 7-2 The Soviet mission to the United Nations, on Avenue de la Paix near the center of Geneva. Dinner on day one of the summit was held in the villa; the meetings on day two in the Administrative Building. (Ronald Reagan Library)

new theme for some time. "I'm sure you do," mumbled McFarlane. "That's right. No question." He was greatly relieved when the dinner came to an end. Hardly had he got back to the American residence for the night when a black limo drew up and a messenger presented him with a box of Russian chocolates.[86]

WEDNESDAY, NOVEMBER 20 was truly the morning after. Reagan was tired and restless—last-minute coaching from Shultz did not go down well—and, according to his biographer, he drank more coffee at breakfast than was good for his bladder before a morning of intense meetings.[87]

At the Soviet mission to the UN, their venue for day two, the president got into a fierce battle with Gorbachev about human rights. It had been agreed beforehand that Reagan would use the initial one-on-one that day to raise this issue. The Soviets knew the Americans wanted to press the matter at Geneva and the Americans knew the Soviets resented this interference in their domestic affairs. So a private meeting was deemed the best way to handle things.[88]

But Reagan piled in with passionate intensity, going on at length about Russian Pentecostals, one of his pet topics. Gorbachev observed testily that the issue of human rights was being used "for political purposes" by some in the administration, "including the president." But he gave some examples of how the USSR was loosening up, for instance over Soviet-American marriages and the treatment of Jews. Having gone through this ritual exchange, he indicated that he was ready to get into the plenary session.

But Reagan had much more to say, bringing up individual cases for Gorbachev to look into. The Soviet leader was now getting hot under the collar. The previous day American civil rights leader Jesse Jackson had needled him about Soviet Jews, during an impromptu encounter in the lobby of the Soviet mission.[89] What about the position of blacks in the United States? Gorbachev asked Reagan. What about women? The president's line, he complained, was always that "there are no rights in socialist countries" whereas "they are in bloom in the democracies."

Reagan argued that concessions on human rights would ease pressure on him back home from anti-Soviet pressure groups and so expedite arms control agreements. "I know what the president can do as a political leader when he wants to," Gorbachev replied scathingly. "When he doesn't want to, he talks about pressure groups, and so on." By the end Gorbachev was interrupting Reagan without listening to the translation, so impatient was he to bring the session to an end.

As on day one this initial private session had grossly overrun: they had been at it for seventy minutes. But whereas the Tuesday tête-à-tête had fostered a good mood, Wednesday's left both men frustrated and angry. Those feelings carried over into the plenary, which finally began at 11:30.

This was supposed to address regional and bilateral issues, but Reagan wanted to pick up on some aspects of arms control for which there hadn't been time the previous afternoon. He read methodically from his talking points, which probably added to Gorbachev's irritation; he was becoming contemptuous of the president's reliance on briefing books and index cards. Eventually the Soviet leader had a chance to respond and he soon pulled the discussion back to SDI. Now very emotional, his language became increasingly blunt. "Do you take us for idiots?" And again: "I think it inappropriate in our conversation to inject banalities more in keeping with press conferences." They went over the same ground again, with Gorbachev talking of the threat of an American first strike and Reagan trotting out his line about a shield not a spear.[90]

"Why don't you believe me when I say the Soviet Union will never attack?" demanded Gorbachev.

Reagan started to respond.

"Please answer me, Mr. President. What is your answer?"

And again, before Reagan could get going: "I want an answer from you. Why won't you believe me?"

Finally Reagan got a word in: "Look, no one can say to the American people that they should rely on personal faith rather than sound defense."[91]

Gorbachev shifted ground. "Why should I accept your sincerity on your willingness to share SDI research when you don't even share your advanced technology with your allies? Let's be more realistic. We're prepared to compromise." Once again he went over the Soviet offer: "deep cuts" in nuclear arsenals if the United States would abandon the "firebird" of SDI.

There was silence. A long silence. At least thirty seconds, Shultz thought. Finally Gorbachev tossed his pencil on the table, sat back in his chair and spread his arms wide. "Mr. President, I don't agree with you, but I can see you really mean what you say." Then very calmly: "Maybe this has all grown a little bit heated. I was just trying to convey to you the depth of our concerns on SDI."[92]

Although the talk went on, the Americans saw this as a turning point in the session: the Russian had blinked. But Gorbachev told his advisors afterward that he decided to cut off the discussion because there was clearly no way at Geneva to persuade Reagan to drop SDI. He said he would try again at future summits rather than risk bringing this one to ruin.[93] Once again, his attitude was very different from Khrushchev's obsessive point-scoring at Vienna. Gorbachev was thinking long, envisaging summitry as a process not an event.

After lunch the two leaders came back all smiles and pleasantries. This final plenary was intended to sum up their summit. Both men played up the positive features, stressing the importance of a continuing dialogue, especially future summits. The Soviets cautiously raised the question of a joint statement and Reagan was now much more forthcoming. He apologized for any "confusion" beforehand, explaining his opposition to anything "pre-cooked," and agreed that such a document might be "worthwhile." The Soviet and American delegations had informally started discussing an outline; their work now moved into high gear while the two leaders had an animated chat.[94]

Yet a few steps away stood their special military aides, each carrying the celebrated "football," a briefcase containing the codes for unleashing nuclear weapons against the other's country. Ken Adelman wondered whether each would acknowledge the other's existence but both officers kept gazing intently at their respective leaders.[95] As with the special communications room for the Americans in the Soviet embassy in Vienna in June 1961, the episode evoked the surrealism of the nuclear age.

Elsewhere in the Soviet mission the two wives were enduring another tea party. Raisa wanted to show off some children's posters on the theme "what the world means to me" and insisted on explaining the meaning of each picture in detail. Nancy found it all very condescending and had to restrain herself from saying "You don't have to tell me what a missile is. I get the message." On this occasion Raisa, usually very chic, had worn a black skirt, white shirt and black tie. A puzzled Nancy later discovered that this was the standard uniform for Russian teachers. It was the only time Raisa would be photographed for Soviet consumption and Gorbachev's wife, though an object of fascination in the West, knew that her manner and wardrobe were fiercely controversial back home.[96]

At dinner that evening at Maison de Saussure, the mood was convivial. The leaders were again on good form and their wives a bit more relaxed. Reagan remarked that he and Gorbachev were meeting for the first time at this level; they therefore had little practice but, having read the history of previous summits, he had concluded that earlier leaders had not accomplished very much. So he suggested, with Gorbachev nodding in agreement, that the two of them should simply say "To hell with the past—we'll do it our way and get something done." When an angry Shultz interrupted coffee to complain that Kornienko, a holdover from the Gromyko era, was blocking agreement on parts of the joint statement, Gorbachev said smilingly to Reagan: "Let's put our foot down." Each took his delegation aside. In fact the Soviet leader leaned harder on his staff to sort things out.[97]

Even so it took most of the night for the two delegations to hammer out the wording, gradually eliminating or resolving the contested passages in their draft. The Soviets had wanted to agree on the resumption of direct flights between the two countries— suspended after KE 007—the quid pro quo for the American program of cultural exchanges. This was where Gorbachev put his foot down. The Americans were also pleased with his promise about "resolving humanitarian cases in the spirit of cooperation." The Soviets for their part secured a statement that both sides "agreed that a nuclear war cannot be won and must never be fought"—a matter of real moment for the Politburo after the 1983 war scare—and also a general commitment to "prevent an arms race in space and to terminate it on earth." Most important, both sides pledged to "place on a regular basis and intensify dialogue at various levels." This process was to include "greater travel and people-to-people contact" and regular meetings between foreign ministers and between heads of other departments. There was also a promise to meet at the summit again "in the nearest future" in Washington and then in Moscow.[98]

At ten o'clock on Thursday, November 21 the statement was issued and the two leaders spoke briefly to the media. Predictably Gorbachev featured the arms control discussions and Reagan the wider American agenda, but both leaders gave optimistic assessments of the good start they had made. Gorbachev then traveled to Prague to meet Warsaw Pact leaders, while Reagan flew to Brussels to brief his Western allies. Again the president presented this first meeting "not as a watershed event in and of itself, but rather an important part of a vital long-term process." Most NATO leaders offered congratulations but Margaret Thatcher was more cautious: "The presentation and style of the Soviet leadership have changed but the substance appears the same." After ninety minutes Reagan flew back across the Atlantic to address a joint session of the U.S. Congress at 9:20 p.m. Washington time, his speech carried live on radio and TV.[99]

Like Nixon in 1972, Reagan wanted to put his own spin without delay on how the summit was interpreted. He admitted there wasn't a "meeting of minds" on ideology or national purpose, but stressed the range and candor of what he called their "fireside summit": five of the fifteen hours had been spent one on one. He also featured their agreement "in the parking lot" for future meetings in Washington and Moscow. The president's speech went down extremely well: "I hadn't gotten such a reception since I was shot," he noted in his diary. It rounded off a day that began twenty hours earlier, showing that the aging president could rise to the occasion when it really mattered.[100]

What was his private verdict? Reagan's hawkish speechwriters—particularly Peggy Noonan and Pat Buchanan—had inserted derogatory comments about the Soviet Union and Gorbachev himself into the speech, but the president took them out. "This has been a good meeting. I think I can work with this guy," Reagan insisted. "I can't just keep poking him in the eye." To communist leaders around the world, Gorbachev played up Geneva as "a real skirmish," claiming that Don Regan had told him afterward that "no one had ever talked so frankly and with such force to the president before." But on the plane home he remarked to his entourage that, although Reagan was "stubborn and very conservative," he was "not as hopeless as some believed." Hardly a ringing endorsement, but Gorbachev felt he had made contact with Reagan and could work with him.[101]

AFTER THE SUMMIT there was bound to be a letdown. In Moscow Gorbachev faced criticism about his lack of achievements at Geneva, not only from old-guard politicians such as Vladimir Shcherbistky, the party boss of the Ukraine, but also Marshal Sergei Akhromeyev, chief of staff of the Soviet armed forces. In Washington, McFarlane resigned as national security advisor, shattered by the high-level feuds. And a weary Shultz had to be dissuaded from going as well.[102]

By the new year the spirit of Geneva seemed to have evaporated. Gorbachev felt he could not go to Washington unless assured of an arms control agreement—one "getting acquainted" meeting was enough—yet Reagan clearly would not give up SDI. For his part the president was now losing confidence in the Soviet leader, who seemed to be backing away from his promise to maintain their dialogue through a summit in Washington. Although on a personal level Gorbachev made a very good impression at Geneva, he had also lapsed frequently into old-style Leninist jargon and fierce denunciations of the United States. This side of Gorbachev seems to have been uppermost in Reagan's mind by early 1986. Moreover Gorbachev's focus clearly remained SDI and arms control, with little attention to other areas of the American agenda, notably Afghanistan and human rights, which the administration regarded as litmus tests of any real change in the Kremlin. Told that there was no movement on the Soviet side, the president said: "Well, let's wait until there is. Then we'll see what we can do."[103]

For Gorbachev too the negatives about Geneva came to obscure the positives. In February he told the leader of the American communist party that Reagan said many things that were frankly "trite." He seemed "so loaded down with stereotypes that it was difficult for him to accept reason. Whenever I brought up specifics the president immediately let Shultz take over. And during our 'fireside chats,' as the president called them, Reagan read prepared texts." Geneva, said Gorbachev, was necessary "simply to explain our positions to each other" and to start a dialogue. But a second summit had to be "a step beyond" and lead to "real progress on the crucial issues in our relations."[104]

Without impetus from the top, the working groups of diplomats and officials set up at Geneva never got going. Arms control, in particular, remained in the hands of conservatives on both sides; they had been haggling for years in Geneva and were set in their positions. "This whole thing smells of mothballs," Gorbachev fumed. "We should give a shake-up to all this old clothing." But Reagan, his interest waning, saw no reason to take the initiative.[105]

Gorbachev was now publicly demanding "new thinking," encouraged by new advisors drawn from outside the Foreign Ministry, notably the policy intellectual Anatoly Chernyaev. His report to the 27th Party Congress in February 1986, though still loaded with criticisms of Western imperialism, broke new ground. It stressed the "interdependence" of the two worlds of capitalism and communism, going far beyond the old rhetoric about peaceful coexistence. And it insisted that security in a nuclear world could only be "mutual," satisfying both sides rather than being a zero-sum game. But even more than in Washington "new thinking" had yet to permeate the middle layers of the bureaucracy. This became clear in April with the explosion at the Chernobyl nuclear reactor in the Ukraine. Although only two people died immediately, the disaster demonstrated the appalling dangers of any kind of nuclear discharge and proved, even more than the KE 007 affair, the inefficiency and secretiveness of the Soviet bureaucracy. New slogans began to feature in Gorbachev's vocabulary: *glasnost,* signifying "transparency" or "openness," and *perestroika,* meaning "restructuring." He had not given up on communism or the party, but the 1985 rhetoric about simply speeding up the old system— *uskorenie*—faded away. His goal now was radical reform.[106]

Two visitors that summer—François Mitterrand and Richard Nixon—helped rekindle Gorbachev's ardor for summitry. Mitterrand was not only socialist but also French, and therefore doubly unlikely to admire Reagan. As the president rambled anecdotally during their first G7 summit in July 1981, Mitterrand wondered: "What planet is this man living on?" But after reflection he offered shrewd, if condescending, approval: "This is a man without ideas and without culture . . . but, under the surface, you will find someone who is not stupid, who has great good sense, and who is profoundly well-intentioned."[107]

In July 1986 Mitterrand met both superpower leaders in quick succession, trying to act as an intermediary. Reagan agreed with Mitterrand that Gorbachev was the first Soviet leader to behave like "a modern man." But, he went on, "Can we believe that he means to abandon the fundamentals of their foreign policy, namely expansion and global communism? Up to now, Gorbachev has not said that. And as long as they are like that, we cannot sign verifiable treaties." In Moscow, three days later, Gorbachev fumed that Reagan was just a tool of the American military-industrial complex, but Mitterrand stopped him short. Yes, Reagan was under its influence, but he also entertained very different ideas and took a "prophetic position" of his own. Despite his political past, Mitterrand continued, Reagan was "intuitively striving to find a way out of the current tension. He's not an automaton, he likes to laugh and, more than the others, is responsive to the language of peace." Mitterrand's sense of Reagan's contradictions struck Gorbachev forcibly. "This is extremely important," he said, "and I'm taking special note of it."[108]

Ten days later the Soviet leader was told much the same thing by an American VIP. Former President Richard Nixon insisted that Reagan was sincere about peace and viewed the Soviet-American relationship as "his personal responsibility." Nixon emphasized that Reagan was a conservative and therefore in a position, unlike any Democratic president, to make an agreement stick. Failure to reach an accord while Reagan was in office could provoke a powerful backlash. Nixon sent Reagan a report of his visit to the Kremlin, stressing Gorbachev's skill, subtlety and goodwill. Like Mitterrand, the veteran summiteer saw himself as Pandarus, trying to bring the reluctant couple together again.[109]

In August, while vacationing on the Black Sea, Gorbachev mulled over this advice from Mitterrand and Nixon as he read with distaste a Foreign Ministry outline for a future meeting with Reagan. Chernyaev agreed: "It's no good." Gorbachev, more bluntly, said it was "simply crap." He fumed about how the Foreign Ministry had still not learned to "think big": they got caught up in details, they were afraid to lose face. He told Chernyaev he wanted the Foreign Ministry to prepare a letter proposing that the two leaders meet "in late September or early October either in London or"—a slight pause—"Reykjavik."

"Why Reykjavik?" asked Chernyaev.

"Halfway between us and them, and none of the big powers will be offended."[110]

The letter was finally delivered by Shevardnadze in Washington on September 19. Gorbachev set out an array of recent problems in the talks about "space weapons," intermediate nuclear forces in Europe, and nuclear testing, making clear that he blamed U.S. negotiators. "In almost a year since Geneva there has been no progress on these issues," he told Reagan; the talks would "lead nowhere until you and I intervene personally." He therefore proposed

a quick one-on-one meeting, let us say in Iceland or in London, maybe just for one day, to engage in a strictly confidential, private and frank discussion (possibly with only our foreign ministers present). The discussion—which would not be a detailed one, for its purpose and significance would be to demonstrate political will—would result in instructions to our respective agencies to draft agreements on two or three very specific questions which you and I could sign during my visit to the United States.[111]

Gorbachev's gambit was classic summitry—a top-level meeting to kickstart negotiations that were stalled lower down.

But once again progress was nearly sabotaged by free-ranging bureaucrats. The FBI, pursuing its own narrow agenda, chose the end of August to mount a sting operation to trap Gennadi Zakharov, an employee at the UN Secretariat. The Bureau was concerned at the number of Soviet agents operating under UN cover and, since Zakharov was not a diplomat and therefore did not enjoy diplomatic immunity, it intended to put him on trial as an example. Absolutely predictably the Soviets retaliated in kind, arresting Nicholas Daniloff, an American journalist in Moscow, on charges of espionage. What started as routine bureaucratic tit-for-tat quickly escalated to the top level. This was just the sort of human case that Reagan focused on—graphic evidence that the Soviet system was still evil at its heart. "I'm mad as hell," he wrote in his diary. Gorbachev was still calling Daniloff a spy despite Reagan's personal assurances to the contrary. (Although the president was strictly correct, Daniloff had been used in the past as an unwitting courier for the CIA. The State Department legal advisor told Reagan there was sufficient circumstantial evidence to convict Daniloff even in a U.S. court.) Eventually the affair was resolved by what Jack Matlock has confessed was "a thinly disguised trade," releasing Daniloff for Zakharov. The Americans could deny it was a direct swap because the Soviets also threw in an imprisoned Soviet dissident. The deal was arranged by Shultz and Shevardnadze, who had to rely entirely on each other's word that they could extract the three men from the tenacious grasp of bureaucratic rivals. Their successful resolution of the affair was a major step in building personal trust.[112]

It also ensured American agreement to meet at Reykjavik. The Icelandic government made available a government conference center, the Hofdi House, for the weekend. Reagan stayed with the U.S. ambassador; Gorbachev used a Soviet ship moored in the harbor. As at Geneva there was a huge media presence—one of whom was the newly released Nick Daniloff. Initially both First Ladies decided not to attend since this was to be a short business meeting. Later on Raisa changed her mind, but Nancy decided not to. She avoided another tea party but conceded all the limelight to her Soviet rival.

Hoping to cut through the bureaucratic logjam, Gorbachev's strategy was to "sweep Reagan off his feet" by a "bold," even "risky" approach to the arms race. Dobrynin and parts of the Politburo felt Gorbachev had become "unreasonably fixated" by SDI—which only encouraged the Americans to keep up the pressure. And Chernyaev urged him to drop any attempts at linkage lest Reykjavik prove "another dead end." But although Gorbachev said on several occasions that "we have to stop being afraid of SDI," he seems to have meant not allowing the Americans to use it as intimidation. His aim at Reykjavik was still to secure an end to SDI in return for even more radical cuts in nuclear arsenals. And he still took little interest in the rest of the American agenda. "New thinking" had not yet prevailed over the old.[113]

American conservatives have been fiercely critical of the administration's "hasty acceptance of a hasty offer for a hasty meeting"; some speak of the Soviets springing a "trap" into which the administration nearly fell.[114] Reagan certainly did not prepare for Reykjavik with the assiduity he had shown before Geneva, perhaps the most carefully prepared event of his presidency.[115] There were, after all, only a few weeks of lead time. The administration set up some planning groups and took the usual astrological advice, but NSC staffers totally failed to anticipate Gorbachev's "bold" approach. They thought him "coy" or even "undecided" about a summit and warned Reagan of the need to "smoke him out."[116] The White House hoped to reach agreement on a few key issues, notably intermediate nuclear forces (INF) in Europe, thereby persuading Gorbachev to set a firm date for the Washington summit. Reagan insisted that he would "not permit the meeting to focus exclusively or disproportionately on arms control" and promised to "ensure that regional, bilateral and human rights issues" were "thoroughly reviewed."[117]

He did try to do that in their opening meeting on Saturday, October 11 but was swept aside by a torrent of words as Gorbachev outlined new proposals for 50 percent cuts in nuclear arsenals and an INF treaty that disregarded British and French nuclear deterrents. Over lunch Reagan's staff drew up some talking points in reply, which the president, much more comfortable with a script, spent most of the afternoon session reading out. Gorbachev was peeved but agreed that, overnight, staffers should try to reconcile their positions. Two working groups were set up, one on arms control, the other on the rest of the American agenda. There was little progress on the latter, but on arms control Marshal Sergei Akhromeyev, chief of the Soviet general staff, cut through the traditional roadblocks with clearcut decisions. The pace was exhilarating but also unsettling. During the night the high-tech Americans found themselves with no access to computers or even a photocopier. They prepared and circulated a new set of proposals, but only with the aid of carbon paper donated by the Soviets.[118]

On the second day, Sunday, October 12, the pace was even more intense. Unlike Geneva, there were no plenary sessions to hold the leaders in check: they talked one to one except for interpreters and foreign ministers. The experts were told to do what their leaders wanted, rather than try to keep them in line. The drafting was feverish. At one point, finding all the rooms occupied, Robert Linhard and Richard Perle put a board across a bathtub to create some writing space.[119]

The result, by 5:30 that afternoon, was a dramatic arms control package. Both sides would adhere to the 1972 ABM treaty for ten years—meaning no deployment of SDI during that time. They would make 50 percent cuts in all "strategic offensive weapons" over the first five years and eliminate all "offensive ballistic missiles" in the remaining five. But Gorbachev was still unhappy on two points. He wanted research on SDI confined "to the laboratory" and he noted that the two five-year periods were not symmetrical. Indeed they weren't. The elimination of all ballistic missiles would leave the United States with vast nuclear superiority in strategic bombers, which is why Weinberger had been pushing the idea for some months as a shrewd negotiating ploy. Yet Reagan—whose grasp of the distinction between "missiles" and "weapons" was fuzzy and who in any case hated all things nuclear—said: "It would be fine with me if we eliminate all nuclear weapons." Gorbachev replied: "We can do that. We can eliminate them." Shultz did not demur. On the contrary he said: "Let's do it." Reagan then said they could turn this over to the arms control negotiators to draft a treaty, which Gorbachev could come to America to sign. The Soviet leader agreed.[120]

This was an astonishing breakthrough. But Gorbachev still wanted SDI research explicitly confined to the "laboratory" and that became the sticking point. "I cannot give in," said the president. "This is my last word," replied the Soviet leader. Both men were now eloquent and impassioned: Reagan needed no prompt cards. He asked whether Gorbachev was going to throw everything away for "one word." I could say the same to you, Gorbachev replied. This was a question of principle for his country. Without such tight restrictions, the Americans could research and test a space-weapons system over the next ten years and then deploy it when the Soviets had scrapped their nuclear arsenal. If he went back to Moscow with that kind of agreement, he would be called an idiot.[121] "I have a clear conscience before my people and before you," Gorbachev declared. "I have done everything I could."[122]

The original American record indicates the conference ended at that point. But so important was this final meeting that a second version of the minutes was produced, trying to give fuller context to the cut and thrust of the debate. This left the last move to Reagan, who stood up on hearing Gorbachev's words. Both men collected their papers and went outside. Gorbachev conveyed his greetings to Nancy Reagan, then "they shook hands and parted." But the Soviet minutes record further exchanges in the room.

"It's too bad to part this way. We were so close to an agreement," Reagan declared, adding that he didn't think Gorbachev wanted an agreement anyway.

Gorbachev replied: "I wanted an agreement and did everything I could, if not more."

"I don't know when we'll ever have another chance like this," Reagan added, "and whether we will meet soon."

"I don't either," said Gorbachev. [123]

In his memoirs Reagan reported an additional conversation as they reached their cars. "I don't know what else I could have done," said Gorbachev. "I do," Reagan replied. "You could have said yes." The precise ending to Reykjavik is almost impossible to discern amid all the spin and the myths.[124]

Afterward the president was too tired to talk to the media. In any case a free-flowing, high-stakes press conference was hardly his forte. So the briefings were done by Shultz in Reykjavik and later, on Air Force One, by National Security Advisor John Poindexter. Both men tried to sound positive but their gray, dejected faces were far more eloquent—"failure" was the message graphically conveyed to the American media. Gorbachev, in contrast, conducted his own press conference a mere twenty minutes after the summit ended. His first instinct had been to blast the Americans for blocking the world's hopes of peace: this had been the contingency plan concocted in Moscow. But as he entered the packed conference hall, he sensed the crowd's genuine anxiety. Overcoming his weariness and frustration, he gave an upbeat assessment, noting the numerous issues that had been agreed. "In spite of all its drama, Reykjavik is not a failure—it is a breakthrough, which allowed us for the first time to look over the horizon." On the plane home NSC staffer Jack Matlock came to the same conclusion, after finally getting hold of the interpreter's notes for the last session. The number of key points agreed on seemed unprecedented: when listed, they filled a full page of a yellow legal pad. He showed this to Regan and Poindexter, but by then Reykjavik had been spun to the American media.[125]

Reagan was widely criticized by liberals in the West for sacrificing world peace on the altar of Star Wars. But some senior Soviet aides, including Akhromeyev and Dobrynin, thought Gorbachev had been too obsessive on SDI.[126] Western conservatives were appalled at what Reagan had nearly given away. Thatcher felt as if there had been "an earthquake" beneath her feet. She raced across the Atlantic to pull Reagan back onto the straight and narrow of mutually assured destruction. And Nixon, repeating his usual refrain about a properly prepared meeting, wrote that "no summit since Yalta has threatened Western interests so much as the two days at Reykjavik."[127]

On one level Reykjavik was prefigured at Geneva, when Gorbachev tried and failed to get Reagan to suspend SDI. By October 1986 he was asking for restrictions on research and testing rather than a total ban, but the essential issue remained the same and there was little likelihood that the president would budge. Yet Reykjavik was a quantum leap beyond Geneva because the two leaders, freed from the grip of advisors in plenary sessions, let their antinuclear radicalism take hold. The result was an outline deal to abolish their nuclear weapons by 1996. Such breathtaking novelty would have been inconceivable outside the heady atmosphere of a one-to-one summit.[128]

Above all the two men began to resolve their previously contradictory views of the other. After their post-Reykjavik bitterness had cooled, each could see how far the other had moved and how radically he could think. The emotional outbursts had exposed each man's deepest convictions to the other and this would never have happened except at the summit. Reagan the optimist confirmed his positive impressions at Geneva, his hunch that the human Gorbachev would win out over the Leninist. And the Soviet leader grasped Mitterrand's point that Reagan's peace-loving intuition mattered more than his formulaic Americanism, his reliance on prompt cards or his tedious anecdotes. Before Reykjavik, Gorbachev could still talk of the president as a "fool and a clown" who was not fit to lead a superpower. Afterwards he never spoke of Reagan in that way. Chernyaev believes this was the moment when Gorbachev became convinced that things would "work out" between him and Reagan. "A spark of understanding was born between them, as if they had winked to each other about the future."[129]

DESPITE THE RECRIMINATIONS after Reykjavik, signs of convergence increased in the following months. The high-profile Soviet dissident Andrei Sakharov was released from internal captivity in December 1986, evidence that the Kremlin was taking seriously America's human rights agenda. The following February Gorbachev dropped his attempts to link all progress on arms control with restrictions on SDI. On this he was finally heeding his advisors but also reacting to new realities in the United States: after the Republicans lost control of the Senate in the November 1986 midterm elections, SDI was not going to enjoy the same lavish funding as before.

The Reagan administration was also seriously weakened by the Iran-Contra affair, which first surfaced a few weeks after Reykjavik and consumed public attention for months. NSC staffers had covertly sold arms to Iran—breaching U.S. law and policy—in the hope of securing the release of American hostages in Lebanon. Then it had used some of the profits for the equally illegal support of the Contra anticommunist guerrillas in Nicaragua. At best Reagan was shown to be an ineffectual manager; at worst possibly an accomplice in a new Watergate. The weakened administration needed a foreign-policy success and it was responsive to Gorbachev's efforts to conclude a treaty on intermediate nuclear forces for signing in Washington.

The bureaucratic fallout from Iran-Contra also helped Shultz consolidate his hold over the bureaucracy. Poindexter resigned as national security advisor and Don Regan, who often had turf fights with Shultz, was also forced out. Their replacements, Frank Carlucci and Howard Baker, proved much better team players as far as Shultz was concerned. William Casey, the anti-Soviet CIA director, was also seriously damaged by the affair; he resigned on health grounds a few months later. Other hawks who left the administration during 1987 included speechwriter Pat Buchanan, Richard Perle at the Pentagon and eventually, in November, Weinberger himself. Shultz's relationship with Shevardnadze, though not totally harmonious, deepened through frequent meetings into real trust. Lower down, their senior assistants such as Rozanne Ridgway and Alexander Bessmertnykh also forged effective working relations. The dialogue promised at Geneva in 1985 was beginning to bear fruit.

Gorbachev finally set foot on American soil at 4 p.m. on December 7, 1987. This was the first Soviet-American summit in Washington for fourteen years and only the third in all (Eisenhower and Khrushchev in 1959, Nixon and Brezhnev in 1973). Gorbachev had come to sign the INF treaty, just finalized by negotiators in Geneva. Although affecting only about 5 percent of their nuclear arsenals, some fifty thousand warheads, this was the first time the superpowers had reduced their stockpiles: the SALT agreements of the 1970s had simply limited expansion. The treaty also eliminated a whole class of weapons, including the cruise, Pershing and SS-20 missiles that had brought Europe close to war in 1983. New procedures for verification underpinned the agreement, including unannounced spot inspections. Here was a massive change of heart for the secretive Soviet Union; on some points in fact the Americans proved less radical.[130]

Verification lay at the heart of any successful arms control regime—it was one reason why détente in the 1970s had collapsed—and the treaty therefore showed the character of the new Soviet-American relationship. Reagan alluded to this at the (astrologically timed) signing ceremony, when he trotted out his favorite Russian proverb: *Doveryai, no proveryai* ("Trust, but verify"). "You repeat that at every meeting," Gorbachev interjected. Reagan nodded and smiled. "I like it." There was laughter all around. Even though the two leaders were now on first-name terms, the summit was not without its friction. Gorbachev was getting tired of Reagan's barbed jokes about the Soviet Union, and their exchanges about human rights were again hard-edged. "You are not a prosecutor, and I am not on trial here," Gorbachev snapped at one point.[131]

For Gorbachev the emotional highlight came on December 10, when he suddenly ordered his chauffeur to stop a few blocks from the White House and plunged into a crowd of onlookers—to their delight and the consternation of the security men. America seemed in the grip of Gorbymania (or "Gorbasm" as disgruntled conservatives put it). For a leader now facing growing criticism at home, the adulation was invigorating. This exposure to American life, however superficial, was also an invaluable by-product of summitry. "In Washington, perhaps for the first time," Gorbachev told the Politburo, "we understood so clearly how important the human factor is in international politics. Before, we were content with a rather banal formula," talking about the value of "personal contacts" but meaning only encounters between the "representatives of two irreconcilable systems." Now he saw that policymakers must also "represent purely human qualities, the interests and the aspirations of common people, and that they can be guided by purely normal human feelings and aspirations." In today's world this was of "enormous importance" and it had "produced specific results." He felt all this in "a very, very clear way" in Washington.[132]

The epiphanies were mutual. At a White House dinner Shultz got talking to Marshal Akhromeyev, at this time a crucial ally for Gorbachev in pushing his arms control projects through an increasingly recalcitrant defense establishment. During the evening Akhromeyev unbuttoned enough to talk about his service as a teenage officer fighting Hitler's Wehrmacht. He was now the last soldier on active duty who had served in World War II. "The last of Mohicans," as he put it to Shultz. The secretary of state was astonished at this turn of phrase: it turned out that Akhromeyev, like many Russians of his generation, had read James Fennimore Cooper's novel in translation. "I'm the Marshal of the Soviet Union," he went on emotionally, "and I have had many honors in my career, but I have never been as proud of anything as when I was a sergeant fighting for my country at Leningrad." Then he added quietly: "Until now. My country is in trouble, and I am fighting alongside Mikhail Sergeyevich to save it. That is why we made such a lopsided deal on INF . . . We want to restructure ourselves and to be part of the modern world. We cannot continue to be isolated." Shultz was deeply moved.[133]

At the end of May 1988 Mr. Reagan finally went to Moscow. Joking about the president's now celebrated liking for Russian proverbs, Gorbachev welcomed him with a maxim that was particularly apt: "It is better to see once than to hear a hundred times."[134] An agreement on intercontinental weapons was not ready, mostly because of conservative opposition in Washington, and it was not in fact signed until 1991. But the symbolism of the summit made up for its lack of substance. Reagan sought to match Gorbachev's walkabout in Washington with a stroll down the Arbat, now a pedestrian precinct, though the effect was diminished by the heavy-handed way Soviet police dealt with the crowds. His personal high point was an address on freedom and democracy at the Gorbachevs' alma mater, Moscow State University, delivered under the stony gaze of a huge bust of Lenin. Laced with allusions to movies and classic Russian authors, and followed by a relaxed question-and-answer session with students, this showed the president at his best. Even though only snippets were shown on Soviet television, it helped soften Reagan's image in the eyes of ordinary Russians. The most poignant moment came during a stroll with Gorbachev through Red Square on May 31, when the president was asked whether he still thought the Soviet Union was an evil empire. "No," he replied firmly. "I was talking about another time, another era."[135]

Even the First Ladies managed to get on better; at one point they were photographed hand in hand. And Raisa deftly gave the president one more Russian proverb: "*Kooi zhelezo poka Gorbachev.*" "Strike iron while Gorbachev is hot."[136]

That indeed was what both men had been doing—seizing a rare moment of convergence in international politics. It was made possible above all by their developing personal relationship. In Moscow Gorbachev told Nancy Reagan that he and her husband had "a certain chemistry," adding: "It's very rare." The president agreed, writing in his memoirs: "Looking back now, it's clear there was a chemistry between Gorbachev and me that produced something very close to a friendship." Although they aired their national and ideological differences, this chemistry, said Reagan, "kept our conversations on a man-to-man basis, without hate or hostility."[137]

Yet the chemical reaction had not come about overnight. Both leaders knew in mid-1988 that they had traveled a long and bumpy road since late 1985. The Moscow summit had "shown how right we were in choosing the path we took in Geneva," Gorbachev said in his final press conference. Reagan remarked that at Moscow they had "established the kind of working relationship I think we both had in mind when we first met in Geneva."[138]

That relationship was not merely personal, like that of some summiteers, but drew in their leading advisors and officials as well. George Shultz was particularly important. Ever since 1983, appealing to the peacemaking side of the president's fractured worldview, he kept coming up with strategies and tactics to help translate Reagan's vision into practical policies. As a skilled manager and bureaucratic infighter he was able to forge a consensus in Washington, holding off his main rivals and eventually building an effective team, especially with Colin Powell, Reagan's last head of the NSC. Powell joked that the national security advisor and the secretary of state had not got on so well since the days when Henry Kissinger held both posts simultaneously.[139]

But Kissinger's highly personal diplomacy could not forge consensus; on the contrary, his methods helped undermine his remarkable achievements. Shultz, in contrast, had the confidence of the president and the support of the diplomatic bureaucracy. Among his key innovations was to reject Kissinger's axiom of linkage. In other words, while pressing hard on its own agenda, the administration did not tie progress on arms control tightly to Soviet movement on, say, Afghanistan or human rights. Without his secretary of state, Reagan would never have left a lasting legacy as a peacemaker. Jack Matlock has called Shultz "one of the most effective statesmen of the twentieth century."[140]

Although Shevardnadze had less influence on Gorbachev, his partnership (and eventual friendship) with Shultz helped maintain and deepen Soviet-American dialogue in the interims between the summits. After the frigid formality of the Gromyko years, businesslike conferences between the Soviet foreign minister and his American counterpart became routine. Shevardnadze said that "Shultz and I lost count somewhere around thirty-five or thirty-seven meetings." Lower-level contacts were equally vital. The way Ridgway and Bessmertnykh handled business summed up for Gorbachev what was meant by "the human factor" in international politics. "They connect at the intuitive level—this should be so, we can do this, we won't worry about that yet, we'll come back to this later, etc. Two reasonable, intelligent people," he said, who'd almost forgotten which side they were on. "Just normal people who know their responsibilities."[141]

The breakthrough involved more than personal chemistry, because the whole physics of Cold War bipolarity had changed. This was largely due to Gorbachev and his advisors, who started with talk about speeding up the Soviet system, then adopted slogans about openness and restructuring, and ended up accepting the essential principles of democracy. Gorbachev's "new thinking" was derived from many sources, particularly social democrats in the West, but his encounters at the summit played an important part. Starting with Thatcher in 1984 and continuing with Reagan, he discovered that the ideologues of capitalism were more complex and more attractive than Marxist-Leninist dogma had allowed. Although the president was frustrating at times, he made Gorbachev think—and also hope, particularly after Reykjavik. Gorbachev developed a deep respect for Shultz—"a truly intelligent and decent person, a real statesman," he observed in April 1988. Aside from negotiating, Shultz had continued his Kremlin tutorials about open societies being the only winners in the information age, and Gorbachev continued to listen. "We should have more of this kind of talk," he remarked.[142]

Above all, these meetings with the Americans convinced the Soviet leader that real security in the nuclear age was mutual, not a zero-sum game. In other words his country could only feel secure if America felt secure, whereas Cold War doctrine assumed that one's side security depended on the other side feeling insecure. Ultimately Gorbachev took this idea much further than the Ameri-

cans, even Shultz, by developing the criterion of "reasonable sufficiency" rather than overwhelming superiority to judge the appropriate size of a nuclear arsenal. Gorbachev "did not lose the arms
race," commented American analyst Raymond Garthoff, "he called
it off." And Russian historian Dmitri Volkogonov, no eulogist of the
Soviet leader, felt Gorbachev did more than anyone in the twentieth century "to remove the threat of global war."[143]

If summitry played a part in the education of Mikhail Gorbachev, it also changed Ronald Reagan. Without those personal encounters, the president's hopeful, idealistic side would probably not
have come to the fore. At Geneva he began to sense the underlying
humanity of his ideological foe; later summits made that clear. And
if he had not loosened up, Gorbachev would not have come to
trust the West, or at least to gamble on its cooperativeness.

Of course the Soviet Union was under pressure from the arms
race; undeniably its command economy was outmoded in the
postindustrial age. But it could have toughed out the 1980s if
Weinberger, Casey and their ilk had called the shots in Washington.
In the longer run, such obduracy would have aggravated the country's structural problems, but it was an entirely possible scenario if
the Reagan administration had not shifted tack in its second term.
The fact that Washington did budge was critical in ensuring a
peaceful outcome to the Cold War endgame.

By 1989 Gorbachev's insistence that the values of humanity took
precedence over those of class and nation persuaded him that the
Eastern Europeans must be allowed to go their own way peacefully.
Unlike Khrushchev in Budapest in 1956, Brezhnev in Prague in
1968 or the Chinese communist regime in Tiananmen Square that
very year, Gorbachev refused to sanction the use of force when reform got out of hand and turned into revolution. He adopted that
position partly on principle but also because he was now confident
that Washington would not exploit the disintegration of the Soviet
bloc.[144]

Mikhail Gorbachev and Ronald Reagan made many mistakes at
the summit. But their personal rapport, the relations forged between their advisors and the tenacity with which both sides kept

talking all show that summitry can make a difference when properly managed. The encounters that began in frosty Geneva in November 1985 helped ensure that the Cold War ended not with a bang or a whimper, but with a handshake.[145]

8

SUMMITRY AS A WAY OF LIFE

From the G7 to Bush and Blair

S UMMITRY CAME OF AGE in the twentieth century. Although top-level meetings had occurred on and off for centuries, leaders tended to avoid such encounters for reasons of both safety and status. And from the sixteenth century resident ambassadors and specialist foreign ministries took over the business of diplomacy. Modern summitry was pioneered by Neville Chamberlain and it flourished during the Second World War and the Cold War. Air travel made it possible, weapons of mass destruction made it necessary, and the mass media made it into household news. But since the 1980s the technologies of travel, weaponry and communications have changed profoundly and with them the imperatives for summitry.

The airplane revolutionized distance. In 1938 it took Chamberlain four hours to reach Munich—sixty years earlier Disraeli had spent four days journeying to Berlin. Jets made travel even faster and more comfortable; Reagan's Air Force One was virtually a flying hotel. But by the end of the twentieth century statesmen did not need aircraft in order to talk. Personal computers and electronic mail made it possible for leaders and their staffs to be in instant written contact with their counterparts in other countries. New satellite and microwave technologies allowed them to talk at will on the phone. And through videoconferencing they could even see each other on screen. A parley at the summit was no longer the only means of person-to-person communication.[1]

Twentieth century summits were made necessary by "weapons of mass destruction." The acronym WMD became popularized, indeed demonized, after the attacks on the World Trade Center and the Pentagon on 9/11 but the strategic bomber that Chamberlain dreaded in 1938 and the nuclear missiles that Kennedy, Nixon and Reagan tried to stop were all weapons of mass destruction. Although the threat they posed was enormous it was also clearly defined: only a few nations possessed such capacity. If their leaders could be placated or deterred, then the threat was under control. But, in the post–Cold War world, the threat from weapons of mass destruction is much less focused. The proliferation of nuclear states, especially in South Asia and the Middle East, makes the arms race more difficult to regulate than in the era of superpower bipolarity. And the development of so-called dirty bombs means that small-scale terrorist groups could set off nuclear or biological weapons in major cities without using missiles or other complex delivery systems. Summitry may play a part in confronting these new threats, but it will not have the global significance for arms control of, say, the 1972 meeting in Moscow or Washington in 1987.

Nor will twenty-first-century summits have the same dramatic impact on public opinion because we have now moved beyond the age of *mass* media. During the Cold War ordinary people around the world had access to information, but only through a few defined channels. Obviously in the Soviet Union these channels were closely controlled by the state but, even in the "free world," governments retained a powerful hold on the flow of news. In 1978, for example, Carter's press secretary, Jody Powell, knew that by spinning a story to the three American TV networks, the press agencies and a few major newspapers, he could shape global perceptions of what was happening at Camp David. In the twenty-first century, however, the media are individuated rather than mass. National TV networks have been broken down and also bypassed by cable and satellite channels. These offer ordinary people a vast choice of where, when and whether they get their news. On the Internet,

Web pages and blogs also offer a huge swirl of independent information, rumor and comment. Governments therefore find it much harder to shape interpretations of a summit or even to make people focus on it as the salient news item.

The conditions for classical summitry, as practiced in that half century from Chamberlain and Hitler to Reagan and Gorbachev, have therefore waned. Parleys at the summit between two or three political leaders no longer have the same global significance or resonance. However, summitry is not a thing of the past. On the contrary it has now become almost routine through institutionalized summitry—groups of national leaders meeting at regular intervals backed by a huge bureaucratic infrastructure. Although it dates back at least to the 1970s, institutionalized summitry has matured during the last two decades. In the post–Cold War era many of the most pressing problems of trade, security and the environment require multilateral rather than bilateral solutions.

TWO IMPORTANT EXAMPLES of institutionalized summitry are the European Council—the twice-yearly meetings of the heads of government from across the European Union—and the Group of Eight (G8) leaders of the advanced industrialized nations, who convene every summer in more or less exotic locations.

Both had their roots in another axis of personal summitry, the one between the postwar leaders of France and West Germany. Their countries had been inveterate enemies, fighting three ruinous wars in three quarters of a century: 1870, 1914–18 and 1939–45. The Prussians won the first round and their new united Germany was proclaimed, to rub it in, at the Palace of Versailles. France ended up on the winning side in the two world wars, but at appalling cost—one and half million dead in 1914–18 and four years of occupation in 1940–4. Germany collapsed economically after the First World War and, despite the triumphs of 1940, suffered occupation and division after the Second. Clearly victory for either side was hollow. What's more, other countries, particularly Belgium and the Netherlands, were caught in the jaws of the Franco-German antagonism. Building a new relationship between France and Germany after 1945 was therefore enormously important for Western Europe as a whole. The European Coal and Steel Community of 1952 and the European Economic Community (EEC) formed in 1958 had at their heart this Franco-German rapprochement. The economic sovereignty of each country was eroded so neither would be able to wage war again. The unspoken motto was "If you can't beat them, join them."

But it was an uneasy reconciliation, thrown into doubt in May 1958 when a military coup brought Charles de Gaulle back to the French presidency with almost dictatorial powers. De Gaulle, who had spent two and a half years in a German POW camp during World War I, led France's military forces against Germany after 1940 and wanted to annex the Rhineland in 1945. He was a passionate nationalist and a noted skeptic about the EEC. In addition his country was on the verge of acquiring nuclear weapons. Konrad Adenauer, the West German chancellor, had staked everything on a policy of binding Germany to the West, tying his part of divided Germany into NATO, the EEC and a new relationship with France. Sensing out the new French leader was enormously important, yet in 1958 Adenauer was reluctant to go to Paris: his defeated countrymen might view that as a Canossa-like humiliation. Eventually de Gaulle proposed an overnight stay in his country home in the remote village of Colombey-les-deux-Églises, several hours east of Paris. That was more acceptable. But as his chauffeur drove him across the old battlefields of Alsace and Lorraine on September 14, 1958, Adenauer still viewed the visit as "necessary" but "not very agreeable."[2]

What followed was a revelation. The invitation to Colombey was itself very significant—no other foreign statesman had ever stayed *chez* de Gaulle.[3] It reflected his admiration for Adenauer's achievements as a strong, democratic leader of West Germany and de Gaulle's conviction that reconciliation between their two countries was essential. The simple but dignified atmosphere of an almost family occasion was intended to convey that message. Adenauer was pleased to find that his host spoke some German and understood much more; the interpreter present throughout the two days had little to do. And he found de Gaulle's nationalism to be "much less virulent than is usually thought"—the French president was "well informed about world affairs and particularly aware of the great importance of Franco-German relations." All in all, Adenauer admitted, "my idea of de Gaulle had been quite different from the man I discovered."[4]

Here was a classic example of a summit with far-reaching implications. Although the honeymoon didn't last long—de Gaulle soon dropped a bombshell demand that NATO be run by a "triple directorate" of America, Britain and France—the marriage proved enduring. Over the next few years the two leaders had regular meetings, culminating in the Franco-German Treaty they signed in Paris in January 1963. Convinced that they were ending a centuries-old rivalry, the two leaders used the treaty to set out organizing principles for the new Franco-German partnership. These included summits at least twice a year and meetings every three months between the foreign ministers and the defense ministers. To root all this at the popular level, there were to be exchanges among schools, youth organizations and the military, as well as intensive teaching of the other's language. The historic Franco-German reconciliation was sealed symbolically and movingly: the two leaders knelt side by side at the high altar at a pontifical mass in the great Gothic cathedral at Reims, rebuilt after German shelling in 1914.

After Adenauer's resignation later in 1963 his successor, Ludwig Erhard, worked to restore relations with the United States. During a visit to America at the end of the year, he was welcomed at President Lyndon Johnson's Texas ranch over the Christmas season, taken hunting and given a huge Stetson. "I love President Johnson and he loves me," declared the chancellor ingenuously, but the schmalz was still significant.[5] Under Erhard West Germany consolidated its transatlantic alliance; his successor, Willy Brandt, forged new links with the Soviet bloc, especially East Germany. Meanwhile de Gaulle's anti-Americanism and Anglophobia drove France into an international isolation that lasted until well after his resignation in 1969. Nevertheless, the Franco-German axis endured.

Valéry Giscard d'Éstaing and Helmut Schmidt breathed life into the regular but now formal Franco-German summits. Giscard, a graduate of France's elite *Grandes Écoles,* was on the center-right of French politics while Schmidt, the illegitimate son of a Jewish businessman, was a German Social Democrat. But having hit it off as finance ministers in the early 1970s, they forged a remarkably close relationship after assuming power in their respective countries in May 1974. They spoke regularly on the phone and had quiet working dinners in Bonn, Paris and at a favorite restaurant, *Au Boeuf,* in the Alsatian town of Blaesheim. The French president famously walked the German chancellor back to his hotel after their first meeting at the Elysée Palace, and on several occasions Giscard visited the Schmidts at home in Hamburg. Ironically their discussions were conducted in English because neither spoke the other's language.[6]

They also revitalized the European Community. De Gaulle's successor, Georges Pompidou, had been the animating spirit behind the Hague summit of December 1969, one of the most far-reaching meetings in the history of the Community. The six heads of government cut through years of deadlock to agree on funding the budget, working toward monetary union and accepting a new British application to join. In June 1972 Pompidou convened another successful summit in Paris, but after that the momentum faltered. The economic crisis of the early 1970s revealed a power vacuum at the top, which the European Commission of bureaucrats and the weak, unelected Parliament could not fill. As soon as he became president of France, Giscard pushed for a new summit of leaders. After meetings in Paris in September and December 1974, the heads of government of the EEC (now enlarged to nine, including Britain) agreed to institutionalize these summits, adopting Giscard's term "European Council." The first meeting was held in Dublin in March 1975. The Council met three times a year (amended to twice in 1985) and comprised the heads of government plus the president of the European Commission. To placate the smaller states, the presidency of the Council rotated every six months; each summit took place in the country that currently presided, or else in

Brussels. During the 1970s Giscard and Schmidt were the dominant figures in the European Council and they shared a set of economic priorities, notably combating inflation and creating new modes of monetary cooperation. Their most substantial achievement was the European Monetary System established in 1978.[7]

Like most institutions, the Council has sluggish periods. Yet it has been at the heart of most subsequent surges of reform within the European Union. The reason is that the EU is based on governments ultimately accountable to their people at the ballot box. All the big decisions about reform ultimately come down to politics—whether or not the national electorates can be brought on board—so they must be made by heads of government. In 1985 the summits at Milan and Luxembourg brought agreement on the Single European Act, intended to break down the remaining barriers to the free movement of goods, labor and money within the EU. And at Maastricht in December 1991 the leaders agreed on the procedures and timetable for full-scale monetary union. Underpinning this was a decisive Franco-German deal: Chancellor Helmut Kohl accepted monetary union and the demise of his country's cherished *deutschmark* in return for President François Mitterrand's consent to rapid German unification after the end of the Cold War. The summit also endorsed further political union of the EU as reassurance that the new, big Germany would remain firmly integrated with its neighbors. To quote Foreign Minister Hans-Dietrich Genscher: "We don't want a German Europe but a European Germany."[8]

So Giscard's European Council proved a significant innovation, wresting some of the power in the Community away from bureaucrats in the European Commission and into the hands of national leaders meeting in regular summits. But the French president was also concerned about lack of cooperation in the West as a whole, in the face of the economic challenges of the mid-1970s. In early 1975 he broached the idea of a summit of the principal Western leaders to resolve the urgent economic problems. Schmidt agreed: "We want a private, informal meeting of those who really matter in the world."[9] Heads of government were in a position to consider economic issues as an integrated whole, rather than fragmented in areas of departmental responsibility. They also had the political authority at home to push through decisions. Sharing the burdens of supreme office with others in similar positions could ease the loneliness of power and inculcate a sense of shared responsibility. Giscard's model was the working group of the Big Five finance ministers who had been meeting regularly and productively for a couple of years. He, Schmidt and George Shultz (then U.S. Treasury secretary) had been founding members, and Shultz's support for Giscard's new idea was critical in winning over President Gerald Ford.

The result of their planning was a meeting at Rambouillet, thirty miles southwest of Paris, on November 15–17, 1975. Despite the grandeur of the sixteenth-century château, now the summer residence of French presidents, Giscard tried to make the event seem like an informal weekend house party. The leaders of the original four, plus Japan and Italy, had plenty of time to socialize as well as to discuss pressing economic problems, particularly how to regulate the new regime of floating exchange rates. Giscard advocated occasional summits—conducted informally and without tight agendas, phalanxes of officials or media spotlight—to build understanding among key leaders. But the Americans took a different line. They favored regular, decision-making meetings, backed by officials, and thought it counterproductive to hold the media at arms' length. After the success of Rambouillet, President Ford hastily arranged another meeting at the El Dorado Beach Hotel near San Juan, Puerto Rico, in June 1976. Canada was now included, making this the Group of Seven, or "G7" for short. Many suspected that Ford's real concern was to boost his image ahead of the autumn U.S. election but at least the momentum was maintained. With President Carter taking a keen interest, at a further meeting in London in June 1977 it was agreed to make these economic summits an annual summer event.

By now a clear pattern had emerged. Each leader chose a senior official to act as his personal representative, known in appropriately Mount Everest parlance as the "sherpa." The sherpa from the upcoming host country would consult with his counterparts, draw up an agenda and rough out possible areas of agreement for an eventual communiqué. The summit was also the occasion for meetings of foreign ministers and finance ministers. To prepare for these each minister appointed a "sous-sherpa"—adding to the complexity. And since the summits were usually convened in capital cities, it became difficult to keep the media at bay or to restrain leaders from grand-standing for public consumption. In an effort to get back to basics, the Canadians held the so-called Ottawa summit in July 1981 at Le Château Montebello, an isolated hunting lodge some fifty miles from the capital. Billed as "the largest log cabin in the world," Montebello could accommodate all the leaders and officials under one roof—which saved time and maximized contact—while leaving the newsmen marooned in Ottawa. "Peace, perfect peace, with loved ones far away," said one jaundiced press officer.[10]

Williamsburg in May 1983 ushered in a new era of remarkable continuity among Western leaders: Reagan, Thatcher, Kohl and Mitterrand would all be present for the next six summits. Under their aegis the G7 remit was enlarged to include political issues as well as economics. Williamsburg was notable for confirming the controversial deployment of cruise and Pershing missiles in Western Europe, while in 1986 Tokyo produced a joint statement on terrorism. And in the early 1990s, these annual summits proved a useful forum for dealing with Eastern Europe's painful transition from communism. Russia became a full member in 1998, turning the G7 into the G8. By the mid-1990s the summits were wrestling with the fallout from globalization such as debt relief and the international drug trade. And in the new century international terrorism and climate change jostled for a place on the crowded agenda.

But the summits seemed increasingly pointless. Communiqués got ever longer: whereas Rambouillet in 1975 issued eleven hundred words, Houston in 1990 generated six thousand. Drafted laboriously over preceding months, they often bore little relationship to what was actually discussed. And they seemed largely rhetoric. A 1992 analysis of communiqués from the first fifteen summits concluded that only a third of 209 promises had been implemented by the governments, with America and France being particularly delinquent.[11] The summits themselves seemed largely a boondoggle. In Genoa in 2001 many of the bloated delegations (the Americans brought 900) had to be accommodated on cruise liners in the harbor. And the events were attracting a vast array of nongovernmental organizations (NGOs) and protesters—some of whom turned violent. Even when the G8 took to the summit (literally) to escape, as in 2003 at the French Alpine resort of Evian, there was several days of rioting in the nearby cities of Geneva and Lausanne.

The keenest would-be reformer among the G8 leaders was Tony Blair of Britain. When he hosted the May 1998 summit in Birmingham the heads of government convened alone, without any supporting ministers. On the middle day they met at a government conference center, Weston Park, well away from the media. The agenda was short and focused—employment, crime and debt relief—and the communiqués relatively short. Birmingham came closer than any previous G7 or G8 summit to "the informal, personal encounter envisaged by the founders," observed one analyst. But the "heads-only" formula and slimmed down agenda didn't last: each summit was shaped by the host nation and most found it hard to keep away the bureaucrats and hangers-on.[12] And G8 meetings were notorious for making big promises that weren't honored: the pledges on aid to Africa made at Gleneagles, Scotland, in 2005 being a conspicuous example.[13]

To its many critics the G8 was little more than a p.r. exercise by a corrupt club. Between them, asserted the environmental organization Greenpeace, these eight countries accounted for only 14 percent of the world's population but controlled 65 percent of global wealth. The G8's ability to act was largely determined by the United States, the biggest and most powerful economy—committed to neoliberal policies on trade and failing to "put its money where its mouth is" on the environment.[14] Critics also pointed to the bill for the summits. On its conference website, the British government calculated the "organisational costs" of Gleneagles at £12.7 million, mostly accommodation, catering and transport for the 2,375 delegates and 2,100 media.[15] But this did not include the policing operation—described as "the largest of its kind ever to be staged in the UK"—which came to £72 million.[16] At a price tag of at least £85 million (or $160 million), critics naturally asked whether such gatherings were worth all the cost and disruption.

The European Council and the G8 are only two examples of the institutionalized summitry that flourishes in the post–Cold War world. The Organization of African Unity, for instance, dates back to 1963. Like the G8, the OAU has had bad press—attacked for its high cost, extensive corruption and reluctance to criticize human rights abuses in member states. But it provides a loose political framework for a continent in which state institutions have proved disastrously weak.[17] The Non-Aligned Movement, created in 1961, has grown from 25 members to 118. Although its summits are convened only every three years, they serve, like those of the OAU, to promote the socialization of new leaders and to encourage common lines of action in the UN General Assembly. And the last two decades have seen a series of global plenary summits, particularly to deal with the environment. The 1992 Earth Summit in Rio de Janeiro, for example, involved forty thousand delegates and observers from 183 states.[18]

OUR WORLD IS THEREFORE LINKED by a web of institutionalized summitry that networks leaders and their officials as never before. Yet classical summitry—a business meeting among two or three heads of government—does continue. Statesmen still feel the need for direct, personal contact. And sometimes these encounters have a global impact akin to that of the conferences described in this book. The most striking case in recent years is the meetings between Tony Blair and George Bush. Arguably the Iraq War grew directly out of Blair's use and misuse of summit diplomacy.

Like many politicians when they reach the top, Blair quickly developed a taste for international summitry when his Labour Party gained power in Britain in 1997. He enjoyed the buzz of mixing with the world's movers and shakers, and the sense of fraternity with other would-be giants who feel pulled down by the pygmies back home. But summitry also appealed to Blair's Christian commitment to make the world a better place and his supreme self-confidence that he was the person to do it. "I am a man with a mission," he told an interviewer in September 2000; in fact the world became his mission field. He was Britain's most zealous crusader since William Ewart Gladstone in the days of Queen Victoria.[19]

Blessed with a fluent tongue and great personal charm, Blair proved an engaging summiteer, getting on famously at first with leaders as diverse as Jacques Chirac and Bill Clinton. Clinton initially functioned like an older brother, tutoring the neophyte British leader in the ways of the world.[20] But Blair soon outgrew any sense of inferiority, partly because of Clinton's sordid affair with Monica Lewinsky, but even more because the president did not share his passion for ethical interventionism. It was Blair, not Clinton, who wanted to use ground troops in the war over Kosovo in 1999, when air attacks on Serbia failed to stop the atrocities against Albanian refugees.

Blair met George Bush for the first time at Camp David on February 23, 2001, a month after the president's inauguration. After the genuine personal rapport between the Blairs and the Clintons, the British were not sure how the prime minister would get on with this hard-line Republican. "I don't expect that they are looking forward to this any more than we are," said Cherie Blair gloomily in the helicopter from Washington to Camp David.[21] But the ice was soon broken and "Tony" and "George" got down to business. Blair was engaging, articulate and informed; he found Bush more incisive and capable than the president's cowboy image and public gaffes suggested. Dinner, a movie and a convivial brunch next morning cemented the bond. Bush was presented with a facsimile of Churchill's draft of the Atlantic Charter of 1941, a calculated evocation of the heyday of Anglo-American summitry.

The two leaders gave a joint press conference at which they gushed about their good relationship. "I can assure you that when either of us gets in a bind," Bush told the media, "there will be a friend at the other end of the phone." Journalists tried to probe the obvious differences in background and outlook. Had the two leaders found "some personal interest" in common, "maybe in religion or sport or music"? There was a pause. "Well," said Bush, "we both use Colgate toothpaste." Embarrassed laughter. "They're going to wonder how you know that, George," Blair joked uneasily. But the answer was simple: Colgate supplied the toothpaste for all the cabins at Camp David. February 2001 became known as "the Colgate Summit."[22] But, although not discussed in public, religion proved the real ring of confidence. The two men's Christianity was very different: Bush was a born-again evangelical who had renounced alcohol, whereas Blair's idiosyncratic blend of Anglo-Catholicism and Christian socialism was a very private creed. Yet their religious faith sustained and inspired them when the world changed dramatically on September 11, 2001.

On that day 2,973 Americans died as a result of the terrorist attacks by Islamic fundamentalists. This was more than at Pearl Harbor sixty years before, a sneak attack with which the assaults on the Twin Towers and the Pentagon were often compared. "We're at war," the president declared bluntly.[23] 9/11 was actually a unique experience for modern America—throughout the Second World War and the Cold War the continental United States had never been under direct attack.[24] September 2001 therefore represented a quantum leap in America's sense of insecurity, making Cold War nostrums of containment or détente seem totally irrelevant. Instead the Bush administration embarked on a "War on Terror," a deliberately vague and dangerously open-ended slogan. 9/11 gave Bush, and also Blair, a new sense of mission. As leaders they soared above the apparent trivia and routine of domestic politics. As Christians they felt engaged in an apocalyptic battle between good and evil. Bush's allusion to a "crusade," though quickly withdrawn because of Muslim sensitivities, was revealing.[25] The administration reverted to strategies of preemptive attack buried in America's nineteenth-century past, claiming that preemption was justified by the nature of the threat.[26] But critics from Gaza to the Balkans argued that 9/11 had simply introduced Americans to the normal insecurities of the modern world.

Bush's initial decision to retaliate against not only Osama bin-Laden's al-Qaeda bases in Afghanistan but also the Taliban regime that hosted them was supported across the Western alliance. Thanks in no small measure to Blair's shuttle diplomacy it was also backed by Russia and Pakistan, Afghanistan's all-important neighbors. "Tony is the great persuader," said one aide. "He thinks he can convert people even when it might seem as if he doesn't have a cat's chance in hell of succeeding." But Blair was not always successful. A striking example occurred on October 31 when President Bashar-al-Assad, Syria's new British-educated leader, used a joint press conference to humiliate Blair with a diatribe about Afghanistan and Israel. "What struck us was the naivety of it," said one British diplomat later. Had the Foreign Office been asked, it would have warned Blair that Assad was bound to play to the domestic gallery. The Damascus fiasco highlighted a growing criticism of Blair's personal approach to diplomacy, both in Britain and abroad. "We get the sense that he needs to be appreciated, to be seen at the heart of the action," said a senior French official. "There is not a single problem that Blair thinks he cannot solve with his own personal engagement—it could be Russia, it could be Africa. The trouble is, the world is a little more complicated than that." But Blair was unrepentant. The world, he would say, is actually a paradoxical place. In some respects modern governments had become much less powerful, but at critical moments they could be "very, very powerful indeed" and "the personal relations between people are of fundamental importance"—far more so than it might seem from the outside. "You need to be able to know that you can trust the other person."[27]

Blair's problems mounted when Bush expanded his War on Terror after the Taliban fell, even though bin-Laden evaded capture. Saddam Hussein's repressive regime in Iraq and its defiance of UN weapons inspectors had long exercised Republicans—Bush's father had missed an apparent chance to topple the regime in 1991 after the American-led coalition had reversed Saddam's invasion of Kuwait. Bush senior, an internationalist by background, had not wanted to stretch his remarkable coalition too far, especially Soviet support. He was also warned that a headless Iraq would fragment into ethnic and sectarian wars, to the ultimate benefit of Iran. But Bush junior was instinctively a unilateralist. His religious sense of good and evil was affronted by Saddam's brutality, and he always seemed alert for ways to go one better than his father. His key advisors were also passionate about Iraq. Neoconservatives such as Paul Wolfowitz at the Pentagon suggested that removing Saddam could begin a wholesale democratization of the Middle East in the American image. Dick Cheney, Bush's powerful vice president, had run the Pentagon during the Kuwait war. By 2001 he had developed an obsession about finishing the issue once and for all.

On November 21, 2001, the president instructed his defense secretary, Donald Rumsfeld, to start working up a war plan for Iraq. Bush raised the stakes dramatically in his State of the Union address on January 29, 2002. He singled out Iraq, Iran and North Korea as an "axis of evil" and linked them, somewhat nebulously, to the support of terrorism and development of weapons of mass destruction. "These regimes pose a grave and growing danger," the president insisted. "I will not wait on events while dangers gather."[28] North Korea was a genuine international problem, with an advanced nuclear program and a demonic regime. Iran was a key player in Middle Eastern politics, teetering between Islamic fundamentalism and Western modernization. But it was Iraq that became the president's fixation. In March he told senior senators: "F—k Saddam, we're taking him out."[29]

Bush's enlargement and redefinition of the War on Terror was predicated on the assumption that you could not negotiate with evil regimes. That was classic Cold War doctrine. But instead of containment his policy was preemptive attack. This split the international coalition forged after 9/11 and Blair became America's sole significant ally in the ensuing war. The simple charge against the prime minister, graphically illustrated in numerous cartoons, is that he acted as Bush's poodle, dutifully doing the president's bidding. But that is a caricature.

In part Blair accepted the recurrent axiom of British foreign policy since World War II—that it was vital to keep in step with the Americans. Whereas the French shouted *"Non!"* loudly and publicly when they disagreed with American policy, the British motto was "Never say 'no.' Say 'yes, but—'" with the "yes" said firmly in public and the caveats made behind closed doors. Blair had no doubts about the wisdom of this approach. "Supporting the Americans is part of Tony's DNA," said one Cabinet minister.[30]

But the special relationship is not the whole story: the prime minister was also a true believer in the cause to topple Saddam. From early in his premiership Blair had been struck by the danger of weapons of mass destruction falling into the hands of "rogue states," especially Iraq: "He got religion about it," according to one American diplomat.[31] In December 1998 Blair and Clinton had mounted a four-day air blitz on Iraq, hoping to force Saddam into cooperating with UN weapons inspectors, but there was no movement. In early 2002 Blair therefore agreed entirely with Bush about the desirability of what the Americans were now calling "regime change." Iraq was not the only country on his wish list: he felt the same about Robert Mugabe in Zimbabwe and the Burmese junta. "Yes, let's get rid of them all," he would say to those who asked why he focused on Saddam. "I don't because I can't, but when you can, you should."[32] Blair's problem was that postimperial Britain could act only when America was willing.

This crusading prime minister had no time for skeptics and paid little attention to details. "You guys sort it out," he would tell his officials.[33] Unlike his political archrival, Gordon Brown, he did not think through policies at great length, nor did he bring to bear a historical sense of time, place and circumstance. Like other can-do premiers he shunned the Foreign Office—whose regional specialists could always offer pragmatic reasons why the status quo was safer than any alternative—and relied heavily on an inner circle. Things were somewhat better than in the days of Neville Chamberlain and Horace Wilson: the prime minister now had not one but two specialist diplomats as foreign policy advisors. But Sir David Manning, who handled the world outside Europe, shared Blair's fix on America and was sympathetic to ethical interventionism.[34] Most of the prime minister's other key advisors were more concerned with domestic opinion and media management. This obsession was summed up by the notorious email from Jo Moore, one of New Labour's legion of Whitehall political advisors, that

9/11 was a "good day to bury bad news."[35] At the top the key figure was Alastair Campbell, a former tabloid editor who had directed Number 10's media operations with ferocious ruthlessness since 1997. Within this cocoon, there was little chance that the prime minister's gut instincts would be subjected to rigorous challenge. Blair was ready to go to war and he intended to resolve the problems this posed at home by parleys with Bush at the summit.

Their alliance was forged at three major summits in 2002–3. When they met at the president's ranch near Crawford, Texas, on April 6, 2002, there was no formal agreement about whether to attack Iraq, let alone when. But Blair came away in no doubt about the Bush administration's thinking and publicly aligned himself with the trend the following day. "We must be prepared to act where terrorism or Weapons of Mass Destruction threaten us," he declared. "If necessary the action should be military and again, if necessary and justified, it should involve regime change."[36] Blair had clearly signed up in principle. However, in the "yes, but" tradition, he sought to extract something in return. According to a Cabinet Office summary, Blair told Bush at Crawford that "the UK would support military action to bring about regime change, provided that certain conditions were met: efforts had been made to construct a coalition/shape public opinion, the Israeli-Palestine crisis is quiescent, and the options for action to eliminate Iraq's WMD through UN weapons inspectors had been exhausted."[37]

Before the Crawford meeting, Manning stressed that Bush, under fire from most of Europe, really wanted Blair's support on Iraq. "This gives you great influence," he told the prime minister:"on the public relations strategy; on the UN and weapons inspectors; and on U.S. planning for any military campaign. This could be critically important." But it seems that Blair never tried to drive a hard bargain at the summit table: his conditions were obscured by declarations of basic support. As Richard Armitage of the State Department told the British ambassador in Washington: "The problem with your 'yes, but' is that it is too easy to hear the 'yes' and forget the 'but.'"[38]

The State Department, led by Colin Powell, was still interested in the "buts." It was in fact using the British to press arguments for which it could no longer get a hearing in the White House. But the Bush administration's heavy hitters—Vice President Dick Cheney and Donald Rumsfeld in the Pentagon—were now moving inexorably to war. Condoleeza Rice, the national security advisor, though close to the president, was not one of the big players. In the view of many Washington insiders, Cheney was "the president's real national security advisor."[39] He weighed in on August 26 with a speech scoffing at the UN inspectors and declaring that "there is no doubt that Saddam Hussein now has weapons of mass destruction." Cheney also insisted that "there is no doubt that he is amassing them to use against our friends, against our allies and against us." Neither the president nor the CIA had ever made such exaggerated claims but, to Powell's fury, the vice president's words were taken as administration policy.[40]

As Sir Richard Dearlove, the head of Britain's Secret Intelligence Service, told Blair after a visit to Washington, military action was "now seen as inevitable. Bush wanted to remove Saddam through military action justified by the conjunction of terrorism and WMD. But the intelligence and facts were being fixed around the policy." Dearlove also warned that "there was little discussion in Washington of the aftermath after [sic] military action." This was a point regularly raised by specialists in the Foreign Office and passed on to Blair.[41]

Alarmed at the race to war without much progress on his conditions, Blair crossed the Atlantic for another summit with the president, held at Camp David on September 7, 2002. As usual he took only Manning, Campbell and others of his inner circle. The Foreign Office was sidelined and the ambassador in Washington, Sir Christopher Meyer, dealt largely with Number 10. At the last minute Meyer learned that Cheney would attend all the meetings, another sign of who was calling the shots. He "just sat there throughout like a lump," recalled one British official—an intimidating presence spoiling the intimacy Blair hoped to foster. According to British insiders the two leaders made a deal: "Bush promised that if the UN did deliver genuine disarmament, he would pursue the diplomatic route. Blair promised that if that failed, he would go to war." Although the documents for this and other Bush-Blair summits remain closed, it seems likely that Blair played his trump card of British military support too early. His pledge strengthened the administration propensity to take him for granted and again blunted the impact of his other "conditions," especially an improvement in the Israel–Palestine situation. Little wonder that a cheerful Bush announced afterward to Blair's mystified entourage that "your man has got *cojones*," which they discovered was Spanish slang for "balls."[42]

Even on the issue of the UN weapons inspectors, a battle royal erupted inside the administration. Cheney and Rumsfeld (who had now penciled in February 15, 2003, as the date for war) were ferociously opposed. The president's speech to the UN on September 12 went through twenty-four drafts before Bush put his foot down and said he would definitely ask for a UN resolution to send in weapons inspectors again. "Blair had a lot to do with it," the president said later.[43]

Although the prime minister got the breathing space he wanted, a gulf was now opening up between Bush and Blair's private reason for war—regime change—and the public one—Saddam Hussein's possession and likely use of weapons of mass destruction. The prime minister was clear that he could not take Britain to war simply to topple another leader, however barbarous. That would not be acceptable in international law or to the British people. Like Anthony Eden in the Suez crisis of 1956, he needed a justification for regime change. In an effort to force domestic opinion into line with what had been agreed at the summit, Number 10 stepped up its propaganda campaign. It leaned on intelligence authorities to reveal unprecedented amounts of secret material and stretched the evidence as far as it thought it could get away with. A fifty-page dossier on "Iraq's Weapons of Mass Destruction: The Assessment of the British Government," published on September 24, 2002, included a line that would become notorious. Blair's foreword stated that Saddam's military planning "allows for some of the WMD to be ready within 45 minutes of an order to use them."[44] This was actually based on intelligence from what the Commons Foreign

Affairs Committee later described as "a single, uncorroborated source."[45]

Despite persistent prevarication in London and Washington, no such weapons were ever found. After the war Blair claimed that he did not realize this claim referred only to battlefield weapons.[46] But an earlier draft of his foreword included this sentence: "The case I make is not that Saddam could launch a nuclear attack on London or another part of the UK (he could not)." This was deleted before publication.[47] It was not in the government's interest to clarify the "threat" posed by Saddam. On the contrary, it did everything possible to exaggerate.

For millions of Blair's critics, the "forty-five minutes" claim proved that he could not be trusted. "BLiar" became a punning nickname, but the charge of calculated self-deception was probably more accurate. "We hoped we were right," said one official. "We *felt* we were right."[48] They also needed to be right: the slide to war, lubricated by Blair's summitry, was gathering speed and WMD were the only acceptable pretext. Hence the government's persistent manipulation of the evidence. We should not forget here Blair's professional training. A lawyer's job is to make the best possible case for his client by selecting and massaging the serviceable pieces of evidence. But in a court of law, there is also a rival lawyer whose task is to make an equally plausible case on the opposite side. As prime minister Blair marginalized dissent and closed his eyes to inconvenient evidence. He was acting as prosecutor, judge and executioner.

After a two-month struggle the UN Security Council was persuaded to pass a resolution on November 8, 2002. It had taken six weeks of bitter haggling—not the expected two—because France and Russia were skeptical of the intelligence evidence and would not give Britain and the United States a blank check for war. So, although UN Resolution 1441 imposed a tough inspection regime on Iraq, it merely threatened "serious consequences" if Saddam failed to comply, and then only after further consultations in the Security Council.[49] Although Saddam let the UN inspectors back into Iraq at the end of November, they asked for more time to complete their complex and difficult investigations. Meanwhile transatlantic relations almost broke down, with France and Germany doing their best to block the race to war and Rumsfeld denouncing them as "old Europe," out of touch with the new global realities.

Blair raced across the Atlantic for his third and final big prewar summit, held at the White House on January 31, 2003. The president was willing to delay the war, but only because the Pentagon needed more time. On the question of a second UN resolution to authorize war, Blair found everyone, even Colin Powell, against him: the struggle would take too long and the vote was unlikely to be unanimous. At the summit Blair pressed the case for a second resolution as a domestic necessity, appealing to Bush as one politician to another. "If that's what you need, we will go flat out to try and help you get it," the president claims he replied.[50] This was not exactly an unconditional yes. And when Bush spoke to the press, he was not particularly helpful: "Should the United Nations decide to pass a second resolution, it would be welcomed if it is yet another signal that we're intent upon disarming Saddam Hussein. But 1441 gives us the authority to move without any second resolution."[51]

On Blair's other principal condition for war—progress on the Palestine question—he had worked hard before the summit to get Yasser Arafat, the autocratic and corrupt Palestinian leader, to agree to appoint a real prime minister. At the meeting Blair believed this had persuaded Bush to issue a "road map" for progress toward a Palestinian state, once the war was over. "Clinton messes you around," he told an aide on the plane home, "but when Bush promises something, he means it." The nature of Bush's promise will only be known when (and if) the summit documents are opened. Yet Blair probably deceived himself in the way that often happens at such meetings, hearing only what he wanted to hear. One official who saw the two men at all their summits recalled the pattern:

> Bush listens politely, agrees that the points being made are good. He says things like: "I'll do what I can." As soon as Tony is in the air on his way back home Bush forgets the conversation and we know he has forgotten. There have been several moments when Tony really

felt Bush had got it. Tony would say things like: "We are really on the same page. Bush has finally clicked." Then a few hours later soberness would set in and he would realise he hadn't.[52]

Ironically Blair could do exactly the same to *his* suitors. According to Paddy Ashdown, former leader of Britain's Liberal Democrat party, he "has a habit of too easily saying what he thinks people want to hear, leaving the impression that agreements have been made which haven't been, or that they haven't been when they have, with subsequent suspicion of bad faith and broken promises."[53] Gordon Brown, Blair's long-time heir-apparent, was jollied along for years in this way. But the prime minister apparently found it hard to see when others were doing the same to him. Or perhaps he could not afford to. Like Chamberlain with Hitler and Churchill with Stalin, he had invested too much in Bush, at too high a price, to be honest about their relationship.

The aftermath of the January 31 Bush-Blair meeting also illustrates the perennial problem of follow-up after a summit. Whatever was said or implied across the table, the crucial power relationships lay in Washington. Cheney and Rumsfeld called the shots and they were pumped up and ready for America to go it alone. Powell and the State Department, temperamentally and institutionally inclined toward international cooperation, were now sidelined. The administration made some effort to seek a second UN resolution but it did not intend to be hamstrung. As for the "road map" for Palestine, Bush's decisions were always going to be shaped by conservative opinion at home, vehemently pro-Israel. Planning to run for reelection in 2004, he could not forget that his father had forfeited a second term by alienating conservatives and allowing a third-party candidate, Ross Perot, to split the Republican vote in 1992. Against these political realities, what was said or implied about the Palestinians in heady moments at the summit soon evaporated.

Bush went to war on March 20, 2003, with Blair his only substantive ally, though the Americans dressed up the logistic support of other nations as a vast coalition. Unlike Eden in 1956, Blair had given both the Cabinet and Parliament the opportunity to discuss the issue, but on the basis of information carefully spun by Campbell's machine. Despite some moments of anxiety, the military campaign was brief—by April 4 U.S. forces had reached Baghdad—and on May 1 the president announced an end to "major combat operations in Iraq." He spoke on the deck of the aircraft carrier *Abraham Lincoln* in front of a banner proclaiming "Mission Accomplished." The White House later blamed the banner on the navy but that line was in the original draft—the speech had been changed but not the backdrop.[54] It was a rare PR mistake by the president's media-savvy entourage, and one that would haunt him as Iraq collapsed into anarchy and the Americans got sucked in. Until that day the war had cost only 139 American lives. By the end of 2006 the death toll exceeded 3,000, more than the total number of fatalities on 9/11.[55] But Bush ploughed grimly on. His request for supplementary appropriations in February 2007 pushed the cost of the Iraq war, in real terms, beyond the amount spent in Vietnam.[56]

America's rush to war had sidelined meaningful planning for peace. Rumsfeld arrogantly imposed his own strategy on his generals, committed insufficient troops, and made little provision to secure key ministries and officials in Baghdad when the city was liberated. The administration seems to have believed its own rhetoric: once the "tyrant" was toppled Iraqis would be "free" and everyone would live happily ever after. Faced with the predictable looting and anarchy, Rumsfeld could only reply: "Freedom's untidy. Free people are free to make mistakes and commit crimes and do bad things."[57] Despite a huge investment of American troops and money, Iraq disintegrated into a civil war whose main beneficiaries were likely to be the Shias and Iran. Reportedly Bush's father, who had seen this danger in 1991, tried and failed to warn his son.[58]

In the face of this incompetent American juggernaut, what could Blair have done differently? He could have decided, like most world leaders, that Bush's case for war was at best unproven, but that would have been contrary to his philosophy of ethical interventionism. He could have asked probing questions about America's postwar planning, but most of the Middle Eastern experts in Whitehall had been cut out of the policymaking process.

He could have refused to go to war, but that would have run against Britain's traditional strategy of supporting U.S. policy in the hope of modifying it from within. In short he would have had to change his whole style and approach. Yet in the 1960s his Labour predecessor Harold Wilson had resisted repeated pressure from Lyndon Johnson to send troops to Vietnam—and Anglo-American relations suffered no lasting damage.

Blair did not derive much advantage from cooperating with Bush. The administration stayed on the UN track for longer than Washington hawks wished, but in the end the British and Americans went to war without UN backing, and they made no progress with the Israel-Palestine impasse. On the other hand, the benefits Blair provided to Bush may have been decisive. Although the United States possessed the military capacity to go it alone, in diplomatic terms Britain's support was invaluable. Having a real ally on the ground helped swing the American public behind the war, particularly given Blair's cult status in America after 9/11. Had he said a firm "no," instead of "yes" with a stuttering "but," Bush might not have gone ahead on his own.

Tony Blair is often compared with Anthony Eden, an earlier British prime minister who took his country into a botched war on false pretences. But his summitry has echoes of another story, told near the start of this book. A well-intentioned leader convinced of his rightness, whose confidence in his powers of persuasion bordered on hubris. Who squeezed out critical professional advice, controlling policy and information from an inner circle, and who played his best hands too early at the conference table. A leader whose rhetoric became increasingly extravagant and deceptive, yet whose apparent naivete may have been the outward face of a man who knew he had gone too far to turn back. Who does all this remind us of? For all their differences, Tony Blair's approach to summitry had a good deal in common with Neville Chamberlain's.[59]

THE SAGA OF BUSH AND BLAIR demonstrates that, even in today's world of institutional summitry, bilateral meetings on the twentieth-century model still matter. What conclusions, even lessons, can we draw from them?

Face to face across the conference table, statesmen can sense each other's needs and objectives in a way that no amount of letters, phone calls or emails can deliver. Summitry can also cut through bureaucratic obstacles that block progress lower down. Yet the potential dangers are also immense. Individual leaders, however able, cannot hope to grasp all the issues at stake. They may develop fundamental misconceptions or blind spots about each other. Nor can they maintain alertness and acuity through hours of conversation, usually distorted by translation and clouded by jet lag. And there are no fallbacks at a summit. When a head of government "makes a fumble," to borrow the metaphor of Truman's secretary of state, Dean Acheson, "the goal line is open behind him."[60] As we have seen, effective summitry depends not only on rapport between leaders but also smooth teamwork with their bureaucrats, both in preparing for the meeting and during the talks. And, although summitry requires secrecy to be successful, it also needs to be grounded in a public political consensus at home. Otherwise the achievements will not last.

That's why *personal summits*, such as Chamberlain and Hitler in September 1938 or Kennedy and Khrushchev in Vienna in 1961, are unlikely to succeed. By itself the chemistry between two leaders is insufficient to set off a sustained chain reaction. Sometimes, as in 1961, it can prove explosive. *Plenary summits*, where the personal encounter is balanced and complemented by the presence of specialist advisors, have more chance of success. Camp David in 1978 and even Yalta in 1945 fall into that category; each in itself was a successful negotiation. But those two conferences rested on false assumptions that in turn undermined implementation of the agreements. They did not become part of a process of negotiations involving leaders and specialists—*progressive summits*. Although Moscow in 1972 was envisaged as the start of such a process, it did not take off, largely because Nixon and Kissinger's secretive, backstabbing methods made the summit possible but undermined domestic support. In contrast Geneva in 1985 began a sequence of meetings that helped bring the Cold War to a peaceful end, due to that rare but vital mixture—rapport between leaders and cooperation with their advisors, with George Shultz playing a leading role as expediter and coordinator.

In a larger sense these summits shed light on the twentieth century as a whole, the era of two world wars and the Cold War. War represents one way of conducting international relations, for which the antithesis is diplomacy—dialogue and negotiation between states.[61] As we saw in chapter one, diplomacy has long antecedents, yet after 1914 it fell into disrepute. Europe's foreign ministries had conspicuously failed to prevent a devastating conflict. In an increasingly democratic age, diplomacy seemed too important to be left to the diplomats. Elected heads of government began to play a larger role. Prefigured at Paris in 1919, this culminated in Neville Chamberlain's solo attempt at peacemaking in 1938. For the next half century statesmen from the leading powers sought to make a decisive contribution to diplomacy. Winston Churchill, who coined the term "parley at the summit," also remarked in 1954 that "to jaw-jaw is always better than to war-war."[62]

The summitry these statesmen practiced was part of a larger debate about the alternatives to war as an instrument of state policy. Chamberlain's concept of appeasement connoted the peaceful satisfaction of grievances through a negotiated settlement. As used by him in 1937–8, appeasement was a familiar and acceptable diplomatic word. Churchill tried to retrieve it as late as 1950, distinguishing between good and bad forms of appeasement, the one conducted from strength, the other from weakness. Appeasement made particular sense for a small power with overextended responsibilities; in a way Britain had been practicing it since the late nineteenth-century.[63] Churchill sought accommodation with Stalin, as did Harold Macmillan with Stalin's successors in the 1950s. And appeasement on the European model was what, in essence, Roosevelt attempted in 1944–5.

But as a result of Munich and Yalta, "appeasement" became a dirty word, especially in the United States. Transferring their black and white image of Hitler's Germany to Stalin's Russia, America's leaders followed George Kennan's advice that Soviet pressure could be "contained by the adroit and vigilant application of counter-force" but not "charmed or talked out of existence" (an obvious dig at Roosevelt). The doctrine of containment, in Henry Kissinger's words, "allowed no role for diplomacy until the climactic final scene in which the men in white hats accepted the conversion of the men in black hats."[64] American skepticism about summitry in the 1950s reflected underlying doubts about the possibility of diplomacy in general when dealing with the evils of communism. It was men steeped in European history—Nixon and Kissinger—who argued in the 1970s that it was feasible for the United States to negotiate with the Soviets, focusing on interests rather than ide-ology. Their goal was a relaxation of tension, détente, based on ac-ceptance of equality between the superpowers. Yet ironically it was one of the Cold War's leading ideologues, Ronald Reagan, who brought the Cold War to an end. This was not because his arms race simply forced the Soviets out of business, as is often claimed in the United States, but because his ideology transcended containment and even détente to envisage a radical transformation of the inter-national political system beyond the madness of nuclear deterrence.

The Cold War would not have ended without an even larger shift on the Soviet side. Back in 1917–19 the Bolshevik Revolution seemed to be spreading across the world, challenging the traditional international system far more radically than democratic diplomacy in the West. Once the revolution ran out of steam, the Soviets set up a Foreign Ministry and forged diplomatic relations with other states. But their foreign policy remained Janus-faced, playing the diplomatic game but also promoting revolution where possible. In the 1930s no statesman handled Hitler effectively but Stalin erred even more grievously than Chamberlain, ending up isolated and nearly annihilated. After 1945 he and his successors created a terri-torial buffer of client states in Eastern Europe and built up Soviet forces, especially nuclear, to prevent another devastating surprise at-tack on the model of June 1941. They saw diplomacy, especially summitry, as a supplementary means of defense: their main object was to neutralize the German threat and gain acceptance of their position in Eastern Europe. These were Stalin's basic aims at Yalta, Khrushchev's at Vienna and especially Brezhnev's at Moscow in 1972. Each in his own way, and on his own terms, wanted détente with the West.

But although Soviet leaders were keener on diplomacy than hard-line Cold Warriors in America, they saw limits to its utility. For all of them the search for a diplomatic settlement in Europe went hand in hand with expanding Soviet influence in the volatile Third World. Stalin's adventurism in Korea, Khrushchev's in Cuba and Brezhnev's in Africa undercut the gains they had made at the summit. It took a visionary even more radical than Reagan to develop a new approach to Soviet security. Gorbachev's radicalism was learned on the job, from his advisors at home and from summit contacts with Western leaders. The transformation he wrought, by effect if not intent, in Soviet foreign policy—with doctrines such as the "common European home," instead of a divided continent and "reasonable sufficiency" in defense, instead of mutually assured destruction—was profound. The jury is still out on its consequences for Russia.

Attitudes to summitry often mirrored attitudes to diplomacy. Although at a tactical level professional diplomats were usually skeptical about the wisdom of letting their leaders loose at the summit, at a philosophical level leaders and diplomats were usually in step. These four approaches to diplomacy—appeasement, containment, détente and transformation—were all illuminated at the summit. And they also throw light on international relations across the twentieth century.

WHAT DO THESE MEETINGS teach us about the business of summitry? A summit involves three distinct phases: *preparation*, *negotiation* and *implementation*. Each phase deserves closer reflection and raises questions that leaders should ask themselves but rarely seem to.[65]

Preparation. When contemplating a summit, ask whether there is scope for real negotiation (no summit is merely a getting-to-know-you session). If the answer is no, don't go. Kennedy should have resisted the temptation in the spring of 1961. If the answer is yes, then decide if negotiation would be better conducted by foreign ministers or ambassadors. Chamberlain should have made more use of Halifax and senior diplomats in 1938. If a summit is deemed appropriate, define your interests and goals. Also your bottom lines: the concessions you cannot afford to make, the concessions from the other side without which the summit is pointless. The words "you" and "your" here are problematic because most leaders find it hard to disentangle their country's national interests from their personal political goals, Richard Nixon being a conspicuous example. Leaders find it even harder to pose these questions about the other side. Yet it is essential to intuit these needs and goals, and it is even more vital to understand the other leader as a political animal, rather than merely a newfound "friend." The ultimate question, more political than diplomatic, is whether a leader feels that in the last resort he can afford to walk away empty-handed from the summit. Menachem Begin's belief that he could, and his accurate perception that the others could not, help explain why he, more than Carter or Sadat, shaped the outcome of Camp David in 1978.

Trying to understand the "other" involves the vexing issue of military and political intelligence. Almost every summit considered here has revolved around intelligence—from Chamberlain's belief that the price of war with Germany in 1938 would be the virtual obliteration of London to Blair's increasingly frantic attempts to find evidence of Iraq's weapons of mass destruction. Effective summits depend on good intelligence, yet summitry is often undertaken because of the inadequacies of intelligence, in the hope that by going to the very top you can soar above the fog and gain a clear view of the other side. In 1961 Kennedy went to Vienna to form his own assessment of Khrushchev; in 1985 Gorbachev could only find out just how serious America was about SDI by confronting Reagan face to face. That is why Kissinger was so valuable to Nixon in 1972. His presummits in Beijing and Moscow clarified the issues and firmed up many of the agreements without committing the president irrevocably. Kissinger was the precursor of G8 sherpas.

This circularity—you need intelligence to go to the summit but often you can only get it by going—is one reason why my neat checklist of questions for summit preparation is somewhat artificial. Another is the difficulty a leader experiences in really clarifying his bottom lines until forced to do so. Such moments of truth are often intuitive as much as cerebral, experienced only under acute pressure. This makes it very hard for either side to calibrate in advance when and where the collisions will occur. This was particularly true for all three leaders at Camp David in 1978. Summitry is genuinely a journey of exploration.

Once at the summit, the business of *negotiation* raises another set of important questions, again rarely addressed with sufficient care by leaders in the rush of events. Is my overall strategy one of coordination or conversion? In other words, are we on common ground and therefore need only to fine-tune the details of our agreement? Chamberlain flew to his second summit at Godesberg on that assumption, only to find Hitler raising his demands. Alternatively, do I need to bring the other man around to my way of thinking and, if so, should I employ threats or rewards? Most politicians avoid blatant threats at the summit, to preserve the personal chemistry, but Khrushchev and Kennedy were reduced to this by the end of their Vienna mismatch. Usually leaders employ a mix of subtle threats and explicit rewards, the precise mix depending in part on the overall power relationship of the two sides. Nixon's ability to craft a summit with Moscow on his own terms was increased by his surprise opening to China. Usually a superpower's capacity to pressure or bribe is much greater than that of a small nation yet, as the Israelis showed in 1978, a resolute minor power can extract a surprising amount from a superpower.

Successful negotiation is also a matter of tactics. Surprise is sometimes a potent weapon. Hitler's theatrical rants unsettled Chamberlain at Berchtesgaden, pushing him into conceding the principle of Sudeten secession. A leader needs to strike a balance between clarifying his goals and maximizing uncertainty about his bottom line. Stalin was particularly adept at this, aided by his ability, unlike Roosevelt and Churchill, to say little and listen hard. It is also important to save up concessions for the optimum moment in order to extract something more important in return. Chamberlain, Sadat and Blair each tended to play his best cards too early and unconditionally.

Personality also matters, and again a fine balance has to be struck. Summitry is predicated on the idea that better personal relations can yield diplomatic benefits. This makes most leaders reluctant to have an open row at the summit—like Gorbachev backing off on SDI at Geneva. Yet the consistent Mr. Nice Guy rarely walks away with much from the negotiating table. Mr. Nasty may do better, but he has to guess how far to go without alienating his opponent, as Khrushchev found to his cost at Vienna. But Churchill's persistence on Germany at Yalta paid dividends, and Begin's alternation between courtesy and obduracy proved masterful at Camp David. The social and business sides of summitry must be held in creative tension.

Chamberlain deliberately went to the summit almost alone, but most subsequent statesmen, learning from his mistakes, have been accompanied by foreign ministers and professional diplomats. Here too there is a balance to be struck. The whole point of the summit is direct contact, so the presence of advisors in key meetings can slow business and impede frankness, particularly about the leaders' political needs. So at most summits heads of government have brought advisors to plenary sessions but also included one-to-one meetings. Yet the latter leave plenty of room for mistakes on key details, as happened when Brezhnev made a mess of the arms control discussions at Moscow in 1972. Kissinger was better informed but even he would have been wise to bring the American SALT negotiators to the summit, rather than trying to hoard all the credit for himself and Nixon. Few leaders, with the exception of Jimmy Carter, have really mastered the issues at stake when they met at a summit. Lower-level negotiations between specialists are therefore essential; they also allow the leader room to repudiate what has been tentatively agreed, which is hard to do if he is directly involved, as Carter discovered.

British and American leaders, from Churchill and Roosevelt to Blair and Bush, have conversed via a common language. Carter, Begin and Sadat also used English at Camp David. But most summits require interpreters, which disrupts the natural dynamics of conversation and intrudes on its privacy. Chamberlain and Nixon were both willing to use the other side's interpreter and note taker in order to maximize the intimacy, but that makes it difficult to ensure precise communication and obtain a clear record. Most of the summits in this book have been conducted via consecutive translation, which further complicates the exchange of ideas. At Geneva in 1985 simultaneous translation was used for the first time at a Cold War summit. This permitted something closer to a normal conversation, with questions and interruptions, and allowed the listener to link words to tone and body language. In many summits, however, the much-desired personal encounter was lost in translation.

Summitry is exhausting. Getting there, even in the age of swift air travel, leaves the leader jet-lagged and short of sleep. That is why the elderly Reagan usually arrived at least a day early. Tony Blair was much younger and had formidable energy, but one wonders how far his capacity for effective negotiation was sapped by such frenzied shuttle diplomacy. Tension and excitement add to the strain at the summit, not to mention the usual digestive problems associated with foreign travel and unfamiliar fare. The most public example occurred in January 1992 when President George H. Bush threw up over Japanese Prime Minister Kiichi Miyazawa during a state dinner, in full view of TV cameras. But many leaders meet at the summit while suffering from what we might euphemistically call serious internal pressures. And after the adrenaline rush fatigue sets in, making it hard to keep alert in the ebb and flow of discussion, when seizing the right moment for assertiveness or concession is so critical. This is particularly difficult when a leader is in severe pain or on drugs, as Kennedy was at Vienna. Mounting exhaustion and the accumulation of domestic political problems make most leaders impatient to finish. At Yalta Roosevelt in particular failed to tie up significant loose ends in the rush for home.

Descending from the summit is not, however, the end of the affair because *implementation* is equally important. How to present the meeting to their publics at home is an overriding concern for leaders, often shaping their whole organization of the summit, as the enormous efforts of White House advance men make clear. Nixon conducted all his summitry in 1972 with an eye on the November election, not just for narrow personal reasons. He saw his second term as essential to set the new relationships with China and the USSR on a firm footing. Both he and Reagan went straight to Congress after their first Soviet summits, to put their own spin on events before the media could strike.

Agreements also need political backing. Chamberlain failed to persuade his Inner Cabinet after meeting Hitler at Godesberg, setting Britain on course for war until the Führer pulled back at the last moment. In 1972 Brezhnev took great pains to build Politburo support for his meeting with Nixon and then used its achievements to reinforce his political position. The summit may even require full-scale ratification as in the case of a treaty in the United States, or at least a statement of approval from the legislature. Churchill and Roosevelt were obsessed with this after Yalta and imprudently oversold their achievements in consequence.

The third aspect of implementation, what we might call execution, is the hardest of all, exposing the cracks papered over at the summit in the hurried search for agreement. Hitler's breach of the 1938 Munich agreements the following spring was a major reason for the British guarantee of Poland and the slide to World War II. The Yalta agreements fell apart in the spring of 1945 as both Churchill and Stalin sniffed betrayal. What Carter saw as Begin's foot-dragging and deception after Camp David poisoned their subsequent relationship. Or else leaders resort to deception in an effort to make domestic political realities conform to what had been agreed at the summit, as with the Blair government in 2002–3. The handshakes at the top mark a brief moment of convergence between leaders. Honoring those promises after the descent back to harsh domestic realities often proves extremely difficult or even politically impossible.

MUCH CAN THEREFORE BE GAINED from analyzing past summits. This book is offered in part to stimulate debate on a subject that scholars have neglected. Many of the protagonists were themselves keen readers of history: Kennedy wrote about the lessons of Munich, Nixon pored over Churchill's account of Yalta. Yet it is not clear that they learned much from the past. For summitry is an existential act, animated by will more than reason. Even when backed up by effective teamwork, it turns on the capacity of individual leaders. They have to decide whether to risk a summit. They need insight, quick wits and stamina to carry it off. And at the edge of exhaustion they must dig deeper still to sell it at home. In doing all this they discover their limits and expose their flaws. That is why some of the stories told here have a touch of classical tragedy about them—Chamberlain's blend of idealism and hubris, which even today has the power to move and to appall in equal measure; Nixon's mix of realism and paranoia that took him to the top and then laid him low.

In 1816 Lord Byron used the figure of the mountaineer to epitomize the Romantic hero:

He who ascends to mountain-tops, shall find
The loftiest peaks most wrapt in clouds and snow;
He who surpasses or subdues mankind,
Must look down on the hate of those below.
Though high *above* the sun of glory glow,
And far *beneath* the earth and ocean spread,
Round him are icy rocks, and loudly blow
Contending tempests on his naked head,
And thus reward the toils which to those summits led. [66]

Mountaineers who scale the Matterhorn or Everest are usually young and at peak physical fitness. Those who tackle the summits of diplomacy are generally old and sometimes infirm. But they too have to push mind and body harder than ever before in the struggle for success, exposing themselves to great risks and harsh criticism on the way. For politicians, like mountaineers, summitry is the ultimate test; that's why Churchill's metaphor was so apt. But climbers risk only their lives and those of a few colleagues, whereas politicians parley at the summit knowing that the fate of millions may lie in their hands. Many of them dream of changing the world. Often this has been a grand illusion—the air at the top is heady—but sometimes they were right, for good or ill. And, as the story of Blair and Bush reminds us, summitry still has the power to shape the course of history.

SOURCES AND
ACKNOWLEDGMENTS

This book has its roots in my teaching at Cambridge University. For several years I have run a course for final-year history students about Churchill, Roosevelt, Stalin and the wartime alliance, based on contemporary documents. As part of their work, I ask the students to do some role-plays of wartime conferences, such as Teheran and Yalta, to help bring the documents to life. Apart from having a good deal of fun (some of our best Stalins have been female—make of that what you will), the performances have often been historically very revealing.

It was Russell Barnes who suggested that my approach could also generate some interesting television. Under his direction and the aegis of Blakeway Productions I have written and presented three films for the BBC about Munich, Vienna and Geneva. Russell is an outstanding director—historically sensitive, artistically creative and also very efficient (a rare combination). Making the films with him has greatly enriched my understanding of these events.

I am also immensely grateful to Janice Hadlow, Controller of BBC 4, for her commitment to history in general and to these films in particular; to her commissioning editor, Richard Klein, who maintains an ideal balance of hands-off and helpful advice; and to Denys Blakeway, our executive producer, who brought to bear an unrivalled experience in making historical documentaries.

Working with the BBC has also opened doors that would otherwise remain shut: I am grateful to the staff of various historic locations for their kind assistance and to assistant producer Andrea Laux for making all the arrangements. It was intensely exciting to film in the Hotels Dreesen and Petersberg at Bad Godesberg and in the former Führerbau in Munich (now the Musikhochschule). In Vienna generous access was allowed to the Russian Embassy and to the U.S. Ambassador's Residence (particular thanks to Ms. Verena Bartl). In Geneva I am indebted to the kindness and hospitality of the current owners of the Villa Fleur d'Eau, Alimenta SA (especially M. Beniamin and Mme. Wiggli-Genoud), to Mr. Maxim Kochtekov at the Russian Mission to the UN, and to Dr. and Mrs. Daniel Pometta for opening their beautiful home La Maison de Saussure.

Although the records of most of these summits are available on the web, this book is based principally on research in various archives. I have been greatly assisted by staff in the following places in Britain, Germany and the United States:

Special Collections, Birmingham University Library
Modern Manuscripts, Bodleian Library, Oxford
The National Archives, Kew
Churchill Archives Centre, Cambridge
British Cartoon Archive, University of Kent
Institüt fur Zeitgeschichte, Munich
Franklin D. Roosevelt Library, Hyde Park, New York
John F. Kennedy Library, Boston, Massachusetts
Jimmy Carter Library, Atlanta, Georgia
Ronald Reagan Library, Simi Valley, California
U.S. National Archives II, College Park, Maryland
Library of Congress, Manuscripts Division, Washington, D.C.
National Security Archive, Washington, D.C.
Ralph J. Bunche Library, U.S. State Department, Washington, D.C.

Most of the primary material in this book comes from official archives and is in the public domain. Documents in the Chamberlain Archives are quoted by permission of Special Collections at Birmingham University Library. Owners and copyright holders of cartoons and illustrations are acknowledged in the relevant places. In those cases where the author and publisher have been unable to trace copyright owners, they will be happy to make due acknowledgment in future editions.

I also wish to thank Professors Alexander Chubarian and Oleg Rzheshevsky of the Institute of Universal History, Russian Academy of Sciences, for making possible a number of visits to Moscow and especially a memorable conference about the Big Three Allies in World War II held in Yalta.

For hospitality in the United States, I am grateful to family and friends, particularly David Ray and Robin Hazard Ray in Massachusetts and Jeff and Martha Melvoin in California. Several colleagues have commented on draft chapters: special thanks to Warren F. Kimball, Fredrik Logevall and Hamish Scott. I am also indebted to my agent Peter Robinson for his efforts on my behalf and for much helpful advice.

In turning the manuscript into a book I have benefited again from the professionalism of Stuart Proffitt and his colleagues at Penguin—a superb house for publishing history—and from Lara Heimert at Basic Books in New York, who came to the project late but with great energy and enthusiasm. British copy-editor Elizabeth Stratford helped me at many points to make the text clearer and more consistent, while Christine Marra and Gray Cutler Americanized the book with remarkable speed and efficiency.

Cambridge University remains a wonderful place to teach and write history. My thanks to the History Faculty for leave to finish the book, to Christ's College for a congenial office and stimulating colleagues, and to the University Library—a copyright library where, uniquely, one can also browse and borrow. Above all, I remain indebted to Margaret and Jim for their interest and support, mixed with a healthy dose of business-as-usual. This book is dedicated to my mother, who watched these summits with fascination from afar and who, in so many ways, made it possible for me to study them as a historian.

ABBREVIATIONS

ABM   Anti-Ballistic Missile
AHR   *American Historical Review*
AIPAC   America Israel Public Affairs Committee

CA   Confidential Annex
CAB   Cabinet Office papers (TNA)
CAC   Churchill College Archives Centre, Cambridge
CCS   Combined Chiefs of Staff (US-UK)
CDSP   Camp David Study Papers (JCL)
CDU   Christian Democratic Party (FRG)
CHAR   Chartwell Papers, pre-1945 (CAC)
CHUR   Churchill Papers, post-1945 (CAC)
CIGS   Chief of the Imperial General Staff
COS   Chiefs of Staff (UK)
CWH   *Cold War History*
CWIHP   *Cold War International History Project*

DBFP   *Documents on British Foreign Policy*
DDEL   Dwight D. Eisenhower Library, Abilene, Kansas
DGFP   *Documents on German Foreign Policy*
DH   *Diplomatic History*
DRV   Democratic Republic of Vietnam (North Vietnam)
DS   *Diplomacy and Statecraft*

EEC   European Economic Community
EHR   *English Historical Review*
EU   European Union

FDRL	Franklin D. Roosevelt Library, Hyde Park, New York
FO	Foreign Office papers (TNA)
fo	folio
FRG	Federal Republic of Germany (West Germany)
FRUS	U.S. Department of State, *Foreign Relations of the United States* (multi-volumes, Washington, D.C., 1861–)
FRUS, Yalta	U.S. Department of State, *Foreign Relations of the United States: The Conferences at Malta and Yalta, 1945* (Washington, D.C., 1955)
G7	"Group of Seven" Industrialized Nations
G8	"Group of Eight" Industrialized Nations
GDR	German Democratic Republic (East Germany)
HJ	*Historical Journal*
HLRO	House of Lords Record Office
HO	Home Office papers (TNA)
IA	*International Affairs*
ICBM	Intercontinental Ballistic Missile
IHR	*International History Review*
JCH	*Journal of Contemporary History*
JCL	Jimmy Carter Library, Atlanta, Georgia
JCS	Joint Chiefs of Staff (USA)
JFKL	John F. Kennedy Library, Boston, Massachusetts
JIC	Joint Intelligence Committee
JMH	*Journal of Modern History*
LC	Library of Congress, Manuscripts Division, Washington, D.C.
MIRV	Multiple Independently Targetable Reentry Vehicle
NA	U.S. National Archives II, College Park, Maryland

NC	Neville Chamberlain papers, Birmingham University Library
NGO	Non-Governmental Organization
NKVD	People's Commissariat for Security Affairs (USSR)
NPMP	Nixon Presidential Materials Project (NA)
NSA	National Security Archive, Gelman Library, George Washington University, Washington, D.C.
NSC	National Security Council (USA)
NYT	*New York Times*
PLO	Palestine Liberation Organization
POF	President's Office Files (JFKL)
POW	Prisoner of War
PPPUS	Public Papers of the Presidents of the United States— The American Presidency Project at http://www.presidency.ucsb.edu/ws/
PREM	Prime Minister's files (TNA)
PSF	President's Secretary's Files (FDRL)
RG	Record Group (NA)
RRL	Ronald Reagan Library, Simi Valley, California
SALT	Strategic Arms Limitation Treaty
SDI	Strategic Defense Initiative
SLBM	Submarine-Launched Ballistic Missile
SMOF	Staff Member and Office Files (NPMP, WHSF)
SPD	Social Democratic Party (FRG)
TNA	The National Archives of the United Kingdom, Kew, Surrey (formerly Public Record Office)
VF	Vertical File (JCL and RRL)
WHSF	White House Special Files (NPMP)
WM	War Cabinet Minutes (TNA)
WP	War Cabinet Papers (TNA)

NOTES

Introduction

1. Robert Rhodes James, ed., *Winston S. Churchill: His Complete Speeches* (New York, 1974), vol. 8, pp. 7944, 8484–5. The Feb. 1950 drafts in Churchill's papers offer no clue as to where the phrase came from; it was in from the beginning. See CHUR 5/32, folios 67, 170, 275, 306 (Churchill Archive Centre, Cambridge). As speculation: three weeks before, the *Times* published an editorial on the pleasures of mountains that included the word "summit" and also William Blake's epigram: "Great things are done when men and mountains meet / This is not done by jostling in the street." It is quite likely that Churchill saw it since another editorial on that page was an extended appraisal of his recent election broadcast: *Times*, Jan. 23, 1950, p. 5.

2. For instance, "Gipfel" (German), "Sommet" (French) and "Vertice" (Italian). The Russians have now taken to transliterating the English term—саммита. "Prelude to the Parley," *Time*, July 18, 1955; *Dept. of State Bulletin*, no. 846 (Sept. 12, 1955), pp. 415, 419.

3. *Titus Andronicus*, Act IV, Scene 4.

4. *Childe Harold's Pilgrimage*, canto III, stanza lxii. Generally, see Marjorie Hope Nicolson, *Mountain Gloom and Mountain Glory: The Development of the Aesthetics of the Infinite* (Ithaca, New York, 1959); Jacek Wozniakowski, *Die Wildnis: Zur Deutungsgeschichte des Berges in der europaischen Neuzeit* (Frankfurt am Main, 1987); and Hugo G. Walter, *Space and Time on the Magic Mountain: Studies in Nineteenth- and Early-Twentieth-Century European Literature* (New York, 1999).

5. Richard Holmes, *Shelley: The Pursuit* (New York, 1994 reprint), p. 339.

6. Simon Schama, *Landscape and Memory* (London, 1995), p. 462.

7. For these two paragraphs on Mallory, see Robert Macfarlane, *Moun-

tains of the Mind: The History of a Fascination (London, 2003), pp. 9, 236, 270–2.

8. Thomas Carlyle, *On Heroes, Hero-Worship and the Heroic in History*, ed. Michael K. Goldberg (Berkeley, 1993), lecture 1, p. 3; Karl Marx, "Der achtzehnte Brumaire des Louis Napoleon" (1852), in Karl Marx and Friedrich Engels, *Werke*, vol. 8 (Berlin, 1972), p. 115. Marx used the noun "Der Menschen" (human beings) not "Die Männer" (men).

9. Quoted in Arthur Bryant, *The Turn of the Tide, 1939–1943* (London, 1957), p. 320.

10. The principal exception is David H. Dunn, ed., *Diplomacy at the Highest Level: The Evolution of International Summitry* (London, 1996), but these essays concentrate on recent summitry. Keith Eubank, *The Summit Conferences, 1919–1960* (Norman, Oklahoma, 1966) was a brief historical survey written before any archives were open. Charles L. Mee, Jr., *Playing God: Seven Fateful Moments When Great Men Met to Change the World* (New York, 1993) ranges from Attila the Hun to the G7 Summit of 1991. David Stone, *War Summits: The Meetings that Shaped World War II and the Postwar World* (Washington, D.C., 2005), reworks the secondary literature on wartime diplomacy without any use of primary sources (p. ix). G. R. Berridge's standard textbook *Diplomacy: Theory and Practice* (3rd ed., Basingstoke, 2005) contains a brief account and analysis of summitry in ch. 10. Henry Kissinger's classic *Diplomacy* (New York, 1994) refers briefly to several of these meetings but it is interesting that "summits" and "summitry" do not appear as conceptual entries in the book's index. But there is a succinct essay on Cold War summitry by the former West German diplomat Wilhelm G. Grewe, *Die Amerikanisch-Sowjetischen Gipfeltreffen seit Roosevelt und Stalin* (Stuttgart, 1987). Some individual summits have received close scholarly attention, for instance Keith Sainsbury, *The Turning Point: Roosevelt, Churchill, and Chiang Kai-shek, 1943. The Moscow, Cairo and Teheran Conferences* (Oxford, 1986); Hans-Joachim Giersberg, et al., *Schloss Cecilienhof und die Potsdamer Konferenz, 1945* (Berlin, 1995); Margaret MacMillan, *Seize the Hour: When Nixon Met Mao* (London, 2006).

Chapter 1: Toward the Summit

1. J. M. Munn-Rankin, "Diplomacy in Western Asia in the Early Second Millennium B.C." *Iraq*, 18 (1956), p. 99; Mario Liverani, *Prestige and Interest: International Relations in the Near East, ca. 1600–1100 B.C.*

(Padova, 1990), p. 286. See also Raymond Cohen and Raymond West-brook, eds., *Amarna Diplomacy: The Beginnings of International Relations* (Baltimore, 2000), esp. chs. 1, 17, 18.

2. Sir Frank Adcock and D. J. Mosley, *Diplomacy in Ancient Greece* (London, 1975), esp. ch. 16; see also D. J. Mosley, *Envoys and Diplomacy in Ancient Greece* (Weisbaden, 1973), esp. pp. 43, 93–5.

3. David Braund, *Rome and the Friendly King: The Character of the Client Kingship* (London, 1984), esp. pp. 165–74.

4. For these two paragraphs see Fergus Millar, "Emperors, Frontiers and Foreign Relations, 31 B.C. to A.D. 378," *Britannia*, 13 (1982), pp. 13–15; Andrew Gillett, *Envoys and Political Communication in the Late Antique West, 411–533* (Cambridge, 2003), pp. 11–26.

5. The phrase of Senarius, veteran emissary of Theodoric the Ostrogoth in late-fifth-century Italy, who called himself a "ceaseless wayfarer of the world" (*mundi sine fine viator*)—Gillett, *Envoys*, pp. 194–5.

6. Jonathan Shepard and Simon Franklin, eds., *Byzantine Diplomacy* (Aldershot, 1992), esp. pp. 16–17, 85, 295–303; François L. Ganshof, *The Middle Ages: A History of International Relations*, transl. Rény Inglis Hall (New York, 1970), pp. 128–9.

7. Ganshof, *Middle Ages*, pp. 36–7, 48–9, 126–8; Peter Munz, *Frederick Barbarossa: A Study in Medieval Politics* (London, 1973), pp. 323–33.

8. For an excellent study of the reality and the myth, see Harald Zimmermann, *Der Canossagang von 1077: Wirkungen und Wirchlichkeit* (Mainz, 1975). Bismarck's words are quoted there, p. 5.

9. For the stories of Duke John and the Picquiny meeting see *The Memoirs of Philip de Commines, Lord of Argenton*, ed. Andrew R. Scoble (2 vols., London, 1906), vol. 1, book 4, chs. 9–10, pp. 268–77.

10. There are brief accounts in J. J. Scarisbrick, *Henry VIII* (Harmondsworth, Middlesex, 1971), pp. 108–13, and Alison Weir, *Henry VIII: King and Court* (London, 2002), pp. 223–31. The standard study is Joycelyne G. Russell, *The Field of the Cloth of Gold: Men and Manners in 1520* (London, 1969).

11. For these two paragraphs see Commines, *Memoirs*, vol. 1, book 2, ch. 8, pp. 121–6.

12. Mattingly, *Renaissance Diplomacy*, esp. pp. 64, 78, 124–5, 145–6, 224–5. For the quotation from Wotton see pp. 64, 314.

13. These three paragraphs, including the quotations from Froissart, Starkey and Hobbes, are derived from the essay by Quentin Skinner "From the state of princes to the person of the state" in Skinner, *Visions of Politics, vol. 2, Renaissance Virtues* (Cambridge, 2002), pp. 368–413.

14. Geoffrey Parker, *The Thirty Years War* (London, 1987), pp. 177–8.

15. Vladimir Matveev, "Summit Diplomacy of the Seventeenth Century: William III and Peter I in Utrecht and London, 1697–8," *Diplomacy and Statecraft*, 11 (2000), pp. 29–48. George Baramy, *The Anglo-Russian Entente Cordiale of 1697–8: Peter I and William III at Utrecht* (New York, 1986), presents the Utrecht meeting explicitly as a "summit" (p. 5).

16. This was because of the addition of some domestic functions, such as management of the Mint and the Census. Although these were dropped during the nineteenth century, the name stuck.

17. H. M. Scott, *The Emergence of the Eastern Powers, 1756–1775* (Cambridge, 2001), pp. 93–4, 147–8, 163, 193–4, 205; also Derek Beales, *Joseph II: vol. I, In the Shadow of Maria Theresa, 1741–1780* (Cambridge, 1987), pp. 284–6. For overviews of diplomatic practice, on which this section also draws, see M. S. Anderson, *The Rise of Modern Diplomacy, 1450–1919* (London, 1993), chs. 1–3, and Keith Hamilton and Richard Langhorne, *The Practice of Diplomacy: Its Evolution, Theory and Administration* (Basingstoke, 1995), chs. 1–4. On the foreign ministry, see G. R. Berridge, *Diplomacy: Theory and Practice* (3rd ed., London, 2005), ch. 1.

18. Alan Palmer, *Alexander I: Tsar of War and Peace* (London, 1974), ch. 8, quoting pp. 137–8; H. M. Scott, *The Birth of the Great Power System, 1740–1815* (London, 2006), pp. 325–6.

19. A point made powerfully by Herbert Butterfield, *The Peace Tactics of Napoleon, 1806–1808* (Cambridge, 1929), p. 263.

20. Roy Bridge, "Allied Diplomacy in Peacetime: The Failure of the Congress 'System,'" 1815–1823, in Alan Sked, ed., *Europe's Balance of Power, 1815–1848* (London, 1979), p. 47 (Metternich quotation); Richard Langhorne, "The Development of International Conferences, 1648–1830," *Studies in Politics and History*, 2 (1981), special issue on "Diplomatic Thought, 1648–1815," pp. 61–91.

21. Hamilton and Langhorne, *The Practice of Diplomacy*, p. 132; Keith Hamilton, *Bertie of Thame: Edwardian Ambassador* (Woodbridge, Suffolk, 1990), p. 60. To avoid expletives, Bertie actually wrote "d——d."

22. There is a succinct account of the negotiations and the setting in Iselin Gundermann, *Berlin als Kongresstadt, 1878* (Berlin, 1978). See also Karl Otmar Freiherr von Aretin, ed., *Bismarcks Aussenpolitik und der Berliner Kongress* (Wiesbaden, 1978), esp. the essay by Imanuel Geiss, "Der Berliner Kongress, 13. Juni–13. Juli 1878," pp. 69–105, and W. N. Medlicott, *The Congress of Berlin and After: A Diplomatic History of the Near Eastern Settlement, 1878–1880* (2nd ed., London, 1963), chs. 1–2.

23. Andrew Roberts, *Salisbury: Victorian Titan* (London, 1999), pp. 198–9.

24. William Flavelle Monypenny and George Earle Buckle, *The Life of Benjamin Disraeli, Earl of Beaconsfield* (2 vols., rev. ed., London, 1929), vol. 2, part 6, ch. 9.

25. Roberts, *Salisbury*, pp. 198–9, 206.

26. John C. G. Röhl, *The Kaiser and His Court: Wilhelm II and the Government of Germany*, transl. Terence F. Cole (Cambridge, 1994), p. 12.

27. Michael Balfour, *The Kaiser and His Times* (London, 1964), p. 257.

28. See Christopher M. Clark, *Kaiser Wilhelm II* (London, 2000), ch. 5, esp. pp. 140–2.

29. On the evolution of state visits, see Johannes Paulmann, *Pomp und Politik: Monarchenbegegnungen in Europa zwischen Ancien Régime und Erstem Weltkrieg* (Paderborn, 2000).

30. Hamilton and Langhorne, *The Practice of Diplomacy*, pp. 114–15.

31. The fullest study of the conference is Raymond A. Esthus, *Double Eagle and Rising Sun: The Russians and Japanese at Portsmouth in 1905* (Durham, North Carolina, 1988).

32. Howard K. Beale, *Theodore Roosevelt and the Rise of America to World Power* (New York, 1962 pbk.), p. 253.

33. "An Appeal to the American People," Aug. 18, 1914, in Arthur Link et al., eds., *The Papers of Woodrow Wilson* (69 vols., Princeton, 1966–94), 30:394.

34. Wilson to House, July 21, 1917, in Link et al., eds., *Wilson Papers*, 43:238.

35. Speech of Jan. 8, 1918, in Link et al., eds., *Wilson Papers*, 45:534–9.

36. Quoted in Daniel M. Smith, *The Great Departure: The United States and World War I, 1914–1920* (New York, 1965), p. 109.

37. John Maynard Keynes, *The Economic Consequences of the Peace* (1919), in *The Collected Writings of John Maynard Keynes, vol. 2* (London, 1971), p. 24.

38. Sterling Kernek, *Distractions of Peace during War: The Lloyd George Government's Reactions to Woodrow Wilson, December 1916 to November 1918* (Philadelphia, 1975), p. 104.

39. Robert H. Ferrell, *Woodrow Wilson and World War I, 1917–1921* (New York, 1985), p. 136.

40. Frank Cobb to Colonel House, telegram, Nov. 14, 1918, in Charles Seymour, ed., *The Intimate Papers of Colonel House* (4 vols., London, 1926–8), vol. 4, pp. 219–21. See also the discussion in Arthur Wal-

worth, *America's Moment, 1918: American Diplomacy at the End of World War I* (New York, 1977), pp. 114–20.

41. Wilson to Senator Key Pittman, Nov. 18, 1918, Link et al., eds., *Wilson Papers*, 53:116.

42. Cf. his press statement, Nov. 18, 1918, in U.S. Department of State, *Papers Relating to the Foreign Relations of the United States, 1919: The Paris Peace Conference, vol. I* (Washington, D.C., 1942), p. 136—henceforth *FRUS*.

43. Arthur Walworth, *Woodrow Wilson* (2nd ed., Boston, 1965), book 2, p. 210. Cf. Wilson to House, Nov. 16, 1918: "I infer that French and English leaders desire to exclude me from the Conference for fear I might there lead the weaker nations against them" in *FRUS: Paris, 1919*, 1:134.

44. Arthur Willert, quoted in Margaret MacMillan, *Peacemakers: The Paris Peace Conference and Its Attempt to End War* (London, 2002), p. 11.

45. Entirely because of his time in Paris, Wilson is recorded as having spent an average of twenty-six days per year abroad during his eight-year presidency, a figure exceeded only by Bill Clinton (thirty days). See *The Economist*, "The World in 2006," p. 60.

46. Quoted in John A. Thompson, *Woodrow Wilson* (London, 2002), pp. 190–1. This book offers a spirited defense of Wilson as a pragmatic politician.

47. A point emphasized in Peter Raffo, "The Anglo-American Preliminary Negotiations for a League of Nations." *Journal of Contemporary History*, 9 (1974), 153–76.

48. The disillusioned words of Harold Nicolson, *Peacemaking, 1919* (London, 1933), p. 42.

49. Lloyd Ambrosius, *Woodrow Wilson and the American Diplomatic Tradition: The Treaty Fight in Perspective* (Cambridge, 1987), pp. 53–4.

50. Michael L. Dockrill and J. Douglas Goold, *Peace without Promise: Britain and the Peace Conferences, 1919–1923* (London, 1981), p. 59.

51. Seymour, ed., *The Intimate Papers of Colonel House*, 4:405.

52. Peter Rowland, *Lloyd George* (London, 1975), p. 495.

53. Robert E. Sherwood, *Roosevelt and Hopkins: An Intimate History* (New York, 1948), p. 227; Doris Kearns, *Lyndon Johnson and the American Dream* (New York 1977 pbk.), p. 358.

54. On these points see Keith Eubank, *The Summit Conferences, 1919–1960* (Norman, Oklahoma, 1966), pp. 10–13, 29–31, though he does not draw the same conclusions.

55. A phrase that reflected not just Nicolson's snobbery but also the

campaign by the Northcliffe press for a vindictive peace. See Nicolson, *Peacemaking*, pp. 63–4.

56. Quoted in B. J. C. McKercher, "Old Diplomacy and New: The Foreign Office and Foreign Policy, 1919–1939." in Michael Dockrill and Brian McKercher, *Diplomacy and World Power: Studies in British Foreign Policy, 1890–1950* (Cambridge, 1996), p. 92. See also Alan J. Sharp, "The Foreign Office in Eclipse, 1919–1922," *History*, 61 (1976), pp. 198–218.

57. Baldwin to Chamberlain, Oct. 15, 1925, and Balfour to Chamberlain, Oct. 16, 1925, Austen Chamberlain papers, AC 37/1b and 37/24 (Birmingham University Library).

58. Letter to Ida, Oct. 31, 1925, in Robert C. Self, ed., *The Austen Chamberlain Diary Letters: The Correspondence of Sir Austen Chamberlain with His Sisters Hilda and Ida, 1916–1937* (Cambridge, 1995), pp. 282.

59. Diary, Oct. 22, 1925, Neville Chamberlain papers, NC 2/21 (Birmingham University Library).

60. There is a useful website at http://www.century-of-flight.freeola.com.

61. Alan Bullock, *Hitler and Stalin: Parallel Lives* (London, 1991), pp. 269–70; cf. Ian Kershaw, *Hitler, 1889–1936: Hubris* (London, 1998), p. 363.

62. Conrad Black, *Franklin Delano Roosevelt: Champion of Freedom* (London, 2003), pp. 238–9; Roy Jenkins, *Franklin Delano Roosevelt* (London, 2004), pp. 60–1.

63. Geoffrey Nowell-Smith, ed., *The Oxford History of World Cinema* (Oxford, 1996), p. 207.

64. Anthony Aldgate, *Cinema and History: British Newsreels and the Spanish Civil War* (London, 1979), pp. x–xi.

65. Aldgate, *Cinema and History*, pp. 158–61.

66. J. A. Ramsden, "Baldwin and Film," in Nicholas Pronay and D. W. Spring, eds., *Propaganda, Politics and Film, 1918–45* (London, 1982), ch. 5, esp. pp. 129–32, 142. The importance of the mass media for modern summitry is a theme of the essay by Wilhelm G. Grewe, *Die Amerikanisch-Sowjetischen Gipfeltreffen seit Roosevelt und Stalin* (Stuttgart, 1987), esp. p. 6.

Chapter 2: Munich 1938

1. For examples see David Chuter, "Munich, or the Blood of Others" in Cyril Buffet and Beatrice Heuser, eds., *Haunted by History: Myths in In-*

ternational Relations (Oxford, 1998), pp. 65–79; also Alex Danchev, "The Anschluss," *Review of International Studies*, 20 (1994), esp. pp. 97–101.

2. Among biographies, Keith Feiling, *The Life of Neville Chamberlain* (London, 1946), remains useful. David Dutton, *Neville Chamberlain* (London, 2001) is a revealing study of the vicissitudes of Chamberlain's reputation, while Robert J. Caputi, *Neville Chamberlain and Appeasement* (London, 2000) looks at the wider currents of historiography. On the diplomacy of the period R. A. C. Parker, *Chamberlain and Appeasement: British Policy and the Coming of the Second World War* (London, 1993) is critical but judicious.

3. Quoted in Ian Kershaw, *Hitler* (2 vols., London, 1998, 2000), 2:89. More generally, pp. 87–125 provide an excellent general account of Hitler's thinking during the Czech crisis.

4. On these concerns, see Adam Tooze, *The Wages of Destruction: The Making and Breaking of the Nazi Economy* (London, 2006), pp. 268–74.

5. This was the message as noted by Ribbentrop after talking with the British ambassador. Halifax's instruction asked the ambassador to warn that in a conflict, the British "could not guarantee that they would not be forced by circumstances to become involved also." See *Documents on German Foreign Policy, 1918–1945*—henceforth *DGFP*—series D, vol. 2 (London, 1950), doc. 186, and E. L. Woodward and Rohan Butler, eds., *Documents on British Foreign Policy, 1919–1939*—henceforth *DGFP*—3rd series, vol. 1 (London, 1949), doc. 250.

6. *DGFP* D/2, doc. 221.

7. See Michael Bloch, *Ribbentrop* (London, pbk. edition, 2003), esp. pp. 16, 120, 125–6, 145.

8. A point developed by Richard Overy, "Germany and the Munich Crisis: A Mutilated Victory," in Igor Lukes and Erik Goldstein, eds., *The Munich Crisis, 1938: Prelude to World War* (London, 1999), pp. 202–3.

9. See *DGFP* D/2, docs. 424, 448: the Verdun references are on pp. 687, 729.

10. François Bédarida quoted in Élisabeth du Réau, *Édouard Daladier, 1884–1970* (Paris, 1993), p. 260. Generally on French policy see Yvon Lacaze, *La France et Munich: Étude d'un processus décissionel en matière de relations internationales* (Berne, 1992); also Peter Jackson, *France and the Nazi Menace: Intelligence and Policy Making, 1933–1939* (Oxford, 2000), ch. 8.

11. Neville Chamberlain to Ida Chamberlain, May 22, 1938, Neville Chamberlain papers NC 18/1/1053 (Birmingham University Library).

12. *DBFP* 3/2, appendix 4, docs. i and iii.

13. Chamberlain to Halifax, Aug. 19, 1938, *DBFP* 3/2, appendix 4, doc. ii.

14. Note of a meeting of ministers, Aug. 30, 1938, CAB 23/94, fos. 289–95 (The National Archives, Public Record Office, Kew—henceforth TNA).

15. CAB 23/94, fo. 296; Neville to Ida, Sept. 3 and 11, 1938, NC 18/1/1066/1068. See also Chamberlain's comments on bluff in *DBFP* 3/2, doc. 744. Cf. Harold Temperley, *The Foreign Policy of Canning, 1822–1827: England, the Neo-Holy Alliance and the New World* (London, 1925). This volume had been sent to Chamberlain by the author after press comments about the similarity of the prime minister's approach to diplomacy with that of Canning. See NC 7/11/31/264-9.

16. Uri Bialer, *The Shadow of the Bomber: The Fear of Air Attack and British Politics, 1932–1939* (London, 1980), especially pp. 14, 130.

17. David Reynolds, *In Command of History: Churchill Fighting and Writing the Second World War* (London, 2004), p. 99.

18. CAB 23/94, fo. 316.

19. CAB 23/94, fos. 305–11. See also John Charmley, *Duff Cooper* (London, 1986), pp. 115–16, and John Julius Norwich, ed., *The Duff Cooper Diaries, 1915–1951* (London, 2005), pp. 255–6.

20. Quoted in A. J. P. Taylor, *English History, 1914–1945* (Harmondsworth, Middlesex, 1970), p. 87 note 1.

21. *Daily Herald*, Sept. 16, 1938. The evidence in this chapter belies revisionist claims that "Horace Wilson was little more than a loyal and efficient civil servant carrying out the Prime Minister's bidding to the best of his ability"—Dutton, *Chamberlain*, p. 203.

22. Quotations from minutes of Aug. 30 and Sept. 7, 1938, Vansittart papers VNST 2/39 (Churchill Archives Centre, Cambridge—henceforth CAC).

23. Quotations from Henderson to Wilson, Sept. 10, 1938, *DBFP* 3/2, Appendix I, and Inskip notes on Munich, Sept. 12, 1938, Caldecote papers, INKP 1 (CAC). See also Parker, *Chamberlain and Appeasement*, p. 159.

24. Max Domarus, *Hitler: Speeches and Proclamations, 1932–1945, vol. 2* (London, 1992), p. 1154.

25. Note for Sept. 12, 1938, Templewood papers, X.5(3) (Cambridge University Library); see also Inskip notes, Sept. 13, 1938, INKP 1 (CAC).

26. Meeting of ministers, Aug. 30, 1938, CAB 23/94, fo. 288.

27. So claimed Neville to Ida, Sept. 2, 1938, Chamberlain papers, NC 18/1/1066.

28. Neville to Ida, Sept. 19, 1938, NC 18/1/1069; see also Cab 38 (38) 1, Sept. 14, 1938, CAB 23/95, fos. 35, 39.

29. Cab 38 (38) 1, Sept. 14, 1938, CAB 23/95, fo. 40. The word "lunatic" is used in Neville to Ida, Sept. 11, 1938, NC 18/1/1068.

30. Ball, memo, June 1, 1938, Chamberlain papers, NC 8/21/8. Constitutionally, the next election had to take place no later than November 1940.

31. Quotations from Erik Goldstein, "Neville Chamberlain, the British Official Mind and the Munich Crisis," in Lukes and Goldstein, eds., *The Munich Crisis*, pp. 277–8—an essay that brings out well this element of hubris.

32. Neville to Ida, Jan. 23, 1938, NC 18/1/1036.

33. Austen was on the Commons benches beside him; Joe's widow and the rest of the family watched from the gallery. Feiling, *Chamberlain*, pp. 204–5.

34. Hilda to Neville, Sept. 16, 1938, NC 18/2/1091, and Neville to Ida, Sept. 19, 1938, NC 18/1/1069.

35. See above, chapter one, p. 32.

36. See his comments in CAB 23/95, fos. 35–6.

37. Inskip notes on Munich, Sept. 8 and 12, 1938, INKP 1.

38. PREM 1/266A, fo. 316 (TNA).

39. Norwich, ed., *Duff Cooper Diaries*, Sept. 14, 1938, pp. 259–60.

40. DBFP 3/2, doc. 862.

41. On the German response to Chamberlain's message see *DGFP* D/2, docs. 469, 480.

42. One should probably discount the Führer's comment, months later, to a foreign diplomat that he could hardly believe his luck at the news: "I've fallen from Heaven" (*Ich bin von Himmel gefallen*). This is quoted without attribution in L. B. Namier, *Diplomatic Prelude, 1938–1939* (London, 1948), 35. That may well have been Hitler's mood after the meeting but, beforehand, he was not so sure.

43. Helmuth Groscurth, *Tagebücher eines Abwehroffiziers, 1938–1940*, ed. Helmut Krausnick and Harold C. Deutsch (Stuttgart, 1970), p. 109, reporting Hitler on Aug. 30, 1938. Goebbels wrote in his diary for Sept. 1, 1938, that Hitler did not believe London would intervene in the Czech crisis and that he was "firmly resolved on action. He knows what he wants and is going straight for his goal." Elke Fröhlich, ed., *Die Tagebücher von Josef Goebbels, teil I, band 6* (Munich, 1998), p. 68.

44. Waclaw Jedrzejewicz, ed., *Diplomat in Berlin: Papers and Memoirs of*

Jósef Lipski (New York, 1968), p. 408—reporting conversation with Hitler on Sept. 20, 1938.

45. Goebbels, *Tagebücher*, I/6, p. 91; Paul Schmidt, *Hitler's Interpreter* (London, 1951), p. 90.

46. *News Chronicle*, Sept. 15, 1938, p. 2. A large sample of press comment on the September crisis may be found in NC 15/8/165–175.

47. Newcastle, *Evening Chronicle*, Sept. 15, 1938.

48. Kordt to Berlin, tel. 422, Sept. 15, 1938, *DGFP* D/2, doc. 486.

49. Quotations from *New York Times*, Sept. 15, 1938, p. 24; Galeazzo Ciano, *Diary 1937–1943*, eds. Robert L. Miller and Stanislao L. Pugliese (London, 2002), Sept. 14, 1938, p. 126.

50. *Daily Mail*, Sept. 15, 1938, p. 10.

51. *News Chronicle*, Sept. 15, 1938, p. 1.

52. *Evening Standard*, Sept. 15, 1938, p. 5.

53. See the article "Chamberlain's Gamp" by Wilson Midgley in the *Star*, Sept. 16, 1938.

54. *Times*, Sept. 16, 1938, p. 10.

55. Strang had good French, plus a reading knowledge of Serbo-Croat and Russian picked up during postings to Belgrade and Moscow. "I ought to have learnt German also," he admitted rather ruefully in his memoirs, "but this I did not do and have never done." Lord Strang, *Home and Abroad* (London, 1956), pp. 30–1, 60.

56. John W. Wheeler-Bennett, *Munich: Prologue to Tragedy* (London, 1948), p. 106, note 1. Horace Wilson's unpublished memoir stated flatly that "neither of us had flown before." Wilson, "Munich, 1938," p. 36, CAB 127/158 (TNA). Strang, *Home and Abroad*, 137, said simply it was Chamberlain's first flight.

57. Neville to Ida, Sept. 19, 1938, NC 18/11/1069.

58. NC 8/26/11–13.

59. "Wife of Premier Prays," *Daily Herald*, Sept. 16, 1938.

60. Quotations in this paragraph from *Daily Express*, Sept. 16, 1938, p. 2.

61. Detail from *Daily Telegraph and Morning Post*, Sept. 15, 1938, pp. 13–14, and *Daily Express*, Sept. 16, 1938, p. 2. Cf. *New York Times*, Sept. 15, 1938, p. 24: "In a startling and almost literal sense, Mahomet goes to the mountain."

62. For background see Kershaw, *Hitler*, 1:282–3, 536, 749 note 11. The Berghof complex was destroyed by Allied bombing at the end of World War II. What tourists visit today is the Kehlsteinhaus, farther up the mountain, which was opened as a teahouse for Hitler in 1939.

63. Lord Birkenhead, *Halifax: The Life of Lord Halifax* (London, 1965), p. 368.

64. Neville to Ida, Sept. 19, 1938, NC 18/11/1069. The "dog" reference is recorded in Inskip notes, Sept. 17, 1938, INKP 1, and Norwich, ed., *Duff Cooper Diaries,* p. 260.

65. Detail and quotations on these preliminaries to the conference come from Neville to Ida, Sept. 19, 1938, NC 18/11/1069. See also Chamberlain's account to the Cabinet on Sept. 17, 1938, CAB 23/95, fos. 71–2. On the ploy, which apparently Hitler himself had approved, see Nevile Henderson, *Failure of a Mission: Berlin 1937–1939* (London, 1940), p. 150; Schmidt, *Hitler's Interpreter,* p. 91.

66. Both Chamberlain's summary of the meeting, based on notes he had taken, and a translation of the fuller paraphrase provided by Schmidt, the German interpreter, are in *DBFP* 3/2, docs. 895 and 896. The latter is a somewhat expurgated version of the German original, printed in *DGFP* D/2, doc. 487, but it probably follows the sequence of the conversation more accurately than Chamberlain's summary. The latter also offers a number of supposedly verbatim quotations. What follows is based on these sources.

67. The claim of three hundred dead was bandied around downstairs, where the rest of the British party was waiting. Wilson repeatedly asked Ribbentrop for confirmation but received none. Back at the Grand Hotel later he phoned the Runciman mission in Prague, who said the story was "nonsense." In the month the mission had been in Czechoslovakia, there had only been twenty-eight casualties, both German and Czech (Wilson, notes, Sept. 16, 1938, *DBFP* 3/2, pp. 353–4). As the FO noted later, there was no reference to three hundred dead in the copy of Schmidt's account of the meeting: "This was obviously expunged from the record as it was such a palpable lie" (M.J. Cresswell, minute, Oct. 11, 1938, PREM 1/266A, fo. 18). The three hundred figure is, however, in Schmidt's original version of what Hitler said. See *DGFP* D/2, p. 788.

68. Chamberlain's notes refer to Slovaks, not Ukrainians. See *DGFP,* D/2, pp. 790–1 and *DBFP* 3/2, p. 340.

69. This direct quote is found only in Chamberlain's account (*DBFP* 3/2, p. 340). As the punctuation suggests, it was probably a compilation of various sayings rather than a verbatim report. But most of the comments appear in various places in the German record, including references to risking world war.

70. *DGFP* D/2, pp. 792–3.

71. *DBFP* 3/2, p. 340.

72. Cf. CAB 23/95, fo. 41.

73. *DGFP* D/2, p. 797; *DBFP* 3/2, p. 341.

74. *DBFP* 3/2, p. 351.

75. Neville to Ida, Sept. 19, 1938, NC 18/11/1069.

76. Cf. *Daily Herald*, Sept. 15, 1938, p. 1; Inskip notes, dated Sept. 15, 1938, INKP 1.

77. *Memoirs of Ernst von Weizsäcker*, transl. John Andrews (London, 1951), p. 150; Wilson, "Munich, 1938," p. 38, CAB 127/158.

78. Schmidt, *Hitler's Interpreter*, pp. 92–3.

79. See CS 5 (38), Sept. 16, 1928, in CAB 27/646, and Cab 39 (38), Sept. 17, 1938, CAB 23/95. Quotations in the text come from the latter document, fos. 77–9.

80. For these two paragraphs see CAB 23/95, quoting fos. 72 and 76 (Chamberlain) and 88–9 (Cooper).

81. CAB 23/90, fos. 70, 80.

82. Inskip notes, Sept. 17, 1938, INKP 1; cf. CAB 23/95, fo. 90.

83. *DBFP* 3/2, doc. 883.

84. *DBFP* 3/2, doc. 928.

85. For the pressure on Czechoslovakia see *DBFP* 3/2, docs. 978–9, 991–3, 1002, 1004, 1007; Wheeler-Bennett, *Munich*, 118–28.

86. Richard Cockett, *Twilight of Truth*, pp. 741–5.

87. On this intricate issue, see Réau, *Daladier*, p. 258; Detlef Brandes, "Eine Verspätete Tschechische Alternative zum Münchener 'Diktat': Edvard Beneš und die sudetendeutsche Frage, 1938–1945," *Vierteljahrshefte für Zeitgeschichte*, 42 (1994), 221–41; Eduard Beneš, *The Fall and Rise of a Nation: Czechoslovakia, 1938–1941*, ed. Milan Hauner (Boulder, 2004), pp. xxii–xxv, 18–19; Hugh Ragsdale, *The Soviets, the Munich Crisis, and the Coming of World War II* (Cambridge, 2004), pp. 98–103.

88. CAB 27/646, fo. 44. Little wonder the British Government refused to make public its message to Prague in the White Paper it published on September 28, setting out its case in advance of anticipated war. See ibid., fo. 105.

89. For these two paragraphs see CAB 27/646, CS (38) 7 and 8, quoting from folios 46–7, 56.

90. Quotations in this paragraph from Kordt's telegram, *DGFP* D/2, doc. 568.

91. For the former view, see e.g., Schmidt, *Hitler's Interpreter*, pp. 94–5; Bloch, *Ribbentrop*, pp. 210–11; for the latter Kershaw, *Hitler*, 2:111. See also the fairly conclusive entry in Goebbels's diary for Sept. 19, indicating that at first "the Führer won't cough up" (*will es nicht herausrücken*) but

that he eventually did so, having revised the text, to resolve what had become a "painful disagreement"—Goebbels, *Tagebücher*, I/6: 99–100.

92. On the haggling, see *DBFP* 3/2, docs. 896, 930, 949, 983, 985; cf. *DGFP* D/2, docs. 522, 532.

93. Henderson, *Failure of a Mission*, pp. 153–4.

94. Ivone Kirkpatrick, *The Inner Circle* (London, 1959), pp. 114.

95. Schmidt, *Hitler's Interpreter*, p. 96. Schmidt's record of the meeting is in *DGFP* D/2, doc. 562, Kirkpatrick's in *DBFP* 3/2, doc. 1033: they correspond closely until near the end when Schmidt's is much less full. In my account I have followed the British version except where indicated.

96. "*Es tut mir fürchtbar leid, aber das geht nicht mehr*" is the phrase quoted in Kirkpatrick, *The Inner Circle*, p. 115. His official transcripts reads: "Herr Hitler said that he was sorry, since these proposals could not be maintained" (*DBFP* 3/2, p. 465).

97. Schmidt, *Hitler's Interpreter*, p. 96. Even allowing for the color added to most memoirs, Schmidt's account of Chamberlain's reaction seems entirely plausible.

98. Kirkpatrick, *The Inner Circle*, p. 116. Kirkpatrick's memoirs are revealing on the dynamics of the meeting but they sometimes telescope or rearrange the sequence of the conversation, for which I have followed the two official transcripts.

99. *DBFP* 3/2, pp. 471, 473. Chamberlain's comment is not brought out so clearly in Schmidt's account and Hitler's does not appear at all. See *DGFP* D/2, p. 879.

100. Goebbels, *Tagebücher*, I/6: 99, 103.

101. This point is brought out perceptively in Kershaw, *Hitler*, 2: 112–13, though he presents it more categorically, whereas I see Hitler as keeping open his options.

102. For the exchanges in these three paragraphs, see *DBFP* 3/2, docs. 1048, 1052-4, 1057. Background draws particularly on Wilson, "Munich 1938," pp. 27–8, 40–2 (CAB 127/158), and Kirkpatrick, *The Inner Circle*, pp. 118–20. There is a detailed chronology of events for Sept. 24, 1938, in Chamberlain papers, NC 8/26/10.

103. This paragraph draws on the inner Cabinet discussions of Sept. 22–23, CS (38) 8–11, in CAB 27/646, quoting esp. from fos. 74–5, 83–4. See also DBFP 3/2, doc. 1038.

104. See CS (38) 10–12, CAB 27/646, quoting Halifax at fo. 86. The final message is in *DBFP* 3/2, doc. 1058, but see also John Harvey, ed., *The Diplomatic Diaries of Oliver Harvey, 1937–1940* (London, 1970), Sept. 23, 1938, p. 194, and the draft telegram in FO 371/21740, fos. 209–10

TNA). Halifax strengthened the draft in several places though, on reflection, he decided to cut a final blunt paragraph warning Chamberlain not to give the impression "that main conclusion of your efforts had been to put further suggestions to Czechoslovak Government in face of complete absence of response from the other side."

105. Kirkpatrick's note of the conversation is *DBFP* 3/2, doc. 1073, Schmidt's is *DGFP* D/2, doc. 583. They are the sources for what follows. Some points appear in one set of notes and not in the other, and they differ significantly in places as the sequence in which points were made. See further comment in the text.

106. Schmidt said that Henderson liked introducing German words into the discussion—*Hitler's Interpreter*, p. 100. These exchanges come out particularly sharply in *DBFP* 3/2, p. 504.

107. The withdrawal is mentioned only in *DGFP* D/2, p. 905.

108. Schmidt says they began "about 11 p.m." and ended "about 1:45 a.m."—*DGFP* D/2, p. 907.

109. Kirkpatrick, *The Inner Circle*, p. 121; similarly in Henderson, *Failure of a Mission*, p. 157.

110. *DBFP* 3/2, p. 508.

111. *DGFP* D/2, pp. 907–8; Schmidt, *Hitler's Interpreter*, p. 102.

112. Kirkpatrick, *The Inner Circle*, p. 122.

113. For the minutes see CS 38 (13), Sept. 24, 1938, CAB 27/646, fos. 90–3, and Cab 42 (38), Sept. 24, 1938, CAB 23/95, fos. 167–92. These are the sources for what follows.

114. CAB 23/95, fo. 179.

115. CAB 23/95, fo. 180. Wilson, "Munich 1938," p. 59 (CAB 127/158) recalled Chamberlain talking as they flew home about the thousands of homes spread out beneath him.

116. Norwich, ed., *Duff Cooper Diaries*, p. 264, Sept. 24, 1938.

117. Wilson to Chamberlain, Sept. 1938, PREM 1/266A, fo. 124.

118. Cadogan, *Minutes*, Sept. 20, 1938, PREM 1/266A, fos. 266–8.

119. David Dilks, ed., *The Diaries of Sir Alexander Cadogan, OM, 1938–1945* (London, 1971), p. 103; Halifax at inner Cabinet, CAB 27/646, fo. 92.

120. Cadogan, *Diaries*, pp. 103–4.

121. For Cadogan's account of Sept. 15, 1938, see Cadogan, *Diaries*, p. 105.

122. CS (38) 13, Sept. 24, 13, 1938, CAB 27/646, fo. 92; Cab 43 (38), Sept. 25, 1938, CAB 23/95, fo. 197. In later notes, "Crisis Sept. 38," p. 7, written for his memoirs, Hoare claimed that in the inner Cabinet "I said

the terms were impossible. The others agreed." That is not borne out by the minutes in CAB 27/646.

123. Cab 43 (38), Sept. 25, 1938, CAB 23/95, fos. 198–200.

124. Ibid., fo. 200.

125. Hickleton papers, A4.410.3.7 (Borthwick Institute, York); also printed in Lord Birkenhead, *Halifax* (London, 1965), pp. 400–1.

126. After one performance a few months later, the Tory MP "Chips" Channon noted that Halifax "fascinates and bamboozles everyone. Is he saint turned worldling, or worldling become saint?" Robert Rhodes James, ed., *"Chips": The Diaries of Sir Henry Channon* (2nd ed., London, 1993), p. 184, entry for Feb. 16, 1939.

127. A point brought out well in Andrew Roberts, *"The Holy Fox": A Life of Lord Halifax* (London, 1991), pp. 115–16. Cf. Peter Neville, "Sir Alexander Cadogan and Lord Halifax's 'Damascus Road' Conversion over the Godesberg terms, 1938," *Diplomacy and Statecraft*, 11 (2000), 81–90.

128. *DBFP* 3/2, doc. 1092.

129. Phipps's message, received at 5:45 p.m.. on Sept. 24, 1938, is printed in DBFP 3/2, doc. 1076. The original and the minutes by Sargent, Sept. 24, and Vansittart, Sept. 27, are in FO 371/21740, C10602/1941/18 (TNA). See also John Herman, *The Paris Embassy of Sir Eric Phipps: Anglo-French Relations and the Foreign Office, 1937–1939* (Brighton, Sussex, 1998), pp. 110–22.

130. *DBFP* 3/2, doc. 1093. See also Réau, *Daladier*, pp. 266–8.

131. Simon, diary for Sept. 1938, p. 10, MS Simon 10 (Bodleian Library, Oxford); Strang, *Home and Abroad*, p. 140.

132. Cab 44 (38), 25 Sept. 1938, CAB 23/95.

133. *DBFP* 3/2, doc. 1111; Cockett, *Twilight of Truth*, p. 82.

134. See *DBFP* 3/2, docs. 1115–16, 1118 (Kirkpatrick's notes) and 1121 (Chamberlain's message); also Schmidt, *Hitler's Interpreter*, p. 103, and Wilson, "Munich 1938," pp. 45–7 (CAB 127/158).

135. What follows is based on the British and German records, printed as *DBFP* 3/2, doc. 1129, and *DGFP* D/2, doc. 634.

136. Wilson's whisper (quoted in English) appears only in Schmidt's account, *DGFP* D/2, p. 965, where it also says that Wilson tried to continue the meeting but Henderson advised him to leave. Kirkpatrick records neither of these points though he does say that Hitler and Wilson had some conversation at the door "which I was unable to catch" (*DBFP* 3/2, p. 567). See also Schmidt, *Hitler's Interpreter*, 104. Wilson's account is in "Munich 1938," pp. 48–50.

137. Jodl, "Dienstliches Tagebuch," Sept. 27, 1938, in *Trial of the Major*

War Criminals before the International Military Tribunal, vol. 28 (Nuremburg, 1948), doc. 1780-PS, pp. 387–8.

138. Cadogan, *Diaries*, p. 107, Sept. 27, 1938.

139. Neville Chamberlain, *The Struggle for Peace* (London, 1939), pp. 274–6.

140. Basil Collier, *The Defence of the United Kingdom* (London, 1957), p. 65.

141. Hoare, memo, "Air-Raid Precautions: The Crisis," Oct. 26, 1938, CAB 16/190, fos. 304–11; see also the review by Home Office Air Raid Precautions Dept., Nov. 10, 1938, fos. 23–5.

142. Draft report of Committee on Evacuation, July 26, 1938, pp. 38–9, in Home Office papers HO 45/17636 (TNA).

143. "The Protection of Your Home against Air Raids," pp. 13–14, copy in HO 45/18144. Hoare personally accelerated distribution of this booklet on Sept. 19. See his minute on Eady to Hoare, Sept. 17, 1938, in same file.

144. Arnold Toynbee to Quincy Wright, Oct. 14, 1938, in Roger S. Greene papers, folder 747 (Houghton Library, Harvard University).

145. *DBFP* 3/2, docs. 1158–9.

146. *DGFP* D/2, doc. 657—phone message at 10:40 a.m., London time.

147. Schmidt, *Hitler's Interpreter*, p. 105; Henderson, *Failure of a Mission*, p.161.

148. Based on Bloch, *Ribbentrop*, p. 213.

149. Goebbels, *Tagebücher*, I/6, p.119, Sept. 29, 1938.

150. Schmidt, *Hitler's Interpreter*, p. 107.

151. See Wheeler-Bennett, *Munich*, pp. 161–7, though at the end he contests the idea that Hitler had really "climbed down" or "lost face."

152. Schmidt, *Hitler's Interpreter*, pp. 106–8; von Weizsäcker, *Memoirs*, pp. 154—Göring said he "knew this from Hitler."

153. Cf. Kershaw, *Hitler*, 2:120.

154. Groscurth, *Tagebücher*, p. 128, Sept. 28, 1938.

155. The fullest account of the plot, on which these paragraphs are based, is in Peter Hoffmann, *The History of the German Resistance, 1933–1945*, transl. Richard Barry (3rd edn, Montreal, 1996), chs. 4–7, esp. pp. 81–94.

156. E.g., von Weizsäcker, *Memoirs*, p. 158. Hoffmann, *German Resistance*, 562–3, rejects this argument, after considering the evidence at length.

157. There are vivid accounts of the scene in Wheeler-Bennett, *Munich*, pp. 167–71. Two of the great political diarists of the era also recorded

it, albeit from very different standpoints. See Channon, *Diaries*, 170–2, and Harold Nicolson, *Diaries and Letters, 1930–1939*, ed. Nigel Nicolson (London, 1966), pp. 368–71.

158. The speech is reprinted in Chamberlain, *Struggle for Peace*, pp. 279–301; cf. *DBFP* 3/2, doc 1172. For the official record see House of Commons, *Debates*, 5th series, vol. 339, cols 1–28.

159. Neville to Hilda, Oct. 2, 1938, Chamberlain papers, NC 18/1/ 1070. It was a sign of the pressure that Chamberlain had been under that he does not appear to have written to his sisters for two weeks.

160. The sheet is preserved among Chamberlain's papers, NC 4/5/25.

161. This paragraph draws on Cadogan, *Diaries*, p. 109, Sept. 28, 1938; Wilson, "Munich 1938," pp. 51–2, 56 (CAB 127/158); Simon diary, Sept. 28, 1938, MS Simon 10; and Wheeler-Bennett, *Munich*, pp. 169–70. There are unresolved discrepancies: Wheeler-Bennett, for instance, speaks of two pieces of paper, and Wilson claims he sent a message urging Simon not to interrupt Chamberlain until the climactic moment. This is not mentioned by Simon and does not accord with the recollection in Lord Home, *The Way the Wind Blows* (London, 1978), p. 63.

162. Nicolson, *Diaries and Letters*, p. 370.

163. Chamberlain, *Struggle for Peace*, pp. 300–1; Neville to Hilda, Oct. 2, 1938, Chamberlain papers, NC 18/1/1070.

164. Wheeler-Bennett, *Munich*, p. 171.

165. Ciano, *Diary*, p. 134, Sept. 29, 1938.

166. The German records are in *DGFP* D/2, docs. 670, 674–5. Wilson's brief account, written from memory, is in *DBFP* 3/2, doc. 1227. He also added some recollections in "Munich 1938," pp. 52–4 (CAB 127/158). On the venue, see Alexander Krause, *Arcissstrasse 12* (Norderstedt, 2004), pp. 38–47.

167. On the lack of consultation see Réau, *Daladier*, pp. 275, 284–5.

168. He was fluent in French and competent in English, but greatly overestimated his skill in German, which often caused serious problems for Italian diplomats because he liked to talk with Hitler alone. See Denis Mack Smith, *Mussolini* (London, 1983), pp. 9, 12, 286–7, 320.

169. Recalled by Chamberlain to the Cabinet on Sept. 30, CAB 23/95, fo. 280. See also Wilson in "Munich 1938," p. 54.

170. Quotations from *DBFP* 3/2, p. 633.

171. Neville to Hilda, Oct. 2, 1938, Chamberlain papers, NC 18/1/ 1070; Strang, *Home and Abroad*, pp. 146–7.

172. Schmidt's record of the meeting is *DBFP* 3/2, doc. 1228; Chamberlain's notes are in NC 8/26/3. See also Feiling, *Chamberlain*, p. 381.

173. Neville to Hilda, Oct. 2, 1938, Chamberlain papers, NC 18/1/ 1070; Schmidt, *Hitler's Interpreter*, 112–14. The account by Douglas-Home, who was there, accords with Schmidt's—Home, *The Way the Wind Blows*, p. 64.

174. Strang, *Home and·Abroad*, p. 148.

175. "Les gens sont fous"—or possibly something more obscene if Sartre is to be believed. See Réau, *Daladier*, p. 285.

176. Neville to Hilda, Oct. 2, 1938, Chamberlain papers, NC 18/1/1070.

177. For these two paragraphs, see Home, *The Way the Wind Blows*, p. 65; *Daily Mirror*, Oct. 1, 1938, pp. 1, 14. The *Daily Sketch*, Oct. 1, 1938, p. 1, quotes Chamberlain saying ". . . that a statesman has come back from Germany . . ."

178. Strang, memo, Oct. 10, 1938, p. 2, FO 371/21659, C14471/42/ 18 (TNA). This was part of the FO's postmortem on the crisis, analyzed in Donald Lammers, "From Whitehall after Munich: The Foreign Office and the Future Course of British Foreign Policy," *HJ* 16 (1973), pp. 831–56.

179. Kershaw, *Hitler*, 2:123.

180. François Genoud, ed., *The Testament of Adolf Hitler: The Hitler-Bormann Documents, February–April 1945* (London, 1961), p. 84.

181. Quotations from John Harvey, ed., *The Diplomatic Diaries of Oliver Harvey, 1937–1940* (London, 1970), Sept. 15, 1938, p. 180, and Nicolson, *Diaries and Letters*, p. 371.

182. As printed in Winston S. Churchill, ed., *Into Battle* (London, 1941), p. 42.

183. Churchill to Chamberlain, Oct. 5, 1938, and Chamberlain to Churchill, Oct. 6, 1938, Chamberlain papers, NC 7/9/38 and /39.

184. Letter to the archbishop of Canterbury, Oct. 14, 1940, quoted in Feiling, *Chamberlain*, p. 455.

185. House of Commons, *Debates*, 5th series, 365:1617, Nov. 12, 1940.

Chapter 3: Yalta 1945

1. Address in Riga, May 7, 2005, text from White House website at http://www.whitehouse.gov/news/releases/2005/05/20050507-8.html. The two main scholarly studies of the conference are Diane Shaver Clemens, *Yalta* (New York, 1970) and Russell D. Buhite, *Decisions at Yalta: An Appraisal of Summit Diplomacy* (Wilmington, Delaware, 1986). The

then U.S. secretary of state, Edward R. Stettinius Jr., published a full-length memoir, *Roosevelt and the Russians: The Yalta Conference* (Garden City, New York, 1949). There are some astute comments on the conference from Stalin's angle in Vojtech Mastny, *Russia's Road to the Cold War: Diplomacy, Warfare and the Politics of Communism, 1941–1945* (New York, 1979), pp. 239–53. See also the stimulating essay on Yalta in Eric Alterman, *When Presidents Lie: A History of Official Deception and Its Consequences* (New York, 2004), ch. 2.

2. John Colville, *The Fringes of Power: Downing Street Diaries, 1939–1955* (London, 1986), p. 624, entry for May 2, 1948.

3. More exactly, 1,161 from Churchill and 788 from FDR. See Warren F. Kimball, ed., *Churchill and Roosevelt: The Complete Correspondence* (3 vols., Princeton, 1984), 1:3. These volumes, and Kimball's overview, *Forged in War: Roosevelt, Churchill, and the Second World War* (New York, 1997), are indispensable on their wartime relationship. Most of their correspondence with Stalin was published by the Soviets as Ministry of Foreign Affairs of the USSR, *Correspondence between the Chairman of the Council of Ministers of the U.S.S.R. and the Presidents of the U.S.A. and the Prime Ministers of Great Britain during the Great Patriotic War of 1941–1945* (2 vols., Moscow, 1957). See also Susan Butler, ed., *My Dear Mr. Stalin: The Complete Correspondence of Franklin D. Roosevelt and Joseph V. Stalin* (New Haven, 2005), based on the documents in the Roosevelt Library but lacking the critical apparatus in Kimball's volumes.

4. On the "wheelchair president," see my essay of that title in David Reynolds, *From World War to Cold War: Churchill, Roosevelt and the International History of the 1940s* (Oxford, 2006), ch. 9.

5. FDR to Churchill, Dec. 2, 1942, in Kimball, ed, *Churchill and Roosevelt*, 2:54, R-224; Harold Macmillan, *War Diaries: The Mediterranean, 1943–1945* (New York, 1984), p. 8, Jan. 26, 1943.

6. Churchill to FDR, April 1, 1942, in Kimball, ed, *Churchill and Roosevelt*, 1:439; air miles calculated by the Churchill Museum, Cabinet War Rooms, London.

7. Martin Gilbert, *Winston S. Churchill*, vol. 7 (London, 1986), p. 217; W. Averell Harriman and Elie Abel, *Special Envoy to Churchill and Stalin, 1941–1946* (New York, 1975), p. 362.

8. As argued by Keith Sainsbury, *The Turning Point: Roosevelt, Stalin, Churchill, and Chiang-Kai-Shek, 1943. The Moscow, Cairo, and Teheran Conferences* (Oxford, 1986), pp. 1–2, 307–9.

9. See, for instance, John Grigg, *1943: The Victory that Never Was* (London, 1980).

10. Jonathan R. Adelman, *Prelude to the Cold War: The Tsarist, Soviet, and U.S. Armies in the Two World Wars* (Boulder, Colorado, 1988), p. 128.

11. David M. Glantz and Jonathan House, *When Titans Clashed: How the Red Army Stopped Hitler* (Lawrence, Kansas, 1995), pp. 141, 214; see also Steven J. Zaloga, *Bagration 1944: The Destruction of Army Group Centre* (Oxford, 1996).

12. Milovan Djilas, *Conversations with Stalin*, transl. Michael B. Petrovich (London, 1962), p. 105.

13. FDR to Arthur Murray, March 4, 1940, Elibank papers, National Library of Scotland, Edinburgh, MSS. 8809, fo. 229.

14. Adolf Hitler, *My Battle*, abridged and translated by E.T.S. Dugdale (Boston, 1933)—copy in Franklin D. Roosevelt Library, Hyde Park, New York, with inscription on flyleaf: "Franklin Delano Roosevelt. The White House. 1933." On stereotypes of "Prussianism" in general, see Christopher Clark, *The Iron Kingdom: The Rise and Downfall of Prussia, 1640–1947* (London, 2006), pp. 670–5.

15. Transcript of conference with Senate Military Affairs Committee, Jan. 31, 1939, in Donald B. Schewe, ed., *Franklin D. Roosevelt and Foreign Affairs, Jan. 1937–Aug. 1939* (14 vols., New York, 1979–83), 13:203–4. For fuller discussion see Reynolds, *From World War to Cold War*, 168–70.

16. At Teheran Stalin disputed FDR's view that Hitler was "mentally unbalanced," saying that although the German leader was "not basically intelligent . . . only a very able man could accomplish what Hitler had done in solidifying the German people whatever we thought of the methods." *Foreign Relations of the United States: The Conferences at Cairo and Tehran, 1943* (Washington, D.C., 1961), p. 513—henceforth *FRUS, Cairo and Teheran*.

17. Forrest Davis, "Roosevelt's World Blueprint," *Saturday Evening Post*, April 10, 1943, p. 21; Richard Law, minute of meeting with FDR, Dec. 22, 1944, FO 371/44595, AN 155/32/45 (TNA). See also John Lewis Gaddis, *The United States and the Origins of the Cold War, 1941–1947* (New York, 1972), p. 41.

18. Eduard Mark, "October or Thermidor? Interpretations of Stalinism and the Perception of Soviet Foreign Policy in the United States, 1927–1947," *American Historical Review*, 94 (1989), esp. pp. 845–51. For an overview see Mary E. Glantz, *FDR and the Soviet Union: The President's Battles over Foreign Policy* (Lawrence, Kansas, 2005).

19. FDR to Churchill, March 18, 1942, in Kimball, ed., *Churchill and Roosevelt*, 1:421.

20. Halifax secret diary, Dec. 18, 1943, quoting account of Teheran by

Sir Archibald Clark Kerr, British ambassador to Moscow, Hickleton papers A 7.8.19 (Borthwick Institute, York). Eden told the British Cabinet that during most of the conversation on Poland "Roosevelt preferred to pretend to be asleep, so as not to be too much committed with his American public." John Barnes and David Nicholson, eds., *The Empire at Bay: The Leo Amery Diaries, 1929–1945* (London, 1988), p. 956, Dec. 13, 1943.

21. "Memorandum of conversations with the President," Oct. 21 to Nov. 19, 1944, pp. 1–2, 7–9, Averell Harriman papers, box 175: chronological files (Library of Congress, Washington, D.C.). See also John Lamberton Harper, *American Visions of Europe: Franklin D. Roosevelt, George F. Kennan, and Dean G. Acheson* (New York, 1994), pp. 26, 40, 50–1, 81, 89, 102–4.

22. Speeches of Feb. 19, 1919 and March 6, 1931, in Robert Rhodes James, ed., *Winston S. Churchill: His Complete Speeches* (8 vols., New York, 1974), 3:2670 and 5:4991.

23. Churchill to Eden, M474/2, Oct. 21, 1942, prime minister's operational files PREM 4/100/7 (TNA).

24. Note by Churchill, probably April 12, 1943, PREM 4/30/11; Lord Moran, *Winston Churchill: The Struggle for Survival, 1940–1965* (London, 1968 pbk.), pp. 160, 162—entry for Nov. 29, 1943.

25. Gilbert, *Churchill*, 7: 664.

26. Speech of Oct. 1, 1939, printed in Winston S. Churchill, *Into Battle* (London, 1941), p. 131.

27. Record of dinner on Nov. 30, 1943, *FRUS, Cairo and Teheran*, p. 584.

28. Ian Jacob, diary, Aug. 14, 1942, JACB 1/17 (Churchill Archive Centre, Churchill College, Cambridge—henceforth CAC); Lord Tedder, *With Prejudice: The War Memoirs of Marshal of the Royal Air Force Lord Tedder GCB* (London, 1966), p. 330; Geoffrey Wilson to Sir Archibald Clark Kerr, May 15, 1944, p. 3, Foreign Office correspondence FO 800/302 (TNA).

29. For fuller evidence and discussion, see Reynolds, *From World War to Cold War*, pp. 240–5.

30. A point emphasized for instance by Sir Frank Roberts: see "A Diplomat Remembers Stalin," p. 7 (TS 1988), in Roberts papers, box 8 (CAC).

31. The phrase is William Taubman's: see his book *Stalin's American Policy: From Entente to Détente to Cold War* (New York, 1982), p. 46.

32. Churchill to Eden, telegrams T318/3 and T320/3, March 17 and 18, 1943, in Chartwell Papers, CHAR 20/108 (CAC).

33. Printed as message C-459 in Kimball, ed., *Churchill and Roosevelt*, 2: 553.

34. Harriman to secretary of state, Sep. 20, 1944, *FRUS 1944*, 4: 997–8, cf. p. 989.

35. Dennis J. Dunn, *Caught between Roosevelt and Stalin: America's Ambassadors to Moscow* (Lexington, Kentucky, 1998), p. 139.

36. Letter to Clementine Churchill, Oct. 13, 1944, in Mary Soames, ed., *Speaking for Themselves: The Personal Letters of Winston and Clementine Churchill* (London, 1998), p. 506.

37. Minutes M 1181/4 and 1209/4, Dec. 3 and 11, 1944, CHAR 20/153.

38. These suspicions are a central theme of Gabriel Gorodetsky, *Grand Delusion: Stalin and the German Invasion of Russia* (New Haven, 1999). See also Christopher Andrew and Julie Elkner, "Stalin and Foreign Intelligence," in Harold Shukman, ed., *Redefining Stalinism* (London, 2003), p. 79.

39. Cf. Winston S. Churchill, *The Second World War* (6 vols., London, 1948–54), 3:49.

40. Vladislav Zubok and Constantine Pleshakov, *Inside the Kremlin's Cold War: From Stalin to Khrushchev* (Cambridge, Mass., 1996), p. 18.

41. Vojtech Mastny, *The Cold War and Soviet Insecurity: The Stalin Years* (New York, 1996), p. 23.

42. Djilas, *Conversations with Stalin*, p. 104. This was before the Labour government took power—Stalin was probably referring to the wartime coalition's takeover of the railways, mines and other key industries.

43. Ivo Banac, ed., *The Diary of Georgi Dimitrov, 1933–1949* (New Haven, 2003), p. 358—entry for Jan. 28, 1945.

44. See text in J. Stalin, *On the Great Patriotic War of the Soviet Union* (Moscow, 1944), esp. pp. 167–73. See also Eduard Mark, "Revolution by Degrees: Stalin's National-Front Strategy for Europe, 1941–1947," Cold War International History Project, working paper 31 (2001).

45. I am following here Taubman, *Stalin's American Policy*, pp. 73–5.

46. FDR to Harriman, Oct. 11, 1944, *FRUS 1944*, 4:1009.

47. E.g., Cunningham to Churchill, Nov. 3, 1944, P/44/53, CAB 120/170 (TNA).

48. Quotations from Clark Kerr to Eden, tel. 2558, Sept. 25, 1944, PREM 3/396/5, fo. 214 (TNA), reporting meeting with Stalin on September 23. Harriman also attended the meeting and reported in the same vein, noting that Stalin "looked more worn out than I have ever seen

him." See *FRUS: The Conferences at Malta and Yalta, 1945* (Washington, D.C., 1955), p. 5—henceforth *FRUS Yalta*.

49. Eden diary, Feb. 2, 1945, printed in Lord Avon, *The Reckoning* (London, 1965), p. 512.

50. Kimball, ed., *Churchill and Roosevelt*, 3:396 and 514.

51. Sarah Churchill to Clementine Churchill, Feb. 1, 1945, quoted in Gilbert, *Churchill*, 7:1170, gave figures of 35 apiece and then 535. The total figure of seven hundred comes from Moran, *Churchill*, p. 242, and W. Averell Harriman and Elie Abel, *Special Envoy to Churchill and Stalin, 1941–1946* (New York, 1975), p. 391.

52. Figures from Joan Bright Astley, *The Inner Circle* (London, 1971), p. 174. Joan Bright, as she then was, handled advance arrangements on the British side.

53. Background from the president's log, printed in *FRUS Yalta*, esp. pp. 549–52.

54. Kathleen Harriman to Miss Marshall, Feb. 1, 1945, copy in Harriman papers, box 176: chronological files (LC). The Harrimans arrived early, having come down from Moscow by train.

55. Astley, *Inner Circle*, p. 191.

56. Memo for Stettinius, Feb. 5, 1945, Record Group (RG) 43, box 2 "Big Three Meeting," folder 1 (NA).

57. Sergo Beria, *Beria, My Father: Inside Stalin's Kremlin* (London, 2001), pp. 92–3; 103–5; Christopher Andrew and Vasili Mitrokhin, *The Mitrokhin Archive: The KGB in Europe and the West* (London, 1999), pp. 175–6; Andrew and Elkner, "Stalin and Foreign Intelligence." p. 83. Cf. the rather uncritical article by Gary Kern, "How 'Uncle Joe' Bugged FDR," *Studies in Intelligence*, 47/1 (2003), pp. 19–31.

58. *FRUS Yalta*, p. 551; Jacob to Churchill, Jan. 10, 1945, CAB 120/174 (TNA).

59. Dr Howard G. Bruenn, quoted in Robert H. Ferrell, *The Dying President: Franklin D. Roosevelt, 1944–1945* (Columbia, Missouri, 1998), p. 37.

60. Moran, *Churchill*, pp. 240—entry for Jan. 30, 1945. See also the similar comments in the diary of Churchill's principal military advisor at this time: Lord Alanbrooke, *War Diaries, 1939–1945*, eds. Alex Danchev and Daniel Todman (London, 2001), pp. 649–50.

61. See Eden's Yalta diary, entries for Feb. 4 and 7, 1945, Avon Papers, AP 20/3/11 (Birmingham University Library).

62. Moran, *Churchill*, pp. 242, 247—entries for Feb. 2 and 4, 1945. In the book Moran also commented (p. 250, entry for Feb. 7, 1945) that "to

a doctor's eye, the President appears a very sick man. He has all the symptoms of hardening of the arteries of the brain in an advanced stage, so that I give him only a few months to live." But this seems to have been a later insertion: it does not appear in the original manuscript diary in Moran papers, K 4/1/2 (Wellcome Institute for the History of Medicine, London).

63. The fullest published set of conference documents comes from the American side in *FRUS Yalta*. This includes minutes (sometimes sanitized) of the plenary sessions and of other meetings in which Americans were involved. The Soviet government printed their minutes of the plenary sessions in *The Teheran, Yalta and Potsdam Conferences: Documents* (Moscow, 1969), pp. 54–146, but they deleted all passages showing Stalin's hard line on Germany and his opposition to a postwar role for France. The original U.S. documents are in RG 43, boxes 2–5 (NA). The British documents may be found in Cabinet papers, CAB 99/31, and in prime minister's papers PREM 3/51/4–6 and /9 (TNA). For documents from the FDR Library see George McJimsey, ed., *Documentary History of the Franklin D. Roosevelt Presidency, vol. 14, The Yalta Conference, October 1944–March 1945* (New York, 2003)—though the most important of these documents have been published in *FRUS*.

64. These comments come from Andrei Gromyko, *Memoirs*, transl. Harold Shukman (New York, 1990), pp. 85, 114.

65. Martin J. Sherwin, *A World Destroyed: The Atomic Bomb and the Grand Alliance* (New York, 1977), p. 133.

66. As noted by Hopkins in his meeting with Stettinius, Villa Lauro, Naples, Jan. 31, 1945, RG 43, box 4, brown binder (NA).

67. *FRUS Yalta*, p. 663.

68. Churchill also expressed "heartfelt thanks." See *FRUS Yalta*, pp. 721–3; William D. Leahy diary, Feb. 7, 1945 (Library of Congress, Washington, D.C.).

69. Cf. Charles F. Bohlen, *Witness to History, 1929–1969* (London, 1973), p. 168. Eden was also concerned to safeguard a separate vote for each of the British Dominions—more genuinely independent than India, but still a gray area. See notes of discussion between Stettinius and Hopkins, Jan. 31, 1945, RG 43, box 4.

70. Stettinius Jr., *Roosevelt and the Russians*, pp. 193–5; *FRUS Yalta*, pp. 734–40, 967–8, 976.

71. Recalled by Alger Hiss in Michael Charlton, *The Eagle and the Small Birds: Crisis in the Soviet Empire from Yalta to Solidarity* (London, 1984), p. 46.

72. Tsuyoshi Hasegawa, *Racing the Enemy: Stalin, Truman, and the Surrender of Japan* (Cambridge, Massachusetts, 2005), pp. 27, 30–37.

73. Here I follow the incisive account in Buhite, *Decisions at Yalta*, ch. 5.

74. Martin Gilbert, *Winston S. Churchill, vol. 7* (London, 1986), p. 1205. On the memoirs see David Reynolds, *In Command of History: Churchill Fighting and Writing the Second World War* (London, 2004), p. 466.

75. Churchill to Eden, minutes M1025/4, Oct. 23, 1944, CHAR 20/153, and M127/5, Jan. 28, 1945, CHAR 20/209 (CAC).

76. *FRUS Yalta*, p. 501; cf. State Department, "Summary Account and Excerpts: United States Wartime Commitments concerning China" [no date, 1949?], pp. 45–9, RG 43, box 2, folder 2 (NA).

77. A point emphasized by Mastny, *Russia's Road to the Cold War*, p. 252, though I do not agree with parts of his argument.

78. For background, I have drawn on Alexei M. Filitov, "The German Issue in Soviet-American Relations at the Final Stage of World War Two," paper for conference on "The Allied Experience of World War II—War Aims, War Results," Roosevelt Study Center, Middelburg, the Netherlands, June 14, 1995.

79. Minutes of meeting on Oct. 9, 1944, PREM 3/434/2 (TNA); Geoffrey Roberts, *Stalin's Wars: From World War to Cold War, 1939–1953* (London, 2006), p. 226.

80. *FRUS Yalta*, pp. 611–16, 624–8.

81. *FRUS Yalta*, pp. 656–7, 660; minute from "VJL" to Clement Attlee, Feb. 12, 1945, CAB 118/14 (TNA).

82. Zubok and Pleshakov, *Inside the Kremlin's Cold War*, p. 31; *FRUS Yalta*, pp. 620–3, 630–3. In his diary, Maisky claimed that that figure of $10 billion for the Soviet Union was hurriedly agreed at the conference during a Feb. 5 huddle between him, Stalin and Molotov—Roberts, *Stalin's Wars*, pp. 249–50—but it is nevertheless clear that the Soviets came to the conference well prepared on reparations.

83. I am developing here the interpretation in Clemens, *Yalta*, p. 138.

84. As discussed in Gromyko, *Memoirs*, pp. 87–8.

85. See Matthews' minutes in *FRUS Yalta*, p. 909, and Stettinius, *Roosevelt and the Russians*, pp. 263–4.

86. *FRUS Yalta*, pp. 921–2.

87. British minutes of 6th plenary meeting, Feb. 10, 1945, p. 4, in PREM 3/51/4, fo. 62 (TNA).

88. *FRUS Yalta*, p. 902; cf. WM 16 (45) Confidential Annex, Feb. 8, 1945, CAB 65/51, fos. 52–4 (TNA).

89. Churchill to Eden, M113/5, Jan. 25, 1945, CAB 120/170 (TNA).

It is worth noting that even Georges Bidault, one of de Gaulle's leading advisors, thought it better not to invite the General to Yalta—see Caffery to State Dept., Feb. 3, 1945, printed in McJimsey, ed., *Documentary History: Yalta*, doc. 38.

90. For the documentation see *FRUS Yalta*, pp. 573, 616–9, 710–11, 899–900; cf. Robert E. Sherwood, *Roosevelt and Hopkins: An Intimate History* (New York, 1948), pp. 858–9; Stettinius, *Roosevelt and the Russians*, p. 262; Harriman, *Special Envoy*, p. 402. The Soviet record of Yalta, published in 1967 when de Gaulle was pioneering détente, omitted all references to France, on which Stalin had taken a notably hard line.

91. *FRUS Yalta*, p. 628.

92. Eden, diary, Feb. 6, 1945, Avon papers, AP 20/3/11.

93. Thomas M. Campbell and Edward R. Stettinius, eds., *The Diaries of Edward R. Stettinius, Jr., 1943–1946* (New York, 1975), p. 214, entry for Jan. 11, 1945.

94. Colville, *Fringes of Power*, p. 555, entry for Jan. 23, 1945.

95. *FRUS Yalta*, p. 677. There was a certain amount of special pleading here by the Russians: the "Curzon Line" was actually an Anglo-French proposal at the Spa conference of July 1920, in an effort to end the Russo-Polish war, and it had set out two possible lines in Galicia, one east of Lwow, the other west. At Yalta the Soviets naturally pushed for the western line. See I. C. B. Dear, ed., *The Oxford Companion to the Second World War* (Oxford, 1995), pp. 907–8.

96. *FRUS Yalta*, pp. 232, 505, 720.

97. *FRUS Yalta*, pp. 907, 980.

98. Beria, *My Father*, p. 106.

99. For the communiqué see *FRUS Yalta*, p. 973. For the situation on the ground see Krystyna Kersten, *The Establishment of Communist Rule in Poland, 1943–1948* (Berkeley, 1991).

100. *FRUS Yalta*, pp. 853, 856, 862–3, 873, 977–8.

101. *FRUS Yalta*, p. 500, foreign ministers' meeting on Feb. 1, 1945.

102. Churchill, *Second World War*, 6:337; William D. Leahy, *I Was There* (New York, 1950), pp. 315–16.

103. Avon, *The Reckoning*, pp. 504 (diary Jan. 4, 1945) and 514; Cadogan, letter to his wife, Feb. 8, 1945, in David Dilks, ed., *The Diaries of Sir Alexander Cadogan, OM, 1938–1945* (London, 1971), p. 706.

104. Letter to Lady Theo Cadogan, Feb. 11, 1945, in Cadogan, *Diaries*, 708–9.

105. Ismay to Mountbatten, Feb. 17, 1945, Ismay papers, 4/24/23 (Liddell Hart Centre for Military Archives, King's College, London).

106. Churchill to Attlee, tel. Jason 551, Feb. 14, 1945, CHAR 20/223.

107. Leahy, Yalta diary, p. 33, entry for Feb. 11, 1945 (LC).

108. Quotations from Sherwood, *Roosevelt and Hopkins*, pp. 860, 869.

109. Stettinius, *Roosevelt and the Russians*, pp. 295, 306; similarly Leahy, *I Was There*, pp. 317–18, 322.

110. Ferrell, *The Dying President*, pp. 104–8; Kimball, *Forged in War*, 339–41; Sherwood, *Roosevelt and Hopkins*, 867; Harriman and Abel, *Special Envoy*, pp. 389–90. On the photographs, see also Robert Hopkins, *Witness to History: Recollections of a World War II Photographer* (Seattle, 2002), p. 154.

111. Buhite, *Decisions at Yalta*, pp. 58–67.

112. Ismay to Churchill, Jan. 1, 1945, PREM 3/51/1, fos. 61–2 (TNA), asked for the prime minister's approval of the idea, adding, "I am assured that they can be completely segregated from our Party, and that they will be reasonably sanitary."

113. Nikolai Tolstoy, *Victims of Yalta* (London, 1974), chs. 2–4; cf. Alistair Horne, *Macmillan, 1894–1956* (London, 1988), pp. 253–6.

114. *FRUS Yalta*, pp. 309–24, 610, 768, 798.

115. Stettinius, *Diaries*, pp. 214, 216.

116. Henry Morgenthau, *Diaries*, vol. 308, pp. 294–5, 310, 315 (FDRL); John Morton Blum, *From the Morgenthau Diaries: Years of War, 1941–1945* (Boston, 1967), p. 305. See also Lloyd C. Gardner, *Spheres of Influence: The Partition of Europe from Munich to Yalta* (London, 1993), pp. 223–4; and, more generally, George C. Herring, Jr, *Aid to Russia, 1941–1946: Strategy, Diplomacy, the Origins of the Cold War* (New York, 1973), ch. 5.

117. Kennan to Bohlen, Jan. 26, 1945, Charles E. Bohlen papers, RG 59 Lot 74 D379, box 1: personal correspondence, 1944–6 (NA). See also Harper, *American Visions of Europe*, pp. 187–90; Bohlen, *Witness to History*, p. 175.

118. Eduard Mark, "American Policy toward Eastern Europe and the Origins of the Cold War, 1941–1946: An Alternative Interpretation," *Journal of American History*, 68 (1981), pp. 316–36; Bohlen, *Witness to History*, p. 176.

119. See *FRUS Yalta*, pp. 606–7, 635.

120. Deputy PM and chief whip to Churchill, Feb. 16, 1945, tel., Fleece 449, copy in CHAR 9/206, fo. 201 (CAC); WM 22 (45) 1 CA, Feb. 19, 1945, CAB 66/51, fos. 77–8 (TNA).

121. Ben Pimlott, ed., *The Second World War Diary of Hugh Dalton, 1940–1945* (London, 1986), 836, entry for Feb. 23, 1945; Colville, *Fringes*

of Power, (cited note 2), p. 562, entry for Feb. 23, 1945; speech draft in CHAR 9/206, fo. 126 (CAC).

122. WM 23 (45) 2, CA, Feb. 21, 1945, CAB 65/51, fo. 82 (TNA).

123. House of Commons, *Debates*, 5th series, 408:1267–95, Feb. 27, 1945, quoting from columns 1283–4, 1294.

124. Churchill, *Second World War*, 6:351; Clark Kerr to Eden, dispatch 772, Nov. 19, 1944, FO 371/40725, U8736/180/70, with Churchill's comments, Feb. 8, 1945, on reverse of folio 355. This minute is often quoted without reference to Churchill's last sentence, thereby fundamentally distorting his meaning: cf. Gilbert, *Churchill*, 7:1196; Michael R. Beschloss, *The Conquerors: Roosevelt, Truman and the Destruction of Hitler's Germany, 1941–1945* (New York, 2002), pp. 178, 188.

125. See correspondence in CHAR 9/206, esp. fos. 192, 201.

126. Churchill, *Second World War*, 6:352; Harold Nicolson, *Diaries and Letters, 1939–1945* (London, 1967), pp. 437, 439; cf. the discussion of the debate in P.M. H. Bell, *John Bull and the Bear: British Public Opinion, Foreign Policy and the Soviet Union, 1941–1945* (London, 1990), pp. 173–83.

127. Daniels to Early, Feb. 13, 1945, Official File OF 4675—Crimea conf. folder 2 (FDRL). See also Robert L. Messer, *The End of the Alliance: James F. Byrnes, Roosevelt, Truman, and the Origins of the Cold War* (Chapel Hill, 1982), pp. 35–64; Ralph B. Levering, *American Opinion and the Russian Alliance, 1939–1945* (Chapel Hill, NC, 1976), pp. 184–90; and Alterman, *When Presidents Lie*, pp. 30–2.

128. Samuel I. Rosenman, *Working with Roosevelt* (London, 1952), pp. 476, 480; Doris Kearns Goodwin, *No Ordinary Time—Franklin and Eleanor Roosevelt: The Home Front in World War II* (New York, 1994), pp. 586–7. I have followed the text in FDR's speech file that shows both what he intended to say and also his ad-libs. This is printed in McJimsey, ed., *Documentary History: Yalta*, doc. 144. The cleaned-up published version is in Samuel I. Rosenman, ed., *Public Papers and Addresses of Franklin D. Roosevelt, 1944–45* (New York, 1950), doc. 138.

129. McJimsey, ed., *Documentary History: Yalta*, esp. pp. 631–3, 638–9.

130. Bevin is quoted in WM 26 (45) 5 CA, March 6, 1945, CAB 65/51, fo. 93; Sargent to Churchill, May 14, 1945, PREM 3/396/12, fo. 585.

131. Kimball, ed., *Churchill and Roosevelt*, 3:613, C-934. This remained Churchill's considered view. In 1950 the preliminary notes for volume six of his memoirs stated that the collapse of the Yalta agreements "probably was not due to bad faith on the part of Stalin and Molotov, but that when they got back home they were held up by their colleagues." See

"Notes on Vol. VI," p. 15, Ismay papers, 2/3/296 (Liddell Hart Centre for Military Archives, King's College, London).

132. Bohlen, *Witness to History*, p. 217; cf. Stettinius, *Roosevelt and the Russians*, pp. 309–11.

133. Harriman, memo of remarks by Anne O'Hare McCormick, Jan. 25, 1954, Harriman papers, box 872: Recollections (LC). Given the date, this remark must be taken with some caution.

134. The messages are printed in Kimball, ed., *Churchill and Roosevelt*, vol. 3; quotation from C-905 on March 8.

135. On March 15, for instance, FDR "approved without change" a State Department reply to Churchill on Poland but only after Bohlen "went over with him the message point by point." On March 29 Stettinius gave FDR drafts of two more messages to Churchill "which the President read with close attention and asked a number of questions on various points. He finally approved and signed both messages without change." Bohlen, memcons, March 15 and 29, 1945, Bohlen papers, box 4: memos of conversation, president, 1945 (NA).

136. Kimball, ed., *Churchill and Roosevelt*, 3:562, C-714; *Stalin-Roosevelt correspondence*, vol. 2, doc. 289; cf. Butler, ed., *Dear Mr Stalin*, doc. 303 (see above note 4).

137. *Stalin-Roosevelt correspondence*, vol. 2, docs. 286–8; Butler, ed., *Dear Mr Stalin*, docs. 300–02; Bohlen, *Witness to History*, p. 209; Winston to Clementine, April 6, 1945, in Soames, ed., *Speaking for Themselves*, p. 522.

138. Kimball, ed., *Churchill and Roosevelt*, 3:630, R-742. Those who believe that FDR was shifting ground cite his message of April 6 to Churchill: "Our Armies will in a very few days be in a position that will permit us to become 'tougher' than has heretofore appeared advantageous to the war effort." But this was drafted by Leahy and given little attention by FDR (ibid, 3:617, R-736). The administration's main aim at the time was to dissuade Churchill from going public about the rift and thereby imperilling the San Francisco conference. Hints of a tougher line in the future might help keep him on side. Cf. Thomas T. Hammond, ed., *Witnesses to the Origins of the Cold War* (Seattle, 1982), pp. 297–8; Robert Dallek, *Franklin Roosevelt and American Foreign Policy, 1932–1945* (New York, 1979), p. 534.

139. Roosevelt to Harriman, tells 229 and 230, April 12, 1945; Harriman to Roosevelt, tel., April 12, 1945; and Harriman to Molotov, letter, April 12, 1945—all in Harriman papers, box 178: Moscow chronological files (LC).

140. As argued for instance by Diane S. Clemens, "Averell Harriman,

John Deane, the Joint Chiefs of Staff, and the 'Reversal of Co-operation' with the Soviet Union in April 1945," *International History Review*, 14 (1992), esp. pp. 303–6.

141. Truman diary, May 22, 1945, quoted in Messer, *End of the Alliance*, p. 82.

142. As perceptively noted by Warren F. Kimball, though I do not entirely agree with his explanation. See his book *The Juggler: Franklin Roosevelt as Wartime Statesman* (Princeton, 1991), ch. 8, esp. pp. 173–5, 181.

143. Churchill to Eden, M/256/5, March 25, 1945, FO 954/26, fo. 591; Clementine to Winston, April 5, 1945, and Winston to Clementine, April 6, 1945, in Soames, ed., *Speaking for Themselves*, pp. 521–3; Mary Soames, *Clementine Churchill* (2nd edition, London, 2002), pp. 406–7; *Stalin-Churchill correspondence*, doc. 418.

144. Bohlen, *Witness to History*, p. 217.

145. Clark Kerr to FO, March 27, 1945, in Graham Ross, ed., *The Foreign Office and the Kremlin: British Documents on Anglo-Soviet Relations, 1941–1945* (London, 1984), pp. 193–9; Harriman to State Dept., April 6, 1945, *FRUS 1945*, 5:821–4.

146. Albert Resis, ed., *Molotov Remembers: Inside Kremlin Politics: Conversations with Felix Chuev* (Chicago, 1991), p. 51, comments of Aug. 15, 1975.

147. On these decisions, see David M. Glantz and Jonathan House, *When Titans Clash: How the Red Army Stopped Hitler* (Lawrence, Kansas, 1995), pp. 249–55.

148. For operational details, see the U.S. official military history by Forrest C. Pogue, *The Supreme Command* (Washington, 1954), chs. 23–24 and map VI.

149. Antony Beevor, *Berlin: The Downfall* (London, 2002), pp. 144–5.

150. Quotations from Beevor, *Berlin*, pp. 145–7.

151. This is a different argument from that of Eric Alterman, who argues that Roosevelt and Churchill "lied" about Yalta to the public whereas Stalin was "a brutal dictator who kept his word." I agree with Alterman that the Western leaders misrepresented the fudges at Yalta when they returned home but believe that Stalin also stretched and twisted those elastic agreements as the correlation of forces seemed to turn against him in March 1945. See *When Presidents Lie*, ch. 2, esp. pp. 23, 27 and 41.

152. The standard studies are Herbert Feis, *Between War and Peace: The Potsdam Conference* (Princeton, 1960); Charles L. Mee, *Meeting at Potsdam* (London, 1975); and Hans-Joachim Giersberg, et al., *Schloss Cecilienhof und die Potsdamer Konferenz, 1945* (Berlin, 1995).

153. McJimsey, ed., *Documentary History: Yalta*, doc. 156; Sherwood, *Roosevelt and Hopkins*, pp. 876–7.

154. Messer, *End of the Alliance*, 122–5; Theoharis, *Yalta Myths*, pp. 19, 31, 36; Alterman, *When Presidents Lie*, pp. 59–66.

155. Harriman, draft tel., April 10, 1945, p. 6, Harriman papers, box 178: chronological files (LC). The draft is marked: "Not sent. Taken to Washington as a memorandum."

156. Kennan, memo, "Russia's International Position at the Close of the War with Germany" [June 1945], *FRUS 1945*, 5:858.

157. Churchill asked his military planners in mid-May 1945 to explore whether Britain and America could wage war with the USSR to get a satisfactory Polish settlement. They showed that the idea was inconceivable. The contingency plan was filed away with the title "Operation Unthinkable." See Reynolds, *In Command of History*, pp. 476–7.

Chapter 4: Vienna 1961

1. David Dilks, ed., *The Diaries of Sir Alexander Cadogan, OM, 1938–1945* (London, 1971), p. 778, Aug. 2, 1945.

2. John Colville, *The Fringes of Power: Downing Street Diaries, 1939–1955* (London, 1985), p. 676, recording comments in Aug. 1953.

3. Keith Eubank, *The Summit Conferences, 1919–1960* (Norman, Oklahoma, 1966), pp. 144, 158–9. For a detailed study see Günter Bischof and Saki Dockrill, eds., *Cold War Respite: The Geneva Summit of 1955* (Baton Rouge, Louisiana, 1955).

4. *New York Times*, Feb. 21, 1950, p. 12.

5. Quotations from Athan G. Theoharis, *The Yalta Myths: An Issue in U.S. Politics, 1945–1955* (Columbia, Missouri, 1970), pp. 93, 142–3.

6. Speech to Congress, March 12, 1947 (PPPUS website).

7. "The Sources of Soviet Conduct," reprinted in George F. Kennan, *American Diplomacy, 1900–1950* (Chicago, 1951), pp. 107–28, esp. pp. 124, 126, 128. This is the celebrated "Mr. X" article first published anonymously in the journal *Foreign Affairs*, July 1947. See also the discussions of containment in John Lewis Gaddis, *Strategies of Containment: A Critical Appraisal of Postwar American National Security Policy* (New York, 1982), chs. 1–3; Henry Kissinger, *Diplomacy* (New York, 1994), ch. 18; and Fredrik Logevall, "A Critique of Containment," *DH*, 28 (2004), pp. 473–99.

8. Speech of Dec. 14, 1950, in Robert Rhodes James, ed., *Winston S.*

Churchill: His Complete Speeches, 1897–1963, vol. 8 (New York, 1974), p. 8143. See generally John W. Young, *Winston Churchill's Last Campaign: Britain and the Cold War, 1951–1955* (Oxford, 1996), and Klaus Larres, *Churchill's Cold War: The Politics of Personal Diplomacy* (London, 2002).

9. Churchill to Eisenhower, May 7, 1953, PREM 11/1074 (TNA).

10. Speech of Oct. 9, 1948, in Rhodes James, ed., *Churchill: His Complete Speeches*, 8: 7708.

11. Peter Catterall, ed., *The Macmillan Diaries: The Cabinet Years, 1950–1957* (London, 2003), May 5, 1955, p. 420 [Yalta and Churchill]; Richard Aldous, *Macmillan, Eisenhower and the Cold War* (Dublin, 2005), pp. 25, 175 note 10.

12. William Taubman, *Khrushchev: The Man and His Era* (New York, 2003), p. 75. This excellent biography is a major source on Khrushchev's side of the story, supplemented by the essays in William Taubman, Sergei Khrushchev and Abbott Gleason, eds., *Nikita Khrushchev* (New Haven, 2000). Aleksandr Fursenko and Timothy Naftali, *Khrushchev's Cold War: The Inside Story of an American Adversary* (New York, 2006) draws on recent Soviet material.

13. Catterall, ed., *Macmillan Diaries*, July 19 and 22, 1955, pp. 452, 456.

14. Carl A. Linden, *Khrushchev and the Soviet Leadership* (2nd ed., Baltimore, 1990), pp. 92–3.

15. Michael R. Beschloss, *Mayday: Eisenhower, Khrushchev and the U-2 Affair* (New York, 1986), p. 195.

16. Quoted in Michael B. Yahuda, *China's Role in World Affairs* (London, 1978), p. 109.

17. Taubman, *Khrushchev*, pp. 329, 331–2.

18. Taubman, *Khrushchev*, pp. 350–3; Fursenko and Naftali, *Khrushchev's Cold War*, p. 43.

19. The phrase of former aide Oleg Troyanovsky in his essay "The Making of Soviet Foreign Policy," in Taubman et al., eds., *Nikita Khrushchev*, p. 217.

20. The struggle with Mikoyan is emphasized in Fursenko and Timothy Naftali, *Khrushchev's Cold War*, pp. 194–217, quoting from p. 201.

21. In Dean Rusk, *As I Saw It* (New York, 1990), p. 227, the words are "Berlin is the testicles of the West" but one doubts that Khrushchev's language would have been so decorous!

22. David Childs, *The GDR: Moscow's German Ally* (London, 1983), pp. 64, 142. For detailed studies of the crisis, see Honoré M. Catudal, *Kennedy and the Berlin Wall Crisis: A Case Study in U.S. Decision Making* (Berlin,

1980), and Michael Lemke, *Die Berlinkrise 1958 bis 1963: Interessen und Handlungsspielräume der SED im Ost-West-Konflikt* (Berlin, 1995).

23. Alistair Horne, *Macmillan, 1957–1986* (London, 1989), p. 117; Aldous, Macmillan, *Eisenhower*, p. 73.

24. Quotations from Taubman, *Khrushchev*, pp. 412, 419–20.

25. Report on Khrushchev's American visit, sent to the Czech communist party, quoted in Petr Lunák, "Khrushchev and the Berlin Crisis: Soviet Brinkmanship Seen from Inside," *Cold War History*, 3 (2003), p. 65.

26. Fursenko and Naftali, *Khrushchev's Cold War*, pp. 289, 340.

27. See the itinerary given in Sonnenfeldt to Kissinger, March 21, 1972, Nixon Presidential Materials Project, WHSF, SMOF, Haldeman papers, box 156: Russia Trip File (NA).

28. *Public Papers of the Presidents of the United States: John F. Kennedy* (3 vols., Washington, D.C., 1962–4), *1961*, pp. 1–3. On the background see Richard J. Tofel, *Sounding the Trumpet: The Making of John F. Kennedy's Inaugural Address* (Chicago, 2005).

29. Michael R. Beschloss, *The Crisis Years: Kennedy and Khrushchev, 1960–1963* (New York, 1991), pp. 17–19.

30. Transcript of Kennedy interview with James McGregor Burns [Aug. 1959], pp. 40–3, in Theodore C. Sorensen papers, box 6: books, *John F. Kennedy* (John F. Kennedy Library, Boston—henceforth JFKL). A sanitized version appeared in Burns' campaign biography, *John Kennedy: A Political Profile* (New York, 1959), pp. 270–3.

31. Speech at University of Rochester, New York, Oct. 1, 1959, reprinted in John F. Kennedy, *A Strategy for Peace*, ed. Allan Nevins (New York, 1960), p. 13.

32. Kennedy, *A Strategy for Peace*, esp. pp. 10–13.

33. Speech in the U.S. Senate, June 14, 1960, in Kennedy, *A Strategy for Peace* (added by publisher at the last minute on unnumbered pages before the main text).

34. As with most of Kennedy's writings, the research was done by others—in this case the press secretary at the U.S. embassy in London, where Kennedy's father was then ambassador. And the title was adapted from the American edition of Churchill's speeches from 1932–8: *While England Slept*. For background see Robert Dallek, *John F. Kennedy: An Unfinished Life* (London, 2003), pp. 61–6.

35. John F. Kennedy, *Why England Slept* (London, 1961 reprint), esp. pp. 7–8, 127–9, 149–50, 154, 171, 177.

36. See, for instance, D. C. Watt, "Appeasement: The Rise of a Revisionist School," *Political Quarterly*, 36 (1965), 191–213.

37. Kennedy, *Why England Slept*, esp. ch. 10.

38. Kennedy, *Public Papers, 1961*, p. 2.

39. Quotations from Dallek, *Kennedy*, pp. 119, 123.

40. See the extensive discussion in Dallek, *Kennedy*, pp. 100–05.

41. Notes in Kennedy Pre-Presidential Papers, box 811: Senate Files: Khrushchev Meeting (JFKL).

42. Kennedy, *A Strategy for Peace*, p. 9.

43. Mikhail Smirnovsky, memo [Aug. 1960], reproduced in Cold War International History Project (CWIHP), Bulletin 4 (Fall 1994), quoting from p. 66.

44. Harriman to Kennedy, Nov. 15, 1960, and memo of meeting with Menshikov, Dec. 14, 1960, in NSF 176, CO: USSR: Gen., 2/15–2/19/61 (JFKL).

45. George F. Kennan, oral history, March 23, 1965, pp. 26–33 (JFKL).

46. Dean Rusk, "The President," *Foreign Affairs*, 38/3 (April 1960), p. 365. In the omitted passage, Rusk heightened the contrast by referring obliquely to the personality and political differences between Eisenhower and Khrushchev, but his basic point was general and structural. To Rusk's embarrassment, he was often asked about this article in the run up to the Vienna summit; e.g., *Department of State Bulletin*, 1131:300–1, 308 (Feb. 27, 1961) and 1135:443 (March 9, 1961).

47. For Stevenson's proposal see his record of a phone conversation with Kennedy, Jan. 13, 1961, *FRUS 1961–3*, vol. 5, pp. 15–16.

48. A translation of the whole text is in President's Office Files (POF) 126A: CO: USSR: Khrushchev Reports (A).

49. Moscow to Washington, tel. 1682, Jan. 19, 1961, NSF 176: CO: USSR Gen., 1/1/61–1/21/61; cf. the analysis in the same file.

50. Quoted in Ralph G. Martin, *A Hero for Our Time* (New York, 1983), p. 351; cf. Beschloss, *Crisis Years*, p. 61 and title to chapter 3, where Martin's quotation is rendered as "our clue to the Soviet Union."

51. Cf. *FRUS 1961–3*, vol. 5, p. 114.

52. Bundy, notes of discussion on Feb. 11, 1961, *FRUS 1961–3*, vol. 5, pp. 63–7; Llewellyn Thompson oral history, March 25, 1964, p. 3 (JFKL).

53. FRUS 1961–3, vol. 5, p. 66; Charles E. Bohlen oral history, May 21, 1964, p. 3 (JFKL).

54. *FRUS 1961–3*, vol. 5, pp. 48, 64; Bohlen, "Points for Consideration," Feb. 18, 1961, copy in NSF 234: Vienna Briefing Book, vol. II (JFKL).

55. Kennedy to Khrushchev, Feb. 22, 1961, *FRUS 1961–3*, vol. 6, pp. 5–6.

56. Bohlen, "Points for Consideration," Feb. 18, 1961, copy in NSF 234:Vienna Briefing Book, vol. II (JFKL).

57. Thompson to Rusk, tells 2135 and 2136, March 10, 1961, *FRUS 1961–3*, vol. 5, pp. 92–4. Beschloss, *Crisis Years*, pp. 66, 80, 87–8, suggests that Khrushchev had now gone cool on the idea of a summit and had deliberately fled Moscow as a snub to Thompson and Kennedy, but this interpretation was based on limited evidence available in 1990–1. My reading is that both leaders wanted a meeting and that arrangements proceeded steadily, except for the hiatus over the Bay of Pigs in April.

58. See Thompson to Rusk, tels 2361 and 2459, April 1 and 11, 1961, and Rusk to Thompson, April 5, 1961, all in NSF 234:Vienna, folder 1 (JFKL).

59. On April 7 the Washington commentator Drew Pearson stated: "It can be reliably reported that Khrushchev has offered to meet President Kennedy in Vienna while Kennedy is in Europe to see DeGaulle. Khrushchev very much wants to see Kennedy. He has passed word via the American embassy that he is ready whenever Kennedy is." Copy in Pierre E. G. Salinger papers, box 128: State Visits, Austria, Personal Briefing papers (JFKL).

60. David Reynolds, *One World Divisible: A Global History since 1945* (New York, 2000), p. 174.

61. Quotations from Walter A. McDougall, *The Heavens and the Earth: A Political History of the Space Age* (New York, 1985), pp. 319–20.

62. For discussion of Kennedy's motives see Dallek, *Kennedy*, p. 362; Aleksandr Fursenko and Timothy Naftali, *"One Hell of a Gamble": Khrushchev, Castro, and Kennedy, 1958–1964* (New York, 1997), p. 88; Arthur M. Schlesinger Jr., *A Thousand Days: John F. Kennedy in the White House* (New York, 1971 pbk.), pp. 241–3.

63. Schlesinger to Kennedy, April 5, 1961, *FRUS 1961–3*, vol. 10, doc. 81.

64. Chapter headings from Lawrence Freedman, *Kennedy's Wars: Berlin, Cuba, Laos, and Vietnam* (New York, 2000), pp. 129, 139.

65. Schlesinger, *A Thousand Days*, p. 271.

66. Richard Reeves, *President Kennedy: Profile of Power* (New York, 1993), p. 95.

67. Texts in *FRUS 1961–3*, vol. 6, docs. 9–11.

68. On Kennedy's motives, I follow Fursenko and Naftali, *"One Hell of a Gamble,"* pp. 105–6.

69. *FRUS 1961–3*, vol. 5, pp. 130–3.

70. Quotations in this paragraph from Freedman, *Kennedy's Wars*, pp. 295, 302.

71. GRU report in Fursenko and Naftali, *"One Hell of a Gamble,"* pp. 113–14.

72. Robert F. Kennedy oral history, March 1, 1964, p. 70 (JFKL).

73. *FRUS 1961–3*, vol. 5, p. 66.

74. Khrushchev to Kennedy, May 12, 1961, *FRUS 1961–3*, vol. 6, doc. 15; Memcon of White House meeting, May 16, 1961, *FRUS 1961–3*, vol. 5, doc. 69.

75. *FRUS 1961–3*, vol. 5, p. 136.

76. Fursenko and Naftali, *"One Hell of a Gamble,"* pp. 117–20.

77. The Soviet evidence undermines claims (e.g., Beschloss, *Crisis Years*, pp. 181, 233) that Khrushchev deliberately used Bolshakov to gull Kennedy into a summit on false hopes of a test ban agreement. It would be more accurate to say that Kennedy deluded himself. Fursenko and Naftali, *"One Hell of a Gamble,"* p. 117. For background see Glenn T. Seaborg, with Benjamin S. Loeb, *Kennedy, Khrushchev and the Test Ban* (Berkeley, 1981), ch. 3.

78. Taubman, *Khrushchev*, p. 493.

79. Fursenko and Naftali, *Khrushchev's Cold War*, p. 354.

80. Paris to Washington, tel. 1577, May 17, 1961, and Washington to Paris, tel. 1642, both in NSF 234:Vienna (1).

81. Bohlen, memcon of phone conversation with the president, May 16, 1961, Charles E. Bohlen papers, box 18: Memoranda of Telephone Conversations, RG 59 Lot 74 D379 (NA).

82. Text as quoted in circular telegrams to U.S. missions, e.g., Washington to New Delhi, tel. 2379, May 18, 1961, NSF 234:Vienna (1). See also *New York Times*, May 20, 1961, p. 2.

83. "Transcript of Background Press and Radio Briefing," May 19, 1961, pp. A4–5, B 7, B10, copy in Salinger papers, box 127: State Visits, Austria, Advance Survey (1) (JFKL). For "size-up" see *Time*, June 16, 1961, p. 13.

84. See correspondence in NSF 234:Vienna (1).

85. Washington to Vienna, tel. 2012, May 19, 1961, NSF 234:Vienna (1); Salinger, talk on "Presidential Advances," no date [late 1961?], Salinger papers, box 127: State Visits, Austria, Advance Survey (1).

86. For background see Salinger papers, box 127: State Visits, Austria, Press Arrangements.

87. "Notes on meeting between the Soviet and USA Representa-

tives," May 23, 1961, Salinger papers, box 128: State Visits, Austria, Advance Survey (2).

88. "Arrangements for the President's Visit," memcon, June 1, 1961, copy in John J. McNally: White House Office staff files, box 4: Travel, Paris-Vienna-London, 1961 (JFKL). See also the comparison of the two advance parties in *New York Times*, June 4, 1961, p. 27.

89. Salinger, talk on "Presidential Advances"; *New York Times*, June 5, 1961, p. 12.

90. Fursenko and Naftali, *"One Hell of a Gamble,"* pp. 120–4; *FRUS 1961–3*, vol. 14, doc. 24.

91. Moscow to Washington, tel. 2887 and 2890, May 24, 1961, NSF 234: Trips, Vienna (1). Only the former is printed in full in *FRUS 1961–3*, vol. 14, doc. 24.

92. Kennedy, *Public Papers, 1961*, doc. 205.

93. Between 1952 and 1966 the Soviet Communist's party ruling Political Bureau (Politburo) was known as the Presidium.

94. Fursenko and Naftali, *Khrushchev's Cold War*, p. 355–9, prints an extended summary of the Soviet records of this meeting. See also Anatoly Dobrynin, *In Confidence: Moscow's Ambassador to America's Six Cold War Presidents, 1962–1986* (New York, 1995), pp. 43–4.

95. G.M. Kornienko, "Upushchennaia Vozmoshnost: Vstrecha N. S. Khrushcheva i J. Kennedi v Vene v 1961g," *Novaia i Noveishaia Istoria*, (March–April 1992), p. 102.

96. Walter Lippmann, "Today and Tomorrow" column, *Washington Post*, April 17, 1961; also Fursenko and Naftali, *Khrushchev's Cold War*, p. 356. Kennedy was belatedly struck at Vienna by the extent to which Khrushchev "believed the communist folklore about Wall Street running the government"—Theodore C. Sorensen, oral history, March 26, 1964, pp. 30–1 (JFKL).

97. Thompson to Rusk, tel. 2898, May 24, 1961, NSF 234:Vienna (1). Thompson called this message a summary of "minor and supplemental items" from his conversation but thought them "worth reporting" in view of the importance of the forthcoming meeting. Bizarrely the U.S. official documents failed to print this revealing text, mentioning the telegram only in a footnote as "a list of minor items." See *FRUS 1961–3*, vol. 14, p. 69.

98. Taubman, *Khrushchev*, esp. pp. 110–11, 155–8.

99. OCI paper 2391/61, "Khrushchev—A Personality Sketch," POF 126: CO: USSR, Vienna Meeting, Background Documents, C; PMK-D/11, "Khrushchev: the Man, His Manner, His Outlook, and His View of

the United States," May 25, 1961, NSF 234A:Vienna Briefing Book, II/4 (both JFKL).

100. State Dept. Bureau of Information and Research, Khrushchev personality sketch, CF 1909, RG 59 Executive Secretariat Conference Files, box 255 (NA).

101. Draft "Talking Points—Berlin and Germany," and Bundy annotations, NSF 234:Vienna, Briefing Book, vol. I, doc. 2a.

102. Moscow to Washington, tel. 2914, May 25, 1961, POF 126: CO: USSR,Vienna Background documents (A).

103. *FRUS 1961–3*, vol. 14, pp. 37–8, 73.

104. Vladislav Zubok, "Khrushchev and the Berlin Crisis (1958–1962)," Cold War International History Project Working Paper (henceforth CWIHP,WP), 6 (1993), pp. 19–20; Hope M. Harrison, "Ulbricht and the Concrete 'Rose': New Archival Evidence on the Dynamics of Soviet-East German Relations and the Berlin Crisis, 1958–1961," CWIHP, WP 5 (1993), pp. 36, 44. Harrison prints Ambassador Pervukhin's letter in full in appendix D.

105. *FRUS 1961–3*, vol. 14, docs. 4, 24–5; *FRUS 1961–3*, vol. 5, doc. 44.

106. *FRUS 1961–3*, vol. 5, pp.141–2, 157, 160, 163. The American press also predicted that Khrushchev wanted a productive meeting and sought common ground, e.g., *New York Times*, June 3, 1961, p. 7.

107. On the summit, see generally the volume of essays edited by Monika Sommer and Michaela Lindinger, *Die Augen der Welt auf Wien gerichtet: Gipfel 1961 Chruschtschkow-Kennedy* (Innsbruck, 2005), which looks at the summit as both a diplomatic and cultural event. The U.S. records are published in *FRUS 1961–3*, vol. 5, docs. 83–9. The originals and supplementary material may be found in State Dept. records, RG 59 Executive Secretariat Conference files, boxes 254–5, CF 1900–1910 (NA).

108. Jean Lacouture, *De Gaulle: The Ruler, 1945–1970* (New York, 1992); Kennedy, *Public Papers, 1961*, p. 429.

109. Reeves, *President Kennedy*, pp. 346–7; Dallek, *Kennedy*, pp. 397–9.

110. Hugh Sidey, introduction to Cecil Stoughton and Chester V. Clifton, *The Memories: JFK, 1961–1963* (New York, 1973), p. 7.

111. Charles de Gaulle, *Mémoires*, edition annotée (Paris, 2000), p. 1107; FRUS 14, doc. 30, pp. 81–2.

112. David Halberstam, *The Best and the Brightest* (New York, 1973 pbk.), p. 95; Sorensen, memo, June 2, 1961, POF 126: CO: USSR,Vienna Background documents (A).

113. Theodore C. Sorensen, *Kennedy* (London, 1965), p. 543.

114. Quoted in Sommer und Lindinger, eds., *Die Augen der Welt*, p. 88.

115. *New York Times*, June 4, 1961, p. 27.

116. Reeves, *President Kennedy*, pp. 158–9, quoting Jacobson's unpublished memoirs. Jacobson and his wife stayed in Room 404 of the Hotel Kummer, well away from the main U.S. hotels: the Bristol and Prinz Eugen. A few White House press technicians were in the Kummer, but two floors below the Jacobsons. See hotel lists in White House Central Files (WHCF) 971: TR9/CO 19: Vienna. On the timing see *New York Times*, June 4, 1961, p. 27.

117. *FRUS 1961–3*, vol. 5, doc. 83, pp. 172–3.

118. Although the standard accounts say that Gromyko was also present for this first session (Schlesinger, *Thousand Days*, 334; Reeves, *President Kennedy*, 159; Beschloss, *Crisis Years*, 194), he is not listed on the official transcript for this first meeting. See *FRUS 1961–3*, vol. 5, doc. 83.

119. This summary of the first session follows the transcript in *FRUS 1961–3*, vol. 5, doc. 83.

120. Kennedy's comment that the U.S. had misjudged the Cuban situation does not appear in the official transcript: it was deleted from the draft based on the interpreter's notes. See *FRUS 1961–3*, vol. 5, doc. 83, p. 178, and the draft transcript of first meeting, p. 9, in Theodore C. Sorensen papers, box 42: Berlin, 1 (JFKL). But Kennedy repeated the admission in the afternoon session and this remark remains in the official transcript (*FRUS 1961–3*, vol. 5, p. 183).

121. Reeves, *President Kennedy*, p. 162. Most of Reeves' evidence for these reactions comes from interviews and should be used with caution because the exact timing is unclear. The exchange with Thompson was noted by Arthur Schlesinger on Dec. 10, 1964—Arthur M. Schlesinger Jr. papers, box W–3: Berlin notes (JFKL)—and printed in Schlesinger, *Thousand Days*, 340, as occurring after the day's meetings. Since Thompson did not attend the afternoon sessions, I agree with Reeves in placing it before lunch.

122. Pierre Salinger, *With Kennedy* (London, 1967), p. 178 [the menu]; Kenneth P. O'Donnell and David Powers, *"Johnny, We Hardly Knew Ye": Memories of John Fitzgerald Kennedy* (Boston, 1970), p. 294 [Gromyko story].

123. *FRUS 1961–3*, vol. 5, doc. 84, p. 179.

124. Reeves, *President Kennedy*, p. 162.

125. This account of the afternoon session follows the transcript in *FRUS 1961–3*, vol. 5, doc. 85.

126. Bohlen, "Line of Approach to Khrushchev" June 1, 1961, *FRUS 1961–3*, vol. 5, doc. 80, p. 165.

127. *FRUS 1961–3*, vol. 5, p.187; cf. Beschloss, *Crisis Years*, p. 202. Soviet bloc commentators attached considerable importance to a concession on this point before the Summit. See *New York Times*, June 4, 1961, p. 27.

128. Thompson, oral history, April 27, 1966, p. 36; Bohlen, oral history, 21 March 1964, p. 5 (both JFKL). In his memoirs, Rusk said that the lack of an "agreed-upon agenda" was "a sure prescription for disaster"—*As I Saw It*, p. 220—though some of that is surely retrospective wisdom.

129. Troyanovsky, "Making of Soviet Foreign Policy," in Taubman et al., eds., *Khrushchev*, p. 231. In the account of Vienna in his memoirs, Khrushchev compared the confident Kennedy favorably with Eisenhower, always being prompted by his advisors, but this must be taken with a pinch of salt: his opinion of the president rose considerably after the Cuban missile crisis and Kennedy's assassination. See Strobe Talbott, ed., *Khrushchev Remembers: The Last Testament* (London, 1974), pp. 497–8.

130. *New York Times*, June 4, 1961, p. 26; Sorensen, *Kennedy*, p. 543; Beschloss, *Crisis Years*, pp. 207–9; Schlesinger, *Thousand Days*, p. 342 [on Jackie].

131. This account of the first session of day two follows the transcript in *FRUS 1961–3*, vol. 5, doc. 87.

132. On testing see *FRUS 1961–3*, vol. 5, doc. 87, pp. 211–16; Seaborg, *Kennedy, Khruschchev and the Test Ban*, p. 68.

133. For their discussion of Germany see *FRUS 1961–3*, vol. 5, doc. 87, pp. 216–25.

134. Salinger, *With Kennedy*, pp. 181–2.

135. This account of the lunch is based on the transcript in *FRUS 1961–3*, vol. 5, doc. 88, pp. 225–8.

136. A copy of the schedule is in WHCF 971:TR9/CO 19:Vienna.

137. Benjamin C. Bradlee, *Conversations with Kennedy* (New York, 1975), 126.

138. *FRUS 1961–3*, vol. 5, doc. 89, pp. 229–30. It is interesting that the original draft of the American record—written up from his working notes by Alexander Akalovsky, the State Department interpreter—reported simply a final, continuous tirade by Khrushchev, without interruption by Kennedy. There was no mention in this draft of the remark about it being Khrushchev who wanted to force a change and/or any sign of Kennedy's "cold winter" punch line. Akalovsky's drafts of all the Vienna conversations were reviewed by the White House and it is not clear when and by whom the revisions were made. The "cold winter"

line is also in the Soviet minutes, and is recalled by interpreter Sukhodrev in his memoirs, but possibly Kennedy made his interventions less forcefully than many American accounts suggest. Akalovsky's draft of this final meeting is in POF 126A: CO: USSR: Vienna Meeting, folder J, and the official version, marked "Approved by White House, 6/23/61," is in folder I. See also V. M. Sukhodrev, *Iazyk Moi, Drug Moi: Ot Khrushcheva do Gorbacheva* (Moscow, 1999), p. 141 and, for the Russian record, Sommer and Lindinger, eds., *Die Augen der Welt*, pp. 54–5.

139. This account follows the interview with Reston in Halberstam, *The Best and the Brightest*, pp. 96–7. Reston later told a similar story, in somewhat different words, to biographer Richard Reeves. See Reeves, *President Kennedy*, 172–3. In both volumes, the talk with Kennedy is said to have taken place at the U.S. embassy, but it may have been at the ambassador's residence, which was more secluded and also where Kennedy was officially supposed to go after the final meeting for a quick change before driving to the airport (see schedule in WHCF 971: TR9/CO 19: Vienna).

140. Fursenko and Naftali, *Khrushchev's Cold War*, p. 364; Beschloss, *Crisis Years*, p. 225.

141. Diary entries for June 4 and 11, quoted in Harold Macmillan, *Pointing the Way, 1959–1961* (London, 1972), pp. 356–7; letter to Queen Elizabeth, Sept. 15, 1961, in Horne, *Macmillan*, pp. 303–4.

142. Transcript of joint press briefing, June 4, 1961, in Salinger papers, box 127: State Visits, Austria, Advance Survey (1); Salinger, *With Kennedy*, p. 182.

143. *New York Times*, June 5, 1961, p. 1; *Washington Post*, June 6, 1961, p. A10; *Time*, June 16, 1961, p. 13; *U.S. News and World Report*, June 19, 1961, p. 39.

144. Copy of decree of June 17, 1961, in CF 1907, folder 2, tab 84, RG 59 Executive Secretariat Conference Files, box 254 (NA).

145. Kennedy, *Public Papers, 1961*, doc. 231.

146. "Report by Chairman N.S. Khrushchev on His Meeting with President John F. Kennedy in Vienna" and accompanying memoranda (New York, 1961), copy in Schlesinger papers, box W-3: Berlin: Reports—Khrushchev speech.

147. Robert F. Kennedy oral history, Feb. 27, 1965, p. 630 (JFKL); Peter Collier and David Horowitz, *The Kennedys: An American Drama* (New York, 1984), pp. 277–8.

148. Reeves, *President Kennedy*, pp. 175–8.

149. A point made bluntly by Bundy to Kennedy, June 10, 1961, NSF 398: Bundy (JFKL).

150. Acheson, report, June 28, 1961, *FRUS 1961–3*, vol. 14, doc. 49, quoting pp. 138–9.

151. On the situation in Berlin see Catudal, *Kennedy and the Berlin Wall Crisis*, pp. 164–5, 184–6.

152. Catudal, *Kennedy and the Berlin Wall Crisis*, esp. pp. 125–6, 187–8, 216, 239. Walt Rostow's claim that Kennedy in early August was explicitly predicting "a wall" (Beschloss, *Crisis Years*, 265) seems like retrospective wisdom. Rostow's earlier version of his talk with Kennedy did not use the term "wall." See Schlesinger, *Thousand Days*, p. 367, and Reeves, *President Kennedy*, pp. 298, 693.

153. Kennedy, *Public Papers, 1961*, doc. 302.

154. Fursenko and Naftali, *Khrushchev's Cold War*, p. 356; Lunák, "Khrushchev and the Berlin Crisis," pp. 72, 74.

155. See Zubok, "Khrushchev and the Berlin Crisis." pp. 19–24; Harrison, "Ulbricht and the Concrete 'Rose,'" pp. 45–51 and appendix H; Michael Lemke, *Die Berlinkrise*, pp. 161–72.

156. O'Donnell and Powers, *"Johnny, We Hardly Knew Ye,"* p. 303; Beschloss, *Crisis Years*, pp. 278–9.

157. Dallek, *Kennedy*, p. 625.

158. Willy Brandt, *People and Politics: The Years 1960–1975* (London, 1978), p. 20.

159. For argument and quotations see Taubman, *Khrushchev*, esp. pp. 506, 541, 583. On nuclear warheads see Steven Zaloga, *Target America: the Soviet Union and the Strategic Arms Race, 1945–1964* (Novato, California, 1993), p. 213.

160. For these two paragraphs see *FRUS 1961–3*, vol. 5, doc. 77, and *FRUS 1961–3*, vol. 7, doc. 28; Dobrynin, *In Confidence*, pp. 96–8.

161. Halberstam, *Best and the Brightest*, p. 97; David Kaiser, *American Tragedy: Kennedy, Johnson, and the Origins of the Vietnam War* (Cambridge, Mass., 2000), pp. 101–2.

162. Schlesinger, *Thousand Days*, p. 505.

163. For samples of the debate see Freedman, *Kennedy's Wars*, pp. 317–19, 416–17; Robert Dallek, "Lyndon Johnson and Vietnam: The Making of a Tragedy," *Diplomatic History*, 20 (1996): 147–62, esp. p. 149, and Dallek, *Kennedy*, pp. 709–10; Robert S. McNamara, with Brian Van-DeMark, *In Retrospect: The Tragedy and Lessons of Vietnam* (New York, 1995), pp. 95–7; and Fredrik Logevall, "Vietnam and the Question of

What Might Have Been," in Mark J. White, ed., *Kennedy: The New Frontier Revisited* (New York, 1998), pp. 19–62.

164. See Dallek, *Kennedy*, p. 399; Beschloss, *Crisis Years*, p. 206.

Chapter 5: Moscow 1971

1. The fullest memoir account of the summit and its background is in Henry Kissinger, *White House Years* (London, 1979), esp. chs. 26 and 28—a massive volume full of insight and detail yet, like Churchill's memoirs, shrewdly written as a preemptive strike on the verdict of history. A useful counterbalance is the even bigger history spiced with memoir by Raymond L. Garthoff, *Détente and Confrontation: American-Soviet Relations from Nixon to Reagan* (2nd ed., Washington, 1994), esp. chs. 3, 5, 9. The relevant official records have now largely been declassified. At the time of my research, they were available at the Nixon Presidential Materials Project (NPMP) in the U.S. National Archives in College Park, Maryland, but eventually they will be moved to the Nixon Presidential Library in Yorba Linda, California. Many of these documents have been published in *FRUS 1969–1976*, vol. 14—also available electronically on the State Department website—and I have cited them from this source wherever possible. But this excellent volume does not include material on the media aspects of the summit and I have cited that from the original files.

2. Nixon, press conference, Feb. 6, 1969, available in *Public Papers of the Presidents of the United States: Richard Nixon* (6 vols., Washington, D.C., 1971–5) and also on PPPUS website.

3. For fuller discussion, on which this section draws, see David Reynolds, *One World Divisible: A Global History since 1945* (London, 2000), chs. 8 and 10.

4. H. R. Haldeman, with Joseph DiMona, *The Ends of Power* (London, 1978), p. 81.

5. Johnson news conference, July 28, 1965, PPPUS website. More generally see Brian VanDeMark, *Lyndon Johnson and the Escalation of the Vietnam War* (New York, 1991).

6. Seymour M. Hersh, *Kissinger: The Price of Power* (London, 1983), p. 65; cf. R. J. Overy, *The Air War, 1939–1945* (London, 1980), p. 120.

7. Nixon to Laird and Rogers, Feb. 4, 1969, *FRUS 1969–76*, vol. 1, doc. 10.

8. David Holloway, *The Soviet Union and the Arms Race* (2nd ed., New Haven, 1984), pp. 58–9.

9. See Archie Brown and Michael Kaser, eds., *The Soviet Union since the Fall of Khrushchev* (2nd ed., London, 1978), chs. 1–2, 9.

10. See Yang Kuisong, "The Sino-Soviet Border Clash of 1969: From Zhenbao Island to Sino-American *Rapprochement.*" *CWH* 1 (2000), pp. 21–52; Elizabeth Wishnick, *Mending Fences: The Evolution of Moscow's China Policy from Brezhnev to Yeltsin* (Seattle, 2001), ch. 2.

11. For a version of this joke, see Arkady N. Shevchenko, *Breaking with Moscow* (London, 1985), p. 166.

12. Richard M. Nixon, "Asia after Vietnam," *Foreign Affairs*, Oct. 1967, p. 121; Chen Jian, *Mao's China and the Cold War* (Chapel Hill, North Carolina, 2001), pp. 238–9.

13. Robert S. Litwak, *Détente and the Nixon Doctrine: American Foreign Policy and the Pursuit of Stability, 1969–1976* (Cambridge, 1984), p. 122.

14. See speeches by Kennedy on Jan. 20, 1961, and June 10, 1963, and by Nixon, Jan. 20, 1969 (PPPUS website).

15. Garry Wills, *Nixon Agonistes: The Crisis of the Self-Made Man* (New York, 1971 pbk.), pp. 30–1.

16. Stephen E. Ambrose, *Nixon* (3 vols., New York, 1987–91), 2:409.

17. Walter Isaacson, *Kissinger: A Biography* (New York, 1992), pp. 127–8. This remains the best overall study but see also Jussi Hanhimäki, *The Flawed Architect: Henry Kissinger and American Foreign Policy* (Oxford, 2004).

18. Roger Morris, *Uncertain Greatness: Henry Kissinger and American Foreign Policy* (New York, 1977), p. 3.

19. *The Memoirs of Richard Nixon* (London, 1978), p. 341.

20. Quotations from Isaacson, *Kissinger*, pp. 193, 367.

21. Isaacson, *Kissinger*, p. 394, 477.

22. Quoted in Hanhimäki, *Flawed Architect*, p. 12.

23. Margaret MacMillan, *Seize the Hour: When Nixon Met Mao* (London, 2006), p. 61.

24. Anatoly Dobrynin, *In Confidence: Moscow's Ambassador to America's Six Cold War Presidents, 1962–1986* (New York, 1995), pp. 199, 201.

25. On the power struggle, see Harry Gelman, *The Brezhnev Politburo and the Decline of Détente* (Ithaca, New York, 1984), esp. chs. 2–3, and Richard D. Anderson Jr., *Public Politics in an Authoritarian State: Making Foreign Policy during the Brezhnev Years* (Ithaca, New York, 1993). For a positive view of Brezhnev's leadership, at least in his early years, see Ian D. Thatcher, "Brezhnev as Leader," in Edwin Bacon and Mark Sandle, eds., *Brezhnev Reconsidered* (London, 2002), ch. 2.

26. State Department biographical note, May 1961, RG 59 Executive Secretary's Conference Files, box 255 CF 1909 (NA).

27. See Dobrynin, *In Confidence*, pp. 129–33, Shevchenko, *Breaking with Moscow*, pp. 145–9, and A. M. Alexandrov-Agentov, *Ot Kollontai do Gorbacheva* (Moscow, 1994), pp. 66–73.

28. Gerard Smith, *Doubletalk: The Story of SALT I* (Lanham, Md., 1985), title and p. 444.

29. Kissinger, *White House Years*, pp. 551–2. There is a detailed chronology of all the Kissinger-Dobrynin meetings about a summit in 1969–71, together with supporting records, in NPMP, NSC, Kissinger Office Files: box 73: USSR, Apex, Top Secret, H.A.K. (NA).

30. Timothy Garton Ash, *In Europe's Name: Germany and the Divided Continent* (London, 1993), pp. 64–6, 466.

31. M. E. Sarotte, *Dealing with the Devil: East Germany, Détente, and Ostpolitik, 1969–1973* (Chapel Hill, North Carolina, 2001), pp. 46–55.

32. *FRUS 1969–76*, vol. 14, doc. 15.

33. Quotations from Nixon, *Memoirs*, p. 462.

34. Kissinger, *White House Years*, pp. 551–7, though cf. Dobrynin, *In Confidence*, p. 207. For the April exchanges see also *FRUS 1969–76*, vol. 12, docs. 150, 152.

35. Gelman, *Brezhnev Politburo*, pp. 127–30; also Sidney I. Ploss, "Soviet Politics on the Eve of the 24th Party Congress," *World Politics*, 23 (1970), pp. 61–82.

36. Garthoff, *Détente and Confrontation*, p. 17; Dobrynin, *In Confidence*, pp. 218–20.

37. Chen Jian, *Mao's China*, pp. 257–62; Kissinger, *White House Years*, pp. 709–10.

38. Li Zhisui, *The Private Life of Chairman Mao* (London, 1996), p. 558; Chen Jian, *Mao's China*, p. 253. See also the essays in William C. Kirby, Robert S. Ross, and Gong Li, eds., *Normalization of U.S.-China Relations: An International History* (Cambridge, Mass., 2006), esp. chs. 2, 5 and 6.

39. H. R. Haldeman, *The Haldeman Diaries: Inside the Nixon White House* (New York: G.P. Putnam's Sons, 1994), p. 271; Kissinger, *White House Years*, p. 834; Kissinger-Dobrynin memcom, April 23, 1972, in NPMP, NSC, Kissinger Office files box 73: Apex. Dobrynin argues (*In Confidence*, pp. 218–23) that Gromyko's hard line on Berlin (against Dobrynin's advice) drove Nixon to visit China before visiting the USSR. But this is not borne out by the American evidence—the China opening was already well advanced—and probably reflects Dobrynin's desire to score some points at the expense of his former boss.

40. Garthoff, *Détente and Confrontation*, pp. 166–8. Privately Nixon also

promised the Soviets that he would seek to end the U.S. trade embargo and sell them grain—Hersh, *Kissinger*, pp. 343–8.

41. Haig to president, July 6, 1971, copy in Kissinger Office files, box 73: Apex, tab 30.

42. *FRUS 1969–76*, vol. 17, docs. 118, 125, 130.

43. Kissinger, memo for the president, July 14, 1971, *FRUS 1969–76*, electronic vol. E-13, doc. 9. Kissinger's own vivid account of the visit is in *White House Years*, ch. 19, where Zhou is upgraded to "one of the two or three most impressive men I have ever met" (p. 745).

44. Jung Chang and Jon Halliday, *Mao: The Unknown Story* (London, 2006), pp. 718–20.

45. Kissinger, memo for the president, July 14, 1971, *FRUS, 1969–76*, electronic vol. E-13, doc. 9.

46. White House tape, July 22, 1971, in *FRUS, 1969–76*, vol. 17, doc. 147, note 2. Conscious of the taping system, Nixon sometimes spoke for posterity. Even so, these comments seem an accurate reflection of his approach.

47. *FRUS 1969–76*, vol. E-13, docs. 7 and 8.

48. Nixon, *Memoirs*, pp. 544–5.

49. Nixon to Kissinger, memo, July 19, 1971, and taped conversation, July 22, 1971, in *FRUS 1969–76*, vol. 17, doc. 147 and note 2. See also Hanhimäki, *Flawed Architect*, p. 144.

50. Dobrynin, *In Confidence*, p. 226. It seems likely that, even on his first visit, Kissinger was already providing the Chinese with high-grade intelligence about Soviet military dispositions: see Hersh, *Kissinger*, p. 376.

51. E.g., Hersh, *Kissinger*, pp. 418–19; MacMillan, *Seize the Hour*, pp. 283, 313; cf. Garthoff, *Détente and Confrontation,* p. 263; William A. Bundy, *A Tangled Web: The Making of Foreign Policy in the Nixon Presidency* (London, 1998), p. 241. Dobrynin told Kissinger in Nov. 1971 that his visit to Beijing had caused "consternation" in Moscow; *FRUS 1969–76*, vol. 14, p. 52.

52. Kissinger-Dobrynin memcon, July 19, 1971, Kissinger Office files, box 73: Apex.

53. Press conference, Oct. 12, 1971, PPPUS website; see generally Kissinger, *White House Years*, pp. 834–40.

54. Chen Jian, *Mao's China*, pp. 269–71, 277; MacMillan, *Seize the Hour*, p. 221; Chang and Halliday, *Mao*, pp. 671–85.

55. Nixon, *Memoirs*, pp. 559–60; Kissinger, *White House Years*, pp. 1054–5.

56. Li Zhisui, *Private Life of Chairman Mao*, pp. 563–4.

57. *FRUS 1969–76*, vol. 17, doc. 194, quoting p. 679; Kissinger, *White House Years*, pp. 1058, 1060.

58. Meeting on Feb. 23, 1972, *FRUS 1969–76*, vol. E-13, doc. 92.

59. Nixon, note, Feb. 23, 1972, in MacMillan, *Seize the Hour*, p. 239.

60. Meetings of Feb. 24 and 28, 1972, in *FRUS 1969–76*, vol. 17, docs. 199, 204, pp. 768–9, 822; Li Danhui, "Vietnam and Chinese Policy toward the United States," in Kirby et al., eds., *Normalization of U.S.-China Relations*, p. 198.

61. MacMillan, *Seize the Hour*, pp. 298–307, 330–4.

62. Nixon, toast, Shanghai, Feb. 27, 1972 (PPPUS); K.A. Hamilton, "A 'Week That Changed the World': Britain and Nixon's China Visit of 21–28 February 1972," *DS*, 15 (2004), p. 117. Chang and Halliday, *Mao*, pp. 705–14, depict that whole affair as a sophisticated con trick in which Nixon the Red-baiter was himself baited, but the main value of the China trip for the president was its impact on Moscow.

63. Nixon, *Memoirs*, p. 433.

64. Kissinger, *White House Years*, pp. 1127–8; Dobrynin, *In Confidence*, pp. 239–40.

65. Chapin, memo for the Russia File, March 16, 1972, NPMP, WHSF, SMOF, Dwight L. Chapin papers, box 15: chronological files (NA).

66. *FRUS 1969–76*, vol. 14, doc. 58.

67. Wladimir S. Semjonow, *Von Stalin bis Gorbatschow: Ein halbes Jahrhundert in diplomatischer Mission, 1939–1991* (Berlin, 1995), pp. 338–9.

68. *FRUS 1969–76*, vol. 14, p. 211.

69. Jeffrey Kimball, *Nixon's Vietnam War* (Lawrence, Kansas, 1998), p. 301.

70. Kissinger, *White House Years*, pp. 1120–1, 1176.

71. For examples in Jan. 1972 of Nixon talking of getting rid of Kissinger, see Isaacson, *Kissinger*, pp. 394–6.

72. *FRUS 1969–76*, vol. 14, pp. 46–7, 61, 210; Kissinger, *White House Years*, p. 839.

73. *FRUS 1969–76*, vol. 14, esp. docs. 94–5, 102, 127.

74. Kissinger, *White House Years*, pp. 1125–6, 1154–5.

75. *FRUS 1969–76*, vol. 14, p. 511. Kissinger presents a colorful picture in *White House Years*, pp. 1137–41.

76. *FRUS 1969–76*, vol. 14, doc. 134, quoting from p. 499; Kissinger, *White House Years*, pp. 1144–6.

77. *FRUS 1969–76*, vol. 14, doc. 139; Kissinger, *White House Years*, pp. 1146–8.

78. *FRUS 1969–76*, p. 486.

79. Haig's actual message said the president "insists that no substance on summit be discussed until Vietnam situation has been fully explored." *FRUS 1969–76*, vol. 14, docs. 136 (Nixon-Haig conversation) and 138 (Haig to Kissinger, April 21, 1972).

80. Kissinger, *White House Years*, pp. 1148, 1154–5.

81. Kissinger, *White House Years*, pp. 1148, 1151; Ilya V. Gaiduk, *The Soviet Union and the Vietnam War* (Chicago, 1996), p. 236.

82. Nixon statement, May 20, 1971 (PPPUS).

83. Garthoff, *Détente and Confrontation,* pp. 180–3; Hersh, *Kissinger,* pp. 340–3.

84. Kissinger, memcon of April 22, 1972, *FRUS 1969–76*, vol. 14, doc. 139, p. 532; Garthoff, *Détente and Confrontation,* pp. 183–7. Garthoff had served on the official arms control delegation, so he wrote with inside knowledge—but also considerable resentment toward Kissinger. Nevertheless his critique is generally judicious and sometimes devastating. See also Hersh, *Kissinger,* pp. 534–41.

85. Smith, *Doubletalk*, esp. pp. 243, 372, 376–7.

86. Haig to Kissinger, April 22, 1972, *FRUS 1969–76*, doc. 146, p. 559.

87. Kissinger was also riled by some Soviet sharp practice. After Brezhnev had left the meeting, Gromyko tried to negotiate on the basis of an earlier, rejected Soviet draft, claiming that Brezhnev would accept no further changes. FRUS 1969–76, vol. 14, doc. 160, quoting p. 620; Kissinger, *White House Years*, pp. 1152–3.

88. Kissinger, *White House Years*, pp. 1131–2, 1150–1.

89. Quotations from *FRUS 1969–76*, vol. 14, pp. 590, 605, 636. See also Haldeman, *Diaries*, pp. 444, 446.

90. Haldeman, *Diaries*, pp. 446–7; Kissinger, *White House Years*, p. 1163.

91. Chapin to Haldeman, April 20, 1972, NPMP, WHSF, SMOF, H. R. Haldeman papers, box 156: Russian Trip File (NA).

92. Quotations from Chapin to Ziegler, April 7, 1972, Chapin papers, box 16.

93. See Chapin-Haldeman cables of April 20–24, 1972, in Haldeman papers, box 156: Russian Trip File; and Chapin to Haig, May 2, 1972, and to Beam, May 3, 1972, Chapin papers, box 16.

94. Nixon, *Memoirs*, pp. 594–5, 599–600; Kissinger, *White House Years*, pp. 1168–74; cf. *FRUS 1969–76*, vol. 14, pp. 361, 375 on cancelling first.

95. *FRUS 1969–76*, vol. 14, pp. 677 (Haig) and 712 ("bravado"). See also Nixon, *Memoirs*, pp. 600–01; Haldeman, *Diaries*, pp. 451–3. Kissinger's memoirs play the whole thing down as a momentary wobble when he

told the president what the latter wanted to hear instead of sticking to his guns: see Kissinger, *White House Years*, pp. 1177–8.

96. Haldeman, *Diaries*, pp. 451–5; Nixon, *Memoirs*, pp. 601–2; *FRUS 1969–76*, vol. 14, p. 746.

97. Nixon, address of May 8, 1972 (PPPUS).

98. Nixon, *Memoirs*, pp. 602–3; Kissinger, *White House Years*, p. 1184–5; Isaacson, *Kissinger*, p. 420–1. For the leaks see Stephen Bull to Haldeman, May 17, 1972, Haldeman papers, box 156: Moscow Trip, May 1972.

99. Kissinger even claims that Dobrynin told him on May 11 that the Americans had "handled a difficult situation uncommonly well." Predictably Dobrynin's account is rather different, with an agitated Kissinger repeatedly asking whether the summit was still on, but the phrase is in an official American minute. Kissinger, *White House Years*, pp. 1192–5; Dobrynin, *In Confidence*, pp. 247–8; cf. *FRUS 1969–76*, vol. 14, doc. 214.

100. Dobrynin, *In Confidence*, p. 248; Bundy, *A Tangled Web*, p. 320).

101. Shevchenko, *Breaking with Moscow*, pp. 212–13.

102. Dobrynin, *In Confidence*, p. 248; Alexandrov-Agentov, *Ot Kollontai do Gorbacheva*, pp. 223–4. Bundy, *Tangled Web*, pp. 321–2, and Sarotte, *Dealing with the Devil*, pp. 136–7, place much more emphasis on the German angle.

103. Isaacson, *Kissinger*, p. 422 (Dobrynin interview); Garthoff, *Détente and Confrontation,* pp. 113–17.

104. This account of the party line draws on an informer's report of a lecture in Leningrad, May 21, 1972, in Moscow embassy to State Department, airgram A-392, May 26, 1972, copy in National Security Archive (NSA), Nuclear History, Berlin Crisis, box 66: May 1972 Summit.

105. *FRUS 1969–76*, vol. 14, pp. 840–1.

106. Mark Feeney, *Nixon at the Movies: A Book about Belief* (Chicago, 2004), p. 347; Nixon, *Memoirs*, p. 609.

107. Ambrose, *Nixon*, 1:519–34; 2:64–5, 106–7.

108. Haldeman, *Diaries*, pp. 461–2; Kissinger, *White House Years*, p. 1205; cf. *FRUS 1969–76*, vol. 14, pp. 926–7.

109. Cf. *FRUS 1969–76*, vol. 14, pp. 89, 91, 243.

110. Nixon, *Memoirs*, pp. 206–7, 609.

111. Kissinger-Brezhnev memcon, April 21, 1972, *FRUS 1969–76*, vol. 14, p. 482.

112. *FRUS 1969–76*, vol. 14, doc. 257; Nixon, *Memoirs*, pp. 609–10; Kissinger, *White House Years*, pp. 1207–9. Kissinger was reduced to the indignity of begging an account of the meeting from Sukhodrev.

113. Nixon, *Memoirs*, p. 610.

114. Nixon, *Memoirs*, pp. 618–19; Kissinger, *White House Years*, pp. 792, 1207. For a slightly different version of the chandelier story in the conference minutes for May 27 see *FRUS 1969–76*, vol. 14, p. 1151.

115. Nixon, *Memoirs*, p. 611; Kissinger, *White House Years*, pp. 1211–14; *FRUS 1969–76*, vol. 14, doc. 259.

116. Garthoff, *Détente and Confrontation*, pp. 342–3. The official record is slightly different. See *FRUS 1969–76*, vol. 14, pp. 999–1000.

117. For these two paragraphs see Nixon, *Memoirs*, pp. 612–14; Kissinger, *White House Years*, pp. 1223–9; Alexandrov-Agentov, *Ot Kollontai do Gorbacheva*, pp. 229–30. The U.S. record is in *FRUS 1969–76*, vol. 14, doc. 271.

118. Kissinger, *White House Years*, p. 1225; Alexandrov-Agentov, *Ot Kollontai do Gorbacheva*, pp. 228–9.

119. *FRUS 1969–76*, vol. 14, pp. 1161–2, 1167–8; Gaiduk, *Soviet Union and the Vietnam War*, p. 240. Kissinger's deviations from the president's line on Vietnam was, however, noted by some of his aides. See John Negroponte to Kissinger, June 6, 1972, Kissinger Office files, box 74: Moscow Summit, folder 1.

120. Kissinger, *White House Years*, pp. 1219–22, 1229. See also *FRUS 1969–76*, vol. 14, docs. 262 and 263, esp. p. 1011 ("be quiet"). For the notes, see Kissinger Office files, box 74: Moscow Summit, folder 2.

121. See Garthoff, *Détente and Confrontation*, pp. 194–5 and note 106; Hersh, *Kissinger*, pp. 545–6.

122. SALT meeting May 25, 1972, 5:20 p.m. in *FRUS 1969–76*, vol. 14, p. 1106.

123. Kissinger, *White House Years*, pp. 1229–30.

124. Garthoff, *Détente and Confrontation*, pp. 212–13, Smith, *Doubletalk*, esp. pp. 407–9, 417–18.

125. Smith, *Doubletalk*, pp. 435–9; Haldeman, *Diaries*, pp. 464–5; Kissinger, *White House Years*, pp. 1244–5. Transcripts of the press conferences are in NSA, Nuclear History, Berlin Crisis, box 66: May 1972 Summit.

126. Smith, *Doubletalk*, pp. 407–9, 432; Garthoff, *Détente and Confrontation*, pp. 208–13, 223.

127. *FRUS 1969–76*, vol. 14, pp. 985, 989, 1187.

128. Kissinger, *White House Years*, pp. 1208, 1250; Garthoff, *Détente and Confrontation*, pp. 43–6, 327. See also Shevchenko, *Breaking with Moscow*, pp. 205–6. For the drafts of April 22 and 24, 1972, see Kissinger office files, box 72: HAK Moscow Trip, April 1972—Exchange of Notes.

129. Garthoff, *Détente and Confrontation*, pp. 333–4.

130. Minute by Brian Fall, May 30, 1972, in G. Bennett and K. A. Hamilton, eds., *Documents on British Policy Overseas*, series 3, vol. 1 (London, 1997), doc. 97, esp. p. 477.

131. This is the argument of Garthoff, *Détente and Confrontation,* pp. 334–5. Dobrynin, *In Confidence*, p. 252, was more dismissive of the document's significance, taking Kissinger's line, but it is likely that their acceptance by the United States ran counter to his advice and, as in other places in his memoirs, he sought to play down a personal defeat.

132. Dobrynin, *In Confidence*, pp. 255–6; Shevchenko, *Breaking with Moscow*, p. 215. "He doesn't have a hobby," Haldeman noted in his diary in December 1968. "His best relaxation is talking shop"—Ambrose, *Nixon*, 2:227. See also *FRUS 1969–76*, vol. 14, pp. 835–6,

133. Dobrynin, *In Confidence*, p. 256; Shevchenko, *Breaking with Moscow*, pp. 214–16.

134. Nixon, *Memoirs*, pp. 619–20; Kissinger, *White House Years*, pp. 1138, 1210.

135. See the analysis of the media in Moscow Embassy to State Department, tel. 5161, May 31, 1972, copy in NSA, Nuclear History, Berlin Crisis, box 66: May 1972 Summit.

136. See Chapin papers, box 16, esp. his memos to Moore, May 21 and 24, and to Schrauth, May 31, 1972; and Haldeman papers, box 156: Russian Trip File, esp. memos from Moore to Chapin, May 22 and 26, 1972.

137. Address of June 1, 1972 (PPPUS—text and audio). On June 18, 1940, after the fall of France, Churchill told the House of Commons in his "Finest Hour" speech that if Britain could stand up to Hitler, "all Europe may be free and the life of the world may move forward into broad, sunlit uplands." If Britain failed, then the whole world would "sink into the abyss of a new Dark Age." Winston S. Churchill, *The Second World War* (6 vols., London, 1948–54), 2:198.

138. Haldeman, *Diaries*, June 2, 1972, p. 469; annotation on Kissinger to Nixon, July 26 , 1972, in NPMP, NSC, President's Trip Files, box 477: Reaction to the Moscow Summit.

139. David Greenberg, *Nixon's Shadow: The History of an Image* (New York, 2003), p. 278; Isaacson, *Kissinger*, p. 437; *New York Times*, June 2, 1972, p. 37 (Reston); Zbigniew Brzezinski, "How the Cold War was Played," *Foreign Affairs*, Oct. 1972, p. 207.

140. Fifty-seven hundred as against twenty-five hundred. This point was carefully ignored by critics such as Richard Perle, who complained about the "gratuitous imbalance" of SALT I. See his essay "SALT I versus SALT II" in Norton T. Dodge, ed., *After the Moscow Summit* (Mechanics-

ville, Maryland, 1974), p. 46; cf. figures in David Holloway, *The Soviet Union and the Arms Race* (2nd ed., New Haven, 1984), p. 59.

141. Nixon, *Memoirs*, pp. 621, 625–6; see also Dobrynin, *In Confidence*, pp. 258–9.

142. Ambrose, *Nixon*, 2:560–3.

143. James T. Patterson, *Grand Expectations: The United States, 1945–1974* (New York, 1996), p. 762.

144. Ambrose, *Nixon*, 3:56–7.

145. Ambrose, *Nixon*, 3:177; Henry Kissinger, *Years of Upheaval* (London, 2000), pp. 294, 300.

146. Hanhimäki, *Flawed Architect*, pp. 291–4.

147. Ambrose, *Nixon*, 3:365–6.

148. Garthoff, *Détente and Confrontation,* p. 481; Ambrose, *Nixon*, 3:370–4.

149. Nixon, *Memoirs*, p. 1036; Henry Kissinger, *Diplomacy* (New York, 1994), p. 741.

150. Kissinger, *White House Years*, pp. 840, 1153, 1243.

151. Haldeman, *Ends of Power*, pp. 192–6; Hersh, *Kissinger*, pp. 314–17; Isaacson, *Kissinger*, pp. 230–3.

152. Henry A. Kissinger, *A World Restored: Metternich, Castlereagh and the Problems of Peace, 1812–1822* (London, 1957), p. 326.

153. As Ehrlichman noted at the time—see Isaacson, *Kissinger*, p. 478.

154. For similar judgments see Bundy, *Tangled Web*, pp. 520–2, 529; Ambrose, *Nixon*, 2:653–7.

155. His new slogan was "peace through strength." Garthoff, *Détente and Confrontation*, p. 604.

156. Quoted in Odd Arne Westad, *The Global Cold War: Third World Interventions and the Making of Our Times* (Cambridge, 2005), pp. 247–8.

Chapter 6: Camp David 1978

1. Quoted from T. G. Fraser, ed., *The Middle East, 1914–1979* (London, 1980), p. 18. The overview in this section is distilled from David Reynolds, *One World Divisible: A Global History since 1945* (London, 2000), esp. pp. 76–80, 234–42, 370–6.

2. Quotations from David Hirst and Irene Beeson, *Sadat* (London, 1981), p. 152. See also Uri Bar-Joseph, "Last Chance to Avoid War: Sadat's Peace Initiative of February 1973 and Its Failure," *JCH*, 41 (2006), 545–56.

3. Robert Slater, *Warrior Statesman: The Life of Moshe Dayan* (London, 1991), p. 334.

4. For a discussion of Kissinger's Middle Eastern diplomacy see Jussi Hanhimäki, *The Flawed Architect: Henry Kissinger and American Foreign Policy* (Oxford, 2004), ch. 14.

5. Carter diary, Jan. 20, 1977, quoted in Jimmy Carter, *Keeping Faith: Memoirs of a President* (New York, 1982), p. 24.

6. Jimmy Carter, *The Blood of Abraham: Insights into the Middle East* (3rd ed., Fayetteville, Arkansas, 1998), p. 25. The book was first published in 1985.

7. Some of these personal roots are discussed in William B. Quandt, *Camp David: Peacemaking and Politics* (Washington, D.C., 1986), pp. 30–2.

8. I have followed the succinct analysis in Quandt, *Camp David*, pp. 34–5; see also Herbert D. Rosenbaum and Alexej Ugrinsky, eds., *Jimmy Carter: Foreign Policy and Post-Presidential Years* (Westport, Conn., 1994), ch. 1.

9. Background from Hirst and Beeson, *Sadat,* quoting pp. 75, 80–1.

10. Hirst and Beeson, *Sadat*, p. 244. On the economic crisis see also Michael N. Barnett, *Confronting the Costs of War: Military Power, State, and Society in Egypt and Israel* (Princeton, 1992), pp. 138–40, 218–25.

11. A point noted by Hermann Eilts, then U.S. ambassador to Egypt, in Rosenbaum and Ugrinsky, eds., *Jimmy Carter: Foreign Policy*, p. 151.

12. Carter, *Keeping Faith*, pp. 282, 284; Douglas Brinkley, *The Unfinished Presidency: Jimmy Carter's Journey Beyond the White House* (New York, 1998), pp. 61 (Basheer), 106.

13. Hirst and Beeson, *Sadat*, pp. 51, 185.

14. Quandt, *Camp David*, pp. 50–3.

15. Sasson Sofer, *Begin: An Anatomy of Leadership* (Oxford, 1988), pp. 111–12, 118, 157. Chs 6–10 of this book provide a good discussion of his worldview.

16. For background see Eric Silver, *Begin: A Biography* (London, 1984), chs. 1–4, quoting p. 29.

17. On their feud see Silver, *Begin*, pp. 119–21.

18. Silver, *Begin*, p. 140; Sofer, *Begin*, pp. 175–6.

19. The article is quoted at length in Hirst and Beeson, *Sadat*, p. 88.

20. Brzezinski to Begin, June 21, 1977, National Security Affairs, Brzezinski, Country files, box 34: Israel (Jimmy Carter Library, Atlanta, Georgia—henceforth JCL).

21. Brzezinski to Carter, June 10, 1977, JCL, National Security Affairs, Brzezinski, Country files, box 34: Israel. Cf. J. Bowyer Bell, *Terror out of*

Zion: Irgun Zvai Leumi, LEHI, and the Palestine Underground, 1929–1949 (New York, 1977), esp. pp. 103, 105, 111, 173.

22. Carter, *Keeping Faith*, pp. 284, 288.

23. Remarks at Clinton, Mass., March 16, 1977. These and other presidential statements are published in *The Public Papers of the Presidents of the United States: Jimmy Carter* (7 vols., Washington, D.C., 1977–81) and electronically on the PPPUS website.

24. [Jordan], memo for the president [no date, probably June 1977], JCL, Chief of Staff—Jordan, box 35: Middle East (Confidential), 1977(2).

25. Ibid.; see also Carter, *Keeping Faith*, pp. 288–9, and Zbigniew Brzezinski, *Power and Principle: Memoirs of the National Security Adviser* (London, 1983), pp. 95–7.

26. Quandt to Brzezinski, "Background on Begin," July 15, 1977, JCL Remote Archive Capture (RAC), NLC-5-6-7-13-9; Carter, *Keeping Faith*, p. 290; Silver, *Begin*, p. 168.

27. Record of Vance-Gromko meeting, Geneva, May 19, 1977, p. 10, copy in National Security Archive, Soviet Flashpoints, box 6: Additional Carter-Brezhnev documents.

28. Quandt, *Camp David*, ch. 5, quoting p. 123.

29. Quandt, *Camp David*, pp. 139–45; Brzezinski, *Power and Principle*, pp. 109, 111.

30. Hirst and Beeson, *Sadat*, p. 255; Quandt, *Camp David*, p. 146.

31. Quotations from Hirst and Beeson, *Sadat,* pp. 265, 275.

32. Sofer, *Begin*, pp. 182–3.

33. Both speeches are printed in *The Camp David Accords and Related Documents* (Beer-Sheva, Israel, 1998), pp. 35–51—a volume published by the Chaim Herzog Center for Middle East Studies and Diplomacy.

34. See for example the comments of Ambassador Eilts in Rosenbaum and Ugrinsky, eds., *Jimmy Carter: Foreign Policy*, p. 184.

35. Silver, *Begin*, p. 179. Begin's plan is printed in *The Camp David Accords*, pp. 57–9.

36. Quandt, *Camp David*, p. 156.

37. Quoting from Carter's twenty-point memo in JCL, Plains papers, box 1: Egypt, 11/77–11/81.

38. Brzezinski, *Power and Principle*, pp. 240–3; Quandt, *Camp David*, pp. 165–71. See also Jordan to Carter, undated memo, in JCL, Plains papers, box 1: Egypt, 11/77–11/81.

39. Carter, *Keeping Faith*, pp. 306–8; Brzezinski, *Power and Principle*, pp. 243–4; Quandt, *Camp David*, pp. 172–5. The original records of this meeting were still closed at time of writing. For the conference schedule

see Tim Kraft to Carter, memo, Jan. 30, 1978, in JCL, White House Central Files, CO–23, CO box 45: Executive.

40. Brzezinski, *Power and Principle*, pp. 246–7; Quandt, *Camp David*, pp. 184–6.

41. For this point see Brzezinski, *Power and Principle*, p. 244, and Quandt, *Camp David*, pp. 176–7, who noted that Carter—interviewed in 1985—was vague on this point.

42. See Mohamed Ibrahim Kamel, *The Camp David Accords: A Testimony* (London, 1986), chs. 10–12.

43. Jordan to Carter, "Middle East," July 10, 1978, JCL, Chief of Staff Papers, Jordan, box 49: Middle East (CF, O/A 414).

44. Brzezinski, *Power and Principle*, pp. 250–1.

45. Poll data cited in CBS News Poll, "Camp David Summit," Sept. 19, 1978, copy in Jordan papers, box 35: Middle East, Camp David, 9/78. See also Betty Glad, *Jimmy Carter: In Search of the Great White House* (New York, 1980), pp. 450–1.

46. Quandt, *Camp David*, pp. 201–2; Jody Powell, *The Other Side of the Story* (New York, 1984), p. 60.

47. Facsimiles of the two letters are available on the Carter Library website, "The Camp David Accords after Twenty-Five Years." See http://www.jimmycarterlibrary.org/documents/campdavid25/campdavid25_documents.phtml.

48. Quandt, *Camp David*, pp. 201–4; Brzezinski, *Power and Principle*, pp. 251–2.

49. Printed in Department of State, Bulletin, no. 2018 (Sept. 1978), p. 43.

50. Cyrus Vance, *Hard Choices: Critical Years in American Foreign Policy* (New York, 1983), p. 218.

51. For background on Camp David see JCL, Plains Papers, Vertical File: Camp David—History—Retreat; also Powell, *Other Side of the Story*, pp. 60–3. Fears of a terrorist attack are in Situation Room memo for Brzezinski, "Noon Notes," Aug. 30, 1978, JCL, RAC, 1-7-6-51-1.

52. Rafshoon to Carter, "Camp David Summit," Aug. 25, 1978, JCL Staff Files, Gerald D. Rafshoon papers, box 10: Camp David Summit, 9/5–9/17/78; Powell, *Other Side of the Story*, pp. 65–6; Martin Schram, "Camp David: A Gamble Carter Is Unlikely to Lose," *Newsday*, Sept. 10, 1978.

53. Powell, *Other Side of the Hill*, pp. 64–7. This paragraph also draws on Jim Purks to Rex Granum, Aug. 10, 1978, JCL Staff Files—Press, Rex Granum papers, box 80: Camp David Summit, Press Concerns; and Anne

Edwards to Rafshoon and Powell, Aug. 30, 1978, and "Notice to the Press," Sept. 4, 1978, both in JCL Staff Files—Press (Advance), Anne Edwards papers, box 3: Camp David Summit (1978).

54. Vance to president, covering letter, and Vance, memo, "An Overview of the Camp David Talks," p. 1, both undated, in JCL, Plains papers, Vertical File: Camp David Study Papers—henceforth VF:CDSP.

55. "A Scenario for Camp David," p. 1, VF:CDSP, and Vance, "Overview," esp. pp. 6, 9–13.

56. "Considerations for Conducting the Summit Meetings," p. 3, VF:CDSP.

57. Vance, "Overview," p. 20; "A Scenario for Camp David."

58. Vance, "Overview," pp. 2, 13–14; cf. Quandt, *Camp David*, pp. 218–19.

59. Carter notes on Vance, memo, "Study Papers for the Camp David Talks"; "Fall-back Options Should Camp David Produce a Deadlock"— both VF:CDSP; Carter, *Keeping Faith*, pp. 320–1; Quandt, *Camp David*, p. 218.

60. Begin, newspaper interview in *Al-Anba*, Aug. 20, 1978, in Israel Ministry of Foreign Affairs, *Israel's Foreign Relations: Selected Documents*, vols. 4–5 (1977–9), doc. 187—accessed on the official website http://www.mfa.gov.il.

61. Vance, *Hard Choices*, p. 217; Sofer, *Begin*, pp. 190–1, quoting delegation member Aharon Barak.

62. On the speech see Bowdler and Saunders to Vance, "Analysis of Arab-Israeli Developments, no. 538, August 18, 1978," JCL, RAC, NLC-6-51-2-1-6.

63. Kamel to Sadat, memo, Aug. 28, 1978, in Kamel, *Camp David Accords*, pp. 273–9.

64. NSC memo for Brzezinski, "Additional Information Items," Sept. 5, 1978, JCL, RAC, NLC-1-7-7-24-0. For the cable from Ambassador Eilts, see Quandt, *Camp David*, p. 215.

65. Brzezinski to Carter, "Strategy for Camp David," [Aug. 31, 1978], Brzezinski papers (donated), box 13: Middle East—Negotiations (JCL)— parts of which are printed in Brzezinski, *Power and Principle*, pp. 253–4.

66. Carter, *Keeping Faith*, pp. 321–5. Timings, here and elsewhere, are taken from the President's Daily Diary in JCL, Plains files, box 11.

67. Carter, *Keeping Faith*, pp. 322–5, 331–2; Brzezinski, *Power and Principle*, p. 254; Ellis Woodward to Phil Wise, "Status of Preparations of Camp David Summit," Aug. 28, 1978, JCL Staff Files—Press, Rex Granum papers, box 80: Camp David Summit, Press Concerns.

68. Ezer Weizman, *The Battle for Peace* (London, 1981), pp. 344–5.

69. Brzezinski, *Power and Principle*, p. 255; Carter, *Keeping Faith*, pp. 338–41.

70. Kamel, *Camp David Accords*, pp. 295–8.

71. For what follows on this first meeting see Carter, *Keeping Faith*, pp. 342–6. Sadat's proposal is printed in Quandt, *Camp David*, appendix D. There were no agreed minutes from Camp David, each side keeping its own notes. No Egyptian and Israeli documents were available at time of writing, and only some of Carter's notes were open. My analysis of his meetings with Sadat and Begin therefore relies heavily on the account in Carter's memoirs, thought not always on his interpretation.

72. Carter, *Keeping Faith*, p. 346.

73. Carter, *Keeping Faith*, pp. 346–50; Weizman, *Battle for Peace*, pp. 355–6.

74. For the meeting see Carter, *Keeping Faith*, pp. 350–5; also Carter, "Notes taken at mtg. Begin-Sadat," Sept. 7, 1978, in JCL, Plains papers, box 28: Mid East: Camp David Summit, President's Working Papers, 10/22/73–9/12/78.

75. Carter, *Keeping Faith*, pp. 350–5; also Carter, "Notes taken at mtg. Begin-Sadat," Sept. 7, 1978, in JCL, Plains papers, box 28: Mid East: Camp David Summit, President's Working Papers, 10/22/73–9/12/78.

76. Carter, notes, "Afternoon, 9/7/78," in JCL, Plains papers, box 28: Mid East: Camp David Summit, President's Working Papers, 10/22/73–9/12/78; Carter, *Keeping Faith*, pp. 355–9.

77. Carter, *Keeping Faith*, pp. 359–60; Kamel, *Camp David Accords*, pp. 306–7; Weizman, *Battle for Peace*, pp. 358.

78. Carter, *Keeping Faith*, pp. 360–3; Kamel, *Camp David Accords*, p. 312.

79. As recalled by Eilts in Rosenbaum and Ugrinsky, eds., *Jimmy Carter: Foreign Policy*, p. 153.

80. Carter, notes of meetings with Begin and Sadat, Sept. 8, 1978, in JCL, Plains papers, box 28: Mid East: Camp David Summit, President's Working Papers, 10/22/73–9/12/78; Carter, *Keeping Faith*, pp. 364–9.

81. Carter, *Keeping Faith*, p. 369; Quandt, *Camp David*, p. 226.

82. Carter, "Necessary elements of agreement, 9/9," in JCL, Plains papers, box 28: Mid East: Camp David Summit, President's Working Papers, 10/22/73–9/12/78; Quandt, *Camp David*, p. 226.

83. See interview with Dayan in *The New Yorker*, Oct. 2, 1978, p. 31.

84. Brzezinski, *Power and Principle*, p. 259; Weizman, *Battle for Peace*, pp. 346–7, 363. According to Brzezinski, the encounter ended one game apiece; Weizman claims that Begin won.

85. Kamel, *Camp David Accords*, p. 321; Moshe Dayan, *Breakthrough: A Personal Account of the Egypt-Israel Peace Negotiations* (London, 1981), p. 155; Weizman, *Battle for Peace*, pp. 342, 359.

86. Carter, *Keeping Faith*, pp. 371–2, 389–90; Dayan, *Breakthrough*, p. 170–1.

87. Transcripts of the daily press conferences are in JCL, Appointments Files, Presidential Diary file, box PD–38, "back-up" folders for each day, quoting from Sept. 7, 1978, p. 10, and Sept. 9, 1978, p. 3. See also *Washington Post*, Sept. 8, 1978, p. A1; Powell, *Other Side of the Hill*, pp. 68–76; Weizman, *Battle for Peace*, p. 358.

88. For coverage see the articles by Hugh Sidey and James Reston in the *Washington Star*, Sept. 10, 1978, and those by Edward Walsh and Jim Hoagland in *Washington Post*, Sept. 11, 1978.

89. Powell, press conference, Sept. 11, 1978, pp. 1, 3 and 5, in JCL, PD-38.

90. Carter, *Keeping Faith*, pp. 372–4.

91. Carter, *Keeping Faith*, pp. 375–9; Quandt, *Camp David*, pp. 228–9.

92. Brzezinski, *Power and Principle*, p. 262.

93. Kamel, *Camp David Accords*, ch. 38, esp. pp. 334–6. In the absence of Egyptian documents, Kamel's book remains an essential source, despite being permeated by a conspiracy theory about how the Americans were seduced and blackmailed by the Israelis.

94. Kamel, *Camp David Accords*, pp. 336–45; Carter, *Keeping Faith*, pp. 383–5.

95. Brzezinski, *Power and Principle*, pp. 263–4; Carter, *Keeping Faith*, pp. 385–7.

96. Carter, *Keeping Faith*, pp. 382–5; Quandt, *Camp David*, pp. 230–2. Quandt's analysis brings out the shift to a split deal much more clearly than Carter's narrative.

97. On the day's discussions see Carter, *Keeping Faith*, pp. 387–8, and Quandt, *Camp David*, pp. 232–3.

98. Carter, *Keeping Faith*, pp. 388–9; Brzezinski, *Power and Principle*, p. 265.

99. Carter, *Keeping Faith*, p. 391; Dayan, *Breakthrough*, p. 174.

100. Carter to Begin and Sadat, Sept. 15, 1978, JCL, Plains papers, box 28: Mid East: Camp David Summit, President's Working Papers, 9/13/78–9/27/78.

101. Carter, *Keeping Faith*, pp. 391–2; Vance, *Hard Choices*, p. 224.

102. This account of the Sadat-Carter confrontation (including the Carter speech) follows Brzezinski, *Power and Principle*, pp. 271–2, recording what Carter told him the following week. Carter, *Keeping Faith*, pp.

392–3, is lower-key, paraphrasing the speech. Sadat's comments to his aides are from Kamel, *Camp David Accords*, pp. 356–7.

103. Quandt, *Camp David*, pp. 240–1.

104. Quandt, *Camp David*, pp. 241–2; Weizman, *Battle for Peace*, pp. 370–1; cf. Carter, *Keeping Faith*, p. 394, which shows Carter's ignorance.

105. Quandt, *Camp David*, pp. 243–5.

106. Carter, *Keeping Faith*, pp. 395–7; Quandt, *Camp David*, pp. 245–7. Quandt says the meeting ended at 1:30 a.m.—the official White House log for Sept. 15, 1978 says 12:20 a.m. (JCL, Plains files, box 11).

107. Memo printed in Quandt, *Camp David*, p. 251.

108. Powell press conferences Sept. 12, 1978, pp. 6, 9, and Sept. 14, 1978, p. 2 (JCL, Appointments Files, Presidential Diary file, box PD–38, "back-up" folders for each day); "The White House News Summary," Sept. 14, 1978, p. 5, and Sept. 15, 1978, pp. 2–3 (JCL Reading Room).

109. Helen Thomas's choice of expletive was not identified in the transcript. See Powell press conferences Sept. 15, 1978, p. 2, and Sept. 16, 1978, p. 1 (JCL, Appointments Files, Presidential Diary file, box PD–38, "back-up" folders for each day); Powell, *Other Side of the Hill*, pp. 79–80.

110. Carter, *Keeping Faith*, pp. 398–9.

111. Quandt, *Camp David*, pp. 253; Carter, *Blood of Abraham*, p. 157.

112. Kamel, *Camp David Accords*, pp. 363–9.

113. A. Denis Clift, *With Presidents to the Summit* (Fairfax, Virginia, 1993), p. 168.

114. Remarks at the White House, Sept. 17, 1978 (PPPUS).

115. "White House News Summary," Sept. 19, 1978, p. 15, reporting Kissinger on the NBC *Today Show* on Sept. 18; CBS News Poll, "Camp David Summit," Sept. 19, 1978, copy in JCL, Chief of Staff, Jordan papers, box 35: Middle East, Camp David, 9/78; *Washington Star*, Sept. 18, 1978, *Washington Post*, Sept. 19, 1978.

116. Eizenstat to Rafshoon and Sanders, Sept. 25, 1978, JCL Staff Files, Rafshoon papers, box 10: Camp David Summit, 9/5–9/17/78.

117. Begin, interview in *Ma'ariv*, Sept. 20, 1978, in *Israel's Foreign Relations: Selected Documents*, vols. 4–5 (1977–9), doc. 197.

118. Quandt, *Camp David*, pp. 24–51. Carter's note of record on settlements, Sept. 20, 1978, is in JCL, Plains papers, box 28: Mid East: Camp David Summit, President's Working Papers, 9/13/78–9/27/78.

119. Brzezinski to Carter, Nov. 30, 1978, Brzezinski papers (donated), box 14: Middle East—Negotiations, 9/7/78–12/78 (JCL); Jordan to Carter, Nov. 30, 1978, JCL, Chief of Staff Papers, Jordan, box 49: Middle East (CF, O/A 414).

120. Quotations from Carter, *Keeping Faith*, p. 426. Quandt, *Camp David*, chs. 10–11, provides a concise account of how the treaty was finally negotiated; see also Robert A. Strong, *Working in the World: Jimmy Carter and the Making of American Foreign Policy* (Baton Rouge, 2000), ch. 7 on his Middle Eastern shuttle diplomacy.

121. Cf. Rosenbaum and Ugrinsky, eds., *Jimmy Carter: Foreign Policy and Post-Presidential Years*, p. 174.

122. Jimmy Carter, *Palestine: Peace not Apartheid* (New York, 2006), p. 89.

123. Sofer, *Begin*, p. 210.

124. As recalled in Clift, *With Presidents to the Summit*, p. 165.

125. Commenting on the initial briefing book, he wrote: "This is the same faulty approach as was presented to me in early preparation for Camp David. In every issue, I need for all of us to have clear what our *maximum* goal is. I'm not going to Vienna just for the opera." Carter to Brzezinski, May 25, 1979, Brzezinski (donated) papers, box 19—Vienna summit (JCL).

126. Eilts in Rosenbaum and Ugrinsky, eds., *Jimmy Carter: Foreign Policy and Post-Presidential Years*, p. 181; Carter, *Keeping Faith*, p. 322.

127. 1983 interview, quoted in Shibley Telhami, *Power and Leadership in International Bargaining: The Path to the Camp David Accords* (New York, 1990), p. 164. Projecting uncertainty is a central theme of Telhami's book.

128. Lewis quoted in Quandt to Brzezinski, "Background on Begin," July 15, 1977, JCL RAC, NLC-5-6-7-13-9.

129. Saunders' quotations from Silver, *Begin*, p. 181, and Telhami, *Power and Leadership*, pp. 182–3.

130. Vance, *Hard Choices*, p. 181; Brzezinski, *Power and Principle*, p. 263.

131. Quandt, *Camp David*, p. 316.

132. Between June 1977 and October 1979, according to CIA estimates, the Begin government spent at least $300 million on settlements, including 31 new ones on the West Bank, bringing the total there to 108. But that was as nothing to the new projects announced in the autumn of 1979, which would cost some $4.7 billion over the next few years. Brzezinski to Carter, memo, Dec. 6, 1979, JCL, RAC, NLC-6-26-3-1-2.

Chapter 7: Geneva 1985

1. For useful overviews of those relations, to which this chapter is indebted, see Raymond L. Garthoff, *The Great Transition: American-Soviet*

Relations and the End of the Cold War (Washington, D.C., 1994), and Don Oberdorfer, *From the Cold War to a New Era: The United States and the Soviet Union, 1983–91* (Baltimore, 1998); Jack F. Matlock Jr., *Reagan and Gorbachev: How the Cold War Ended* (New York, 2004). Oberdorfer and Matlock also provide useful accounts of the Geneva summit, though I differ from them at some points. The American minutes of the conference are in the Ronald Reagan Library, Simi Valley, California (henceforth RRL), but are also available on the Thatcher Foundation website, http://www.margaretthatcher.org/archive/displaydocument.asp?docid= 109185. Other documentary material is now open at the RRL but much more will be declassified in the next few years: my account will therefore need amendment at various points.

2. Raymond L. Garthoff, *Détente and Confrontation: American-Soviet Relations from Nixon to Reagan* (2nd ed., Washington, D.C., 1994), pp. 1059–60.

3. Peter Schweizer, *Reagan's War: The Epic Story of His Forty-Year Struggle and His Final Triumph over Communism* (New York, 2002), chs. 1–8, quoting from pp. 36, 91.

4. Quotations from Beth A. Fischer, *The Reagan Reversal: Foreign Policy and the End of the Cold War* (Columbia, Missouri, 1997), p. 24.

5. Presidential Press Conference, Jan. 29, 1981; speech at Notre Dame, May 17, 1981. All Reagan's public statements are available in printed form in *Public Papers of the Presidents of the United States: Ronald Reagan* (15 vols., Washington, D.C., 1982–91) and also online at the PPPUS website.

6. Speech to National Association of Evangelicals, Orlando, Florida, March 8, 1983: cf. Oberdorfer, *From the Cold War*, p. 23; Robert Lettow, *Ronald Reagan and His Quest to Abolish Nuclear Weapons* (New York, 2005), p. 17.

7. The story is told, for instance, in Martin Anderson, *Revolution: The Reagan Legacy* (2nd edn, Stanford, 1990), pp. 80–3.

8. Speech of March 8, 1983; Lettow, *Ronald Reagan and His Quest*, pp. 35, 133.

9. The titles of two biographies; see Bob Schieffer and Gary Paul Gates, *The Acting President* (New York, 1989) and Lou Cannon, *President Reagan: The Role of a Lifetime* (New York, 1991).

10. Even when Alzheimer's clouded his memory in the final years, Reagan kept coming back to that story: Edmund Morris, *Dutch: A Memoir of Ronald Reagan* (New York, 1999), p. 667; Michael Deaver, *A Different Drummer: My Thirty Years with Ronald Reagan* (New York, 2001 pbk.), pp. 21–2.

11. Cannon, *President Reagan*, p. 216.

12. Oberdorfer, *From the Cold War*, p. 22 (McFarlane); Carlucci is quoted in William Wohlforth, ed., *Witnesses to the End of the Cold War* (Baltimore, 1996), p. 46.

13. Lettow, *Ronald Reagan*, pp. 49–53; Morris, *Dutch*, pp. 428–38; Deaver, *Different Drummer*, pp. 231–2.

14. Adelman, *The Great Universal Embrace: Arms Summitry—A Skeptic's Account* (New York, 1989), p. 27. Similarly, insider journalist Don Oberdorfer has written that "Reagan was of two minds about the Soviet Union, and even some of his closest associates disagreed about which one was dominant"—*From the Cold War*, p. 21. This seems to me a more accurate portrait of Reagan than those accounts suggesting a consistent long-term policy; for instance, Ronald Reagan, *An American Life* (New York, 1990), pp. 13–14, and Matlock, *Reagan and Gorbachev*, pp. xiii–xiv.

15. Caspar Weinberger, *Fighting for Peace: Seven Critical Years at the Pentagon* (London, 1990), p. 233.

16. Shultz statement to Senate FRC, June 15, 1983, in U.S. Department of State, *American Foreign Policy Current Documents, 1983* (Washington, D.C., 1985), doc. 210, esp. pp. 513–14.; also George P. Shultz, *Turmoil and Triumph: My Years as Secretary of State* (New York, 1993), pp. 162, 488–9.

17. Jack Matlock, in Wohlforth ed., *Witnesses to the End of the Cold War*, p. 113.

18. Oberdorfer, *From the Cold War*, pp. 41–2, 490.

19. Richard Allen (1981–2), William Clark Jr. (1982–3), Robert McFarlane (1983–5), John Poindexter (1985–6), Frank Carlucci (1986–7) and Colin Powell (1987–9).

20. Seymour Hersh, *"The Target is Destroyed": What Really Happened to Flight 007 and What America Knew About It* (London, 1986), quoting the senior U.S. delegate to the UN on p. 134.

21. Christopher Andrew and Vasili Mitrokhin, *The Mitrokhin Archive II; The KGB and the World* (London, 2006), p.16.

22. I still vividly remember first hearing this celebrated perestroika joke during a private dinner in Moscow in 1988.

23. Michael R. Beschloss and Strobe Talbott, *At the Highest Levels: The Inside Story of the End of the Cold War* (Boston, 1993), p. 6.

24. Christopher Andrew and Oleg Gordievsky, *Instructions from the Centre: Top Secret Files on KGB Operations, 1975–1985* (London, 1991), ch. 4, and Vladimir E. Shlapentokh, "Moscow's War Propaganda and Soviet Public Opinion," *Problems of Communism*, 33/5 (Sept.–Oct. 1984, pp. 88–94).

25. Diary entry quoted in Reagan, *American Life*, p. 585. The impact of these events in late 1983 on the president's policies is highlighted by Fischer, *Reagan Reversal*, ch. 5, though, in my judgment, she understates his earlier inclinations towards conciliation.

26. Presidential address, Jan. 16, 1984 (PPPUS).

27. *New York Times*, Sept. 26, 1985, p. B8. See also Massie's website at http://www.suzannemassie.com/index.html and NSC, Coordination Office files on meetings with Suzanne Massie, in boxes 90876, 90912, 91210, 91948, 91962 and 91968 (RRL).

28. Garthoff, *Great Transition*, pp. 159–60; Anatoly Dobrynin, *In Confidence: Moscow's Ambassador to Six Cold War Presidents, 1962–1986* (New York, 1995), p. 550.

29. Mikhail Gorbachev, *Memoirs* (London, 1996), p. 165.

30. Quoted in Dmitri Volkogonov, *The Rise and Fall of the Soviet Empire: Political Leaders from Lenin to Gorbachev*, trans. Harold Shukman (London, 1998), p. 498.

31. I follow here the argument of John Miller, *Mikhail Gorbachev and the End of Soviet Power* (London, 1993), pp. 64–7.

32. On the visit see Archie Brown, *The Gorbachev Factor* (Oxford, 1996), pp. 77–8.

33. Reagan-Thatcher meeting, Dec. 22, 1984, memcon, NSC European & Soviet Affairs Directorate: Thatcher Visit, Dec. 1984 [1], box 90902 (RRL); text available at Thatcher Foundation website, http://www.margaretthatcher.org/archive/displaydocument.asp?docid=109185.

34. A point stressed, for instance, by Rozanne Ridgway, then assistant secretary of state for European and Canadian affairs, in Wohlforth, ed., *Witnesses to the End of the Cold War*, p. 17.

35. Reagan to Gorbachev, March 11, 1985, NSC Executive Secretariat, Head of State File: USSR, box 39, 8590272 (RRL).

36. Notes taken by Kenneth Adelman and quoted in his memoir *The Great Universal Embrace*, pp. 121–2.

37. Minutes of Gorbachev's meeting with secretaries of the Central Committee, March 15, 1985, available in translation in National Security Archive (NSA) electronic briefing book, no. 172, "Toward the Geneva Summit," posted Nov. 22, 2005, document 5: http://www.gwu.edu/~nsarchiv/NSAEBB/NSAEBB172/index.htm.

38. Alexander Yakovlev, "About Reagan," March 12, 1985, NSA, "Toward the Geneva Summit," doc. 3.

39. Gorbachev to Reagan, March 24, 1985, NSC Executive Secre-

tariat, Head of State File: USSR, box 39, 8590336 (RRL). The documentary record therefore does not bear out claims that "Gorbachev was interested in a summit with Reagan at the earliest possible moment," Schweizer, *Reagan's War*, p. 246.

40. Eduard Shevardnadze, *The Future Belongs to Freedom* (New York, 1991), p. 39; Shultz, *Turmoil and Triumph*, pp. 571–2.

41. Shultz, *Turmoil and Triumph*, p. 571.

42. Oberdorfer, *From the Cold War*, p. 120.

43. Shultz, *Turmoil and Triumph*, pp. 573–4.

44. State Dept. to Bucharest and other embassies, telegram, Aug. 6, 1985, National Security Archive, Malcolm Byrne Research Files, box 41: Shultz-Shevardnadze, 7/85.

45. Donald T. Regan, *For the Record: From Wall Street to Washington* (London, 1988), pp. 260–1. More generally, see Geoffrey Hartman, ed., *Bitburg in Moral and Political Perspective* (Bloomington, Indiana, 1986).

46. Regan, *For the Record*, pp. 4, 299–301; Joan Quigley, *"What Does Joan Say?": My Seven Years as White House Astrologer to Nancy and Ronald Reagan* (New York, 1990), chs. 10–13. See also William Henkel to Donald T. Regan, "Potential Presidential Residences in Geneva," July 26, 1985, Dennis W. Thomas papers, CFOA 582: Geneva—Safe [3] (RRL). Daniel and Darianne Pometta generously showed me the house and recalled the Reagan's visit when we filmed there on April 23, 2007.

47. McFarlane quoted in Cannon, *President Reagan*, pp. 748–9. See also Matlock, *Reagan and Gorbachev*, pp. 132–4.

48. Matlock, *Reagan and Gorbachev*, pp. 134–5; Matlock to William F. Martin, "Soviet Films for the President," Nov. 7, 1985, NSC Coordination Office, box 90538: 156 to Geneva, 2 [5] (RRL). *Moscow Doesn't Believe in Tears* won an Oscar for the best foreign film of 1980.

49. Shultz's memoirs snipe away at McFarlane and the NSC, while Matlock does his best to defend them; for examples see Shultz, *Turmoil and Triumph*, pp. 572, 575 and Matlock, *Reagan and Gorbachev*, pp. 74–5, 126–7. Dobrynin, *In Confidence*, p. 580, also offers a more positive view of McFarlane.

50. Gorbachev to Reagan, Oct. 12, 1985, Platt to McFarlane, Oct. 31 with notes by Matlock and McFarlane, and Reagan to Gorbachev, Nov. 1, 1985—all in NSC, Executive Secretariat, Head of State File: USSR, box 40, 8591143.

51. Dobrynin, *In Confidence*, pp. 581–3.

52. Notes of Shultz-Shevardnadze meetings, Nov. 4, 1985, quoting from afternoon meeting, p. 5; memos on "Geneva Meetings Scenarios"

and "Status of Issues"—all in Robert E. Linhard papers, box 92178: Summit Nov. 19–21, 1985, folder 1 (RRL). Kvitsinsky is quoted in Shultz, *Turmoil and Triumph*, p. 587.

53. There are detailed accounts in Shultz, *Turmoil and Triumph*, pp. 589–95, which I have followed here, and in Oberdorfer, *From the Cold War*, pp. 130–8, for which the main source seems to have been Shultz. See also Robert C. McFarlane, with Zofia Smardz, *Special Trust* (New York, 1994), pp. 315–16.

54. Shultz, *Turmoil and Triumph*, pp. 586–9, 591.

55. Richard Judy, "Computing in the USSR: A Comment," *Soviet Economy*, 2 (1986), esp. pp. 362–3; more generally, David Reynolds, *One World Divisible: A Global History since 1945* (London, 2000), pp. 506–19.

56. The seven-digit numbering of Reagan-Gorbachev messages (e.g., note 50) reflected the IT structure. 85 stood for the year, 9 indicated that this was a System II document classified as "secret" or "top secret" (there were five "systems" or layers), while the remaining four digits represented the document number, allocated in chronological sequence. I am grateful to archivists at the Reagan Library for helping explain this system to me.

57. For background see Igor Korchilov, *Translating History: The Summits that Ended the Cold War as Witnessed by Gorbachev's Interpreter* (London, 1997), pp. 21–2, 48, and Pavel Palazchenko, *My Years with Gorbachev and Shevardnadze: The Memoir of a Soviet Interpreter* (University Park, Pennsylvania, 1997), pp. 31–3.

58. Shultz, *Turmoil and Triumph*, pp. 573–4, 587; for Taransenko see Wohlforth ed., *Witnesses to the End of the Cold War*, p. 19.

59. Shultz, talking points, "Meeting with the President, Nov. 6 [1985]," Linhard papers, box 92178: Summit Nov. 19–21, 1985, folder 1 (RRL). Shultz, *Turmoil and Triumph*, pp. 595–6, treats Dobrynin's message as virtually "an apology." For a different, and more plausible, account, see Dobrynin, *In Confidence*, p. 584, who says "Shultz was satisfied, even relieved."

60. Richard Nixon, "Superpower Summitry," *Foreign Affairs*, 64/1 (Fall 1985), quoting pp. 1, 10.

61. Dobrynin, *In Confidence*, pp. 583–4; Palazchenko, *My Years with Gorbachev*, pp. 41–2.

62. Oberdorfer, *From the Cold War*, pp. 151–2; Dobrynin, *In Confidence*, pp. 584–5. Cf. the rather disingenuous account in Shultz, *Turmoil and Triumph*, pp. 595–6.

63. Oberdorfer, *From the Cold War*, pp. 128–9, 138–9; Shultz, *Turmoil and Triumph*, p. 594.

64. Presidential news conference, Sept. 17, 1985.

65. *Time*, Nov. 18, 1985, p. 26; cf. Matlock in Wohlforth ed., *Witnesses to the End of the Cold War*, p. 114; Regan, *For the Record*, p. 303.

66. Henkel, memo, "Updated Information for the Trip of the President to Geneva," Nov. 14, 1985, Dr. T. Burton Smith, memo, "Medical Information," Nov. 12, 1985—both in Jack F. Matlock Jr. papers, box 45: Geneva Files, File Index Nov. 1985 (RRL). See also Quigley, *"What Does Joan Say?"* p. 145, Oberdorfer, *From the Cold War*, p. 140, and Morris, *Dutch*, pp. 547–50.

67. Matlock, *Reagan and Gorbachev*, pp. 134–5; Morris, *Dutch*, p. 554; cf. Nancy Reagan, with William Novak, *My Turn: The Memoirs of Nancy Reagan* (London, 1989), pp. 266–7. "Let Ronnie be Ronnie," she told the staff.

68. *New York Times*, Nov. 18, 1985, p. A6, and Nov. 19, 1985, p. A15.

69. Morris, *Dutch*, pp. 555–6; Dobrynin, *In Confidence*, p. 587; Regan, *For the Record*, pp. 304–5. RRL photo c31977–17 (available on the Reagan Library website) shows the president standing near the window just before he went out, wearing a coat and scarf.

70. The following account is based on the Memcon of First Private meeting, Nov. 19, 1985, 10:20–11:20. See also Morris, *Dutch*, pp. 558–60 and Dobrynin, *In Confidence*, pp. 587–8. Transcripts of all the meetings may be found in Matlock papers, box 52: Geneva Meeting, Memcons of Plenary and Tete-a-Tete [2] (RRL). Almost all are available in the NSA electronic briefing book 172. I have turned reported speech into direct speech at some points.

71. Shultz, *Turmoil and Triumph*, p. 600; Morris, *Dutch*, p. 558.

72. Regan, *For the Record*, pp. 3067; Morris, *Dutch*, p. 560. On the table, see also *Time*, Nov. 18, 1985, p. 22.

73. Memcon of First Plenary Session, Nov. 19, 1985, 11:27 a.m–12:15 p.m.; Regan, *For the Record*, p. 307; Morris, *Dutch*, p. 562–3. The memoirs provide useful color but they are frequently inaccurate on timing and details; Regan, for instance, claims that the plenary session was conducted via consecutive interpretation—and events from one session are sometimes shifted to another.

74. Memcon, Second Plenary Meeting, Nov. 19, 1985, 2:30–3:40 p.m. Sharper versions of the interchanges may be found in the "Summary Record" in Matlock papers, box 52: Geneva Memcons (Reagan-Gorbachev Meetings), folder 2, and in the notes in Linhard papers, box 92178: Geneva Summit records (2). On Gorbachev's style, see Korchilov, *Translating History*, p. 40.

75. Gorbachev, *Memoirs*, pp. 405–6, though he cites as evidence their first private meeting. It seems to me that the second plenary meeting is when the gloves came off.

76. Regan, *For the Record*, p. 310; Memcon, Second Private Meeting, Nov. 19, 1985, 3:40–4:45 p.m., p. 1; on Arbatov, cf. President's Remarks about the Anglo-Irish Agreement, Nov. 15, 1985.

77. Reagan told this joke—one of his favorites—at Geneva but it is not clear when. Cf. his remarks to the North Atlantic Council in Brussels, Nov. 21, 1985, p. 13, copy in Linhard papers, box 92178: Geneva Summit Records (4).

78. "Summary Record," pp. 8, 10–11, Matlock papers, box 52: Geneva Memcons (Reagan-Gorbachev Meetings), folder 2; see also the three cables from Ronald F. Lehman, Nov. 19, 1985, in Linhard papers, box 92178: Summit (2). Shultz, *Turmoil and Triumph*, pp. 600–1, describes the exchange but locates it, wrongly, in the morning plenary.

79. The following account is based on Memcon, Second Private Meeting, Nov. 19, 1985, 3:40–4:45 p.m.

80. Reagan, *An American Life*, p. 631; Regan, *For the Record*, pp. 310–11.

81. Actually tropes of language, but Carter had been similarly excited by God-talk from Brezhnev at Vienna in 1979. Cf. Jimmy Carter, *Keeping Faith* (New York, 1982), pp. 245, 248.

82. For this paragraph see Morris, *Dutch*, pp. 568–9, 823; Gorbachev's postsummit comments are noted in the diary of Anatoly S. Chernyaev, Nov. 24, 1985, translation available on the National Security Archive website at http://www.gwu.edu/~nsarchiv.

83. Memcon, Dinner Hosted by the Gorbachevs, Nov. 19, 1985, 8–10 p.m., p. 4.

84. Peter Roussel, memo for Regan, McFarlane and Speakes, Sept. 24, 1985, in Matlock papers, box 52: Geneva Meeting: Mrs. Reagan's Schedule (RRL).

85. Regan, *For the Record*, pp. 31–14. See also memcons of "Mrs. Reagan's Tea for Mrs. Gorbachev," Nov. 19, 1985, 3:34–4:30 p.m., and of "Dinner Hosted by the Gorbachevs," Nov. 19, 1985, 8–10 p.m.

86. McFarlane, *Special Trust*, pp. 320–1.

87. Morris, *Dutch*, p. 569.

88. For the account that follows see memcon, Reagan-Gorbachev Morning Tête-à-Tête, Nov. 20, 1985, 10:15–11:25 a.m., Matlock papers box 52: Geneva Memcons, (Reagan-Gorbachev Meetings), folder 2. This memcon is not available in the NSA electronic briefing book.

89. *New York Times*, Nov. 20, 1985, p. A1.

90. Memcon, Third Plenary Meeting, Nov. 20, 1985, 11:30 a.m.–12:40 p.m.

91. This account follows Oberdorfer, *From the Cold War*, p. 149, who relied mainly on Shultz and McFarlane's recollections. Morris, *Dutch*, p. 570, apparently based on notes by Regan, renders the exchange as much more two-way, but the summary in the memcon, p. 6, suggests that Oberdorfer is more accurate.

92. Again I have followed Oberdorfer, *From the Cold War*, p. 149, whose account again squares with the summary in the memcon, p. 7. Gorbachev's final lines are confirmed by Dobrynin, *In Confidence*, p. 590. Once more Morris, *Dutch*, p. 570, renders Gorbachev's words differently.

93. Dobrynin, *In Confidence*, p. 590.

94. Memcon, Fourth Plenary Meeting, Nov. 20, 1985, 2:45–3:30 p.m.

95. Adelman, *Great Universal Embrace*, p. 146.

96. Memcon, Mrs. Gorbachev's Tea for Mrs. Reagan, Nov. 20, 1985, 4:00–5:15 p.m.; Nancy Reagan, *My Turn*, pp. 339–40.

97. Memcon, Dinner Hosted by President and Mrs. Reagan, Nov. 20, 1985, 8–10 p.m.; Gorbachev, *Memoirs*, p. 410; cf. Shultz, *Turmoil and Triumph*, pp. 603–5.

98. The Joint Statement, Nov. 21, 1985, is on the PPPUS website. A copy of what had been agreed at 12:15 a.m. is in Linhard papers, box 92178: Geneva Summit Records (1). See also Dobrynin, *In Confidence*, pp. 590–1.

99. The leaders' remarks, Nov. 21, 1985, are on the PPPUS website. A memcon of the special session of the North Atlantic Council in Brussels, Nov. 21, 1985, is in Linhard papers, box 92178: Geneva Summit Records (4).

100. Reagan's address to Congress, Nov. 21, 1985 (PPPUS); for his diary comment, see *An American Life*, p. 641.

101. Matlock, *Reagan and Gorbachev*, p. 164; Volkogonov, *Rise and Fall of the Soviet Empire*, p. 492; Dobrynin, *In Confidence*, p. 592.

102. Oberdorfer, *From the Cold War*, pp. 157, 490.

103. Matlock, *Reagan and Gorbachev*, pp. 175–6, 190–1.

104. Anatoly S. Chernyaev, *My Six Years with Gorbachev*, translated and edited by Robert D. English and Elizabeth Tucker (University Park, Pennsylvania, 2000), pp. 52–3.

105. Chernyaev, in Wohlforth, ed., *Witnesses to the End of the Cold War*, p. 166; Matlock, *Reagan and Gorbachev*, p. 190.

106. Garthoff, *The Great Transition*, pp. 253–65; Miller, *Mikhail Gorbachev and the End of Soviet Power*, pp. 75–80; Brown, *Gorbachev Factor*, pp. 217–20.

107. Pierre Elliott Trudeau, *Memoirs* (Toronto, 1993), p. 332; Jacques Attali, *Verbatim* (3 vols., Paris, 1993–5), 1:104, recording Mitterrand's comments to Helmut Schmidt in Oct. 1981.

108. Attali, *Verbatim*, 2:109–13, recording conversations on July 4 and 7, 1986; Chernyaev, *My Six Years with Gorbachev*, pp. 75–6.

109. Chernyaev, *My Six Years with Gorbachev*, pp. 76–7; Stephen Ambrose, *Nixon* (3 vols., New York, 1987–91), 3:562–3.

110. Chernyaev, *My Six Years with Gorbachev*, p. 78.

111. Gorbachev to Reagan, Sept. 15, 1986, NSC Executive Secretariat, Head of State file, box 40: USSR, doc. 8690659 (RRL).

112. Oberdorfer, *From the Cold War*, pp. 174–82; Reagan, *An American Life*, p. 667; Matlock, *Reagan and Gorbachev*, pp. 210–11.

113. Chernyaev, *My Six Years with Gorbachev*, pp. 81–2; Dobrynin, *In Confidence*, p. 591, 620–1; Wohlforth, ed., *Witnesses to the End of the Cold War*, pp. 36–7.

114. Adelman, *Great Universal Embrace*, p. 26; Schweizer, *Reagan's War*, p. 262. Margaret Thatcher, similarly, uses the word "trap" in her memoir *The Downing Street Years* (London, 1993), pp. 470–1.

115. Cannon, *President Reagan*, pp. 748, 764.

116. Quotations from NSC memo by Stephen Sestanovich, Oct. 4, 1986, copy in NSA Reykjavik File, doc. 6.

117. National Security Directives, NSDD 244 and 245, Oct. 3 and 7, 1986 (RRL); Regan, *For the Record*, p. 344; Quigley, *"What Does Joan Say?"* ch. 14.

118. Adelman, *Great Universal Embrace*, p. 53. Oberdorfer, *From the Cold War*, pp. 189–205, provides another view. The Reykjavik memcons are available in the RRL NSC Executive Secretariat, System File 8690725 (Reykjavik) and the Thatcher Foundation website at http://www.margaretthatcher.org. A further set of transcripts, both American and Soviet, was made available as "The Reykjavik File" on the National Security Archive website for the twentieth anniversary of the conference: http://www.gwu.edu/~nsarchiv.

119. Oberdorfer, *From the Cold War*, pp. 200–1.

120. U.S. memcon of meeting, Oct. 12, 1986, 3:25–6 p.m., esp. pp. 9–10.

121. U.S. Memcon of meeting, Oct. 12, 1986, 3:25–6 p.m., esp. pp. 10–15.

122. Soviet memcon, Oct. 12, 1986, p. 7, NSA Rejkjavik File, doc. 16.

123. Revised U.S. memcon of meeting, Oct. 12, 1986 (dated Oct. 15, 1986, one day after the first version); Soviet memcon, Oct. 12, 1986, p. 7.

124. Reagan, *American Life*, p. 679, supported by Shultz, *Turmoil and Triumph*, pp. 773–4. Gorbachev, *Memoirs*, p. 419, says that Reagan reproached him for planning from the start to put him in this situation, which Gorbachev says he denied. "I am really sorry," replied Reagan. Dobrynin, *In Confidence*, p. 621, reports a different exchange near the cars, for which he acted as "impromptu interpreter," with Gorbachev telling Reagan he had missed the chance to go down in history as the leader who paved the way for nuclear disarmament. "That applies to both of us," Reagan replied. Another American version has Gorbachev saying plaintively, "Can't we do something about this?" to which Reagan replied: "It's too late." But this came from an indirect source. See Cannon, *President Reagan*, pp. 769, 888.

125. Gorbachev, *Memoirs*, p. 419; Chernyaev, *My Six Years with Gorbachev*, p. 86; Matlock, *Reagan and Gorbachev*, pp. 237–9. I find Matlock's claim, that Gorbachev never accepted the idea of eliminating ballistic missiles, difficult to square with the memcon.

126. Shultz, *Turmoil and Triumph*, pp. 774–5 (on Akhromeyev); Dobrynin, *In Confidence*, p. 622.

127. Thatcher, *Downing Street Years* (London, 1993), pp. 471–3; Richard M. Nixon, *1999: Victory without War* (New York, 1988), p. 191.

128. Even Kenneth Adelman, a vehement critic of Reykjavik, writes that this was "superpower summitry at its worst and its best, with the two world leaders making historic mistakes and historic advances"—*Great Universal Embrace*, p. 17.

129. Chernyaev, *My Six Years with Gorbachev*, pp. 85–6.

130. Garthoff, *Great Transition*, p. 327.

131. President's remarks at INF signing ceremony, Dec. 8, 1987; Gorbachev, *Memoirs*, p. 447. See generally Oberdorfer, *From the Cold War*, pp. 257–71.

132. Notes of Politburo meeting, Dec. 17, 1987, quoted by Chernyaev in Wohlforth, ed., *Witnesses to the End of the Cold War*, p. 49.

133. Shultz, *Turmoil and Triumph*, pp. 1011–12; he gave a slightly different rendition in Wohlforth, ed., *Witnesses to the End of the Cold War*, p. 91. Later Akhromeyev came to believe that Gorbachev was destroying the Soviet Union. He was implicated in the failed coup of August 1991 and took his own life. But that does not impugn the sincerity of what he said to Shultz in December 1987.

134. Gorbachev's remarks at the opening ceremony, May 29, 1988, in Novosti Press Agency, *USSR-USA Summit: Moscow, May 29–June 2, 1988—Documents and Materials* (Moscow, 1988), p. 30.

135. Joseph G. Whelan, *The Moscow Summit, 1988: Reagan and Gorbachev in Negotiation* (Boulder, Colorado, 1990), pp. 41. Though able to use only the published materials, this remains a useful study of the summit.

136. Korchilov, *Translating History*, p. 183.

137. Nancy Reagan, *My Turn*, p. 355; Reagan, *American Life*, p. 707.

138. Quotations from Whelan, *The Moscow Summit*, pp. 78, 80.

139. This was at a farewell dinner in January 1989. "Everyone roared," said Shultz, "including Henry." Shultz, *Turmoil and Triumph*, p. 1138.

140. Matlock, *Reagan and Gorbachev*, p. 25. For similar assessments of Shultz's importance see Oberdorfer, *From the Cold War*, p. 480, and Fred I. Greenstein's useful essay "Ronald Reagan, Mikhail Gorbachev, and the End of the Cold War: What Difference Did They Make?" in Wohlforth, ed., *Witnesses to the End of the Cold War*, p. 217.

141. Shevardnadze, *The Future Belongs to Freedom*, p. 83; Chernyaev, *My Six Years with Gorbachev*, p. 144.

142. Quotations from Chernyaev, *My Six Years with Gorbachev*, pp. 143–4; on the continued tutorials see Shultz, *Turmoil and Triumph*, pp. 887–93.

143. Garthoff, *Great Transition*, p. 775; Volkogonov, *Rise and Fall of the Soviet Empire*, p. 435.

144. On the importance of this feature of Gorbachev's thinking see the valuable article by Vladislav M. Zubok, "Gorbachev and the End of the Cold War: Perspectives on History and Personality," *Cold War History*, 2 (2002), esp. pp. 81–4.

145. Of course explanations of the end of the Cold War remain highly contentious. For an introduction to the debate see the essays in Silvio Pons and Federico Romero, eds., *Reinterpreting the End of the Cold War: Issues, Interpretations, Periodizations* (London, 2005). My own views are set out in more detail in Reynolds, *One World Divisible*, chs. 13–15.

Chapter 8: Summitry as a Way of Life

1. For these technological changes, and others discussed in later paragraphs, see the general discussion in David Reynolds, *One World Divisible: A Global History since 1945* (London, 2000), chs. 14 and 17.

2. Hans-Peter Schwarz, *Adenauer: Der Staatsman, 1952–1967* (Munich, 1993), p. 443.

3. Charles Williams, *The Last Great Frenchman: A Life of General de Gaulle* (London, 1993), p. 2. Though de Gaulle did extend such an invita-

tion to Winston Churchill in 1948. See David Reynolds, *In Command of History: Churchill Fighting and Writing the Second World War* (London, 2004), p. 168.

4. Schwarz, *Adenauer*, p. 452; Jean Lacouture, *De Gaulle: The Ruler, 1945–1970* (New York, 1992), p. 216.

5. Quoted by Thomas A. Schwarz, "The United States and Western Europe in the 1960s," in Diane B. Kunz, ed., *The Diplomacy of the Crucial Decade: American Foreign Relations during the 1960s* (New York, 1994), p. 134.

6. Haig Simonian, *The Privileged Partnership: Franco-German Relations in the European Community, 1969–1984* (Oxford, 1985), pp. 367–9; cf. Robert Gildea, *France since 1945* (Oxford, 1996), pp. 258–9.

7. Derek W. Urwin, *The Community of Europe: A History of European Integration since 1945* (London, 1991), ch. 12; Annette Morgan, *From Summit to Council: Evolution in the EEC* (London, 1976).

8. Genscher was quoting the novelist Thomas Mann. See Hans-Dietrich Genscher, *Unterwegs zur Einheit: Reden und Dokumente aus bewegter Zeit* (Berlin, 1991), p. 261. See also Keith Middlemas, *Orchestrating Europe: The Informal Politics of European Union, 1973–1995* (London, 1995), ch. 5, esp. p. 157.

9. Quoted in Robert D. Putnam and Nicholas Bayne, *Hanging Together: Cooperation and Conflict in the Seven-Power Summits* (2nd ed., London, 1987), p. 29. This book is the standard survey of the G7 summits, on which this section is heavily based.

10. Quoted in Robert Armstrong, "Economic Summits: A British Perspective," Bissell Paper, no. 4 (May 1988), p. 2 (Center for International Studies, University of Toronto), copy available on http://www.g7.utoronto.ca/scholar/armstrong1999/index.html.

11. Peter I. Hajnal, *The G7/G8 System: Evolution, Role and Documentation* (Aldershot, 1999), pp. 93–4; George M. von Furstenburg and Joseph P. Daniels, *Economic Summit Declarations, 1975–1989: Examining the Written Record of International Cooperation* (Princeton, 1992), esp. ch. 6.

12. Nicholas Bayne, *Staying Together: The G8 Summit Confronts the 21st Century* (Aldershot, 2005), chs. 1 and 3, quoting from p. 43.

13. With the partial exception of Britain. See *The Times*, April 4, 2007, p. 43.

14. Greenpeace, "G8 Rules the World: Who Rules the G8?," June 2, 2003, on http://www.greenpeace.org/international/news/who-rules-the-g8.

15. UK government website "G8 2005 Gleanagles: Summit Facts and

Figures" at http://www.g8.gov.uk/servlet/Front?pagename=OpenMarket/
Xcelerate/ShowPage&c=Page&cid=1134648207862.

16. For this information, one has to consult the report by the Scottish
Executive's Justice Dept., "Policing the G8," Dec. 2005, available at
http://www.scotland.gov.uk/Topics/Government/International-
Relations/G8/costofpolicing.

17. See Richard Hodder-Williams, "African Summitry" in David H.
Dunn, *Diplomacy at the Highest Level: The Evolution of International Summitry* (London, 1996), pp. 132–46; and Peter J. Schraeder, "African International Relations" in April A. Gordon and Donald L. Gordon, eds., *Understanding Contemporary Africa* (2nd ed., Boulder, Colorado, 1996), pp.
135–40.

18. See Dunn, ed., *Diplomacy at the Highest Level*, chs. 8, 10, 14, esp. pp.
121, 220.

19. Quotation from James Naughtie, *The Rivals: The Intimate Story of a
Political Marriage* (London, 2001), p. 262.

20. Peter Riddell, *Hug Them Close: Blair, Clinton, Bush and the "Special
Relationship"* (London, 2003), pp. 61–2.

21. Christopher Meyer, *DC Confidential* (London, 2005), p. 171.

22. Bush-Blair news conference at Camp David, Feb. 23, 2001 (PPPUS
website).

23. Bob Woodward, *Bush at War* (2nd ed, London, 2003), p. 17.

24. If one discounts a few shells from Japanese submarines and some
stray parachute bombs on the West Coast during the Second World War.

25. Exchange with reporters, Sept. 16, 2001. Bush did use the term
again during remarks in Anchorage, Alaska, Feb. 16, 2002 (both citations
from PPPUS).

26. John Lewis Gaddis, *Surprise, Security, and the American Experience*
(Cambridge, Mass., 2004).

27. Quotations in this paragraph from John Kampfner, *Blair's Wars*
(2nd ed, London, 2004), pp. 127–8, 135–7.

28. Bob Woodward, *Plan of Attack* (London, 2004), pp. 1–2, 9, 25–6, 92.

29. Michael Elliott and James Carney, "First Stop, Iraq," *Time*, March
31, 2003.

30. Kampfner, *Blair's Wars*, p. 33. On the "yes, but" tradition see my essay "A 'Special Relationship'? America, Britain and the International Order since 1945," in David Reynolds, *From World War to Cold War: Churchill, Roosevelt, and the International History of the 1940s* (Oxford, 2006), pp.
310–11.

31. Riddell, *Hug Them Close*, pp. 91–2.

32. Peter Stothard, *30 Days: A Month at the Heart of Blair's War* (London, 2003), p. 42.

33. Private information. I have benefited from off-the-record conversations with several Whitehall insiders.

34. Kampfner, *Blair's Wars*, p. 92–3.

35. Anthony Seldon, *Blair* (London, 2004), p. 308.

36. Blair, speech at College Station, Texas, April 7, 2002 (http://www.pm.gov.uk).

37. Cabinet Office note, July 2002, printed in Meyer, *DC Confidential*, pp. 245–6.

38. Manning memo for prime minister, "Your Trip to the US," March 14, 2002, text on http://www.downingstreetmemo.com/manningtext.html; Seldon, *Blair*, p. 574; cf. Meyer, *DC Confidential*, pp. 247–8.

39. James Risen, *State of War: The Secret History of the CIA and the Bush Administration* (New York, 2006), p. 64.

40. Woodward, *Plan of Attack*, pp. 163–4.

41. Rycroft to Manning, "Iraq: Prime Minister's Meeting, July 23, 2002," and (for FCO doubts) Jack Straw, memo to Blair, PM/02/019, March 25, 2002, both on http://www.downingstreetmemo.com.

42. Seldon, *Blair*, pp. 577–8; Kampfner, *Blair's Wars*, pp. 197–8.

43. Woodward, *Plan of Attack*, pp. 180–5.

44. "Iraq's Weapons of Mass Destruction: The Assessment of the British Government," Sept. 2002, p. 4, available at http://www.number-10.gov.uk/output/Page284.asp.

45. House of Commons, Foreign Affairs Committee, *The Decision to Go to War against Iraq*, HC 813–1, July 7, 2003, p. 27, para. 70.

46. Lord Butler et al., *Review of Intelligence on Weapons of Mass Destruction*, HC 898, July 14, 2004, p.139, para. 504.

47. As noted even by Lord Hutton, *Report of the Inquiry into the Circumstances Surrounding the Death of Dr David Kelly C.M.G.*, Jan. 28, 2004, ch. 6, para. 209—a report that generally turned a blind eye to evidence unflattering to the government. See http://www.the-hutton-inquiry.org.uk/content/report/chapter06.htm#a39.

48. Kampfner, *Blair's Wars*, p. 207.

49. Riddell, *Hug Them Close*, p. 222.

50. Woodward, *Plan of Attack*, p. 297.

51. Meyer, *DC Confidential*, p. 262; Bush-Blair news conference, Jan. 31, 2003 (PPPUS).

52. Kampfner, *Blair's Wars*, pp. 263–4.

53. Paddy Ashdown, *The Ashdown Diaries, vol. II, 1997–1999* (London,

2001), p. 503. Ashdown also remarked ruefully that Blair "always meant it when he said it"—Riddell, *Hug Them Close*, p. 12.

54. Bob Woodward, *State of Denial* (London, 2006), pp. 186–7.

55. *The Times*, Jan. 2, 2007, p. 28; *Washington Post*, March 19, 2007, p. A14. See also the table and chart at http://www.icasualties.org/oif/US_chart.aspx.

56. *The Times*, Feb. 5, 2007, p. 34.

57. David L. Phillips, *Losing Iraq: Inside the Postwar Reconstruction Fiasco* (New York, 2006), p. 136. The failures of planning are documented in Woodward, *State of Denial*, a disillusioned postscript to his originally supportive insider accounts of Bush's war on terror.

58. Risen, *State of War*, p. 1; Woodward, *Plan of Attack*, pp. 159–60, and Woodward, *State of Denial*, p. 114.

59. Just to be clear: this is not to imply any parallels on the other side. The president saw Saddam as another Hitler and was profoundly convinced of his moral rectitude in overthrowing the Iraqi regime.

60. Dean Acheson, *Present at the Creation: My Years in the State Department* (New York, 1969), p. 480.

61. See, for example, Adam Watson, *Diplomacy: The Dialogue between States* (London, 1982), pp. 10–11.

62. Quoted in Klaus Larres, *Churchill's Cold War: The Politics of Personal Diplomacy* (New Haven, 2002), p. 380.

63. As argued by Paul Kennedy, *Strategy and Diplomacy, 1870–1945* (London, 1983), ch. 1.

64. "The Sources of Soviet Conduct, in George F. Kennan, *American Diplomacy, 1900–1950* (Chicago, 1951), p. 120; Henry Kissinger, *Diplomacy* (New York, 1994), p. 471.

65. I am adapting here the typology of Richard Ned Lebow, *The Art of Bargaining* (Baltimore, 1996). See also Jeff Rubin & Burt Brown, *The Social Psychology of Bargaining and Negotiations* (New York, 1975) and Dean G. Pruitt, *Negotiation Behavior* (New York, 1981).

66. George Gordon, Lord Byron, *Childe Harold's Pilgrimage*, canto III, stanza xlv.

INDEX

Page numbers in **bold** denote text graphics.